THE
OLYMPIC
GAMES

THE OLYMPIC GAMES

80 Years of People, Events and Records

Edited by
Lord Killanin and John Rodda

BARRIE & JENKINS
COMMUNICA - EUROPA

First published by
Barrie & Jenkins Ltd
24 Highbury Crescent
London N5 1RX
1976

ISBN 0 214 20091 4

This book was designed and produced by
Rainbird Reference Books Limited
Marble Arch House, 44 Edgware Road, London W2
House Editor: Perry Morley
Designer: Jonathan Gill-Skelton

The text was filmset and colour originated
by Jolly & Barber Limited, Rugby

Printed and bound in the U.S.A.

Contents and Colour Plates

Colour Plates

Contributors

Harold Abrahams, CBE. Represented Great Britain in the Olympic Games, 1920 and 1924, winning the 100 metres at the latter; Captain, British Athletic Team, Olympic Games, 1928; Chairman, British Amateur Athletic Board 1968–75; past Chairman, International Amateur Athletic Federation Technical Committee; Athletics Correspondent, *Sunday Times* (London) 1925–67; broadcaster since 1924. His many publications on athletics include works on the 1928 and 1936 Olympic Games; *Track and Field Olympic Records* (1948); *The Olympic Games, 1896–1952* and *1956; The Rome Olympiad* (1960).

Neil Allen. Watched his first Olympic Games as a schoolboy in 1948; at Melbourne in 1956 was the youngest accredited reporter from anywhere in the world. Since then he has covered all the Summer Olympics for *The Times* (London) as its chief correspondent and specialist in athletics, boxing and swimming. President, Athletics Commission of the International Sports Writers' Association (AIPS). Author of *Olympic Diary 1960* and *Olympic Diary 1964*.

Don Anthony. Principal Lecturer in Physical Education, Avery Hill College of Education, London; teacher, Faculty of Education, London University; sports consultant to UNESCO and to British Airways. Founder, Amateur Volleyball Association of Great Britain and Northern Ireland in 1955; President, English Volleyball Association. Author of *Volleyball – Do It This Way* (1964) and *Success in Volleyball* (1973). Competed for Britain in the 1956 Olympic Games in the hammer event.

Professor Arnold Beckett. Professor of Pharmaceutical Chemistry and Head, Department of Pharmacy, Chelsea College (University of London). Member, IOC Medical Commission, since 1968. Co-author, *Practical Pharmaceutical Chemistry* (1962); founder and co-editor, *Journal of Medicinal Chemistry*. Chairman, Board of Pharmaceutical Sciences for the Fédération Internationale Pharmaceutique.

Monique Berlioux. Born in Metz, France and educated at the Lycée Fénelon and Faculté des Lettres in Paris, Master of Arts, was a journalist and TV Director 1947–61 and Head of the Press Service, Ministry of Youth and Sports, 1961–6. Is now Director, International Olympic Committee, which she joined in 1967 as Director for Press and Public Relations and Administration. Was swimming champion of France and semi-finalist in the 1948 Olympic Games. She has written several books, *La Natation* (1947); *Mon Séjour chez Mao Tsé Toung* (1955); *Olympica* (1956); *Femmes* (1967); awarded the Chevalier de la Légion d'Honneur and

Chevalier des Arts et des Lettres. Other sports activities include horse riding, cycling, motor racing, etc.; member of the Racing Club de France.

Jenő Boscovics. Chief correspondent, Hungarian News Agency. Began to write about weightlifting in 1960; has covered all the European and World Championships since 1961 and the 1972 Olympic Games. Secretary, since 1969, weightlifting section of the International Sports Writers' Association (AIPS).

Richard Desborough Burnell. A second-generation Olympic gold medallist, he won the double sculls title in the 1948 Games (with Herbert Bushnell); his father, C. D. Burnell, won the eight-oar title in 1908. Rowing Correspondent, *The Times* (London), 1946–67; now Rowing Correspondent, *Sunday Times*; contributor to BBC sports programs and many publications. Author of *The Oxford and Cambridge Boat Race* (1954); *Henley Regatta* (1957); *Races for the America's Cup* (1965); *The Complete Sculler* (1973).

Jacques M. Caryotakis. Former President, Greek Amateur Wrestling Federation; Director General, Athens City Gas Company; author of a history of the heavy sports in ancient Greece.

James Coote. Sports correspondent, *Daily Telegraph* (London). His books include *Olympic Report 1968; Olympic Report 1972; History of the Olympics in Pictures* (1972).

S. E. Crisp. Sports writer specializing in archery. Made his first bow and shot his first arrows at the age of seven; nearly fifty years later became a founder member of the Association for Archery in Schools in 1963; now the Hon. Secretary of that association. Has reported all recent World Championships for Target Archery and the 1972 Olympic Games. Regular contributor to *The British Archer*.

Brian Crowther. Swimming correspondent, *Guardian* (London and Manchester), since 1961. Attended the Olympic Games in 1960, 1968 and 1972, three European Championships and four Commonwealth Games. Member, British Swimming Writers' Club and the Sports Writers' Association.

Dr H. C. Willi Daume. German industrialist. President, National Olympic Committee for Germany; President, Organizing Committee for the Games of the XXth Olympiad in Munich, 1972; Vice-President, IOC (Member since 1956); Hon. President, the German Sports Federation (Deutscher Sportbund). Has been awarded decorations and honours by several countries.

Sándor Dávid. Past member of Hungarian champion sabre team; has written on fencing for 15 years; columnist of Hungarian daily *Népsport* (People's Sport). Has covered all the World Championships and Olympic Games since 1963 except for the 1964 Games in Tokyo.

J. W. Dudderidge, OBE. President, British Canoe Union; past Vice-President and currently Member for Europe on the Board of the International Canoe Federation. Successively competitor, Team Manager and Technical Official at Olympic Games, 1936–72.

K. S. (Sandy) Duncan. British international in the long jump 1932–8; Chef de Mission of twelve British teams to the Olympics 1952–72. General Secretary, British Olympic Association, 1948–74; now Director of International Affairs. A member of the IOC/NOC Commissions on the Olympic Program and Solidarity; editor of the IOC booklet, *The Administration of an Olympic Games* (1969).

HRH the Prince Philip, Duke of Edinburgh. Competed successfully in jumping and throwing at school from the age of ten and ended his athletic career throwing the javelin at inter-command championships in the Navy. After World War II was diverted first to cricket and then to polo but after his marriage to the then Princess Elizabeth found himself becoming increasingly involved in the administrative side. In 1955 he was invited to become President of the British Commonwealth Games Federation and has attended each of the Games ever since. He attended the Olympic Games in Helsinki in 1952, and in 1956 he opened the Olympic Games in Melbourne and attended the Equestrian Olympics in Stockholm.

In 1964 he was elected President of the International Equestrian Federation (FEI) for four years and was re-elected in 1968 and 1972. In that capacity he attended the Mexico and Munich Games and made preliminary visits to the Equestrian Olympic sites in Munich and Montreal to approve the plans and preparations. He has travelled widely in connection with the FEI, including visits to Hungary, the USSR and the United States. In 1973 he addressed the Olympic Congress in Varna.

Marie-Thérèse Eyquem. Concerned particularly with women's sports, she has gradually achieved equal treatment for women in sport in France. Elected President, International Federation of Women's Physical and Sporting Education in 1961. Her books include *La Femme et le Sport* (Woman and Sport); and *Pierre de Coubertin, l'Epopée Olympique* (Pierre de Coubertin, the Olympic Pope); the latter won the Grand Prix de Littérature Sportive. Has also written a play, *Marie-Louise* *d'Orléans*, which won a literary prize. A town councillor; founder President of the rural *foyer* of her town (Moustier-Ventadour, Corrèze); member, Executive Committee, and National Secretary, French Socialist Party.

Doug Gardner. Deputy Editor, *Sportsworld*, the official magazine of the British Olympic Association, for which he has worked since 1954. Reported his first Olympics in 1948 and in 1963 succeeded the late Dr Willy Meisl as the magazine's expert on international association football. Particularly interested in the political aspects of sport and has regularly attended IOC and FIFA Congresses. Author, *Jackdaw Guide to Football* (1970) and a pocket *History of Football* (1971); edited the British Olympic Association's Official Reports of the 1964 and 1972 Olympic Games; is the first man to write on international sport for the *Annual Register of World Events*.

Alan Gayfer. Active racing cyclist since 1948. Has reported cycle racing throughout Europe, on road and track. Contributor to *Encyclopaedia Britannica*, British national newspaper and international cycling magazines.

Doug Gilbert. Competed in athletics (200 metres and 400 metres) in Canada and at Northwestern University, near Chicago, on a US athletic scholarship (1957–61). Worked at the *Winnipeg Tribune* (Canada) 1962–4; continued as a sportswriter in Chicago, 1964–9; returned to Canada in 1970, taking responsibility for the *Montreal Gazette*'s Olympics coverage after the city's successful application to stage the 1976 Games. Author of a comprehensive comparative study of approaches to élite sport and physical education in Canada, the German Democratic Republic and the USSR, 1973–4.

Włodzimierz Gołębiewski. Failed to win a place in Poland's Olympic cycle team for 1936 but his father sent him to Berlin for a few days to watch the competition. That began a long and valuable association with Olympism. Attended all the summer Olympics from 1952 as Sports Editor of *Trybuna Ludu* (Tribune of the People). Vice-President, International Amateur Cycling Federation; member of the Jury of Appeal. President, Polish Cycling Federation; organizer of the Tour de Pologne and the Peace Race.

John Goodbody. Formerly athletics and swimming correspondent, *Evening News* (London); covered the 1968 and 1972 Olympic Games. Has made a speciality of judo on which he has written several books. Was a member of Britain's National Judo Squad and won a light-heavyweight bronze medal in the 1969 Maccabiah Games.

Jean Grenier. Past President, Quebec Speed Skating Federation; Vice-President, Canadian Amateur Speed Skating Association; Chairman, Indoor Speed Skating Subcommittee of the International Skating Union.

John Hennessy. Sports Editor of *The Times* (London) since 1954. Covered 1960 Olympics in Rome, but realized that his place on such occasions was at base and has not attended a Summer Olympics since. He has specialized in winter sports since 1959 (covering all Winter Olympics since 1964) and IOC Sessions (covering the last ten, except the one at Mexico City, 1972).

Richard Lynton Hollands. Sports writer specializing in hockey and cricket. Contributor at various times to many British newspapers including the *Daily Telegraph* and *Evening Standard*. Managing Editor, *Hockey News*, 1951–71; co-author, with the late R. Y. Fison, of *Hockey* (1951).

Erich Kamper. Sports journalist since 1931. Has been particularly interested in the Olympics since his schooldays, beginning then to establish his sports library, which 40 years of research has made one of the world's best. Since 1948 has contributed to several Olympic books; achieved international recognition with his *Encyclopaedia of the Olympic Winter Games* (1964). In 1969 became an Hon. Member of the International Olympic Academy. His *Encyclopaedia of the Olympic [Summer] Games* (1972) has been highly acknowledged. His *Who's Who at the Olympics* (1975), containing nearly 12,000 brief biographies of all Olympic medal winners since 1896, completes his Olympic trilogy.

John Kerr. Equestrian Correspondent, *Guardian*, for ten years; saw his first horse show (sent there because he knew 'something about racing') in 1952, a few weeks after Britain's only gold medal at Helsinki had nudged show jumping into the sporting scene. Has contributed arts columns, with an all too evident bias towards the cinema (of which he is a lifelong devotee) to the *Irish Times* and still reports annually on the London Film Festival.

Boris Khavin. Took part in athletics and volleyball during his schooldays. After World War II he finished studying journalism and became a sports journalist. Since 1960 he has been editor of the Moscow review *Sport za Rubezhom* (Foreign Sport). He is the author of works on the history of the Olympic Games and on various problems of the Olympic Movement.

Lord Killanin. Became an International Olympic Committee Member, 1952; elected Vice-President 1968 and succeeded Avery Brundage as President 1972. See *Who's Who in the Olympic Games*, page 201.

Karl Heinz Lanz. Editor, *Deutsche Schützenzeitung* (German Shooting Times) since 1954; editor *UIT Journal* (Journal of the International Shooting Union) since 1961. Has attended five Olympic Games as reporter and radio and television commentator; was captain of the German shooting team in 1968.

Nadjeda Lekarska. Secretary, Bulgarian Olympic Committee, 1954–68; Bulgarian Olympic Attaché at the 1960 Olympic Games, at Rome and Squaw Valley, the 1964 Games at Tokyo, and the 1968 Games at Mexico City and Grenoble. Member, IOC Joint Commission on the Olympic Program, as representative of the Bulgarian NOC, and has been one of its delegates to the IOC several times. Author, *Essays and Studies on Olympic Problems* (1973); chief editor since 1972, Bulgarian NOC's *Bulletin of the BOC*.

Peter Lunn, CMG, OBE. Son of Sir Arnold Lunn, who invented Alpine ski racing. Competed in World Ski Championships (Downhill and Slalom) 1931–7, finishing in first ten 1934, 1935 and 1936. Captain of British Olympic Team in 1936 when he finished twelfth. Still an active skier.

Tom McNab. British National Athletics Coach since 1963. Author, *Illustrated Teach Yourself Athletics (Track)* (1972); *Illustrated Teach Yourself Athletics (Field)* (1972); *Modern Schools Athletics* (1968); *Guide to British Track and Field Literature 1275–1968*, with Peter Lovesey, (1968); *Munich 1972* (1971). Originator of the Five Star Award Scheme, an elementary incentive test of athletic ability widely used by schools.

Gaston Meyer. French sports journalist, first at *L'Aéro-Sport* in 1929, then athletics correspondent at *L'Écho des Sports* in 1931. The same year he became sportswriter for *Petit Journal*; athletics correspondent, *L'Auto*, 1933; he founded *Élans*, 1946; after that journal merged with *L'Équipe*, he became deputy editor (1946), then editor, 1954–70. Founded the French Athletics Club. Author of several books including *Le Phénomène Olympique* (1959); *L'Athlétisme, Langage Universel* (1962); *Les Jeux Olympiques* (1963). Knight of the Legion of Honour, 1959, and an officer, 1970. In 1972 he received the 31st Olympic Diploma of Merit.

Andy Mezey. Former member of Hungarian National Handball Team; introduced handball to the Province of Quebec, founded the Quebec Olympic Handball Federation and was its President until 1970; Playing coach of Canada's national team 1963–70. President, Canadian Team Handball Federation, 1974.

Vernon Eversfield Morgan, OBE
Competed in the 1928 Olympic Games in the 3,000-metres steeplechase. Sports Editor, Reuters, for 35 years, covering all major world sports events including 17 Olympic Games (nine Summer and eight Winter). Attended all IOC Plenary Sessions during the Olympiads and many in non-Olympic years. Former member, IOC Press and Public Relations Committee; Hon. Member, International Olympic Academy. Vice-President, British Olympic Association. Has been awarded the Olympic Diploma of Merit and Diploma of the AIPS (International Sports Writers' Association) for Distinguished Services to Sports Journalism.

The Rt Hon. Philip J. Noel-Baker, PC. Hon. Fellow, King's College, Cambridge, where, in addition to many other academic distinctions, he obtained a first-class honours degree in Economics and the Whewell Scholarship in International Law. Member, British Olympic Track Team, 1912, 1920 (silver medal 1,500 metres), and 1924, and captained it in 1920 and 1924; Life member, British Olympic Association; Commandant, British Team in Helsinki, 1952. Awarded the Diploma of Olympic Merit, 1975. Member of Parliament 1929–31 and 1936–70; held ministerial offices for ten years and was a member of the Government for 23 years. In his work for peace and disarmament he has published numerous books; awarded the Nobel Peace Prize in 1959.

Terry O'Connor. Correspondent, *Daily Mail* (London); a sports writer since 1948, he has covered seven Olympic Games. Also a leading Rugby writer; has reported more than 300 internationals and Test matches all over the world. Apart from journalistic work, he has successfully promoted a number of athletics meetings in Britain.

Cleanthis Palaeologos. Elected Professor of the Academy of Physical Education of Athens, 1932; Director, National Academy of Physical Education, 1950–62. For his long, successful and creative work was awarded the title of Hon. Director of the National Academy of Physical Education on his retirement. Member of Hellenic Olympic Committee since 1974. Hon. Secretary, International Track and Field Coaches' Association 1959-69. His books include *The Legends of Olympia* (1973).

Dr Henri Pouret. Author and broadcaster, specializing in the relationship between art and sport; Member, International Olympic Academy; Member, French Academy of Sports. Has been awarded many French and international distinctions for his broadcasts on Aesthetics and Olympism.

John Clinton Rodda. Sports journalist for 30 years; first associated with the Olympic Movement during the Games of 1948, when, as a young reporter, he covered the cycling events at Herne Hill, London. He became a writer for the *Manchester Guardian*, 1950; joined the *Guardian* (as it then became), 1959, and has covered every Summer Olympic Games from 1960 and extended his interest to writing about the IOC from 1964 onwards. In his sporting days, he swam for Beckenham Swimming Club, played Rugby football at school; now a jogger.

Sir Stanley Rous, CBE, JP. Secretary, Football Association, 1934–61, now Hon. Vice-President; President, Fédération Internationale de Football Association, 1961–74; now Hon. President. His publications include *The Football Association Coaching Manual* (1938); *Recreative Physical Exercises* (1940); *Handbook for Referees' Instructors* (1973); *A History of the Laws of Association Football* (1974). Awarded the Diploma of Olympic Merit, 1975.

John Samuel. Sports Editor, *Guardian* (London and Manchester) since 1968; Sports Editor, *Observer*, 1960–1; has attended and covered the Winter Games of 1964, 1968 and 1972 and the Summer Games of 1968 and 1972. Specialized in ski and other winter sports subjects; he has attended three world ski championships. Among publications, he has contributed the Alpine and Nordic ski sections and Cresta Run to *The Oxford Companion to Sports and Games* (1975) and is consultant editor, *Ski World*.

James Hugh Miller Somerville. Yachting writer since 1949; associated with *Yachtsman* 1949–58, editor 1959–64. Yachting correspondent, *Sunday Times* (London), since 1954. Contributor to *Yachting* (USA), *Field*, *Scotsman*, *New York Times*, etc. His books include *Yacht and Dinghy Racing* (1957); *Yacht Racing Rules Simplified* (1955–61); *Sceptre* (1958); *Leisure Guide Sailing* (1974).

Otto Szymiczek. Technical Adviser, Hellenic Olympic Committee. National and Olympic Track and Field Coach of Greece, 1930–61; Member of the Hellenic Mission to the Games from 1932 to 1972; Member of Board of Directors of the International Olympic Academy since 1961; Dean and Regular Lecturer of the IOA since 1962. President, International Track and Field Coaches' Association since 1956. Has lectured extensively and written many articles on the Olympic Movement and track and field athletics.

Jakob Vaage. Director, Ski Museum, Holmenkollen, Norway, since 1946. An active skier; Norwegian Junior Champion 1924; first chairman of the Norwegian slalom committee in the 1930s; coach to the Norwegian Olympic slalom team 1936; a ski-jumping judge at the 1960 Winter Games at Squaw Valley; member for ten years of the FIS Jumping Judges Committee and Tables Committee. His publications on skiing include *Slalom Downhill* (1939), *Norwegian Skis Conquer the World* (1952) and *The Holmenkollen Ski Jumping Hill* (1968).

Dezső Vad. Competed in ten different sports as a teenager; his favourite being lawn tennis; played twice at Wimbledon, reaching the final of the junior event in 1948 and playing for Hungary in the Davis Cup competition. Became a sports commentator for Hungarian radio in 1950 and joined the daily *Népsport* (People's Sport) in 1957; now International Editor. Has covered three Olympics. Foreign Correspondent, *Sports Zürich* and *Deutsches Sportecho* (Berlin).

Peter Wilson, OBE. Educated Harrow and Fleet Street; worked first for *The Times* (London) and Exchange Telegraph news agency; *Daily Mirror*, 1935; *Sunday Pictorial* (now *Sunday Mirror*) 1938–50; 1943–6 with British Army Newspaper Unit (North Africa, Sicily, Italy, Greece) after being commissioned in infantry, 1941; with *Daily Express* 1950–3; rejoined *Daily Mirror* 1953. Covered eight Olympic Games, 1936–72, and over 100 world boxing championships at all weights; attended every Wimbledon final except two since 1929. Received British Sportswriter of the Year Award, 1966. Retired from regular journalism after Munich Olympic Games, 1972; still covers Wimbledon and certain other big lawn-tennis events for *Daily Mirror*. Awarded OBE 1975.

Ken Wlaschin. Program Director, National Film Theatre, London, and London Film Festival. Author of articles and books on the cinema and novels, mainly thrillers, as well as non-fiction and poetry. Presented season of Olympic films at National Film Theatre in 1972 in connection with the Munich Games.

Paul Zimmerman. Writer for over 40 years; including 12 years with the Associated Press at St Louis, Albuquerque and Los Angeles, before joining the *Los Angeles Times* in 1939, serving as that newspaper's sports editor for over 30 years. Contributor to many magazines including *Esquire* and *Look*. Author, *Los Angeles Dodgers* (1960). Past director, Helms Athletic Foundation. National President, Football Writers' Association of America, 1959.

Introduction   *Lord Killanin*

In 1971 I approached George Rainbird, for whom I had previously co-edited and written a book, with the suggestion that there was a lack of Olympic literature in English. My original suggestion was for an encyclopedia. When I made this proposal I was a Vice-President and also Chairman of the Press and Public Relations Committee of the International Olympic Committee. My term of office was due to end at the Games of Munich in August 1972. I believed that after the Games I would have a good deal of spare time to devote to such a book. I had no idea that at Munich I should find myself succeeding the most distinguished Olympic figure after Baron Pierre de Coubertin – Avery Brundage – as President of the IOC. Although a few approaches had been made to me regarding the presidency, I had not taken them very seriously, especially as I had never canvassed for election either to the Executive or to the Vice-Presidency.

When I found myself President of the IOC, I still felt that a book of a wide-ranging nature on the Olympic Movement would be a considerable asset. Olympic literature is considerable in other countries, especially in Germany where much work was done by the Carl Diem Institute.

The task of assembling this book would not have been possible had it not been for John Rodda, a journalist whom I have known well because he has for many years taken a thorough interest in the Olympic Movement and has attended most of the Sessions of the IOC during the years I have myself been active.

We set out to make this the most comprehensive work on the Olympic Games in the English language, taking into account the strictures on space. I find something new in the article on their founder by Madame Marie-Thérèse Eyquem, whose work shows the man's mental and physical energies and above all his vision; she lays the myth held, I am afraid, fairly widely that Coubertin was an aristocrat bent on preserving sport for his class.

For the celebrations of each Games we have sought reporters of international standing who may not all like the ways of the IOC but have shown a joy in their reporting of the Games; cramming one celebration into the length we could allow provided an exercise in discipline but all of them, I feel, have achieved a précis which would never be possible in their daily reports from the Games arenas.

We were delighted to have the amazingly sharp memory of Philip Noel-Baker, who, sixty-three years ago this year, ran in the Games of Stockholm; we were sad that Sir Arnold Lunn, the father of Alpine skiing, did not live to complete his contribution to the Winter Games.

Apart from the contributors, many other people and organizations, including National and International Sports Federations and National Olympic Committees, have provided help without which this book would not have been possible; the eagerness with which so many people have responded to our letters and questions to clear up queries and contradictions has certainly bolstered the belief that we have had from the beginning of a need for such a book. We thank them all. On page 268 there is a specific reference to our supporters. I would like to add the name of Perry Morley, House Editor at Rainbird, whose enthusiasm and drive has been invaluable in a multitude of aspects, not least in ensuring that every Olympic area has been explored for consideration in this book.

It is my hope, both as the originator of the book and now as President of the IOC, that it will fulfil a useful function. However, I would like to make it absolutely clear that in no place whatever has there been any form of censorship or directive given to any contributor. Each one has had his freedom and each one has contributed according to his knowledge and opinions. There are certain views which may not be considered strictly in line with conventional Olympic thought, but these are views of individuals and I believe it is more important that views should be expressed than suppressed.

The Olympic Movement has always come in for criticism – ever since Coubertin first breathed word of the idea. This has increased in recent years, chiefly due to the growth and sophistication of communication and the great expansion and success of the Games. It has also coincided with a redistribution of wealth and a new social approach to sport and leisure time. Sporting activities are now no longer the privilege of the few but the opportunity of practically everybody. The number of viewers and critics has increased to such proportions that one cannot but compare the present situation with the spectators in Rome just before the Fall of the Empire. Television has made many people experts in particular sports and I can assure you that there is no shortage of advice on what the IOC and I must do.

The future of the Olympic Movement is, I believe, assured, although we shall always have our problems. Among these are the immense growth of the Games; amateurism and eligibility; political interference; and the use of scientific advances in medicine. We hope that some light or new perspective on these subjects is revealed in this book.

During my Olympic life, which began when I was elected President of the Olympic Council of Ireland in 1950 – and to the IOC in 1952 – there have been many changes. The Games of Helsinki and Melbourne were the last of an intimate nature. Subsequently we went to the large metropolises of Tokyo, Mexico City and Munich, where money for the promotion and presentation of the Games seemed to be no object. The Games have also attracted more and more political attention. The arenas and the Village have become a platform for expressions of those seeking new freedoms and self-determination within our society. Coming from a country, part of which separated from the United Kingdom in my own lifetime, this is something of which I have been fully aware; yet in spite of political differences, sport frequently overrides political divides. This has been true of my own country which has been ravaged by political and sectarian strife during recent years but this has not affected the sporting outlook of the Irish people as a whole.

The readers of this book will find an immense amount of fact as well as divergent expressions of opinion. I sincerely hope that it becomes a really useful book of reference. There are areas of Olympic history, unhappily, where there can be no certainty of the facts but we have corrected many misconceptions. No one can be infallible, as we have discovered in reading Olympic historians of the past, and it is possible that errors will have found their way into this book. We should be only too grateful to receive any corrections. In the meantime, I very much hope that this volume will find its way into the collections of sports enthusiasts throughout the world, and promote the Olympic ideals with the motto *Citius, Altius, Fortius* and the motto of the Olympic Congress in Varna in 1973 – 'Sport for a World of Peace'.

Killanin

Dublin
January 1975

The History of The International Olympic Committee   *Monique Berlioux*

The organization of the International Olympic Committee was envisaged as a complete structure by Pierre de Coubertin.

The International Congress of Paris for the Re-establishment of the Olympic Games was convened in June 1894 in the amphitheatre of the Sorbonne – at the very heart of the French university so opposed to sport. Its success surpassed Coubertin's hopes. The opening ceremony began with the hymn to Apollo which had just been discovered in Delphi; this epic anthem created the atmosphere he needed.

On 23 June, the Congress, with the unanimous support of the seventy-nine delegates and forty-nine sports associations from twelve countries present, agreed to re-establish the Games, choosing to hold them in true Hellenic tradition at Athens in 1896.

The principles and details of the Olympic Movement, concerning the Committee, national and international associations and formalities, had already been scrupulously prepared by Coubertin. A passionate Hellenist, he had long studied the administration of the ancient Games as they were held during the period of Pericles (fifth century B.C.). At that time, the judges were elected, wealthy citizens were responsible for the financing, the trainers were unpaid and often had to share the expenses. The athletes themselves arranged and prepared the grounds on which they were to compete at Olympia. The religious tradition was maintained through the worship of the Olympian Zeus.

From the outset, Coubertin laid down the structure of the organization of the Games. Once he had determined the principles and regulations, he was only involved with the main points. He wanted a group of people who would define general policy and be the guardian of the concept. This society was to be independent, international, sovereign and assured of perpetuity. It came into being from the Paris Congress, under the title of 'International Olympic Committee'. Coubertin selected the first members of this committee, which, including himself, totalled fifteen men from twelve nations.

The IOC has unquestionable powers as guide, guardian and arbiter. It is the supreme body in the Olympic Movement, the rock, the foundation stone.

The Olympic Movement comprises in addition the International Sports Federations, which are responsible for the management, administration, techniques and promotion of their respective sports; the athletes, who illustrate Olympism in action; the National Olympic Committees, which represent the IOC and are delegated by it to promote the Olympic Movement within their respective territories and to see that the IOC's regulations are respected there.

The IOC has three aims:

1. Ensuring the regular celebrations of the Games;
2. Making these Games increasingly perfect, more and more worthy of their glorious past and in keeping with the high ideals that inspired those who revived them;
3. Encouraging or organizing all events and, in general, taking all steps likely to lead modern athletics along the right lines.

The IOC is a self-recruiting body. The members are co-opted. Coubertin set out what he expected of them in *Mémoires Olympiques*:

[The Committee] was a 'self-recruiting body', with the same type of management structure as that for the Henley [Royal] regattas. But it was already ... composed of three concentric circles: a small core of earnest and hard-working members; a nursery of willing members ready to be taught; finally, a façade of more or less useful people whose presence satisfied national pretensions at the same time as it gave prestige to the Committee as a whole.

He wanted members to be 'trustees' of the Olympic idea. They would be selected for their knowledge of sport and their national standing, since, according to Coubertin's principle of a 'delegation in reverse', an IOC member is an ambassador from the Committee to his own country and not an ambassador of his country to the IOC.

There was no oath for members until 1955. Since then, all members say, on being introduced to the Committee:

Recognizing the responsibilities that go with the great honour of serving as (one of) the representative(s) of the International Olympic Committee in my country, (. . .), I bind myself to promote the Olympic Movement to the best of my ability and to guard and preserve its fundamental principles as conceived by the Baron Pierre de Coubertin, keeping myself as a member free from all political, sectarian and commercial influence.

The candidates to the IOC, who are numerous, are considered by the Executive Board which makes a recommendation to the General Assembly; the Executive Board's judgment is almost always accepted.

Until 1966, the IOC members were elected for life. They could, at their request, be elected honorary members, able to attend Sessions without voting rights, but those elected after 1966 must retire at the age of seventy-two. Some of course retire before that age, and in extreme cases the Committee is entitled to dismiss them.

From 1974, honorary members cannot attend Sessions and their only privilege is a reserved seat at the Games. Members must reside in their country; because of this ruling, King Constantine of Greece, elected in 1963 when he was Crown Prince, had to resign in 1974. He took up honorary membership.

There are some unwritten rules. When the Committee was constituted, the founder nations were entitled to several representatives. There were up to four members for France and for the United States. In 1966 this figure was reduced to three; today it is two for countries which have staged the Olympic Games, or those with a long Olympic tradition, or those whose territory spreads over a large area. The tendency has been to bring IOC representation on a national scale down to one wherever possible, as has been done in the case of Belgium and the Netherlands, both having staged the Games.

From fifteen in 1894, the IOC's membership increased to forty-eight on the eve of World War I, sixty-seven in 1936 and seventy-two in 1951, the year when the President, Sigfrid Edström, nominated for ratification by the Session the first member from an eastern European country, Constantin Andrianov of the USSR.

In 1974, the IOC had seventy-eight members in sixty-two countries, spread over the five continents as follows: Africa eleven, Asia twelve, America seventeen, Europe thirty-five, Oceania three. Thirty-three of these members have been chosen from the 'third world'. Their social origins are extremely varied, their professions run from head of state to ambassador and from professor of physical education to doctor. Six heads of state have or have had a seat on the IOC: two presidents of the Argentine Republic, Manuel Quintana and Marcelo T. Alvear; Prince Franz-Josef of Liechtenstein; Grand Duke Jean of Luxembourg; Prince Rainier III of Monaco; and the former King of the Hellenes, Constantine II.

There have been over three hundred members since the Committee's creation, of whom about fifty have taken part in the Games as athletes. Of these, ten or so have won gold medals, among them the Marquess of Exeter (Great Britain; 400-metres hurdles, 1928), Masaji Kiyokawa (Japan; 100-metres backstroke, 1932), Julian K. Roosevelt (United States; yachting 6 metres, 1952), Sven Thofelt (Sweden; modern pentathlon, 1928).

At the outset and in the early years Coubertin was completely against any participation of women in Olympic events. Moreover, the founder of the Modern Games could never have imagined women playing a part in the conduct of Olympic affairs at any level. Since Lord Killanin's accession to the presidency, the idea of seeing women in the IOC has been accepted and it is likely that two or three women members will be elected at Sessions in the near future.

The General Assembly usually meets once a year and twice in the year of the Games, just before each one is celebrated. These meetings are called Sessions. It is here that the development of the Movement and its problems are discussed. The program of the Session, usually heavy, is governed by an agenda including the following main points: elections, co-option of new members, amendments to the Rules and Regulations, changes in the program of the Games, relations with the International Federations, the National Olympic Committees and the discussions in the commissions. There are sixteen permanent commissions dealing with such matters as finance, medicine, eligibility, press and publicity, and others which are created from time to time.

The Assembly usually adopts recommendations from the Executive Board with a show of hands. A simple majority is sufficient except for changes in the Rules, for which a majority of two-thirds (the quorum being thirty-five) is required. For elections, an absolute majority is necessary.

Every four years the Session has to select the cities which will organize the Summer and Winter Games. The voting is secret, sometimes with several ballots in between sharp and lively debates. During the three other years, the working reports given by the Organizing Committee of the elected cities are studied in great detail. All these Sessions are accompanied by a certain pomp and ceremony. At the seventy-fifth Session in Vienna in 1974 the solemn opening ceremony included speeches by the President of the Austrian Republic, Rudolf Kirchschläger, the President of the NOC and the President of the IOC. The Olympic anthem was played. Music by Schubert and Mozart completed the ceremony, bearing the stamp of national tradition. This was followed by the presentation of the members to the head of state. There are always a number of receptions, at which the debates of the conference table often continue in a more relaxed, informal manner.

In 1921 Coubertin appointed the first Executive Board, consisting of five members. It has grown in size and stature; it now consists of nine members, elected in full session. They are: the President, elected for eight years, then eligible for re-election for successive periods of four years; the first, second and third Vice-Presidents, elected for four years, who are not eligible for re-election and who advance by seniority of election; five members, elected for four years, eligible for re-election after one year of absence.

Apart from its task of directing the IOC, the Executive Board prepares the work of the Sessions, maintains a constant link with current problems which the Olympic Movement faces, and meets, apart from the Sessions, at least once a year.

Administrative work and research are dealt with by the general secretariat, whose headquarters are in Lausanne, Switzerland. At the head of the general secretariat is a director, assisted by a technical director and a staff including translators, interpreters and librarians.

The Board is also responsible for meeting the International Federations every other year and the NOCs to discuss problems and development, thus ensuring the necessary unity and coordination within the Movement.

Legends always die hard, especially where the IOC is concerned. It has been dubbed 'a closed body', but, particularly since the accession of Lord Killanin as President, every important Olympic decision has been the subject of methodical cooperation between the committee and external sports figures. This has not always been the case and arbitrary decisions, often based upon flimsy evidence or taken hastily, have damaged the image of the IOC, giving it the reputation of being out of step with sports development in modern society. The philosophy of working with external organizations was encouraged by setting up IOC commissions. Since Lord Killanin became a vice-president, the work of these commissions has widened; they have provided a way of bringing people with a particular expertise who are not IOC members into much closer touch with the Assembly. The President has the prerogative of creating the commissions and appointing the chairman and members.

The original rules of the IOC stipulated that the registered office of the society should be moved every four years to the country staging the next Olympic Games. But World War I brought a change. Although he was fifty-one when hostilities broke out, Coubertin enlisted in the Army and told his fellow members that he felt it was wrong that the Committee should be presided over by a soldier. He asked Baron Godefroy de Blonay, a Swiss, to take over the Presidential duties.

For a long time the Founder had been attracted to the quiet city of Vaud, Lake Geneva. This, together with the primary concern of protecting the Olympic institution by establishing it in a country outside the world conflict, was the key to Coubertin's decision – to install the IOC headquarters at Lausanne. He decided to override objections from the members and, on 10 April 1915, in the conference room at Lausanne Town Hall, signatures were exchanged establishing the world administration centre and the archives of the renovated Olympism in that town.

After the 1918 armistice, Coubertin was certainly very pessimistic about the duration of the peace. It therefore seemed necessary to him that the IOC should keep its headquarters in Switzerland, 'a country with permanent neutrality'. It was not until 1922, however, that the IOC actually took up its quarters in Lausanne, occupying a floor of Mon Repos manor, a comfortable mansion in which Coubertin occupied a few rooms towards the end of his life.

In 1968 the IOC moved to the Château de Vidy, a big country house on the shores of Lake Geneva.

Strangely, the IOC has no legal status. Coubertin and his successors, including Brundage, cherished the freedom of this position. However, it does present certain difficulties in modern society, for example, in entering into contracts.

The IOC flag has five interlaced rings, of which the respective colours from the pole end are blue, yellow, black, green and red, on a white background. The yellow and green rings are lower than the other three. The yellow ring links the blue and the black ones; the green links the black and red ones. Coubertin found this emblem at Delphi in 1913. 'These five rings', he wrote, 'represent the five parts of the world won over to Olympism and ready to accept its bountiful rivalries. The six colours combined in this way represent those of every nation without exception.' The IOC flag flew for the first time in Paris, in June 1914, at the Congress marking the twentieth anniversary of its foundation.

The motto adopted by the IOC, *Citius, Altius, Fortius* ('Faster, Higher, Stronger'), made its appearance at the Antwerp Games. Its inventor was a Dominican monk, Father Henri Didon. This teacher, who had a great influence on Coubertin, was prior of Arcueil College, Paris. He wanted all his pupils to practise sport and at their first meeting in the open air he announced, 'Here is your watchword – *citius, altius, fortius.*'

In a way the IOC has a second motto. A religious service in St Paul's Cathedral, London, on 19 July 1908, marked the Games of the fourth Olympiad. The Bishop of Pennsylvania preached a sermon of which one phrase dazzled Coubertin: 'the important thing in the Olympic Games is not so much to have been victorious as to have taken part'.

A few days later, paying tribute to the author of this idea, Coubertin said in a speech:

> The most important thing in the Olympic Games is not to win but to take part, just as the most important thing in life is not the triumph but the struggle. The essential thing is not to have conquered but to have fought well.

These words now appear on the electronic scoreboards at opening ceremonies of the Games.

An Olympic hymn of slow and solemn beauty and classical inspiration was composed in 1896 by the Greek Spyros Samaras to words by his colleague Costis Palamas. In the 1950s there were calls for a change but the attempts to provide something better were unsuccessful and Samaras's cadences have since been linked to every Olympic festival.

Coubertin had a very broad outlook. From his younger days he wanted the Olympic Games to take the form of a pyramid, with national Games at the base, then continental Games. This idea did not begin to evolve until after World War I, when the IOC granted its patronage to the Latin-American Games in 1922, then the African Games in 1925 (which, however, were cancelled). Since then other continental and regional Games have flourished, such as the Pan-American, Asian, Mediterranean, African, World Student Games, and many others.

The cooperation between the IOC and the twenty-six International Sports Federations at present represented on the Olympic program must remain close. When the Movement was founded, confusion reigned in the technical rules as well as in the organization of competition sports. At that time few sports had international associations or rules and very often within single countries there were a variety of styles and laws. The emergence of the Olympic Movement, and the desire of sportsmen to compete in the Games, gave international formalization and impetus that would not otherwise have occurred. Today sports within the Olympic program are all properly controlled and regulated. But in the early years of the Movement Coubertin and his colleagues had to contend with a chaotic jumble of disputes; the Olympic Movement, though, provided a point of understanding, of a realization that compromises could be found. The first Games, together with the IOC's efforts, enabled rapid and great progress, leading to the creation of national and international federations. From the beginning, their precise powers were laid down by Coubertin:

> The IOC members were the trustees of the Olympic idea and were responsible for imbuing the Games' quadrennial competitions with it, but this did not qualify them to replace technicians in the running itself of these competitions. *(Mémoires Olympiques)*

In the early 1960s many sports federations were dissatisfied with some of the IOC's actions and decisions, particularly in relation to amateurism. They felt they should have a more significant voice and a large number (though not the powerful International Amateur Athletic Federation) formed the General Assembly of International Federations in 1967.

Coubertin was always afraid that the IOC might become isolated. Hence the National Olympic Committees (NOCs), which he wanted to establish as branches of the IOC in all countries, so as to simplify and discipline the participation in the Games of athletes from all over the world. Here too, he was not slow in defining their function nor their dangers. In July 1903 he wrote in the *Olympic Review*:

> The NOCs must not be an emanation of the main sports federations or associations of the country. . . . There is every advantage in these Committees being permanent. . . . One cannot insist too strongly on the danger of making a National Olympic Committee the main guiding cog in the sporting activity of a country.

The use of the NOC in some countries for the development of sport for political and other purposes began to worry the IOC fifty years after those words were written and still does. In 1954 the IOC laid down, in Rule 24, the conditions governing the existence of the NOCs. They must consist of representatives of at least five sports federations recognized by the corresponding international federations. Members of the IOC from the country concerned are automatically members of the NOC. The IOC recognizes an NOC only after approving its statutes. Any recognition is revocable, as in the case of South Africa, excluded from the Olympic Movement in 1970.

P Année – Nº 1.   Janvier 1896.

BULLETIN DU COMITÉ INTERNATIONAL
DES
JEUX OLYMPIQUES
PARIS, 229, Rue Saint-Honoré   *Citius – Fortius – Altius*   Rue Saint-Honoré, 229, PARIS

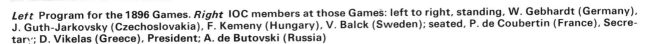

Left Program for the 1896 Games. **Right** IOC members at those Games: left to right, standing, W. Gebhardt (Germany), J. Guth-Jarkovsky (Czechoslovakia), F. Kemeny (Hungary), V. Balck (Sweden); seated, P. de Coubertin (France), Secretary; D. Vikelas (Greece), President; A. de Butovski (Russia)

Coubertin abhorred parliamentary government. He would have found an Olympic Congress held at regular intervals unbearable. Recruited by co-option, the IOC was intended to be dependent on nothing. He was perceptive enough though to realize the need for solid external support for his fragile institution. About two thousand people belonging to sports associations, universities and business circles, representing thirteen nations, attended the first Congress. The second, held with calculated modesty at the Town Hall in Le Havre (the Norman port was one of the cradles of Coubertin's family) welcomed a smaller but equally select committee. The accent was laid on the philosophical, moral and educational originality of the Olympic Movement. The next Congress was not held until 1905, at the Palais des Académies in Brussels. The organizer was the young Comte Henri de Baillet-Latour, who had then been a member of the IOC for two years. There were 210 participants, from twenty-one countries. An essential innovation gave the International Federations (IFs) five representatives each. In May of the following year in Paris, about sixty celebrities from the worlds of art and sport studied how the Arts and Letters could be brought into the Olympic Games. This led to the introduction of the cultural program at Stockholm in 1912. This was not officially a Congress but a 'Consultative Arts, Letters and Sports Conference'. The discussions were widely talked about; Olympism was becoming highly fashionable.

Then came, in March 1913, the Lausanne Congress devoted to sports psychology and physiology, and, in June 1914, the important Olympic Congress on the Olympic Regulations, held in Paris. For the first time the NOCs participated *en masse* in the Congress but World War I broke out before the minutes were finalized. The same questions had to be discussed again at a new Olympic Congress on the Olympic Regulations, held in June 1921 in Lausanne. Besides the IOC, seventy-eight delegates from the NOCs and IFs discussed everything concerning the Games – competitors' qualifications, the program, technical regulations, etc. and serious misunderstandings were overcome between the IOC and the IFs. Differences of opinion existed but they were just as deep between the various IFs, and between the NOCs, as between the IOC

and the individual interests of other sports institutions. Coubertin probably wondered whether revealing these divisions did not do more harm than good, but their appearance through these Congresses, before they were entrenched by tradition and time, was an important part of growing up.

Four years later and after several requests, the IOC agreed to a double Olympic Congress at Prague in May 1925, dealing on the one hand with the regulations and on the other with the educational role of sport. Amateurism, the reduction of the program of the Games, the NOCs' powers, women's participation in Olympism, and a number of other subjects were discussed at length.

By 1930 Coubertin's fears of a clamouring for power from beneath began to manifest themselves. As the IFs and the NOCs were eagerly pressing for a new Congress, one was held, on Olympic regulations, in May, at the Herrenhaus in Berlin, the former House of Lords of Prussia. A new definition of amateurism was adopted, as well as various modifications to the general rules of the Games and to the protocol. However, grappling with conflicting interests, often antagonistic terms of reference, and the personal and national rivalries of the IF and NOC delegates, the IOC feared that by allowing a succession of Olympic Congresses, there would be disorder, paralysis and finally ruin. With World War II looming after the Games of Berlin, and then in 1946 a new zest to pick up the pieces and begin competition again, the next Olympic Congress was a long way off. Perhaps, however, the troubles of the 1950s and 1960s might have been diffused had there been a Congress.

The tenth Congress was held at Varna, Bulgaria, after a gap of forty-three years. It was to consider three fundamental themes: redefinition of the Olympic Movement, relations between the IOC, the IFs and the NOCs, and the pattern of future Olympic Games. Besides the participants, several observers were invited to attend the discussions, among them recent Olympic medal winners, journalists, a representative of Coubertin's family and delegates from the International Federations recognized by the IOC but whose sports were not on the program of the Games. There was no vote to sanction the discussions, but a report of the debates was published.

Left Olympic stamps issued by Greece (1896); Mexico (1968); Germany (1936); German Federal Republic (1972). *Right* G. de Blonay (above) and H. de Baillet-Latour (below), third and fourth IOC Presidents

Since its foundation, the IOC has had seven Presidents: Demetrius Vikelas, Coubertin, the Baron Godefroy de Blonay (who took over from Coubertin during World War I),the Comte de Baillet-Latour, Sigfrid Edström, Avery Brundage and Lord Killanin.

Demetrius Vikelas, a Greek, was the first, in 1894, while Coubertin reserved for himself the position of Secretary-General. Vikelas, a prominent Athenian writer and historian, managed to overcome Hellenic scepticism and pioneered the organization of the first Games in Athens in May 1896. The rules then stipulated that the President should come from the country organizing the next Games, and since these were entrusted to Paris, the leadership of the IOC naturally fell to Coubertin from 1896. His colleagues 'forced him' to remain in office until 1925 and he remained a member until his death.

Henri de Baillet-Latour, of Belgium, who became an IOC member in 1903, was a natural successor to Coubertin in that from the ashes of World War I he had taken on the organization of the Games at Antwerp in 1920 with only a year to prepare. He also bore the burden of the Olympic celebrations in Germany.

While each Games has its own character, its own reflection of national and ethnic standing, the Games of the eleventh Olympiad in Berlin and Garmisch-Partenkirchen marked a crucial point, almost a new beginning for modern Olympism. The Games of Nazi Germany were grandiose and oppressing, they caused bitter resentment but widened the awareness of the Olympic Movement.

What is often overlooked is that these Games were awarded to Berlin in May 1931 by a postal vote of forty-three to sixteen, with eight abstentions. Berlin defeated Barcelona, Rome and Budapest having withdrawn shortly before in favour of the German capital. The German Olympic Committee, according to the rule existing at the time, declared that it also wanted to stage the Winter Games and selected the site of Garmisch-Partenkirchen. In 1931 the IOC placed its trust in the Weimar Republic, which was Nazism's enemy.

Adolf Hitler acquired power on 30 January 1933. The thirty-first Session of the IOC was held in Vienna on 7–9 June of that year. Baillet-Latour officially asked the representatives of the Reich to guarantee their country's observance of the Olympic Charter or to forgo the Games. They gave the requested guarantee. The Vienna Session noted the fact that 'in principle, the German Jews would not be excluded from the Games of the XIth Olympiad'. Of the two German members of the IOC, one, Theodore Lewald, half Jewish by birth, was President of the Organizing Committee of the Berlin Games; the other, Dr Karl Ritter von Halt, was President of the Organizing Committee of the Garmisch Games. Von Halt, born in Munich in 1891 and son of a locksmith, had taken part in the Games of the fifth Olympiad in Stockholm. Knighted during World War I, the tall and statuesque Bavarian became an IOC member in 1929.

Hardly had the thirty-first Session closed when Hitler decided to replace Lewald and von Halt at the head of the two Organizing Committees by the State Director of Sport he had just appointed, Hans von Tschammer und Osten. Baillet-Latour immediately requested an audience with Hitler, who felt obliged to comply. 'It was in consideration of the statures of His Excellency Dr Lewald and Ritter von Halt that the IOC granted the organization of the Games to Berlin and Garmisch,' the IOC President told the German Führer. 'If our two colleagues should cease to be Presidents of the Organizing Committees, the IOC would be obliged to withdraw the Games from the two cities conditionally elected and to award them to other candidates.' Hitler gave in.

The campaigns against staging the Games in two cities of the Third Reich nevertheless grew to a frenzy. Baillet-Latour invited von Halt and Lewald to confirm publicly their promises regarding the observance of the undertakings they had made in Vienna on behalf of Germany. The two delegates repeated their statements on the Third Reich's 'loyalty' towards German Jewish athletes who, according to them, were in no way at a disadvantage compared with their 'Aryan' comrades. Certainly at that time, racial persecutions were proliferating, giving a faint hint of the horrors to come in 1938–45. But the systematic killings had not begun; the world's strange passivity towards the regime was to continue for several years.

Baillet-Latour was careful to make his own inquiries at the source. On 6 November 1935 he said in Berlin that after a conversation with the German Chancellor and inquiries he had made he was convinced that nothing stood in the way of maintaining the Games at Berlin and

Garmisch. 'The conditions required by the Olympic charter have been respected by the German Olympic Committee.'

His remarks caused a great stir and in no way quelled the opposition. The argument and debate shook the IOC itself. Ernest Lee Jahncke, the member for the United States, violently opposed American participation. In doing so he made a stand against Avery Brundage, then President of both the US Olympic Committee and the Amateur Athletic Union. Brundage accused the opponents of American participation in the Games of 'betraying the athletes of the United States'. On 15 September 1935 Hitler proclaimed the 'Nuremberg laws' which made Jews 'sub-humans' and these were followed by a mass of persecutions. Thus Jahncke found his cause encouraged and he continued his campaign against sending a team from the United States. The intensity of his opposition reached a peak when he said that he despised the IOC's massive support for Baillet-Latour's position. The Executive Board called upon Jahncke to retract as he 'was betraying the IOC's interests, contravening its statutes and failing in good breeding towards his colleagues'.

Jahncke refused to apologize and, in a letter which soon became public knowledge, also refused to attend the thirty-fifth Session which was to be held in Berlin immediately before the Games. Upon Baillet-Latour's proposal, on 30 July the IOC agreed to Jahncke's expulsion from the IOC. It was a unanimous decision except for the abstention by the second United States delegate, W. M. Garland. Brundage was immediately elected to replace Jahncke.

At the foot of the Zugspitz the two villages of Garmisch and Partenkirchen were arranged with characteristic Bavarian *Gemütlichkeit*. But signs 'Dogs and Jews are not allowed' had been placed outside the toilet facilities at Olympic sites. Baillet-Latour saw them and again requested an interview with Hitler. After the customary courtesies, he said, 'Mr Chancellor, the signs shown to the visitors to the Games are not in conformity with Olympic principles.' Hitler replied, 'Mr President, when you are invited to a friend's home, you don't tell him how to run it, do you?' Baillet-Latour thought a minute and replied, 'Excuse me, Mr Chancellor, when the five-circled flag is raised over the stadium, it is no longer Germany. It is Olympia and we are masters there.' The signs were removed.

The Belgian President died suddenly in 1942, shortly after hearing that his son had been killed while training with the Free Belgian forces in the United States.

Sigfrid Edström, a Swede, took over the leadership in his double role of vice-president and native of a neutral country. He assumed his functions officially after the Session of Lausanne in 1946. Only twenty-six members were present. Edström put the wheels in motion, filled in the gaps and chose as his successor Brundage. Well prepared, the American was elected in 1952. Edström died in his ninety-fourth year between the Innsbruck and Tokyo Games of 1964.

Brundage, strong and single-minded, set out to 'make the Olympic Games the greatest social force of our time'. Often acting with despotic firmness, this Chicago builder succeeded in equipping the IOC with universal prestige and in safeguarding its unity. Under his presidency, Olympism was confronted with vast and complex problems, among them those of the two Germanies, then China, and apartheid. Brundage held the office of President for twenty years and died on 7 May 1975.

The affair of the two Germanies gives a good example of the IOC's capability of achieving more in the fields of recognition than any other international body.

When the Third Reich fell, von Halt and the entire Executive Committee of his NOC were sent by the Russians to a concentration camp. The IOC did everything possible to liberate the unfortunate group but von Halt was detained for five years and when he came back his health was irreparably impaired. His prime objective was the recognition of the new 'National Olympic Committee of Germany'. It should be noted that in the eyes of the Assembly, both von Halt and the other German IOC member, Duke Adolph-Friedrich of Mecklenburg-Schwerin, 'never ceased to belong to the IOC' in the words of President Edström.

At the Vienna Session of 1951 the two Germans were able to present the application of the German Democratic Republic. At this point the IOC was just coming to terms with a newly shaped, communist eastern Europe. The Soviet NOC was admitted to membership and the IOC considered this an appropriate moment for all candidate delegations to countersign a statement reminding them of the Olympic principles and the obligation to respect the Rules and Regulations of the IOC. Hong Kong and the German Federal Republic were recognized but the German Democratic Republic failed, an unhappy indication that the members were worried about the implications of granting membership to a state which was not recognized in a large part of the world.

Von Halt then turned to promoting the reunion of the two separated parts of Germany under one flag: a fanciful idea in the middle of the cold war but there was a deep personal esteem which linked the former inmate of the Soviet camps and Dr Heinz Schöbel, President of the East German NOC and future member of the IOC, to which he was elected in 1966.

Dr Schöbel made a new request for the East German Committee at the Oslo and Helsinki Sessions in February and July 1952. But he failed on both occasions. At the Helsinki Session, the Assembly decided to put the question of the admission of the German Democratic Republic on the agenda for 28 July but the Session ended on 27 July. There was, though, a glimmer of light, for the Assembly requested von Halt to negotiate the readmission of the East Germans into the Olympic circle. It took time to find an acceptable formula but finally at the Paris Session in 1955 the following agreement was adopted:

> It was decided by twenty-seven votes to seven that the Olympic Committee of the People's Democratic Republic of Germany (East) be recognized provisionally on the understanding that, should it prove impossible to form a unified team from both Germanies to be sent to the Melbourne Games, this recognition would lapse automatically.

Von Halt then had four interviews with the delegations of his former compatriots. Finally they came to what is known as 'the miraculous agreement'. The East German NOC was recognized on 25 January 1956 at Bonn under this title. Bonn and Pankow sent one delegation to Cortina and to Melbourne. The flag, emblem, uniform and living quarters were the same. The *chef de mission* (team leader) was chosen by the group with the greater number of athletes.

The agreement between the two Germanies lasted until the Mexico Games. It was at the Session preceding those Games that Dr Schöbel obtained, with the consent of his colleagues from the German Federal Republic, the recognition that the long separation of the two Germanies should be written into all Olympic documents in the future. On 1 November 1968 the name of the East German NOC became the NOC of the Democratic Republic of Germany (Nationales Olympisches Komitee der Deutschen Demokratischen Republik).

From the 1950s onwards the entry of nations of the third world and especially black Africa to the Olympic family lent momentum to the criticism of apartheid in South Africa. Its team at the Rome Games in 1960 was solely white and that escaped nobody's notice. In the following year South Africa left the British Commonwealth and set itself up as a republic, strengthening its racial laws in a country ruled by a small white minority. Some IOC members launched their offensive through Constantin Andrianov, of the USSR. The decisive charge came at the Baden-Baden Session in 1963. Referring to that section of the Olympic charter which states 'No discrimination in them [the Games] is allowed against any country or person on grounds of race, religion or politics', the IOC called upon the South African Olympic Committee (SANOC) to oppose publicly, and in reality, all racial discrimination in sport and competition. At Innsbruck in January 1964 the IOC noted that the SANOC had not complied and withdrew its invitation for Tokyo. The South Africans' long Olympic absence had begun.

The Supreme Council for Sport in Africa (SCSA), an organization composed of members from African states, was not satisfied with the position and demanded South African exclusion from the Movement. In Teheran in 1967 the Assembly decided to send a commission of inquiry, presided over by Lord Killanin and composed of Sir Ade Ademola, Chief Justice of Nigeria, and Reginald Alexander, a member of a British family long established in Kenya, to South Africa in 1967. The Commission's detailed report consisted of a multiplicity of facts. Following tradition, they left the conclusions to be reached by the IOC members.

At Grenoble on 2 February 1968 during the Winter Games, the IOC members present considered they were too small a group to make an immediate decision and so agreed that South Africa's fate should be settled by a postal vote. The examination of the votes thirteen days later showed a small majority in favour of maintaining the SANOC within the Olympic Movement on condition that its next delegation was incontestably multi-racial, with all its athletes enjoying complete equality of treatment. Led by Abraham Ordia and Jean-Claude Ganga, the President and Secretary-General of SCSA, the sports leaders of black Africa opposed this decision and set in motion a worldwide campaign against the IOC's decision. With the South African government maintaining apartheid, the Mexican Organizing Committee became alarmed on several counts: they believed that the South African team might only be multi-racial on the surface and that there might be demonstrations. 'For every athlete we will provide a policeman' was the offer of General José de Clark of Mexico, a member of the Executive Board, and Chairman of the Organizing Committee – an ironic remark in view of the bitter internal struggles Mexico was to suffer in the weeks before the Games began. But there was another more tangible threat to the Games presented by the South African problem. At one point there was a threat that forty countries, more than a third of the members, would boycott the Mexico Games. General Clark called for the Executive Board to examine the question. Brundage, on his way to Lausanne, flew to South Africa and spent two days discussing the position. In turn at the Château de Vidy the debate lasted two days. Finally, Brundage, almost crushed by over a hundred newsmen and television personnel, stood on the steps at the back of the Château and announced:

> In view of all the information on the international climate received at this meeting, the Executive Board is unanimously of the opinion that it would be most unwise for a South African team to participate in the Games of the XIX Olympiad – therefore, the Executive Board strongly recommends that you endorse this unanimous proposal to withdraw the invitation to these Games. This postal vote is submitted under Rule No. 20. Please reply immediately by cable CIO Lausanne.

This second ballot gave forty-seven votes for the withdrawal of the invitation, sixteen against and eight abstentions.

However, SCSA's allies within the IOC continued to demand expulsion. The Assembly decided, before taking an implacable decision, to hear the two parties once more in full Session. This took place in May 1970 in Amsterdam, and, after years in which SANOC's representatives had shown a personal desire to meet the IOC's requests there was a surprising shift of position. SANOC's representative, in what many members regarded as an abusive speech, talked about IOC interference in South Africa. Those who had tried to keep open the door felt their cause was lost; South Africa was expelled by a narrow majority.

This was not the end of the problem of apartheid. Ordia and Ganga had asked the IOC to deal with the question of Rhodesia at the same time as the SANOC, since apartheid in sport was believed to exist there, too.

The IOC considered the position in Luxemburg in September 1971. It decided that the Rhodesians could only take part in the Munich Games on condition that they had the same flag (the Union Jack) and the same anthem ('God Save the Queen') as in Tokyo. Surprisingly, the Rhodesian NOC accepted, adding that in order to participate it was prepared to take even the boy scout emblem – a remark not appreciated. A fortnight before the official opening of the Munich Games, the row started again. Although Rhodesia's team had already arrived and was composed of whites and blacks, the critics still alleged that apartheid existed in Rhodesia and almost twenty countries threatened to withdraw their teams if the Rhodesians were allowed to attend the opening ceremony and compete. The revolt spread. A movement grew among the Blacks of the United States team that they, too, should refuse to take part. After several consultations and in spite of his deep reluctance, President Brundage had to agree to the IOC's coming to a decision on the withdrawal

Left to right S. Edström, A. Brundage and Lord Killanin, fifth, sixth and seventh IOC Presidents

of the Rhodesian participants. By thirty-six votes to three and three abstentions, the Assembly withdrew the invitation extended to the Rhodesians, which was a relief to everybody – except the athletes from Rhodesia.

For the first time since the creation of the modern Olympic Movement, an NOC duly recognized by the IOC, saw its athletes prevented from taking part in the Games, and this due to political pressure.

At the end of World War II, the IOC had two members for China: Dr Cheting T. Wang, a supporter of Chiang Kai-shek, elected in 1922, and Dr H. H. Kung, elected in 1939. They disappeared from the Olympic scene in 1957 and 1955 respectively, very seldom attending Sessions. In 1947 the IOC, in view of the difficulties of the situation, gave China a third representative: Shou Yi Tung, a sports educationalist. Shortly afterwards he went over to the side of Mao Tse Tung and moved to Peking.

In 1951, the Chinese Olympic Committee recognized by Lausanne retreated to Formosa. The following year, Peking and not Formosa sent athletes (thirty-eight men and two women) to the Helsinki Games. In spite of their doubtful position (their country had no NOC) they were allowed to compete. In 1954, a new NOC formed in Peking was recognized by the IOC under the name of 'Olympic Committee of the Republic of China'. The Olympic Committee with its headquarters in Formosa was also still recognized. In November 1956, at the fifty-second Session of the IOC in Melbourne (where athletes from China and Formosa did not compete), Shou Yi Tung was asked to see how a mixed team from the two Chinas could be formed, on the lines of that of the two Germanies, to take part in the Rome Games in 1960. In 1957, Tung reappeared at Sofia for the fifty-third Session. He asked for his country to be called 'The People's Democratic Republic of China', a request which was accepted. A few outspoken declarations of political faith by Tung obliged Brundage to call him to order, after which calm seemed to reign between the IOC and Peking.

But the continued recognition of the regime in Formosa agitated Peking, and in August 1958 the Olympic Committee of the People's Democratic Republic of China

withdrew from the Olympic Movement. Tung submitted his resignation to the IOC, accompanied by a long diatribe. The IOC could only take note. Simultaneously, the Chinese federations withdrew from the international federations of athletics, basketball, association football, wrestling, weightlifting, swimming, shooting and lawn tennis.

In May 1959, at Lord Killanin's proposal, the IOC notified the Chinese Olympic Committee in Formosa that it could 'no longer be recognized under this name, in view of the fact that it does not administer sport in China'. This left the door open to the other China. Formosa adopted the name 'Olympic Committee of the Republic of China'. The IOC officially accepted this name in 1968.

Killanin's step within the IOC was a semi-public support for some private overtures which were going on between individual members of the IOC and influential people in Peking. Links had been established and ways and means of bringing back the representatives of the most populous country in the world were being worked out.

But this diplomatic campaign came to a grinding halt at Amsterdam in 1970 when Henry Hsu from Formosa was elected to the Assembly. His name was presented by Brundage to the Executive Board who performed its traditional role of vetting and rejected Hsu, not on any ground of personal integrity but in the belief that his election would do damage to the attempt to bring mainland China back to the Movement. Contrary to the unwritten rule to elect only those people approved by the Executive Board, Brundage put forward Hsu's name to the Assembly and he was accepted.

Since 1973–4, mainland China has had many contacts with international sports officials, and before competing in the Asian Games in 1974, won recognition by nine international federations for its corresponding national federations.

The Mexico Games brought unusual burdens for the IOC and the Organizing Committee: in addition to the crisis over South Africa, there was the problem of altitude and riots in the city over the four months before the Games.

When Mexico City was awarded the Games at the Session in Baden-Baden in 1963 there was an outcry from some countries that competition at an altitude of 7,415 ft (2,260 m) would be unfair in some events. At that height the air is thinner and in endurance events – those that last more than a minute – competitors who normally live in the lowlands are at a disadvantage. The objections grew, backed by physiological evidence. Several countries sent teams of doctors and athletes to Mexico to undertake research and finally the IOC agreed that competitors could train at altitude for a period of six weeks before the Games. This helped but it did not bring parity between the lowlanders and those who normally lived and worked at altitude, and the results of the Games bear this out. While there was a degree of unfairness, much useful research on the subject was done.

Although the Russian suppression in Budapest twelve days before the Games of Melbourne had brought the withdrawal of several countries which would not allow their teams to compete against Soviet athletes, Mexico was the first city in which internal strife threatened the Games and the participants.

There had been unrest within the country for several months, largely among students, who felt that a country with so much poverty should not be spending millions on the Games; they used the focus of world publicity on their capital as a platform for their own cause.

There had been demonstrations at the University and at meetings in the city at which people had been killed and injured during the last month before the Games opened. Photographs of tanks opposite the main stadium had caused unease in many countries. Then on 2 October, ten days before the Games were due to open and after several days at which meetings had passed off without any violence, there was the most brutal and bloody confrontation between students, academics, trades unionists and the army. At a meeting in the Plaza de las Tres Culturas, attended by over 10,000 people (not only students), there was a call for the overthrow of the Government. Suddenly, at a given signal, a green Very light, the army opened fire; with students armed and ready for such an eventuality, a battle raged for nearly five hours. No accurate figure of the dead is known but it is certainly over 260, while another 1,200 were wounded. The effect was that opposition to the Government was utterly smashed, and the guarantee from President Diaz Ordaz that there would be no interference with the Games or those taking part was met.

Under the slogan *Todo es posible con la Paz* ('Everything is possible with peace'), the Games, opening on 12 October, had a huge, lasting success. Many of the athletes' performances exceeded those at the previous Games.

The most terrible drama in Olympic history began at the Games of Munich, in the Olympic Village at 4.30 a.m. on 5 September 1972, the eleventh day of the Games. Eight members of the Black September organisation broke into 31 Connollystrasse, the building where the Israeli delegation was housed. The terrorists intended to seize the twenty-one athletes and officials staying there. One man, in raising the alarm, was killed, but enabled eight of his colleagues to get away; one more managed to escape. The eleven remaining Israelis were held hostage until just after midnight on 6 September when, together with five of the terrorists, they died. The three surviving Palestinians were captured. They were released by the Germans on 29 October, following a threat from a Palestinian commando who had hijacked a Lufthansa plane.

From the moment a city has received the responsibility of staging the Olympic Games, it is to its Organizing Committee that the IOC delegates its powers to run the Games, but the IOC retains its supreme authority. It was therefore logical for the representatives of all the institutions concerned to meet as soon as possible after learning of the unprecedented tragedy which had begun. At 7.15 a.m., these representatives decided to set up a 'Crisis Committee', with the Bavarian State's Minister for the Interior, Bruno Merck, at its head. Brundage was one of the first to hear of the tragedy and, without informing his colleagues, left his hotel at 6.30 a.m. to go to the Village. He became a member of the Crisis Committee. Just before 4 p.m. the Organizing Committee released a communiqué written and signed by Brundage and Willi Daume, Chairman of the Organizing Committee:

> The Olympic peace has been broken by an act of assassination by criminal terrorists. The whole civilized world condemns this barbaric crime, this horror. With deep respect for the victims and as a sign of sympathy with the hostages not yet released this afternoon's sports events are being cancelled. The IOC and the Organizing Committee will hold services in commemoration of the victims in a ceremony which will take place tomorrow, 6 September 1972, at 10 a.m. in the Olympic stadium. This ceremony will demonstrate that the Olympic idea is stronger than terror or violence.

An hour later, Brundage said:

> The IOC will not allow participants in the Games who are guests in the Olympic Village to be kidnapped by terrorists and taken outside the Federal Republic.

But the German authorities were later to put into operation an ill-fated plan for terrorists and hostages to leave Germany.

The first Vice-President, Lord Killanin, who had already been elected to succeed Brundage at the head of the IOC but was not to take office until the day after the end of the Games, returned from Kiel, where he had been attending the Olympic regattas, with two other members of the Executive Board, Jonkheer Herman A. van Karnebeek and Prince Takeda. Killanin and the majority of the Executive Board regretted that Brundage had delayed so long in consulting his colleagues, but they approved the idea of a commemorative ceremony and felt that an extraordinary Session should be held that same day.

This began at 10.10 p.m. in the large dining room of the Hotel Vierjahreszeiten, with all members present in Munich attending. They decided that whatever the turn of events the Games would carry on to the end. At 11.45 p.m. Daume told the seventy-one members present what the official German Federal Republic's government spokesman, Conrad Ahlers, had just confirmed over the telephone: all the terrorists had been either killed or captured; the Israeli hostages were all alive. The gathering joyfully passed a vote of congratulations to Brundage and Daume, also to the Federal Republic's government, and split up towards midnight.

Terrorist on the balcony of the Israeli quarters in 1972

But in the early hours of the morning this news was found to be false and only compounded the horror that was unfolded, eventually, to the world's Press. The hostages and terrorists had been taken by helicopters to a military airfield where there was a waiting plane. The terrorists thought they had been tricked; firing began, hand grenades exploded, all the competitors and a policeman were killed and all but three of the terrorists, who were caught.

At 10 a.m., under the weight of the awful truth, the memorial ceremony in honour of the victims opened in the packed Olympic stadium to the strains of the Funeral March from Beethoven's *Eroica* Symphony. From all parts of the world came requests to halt the Games. It was in this atmosphere that after the addresses of Daume, the head of the Israeli delegation, Shmuel Lalkin, then the Federal President Gustav Heinemann, that Brundage said:

Every civilized person recoils in horror at the barbarous, criminal intrusion of terrorists into peaceful Olympic precincts. We mourn our Israeli friends, victims of this brutal assault. The Olympic flag and the flags of all the world fly at half mast. . . We have only the strength of a great ideal. I am sure the public will agree that we cannot allow a handful of terrorists to destroy this nucleus of international cooperation and goodwill we have in the Olympic Movement . . .

The Games of Munich were completed.

The ancient Greeks gave the name Olympiad to the period of four years between the Games. Coubertin adopted this idea. Athens was chosen to celebrate the Games of the first Olympiad (1896), Paris the second (1900) and so on to the Games of Montreal (1976), the twenty-first. He also decided that if Games were not held the number of the Olympiad would remain. Thus when the Games of the sixth Olympiad in 1916 did not take place, the Games of 1920 were held as the seventh.

It was also Coubertin who wanted to maintain the tradition of the ancient Games, of holding all the events in one city. A major task of the IOC consists of nominating, six years in advance, the cities that will have the honour of staging the Games.

Of course, candidatures for the celebration of an Olympiad lead to rivalry and ambition, but the more noble passions and the many expressions of voluntary dedication should also be emphasized. To compare the choice of an Olympic city with a game of grab, as some have done, is a gross misstatement. The Olympic ideal is a fact.

The choice of organizing cities for the 1980 Summer and Winter Games was made, according to the rules, by secret ballot, in 1974. Towards the middle of 1973, a circular letter was sent out to each of the 129 National Olympic Committees asking them to inform the General Secretariat before the end of that year if they would be presenting a candidature. A country is only allowed to put forward one city for any given Games.

For the Summer Games, there was competition between two giants, Moscow and Los Angeles. Both were losing candidates for the Games of 1976; Los Angeles staged those of 1932.

Vladimir Promyslov, the Mayor of Moscow, sent an official letter of application to the IOC General Secretariat. At the same time, Constantin Andrianov, President of the USSR Olympic Committee, made his approval of the candidature known to the IOC headquarters.

The standard series of questionnaires was sent to the USSR Olympic Committee and to the Mayor. These are in three parts, covering general matters, technical information, and radio and television. The particulars required are detailed, for example, a city is asked:

Can you guarantee the use of a film laboratory to develop colour and black-and-white pictures? What is its capacity? What is its capacity for printing colour? Black-and-white?

Moscow also furnished the IOC with the compulsory 'sovereign letter' from Mikhail Yasnov, Vice-President of the Praesidium of the Supreme Soviet of the USSR. This letter formally guaranteed that should the Games of the twenty-second Olympiad be granted to Moscow they would be held according to the Rules and Regulations of the IOC.

Meanwhile Los Angeles completed the same procedure. Once the candidatures had been accepted, the propaganda from the two cities increased its momentum. Anyone or any place with indirect or direct influence on the final vote received brochures, circulars, magazines and invitations to film shows. Lectures, receptions, newspaper and magazine articles reached a peak. As in all other competitions of this kind since the 1920s, the two rival candidates did not resist the temptation of offering first-class return tickets to VIPs and their wives to see the city. In 1964 Killanin had attempted to introduce a rule prohibiting excessive entertaining by the candidate cities. Even though the IOC did not adopt the Irishman's proposal, the warning was heard – though not apparently taken to heart.

According to the traditional procedure, the final stages of the Moscow–Los Angeles duel took place at the IOC Session on 21–24 October 1974. In the monumental, baroque Rathaus of the former Hapsburg capital of Vienna, each delegation put on an exhibition of slides, photographs, music, glossy magazines, models, maps, posters, and so on. Hostesses, interpreters, technicians and well-known personalities worked nonstop.

The day finally came for the official presentations of the candidate cities, the afternoon of 22 October. The Presidents and Secretaries-General of the International Federations attended with the IOC members. A draw had already decided that Los Angeles would make its presentation first.

Each delegation from a candidate city consists of a maximum of six persons, normally including the Mayor, the President of the NOC and the President of the promoting committee of the city. The presentation, which should not last more than thirty minutes, may be used in any way but a film show is the most fashionable method, followed by brief explanations. Once the case has been presented the IOC members may ask questions.

The following day, the IOC members returned to the Session room, alone, and the vote took place. Killanin reminded them of the main points, urging them to consider the future of the Olympic Movement; Moscow won. The ballot was secret and voting figures were not disclosed.

The IOC considers itself a non-profit-making organization. It was born and nurtured in the era of sporting patronage. Coubertin devoted his fortune to it. And without the generosity of several members – so often criticized for their wealth or their birth – the Olympic institution would not have been able to function properly.

By the end of World War II the IOC's expenditure exceeded its income, which came only from the members' subscriptions and increasingly rare donations. So the Organizing Committees of the 1948 Games were asked to allocate to the IOC a contribution fixed at £2,000 for St Moritz and £5,000 for London.

The 1952 and 1956 contributions remained modest, while the obligations and expenses of the Lausanne headquarters and members were rapidly increasing.

Television rights should have been taken into account from Melbourne onwards. But the companies of this formidable growing industry wanted to take too much and give too little. Television rights were levied by the Organizing Committee for the first time in 1960. Out of these the two Organizing Committees paid a modest contribution, divided equally between the IOC and the International Federations. In 1970 the IOC belatedly took a decisive step by modifying Rule 21, which stated:

The Committees entrusted with the organization of the Olympic Games and the Winter Games must pay to the International Olympic Committee the sums decided by it.

The following paragraph was added:

All payments for TV rights and financial contributions in connection with television belong to the IOC who will dispose of certain portions to International Federations, National Olympic Committees and Organizing Committees.

The monies paid by the television companies therefore belong by right to the IOC. The IOC has the responsibility of dividing these sums between the Organizing Committee, the International Federations, the National Olympic Committee and itself.

The world television royalties from Munich totalled DM 43 million. It was decided that DM 27 million would go to the Organizing Committee; the remaining DM 16 million, about $5\frac{1}{2}$ million, was divided into three equal parts, shared by the IOC, IFs and NOCs. Thus the IOC received nearly $2 million which, added to the proceeds from Sapporo, the venue for the Winter Games, enabled it to wipe out its heavy debts and to keep its administration going until the Games of 1976.

But how was the Olympic manna to be shared among the IFs? The Marquess of Exeter's proposal was adopted: half to be shared equally among all Federations represented at the Games, the other half to be allocated to them according to the number of paying spectators. For the NOCs – 129 at that time – the problem was a much more complicated one. Finally, the President, Killanin, Herman van Karnebeek (Netherlands) and Giulio Onesti (Italy) worked out a new scheme into which these funds could be paid. An Olympic Solidarity commission was set up to give aid – not financial but technical – in the form of scholarships and seminars, organized initially by the IOC Secretariat for people nominated by their NOCs. This aid program represents a vast field of action for the IOC. In 1974 $400,000 was spent in this way.

The IOC installed its seventh President, Killanin, on 22 August 1972. Irish, Catholic, liberal, jovial, the iron hand in the cashmere glove, he boxed and rowed at Cambridge and was a competent rider. He had been chairman since 1950 of the Olympic Council of Ireland and was elected to the IOC in 1952. As President, he is an energetic helmsman, accustomed to storms. The motto of his family, Morris, is *Deus nobiscum quis contra nos* ('If God is with us, who is against us?').

The IOC does not feel that there is any reason so far to regret the amazing success of the Summer and Winter Olympics. Nevertheless, because of the enormous growth of the Games in size and complexity, Killanin intends to reorganize to some extent the program, the number of competitors and the ceremonies. He is also vigilant against excessive nationalism; as he said at the opening of the 1974 Session in Vienna:

On behalf of the International Olympic Committee I appeal to every single sportsman and woman not to come to the Olympic Games if they wish to make use of sport for political purposes. This is something on which both sportsmen and administrators must unite on a common front. . . . We all have our own beliefs; we all have our friends and enemies; but the aim of the Olympic Movement is to subjugate these in the fellowship which is enshrined in the intertwining Olympic rings representing the five continents of the world, wedded together in sport, peace and friendship. If this is not accomplished then the Olympic Movement and all sport, whether amateur or professional, is doomed. Instead of progressing towards the common ideals, we shall retreat into barbarism.

Opposite, above Enriqueta Basilo, the first woman in the history of the modern Olympics to light the flame, runs up the steps at the opening of the 1968 Games at Mexico City. Below: A general view of the packed Mexico stadium during the opening ceremony the same year

The Ancient Olympic Games   *Cleanthis Palaeologos*

The origin of the ancient Olympic Games is lost in the mist of prehistory, but for many centuries they were a festival of the Greek people.

The first historical mention of the Games of Olympia occurred in 776 B.C. and the Olympiad celebrated that year was considered as the first and was used to date subsequent historic events. But religious ceremonies and games were held in Olympia before that time. The oldest sanctuary of Greece was there, the altar to the great Mother of the Gods, Rhea (Earth). On the day of the feast, the priest stood in front of the altar, ready to perform a sacrifice. Young men from the region waited at a distance of one stadium (about 200 yards). As soon as a signal was given they ran and the first to arrive at the altar received the torch from the priest's hand and lit the sacrificial fire. Excavations have revealed the sanctuary's age which, according to archaeologists, goes back to the geometric period and even earlier, earlier than the thirteenth century B.C.

Even in those ancient times there were traditions and legends concerning the establishment of the sanctuary and the Games. This was natural since the Olympic Games, the 'Olympia' as they were called in antiquity, were not suddenly established and there were no founders as such. They evolved with time from a simple religious ceremony to become the most magnificent and grandiose sports festival of antiquity.

Innumerable legends have sprung from the region of Olympia to give weight to the event. Here, the legends say, Zeus fought against his father Kronos, the child-eater, in order to take the throne away from him. Here, Apollo defeated Hermes in the race and Ares in boxing. The Curetes, five brothers from Crete who were entrusted by Rhea with the safekeeping and education of Zeus, came to Olympia and competed in the sprint race; Herakles, who won, stipulated that thenceforward the race would be *pentetirikos*, held every four years, at the beginning of the fifth year; he called the Games and celebration 'Olympic'.

After Herakles, his descendant Klymenos, also from Crete, held the Games. Then they were celebrated by Aethlius, first King of Elis, son of Zeus and Protogenia, the daughter of Deucalion, founder of the race of men. It is, according to Eusebius, from Aethlius' name that competitors were called *athletes* and events *athla*. After Aethlius, his son Endymion, the latter's son Epeius, and after him the son of Epeius' sister, Elius, all kings of the area, celebrated the Games in their turn. Augeas, Elius' son, is associated with one of the labours of the demi-god Herakles, who cleaned his stables in a day by diverting a river through them. Herakles overthrew Augeas, gave the throne to his son Phyleas, and founded the Games to commemorate his victory. The names of other founders are also mentioned by Eusebius: Peisus, grandson of Aeolus, husband of Olympia; Oenomaus, son of the god Ares, father of Hippodamia; Pelops, the winner of a legendary chariot race, who won Hippodamia's hand and the throne of Elis; and there were Amythaon, Pelias, Neleus, and Oxylos, whose name is connected with the descent of the Dorians, and many others.

Historic material on the religious and athletic festival of Olympia first appears at the end of the ninth century, when Iphitus reigned over Elis. He was a progressive ruler and wanted to give a pan-Peloponnesian character to the festival for the benefit of his country. He therefore not only renewed the religious ceremonies but organized the Games on a grander scale and ensured that they could be freely celebrated every four years, by means of the remarkable, for those times, institution of the truce (Gr. *ekeheirea*). This was the agreement for the cessation of hostilities during the ceremonies and Games which was signed by the King of Elis, Iphitus, the legislator of Sparta, Lycurgus and the archon (chief magistrate) of Pisa, Cleosthenes. Pausanias says that the agreement was carved, in 884 B.C., on a bronze disc; it is also mentioned by Plutarch. The disc was preserved until the days of Pausanias (second century A.D.). The year 884 B.C. is mentioned by Polybius, Diodorus of Sicily, Julius the African, Aristodemus of Elis, Phlegon and others.

The names of the winners of these Games, which were held every four years from the days of Iphitus, have not been preserved. The Elian writers, Paraballon and Evanoridas, were the first to mention the names of Olympic victors; later Hippias numbered the Olympiads and Aristotle completed his task. The Olympiad, i.e. the quadrennial period, was defined by the serial number and by the winner of the stadium race. Dating began from the year 776 B.C., that Olympiad being called the first. The winner was the Elian Koroebos whose grave had been seen by Pausanias at the border of Arcadia and Elis, by the river Alpheus. In this way, the religious ceremony of minor importance slowly evolved into a splendid festival attended by all the Greek world.

Olympia flourished and became a religious, athletic and artistic centre of pan-Hellenic importance and incredible fame, especially from the end of the sixth century B.C. This period coincided with that of the Persian Wars (510–450 B.C.), which brought great glory to the country, gave birth to significant ideas and provided the necessary means for the development of an art which expressed the true meaning of beauty and opened the way to the 'classical' era. Art tested new forms in Olympia with the sculptures of Pheidias in the temple of Olympian Zeus (472–456 B.C.). This experiment proved so successful that it spread from Olympia to the whole country, Athens in particular. Under the influence of Pericles' genius Athens became the centre of Greek classical art and Olympia the centre of the Greek world.

From 776 until 724 B.C. there was only one event in the Olympic Games, the stadium race. In 724 a second event was included in the Games, the *diaulus* race, run on a length of two stadia. In 720 the *dolichus* race (24 stadia or approximately 4.5 km) was added. In 708 the wrestling and pentathlon events were held for the first time, the latter consisting of a race and competitions in discus, jumping, javelin and wrestling. In 688 boxing was added, in 680 chariot races began with the quadriga race, and finally, in 648, the *pancratium* was added, a combination of wrestling and boxing. From that time onwards, the Olympic program grew, reaching a total of twenty-three events though they were never held all together since new ones were added as others were abandoned. The following events were held at various times in Olympia: the stadium race, diaulus, dolichus, wrestling, pentathlon, boxing, quadriga race, pancratium, colt races, boys' stadium race, boys' wrestling, boys' pentathlon (held only once, during the thirty-eighth Olympiad in 628 B.C.), boys' boxing, hoplite race (for heavily armed soldiers), *apene* race (for chariots drawn by two mules), *synoris* race (for chariots

Above Runner in start position, a bronze statuette dedicated to Zeus by a winner in *c.* 480-470 B.C.
Below Starting line in the stadium at Olympia, where the ancient Games were held

drawn by two young horses), quadriga race for chariots drawn by four young horses, races for young horses, boys' pancratium, and *kalpe*, in which the rider ran the last bend of the hippodrome leading his mare by the reins. Races involving mules were discontinued after the eighty-fifth Olympiad because they were difficult animals and more suited to work than sport.

During the ninety-sixth Olympiad (396 B.C.) contests for heralds and trumpeters were introduced.

The prize for victors at the Olympic Games was a branch of wild olive, as the Greeks believed that through the branch the vitality of the sacred tree was transmitted to the recipient. In more ancient times, prizes had included useful gifts and sums of money. Later, prizes lost their material value and retained only their moral value.

The athletes had to come to Elis one month before the beginning of the Games and it is believed that during this period competitors prepared both morally and physically for the events. Training was carried out under the supervision of the Elian judges and the organizers of the Games had ample opportunity to assess the athletes, their aptitudes, morals, fortitude and skill and to select those whom they considered able to give a performance worthy of the history and fame of Olympia.

Throughout most of the period the athletes usually wore no clothes during the events. The Spartan Acanthus,

winner of the dolichus race in the fifteenth Olympiad (720 B.C.) is said by Dionysius of Halicarnassus to have been the first athlete to run naked. But, according to Pausanias and Thucydides, during the same Games, the *zoma* (shorts) worn by Orsippus, winner of the stadium race, fell from his body and from that time onwards the zoma was abolished and athletes competed in the nude. Pausanias suspected that Orsippus let his zoma fall on purpose in order to be able to run more freely.

The reason women were not allowed to watch the Games remains obscure. According to Pausanias, only one woman, the priestess of the goddess Demetra Chamyne, attended the Games, seated on an altar. He suggests that virgins were allowed to watch the Games, but this seems improbable. Perhaps he meant that they could visit Olympia when the Games were not being held. On the other hand, hippodrome events were watched by women as well as by men, since the hippodrome was located outside the sacred precinct of Olympia.

Up to the twenty-second Olympiad (692 B.C.), the Games lasted for only one day. Later, a second day was added, with the introduction of the boxing event and quadriga race. From 632 B.C., after the boys' events had been added, the Games and ceremonies lasted five days: the first day was devoted to sacrifices, the taking of the oath, the registration of athletes, and so on. The various events were held on the next three days and on the final day prizes were awarded and thanksgiving sacrifices offered to the gods.

The Games provided a magnificent spectacle and for this reason Olympia soon became famous. In its arena the nobility and greatness of man were extolled. Victory at the Stadium of Olympia was tantamount to the victory of beauty and the attainment of beauty was the pursuit of any man wishing to acquire virtue. True beauty encompassed the perfection and grace of the body, a rational and brilliant mind and a pure conscience.

Olympia knew days of great glory. Huge crowds gathered there from all regions of Greece and its colonies, Ionia, Italy, Sicily, Egypt, Libya, from the farthest corners of the Mediterranean, and even from the Dnieper, in order to admire the statuesque men, nimble boys and fleet horses.

Plato was already seventy years old when he first came to Olympia. Thales of Miletus, at an advanced age, died from the hardships of the trip and the sage Chilon of Sparta was an old man when he died in the stadium, after embracing his son, winner of the boxing event. Great philosophers, like Pythagoras, Anaximenes, the cynic Diogenes, the orator Demosthenes, the great Themistocles, Pindar, Simonides, Hippias, Prodicus, Polus, Gorgias, Lucian, who boasted of having travelled to Olympia seven times, all made the trip to Elis. Here, in Olympia, in 444 B.C. during the eighty-fourth Olympiad, when Crisson of Himera in Sicily won the stadium race for the second time (he was to win it for a third time in 440 B.C.), the father of history, Herodotus of Halicarnassus, read some passages of his *History* to the public gathered there for the Games; Thucydides, then a young man, was one of the spectators.

Artists exhibited their work in Olympia, poets recited their poems and epics. All forms of Greek classical art flourished there. Praxiteles carved a god in marble, Paeonius created his winged victory and Pheidias used marble as a medium to express the ideological and moral content of the games of Olympia. Here, Greeks offered to the gods votaries and sanctuaries, athletes erected their statues and Militiades, the winner of the battle of Marathon, offered the helmet he had worn during this historic and glorious battle. Olympia expressed every Greek's ideas. Spectators booed King Philip of Macedon there because they believed he was preparing to conquer Greece. It was in Olympia that the rhapsodists sent by the tyrant of Syracuse, Dionysius, to present his poems were interrupted by the shouting of the crowd. Their outburst was made because they were aware that Dionysius was arranging with the Persians for the conquest of Greece. Here again, in 324 B.C. during the 114th Olympiad, Alexander the Great announced that there would be peace among Greek cities and all Greeks united under his shield.

Athletes whose names have become immortal competed in Olympia and the moral teaching of Olympia cultivated the common conscience of the Greeks, their mind and soul. So great was the fame of the Games, that for many centuries it was believed that this was the greatest event any man could witness.

The names of numerous athletes have been handed down. Leonidas of Rhodes won the three racing events, stadium, diaulus and dolichus races, in four consecutive Olympiads (154th, 155th, 156th, 157th), i.e. from 164 to 152 B.C., and twelve Olympic prizes in all. Hermogenes of Xanthe won all the racing events during two Olympiads (215th, 217th) and won the diaulus and hoplite race during the 216th Olympiad.

Polites of Keramos, Caria (Asia Minor) won, on the same day, the stadium, diaulus and dolichus race (212th Olympiad, A.D. 69). Other triple winners included Phanas of Pellene (512 B.C.), Chiones of Sparta (664–656 B.C.) and Astylus of Croton.

Triple winners are also mentioned for the wrestling, boxing and pancratium events. Their names include some famous athletes such as Hipposthenes, Timasitheus, Milon, Amesinas, Keras, Glaucus, Diagoras, Moschus, Tissandrus, Lygdamis, Polydamas, Promachus and Cleitomachus.

Theagenes from Thassos won during the seventy-eighth Olympiad (468 B.C.) the three events, wrestling, boxing and the pancratium; during the seventy-fifth Olympiad he won the boxing event, and the pancratium and boxing events in the seventy-sixth and seventy-seventh Olympiad respectively. He was also declared winner of three events at the Pythian Games, nine times winner at the Nemean and ten times winner at the Isthmian Games. These three Games were the most important sacred Games and major festivals in ancient Greece after the Olympic Games. Pausanias says that he won a total of 1,400 wreaths.

Cleitomachus from Thebes, a famous boxer and pancratist, won both events during the 141st Olympiad (216 B.C.). At the Pythian Games he won the pancratium event three times and at the Isthmian Games he won once all three events, wrestling, boxing and pancratium. There were eight more athletes who won both the boxing and pancratium events at Olympia, among them Caprus of Elis, Aristomenes of Rhodes, Protophanes of Magnesia and Straton of Alexandria. The boxer Melagomas from Caria, Asia Minor, should also be mentioned. He forced his opponents to admit their defeat without blows being

Athlete's hand-held jumping weight. The inscription shows that it belonged to a pentathlon winner.

exchanged, because, he said, 'to hit, to wound and be wounded was not bravery'. His opponents therefore accepted defeat and withdrew.

The infinite glory of the Olympic Games was followed by decline and degradation and they finally disappeared.

Philosophy, rhetorics and prose gradually became the ideals of youth and athleticism was superseded by learning and studying. The main accusation that was hurled against Socrates was that he introduced unworthy temptations and corrupted the young, drawing them away from the gymnasia and physical exercise to make them 'talkers'.

Then came the Macedonians. A warlike people cannot be content with peaceful contests. Alexander the Great never wished to take part in the Games. He brought Hellenism to the East, but the East took its revenge on the conquerors by laying its stamp on their customs.

The Romans followed. They were also soldiers and they converted the stadia into amphitheatres. In the place of free athletes, slaves competed, hoping to win their lives, no longer against noble opponents, but against wild animals. The people rejoiced in the bloodshed. Victory was bought and sold and degradation took over.

The last blow to the Games of Olympia was given by the ascetic ideas of the early Christians, who considered the body to be merely the prison of the soul; through fasting and privation it must be punished so that death, deliverance, could occur more quickly. This rapidly brought about contempt and decline; the violent end of both athleticism and the Games soon followed. The heart of Greece which beat in Olympia suddenly stopped in A.D. 394 when Emperor Theodosius the Great prohibited, by decree, the celebration of the Olympic Games. Since the time of King Iphitus, Olympia had nourished Greek life and Greek national unity. It had beat 320 times, once every four years, but A.D. 393 had been the last time.

From 395 onwards the fall of Olympia was very rapid. In that year the first damage was caused by the invasion of Alaric's barbarians. A year earlier the famous chryselephantine statue of Zeus had been taken to Constantinople. It was destroyed in 475 during the great fire. Following the attacks of the Goths, a fire destroyed the temple of Zeus; earthquakes in 522 and 551 and the most severe of all in 580 brought down whatever had remained standing. Then came flooding of the river Cladeus; the river Alpheus was diverted and Mother Earth gradually covered, to protect it, everything that had escaped plundering and robbing. Glory had vanished and of the vast riches there were now left but a few ruins and the name of Olympia. Something immortal remained, however: the Olympic spirit.

The Modern Celebrations

I ATHENS 1896 Otto Szymiczek

Although the Olympic Games of Greece finally were extinguished after A.D. 393, their beauty and greatness lingered through the poems of Pindar and Pausanias. The interest in classical Greece in the seventeenth and eighteenth centuries brought the history of the Games to light again. Robert Dover started the Cotswold Olympic Games in England in 1636 which were held for over 200 years. In 1850 the Much Wenlock Olympic Society was founded by Dr Penny Brooke, who was later to meet Baron Pierre de Coubertin. A German archaeologist, Ernst Curtius, who did much work at Olympia, suggested in a lecture in 1852 that the Games should be revived, and Coubertin's visits to England, where he saw and understood the value of the English public-school system and of the Olympian Societies, fired him to initiate the revival of the Olympic Games.

The modern Olympic Games began, as they were to continue in many instances, in a major political and social uproar. Although the Greek people enthusiastically welcomed Coubertin's idea of reviving the ancient Games, the Greek Government, struggling with huge financial difficulties and on the verge of bankruptcy, refused any commitment to them. The idea that Athens should put on the Games was in danger of being abandoned and the Committee which Coubertin set up in November 1894 to organize the events made little progress.

It was then that the heir to the Greek throne, Constantine (1868–1923), grandfather of the Crown Prince Constantine who won a gold medal in sailing (Rome, 1960), set up a twelve-member committee, under his chairmanship, which met for the first time on 13 January 1895, the date considered as that on which the Hellenic Olympic Committee was formed. By April 1895 the committee had issued special bulletins in English, French, German and Greek, containing the rules of the events, the definition of sportsmanship and instructions for the officials of the Games.

Collections were made both in Greece and among Greeks living abroad, to obtain the necessary funds for the organization of the Games and for building sports facilities. The response was remarkable. Georgios Averoff (1818–99), one of Greece's wealthiest businessmen, donated 920,000 drachmae in gold for the reconstruction of the Panathenean Stadium in marble and the architect Anastasios Metaxas prepared the plans.

The issue of the first stamps dedicated to the Olympic theme, brought in 400,000 drs. Much of the required money was provided by the distribution of commemorative medals and the sale of tickets. A special velodrome was built at Neon Phaliron and a shooting range at Kallithea, as well as many other sports installations.

The first modern international Olympic Games began in Athens on Easter Sunday, 24 March 1896 (5 April by the new calendar), with the unveiling of the marble statue of the principal benefactor, Averoff, which had been erected in the square in front of the Panathenean Stadium.

The following day, a Greek national holiday, 80,000 people gathered in the stadium on the seats and tiers and in the surrounding hills, or crowded on the square in front of the stadium and in adjoining streets.

After the arrival of the King and Queen, Crown Prince Constantine, President of the Organizing Committee, delivered an inspired speech. King George I (1845–1913) opened the Games with the following words: 'I declare the opening of the first international Olympic Games in Athens.' Then the Olympic Anthem, composed by Spyros Samaras (1863–1917) to a poem of the National Poet Costis Palamas (1859–1943), was played. This hymn, by decision of the IOC Congress in Tokyo, in 1958, has been recognized as the official Olympic anthem. The composer himself conducted the huge choir and the bands of the Army, Navy, the Municipality of Athens and the provinces. The anthem made such an impression on the audience that it demanded an encore.

The sound of trumpets announced the arrival of the competitors and the beginning of the events. The American James Connolly won the triple jump with 13.71 m (44 ft 11¾ in), to become the first Olympic victor of modern times. His record was inscribed on a special board and the American flag was hoisted on a high pole before the entrance of the stadium.

During these first Olympic Games, only the first and second in each event received prizes: the first, a diploma, a silver medal and a crown of olive branches; the second, a diploma, a bronze medal and a crown of laurel. All competitors received a commemorative medal. The victors' medal had been designed by the French sculptor Jules Chaplain and the commemorative medal by the Greek painter Nikephoros Lytras (1832–1904); the diploma by the famous Greek painter Nicolaos Gyzis (1842–1901). King George I awarded all the prizes on the last day of the Games (3 April, or 16 April by the new calendar).

The 311 athletes who attended those Games came from 13 countries: Australia (1), Austria (4), Bulgaria (1), Chile (1), Denmark (4), Germany (19), France (19), Greece (230), Great Britain (8), Sweden (1), Switzerland (1), Hungary (8), United States (14). Most of them came to Athens on their own initiative and at their own expense. The program of events included nine sports and 43 events among which two were held for the first time, the marathon race, proposed by the Frenchman Michel Bréal (1832–1915) and the discus.

When it was announced that the marathon was to be included in the program, the Greek people were touched and excited; they considered it a matter of national pride to compete in and win this very Greek event, which revived the past glory of their history. Every village began to look for outstanding runners. Two preliminary races were held, on 10 March 1896, at the Greek Championships, when there were twelve participants (only club members could take part), and on 24 March, when the entry was open to non-club members as well. In this second race thirty-eight runners entered, among them Spyros Louis, the eventual winner of the Olympic marathon, who was placed fifth.

In the Olympic marathon itself, held on 29 March in cool and cloudy weather, sixteen runners competed, including four non-Greeks, Albin Lermusiaux (France), who had previously competed in the Olympic 800 metres and had been third in the 1,500 metres, Edwin Flack (Australia), the winner of the 800 metres and 1,500 metres, Arthur Blake (United States), who had come second in the 1,500 metres, and Gyula Kellner (Hungary). At the beginning the foreigners were in the lead, but Blake dropped out in the twenty-third kilometre,

1896. Greek children find a rooftop perch to watch the start of the marathon.

Lermusiaux after the thirty-second and Flack after the thirty-seventh. Of the non-Greeks, only Kellner finished the race, in fourth place. He was awarded a special bronze medal, as the first and only foreign runner to finish.

Louis's success caused tremendous excitement. The spectators threw their straw hats in the air. Prince George ran beside Louis on the last straight from the entrance of the stadium to the finish line, and near the finish line Prince Nicholas joined them too. A Greek barber had promised to shave the winner free for life if he were Greek and a restaurant owner promised to give free meals for life, among other offers recorded.

After the Olympics, King George I asked Louis what he would like as a gift and the marathon winner asked for a horse and cart to carry water from his village, Amaroussion, to Athens because the Athens water supply was very poor and the Athenians were buying cool well water from the village. This story indicates how Louis was able to beat the well-known athletes of the time. Besides cultivating land, he had also been selling water to the

Athenians, carrying his barrels on a mule from Amaroussion to Athens twice a day. Thus, without being aware of it, he was using the most modern training methods, with two sessions a day, running beside the mule at least 14 km (the distance between the village and Athens) each time, assuming that he rode his mule on the return journey. He never took part in competition after this Olympic marathon.

Track and field, weightlifting, gymnastics and wrestling events were held in the Athens Stadium. Fencing was held in the Zappeion building, shooting at the Kallithea shooting range, swimming in the Zea Bay of Piraeus, bicycling in the velodrome of Neon Phaleron and lawn tennis on courts which had been hastily arranged by the temple of Olympian Zeus. Rowing and sailing events were cancelled because of bad weather and cricket was not held because there were no participants. All events were held before enthusiastic crowds, with the main stadium filled on every day of the Games.

Various artistic events were also organized during the period of the Games: performances of ancient drama (*Medea, Antigone*), a torch race, receptions and concerts. The city of Athens was lavishly illuminated at night.

The first international Olympic Games of Athens proved so successful that its near-cancellation during the preparatory phase was easily forgotten. Pierre de Coubertin now witnessed the realization of his dream and with renewed ardour planned the future of the Games. If one compares the performance of today's athletes with that of competitors during the Athens Games, one sees that the first modern Olympics was quite primitive. It is, however, doubtful whether the world will again witness the sincere enthusiasm and exultation of Greek crowds who, during these days of March–April 1896, relived their historic past, of 2,500 years before.

Athens, in 1896, had given the most brilliant start to the history of the modern international Olympic Games.

1896. A competitor in the high jump

II PARIS 1900 Gaston Meyer

At the end of the 1896 Games in Athens, the King of Greece, advised by an eager and successful administrator, Timoleon Philemon, claimed for Greece the exclusive right to organize future Games. Coubertin wavered for a moment but quickly realized that agreement would mean signing the death warrant of the newborn Olympic Movement.

The Greek ideal received unexpected help from the American athletes, who signed a petition asking that Athens should be the permanent home of the Games. During the closing banquet, King George developed his idea and suggested to Coubertin that he should give his consent – or resign. The Frenchman, pretending not to understand, addressed an open letter to the King; he thanked him 'and also the city of Athens and the Greek people, for the energy and the enthusiasm with which he had replied to the appeal in 1894' but confirmed that the Games of the second Olympiad would be held in Paris in 1900. There was no royal loss of face for the Crown Prince later realized the financial impossibility of monopolizing the Games for the benefit of Athens.

It was therefore in Paris that the second Olympiad was celebrated. But Coubertin said secretly to his friends: 'It's a miracle that the Olympic movement survived that celebration!'

Disappointments and difficulties were to begin after the IOC Congress at Le Havre at the beginning of 1897. Sometimes they had nothing directly to do with the Olympic Games; Coubertin's French enemies, officials of the Union of French Athletic Associations (USFSA), of which he had become secretary-general in 1890, were stubbornly contemptuous of the Games and showed their hostility on principle to the Baron's every move. He finally gave up depending on the USFSA to organize the Games. Unfortunately he had the idea of grafting the Olympic Games onto the Universal Paris Exposition of 1900, whose organizer, Alfred Picart, was a conservative official who believed sport to be a useless and absurd activity. He resented 'having an idea thrust on him' and that of incorporating the program of the second Games within the framework of the Exposition upset him.

Before the Congress of 1894 in Paris, Coubertin had proposed a grandiose project to the directors of the 1889 Universal Exposition. He planned to reconstruct the Altis of Olympia, with its temples, statues, gymnasia and stadia. Documents and works of art would be displayed there, landmarks in the history of sport, from ancient times to the present. Outside the Altis would be reproductions of the Roman baths and the Athletic Club of Chicago. The sporting events would take place in these prestigious surroundings. Picart, who succeeded the directors of the Expo 89, thanked Coubertin, filed his plan – and buried it.

But Picart, after an ineffectual move by Alexandre Ribot, former president of the Council, agreed to include 'exhibitions of physical exercises and sports' scattered among the sixteen sections of the Expo, from the Champs-de-Mars to the Cours-la-Reine, and even at Vincennes, which was reserved for the less popular activities. The arrangements were chaotic: skating and fencing came under cutlery, rowing under life-saving, athletics under provident societies!

Coubertin reacted by setting up an organizing committee to establish 'international competitions for the élite'. His mistake was in assembling a committee, the majority of which were counts and marquises, presided over by the Vicomte de la Rochefoucauld. Forty members, of whom eighteen were designated stewards and placed in charge of the various sports, published the program on 29 May 1898; they repeated the program of the Athens Games, augmented by boxing, football and polo; shooting was replaced by archery because it was thought to be more athletic.

This was welcomed enthusiastically, in France and in other countries. Henri Desgrange, who was to found the sporting daily L'Auto, and was at the time director of the cycle-racing stadium of the Parc des Princes at the Auteuil Gate, wrote to Coubertin: 'I have a field of 26,000 square metres, a cycle track of 666 metres, all you need for running and for tennis. I can give you everything except the Seine. . . .' Pierre Giffard's Petit Journal offered to take charge of the swimming competitions, and Pierre Laffitte's Vie au Grand Air offered its columns.

The crash came. On 9 November 1898, the USFSA declared that it would have nothing to do with the organization of a private sports meeting in 1900 but reserved its right to lend its support to an official meeting if undertaken by the State and the City of Paris.

This was echoed by the municipal councillors of Paris, who denounced the 'society of counts and marquises'.

An additional complication arose: the American section of the Exposition sent to Coubertin a high-ranking military man. He wanted Picart's permission to build, in the area reserved for the United States, a stadium in which athletes from the other side of the Atlantic would compete to 'show the other nations what real sport is'. He was unsuccessful; Picart was backed up by the American member of the IOC, William M. Sloane, who disapproved of his fellow countrymen's move.

Eventually, Coubertin resigned from the USFSA. On 22 April 1899, after petty squabbling, the Vicomte de la Rochefoucauld also resigned and the committee voted to dissolve itself.

Twelve months were left before the opening of the Games!

On 19 February 1899, Picart had decided to nominate Daniel Mérillon, president of the Shooting Federation, which was a member of the USFSA, as director-general of the sporting contests at the Exposition. Mérillon finally obtained approval of the plans at the beginning of June 1899.

Coubertin undertook a European tour, to counter suspicions, first from the Germans, who feared hostile demonstrations, then from the British (before the settlement of the 'Fashoda incident' in the Sudan, which had strained relations between the two countries), and also to calm down those who were disconcerted by the incompetence shown by the official sources, which were putting out nothing more than endless rules, regulations and memos.

Finally, it was decided to abandon all the grandiose plans, notably that of using the park of a huge château at Courbevoie, and to go right back to the beginning, to the 1898 plan that the administration had considered at the time to be 'mean and unworthy of the nation'.

The athletic events would be held on the turf of the Racing Club de France, at Croix-Catelan, in the Bois de

Boulogne, and the other competitions in already existing stadia or cycle tracks. Coubertin concluded: 'There was [for these Games] much goodwill but the interesting results had nothing Olympic about them. We have made a hash of our work.'

Born in confusion, the Games rolled on from 20 May to 28 October, comprising an unbelievable muddle of sports, some officially recognized, some not recognized, world amateur championships and professional championships, scattered over the four corners of the capital. Athletics were held in the Bois de Boulogne, swimming at Asnières, yachting at Meulan, fencing at the Tuileries (Palais des Expositions), lawn tennis at the Île de Puteaux, gymnastics at Vincennes, equestrian events at the avenue de Breteuil, cycling at the Parc des Princes, shooting almost everywhere.

There was even a Rugby football match between France and Germany at Vincennes, which made the police work overtime. But the public, forgetting the French defeat in the Franco-Prussian War, applauded both victors and vanquished, all the more happily because the French won, 25–16, or 27–17, depending upon which French newspaper you read the next day. Sophistication in press facilities at the Games did not arrive until several Olympiads later.

There was constant confusion. The public couldn't make head or tail of the events, and nor could the reporters. Even today it is extremely difficult to sort out the wheat from the chaff among the prizewinners. That is why reference books give the yachting results as if they were all entirely official. Association football, polo and Rugby appear only as titles of contests in the official program. Cricket, croquet and golf, if one believes the final decisions of the IOC, were the only official events; there was no boxing; wrestling had disappeared and so had weightlifting.

The number of contestants had increased to 1,319 (including eleven women) as against the 311 at Athens; the number of countries competing had risen to twenty-two from thirteen.

Athletics, which were the main attraction – on average drawing 3,000 spectators each day – were held on the 500-metre grass track of the Croix-Catelan, with very light soil. Although trees got in the way of the discus and hammer, performances achieved a respectable level.

One serious incident marred the beginning of the international competitions scheduled for 14 July, Bastille Day, a national holiday in the Republic. It was feared that spectators would stay away and, without consulting the foreign delegations, the organizers decided to put off the finals planned for 14 July to the next day, a Sunday. Some Americans protested vigorously, on the grounds that it was the Lord's Day. Two of the American competitors in the 1,500 metres withdrew and the United States did not take part in the Prix des Nations, i.e. the 5,000-metres team event.

On 14 July, in the long-jump heats, Myer Prinstein cleared 7.175 m (23 ft 6½ in). He had set the world record of 7.50 m (24 ft 7¼ in) at Philadelphia in June. On that day he beat his great rival, Alvin Kraenzlein, who had held the record in 1898 of 7.24 m (23 ft 9 in), and had jumped 7.43 m (24 ft 4½ in) in 1899.

Because the next day was Sunday, Prinstein was absent, and Kraenzlein won the competition with 7.185 m

(23 ft 6¾ in). On the Monday, Prinstein, learning of this 'betrayal', was so angry that he attacked his rival and hit him with his fist. He consoled himself by taking the triple jump with 14.47 m (47 ft 5¾ in), defeating the victor of the 1896 Games, his compatriot James B. Connolly, later a celebrated journalist and war correspondent of *Collier's*.

Kraenzlein remains, for history, the great star of the 1900 Games. In athletics he took the 60 metres, the 110- and 200-metres hurdles, as well as the long jump.

The other American star of those Games, Ray Ewry, also holds the all-time record for Olympic victories. No fewer than ten from 1896 to 1908 (including 1906) in the standing jump, which was then discontinued. In Paris, he easily took the standing high jump, the standing long jump and the standing triple jump (1.65 m/15 ft 5 in, 3.21 m/10 ft 6½ in, 10.58 m/34 ft 8½ in respectively), each time from the Sioux, Irving Baxter, winner of the running high jump (1.90 m/6 ft 2¾ in) and the pole vault (3.30 m/10 ft 10 in) in the absence on that Sunday of his fellow countrymen Orton and Dvorak, who defeated him easily a few days later. The latter was the first man to use a bamboo pole.

Altogether, the Americans took seventeen of the twenty-three titles. Over 100 metres, the hot favourite Arthur Duffey was beaten by Frank Jarvis (USA) (11.0 sec) from Walter Tewksbury, the winner of the 200-metres (22.2 sec) and the 400-metres hurdles (57.6 sec). Over 400 metres, the crowd were confident of a French victory. But the winner was the American Maxey Long who, that autumn, had at Travers Island lowered the world record for 440 yards to 47.8 sec and then, on the racing track at Guttenberg, New Jersey, that for 440 yards straight to 47 sec.

The middle-distance events were British successes, with Alfred Tysoe over 800 metres, and Charles Bennett over 1,500 metres, the latter threatened by the Frenchman Henri Deloge. In this 1,500 metres, two of the favourites, the Americans Alexander Grant and John Cregan, withdrew. Great Britain completed its success, which became a tradition after that, with the 4,000-metres steeplechase and the team 5,000 metres. Charles Bennett, first in this event, established an official world record for 5,000 metres of 15 min 29.2 sec.

In the throwing events, only the Hungarian Rudolf Bauer, in the discus, provided competition for the Americans. The American John Flanagan, of Irish origin (like Patrick O'Callaghan and John Connolly later), who won the hammer event with 49.73 m (163 ft 2 in), was to be crowned twice more and hold the world record of 56.19 m in 1909.

At last a Frenchman won an event, the marathon. In fact, the winner, Michel Theato, did not learn until twelve years later that he had become an official Olympic champion! He recalled then that in 1900, in suffocating heat, he finished first in a marathon, run through the back streets and mews of Paris in 2 hr 59 min 45 sec. Because of scheduling errors, the course had been obstructed several times and had not been the best organized. An American, Dick Grant, who finished sixth, brought an unsuccessful lawsuit against the IOC, claiming that a cyclist had knocked him down as he was about to overtake the Frenchman.

There were also athletics events for 'non-amateurs'. The famous American Mike Sweeney, who held the high-

1900. *Above* Refreshment for a marathon competitor. *Right, above* Charlotte Cooper (Gt Britain), first woman to win an Olympic title. Below Alvin Kraenzlein (United States), winner of three first prizes.

jump record with 1.97 m (6 ft 5½ in), won the 100 metres, high and long jumps, each endowed with 250 Fr. for the winner) and also the handicap events. And the 400-metres hurdles Olympic champion, Walter Tewksbury, benefiting from a handicap of 4 m, could not keep up with the Indian Norman Pritchard, who, with a 15-m handicap, won in 56 sec.

In about 1965, the French Olympic Committee, in an attempt to count its living Olympic medal holders, and going by a Hungarian book by Dr Ferenc Mező, sponsored by the IOC, discovered that a certain Vasserot, ranked second in the speed cycling event, was still alive. When questioned, the veteran vaguely remembered that he had raced in 1900 on the track at Vincennes. No one had told him at the time that he had taken part in the Olympic Games. He died in 1968 as a 'silver medallist'. More thorough research, undertaken by the Austrian Erich Kamper, confirmed that the gold medal went to the Frenchman Georges Taillandier in that speed event from another Frenchman named Sanz and an American named Lake, the latter having eliminated Vasserot in the semi-final. It is conflicting evidence of this kind which unhappily leaves so many uncertainties in Olympic history.

It is very difficult to place much faith in a roll of honour painfully reconstructed in 1912 and even to take seriously certain competitions like swimming held in the muddy waters of the Seine at Asnières, in a current which swept the champions all over the place.

As for the rowing, this is how the reporter from *Sport Universal* described it: 'This sport was only practised by coarse fellows, noisy, rowdy, who, under the name of boatmen, spread terror among the peaceful riverside inhabitants . . .'

Only gymnastics, in which the Swedes distinguished themselves, found favour with the press, which otherwise hardly mentioned the events.

Monique Berlioux concluded, in her remarkable book *Olympica*, 'The name of Pierre de Coubertin was not mentioned once, by journals or by officials.'

However, during those 1900 Games, in which only the French competed in many events, women's sports made a very timid appearance. Thus, the British Charlotte Cooper, in winning the women's singles lawn-tennis tournament, became the first woman Olympic champion. The runner-up in the final was the French Hélène Prévost, whom Charlotte Cooper defeated 6–1, 6–4. Paired with the famous Reginald Frank Doherty, Charlotte Cooper also won the mixed doubles, from Hélène Prévost and Harold Mahony.

III ST LOUIS 1904 Gaston Meyer

As early as 1894 it had been tacitly agreed that the third Olympic Games should be offered to the young America. On 13 November 1900, the *New York Sun* informed its readers that the Games would be held in Chicago. But James Sullivan, secretary-general of the Amateur Athletic Union, intervened to stop the Games going to Chicago. Sullivan was secretly annoyed that he had not been chosen as a member of the IOC.

Coubertin's French enemies, supporting Messrs de Saint-Clair and Roy in their aim of laying the foundations of an 'International Union', designed to supplant the IOC and to promote future Games, had rallied Sullivan to their cause. Their Games were to take place in 1901 at Buffalo within the framework of the Pan-American Exhibition of which Sullivan was the sports organizer. After Sullivan's pronouncements, Coubertin decided to question, in writing, the people consulted by the American, among them certain members of the IOC. They all supported Coubertin; that was the end of dissidence and of Buffalo's candidature.

The fourth Session of the IOC, held at Paris on 21 May 1901, had therefore to choose between two American candidates, St Louis and Chicago. Before it, William M. Sloane, the American member, obtained from Coubertin an agreement that he would accept the presidency for ten years to strengthen the still frail Olympic Movement.

The IOC was unanimously in favour of Chicago. The Committee decided that the Games should last only twelve days, from 10 to 25 September 1904, and (strangely) 'that the professional events, if there are any, shall be of less importance than the amateur events'.

Meanwhile, St Louis, which was preparing to organize a giant World Fair in 1903, was forced for financial reasons to put it off until 1904. Fearing a clash with the Games at Chicago, it asked for them to be transferred to St Louis, threatening if refused to stage important athletic competitions of its own. Chicago replied in 1902, suggesting that the Games should be put off until 1905, but this Coubertin would not accept. Finally, both parties took the matter to the arbitration of the new president of the United States, Theodore Roosevelt, who was very interested in sport. He opted for St Louis; the IOC agreed, nevertheless regretting that the Games would again be attached to a World Fair, in spite of the very trying experience of 1900.

1904. A crowded 400-metres final, for which the starter perches on a fence for a better view of the field

Was that the reason that Coubertin did not attend the 1904 Games and did not call a Session at St Louis? Or was it because of the difficulties and time taken in travelling? Or was it because of certain problems of protocol? The Americans, dazzled by the aristocracy of old Europe, had virtually insisted upon the presence at St Louis of all those princes, dukes and counts in the IOC, a presence likely to flatter the newly rich. Or perhaps Coubertin felt disappointed, after his first visit, at not encountering the kind of characters and society that his reading of Fenimore Cooper had led him to associate with Missouri and Mississippi.

The third Games suffered a serious setback in the number of participants, both in nations and individual competitors: twelve nations instead of the twenty-two at Paris, 617 athletes as against 1,319. Most of these were Americans, no fewer than 525; there were only ninety-two foreigners, of whom forty-one were from neighbouring Canada. And even these figures include those who took part in demonstration or exhibition matches, notably in basketball, baseball, lacrosse, roque, and motorboating.

St Louis, the cotton capital, founded by French traders, was celebrating the hundredth anniversary of the acquisition of Louisiana by President Thomas Jefferson from Napoleon I for $15 million. In 1904 the city already had a population of 600,000.

That year the world was on the alert. The British navy was mobilized because navigation through the Suez Canal was threatened by the prolonging of the Russo-Japanese War. In that atmosphere, the Olympic celebration did not carry much weight. It even left the rest of the world indifferent. The British sent only one athlete and he was in fact Irish.

The winners of the team sports were: basketball (exhibition), the Buffalo German YMCA (United States); association football, the Gait F.C. of Ontario (Canada); lacrosse, the Shamrock Team of Winnipeg (Canada); water polo, the New York A.C. (United States) – hardly a national selection.

This time, as was to be the case in later years, athletics monopolized attention from 29 August till 3 September. In the pleasant, harmonious surroundings of Washington University, at least 2,000 spectators watched the exploits of the American athletes, under technical conditions which were at last acceptable and on a track of sufficiently good quality, 536.45 m ($\frac{1}{3}$ mile) in length, with a straight stretch of 220 yards.

There was a full program: no fewer than twenty-five competitions, of which one was a team 4-mile (6,437.32-m) event, won by the New York A.C. from the Chicago A.C., and the tug-of-war, won by the Milwaukee A.C. There were only two winners who were not American, the French Canadian policeman from Montreal, Étienne Desmarteau, who won the 56-lb (25.4-kg) weight from New York policeman John Flanagan, and the Anglo-Irishman from the Irish-American Athletic Club of New York, Thomas Kiely, who won the 'all-rounder' championship, forerunner of the decathlon; its program, in one day, consisted of, in succession, 100 yards (91.44 m), shot, high jump, 880-yard walk, hammer, pole vault, 120-yard hurdles, 56-lb weight, long jump and mile! Kiely won the walk in 3 min 59 sec, the 120-yard hurdles in 17.8 sec, the 56-lb weight and the hammer with, respectively, 8.915 m (29 ft 3 in) and 36.75 m (120 ft 6$\frac{1}{2}$ in).

Art in the Olympic Games has been no more widely expressed than through posters

- VIIᵉ OLYMPIADE -
ANVERS (BELGIQUE)
1920 AOUT-SEPTEMBRE 1920

1928
IXᵉ OLYMPIADE
AMSTERDAM

GERMANY
BERLIN-1936
1ᵉ-16ᵉ AUGUST

OLYMPIC GAMES

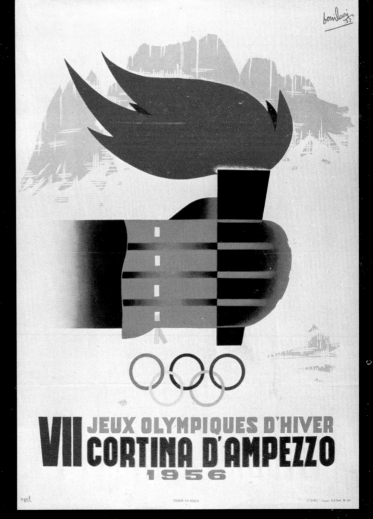

VII JEUX OLYMPIQUES D'HIVER
CORTINA D'AMPEZZO
1956

John Flanagan kept the hammer title, which he had won four years earlier in Paris. Another winner of the preceding Games won again at St Louis: the famous Ray Ewry, champion of all three standing jumps with 1.50 m (4 ft 11 in) in the high jump, 3.47 m (11 ft 4½ in) in the long jump and 10.55 m (34 ft 7½ in) in the triple jump.

There were three other triple winners of these 'American' Games at St Louis: Archie Hahn, known as the 'Milwaukee Meteor', assured himself of the 60 metres (7 sec), the 100 metres (11 sec) and in particular the 200 metres (21.6 sec); in that event, according to the regulations in force at the time, his opponents were all penalized by one yard for committing false starts. But Hahn cleared the line three metres ahead!

James Davies Lightbody, from Chicago but of Scottish origin, only 18 and originally a sprinter, dominated the middle-distance events. On 29 August he won the steeplechase (over 2,500 m) in 7 min 39.6 sec; on 1 September he took the 800 metres in 1 min 56 sec, and finally on 3 September the 1,500 metres in 4 min 5.4 sec, beating Charles Bennett's world record, established in Paris, a performance intrinsically inferior compared with the amateur mile record of Tom Connell (4 min 15.6 sec in 1895) and above all the 4 min 12.75 sec of Walter George, a professional, in 1884.

Harry Hillman, third 'triple winner', assured himself of, in succession, the 400 metres in 49.2 sec, the 200-metres hurdles in 24.6 sec and above all the 400-metres hurdles in 53.0 sec (a 400-metres hurdles, with the obstacles only 76 cm (30 in) high). In that race, George Poage, third, became the first black Olympic medallist.

Two losers of 1900 in Paris gained their revenge in St Louis. Myer Prinstein, with 7.34 m (24 ft 1 in), took the long jump after winning the triple jump with 14.35 m (47 ft 1 in). The absence of the world-record holder, the Irishman Peter O'Connor, was regrettable. His 7.61 m (24 ft 11¾ in) would have been astounding up to Bob Beamon's 8.90 m (29 ft 2½ in) in 1968. When Prinstein and O'Connor met in 1906 in Athens, on the occasion of the tenth anniversary of the revival of the Games, Prinstein outdid his rival, clearing 7.20 m (23 ft 7½ in) against the Irishman's 7.025 m (23 ft 0½ in). Charles Dvorak jumped 3.50 m (11 ft 6 in) in the pole vault. But that was in the absence of the two world-record holders, the American Norman Dole and the Frenchman Fernand Gonder, who had cleared 3.69 m (12 ft 1½ in) the same year. In 1905 Gonder took his record to 3.74 m (12 ft 3½ in).

Another absent Frenchman, Marius Eynard, world-record holder for the discus of 1.923 kg (4¼ lb) with 43.21 m (141 ft 9¼ in) since 1903, relinquished his title to Martin Sheridan. The latter, level with Ralph Rose, a 2-m and 120-kg (264-lb 8-oz or 18-stone 12-lb 8-oz) giant, winner of the shot, defeated him in a throw-off by about five feet (1.52 m) – the only time in Olympic history that a throw-off has decided this event.

Finally, the marathon event, marked with choice incidents, filled the officials with confusion. The contestants numbered thirty-one, nearly all Americans, except the Greek Demeter Velouis (sixth) and the Cuban Felix Carvajal (fifth), who led the race until the twenty-fifth kilometre but then fell behind.

In the stadium, the wait was feverish and the runners behind schedule. In blistering heat, Fred Lorz arrived uncannily cool, hardly a speck of dust on him. He was acclaimed, carried in triumph, and photographed with Alice Roosevelt, daughter of the American President. He appeared a little bewildered by all this ceremony. A quarter of an hour later, the second man appeared, staggering and covered in dust, another American, Thomas Hicks. Second? When the results were announced, the judges and the timekeepers who had followed the course in cars rushed at Lorz. He was vilified, disqualified, struck off the lists, and Hicks was justly acclaimed. Lorz had dropped out of the race at the fifth kilometre; a truck had given him a lift but it had broken down and Lorz, having recovered from his cramp, decided, for a joke, to continue on foot. His story was ultimately believed, and a year later he was allowed to compete again and became US marathon champion in 1905.

As for Hicks's time: 3 hours 28 min 53 sec for 40 km, no better than that of Louis or Theato. Many people realized that Hicks was doped with sulphate of strychnine and cognac, but no one, at that time, dreamed of protesting.

The swimming pool was an asymmetrical lake used in the World Fair and the starting signals were given from a raft. The distances were chaotic and the performances hardly worthy of beach swimmers today. There were peculiar strokes as well, and the plunge for distance, which the American W. E. Dickey won with 19.05 m (62 ft 6 in).

In boxing, the weight categories were indicative of future regulations. Only the Americans took part. It was the same with wrestling.

Coubertin was told of the progress of the Games by the Hungarian Ferenc Kemény, who joined him at Bayreuth. After emphasizing the fine organization, the well-arranged grounds, the respectable performances, but sparse attendance and total misunderstanding of the Olympic spirit, he went on to say: 'I was not only present at a sporting contest but also at a fair where there were sports, where there was cheating, where monsters were exhibited for a joke'. This last was an allusion to two days, called the 'Anthropological Days', on which the competitions were parodied by opposing Patagonians, Filipinos, Ainus, Turks, Coropas from Mexico, American Sioux and Syrians. With a gigantic effort, a pygmy dispatched the regulation weight three metres.

1904. A sponge for Thomas Hicks (United States), the marathon winner. But is Hicks being supported?

1904. Victory in the pole vault for Charles Dvorak (United States) at 3.50 m (11 ft 6 in)

Coubertin, less upset than his informant, made excuses for the Americans, who like children, were seeking sensation rather than the development of sport through the Olympic spirit. He is supposed to have said: 'As for that outrageous charade, it will of course lose its appeal when black men, red men and yellow men learn to run, jump and throw, and leave the white men behind them.'

There was no Olympic Session at St Louis. The sixth Session was held in the banqueting room at the Mansion House, London, put at the disposal of the IOC by the Lord Mayor of London from 20 to 22 June 1904, under the patronage of HM King Edward VII. By a unanimous and solemn vote, after the withdrawal of Berlin's candidature, Rome was announced as the venue for the Games of the fourth Olympiad. But Rome's turn to stage the Games was delayed for over half a century as the Italians had to withdraw their offer.

ATHENS 1906 John Rodda

The gathering of sportsmen in Athens two years after the St Louis Olympics became known as the Interim or Extraordinary Games or the Athenian Games. They do not take an official place in the history of the Movement but they were significant in the slow process of bedding the foundations of modern Olympism.

Coubertin had opposed the Greek plan to have every Olympic Games at Athens but as a compromise he supported the Interim Games (which were also to be held in 1910) but did not give IOC patronage to them.

Coubertin and his committee, unhappy at events in the Games of Paris in 1900 and dismayed at some of the events which came into the Olympic program in St Louis, needed a change of fortune and a reassurance in their aims; the Games at Athens in some ways provided it. But they turned out to be as disappointing as those in St Louis which so many Europeans had missed, for many events were not contested; the program included athletics, weightlifting, wrestling, gymnastics, lawn tennis, association football, fencing, swimming and diving, rowing, shooting (in which there were twelve events) and cycling.

However, it was during the Games in Athens (22 April to 2 May 1906) that the Italians made it known that they would be unable to stage the Olympics in 1908. It was here, at the IOC meeting, that Britain was invited to take over the organization of the 1908 Games and the invitation was accepted. In fact, the British had planned an international sports meeting and it was the organizational structure for this event, much embellished through the birth of the British Olympic Association in 1905, that undertook the work.

1906. The Interim Games. Georgios Aliprantis (Greece) wins the rope climbing.

IV LONDON 1908 John Rodda

The Games of the fourth Olympiad were a significant point of development in the Movement. After the enthusiasm at Athens, the disappointment of Paris and the farce of St Louis, it needed Edwardian England, with its stability and confidence from the bedrock of a flourishing Empire, to restore dignity and credibility.

It was originally intended that the Games should be staged in Rome. Instead the Italians let it be known that they could not sustain their offer and, at Athens in 1906, Lord Desborough was asked by the International Olympic Committee if London could, with only two years remaining, stage the Games. His Lordship soon discovered, through the members of the British Olympic Association, that Britain and London were ready to discharge the task. In fact, the decision to go ahead was taken on 19 November 1906 and the Games opened at Shepherd's Bush on 13 July 1908.

To build a stadium (in which athletics, cycling, swimming, fencing, gymnastics and wrestling took place) within that period and organize the twenty-one sports on the program approved by the IOC was a remarkable feat for that time. But no other country in the world had such a vast sporting expertise. The Amateur Athletic Association had been in existence for thirty years, Henley Royal Regatta much longer, and in these two sports alone there was an organizational experience upon which the Games were to flourish.

The Games provided the first real step towards the competition of women, who had already been playing in the lawn-tennis events but now took part in a demonstration of gymnastics. There was, too, for the first time a winter sport – ice skating.

The British Olympic Association had one piece of good fortune, in coming to an agreement with the organizers of the Franco-British Exhibition who agreed to build an arena for most of the sports. If this was a worthwhile financial arrangement, the Games, in a country which already had the Boat Race, the Derby, Cup Final, Henley, the AAA Championships and the All England (lawn tennis) Championships, were not to find a sporting appetite. The charges for the stadium were initially too high and the publicity the Games received insufficient to bring response. But gradually the news travelled and on the final day, when the marathon was run – one of the hottest days of the English summer as it turned out – there were about 90,000 people in the stadium. Olympism was realized, a little late.

The work of preparation was massive. There were twenty-one separate competitions, each with separate books of rules which had to be translated into French and German; the working out of each program, accepting the correct definitions of amateurism for each sport and defining what was meant by the term 'country' – all these were in those days the responsibility of the Organizing Committee; even the use of the metric system in a place where the Imperial measure was king presented difficulties.

The pace and efficiency of the British Olympic Association's work impressed the IOC at its meeting in The Hague in May 1907. Many decisions were taken then, two of lasting significance, that a gold medal should be awarded to each winner, and 'the principle of English

judges, with power to appoint foreign assistants was carried unanimously'. Coubertin was a supporter of this idea and came to rue it. The belief that the British, judges and adjudicators in so many facets of life, could be impartial in sport was destroyed in many eyes at these Games. The Americans believed that they were particularly hard done by and on their return home criticism of the British was flowing. The bitterness reached a point where the British published a book, *Replies to Criticism of the Olympic Games*.

At this period there was great animosity between many British and American institutions, with one regarded as a young, brash, boasting country and the other staid, snobbish and second best at most things.

James Sullivan, the leading American official, led the foray: 'They [the officials] were unfair to the Americans, they were unfair to every athlete except the British but their real aim was to beat the Americans. Their conduct was cruel and unsportsmanlike and absolutely unfair.' And one American newspaper greeted the victorious Americans on their arrival with 'despite the foul play of the British'.

The sixty-page book published by the British Olympic Association to reply to the tirade which came across the Atlantic dealt mostly with the Halswelle affair (see below) but it was set out with quotations from the Americans on one side of the page and dignified British replies on the other. Relationships between the athletic associations of the two countries were, as a result, broken off.

The restrictions of sports and entries were by today's standards of a curious kind. In most individual sports twelve was the maximum number of entries allowed for any one country. Cricket was removed from the program 'for it is not widely played' but there were positive reflections of the Victorian and Edwardian sporting order, rather than Coubertin's educative objectives. Polo, rackets and *paume* (tennis, as distinct from lawn tennis) were included, but the antithesis of the Coubertin spirit was surely to be discovered in Southampton Water – with motorboat racing. There were apparently seven boats racing for three gold medals. In fact racing was postponed from the middle of July to the end of August because the Duke of Westminster's crack 40-footer *Wolseley-Siddeley* (a commercial name which would not be tolerated in present-day Games) was in the United States racing for the British International Cup. However, the delay did not bring the Duke his Olympic gold medal. After one race was abandoned because of bad weather, three boats went from their moorings for the last race of the competition. *Daimler II* gave up before the start with engine trouble. *Wolseley-Siddeley* got away to a sound start and, after two laps of the course, was leading *Camille* (France), which started late, by almost a lap. The Duke's gold medal seemed safe but then on the third circuit His Grace went too close to Hamble Spit and 'went high and dry on the soft mud' and so *Camille*, at a speed of 18.3 knots in poor weather, went on to win.

There was, however, a far more serious contribution to the development of sport and the Olympic Movement in the Games of 1908. Events at the stadium at Shepherd's Bush were dramatic, held in the presence of members of the Royal Family, and provided an indelible piece of Olympic history in the disqualification of Dorando Pietri (Italy) in the marathon.

1908. Banquet for Olympic competitors and officials at the Holborn Restaurant, London

Dorando, who had always been close to the leaders and saw several of them pass him and then drop out, reached the stadium in an exhausted state. The large crowd had expected to see the figure of Charles Hefferon (South Africa) come on to the track, but he had been overtaken by Dorando just outside the stadium. The Italian's equilibrium was broken apparently by the change from running on the flat ground to the slope into the stadium; this, and the fact that he turned right into the arena rather than left, took his distress to the point of collapse. The fact that like many competitors he had probably taken some form of strychnine was a contributory factor towards the collapse. Doctors attended him on the track and he was revived, but the enormous well of feeling for a man who had undergone such an ordeal precluded his immediate disqualification by removal from the track, which should have happened. Instead Dorando tottered to the line, again receiving help, to tremendous applause.

The second man to finish was John Joseph Hayes of the United States, who had also overtaken Hefferon, and the Americans duly lodged an objection which, surprisingly, took some time to consider because of conflicting evidence. But Hayes was declared the winner, while for two and a half hours Dorando was close to death. He recovered and later received an enormous gold cup from Queen Alexandra, whose gesture expressed the feelings of most spectators. The event and its attendant publicity caused a spate of marathon contests in the years that followed.

The 400 metres produced a disqualification and a sad final, twenty-six-year-old Wyndham Halswelle taking part alone in a re-run of the final after J. C. Carpenter, one of three Americans in a four-man final, had been disqualified for obstruction. Entering the final straight, Halswelle challenged to take the lead but Carpenter moved out, from the inside edge, preventing Halswelle from passing and making the British runner move across the track. Part of the acrimony which arose from this incident – the three Americans declined to take part in the re-run – was due to the difference in racing rules between the countries, an anomaly which was to be removed in international competition by the formation of the Inter-

national Amateur Athletic Federation four years later. Halswelle was probably the best runner in the field, for having recorded 48.4 sec in winning the AAA title, he repeated the time in the second round of the Games competition to set an Olympic record.

Forrest Smithson (United States) gave an indication of reaching a peak for a specific event. Before the Games he had not recorded times as fast as his American rivals, but at Shepherd's Bush he ran 15.8 sec, 15.4 sec and then 15.0 sec, a world record, in winning the 110-metres hurdles title. The 400-metres hurdles was of similar quality, Charles Bacon bringing the United States another gold medal with a time of 55.0 sec, which was then superior to the Imperial distance record, 56.1 sec. Melvin Sheppard (United States) became the only double gold medal winner in individual athletics events at the Games by taking the 800 metres by the convincing margin of nine yards and the 1,500 metres.

One event in which British traditions were upheld was the 3-mile team race, where six of the first seven men to finish were Britons. Joe Deakin, the winner, lived in London and was still running up to the week of his death, aged 93, in 1972.

In the field events Ray Ewry added to his collection of gold medals with two from the standing broad jump and standing high jump, and the only non-American winner in the field was Timothy Ahearne of the United Kingdom in the running hop, step and jump. John Flanagan kept the hammer title he won in St Louis, beating his own Olympic record with 51.92 m (170 ft 4¼ in). There were more disgruntled Americans after the first round of the tug-of-war, an event with which they were not familiar. In their heat against the Liverpool Police, at the word 'heave' the Americans were, to quote a correspondent, 'pulled over with a rush'; they then withdrew from the competition. Some Americans thought that the heavy boots which the British team wore produced an unfair advantage. There was a protest but it was not upheld. However, if heavy boots were within the Olympic spirit, was the fact that the winning British team (City of London Police) had been training together for five months?

Swimming advanced to an international orderliness as the result of the Games. The pool, specially erected in the middle of the main stadium, was 100 metres long. The program was of six races, two diving competitions and water polo. Many of the countries taking part met during the Games to form the International Swimming Federation. One of the best races was the 400 metres, in which Frank Beaurepaire (Australia) stayed with Henry Taylor (Great Britain), who had been second at Athens in 1906, but finally was beaten by three yards. Taylor also won the 1,500 metres and took a gold medal in the 4 × 200-metres relay.

The attitudes and spirit of the day among the competitors were reflected in a diving incident. D. F. Cane, of Great Britain, one of the best divers, fell flat into the water in his semi-final stage, having attempted a double somersault. He was so badly shaken that he spent several days in bed and could not complete the competition; yet the Swedes, to indicate their belief in his talents, presented him with a silver cup.

The supremacy of British rowing was seen at Henley where all the gold medals in the four races were won by

1908. 200-metres breaststroke final in the swimming pool set in the middle of the athletics arena

oarsmen of the host country. There were plenty of exciting moments for the large crowds. In the sculling final, Harry Blackstaffe overcame Alexander McCulloch, also of Great Britain, but it was not until the last 50 yards of the lengthened course – 1½ miles (2,414 m) as against the traditional Henley one of 1 mile 550 yards (1,198 m) – that Blackstaffe got away. It was a remarkable peak to a career, for his first sculling success, winning the London Cup, had been achieved eleven years earlier, and he had won most of the sculling prizes including the Diamonds and the Netherlands Championship. In the year of his Olympic victory he was forty.

Perhaps one of the more poignant events of the Games was the final of the eights, which still holds its place as one of the great contests over this famous stretch of water. A Leander crew of experienced men faced Belgium, which in the two previous years had won the Grand in such fashion as to challenge the very concept of British rowing. In that Leander crew was Charles Burnell, whose son (a contributor to this book) was to win a gold medal at the 1948 Olympics. In the bow of the umpire's launch was Coubertin. Leander led from the first stroke, but the attack and counter-attack of the race went on with such rapidity that many observers in the grandstands thought that one crew would crack completely; eventually the Belgians conceded when really they had nothing left, but defeat by two lengths sounds unjust to their ability and application.

The boxing was heavily dominated by the British, who won all the gold medals and all the silver except one, won by Reginald Baker (Australia) in the middleweight division. Dick Gunn, at the age of thirty-eight, won the featherweight title, having taken the ABA championships of 1894, 1895 and 1896 when he retired to serve on the ABA Council. But if the eight-year rest had cost him hitting power none of the skill was missing.

The weather of July 1908 was often worse than its normal brutishness for an English summer; the cyclists suffered, lawn-tennis players slipped about the All England courts and in fact transferred to indoor courts, and if there were those who returned home dissatisfied, London's contribution had shown the Olympic Movement the enormity of the tasks which lay ahead. The 1908 Games were the first in which entries were restricted, but there was still a need for administrative regulations relating to entries and closing dates, and, above all, international regulations which were understood and accepted generally. London, though, as it was to do in even more bleak circumstances forty years later, had provided an Olympic Games which were an important juncture in the Movement's life. Stockholm and Sweden learned much from the events at Shepherd's Bush in the summer of 1908; they had four years in which to prepare for the next Games and solve many of the problems.

1908. Dorando Pietri (Italy), who was to be disqualified, running through Willesden during the marathon

V STOCKHOLM 1912 The Rt Hon. Philip Noel-Baker

The Stockholm Games were an enchantment – the word was Coubertin's, in the speech with which he brought them to a close. As a competitor, I thought them an enchantment and looking back, six decades, two World Wars and twelve Olympiads later, my memories enchant me still.

Partly, no doubt, it was discovering Sweden. Landing in Gothenburg, soon after the dawn of a lovely summer day, travelling by train through woods and lakes and past smiling Scandinavian farms, the charm and the excitement of our adventure grew upon us hour by hour. But it was the Games themselves, the great concourse of the teams from all the continents, the thrill and fascination of the contests, the sheer beauty of the spectacle they offered – it was these that captured our imaginations and our hearts. We went to Stockholm as British athletes; we came home Olympians, disciples of the leader, Coubertin, with a new vision which I never lost.

In 1912 not everything was as it is today. There was no Olympic Village. The teams lived in different quarters scattered around the town. The Americans were in the transatlantic liner which had brought them from New York; we thought the ship was marvellous when we went to visit them; they thought it far too cramped and small.

The British team were in a two-star hotel which formed one side of a rocky canyon, through which electric trams began to thunder at 5 a.m. We slept several in a room. The meals were ample, nourishing, but not exciting, as Scandinavian menus almost always are.

None of this mattered to us in the least. We were young; we were comfortable enough; there were no complaints to worry the managers of the team. And the moment we walked out of the hotel, we found that Stockholm had a powerful attraction that was all its own – grass and roses at almost every turn; the lovely waterfront, bathed, as I remember, every day in glittering sun; the Royal Palaces; Skansen, to us a new kind of national park; and not least the forest, then close around the city, where we went in the evenings to dance with sedate but friendly and very pretty Swedish girls. Everyone in Stockholm was eager to give us help. The Games were Sweden's great chance in international affairs, and every Swede was resolved to do his share.

There was another reason why the Stockholm Games were an enchantment, and why they remain a landmark in Olympic history. In his opening speech, in the Swedish Parliament, and with the Crown Prince of Sweden in the chair, Coubertin spoke with sharp resentment of the 'unjustified and mischievous opposition' which the IOC had had to face for many years. He said that even in Stockholm he could find 'traces of a last ditch which a belated hostility sought to dig beneath our feet'.

In London in 1908 there had been 'incidents', errors by officials, which the vultures of the chauvinist Press had been able to exploit. In Stockholm there were no incidents, no protests, nothing to allow disloyal critics to pretend that quarrels had occurred. Before the Games had ended the opposition to the Olympic Movement largely died away. The Games were what Coubertin had planned and believed that they would be – a great international festival of sporting friendship and goodwill.

In London, four years before, teams from twenty-two countries had taken part; the competitors numbered 2,035. In Stockholm, there were teams from twenty-eight countries; and the teams were larger. According to the official Swedish records of the Games, there were 3,889 competitors, a figure which includes the gymnasts of Sweden and other Scandinavian countries whose demonstrations helped to spread gymnastics around the world. This increase since the Games in London shows the great momentum which the Olympic Movement had begun to gain. In every sport in the Stockholm program the performance of the teams reflected this notable advance.

As at each celebration of the Games, athletics, for the competitors and for the public, took pride of place. The stadium had been specially built; it was used for the first time in May 1912. We thought it beautiful, as it still is, and technically perfect in plan. The cinder track, and the jumping pits and throwing circles, were designed and laid by a veteran British groundsman, Charles Perry, who had also laid the track in Athens for the 1896 Games and many others. The performances in the Games were worthy of these preparations. There were new records, and splendid contests, in almost every track and field event.

There were many men whom I recall as splendid athletes. But one runner, by his achievements, stood above the rest: Hannes Kolehmainen of Finland. Kolehmainen, in the space of a few days, won his heat and the final of the 5,000 metres; the 10,000 metres, for which no heats were run; the 8-kilometre cross-country race; and his heat of the 3,000-metre team race (the first three runners home to count). Finland did not qualify for the final of the team

1912. The most dramatic finish of the Games. Hannes Kolehmainen (Finland) about to overtake Jean Bouin (France) in the last 30 metres of the 5,000 metres

race, or no doubt Kolehmainen would have won that, too.

Sometimes a single race can ensure the triumph of an athletic meeting. This happened with the 5,000-metres final in the Stockholm Stadium. Kolehmainen was happy and smiling, a generous competitor and a modest winner. Jean Bouin was a handsome, jolly young Frenchman, already, as was evident, on cordial terms with Kolehmainen. The Swedish public took them both to their hearts. In the 5,000-metres final, these two raced away together from the gun; there was soon a large gap between them and the remainder of the field. All the way, for twelve and a half laps, they ran together, passing and repassing one another, as each tried in vain to break away. When the bell rang for the last lap, the great crowd, cheering both of them, were delirious with excitement; when they reached the final straight, Scandinavian solidarity prevailed, the spectators roared a thunderous encouragement for the Finn. Down the straight they ran side by side, first one and then the other pulling a few centimetres ahead. Perhaps my personal affection for Kolehmainen makes me remember that 5,000 metres as the most exciting race I ever saw.

I remember something else about it. In London the Finnish team had not been allowed to carry a flag in the opening parade. Finland was still part of the Russian Empire, and the Tsarist Government had insisted that they must carry the Russian flag – or none. They carried none.

In Stockholm, the Russian flag still went up for Kolehmainen's victory; and, as I shook his hand and thumped him on the back after the 5,000 metres, he turned and pointed at the flagpole and said: 'I would almost rather not have won, than see that flag up there.' He was wrong. What flag it was they hoisted was instantly forgotten; his glorious race with Bouin had struck a resounding blow for the nationalism, and in due course for the independence, of the Finns.

There were other outstanding people on the track in Stockholm: Ralph Craig, who won both the sprints, and who turned up again in London in 1948 as the Captain of the US yachting team; Hans Braun, of Munich, who was beaten by inches in the 400 metres, and who, with luck, might have won the 800 metres; he was a marvellously graceful runner, a very gifted sculptor; he survived three years in the trenches in France and Flanders, only to be shot down and killed in a fighter aircraft in the last month of World War I; Ted Meredith, a Philadelphia schoolboy, who won the 800 metres in a new world-record time; Ralph Rose, who weighed 250 lb (113.40 kg), who won the two-handed shot for the United States, and who was popularly reported to eat two pounds of steak for breakfast, together with six eggs in their shells. Arnold Strode-Jackson, an Oxford undergraduate in his second year, who had run hardly any first-class races before he came to Stockholm, won the 1,500-metres final; he defeated a team of world-record-beating American milers, in a new Olympic time. Jackson was a man of immense courage and iron will-power; in World War I he was wounded four times; four times he was awarded the Distinguished Service Order for exceptional gallantry in action. On both sides of the Atlantic, he became a legendary figure for his feats on the track and on the battlefield.

There was, too, another man who was to become a legend in his own lifetime, Jim Thorpe, an Indian whose

1912. Jim Thorpe (United States), who won the pentathlon but was later disqualified

mother was from the Potawatome tribe and named her son Bright Path and whose father was from the Sac and Fox tribe. Thorpe made a great impression on my mind and fully deserved the accolade of the greatest all-round athlete. He won the pentathlon by a massive margin, finishing first in four of the events, and then the decathlon with a score of 8,412.96 points, nearly 700 more than the second man. 'Sir,' said the King of Sweden, when presenting him with his prize, 'you are the most wonderful athlete in the world.' Thorpe's running, jumping and throwing seemed to me those of a superman.

But I remember, too, the indignation I felt when, on what I thought was a purely technical offence, he was disqualified in January of the following year and declared a professional, his name being removed from the Olympic records. It was discovered that he had been paid for playing baseball – $60 for a month. But when confronted with this sin against Olympism, Thorpe, a quiet, unassuming man, did not deny it. In fact, he did not believe he had done anything wrong. 'I did not play for the money, I played because I liked baseball,' he said.

Nothing like the track and field events in Stockholm had ever happened in athletic history before. They gave a golden glamour to the Games in the eyes of all men and women in every land. Next in prestige to athletics was the association football tournament. It was after Stockholm, and thanks to its exciting matches and the teams' demonstrations of football skill, that the game spread rapidly around the world – first in Scandinavia, but soon elsewhere – only twelve years later the Olympic champions came from Uruguay.

In Stockholm there were eleven teams, all from Europe. Britain and Denmark were notably stronger than the rest, and they fought out the final before 25,000 spectators, Britain winning by 4 goals to 2. Each side had a player of worldwide renown. Vivian Woodward, England's Captain, had already, as an amateur among professionals, earned a reputation, first with Tottenham Hotspurs, and then with Chelsea, as the finest centre-forward in the world. His artistry, and his deadly shooting, were a feature of every game. Nils Middelboe of Denmark showed a skill and versatility that were rare; he moved up from half-back to centre-forward in the final, and beat the British goalkeeper with a brilliant goal. When these tournaments were finished, association football and FIFA were on their way to their present universality and fame.

The same was true of gymnastics, which after Stockholm were firmly established as a major Olympic sport. Thirteen nations entered teams totalling 1,275 men and women gymnasts. Five days were allotted to the contests and the displays, which all took place in brilliant sunshine in the athletics stadium.

All the Scandinavian countries, Italy, Germany and others sent large and well-trained teams of men. Among the contests were obligatory exercises on the parallel bars, on the horizontal bar, on the pommelled vaulting horse, and on the rings. The men performed prodigies of skill and strength on all this apparatus; Italy won the gold medals, in the individual (Alberto Braglia) and the team events.

I was deeply impressed by the magnificent physique of the men gymnasts, and by their strength, their skill, their discipline. But, as so often in gymnastics, it was the women who stole the show. I remember the teams of Scandinavian girls, dressed in colourful and lovely costumes, who gave displays of disciplined collective movement which had the beauty of the ballet, and which seemed somehow imbued with the glorious national spirit of the free and democratic nations of the North. It was not surprising that in the following years the gymnastic system of the Swedish master, Per Henrik Ling, 'based upon the sports and pastimes of the Swedish Vikings', spread rapidly to many other countries, far and near.

In Stockholm swimming also came into its own. The sensation of the swimming pool was a competitor from Honolulu, Duke Kahanamoku. He only won a single gold medal, for the 100-metres freestyle sprint. He also swam as anchor man for the United States in the 4 × 200-metres relay. But his truly magnificent physique, the perfection of his sophisticated crawl, his victory by a wide margin and his exuberant and friendly character, made him a most popular figure in the pool, in the stadium and in the streets of Stockholm.

Swimming was more truly international than it had been before. There were eighteen national teams and 313 swimmers; the swimming pool was popular with the public, and the Olympic contests had gained in 'atmosphere' and in prestige.

In the men's races, it became apparent that Australia and Japan would be bringing strong teams to future Games. In Stockholm, too, women, for the first time, were allowed to swim; their participation was a huge success, with the competitors and the public alike. In the platform diving, Swedish women took seven of the first eight places; an English girl (Isabelle White) broke the sequence.

In wrestling there were teams from seventeen nations; the official Swedish Report of the Games said that the entries were 'simply enormous' and that 'the modern technique of wrestling has been going up enormously during the last few years. Everybody following the wrestling of the 1912 Games can testify to the truth of this assertion.'

The Finns were very much 'top nation' in the wrestling contests. They took three gold medals out of five. In the fifth event, the light heavyweight, a Swede, Anders Ahlgren, wrestled with a Finn, Ivar Böhling, for nine hours, without either of them being able to get a fall. At that point the Judges declared the match a draw, and awarded no gold medal, but two silvers instead.

The modern pentathlon was a new event in the Olympic program, introduced at the instance of Coubertin. The five contests were shooting; swimming (300 metres); fencing; cross-country riding; and cross-country running (4,000 metres).

As the contests were spread over five days, they were, for well-trained men, more a test of widely differing skills than of great physical endurance. In the first event, shooting, the Swedes swept the board, taking the three first places. In the swimming race in the Olympic pool, Britain was first and sixth, but there were three Swedes in between. The fencing was spread over two days, but even so, it was a strenuous affair: a Swede was first, with twenty-four wins (that is twenty-four separate fights!); a Frenchman second with twenty-three. In the cross-country riding, the Swedes took the first five places, and they did almost as well in the cross-country running.

1912. The first photo-finish equipment to be used at the Olympic Games

1912. More women in the Olympic arena. A display by Finnish women gymnasts

As the final placings in the modern pentathlon depended on the results of the running, and as the start and finish were in the stadium, it might have been an exciting and exhilarating spectacle. Some of the drama was taken out of it, however, by the decision that the competitors should start at one-minute intervals. The first man home was Gösta Åsbrink of Sweden, who covered the 4-kilometre course in 19 min 01 sec. Swedes were second and fourth, with George Smith Patton of the United States (who later became a famous General in World War II) third, exactly 60 sec slower than Åsbrink.

In the light of what is said above, it is not surprising that Sweden took all the medals. But the order of these medallists was surprising; first was G. M. Lilliehöök, whose best individual placings were fourth in the riding, and fifth in the cross-country run. The silver medallist was Åsbrink, and the bronze was Georg de Laval.

There were no track cycle races but a road time trial which the Swedish Official Report called 'a veritable epoch in the history of cycle racing'. The course chosen was that of an annual Swedish event – 320 kilometres (199 miles) long. There were 121 starters, of whom ninety-three finished the course. They were dispatched at 2-minute intervals, the first at 2 a.m., the last precisely 5 hours later, at 7 a.m. The individual winner was Rudolf Lewis of South Africa in 10 hr 42 min 39.0 sec.

Towards the end of the Games, the visiting teams were amazed to see the stadium converted, in a single night, into an arena for the equestrian events – hedges, ditches, gates and all the rest. It was a demonstration of the thoroughness and the efficiency with which the Swedish Olympic Committee had prepared the Games. Much of the satisfaction which the teams derived from their events, and much of the general harmony that prevailed, was due to the care and the imagination of the Swedish hosts.

The equestrian cross-country course was thirty-three miles long; the weather was hot, and the ground was hard. But by good fortune all went well. In the three-day event, in the dressage, in the show jumping, the Swedes almost cleared the board. They captured four gold medals out of five; a Frenchman, Jean Cariou, got the fifth.

The Stockholm Games were everything that Coubertin had desired that they should be. There were no 'incidents' or protests. The endemic chauvinist hostility, which for twenty years had been a festering sore, was temporarily silenced. In the stadium, in the pool, in every sports hall, the Olympic spirit had begun to live. The athletes had begun to know each other, and to fraternize. The officials of the national teams and of the international sporting federations had begun to form a close and powerful community of friends. Sweden had done the Olympic Movement proud; the Olympic Movement had brought Sweden an added prestige and an added glamour in the world society of states.

All this made Stockholm 1912 a decisive milestone in the history of the Olympic Games. On the last night of the Games, the Swedish organizers gave the teams and their leaders and officials a magnificent banquet in the stadium where the athletics, the gymnastics and the equestrian events had taken place. It was a fitting climax to the greatest Olympiad there had been. It furthered, as it symbolized, the unity and the fraternity of the sportsmen of the world.

It was at this banquet that Coubertin made his closing speech. As was his custom, he ended by saluting the nation who would be the hosts of the next Games:

A great people [Germany had been chosen for 1916] has received the torch of the Olympiads from your [Swedish] hands, and has thereby undertaken to preserve, and, if possible, to quicken its precious flame . . . . May it [the sixth Olympiad] contribute, like its illustrious predecessors, to the general welfare and to the betterment of humanity! May it be prepared in the fruitful labours of peaceful times! May it be celebrated, when the day comes, by all the peoples of the world in gladness and concord.

There was a transcendent purpose in that great man's mind, which, to those who understood the facts of the international situation of 1912, and who saw the gathering storm clouds, shone out like a beacon through our golden Stockholm days.

VI BERLIN (Cancelled) 1916 John Rodda

At that point where modern Olympism had begun to walk with a firm step – at Stockholm for the celebration of the fifth Olympiad in 1912 – Europe moved towards turmoil.

The candidates for the sixth Games were Berlin, Budapest and Alexandria; Coubertin, and other members of the IOC, aware of the clouds of war and of Germany's navalism and militarism believed that if Berlin were to be awarded the Games war might be averted. Coubertin was aware that there were strong forces in Germany which wanted peace and that, while the Kaiser liked the idea of military power, he had a personal aversion to the thought of war. The Games at Stockholm had brought the Swedes vast, prestigious publicity. The Games for Berlin, Coubertin felt, might help the Kaiser to find support for his more peaceful inclinations.

Thus at the IOC session in Stockholm during the Games, when the candidates for the next Games came up for discussion, Coubertin's influence was seen. Jules de Muzsa, the member in Hungary, waived claim in favour of Germany; he was supported and Berlin was adopted unanimously.

The Germans, like their opponents, believed that the war would be short and in 1914 they did not withdraw from staging the Games. But as time passed the hopes of a Games in Berlin diminished. First Coubertin came under pressure to have the Games in either Scandinavia or the United States, but he declined to take this sort of initiative so long as Germany had not given up the mandate because he believed that it would further damage the Olympic Movement. He established that if an Olympiad was not celebrated it would, like the Ancient Games in Greece, still maintain its number.

War, of course, cut deep into Olympic loyalties. Theodore Cook, an IOC member in Britain, asked that the German members be expelled from certain international academic and scientific groups. Coubertin felt that this would be unwise and after consulting other members rejected the motion and Cook resigned. It was an uneasy time for the IOC for its role and future seemed uncertain. Coubertin wanted to give up the presidency but when war came he decided to stay on; in fact he took a most useful, positive step in 1915, setting up the headquarters of the Movement in Lausanne, where he had a home.

As early as its meeting in June 1914, the IOC had considered Antwerp as a candidate for 1920, which, as the carnage of man's nobility dragged on, was seen as the most appropriate place for the youth of the world to gather in more peaceful ways.

VII ANTWERP 1920 The Rt Hon. Philip Noel-Baker

Coubertin was deeply afflicted by the tragedy of the war, and by the blank Olympiad of 1916. 'Berlin' was written on his heart. But defeat never made Coubertin defeatist. He resolved that, although the date would be barely twenty months after the end of World War I, the seventh Olympiad should be celebrated at the due and proper time. A few weeks after the guns were silenced, he assembled the International Olympic Committee in Lausanne, and they decided that the Games should be in Antwerp in August 1920.

The decision was, of course, intended as a tribute of honour to the gallant Belgians, who had been the victims of unprovoked aggression five years before; it was universally popular throughout the world. But it imposed a heavy burden on the Belgian organizers. Belgium had by no means recovered from the war. After four years of struggle and of enemy occupation, they had not even in 1920 repaired the damage in the battle zone, where lovely, medieval towns like Ypres and Furnes had been totally destroyed. To prepare the stadia and the sports halls needed for the various Olympic sports, to provide for the accommodation of the teams, to arrange the social and ceremonial occasions, including royal visits, and to do all this within eighteen months of the armistice and national reconstruction, was a truly Herculean task.

By Herculean efforts, it was admirably carried out. With great difficulties to overcome, the Belgian organizers built a splendid stadium for the athletics and association football; excellent pools for the swimming and the diving; excellent grounds or sports halls for the contests; and they provided accommodation – living quarters – for the teams which I remember with lively pleasure still.

The accommodation was in the Antwerp City Schools. The catering and the food – to athletes most important – were very good; the Belgian personnel who served us were kind and willing; we were given – again important – admirable beds, eight to a classroom. It has always been a happy memory that I slept next to Bevill Rudd – he was South African, but he chose to live with the British team. The cheerful temper of the team, in our bedrooms, and at meals in the school assembly hall, made our communal life very pleasant and very welcome to us all.

The Commandant of our British team, Brigadier Kentish, D.S.O., managed to provide us with some Scottish pipers. Clad in their kilts, they performed on their bagpipes on all probable and improbable occasions. They were a source of pride to us, and of delight to all our foreign visitors.

Even more important, the Brigadier found a first-class dance band. We invited teams from other countries to evening parties, at which the school playground was our dance floor. I remember in particular a splendid evening with the Swedes, which helped me to forget the worry of the 1,500-metres heats on the following day.

There was the same feeling of relief, of release, that there was to be at Wembley after World War II. The four endless, wasted years of battle were behind us. The world had turned, and we turned with it, to better, happier things. So we all greatly enjoyed ourselves in Antwerp. But we treated our Olympic contests with the serious concentration which they required and deserved.

1920. Charley Paddock (United States) begins celebrating his 100-metres win before reaching the finish.

As always, the Opening of the Games drew an enormous crowd to the stadium. The ceremony was performed by the King of the Belgians, King Albert, an ardent mountaineer, who lost his life in a climbing accident in 1934. His wife, Queen Elizabeth, was by his side and Cardinal Mercier was there, too, to bless the Games. They were all three held in such esteem throughout the world that their presence gave a special distinction to the day. Cardinal Mercier also held a Requiem Mass of Remembrance in Antwerp Cathedral for those who had lost their lives on active service in the war.

The parade of the teams was as colourful as that in 1912, and a great deal smarter. Many competitors had learned of marching during the preceding years.

Anyone who now judges the performance in the running events should make allowance for the track. The Belgians had worked miracles in the preparation of the Games but they had not succeeded in laying the world's fastest track. The track was slow and heavy. When it rained, there were ruts and depressions in its surface; it was a constant worry to the runners from first to last.

To those who had been in Stockholm, there were tragic gaps in the ranks of the athletes – many, like the great Jean Bouin of France, and the great Hans Braun of Germany, had lost their lives on active service.

But there were some survivors. Among them, Hannes Kolehmainen was most eminent. Eight years after Stockholm, he rounded off his magnificent career by a victory in the marathon. Nobody had expected that he could win. There was a strong field; among the most fancied were Christian Gitsham (South Africa), who had been second in Stockholm, Yuri Lossman (Estonia), and Valerio Arri (Italy).

Kolehmainen showed his serious intentions from the start. He was running second at 5 kilometres, and again at 15 kilometres; between those distances he was never further back than fourth; at 30 kilometres, he took the lead, and held it to the tape. His was, I think, the most popular victory in Antwerp; I remember still the cheers that he received when he came first into the stadium. Apart from him, the experts had not been so wrong: the Estonian, Lossman, came next, outsprinting Arri for second place; Arri, to show how fresh he was, turned three somersaults on the track as he crossed the finishing line.

There were other Finns in Antwerp, worthy to belong to Kolehmainen's team. There was Paavo Nurmi, paradoxically, on his first appearance, defeated. A Frenchman, Joseph Guillemot, followed close behind him in the 5,000 metres until they were half-way down the final straight; then he gained a lead with a sudden spurt which Nurmi could not overtake. Guillemot, who had been the victim of poison gas in the war, thus avenged France for the defeat of Bouin in Stockholm eight years before.

But that was neither the end of Nurmi nor of the Finns. Three days later, Nurmi won the 10,000 metres, doing to his conqueror, Guillemot, precisely what Guillemot had done to him. Then he won the individual title in the 8-kilometre cross-country race, and with his compatriots won the team cross-country championship for Finland as well.

Another Finn, Eero Lehtonen, took first place in the pentathlon – long jump, javelin, discus, 200 metres, 1,500 metres (no longer on the program). Lehtonen was to win the same event again, with better performances, in Paris in 1924. Finland took all three medals at Antwerp in the javelin – such a thing had never happened in any field event before.

In the discus, and in the shot again, Finns were first and second. The names of Elmer Niklander, Armas Taipale and Ville Pörhölä were to be famous later on. Antwerp was the start of Finnish pre-eminence in track and field, which reached its zenith eight years later at the Games in Amsterdam.

The United States also had its share of track and field successes. Almost as a matter of course, Americans were first and second in both the sprints: Charles William Paddock, Allen Woodring and Morris Marshall Kirksey. Likewise they won the 4 × 100-metres relay. They could claim six medals out of six for the two hurdle races: the 110 metres and 400 metres. All the six hurdlers were trained and educated in the United States, although one of them, Earl Thomson, who won the 110-metres hurdles and had learned everything he knew at Dartmouth College, N.H., had chosen to run instead for Canada, where he had been born.

The United States also won the 3,000-metres team race: it came second in the 800 metres (Earl Eby from Philadelphia) and in the steeplechase (Patrick Flynn); third in the 1,500 metres (Lawrence Shields, the US University Champion). Americans were first and second in the high jump; first and third in the pole vault; first and third in the hammer; second in the decathlon; second in the long jump.

Any other nation would have been immensely proud of such results. The Americans thought it a rather moderate success. But the standard of their achievement was shown by the fact that every athlete of any other nationality

1920. Two medal-winning children: fourteen-year-old Aileen Riggin (United States) took the springboard diving and Nils Skoglund (Sweden), thirteen, the silver in the plain high diving.

thought that, if he had beaten an American in his event, he had not come to Antwerp in vain.

As in Stockholm, other Scandinavians besides the Finns did well. The Swedes were prominent in almost everything; their most distinguished track success was achieved by Nils Engdahl, who won the bronze medal in the 400 metres, beating all the Americans. They were first and third in the long jump (William Pettersson and Erik Abrahamsson); third (the famous Bo Ekelund) in the high jump; and gained medals in other field events.

The Italians had two splendid walkers, Ugo Frigerio and Donato Pavesi. Frigerio won the gold medals for both the 3,000- and the 10,000-metres walks. He was to win the 10,000 metres again in Paris in 1924 – there was no 3,000 metres then. I saw Frigerio in other competitions besides the Olympic Games. His times in Antwerp were not world records, but I have always thought him the most perfect stylist among all the walkers I have ever seen. His grace and rhythm as he moved were beautiful to watch.

One of the outstanding competitors was H. F. V. (Harry) Edward, a West Indian sprinter – a man whom many other great West Indians were to emulate in years to come. Edward won bronze medals in both the 100 and 200 metres. In the 100 metres, he was the victim of grievous ill-

luck. Owing to a misunderstanding of the officials' orders at the start, Edward, and two other finalists from the United States and France, had relaxed, with their back knees on the track, when the starter's gun was fired. Yards behind, Edward made a splendid effort to come third. I admired no less his cheerful, sporting spirit when a committee decided that the race must stand.

Another was Albert Hill of Britain, a railway guard, and thirty-six years old. Before the war, he had won a British 4-mile championship. He had served in the Army for the full four years of the war. In Antwerp he won both the 800 and 1,500 metres. He had a marvellous temperament, which other runners of all nationalities envied. Before a race, while others were counting aches and pains, and biting nails, Hill would have an early lunch, and then sleep soundly for three hours. This power of sleep must have helped him to win five races in five days – three rounds of 800 metres and the heat and the final of the 1,500 metres.

Both finals were exciting races, and in both he showed that he was past master in the tactics of the track. In the 1,500 metres he stayed at the rear of the leading group, but at the bell, with 400 metres still to go, he flashed into the lead and held it to the end. His was the finest double of the Games.

A third was Bevill Rudd of South Africa. He had had a very strenuous and very exacting war. He was an officer in the first tanks ever to be sent to attack enemy lines. On one of their raids, his tank broke down; he was stuck for hours between the lines, and escaped miraculously with his life. His character was strong, but so generous, and so understanding of others that it was said that 'no one ever lost a race against Bevill without feeling that he had won a friend'. He could do 10 seconds for the 100 yards, and could beat almost any miler of his day. In the 800-metres final in Antwerp, he led into the last straight; then by ill-fate he put a foot in a 'depression' in the track; he wrenched his ankle so badly that he did well to finish third, and it seemed doubtful whether he could start in the 400 later in the week. But start he did, and won the gold medal.

There was much in the Antwerp Games besides athletics to excite and to entertain the teams, the Press reporters, and the general public.

Association football was very popular. Teams from fifteen nations – fourteen from Europe, one from Egypt – took part. Britain swiftly lost the title won in Stockholm, defeated in the first round by Norway 1–3. In the final there was a scene I have never witnessed before or since. When the home team, Belgium, came on the field, it was loudly hooted by the crowd. Embarrassed Belgians told us that the Antwerp Press had bitterly attacked the selectors, because distinguished local players had been left out of the national team.

The game which followed was an unhappy episode in Olympic history. Soccer was in its infancy in Europe and Latin America; the high standards of sportsmanship and fair play in the Olympic championship had not yet been built up. The referee's decisions were constantly disputed; the Czech team walked off the field in protest and a crowd of 40,000 dissatisfied spectators saw the Belgians become the victors by the disqualification of their opponents.

In 1920 lawn tennis was still an Olympic sport. The

tournament was played on courts next door to the stadium, so it was very easy to watch. What most people remember is their first view of Suzanne Lenglen, who won the women's singles and, with Max Decugis, the mixed doubles. It was the beginning of nearly twelve years of French pre-eminence in the game. Suzanne Lenglen seemed to us the greatest player, man or woman, we had ever seen; some would have added: 'or whom we shall ever see'. In every stroke she had the power of 'Little Mo' – Maureen Connolly of California; but Suzanne had something else as well: her every movement was like a lovely ballerina's, and the ballet, quite as firmly as her tennis, stayed in the beholders' minds. There were other famous players in the Antwerp tournament; it was notable that the runners-up in the men's doubles were Ichiya Kamagai and Seiichiro Kashio, a brilliant couple from Japan. But 'Antwerp tennis' meant 'Suzanne Lenglen' in the impartial spectator's mind.

The modern pentathlon – Coubertin's event, to which he attached a great importance – was stoutly contested in the Antwerp Games. Again, as in Stockholm, the Swedes were very much on top, and one of them, Gustav Dyrssen, eventually won – a worthy successor to his compatriot Gustaf Lilliehöök who had triumphed eight years before.

In the swimming pools, there was an even stronger reminder of what Stockholm had produced. The picturesque swimmer from Honolulu, Duke Kahanamoku, was there again. His ebullient and attractive personality drew delighted attention wherever he chanced to go. Again he won the 100-metres freestyle for the United States, followed by his comrade from Honolulu, Pua Kela Kealoha. Again he helped the United States to win the 4 × 200-metres relay, while Warren Kealoha (Pua Kela Kealoha's brother) won the 100-metres backstroke.

There was a pointer to the future in the diving – two children: Aileen Riggin of the United States, who won the springboard diving, and Nils Skoglund of Sweden, who was second in the men's plain high diving.

The wrestling and the boxing drew their usual crowd of fans. In the freestyle competition, honours were fairly evenly divided. Finland took two gold medals, but Sweden, the United States and Switzerland each got one. The Greco-Roman contests were again a purely Scandinavian affair – Finland took three of the gold medals, Sweden the other two. The wrestling was of a higher standard than it had been eight years before.

Boxing was a more international affair. There were eight classes, from flyweight to heavyweight. The United States won three titles (Frank De Genaro, Samuel Mosberg and Edward Eagan); Britain two (Harry Mallin and Ronald Rawson, who were both to be heard of again); France, South Africa and Canada took one title each. I remember no trouble in the ring, but people began to say that the International Federation should clean up the rules.

The rowing people, like the boxers, were a happy band of brothers. Britain, which had still led the world till then, was severely routed. Jack Beresford began his wonderful career by reaching the final of the single sculls; but he was beaten by Jack Kelly of the United States. American crews took two of the other races; Switzerland and Italy took one each.

The equestrian events were, once again, almost a clean sweep for Sweden. An Italian officer, Lieutenant Tommaso Lequio, won the individual show jumping; for the rest, the Swedes were in a class by themselves.

So were the Italians in the fencing. They took two individual titles (Nedo Nadi won the foil and sabre), and all three team events, foil, épée and sabre. A Frenchman, Armand Massard, won the individual épée. The rest of the world seemed to be nowhere. In fact, that was an illusion; there were other strong teams in Antwerp besides the Italians and the French; and it became clear in Antwerp that fencing was then firmly established as an Olympic sport.

The gymnastics, not yet developed as they are today, belonged, like the fencing, to Italy; Italians won both the individual (Giorgio Zampori) and the team event.

All the cycling races were exciting – there were six of them, and six nations won one race each. A Swede, Harry Stenqvist, won the individual title in the 175-kilometres road race; but France won the team race, beating the Swedes by over six minutes on the aggregate of their riders' times, while the Swedes had an advantage over the Belgians of more than five minutes. I remember it as a close race and as a truly magnificent event.

The Antwerp Games were very much what I have called them, a postwar affair. They were an important factor in the world's psychological recovery from the war. They showed that not even a world war, lasting more than the period of a whole Olympiad, could break or weaken the Olympic Movement. Beyond question, it emerged from Antwerp stronger than it had been before. In a speech delivered in Antwerp Town Hall to the IOC, and in the presence of King Albert, Coubertin said:

This is what the seventh Olympiad has brought us: general comprehension; the certainty of being henceforward understood by all . . . These festivals . . . are above all the festivals of human unity. In an incomparable synthesis the effort of muscles and of mind, mutual help and competition, lofty patriotism and intelligent cosmopolitanism, the personal interest of the champion and the abnegation of the team-member, are bound in a sheaf for a common task.

1920. Part of Rugby union football's brief contribution to the Games. United States beat France, 8-0.

VIII PARIS 1924 Vernon Morgan

Paris, having held the second Games in 1900, became the first city to celebrate them a second time. The Games of 1924 were held there at the express wish of Coubertin, who wanted to eradicate the fiasco of the 1900 Paris Olympics and to end his term as IOC President with the staging of his Games in his own country. He got them but not without reservations. Lack of cash and facilities were such that an appeal had to be made to Los Angeles to find out if it could take over the Games should Paris have to withdraw; it said it would. The financial problems in Paris eased but then the Games looked like floundering on another disaster when the Seine overflowed its banks during the winter of 1923 and much of the city was flooded.

However, the effect on Paris did not permeate to the Games and the city staged not only a celebration in which the Baron could take pride but a Games which marked the beginning of a new era in the Movement.

The previous Olympics in Antwerp had been of necessity somewhat austere, coming shortly after the end of World War I. In Paris, records of every kind were established. There were forty-four nations competing as against the previous record of twenty-nine in Antwerp and although there were three fewer events (seventeen as against twenty) there were some 500 more participants with a tally of over 3,000, more in fact than took part in the 1928 Olympics in Amsterdam. In track and field events held in the famous Colombes Stadium, six new world records were set and fifteen Olympic records equalled or bettered. In the Tourelles pool the swimmers set two world records and equalled or beat ten previous Olympic marks.

Paris provided the first collective accommodation for athletes – huts gathered round the Colombes Stadium – but the first Olympic Village, with all the facilities which that term implies, was not built until the Games of 1932 in Los Angeles. In Paris, too, women competed in fencing for the first time; lawn tennis and Rugby football were seen at the Olympics for the last time; polo made its penultimate appearance.

The Olympic motto *citius, altius, fortius* (faster, higher, stronger) was coined for these Games by R. P. Didon, a French schoolmaster who was dedicated to sport and stressed its value to his pupils.

Huge profits were made by speculators buying and selling tickets for the opening ceremony. For not only did all Paris want to see President Gaston Doumergue open the Games, but most of France, as well as people from other European countries. It was an impressive ceremony but, like others of its time, austere compared with the huge colourful opening ceremonies of the 1970s. Never before had there been a Games staged in such terrific heat; never has there been since. Colombes was variously described as a 'cauldron' and a 'furnace', and one of the refreshment stalls was dubbed *La Bonne Frite* ('the good fry'). Although there was at least one storm to relieve the intense heat, it was 45 °C (113 °F) on some days, notably when the 10,000-metres cross-country was run. It is not surprising that only twenty-three of the thirty-eight starters finished the gruelling course, most of them in a poor physical condition. But the winner, Paavo Nurmi, was unaffected by the conditions.

Nurmi, then twenty-seven, was the hero of the Games. Not only did he win the cross country, but three other golds: in the 3,000-metres team race (no longer held), the 1,500 metres and the 5,000 metres, the last two races on the same day within one hour of each other.

In those days runners did not have the aid of either official or unofficial times being called out at the completion of each lap. But Nurmi was as ahead of his time in his thinking about running as he was in the quality and quantity of his training and he realized that an even race was an essential economy in long-distance running. So he carried a watch in his left hand during training and competition. I'll never forget his annoyance when in the 3,000-metres steeplechase in Amsterdam in 1928 (I also took part) he fell in the water jump and damaged his watch. He would never say whether this cost him the race, in which he finished second to his team mate Toivo Loukola.

Nurmi was not the only Finn to defy the heat and show the world they had more like Hannes Kolehmainen. Ville Ritola won the 10,000 metres and the steeplechase, Albin Stenroos took the marathon, Eero Lehtonen the pentathlon (its last appearance on the Olympic program) and Jonni Myyrä the javelin.

The world long-jump record was broken but not in the long-jump competition. The new figures were set in the pentathlon! Robert LeGendre was annoyed that he had not been picked to jump for the United States. So he was not amused when William De Hart Hubbard won the gold medal for the United States with a leap of 7.445 m (24 ft 5 in). On taking the track for the pentathlon LeGendre was reported as remarking, 'I'll show them who their best long jumper is, and what's more I'll set a new world record.' Though taking only the bronze in the pentathlon, LeGendre was as good as his word. His best leap of 7.765 m (25 ft 5 in) was over a foot further than Hubbard's winning Olympic jump, and it duly broke the world record.

Who will ever forget the great win of Harold Abrahams, the only Briton ever to have won the Olympic 100 metres, and with a new Olympic record? Eric Liddell, from Scotland, set not only an Olympic but a world record by taking the 400 metres in 47.6 sec. He took the bronze in the 200 metres but withdrew from the 100 metres, in which he had a strong chance of winning, because the heats were run on a Sunday.

Then there was Douglas Lowe (Gt Britain) in the 800 metres. Timing his effort as superbly as always, he just got home ahead of Paul Martin (Switzerland). Lowe was to repeat this performance four years later in the Amsterdam Olympics. Britain won a gold in the swimming pool too. This was through Lucy Morton in the 200-metre breaststroke.

Two gold medals came Britain's way in the boxing through the two Harrys, Mallin and Mitchell, the former winning the middleweight title and the latter the light heavyweight. Mallin was involved in the most infamous incident of the Games, being bitten in the shoulder by his French opponent, who was subsequently disqualified. The Olympic tournament was held with the referee officiating outside the ring for the first time and critics of this novel Olympic procedure said some boxers took advantage of this.

Britain won another two golds in the rowing events on the Seine, in the single sculls and coxless fours. The victory of Jack Beresford in the single sculls was one of sweet revenge. In 1920 in Antwerp he had been pipped at the post by Jack Kelly (United States). Beresford was eager for revenge in Paris but his final opponent was not Kelly but the sculler who had beaten him for the US title, William Gilmore. The Briton showed consummate skill in a cat-and-mouse affair to win comfortably.

The Rugby football tournament went to the United States with France and Romania the only other contestants.

The United States won both lawn-tennis singles titles in this other sport for which these Games in Paris were the last. Vincent Richards beat Henri Cochet, the local hero, in five tough sets in the men's event and Helen Wills beat Jeanne Vlasto of France in the women's without much trouble. Suzanne Lenglen, her formidable French rival, had withdrawn from the tournament at the last minute through 'indisposition'.

Even in those days they had 'unofficial' medals tables. The United States was an easy leader with forty-five medals, then came Finland with fourteen and France with thirteen. Britain came next with ten.

The American successes came in nine of the seventeen sports. They won thirteen golds in the swimming, seven by their men and six by their women; twelve in track and field; five in shooting and lawn tennis in which they swept the board, winning every title; four in wrestling, two each in rowing and boxing and one in gymnastics. They also won the Rugby football title. Only in gymnastics did any other country win more golds in the above events.

In track and field they won the 200 metres, both hurdles, both relays, the high jump, long jump, shot, hammer, discus, pole vault and decathlon. They were responsible for three of the six world records established.

In the men's swimming events they won the 100- and 400-metres freestyle, the 100-metres backstroke and 200-

1920. A pacemaker of athletic history consults his watch. Paavo Nurmi on his way to win the 5,000 metres

metres breaststroke, the 4 × 200-metres relay and both dives, setting a new world figure in the relay and new Olympic times in three other swimming titles. The women won the 100- and 400-metres freestyle, the 100-metres backstroke, the 4 × 100-metres relay and both dives. World records were established in the 200-metres freestyle and relay.

Their shooting victories came in the free rifle (600 metres), free pistol (25 metres), running deer and, in the team events, in free rifle and clay pigeon. In wrestling the golds came in the featherweight, lightweight, light heavyweight and heavyweight divisions; in boxing, the flyweight and featherweight; in rowing the double sculls and eights, and in gymnastics, the long-horse vault.

Two gold medallists of the United States boxing team later went on to win professional world titles. They were Fidel LaBarba who became the world flyweight champion, and Jackie Fields, the Olympic featherweight champion, who took the world welterweight title in 1929.

There were greats in the swimming events too, like Johnny Weissmuller (of later Tarzan fame) and Duke Kahanamoku. With Andrew Charlton, Australia began its bid to overcome the supremacy of the United States. Weissmuller's success in Paris was the more remarkable in that he was regarded during infancy as a weakling and was thought to have a heart trouble. Yet he became the first man to win the 100 metres in under a minute. Earlier that year in Miami he had broken the world record with 57.4 sec. These were great Games for the Americans in swimming and diving. They won all but three of the titles in both men's and women's events, and in six took all three medals. The three events they lost were the 1,500 metres, won by Australia's Andrew Charlton, the men's plain high diving, won by Australia's Richmond Eve, and the 200-metres breaststroke for women, won by Britain's Lucy Morton, the first and the third in new Olympic times. Charlton also set a new world record.

More than half of the French medals came from cycling and fencing, sports at which the French have always excelled. Sprint gold medallist Lucien Michard went on to win the world professional title, and there has never been an easier winner of the road race than Armand Blanchonnet, who crossed the finishing line more than ten minutes ahead of his nearest rival. The French fencing ace was Roger Ducret, who took three golds and two silvers. The French were particularly delighted that in these, their Games, they were able to avenge themselves on their chief rivals and neighbours, the Italians. In the previous Olympics in Antwerp, the Italians had swept the board, winning five titles to one by France. In Paris the score was France three, Italy one.

History was made in the shooting. Finishing third in the Swedish team in the running-deer (double-shot) team event, won by Norway, was Alfred Swahn. This was his ninth Olympic medal, gained at the age of forty-five. His tally in the Olympics of 1908, 1912, 1920 and 1924 was three golds, three silvers and three bronzes. And it would certainly have been more had it been possible to hold the Games of the sixth Olympiad in 1916.

What is even more remarkable is that his father Oscar not only competed with his son in 1912 and 1920, as well as in 1908, but took six Olympic medals. Between them the Swahns won six golds, four silvers and five bronzes, a total of fifteen, a record likely to stand for all time.

IX AMSTERDAM 1928 The Rt Hon. Philip Noel-Baker

Coubertin was prevented by illness from being present at the ninth Olympic Games. So he sent a message 'to the athletes and all those taking part at Amsterdam in the Games of the ninth Olympiad'; foreseeing that he might be unable to be at Los Angeles for the tenth Olympiad in 1932, he said in his message: 'I should be wise to take the present opportunity of bidding you farewell.'

It was a harsh moment for him when he wrote those words and a grievous moment for the Olympic Movement. But in his message he called on the athletes and others at Amsterdam 'strongly and faithfully [to] keep ever alive the flame of the revived Olympic spirit and maintain its necessary principles . . . The great point is that, everywhere everyone from adolescent to adult, should cultivate and spread the true sporting spirit of spontaneous loyalty and chivalrous impartiality.' And he ended: 'Once again, I beg to thank those who have followed me and helped me to fight a forty-year war, not often easy and not always cleanly fought.'

That he should end his farewell message to the athletes and to his Olympic friends with these bitter words, shows how sharply and how deeply he had been wounded by the venomous hostility of the chauvinists who had constantly attacked him from the first moment when he proposed the revival of the ancient Games. Many of these enemies were pure chauvinists and nothing more – they found such phrases 'international good understanding' and 'festival of human unity' repellent – and, of course, 'utopian' as well. But there were others; I knew them and hated them with a youthful zest which has in no way abated today – a zest of

1928. The first women's 800 metres in the Olympics. Lina Radke (Germany), number 762, was the winner.

which, I feel sure, the generous Coubertin would himself have been ashamed.

There were newspaper proprietors who hoped they could increase their circulation by exploiting or inventing quarrels and 'incidents' in international sport. There were journalists – 'sports writers' – who had never in their lives perspired for an hour from any kind of sport, but who were always ready to make trouble for those who did. There were even would-be 'intellectuals', who boasted that they found the very thought of physical effort abhorrent. These persons – I do not call them 'men' – had indeed made 'war' on Coubertin for forty years. They had done so with venom and with disloyalty which he was fully entitled to resent.

There are still such persons in the world today. In 1972, during the Munich Games, there was a brief, grotesquely foolish, and quickly stifled recrudescence of the chauvinistic attacks. Even the editors of some leading British papers thought it might pay them to join in.

Such persons no longer matter; they only show themselves to be absurd. And, indeed, they did not matter any more at Amsterdam in 1928. Coubertin's 'forty-year war, not often easy and not always cleanly fought' had in fact been won. The chauvinists had been routed, and were in disorderly and disreputable retreat.

No one said any longer that the Amsterdam Games would be 'the last'. In London, in 1908, twenty-two countries had sent national teams. The competitors numbered 2,034. Twenty years – and a world war – later, the countries were to number forty-eight, and the competitors were to be a thousand more. Coubertin had won. The Games were impregnably established; the Olympic Movement had taken sport around the world, and the world replied by giving the Olympic Movement its solid and unwavering support.

Only those who had lived, as I had, through the doubtful, crucial years, and had heard the lying slogans, as I had, naïvely mumbled by Prime Ministers and Foreign Secretaries and such, could fully understand the sense of victory we felt in Amsterdam. Something virile, noble and infinitely important had been brought to triumph. For a full month we enjoyed that triumph in famous and beautiful Amsterdam.

I saw the Games in Amsterdam from a new and different angle. I had twice been Captain of the British track team; in Amsterdam I was Deputy Commissioner for the whole British contingent. This was a most honourable appointment which I greatly valued; it carried responsibilities of various kinds.

One morning I received an urgent message from the Commissioner. Would I please be at the swimming pool at 11 a.m.? Britain was to play the Netherlands at water polo; Queen Wilhelmina of the Netherlands would be there, and it was essential that the British team should not be guilty of any fouls. I would be responsible, if there were trouble; it was my job to see there was none.

Knowing something of how water polo was too often played, I approached the pool with trepidation, not to say alarm. I assembled the British team, and gave them the lecture which the Commissioner had ordained. During the first session in the water, the referee penalized and warned several members of the British team; and the crowd – the arena was packed – began to groan. At the next interval I told the team that, if there were even one more infringement of the rules, I should carry out the Commissioner's instructions, and tell the referee that Britain had 'withdrawn'. In spite of the inhibitions I imposed upon them the British team were victorious by 5–3. But in the next round they met Germany, the ultimate victors in the competition. My admonitions were no less vigorous; Britain lost. Decades later, at an Olympic party in No. 10 Downing Street, I met a burly someone whose face I thought I recognized; most certainly *he* had recognized *me*! 'Ah,' he said, 'you're the chap that lost us the gold medals for water polo in Amsterdam!' That was rose-tinted speculation.

The Olympic Movement (with help from the British Empire) had taken sport around the world. In Amsterdam: Uruguay was Olympic association football champion; Argentina won two gold medals and two silver in the boxing, a gold in the swimming, and elsewhere did well; a runner from Chile was second in the marathon; India won the hockey, 3–0, against the host country, the Netherlands; 50,000 people came to see the match, and predicted that India would remain for long on top; Japan won a gold medal for the triple jump (Mikio Oda), another for the 200-metres breaststroke in the swimming, and did well elsewhere; Egypt won a gold medal in the Greco-Roman wrestling (Ibrahim Mustafa); Haiti's Silvio Cator was second in the long jump; South Africa sent Sid Atkinson to win the 110-metres hurdles, and George Weightman-Smith to break the world record in a semi-final of the same event; New Zealand's Edward Morgan won the welterweight title in the boxing.

The net of organized athletics and of other sports had indeed spread far and wide around the world. There were still no Russians and no Chinese in Amsterdam but the 'Central Powers' had returned – the ex-enemies of World War I, Germany, Austria, Hungary and Bulgaria. It was sixteen years since they had last taken part in the Olympic Games. Considering that fact, they did extremely well.

Germany in particular, was prominent almost everywhere, winning gold medals in the equestrian events, wrestling, water polo and swimming, and several silver and bronze medals in track events.

Lina Radke won the 800-metres women's race in 2 min 16.8 sec. However, the race was not a pleasant sight; several runners collapsed either before or after the finish, and immediately officials from other countries rounded on me, from Britain, for this frightful episode. Four years before Britain had vigorously defended the inclusion of women's athletic events. The trouble with this 800 metres was that the competitors had not been properly trained; thirty-six years later Ann Packer showed the grace and beauty women could bring to this event when she won a memorable race in Tokyo.

Hungary's contribution to the Games was impressive. In the boxing, Antal Kocsis won a gold medal in the flyweight class; Lajos Keresztes won a gold in the lightweight class of the Greco-Roman wrestling; Ödön Tersztyánszky won the individual sabre in the fencing; and with other Hungarians he won the sabre team event. ('The sabre is a magnificent weapon,' Coubertin had said.)

Participation in the Games was still not universal. But the contribution of the distant continents, of the 'developing' nations, and of the 'ex-enemies' of ten years before, added greatly to the richness of the program and to the worldwide interest it evoked.

The sensation of the Amsterdam athletics lay in the fantastic successes of the Finns – and perhaps also the comparative non-success of the United States. The United States won no gold medal on the track for the first five days. Then Raymond Barbuti took the 400 metres. It was to be the only American individual gold medal on the track and he only won it because James Ball of Canada made all the mistakes it is possible for a runner to make in such a race. Ball apparently forgot that, as was the practice in the 400 metres in those days, he could break from the lanes in the back straight. Instead, he carried on in his lane and must have run several yards further than anyone else. Ball was beaten only by inches, and photos show him at the tape looking so wildly and so abstractedly over his left shoulder that that alone must have cost him his first place. Ball never came to the Olympic Games again; but I remember him as one of the most gifted quarter-milers there ever were.

The United States won the two relays, 4 × 100 metres and 4 × 400 metres, a very satisfying compensation. They got two places in each of the hurdles races; but Sid Atkinson of South Africa won the 110-metres high hurdles, and Lord Burghley won the 400-metres hurdles. To crown it all, Finland took the first two places in the decathlon, leaving a lone American (John Kenneth Doherty) with the bronze.

In the field events, jumping and throwing, the United States took thirteen medals out of twenty-four, including five gold. The Finns did less well in these events than they had done in Antwerp; second in the discus, third in the triple jump, was all they had to show. But their successes on the track wiped out whatever disappointment their field-events enthusiasts might have felt. They were first and third (Harri Larva and Eino Purje) in the 1,500 metres. They were first and second (Ville Ritola and Paavo Nurmi) in the 5,000 metres. They were first and second (Nurmi and Ritola – Nurmi's revenge) in the 10,000 metres. They took all three places in the 3,000-metres steeplechase (Toivo Loukola, Nurmi and Ove Andersen, first, second and third respectively). They got third place (Martti Marttelin) in the marathon.

All of these, beginning with the 1,500 metres, are events in which endurance and will-power count. The Finns have a word which combines the meaning of both endurance and will-power – *sisu*. I heard much of *sisu* when I went to visit Finland, and the Finnish Army in the line, during their 'Winter War' against the USSR in 1940. Field Marshal Mannerheim told me that *sisu* was the most important factor in the resistance they put up. I saw much of Finnish *sisu* in Amsterdam in 1928, and again in Munich eleven Olympiads after that.

But what had hit the Americans in the short events? Some whirlwinds, from quarters they did not expect.

There was a nineteen-year-old schoolboy, Percy Williams from Vancouver. He had hitch-hiked his way across Canada from west to east to take part in his country's trials for the Olympic Games; he was rewarded by a double victory in the sprints. He repeated his double victory in the 100 and 200 metres in Amsterdam. Dutch doctors and researchers had asked the 3,000 athletes in the Games to fill in forms giving measurements of their limbs, their chest, their waist, their biceps, etc., and to undergo tests of breathing, chest expansion, lifting weights and so on. I never understood the nature, perhaps the magic, of this

1928. *Above* The association football final. Uruguay defeated Argentina 2–1. *Below* The water polo final. Germany beat Hungary 5–2.

mand of the proceedings from first to last. He went into his finishing sprint around the bottom bend, led into the straight and won with an ample margin of metres to spare, in 1 min 51.8 sec, an Olympic record.

A German runner, Otto Peltzer, had beaten Lowe at Stamford Bridge in London in 1926 in a new world record time. In Amsterdam, Peltzer had been injured, was below his proper form and was eliminated in the second round. So Lowe, the most chivalrous of men, accepted an invitation to go a month later to Berlin and give Peltzer a second chance to win. The race was naturally a sensation; Peltzer had recovered and ran extremely well. But Lowe won by a narrow margin, and in a time faster than Peltzer had recorded in London the year before. This was the end of Lowe's career. He was the perfect Olympic champion, and the perfect artist on the track. He remains the most lovely mover I have ever seen.

In the equestrian events there was what amounted to a revolution. In Stockholm and in Antwerp the Swedes had virtually swept the board; in Paris, they had done extremely well, winning the individual dressage, and the team jumping – two golds out of five, the Netherlands (Adolph D. C. van der Voort van Zijp) had taken two and Switzerland (Alphonse Gemuseus) had taken one.

In Amsterdam, Sweden almost disappeared from view. A brilliant new star, Lieutenant Ferdinand Pahud de Mortanges of the Netherlands, won the individual three-day event; with his Dutch comrades, he won the three-day team event as well. The Germans (Carl Friedrich Freiherr von Langen) did the same for the individual and the team dressage. Captain František Ventura of Czechoslovakia was first in the individual jumping; Spain took the team jumping. In six equestrian events, Sweden got just two *bronze* medals, while Germany, Czechoslovakia, Norway, Poland and other new equestrian competitors were doing well. Neither the United States nor Britain won any medal at all. Later Olympiads were to continue the process which Amsterdam began, and to show that skill with horses is widely distributed around the world.

The modern pentathlon was some comfort to the Swedes. The ultimate winner was Sven Thofelt of Sweden, whose best event was the 300-metres freestyle swimming, in which he was second to Eugenio Pagnini of Italy. The 5-kilometre cross-country riding was won by another Swede, Ingvar Berg. The cross-country running was won by a Pole, Stefan Szelestowski; the fencing by a Dane, Helge Jensen; the revolver shooting by a German, Heinz Hax. So a Swede won this important gold medal; if the contest had been treated as a team event, the three Swedish competitors would have been first again, with Germany second, and the Netherlands third.

The rowing, spread over nine days on the Sloten canal, brought a revival by the British oarsmen. In the coxswainless fours, the British crew (First Trinity, Cambridge) won gold medals. In the coxswainless pairs, Britain (Terence O'Brien and Robert Archibald Nisbet) were second; in the single sculls, the best Briton, Theodore David Collet, came third. The race which gave them most satisfaction was the eights: the British crew (the Thames Rowing Club) was only beaten by the United States by a short half-length in extremely fast time. Two famous men were in the crew: Jack Beresford, who won the single sculls in Paris, at 'two', and 'Gully' Nickalls at 'seven'. The US crew were from the University of California, where there

exercise. But I was not much surprised when they revealed that, according to their tests, Percy Williams, out of the 3,000 in all the various sports, was the perfect athlete in Amsterdam.

Britain, too, produced a whirlwind – Jack London, a black medical student at London University. His homeland was British Guiana but he was universally acclaimed as 'Mr London of London'. He was a red-hot second in the 100 metres, and many people thought he might have beaten Percy Williams, if he had been entered in the 200 metres as well.

For the third places in the sprints, there were the Germans, Georg Lammers and Helmut Körnig. Joachim Büchner of Germany took the third place, after Barbuti and Ball, in the 400 metres; Hermann Engelhard of Germany was third in the 800 metres, in which Erik Byléhn of Sweden was second, and Douglas Lowe of Britain first.

Lowe had won the 800 metres in Paris, and not many people thought that, after four years of pretty strenuous competition, he could win again. In fact, in Amsterdam he was at the very zenith of his glorious career; he coasted through the first two rounds and in the final was in comis sunshine all the year; they had in fact been rowing together for three years.

In this Amsterdam regatta, Australia (Bob Pearce) won the single sculls; the United States (Paul Costello and Charles McIlvaine) the double sculls; Switzerland the coxswained pairs; Italy the coxswained fours – a wide allocation of top honours around the world.

The swimming pools in Amsterdam no longer had the charming personality of Duke Kahanamoku of Honolulu. He had been beaten in Paris into second place in the 100-metres freestyle race by a new star, who shone brightly again in Amsterdam. This was none other than Johnny Weissmuller, who won the 100-metres freestyle again, and was a member of the US team in the 4 × 200-metres relay.

As always, the United States took plenty of medals in the swimming; but besides the German, the Japanese, and Alberto Zorilla (Argentina), a Swede, Arne Borg, took a gold medal in the 1,500-metres freestyle, Japan took second place in the 4 × 200-metres relay, and third place behind Weissmuller in the 100 metres; an Egyptian, Farid Simaika, took a silver medal in the high diving and a bronze in the springboard diving. The United States took the remainder of the men's events and the women's 4 × 100-metres freestyle relay, springboard and the high-board diving.

The gymnastics began to take on the glamour and the beauty that they have today. But the top places were changing hands. The Swiss took nearly everything; a Czech (Ladislav Vácha) won the parallel bars, a Yugoslav the rings; among the women's teams, who were competing for the first time in the Olympic Games, the Netherlands came first.

Italy did well in boxing and in fencing. In boxing Italians took three Olympic titles, Argentina took two, Hungary, the Netherlands and New Zealand one each. In fencing Italy took the team events, foil and épée. Hungary took both individual and team sabres.

Association football had more than its usual success: more than a quarter of a million spectators paid for entrance to the matches. Uruguay narrowly defeated Argentina in the final, 2–1. Italy defeated Egypt for the bronze medals 11–3.

In a month we had time to see something of Amsterdam – the picture galleries, the marvellous housing projects, the reclamation of the Zuider Zee, ten times as large and glorious as Mussolini's draining of the Romagna swamps, about which there was so much sycophantic talk.

But nothing diverted us for long from the greater glory of the Games. Not long before they started, Coubertin wrote the following words about the 'celebration' of Amsterdam:

> If among the great majority of the competitors each one on the last day can give himself credit for having striven in all honour, without failing for a single instant . . . then the moral gain will be won, and the IXth Olympiad will be a noble and happy milestone on the path of chivalrous progress. May it be so. It is my wish and my conviction.

It *was* so. When I left Amsterdam, I had only one regret: that Coubertin had not been there himself to see the noble, happy milestone, and to know that his great Movement was destined to grow yet greater, and most surely to endure.

X LOS ANGELES 1932 Paul Zimmerman

The year was 1932. The world was in the throes of a deep depression. The stock-market crash had driven many a financier to his grave and others to selling apples in the streets. The national bank holiday was just around the corner. It was under such inauspicious circumstances that the summer games of the tenth Olympiad took place.

The wonder is that the Los Angeles Organizing Committee was able to keep the Olympic flame ablaze. The accomplishment must go down in the history of the Movement as one of its finest hours. Under the astute and bold leadership of William May Garland the summer Games of 1932 was one of the most artistic and financially successful ever staged. When it was over and a final accounting was made it showed sixteen world records shattered, two equalled and thirty-three new Olympic marks.

The Games attracted more than $1\frac{1}{4}$ million spectators and when the final audit was made it disclosed that the Los Angeles Organizing Committee had accumulated almost $1 million surplus.

When Los Angeles first sought the Games the world was still riding post-World-War-I prosperity. There was still no hint of a financial calamity when the International Olympic Committee, in its 1923 meeting in Rome, brought Garland's long-time dream to fruition with the awarding of the games to Los Angeles for 1932.

Armed with an official letter of invitation from the mayor, Garland first appeared before the IOC at Antwerp in 1920. His quest was for the 1924 games or the 1928 games at the latest. Garland was told that Paris was the choice for 1924, with Amsterdam standing in the wings for 1928. The IOC members were so impressed with this persuasive man from the shores of the Pacific, however, that they elected him to membership and suggested Los Angeles bid for 1932.

Once the bid succeeded in 1923 Garland returned home and went to work. He headed a group of civic leaders known as the Community Development Associ-

1932. The first specially designed Olympic Village, at Los Angeles

1932. Duncan McNaughton (Canada) winning the high jump with a height of 1.97 m (6 ft 5½ in)

ation which erected a huge stadium. Its seating capacity was enlarged to over 100,000 by the time the games were held.

This association became the nucleus of the Organizing Committee. In the face of growing evidence of a world financial crisis it went stubbornly about the business of preparing to stage the games. In spite of mounting pessimism, early in 1930 it sent out embossed invitations to National Olympic Committees the world over. Aware of the growing fear around the world that the expense of sending athletes such a distance would prove prohibitive, Garland and his committee developed a bold plan.

Appearing before the Olympic Congress at Berlin in the summer of 1930, the Los Angeles representative announced that it was prepared to feed, house, entertain and locally transport every competitor for $2 a day.

With the arranged reduced steamship and railroad fares this meant, for example, that athletes from Europe could make the thirty-day round trip for only $500 each – a third of the anticipated cost. On the basis of such a promise, reservations began to roll in. However, it was not until months later, when the first of the larger contingents began to disembark at United States ports, that Garland and his staff would heave a sigh of relief.

The result of that bold stroke was that 1,500 athletes from thirty-four nations found their way to Los Angeles.

To accomplish the low cost the committee developed a novel plan. The athletes would be housed in an Olympic village, living in common bond; a plan discussed before but never implemented until the Games of 1932.

Located on a hilltop, cooled by ocean breezes and only ten minutes from the Olympic stadium, the village consisted of two-room Mexican ranch-style cottages built in a circle on 250 landscaped acres. Separate dining rooms with cuisines to accommodate every world taste, a hospitality house, recreation area, hospital, fire department, and an independent policing system were included in the fenced-in privacy of the village. Women

athletes were given the exclusive run of the spacious Chapman Park hotel on Wilshire Boulevard. Viewed with scepticism by some of the larger nations at the outset, the village plan was so successful and popular it has been a part of the protocol of every Olympics since.

There were other innovations. For the first time an electric photo-timing device for races was introduced; a forerunner of today's methods. Hand timing remained official but the system was used as a backstop. Very early in the Games it helped the judges determine the victor in the 100-metres dash, in which Eddie Tolan (United States) and Ralph Metcalfe (United States) finished inches apart.

The victory stand had its beginning in Los Angeles – the ceremonies of awarding medals were accompanied by the playing of national anthems while flags of the winners' countries were unfurled. Another first was the use of teletype communications between venues for the press. Each newspaper and press association had at its location in the Olympic stadium press section a private automatic printer that spewed out results from all the other events in progress; a forerunner of the refinement introduced at Tokyo where closed-circuit television receivers were installed. A free bus service supplied transport everywhere.

Under a cloudless sky on 30 July 1932, 101,000 spectators filled the Olympic stadium to capacity, cheering the world's greatest athletes as they paraded onto the field and revelling in the pomp and splendour of the opening ceremonies. For once the woes of the world were forgotten. Vice-President Charles Curtis intoned the speech of welcome and the Games many had thought never could be staged were on. After they had run their spectacular course, another capacity throng filled the Olympic stadium for the closing ceremony. At the end, with the sun setting over the Pacific, the thousands stood and joined in the haunting Hawaiian song of farewell – *Aloha*.

Detractors had said the dry, subtropical climate would prove enervating to the athletes. This fear was quickly dispelled when the program of fourteen sports began with competition in athletics. Before the largest crowds ever attracted for track and field, record-breaking performances became the rule – not the exception.

Perhaps the most startling of the many surprises in athletics was the break in Finland's dominance in the distance races. Where the Finns had taken everything from the 1,500-metres run to the marathon at Paris in 1924 and followed this with four victories in five races at Amsterdam, they were fortunate to glean two gold medals at Los Angeles.

In this, the competitors were aided and abetted by the International Amateur Athletic Federation, which, a few days before the Games opened, had decided that Paavo Nurmi was guilty of charges of professionalism. So the great runner, winner of three gold medals and two silver at Paris and Amsterdam, was relegated to the stands as a spectator.

Beginning with the 1,500-metres run, the erosion of Finland's dominance was heralded. Harri Larva, victor at Amsterdam four years before, ran well back in the pack as Luigi Beccali (Italy) added a burning sprint finish to a withering early pace and crossed the finish line strides ahead of John Cornes (Great Britain) and Philip Edwards (Canada) in 3 min 51.2 sec for an Olympic record.

Only through the good graces of the judges was Lauri

Lehtinen awarded the gold medal in the 5,000 metres. In a surprising performance Ralph Hill (United States) was close on the Finn's heels off the final turn down the finish stretch. As the American put on a sprint to pass, Lehtinen swerved into the second lane to cut him off. Hill then tried to go by on the inside. Lehtinen swung back, thwarting him.

The crowd gave vent to its indignation before the calming voice of the announcer, Bill Henry, saved the day for the Finn.

'Remember, please,' he implored, 'these people are our guests!'

The uproar subsided to a murmur. Hill had to be content with second place, a stride back. Since there was no official protest nor charge of foul, the judges let the victory stand. Lehtinen's time of 14 min 30.0 sec was an Olympic record.

Another setback for the Finns came in the 10,000 metres. Here Janusz Kusociński (Poland) clearly demonstrated his superiority as he ran away from Volmari Iso-Hollo and Lauri Virtanen in the Olympic record time of 30 min 11.4 sec. This was only 5.2 sec under Nurmi's world mark.

The marathon produced a similar story. Little Juan Zabala (Argentina) stayed up with the leaders through the early going. A few miles out of the Olympic stadium he forged to the front.

Although he never held a commanding lead, the diminutive South American clung to his advantage as the leaders took their final lap around the track and even had enough for a finishing spurt. His time of 2 hr 31 min 36 sec was only 19 sec faster than that of Great Britain's Sam Ferris, who came second. Armas Toivonen (Finland), who won the bronze, was only 36 sec behind the winner.

This was the race everyone had expected Nurmi would run to close a spectacular career.

Iso-Hollo salvaged the second gold medal for Finland in the steeplechase. This was an unusual race because the clerk of the course in charge of the lap cards became confused and every competitor ran an extra lap over the hurdles and water jumps.

There was no question of Iso-Hollo's superiority. He was far out in front at what should have been the regulation 3,000 metres and had enough left to extend this advantage over his faltering competition. Thomas Evenson (Great Britain) held off Joseph McCluskey (United States) for second. Iso-Hollo's time for the 3,460 metres was 10 min 33.4 sec compared with the Olympic record of 9 min 14.6 sec he established in the preliminaries over the correct distance.

The United States dominated the sprints as expected. Eddie Tolan became the only double victor in athletics by winning the 100 metres and 200 metres from team mates Ralph Metcalfe and George Simpson. Tolan's time of 10.3 sec for the short dash equalled the world record.

A fast starter, Tolan barely held off the closing surge of Metcalfe. The finish was so tight the judges waited until the new photo-finish pictures could be developed and viewed. Little Eddie had no trouble taking the 200-metres dash from Simpson, with Metcalfe third. His time around the turn was 21.2 sec for another Olympic mark. This trio gave way to four other sprinters in the short relay – Robert Kiesel, Emmett Toppino, Hector Dyer and Frank Wykoff. Their time of 40.0 sec, a world record, was

nine-tenths of a second faster than that of Germany's quartet and emphasized the superiority of American sprinting at its best in California.

Many thought the most spectacular performance came in the 400-metres dash. Here William Carr (United States), with a sensational straightaway burst of speed, beat his team mate Ben Eastman by four yards as he cut eight-tenths of a second off the world record with a time of 46.2 sec.

Leading from starter's gun to tape, Tom Hampson (Great Britain) captured the 800-metres run in the world's fastest time of 1 min 49.7 sec (since middle-distance races were officially timed to one-fifth of a second in 1932, his record was rounded off to 1 min 49.8 sec). Hampson superbly judged his strength and pace as he held off the sprint finish of Alexander Wilson (Canada).

Lord Burghley (the Marquess of Exeter and for long an IOC member) travelled to Los Angeles to defend his 400-metres hurdles title and other races as well. In an ambitious program that would require him to run eight races in the span of a few days, Lord Burghley also entered the 110-metres hurdles and 4 × 400-metres relay. He decided to miss the parade at the opening ceremony, but when he learned that his leading rival in the 400-metres hurdles, Morgan Taylor, had been chosen to carry the United States flag, he also marched in the parade, in a gesture of fine sportsmanship.

All this was too much: Burghley was fifth in the high hurdles which was won by George Saling (United States) in 14.6 sec; in the 400-metres hurdles there was a surprise winner: Burghley and Taylor had been expected to battle for the gold medal but instead an Irishman, Robert Tisdall, won in 51.7 sec (officially rounded up to 51.8 sec) which would have been a world and Olympic record had he not knocked down a hurdle.

Two strides back, less than a foot apart, came Glenn Hardin (United States), Taylor and Burghley, in that order. His Lordship helped Britain take the silver medal in the 4 × 400-metres relay. In this, led by the amazing William Carr, the United States ran away from all opposition, shattering the world record with 3 min 08.2 sec.

The ways things went, only three events – the long jump, high jump and hammer – escaped the record-breaking onslaught. Only one athletics champion at Amsterdam four years before was able to win again in Los Angeles. He was the sturdy Irishman, Dr Patrick O'Callaghan, in the hammer.

A traditional American gold medal was endangered in the pole vault, in which Shuhei Nishida (Japan) kept pace with the three United States stars all the way to the top. William Miller had to set a world record of 4.315 metres (14 ft 1⅞ in) to beat the doughty Japanese vaulter and then only by a fraction of an inch; Nishida's 4.30 m (14 ft 1¼ in) put him well ahead of the other two Americans George Jefferson and William Graber.

The greatest story in the women's athletics concerned Mildred (Babe) Didrikson. This slender eighteen-year-old high-school girl from the wide-open spaces of Texas set two world records and was deprived of equalling a third through an unusual disqualification.

She began by winning the 80-metres hurdles, the first year this women's event was held, in 11.7 sec, beating her American colleague Evelyne Hall by inches. In the javelin she achieved a distance of 43.68 m (143 ft 4 in) to beat the two German favourites, Ellen Braumüller and Tilly Fleischer.

In the high jump she and Jean Shiley, who had represented the United States at Amsterdam, tied at the record height of 1.67 m (5 ft 5¼ in). To break the tie the bar was lowered to 1.65 m (5 ft 5 in) for a jump off. First Shiley and then Didrikson cleared the bar. At that juncture the judges went into a huddle and ruled that Miss Didrikson was disqualified for diving across the bar. So the victory went to Shiley with Babe placed second.

Just as the United States dominated track and field, the Japanese men took charge in swimming. Had it not been for Clarence Crabbe they might have won the five races. Crabbe salvaged a gold medal for the United States, taking the 400-metres freestyle in the Olympic record time of 4 min 48.4 sec.

With their buoyant style of swimming, high in the water, the Japanese started off when Yasuji Miyazaki and Tatsugo Kawaishi took the gold and silver medals in the 100-metres freestyle. Miyazaki's 58.0 sec in the semi-final was an Olympic mark.

Next came Masaji Kiyokawa (he became an IOC member in 1968) who led a Japanese sweep of the 100-metres backstroke. Japan finished first and second in the 200-metres breaststroke in which Yoshiyuki Tsuruta touched first, and again in the 1,500-metres freestyle, Kusuo Kitamura winning in a new Olympic time of 19 min 12.4 sec.

The Japanese 4 × 200-metres relay team made a shambles of the world record which they improved by 37.8 sec with a mark of 8 min 58.4 sec.

The United States girls salvaged the country's pride with Helene Madison, their outstanding swimmer. She achieved a world record of 5 min 28.5 sec in the 400-metres freestyle after setting an Olympic mark of 1 min 06.8 sec in the 100 metres. Her third gold medal came on the anchor leg of the 4 × 100-metres relay in which the Americans covered the 400 metres in 4 min 38.0 sec, a world record.

Eleanor Holm followed Miss Madison to the victors' podium by winning the 100-metres backstroke in 1 min 19.4 sec after setting a new Olympic best of 1 min 18.3 sec in the first heat. Only Claire Dennis of Australia prevented an American sweep, with an Olympic record swim of 3 min 06.3 sec in the 200-metres breaststroke.

There was a wide distribution of laurels among the nations in other sports. French weightlifters; Swedish wrestlers; Italian gymnasts and cyclists; French, Hungarian and Italian fencers; and South African, Argentinian and United States boxers all won titles.

In rowing the United States' eight withstood a valiant closing spurt by Italy, inching to a two-tenths-of-a-second victory. It had been a three-boat race for first place, with Canada less than a length behind the United States and Italy. Great Britain was only another length behind in fourth place. The other outstanding feature of the rowing was the Australian Henry Robert Pearce's successful defence of the single sculls title he won at Amsterdam.

When all the events were over and the records complete, the Games of the tenth Olympiad, which many had despaired of ever taking place because of the ominous clouds of a world financial crisis, had earned for themselves a rightful place as one of the finest in the history of the Olympic Movement.

XI BERLIN 1936 Peter Wilson

They say first impressions are the most lasting – and the Berlin Olympic Games of 1936 were not only the first I had reported but the first I had seen. And the first impression I had of those first Games was of sitting in a hotel lounge, that of the Excelsior I think, fidgeting under the bleak gaze of three half-lifesize colour pictures of the unholy trinity of Hitler, Goering and Goebbels; it was obvious that these were to be the most political Games to date.

In 1936 there were few dictatorships. The Spanish Civil War had been in progress only two weeks by the time the Games started in Berlin on 1 August. Italy had long been under the domination of Benito Mussolini, destined to turn out a sawdust Caesar. But you needed visas, as far as I know, for no European countries apart from Russia – and you never met anyone who had been to the USSR.

But we had read accounts of German anti-Semitism and of its corollary, a colour bar which was second only in viciousness to that in force, at the time, in the Deep South of the United States. There were indeed many requests to remove the Games from Berlin, mainly from Jewish and American organizations.

Therefore it was deliciously ironic that *the* figure of the 1936 Olympic Games should be an American Negro. He was James Cleveland Owens; a condensation of his initials 'J.C.' produced the 'Jesse' by which Owens was universally known.

Owens won the 100 metres, the 200 metres, the long jump and gave the United States a winning medal in the 4 × 100-metres relay. I do not think I have ever seen such a graceful sprinter as Owens. By a trick of the eyes those legs never seemed to be coming down on the track but always rising from the cinders. The nearest approach to him I can recollect was Bobby Morrow, who, in the Melbourne Games of 1956, also won both the individual sprints and anchored the sprint relay.

But whereas Morrow flowed along the track, Owens seemed to be literally spring-toed. In none of his races was there any great drama, for his superiority was so effortless and inevitable that it reduced the excitement; but if that was a loss in his races the excitement was there in the long-jump competition.

A year earlier Owens had set the world record with a leap of 8.13 m (26 ft 8¼ in) which was destined to stand for almost a quarter of a century until Ralph Boston added just 8 cm (3 in) to it in 1960. But in Berlin, Owens, who

1936. Hitler at the opening of the 1936 Games at Berlin

only qualified for the final jump-off with his last leap because of a mix-up, could not throw off the German, Luz Long. After four of the six jumps the Negro and his supposed hated Aryan 'superior' were tied at 7.87 m (25 ft 9¾ in). But it was Owens, not the blond Aryan, who was to prove the Superman. For, with his final jump, Owens covered a magnificent 8.06 m (26 ft 5¼ in).

Long proved himself as good a loser as Owens was a magnificent winner by walking around the infield with his conqueror after the competition was finished, showing, as was often to happen later, that whatever the politicians felt, some of the athletes, despite barriers of language, customs and background, could achieve a rapport through the *lingua franca* of sport.

Unfortunately, Hitler was no sportsman. Early in the Games the German leader had summoned to his box the first two Germans to win medals in the Games so that he could personally congratulate them. But, markedly, there were no congratulations for Owens or any of the other black athletes who were so patently and embarrassingly proving the fallacy of the theory of Aryan supremacy.

Richard D. Mandell, in *The Nazi Olympics* (1972), explains that after Hitler's original personal congratulations:

Count Baillet-Latour, president of the International Olympic Committee, sent word to Hitler that he was merely a guest of honour at the Games. He should congratulate all or none. Hitler chose to congratulate none – in public at least. (Thereafter, he did warmly felicitate German victors, in private however.)

But in Goebbels' newspaper *Der Angriff* (The Attack) the American black athletes were referred to as 'black auxiliaries' of the American team, and their medal-scoring feats were excluded from *Der Angriff*'s scoring chart.

Obnoxious as this was, with the air of general suspicion – the rooms of journalists supposed to be antagonistic were searched and the Press box at the main stadium was infiltrated by temporary occupants who were there, quite obviously, not to report on what was happening in the arena but on what was being said among foreign newspapermen – there was a reverse side to this base coin.

The Olympic Games *are*, after all, the greatest sporting event on earth and not even Hitler could completely destroy the charisma of the Games and the superb performances which were put up.

There was, for instance, the 1,500-metres final which, with Chris Chataway's world 5,000-metres record against Vladimir Kuts in London in 1954 and Herb Elliott's Olympic 1,500-metres triumph in Rome in 1960, remains one of the three greatest foot races I have ever seen.

The five men who had filled the first five places in the 1932 Los Angeles Olympic Games had qualified for the final in Berlin. They were Luigi Beccali (Italy), who four years earlier had set up a new Olympic record of 3 min 51.2 sec, Jerry Cornes (Great Britain), Phil Edwards, a black Canadian, barrel-chested Glen Cunningham who, on the voyage over, had been voted the most popular member of the American team, and Eric Ny (Sweden).

Yet none of these was to win this race. That honour was reserved for a slim New Zealander, Jack Lovelock, an above-average lightweight amateur boxer whose running

1936. *Above* Jesse Owens (United States) wins the long jump with a leap of 8·06 m (26 ft 5¼ in). *Below* The Olympic Stadium and swimming pool (left)

career was nearly cut short years before, when he broke a leg playing Rugby football for the University of Otago in his native New Zealand. By a strange coincidence, Lovelock qualified as a doctor at St Mary's Hospital, London, to which some twenty years later, Dr Roger Bannister, the world's first sub-four-minute miler, was to be attached.

Only one thing detracted from this being the 'perfect' race and that was the absence of the wispy Sidney Wooderson (Great Britain), a perpetual and often successful rival of Lovelock's. Sadly, Wooderson had injured his left ankle and failed to qualify for the final – a disaster for the man who, in the next two years, was to hold the world records for the 800 metres, the half mile and the mile, and was, as far as looks were concerned, the most unlikely athlete ever to bring track fame to Britain.

Jerry Cornes, acting the hare, was first away, with Beccali, the title-holder, close on his heels and Fritz Schaumburg, the German champion, giving the crowd something to cheer about. At 400 metres, Cornes, running a brave race, was still in the lead, with Schaumburg and Ny coming up fast. A hundred metres later and the massive American, Cunningham, had forced his way into the lead. He was still there at 800 metres, with Ny second, Lovelock, who had moved up from sixth place, behind the Swede, and Beccali still dangerous in fourth position.

At 1,000 metres Cunningham was still ahead with Ny on the outside and Beccali pressing behind. When the bell pierced the continuous roar of the crowd, like an express train hurtling through a tunnel, the order was Ny, Cunningham, Lovelock and Beccali, but the Swede withered and faded as the field whirled into the back straight for the last time.

It was here that the race was won, for Lovelock, in the black, fern-emblazoned singlet of New Zealand, his blond hair rising like some golden helmet as he made his supreme effort, apparently extended his legs telescopically as he swept to the front. He won by a good four yards in 3 min 47.8 sec from Cunningham. Statistics are dull things but the value of this epic race was proved by the times of the first six competitors. Lovelock and Cunningham both beat the world record, held by American Bill Bonthron; Lovelock by a full second, Cunningham by 0.4 sec. Beccali, who finished third, clipped two seconds off the time which had won him the gold medal at Los Angeles four years earlier. In fact, the first five runners – young Archie San Romani (United States) was fourth and Phil Edwards fifth – broke the Olympic record, and Jerry Cornes, who finished sixth, still ran 1.2 sec faster than he had to win the silver medal at Los Angeles!

So gripping was this race that even that doyen of athletics broadcasters, Harold Abrahams, performing for a then much more sober-sided BBC, so far forgot the traditional neutrality of a commentator that, as Lovelock slid into the lead, he discarded his professional sang-froid to shout:

. . . 300 metres to go, Lovelock leads. 300 metres to go, Cunningham's gone up into second position, Lovelock!! Lovelock's out on his own about four yards ahead, Cunningham's fighting hard! Lovelock leads. Lovelock! LOVELOCK! Cunningham's second, Beccali, third. Come on, Jack. 100 yards to go. Come on, Jack. My God, he's done it!! Jack, come on. Lovelock wins. Five yards. Six yards. He wins. He's won. Hooray. Lovelock's passing the tape. Cunningham, second, Beccali, third, San Romani, fourth, Edwards, fifth, Cornes, sixth . . .

For Harold, who won the gold medal for the 100 metres in the 1924 Games, things could not have been easy in Berlin, for he is Jewish. But I think that 1,500-metres race must have made up for a lot.

For me 1936 was the start of an unsuccessful love affair with the toughest of all track-and-field events, the marathon of 42,195 m (26 miles 385 yd). Not, I hasten to add, that I ever even contemplated running in that murderous race. But I did hope that I would see a British runner pull it off in the Olympic Games. Alas, it was not to be. In 1936, in one of the more memorable marathons, Ernie Harper (Great Britain) was second to Kitei Son, of Korea, who ran with the Rising Sun of Japan on his chest as Japan had occupied his country. Afterwards Harper told me how, through sign language, he had indicated to Son that he was going too fast too early in the race.

Now that is the sort of remark which some disappointed athletes might make after being beaten out of first place, as though to indicate that had it not been for their own sportsmanship they might have captured the first prize. But I remember at the time I completely believed Harper. And I am glad I did so for in Leni Riefenstahl's magnificent film of the 1936 Games Harper is seen gesturing to Son to slow down.

1936. Jack Lovelock (New Zealand), number 467, moves up at the end of the second lap of the 1,500 metres.

Inevitably, as I maintain they should, for they are the very spine of the Olympic Games, events on the track and field remain most vividly stamped in the memory after some four decades. There was the amusing sight of Cornelius Johnson and Dave Albritton, two lanky American blacks who only bothered to remove their track suits after a number of other competitors had been eliminated from the high jump, apparently killing time between their leaps by shooting craps against each other. In the end both did strip for action and Johnson cleared 2.03 m (6 ft $7\frac{7}{8}$ in), 3 cm ($1\frac{1}{4}$ in) higher than Albritton and 4 cm ($1\frac{7}{8}$ in) lower than the world record which they had jointly established a month earlier in New York.

The pole vault was another compelling competition. It lasted for nearly twelve hours before, round about 10.30 p.m. by floodlight (not taken for granted as it is today), Earl Meadows (United States) was finally declared the victor, having cleared 4.35 m (14 ft $3\frac{1}{4}$ in). Two Japanese, Shuhei Nishida and Suoe Oe, finished in second and third places, each having cleared 4.25 m (13 ft $11\frac{1}{4}$ in) and it was reported that they decided to share the silver and bronze medals by sawing them in half.

Without being unduly parochial, we were naturally anxious for some British successes and in fact the British did considerably better than at some subsequent Olympic Games. A gold medal went to Harold Whitlock, a motor mechanic, in the 50,000-metres walk. Outstanding on the track was Godfrey Brown, but he could not quite win the 400 metres, finishing a fifth of a second behind Archie Williams (United States) who had set a world record for the event only two months earlier. But in the 4 × 400-metres relay Brown anchored the British team of Fred Wolff, Godfrey Rampling – who ran the race of his life – and Bill Roberts into a magnificent gold-medal victory over the Americans, who had won this event every time except once since it had been included in the Olympics.

Nor can Don Finlay be overlooked. Four years earlier at Los Angeles he had won a bronze medal in the 110-metres hurdles and in Berlin he improved on this, a storming finish bringing him second only to the American Forrest Towns, who had already equalled his own world record of 14.1 sec in a preliminary heat. Although Finlay, a beautiful stylist, never won an Olympic or world title he stayed in the top class for year after year and no one who saw his grey head – he was then forty – pass the tape first in 1949, to win his eighth AAA high-hurdles championship, will ever forget the indomitable veteran.

But while Finlay went on for years, there was one British girl who stayed at, or near, the top for literally generations. She was Dorothy Odam, later Mrs Tyler, and if ever there were a hard-luck story in athletics it was hers.

Dorothy was only sixteen in 1936, when she finished second, with the same height, 1.60 m (5 ft 3 in), to the Hungarian, Ibolya Csák. If the rules currently in operation for deciding ties had then been in force she would have won the gold instead of the silver medal. As though that were not a bitter enough disappointment, she again tied for first place in the London Olympics twelve years later – and was again placed second. I saw her again in the Helsinki Games of 1952 when she finished equal seventh, but the gold medallist's winning leap was a quarter of an inch less than Dorothy had achieved in 1948. Her final Games was in 1956 at Melbourne, when she was still good enough to finish equal twelfth.

In association football, after having quite a task to beat China, the British were defeated by Poland, even a powerful centre half called Bernard Joy being unable to stop the scoring efforts of God – one of the Polish forwards.

The swimming events, held in the magnificent pool attached to the main Olympic stadium, were dominated by the Americans and Japanese in the men's events and the Dutch girls.

The Japanese challenge to the United States, at the Games at Los Angeles, four years earlier, had been taken up, for the Americans had organized the training of their team of sixteen to a degree that had not been seen hitherto. Technically, too, they had the edge, for in freestyle their men, particularly, swam with the body in a constant horizontal position. The 100 metres, though, produced the surprise of the competition, with Ferenc Csik of Hungary winning in 57.6 sec from an outside lane and the Japanese occupying the next three places. The 400 metres produced a close contest. Shumpei Uto, like the rest of his Japanese colleagues, displayed mastery of even-paced swimming and stayed just ahead of the American champion Jack Medica. Then with about fifteen metres remaining, the American began to surge through to win by just over a second. In the 1,500 metres Noboru Terada achieved revenge for his country with a decisive win over Medica.

The most definite winner, however, was Adolf Kiefer (United States), who sliced 2.7 sec from the Olympic 100-metres backstroke record in winning a race he led from the start by more than two seconds. The closest contest came in the women's 100 metres, in which Hendrika Mastenbroek, in fourth place towards the end of the final length, swept through to set an Olympic record of 65.9 sec. Similar tactics brought her victory in the 400 metres, although she was a more decisive winner in this event.

Boxing produced the largest entry at an Olympics, thirty-eight nations sending representatives. The original entry of 251, however, receded to 191 because the International Federation decided upon weighing in the boxers on the day of the contest for a second time, and because several countries had trials in Berlin just before the competition. The use of two rings in one hall for the elimination bouts was not satisfactory, with the crowd moving from one end of the hall to the other and the gong used for one contest distracting the competitors in the other ring. The titles were well spread, however, only Germany and France taking two gold medals, and thirteen countries represented in the first three places.

One sport which produced controversy that went on long after the Olympic flame had been extinguished was equestrianism. The course for the three-day event many thought was far too tough. Three horses had to be destroyed, ending the chances of Denmark, Hungary and the United States in the team event. Of the fifty horses, twenty-seven completed the cross-country course and the notorious pond took heavy toll. Here the horse had to jump a fence into water and the depth was clearly uneven. Of the forty-six who attempted this, eighteen fell and ten horses unseated their riders. Some were more fortunate than others, for, as the crowd grew to watch these spectacular landings, it blocked the horses' escape from their riders.

In all this, the winning horse was appropriately named Nurmi, ridden by Ludwig Stubbendorf (Germany) who also took the team prize. The Danes were hardest hit by the failure of their third steed to finish since they placed the third and fourth rider.

The French achieved a breakthrough in cycling, providing the first two men home in the road race, Robert Charpentier and Guy Lapébie, who, with Robert Dorgebray, sixth, enabled them to win the team title as well. Charpentier and Lapébie were also first and second in the 4,000-metres team pursuit in which France was also successful.

Even by standards of the post-World-War-II era, the Berlin Olympics were a massive organization. Hundreds of thousands of people from every sphere of life were involved, and, for the first time, military organizations played a crucial part in the running of the Games. For example, at a festival play, on the periphery of the Games, 10,000 people were involved. The detailed organizational framework can be judged from the news bulletins which were distributed as propaganda for the Games: 3,690 newspapers and magazines received these bulletins, over 3,000 of them outside Germany; to begin with the bulletins were in five languages but ultimately fourteen languages were used. Altogether, 3,000 journalists attended the Games and there were over 150,000 foreign visitors, many of whom took back home fears that the Gathering Storm was indeed gathering.

This was also the first Olympic Games to be broadcast and televised. Television was on a closed-circuit system to halls (twenty-five in Berlin) throughout the country and over 160,000 people watched the daily transmissions from the four main Olympic sites.

Sadly, though, the overall memory of the 1936 Games was the 'Deutschland über alles' atmosphere engendered by Hitler and the Nazis. Everywhere the eye was affronted by flags upon flags, bearing the crooked cross, like so many weeds among the flower beds of less provocative devices; everywhere the ear was assailed by loudspeakers playing martial music or relaying the hysterical Sieg heil responses of the thoughtless multitudes to the appearance of the Führer. There have been other Games where tragedy has intruded – but never again, I hope, will there be a world festival of sport where the prevailing air was so odiously chauvinistic and military.

XII TOKYO/HELSINKI (Cancelled) 1940
John Rodda

In 1936 the International Olympic Committee awarded the Games of the twelfth Olympiad to Japan, Tokyo to stage the summer events and Sapporo those of the winter program. It was another crucial step forward for the Olympic Movement, giving the Games to a country in Asia and one, at that time, which to much of the Western world, still had a mystique and romanticism about it. The Japanese Olympic Committee began preparations immediately and many of the technical experts who had worked on the Games in Berlin accepted invitations to help them.

By 1938 the IOC was calling upon the Japanese to give assurances that the Games could go on unimpaired, for the Indo-China War had begun. The Japanese Olympic Committee refused to resign their intentions until their government stopped their preparations. By that point sixteen sites had been built or reserved in Tokyo for a program of eighteen sports and art competitions which were to have been held from 24 August to 8 September.

The IOC turned to Helsinki; the Finns accepted and began to prepare, only to be overtaken by war.

The IOC, having already nominated St Moritz to stage the Winter Games, met in London in June 1939 and, reflecting the optimism of the time, moved the Winter Games on to Garmisch-Partenkirchen when the Swiss would not maintain an undertaking relating to the skiing events. The Swiss supported the International Ski Federation (FIS) which refused to compete in Alpine skiing because the IOC did not regard skiing instructors as amateurs. The decision showed the IOC to be completely insulated from the political events within Germany and the strong overtones produced at the Berlin Games. In fact, the Germans continued their preparations at Garmisch until 22 November 1939, two months after war in Europe had begun. Helsinki's hopes lasted until May 1940, when it asked the IOC President, Baillet-Latour, to inform all the Federations that it was unable to stage the Games, but wished '. . . to express the sincere hope that Finland will be given the privilege to organize the next Olympic Games'.

XIII LONDON (Cancelled) 1944
John Rodda

The International Olympic Committee had received candidates for the 1944 Games from Budapest, Lausanne, Helsinki, Athens and London for the Summer Games, and St Moritz and Oslo for the Winter Games; Belgrade had also indicated willingness to stage the Games of 1948. At the IOC Session in June 1939, London was awarded the Games over Detroit, Lausanne and Rome. The Winter Games went to Cortina d'Ampezzo. But both were cancelled.

In 1942 the President of the IOC, the Belgian Comte Henri de Baillet-Latour, died; the office passed automatically to Sigfrid Edström who, as a Swede, was conveniently from a neutral country. In 1946 the IOC members, by a postal vote, awarded the Games of the fourteenth Olympiad to London and St Moritz.

XIV LONDON 1948 Harold Abrahams

Soon after the end of World War II, the International Olympic Committee decided that it would be possible to hold the fourteenth Games in 1948, and early in 1946 the Games were awarded to London. In spite of five years of war and enormous difficulties produced by shortage of materials, rationing of food, clothes and other essentials, the organization met with universal approval. The number of countries represented, fifty-nine, and the number of competitors, almost 4,500, were the highest to date. Of these countries, forty-two placed at least one competitor in the first six. Improvisation was the theme – a special temporary track was laid at Wembley Stadium for the athletics; many of the buildings from the 1924 Empire Exhibition were adapted for Press, radio and television, while the athletes were housed in school buildings and in service camps in Uxbridge and Richmond Park. The expenditure amounted to under £600,000 which included about £200,000 for the temporary work at Wembley and other venues and services provided by government departments. Receipts from 'gates' – there were often over 80,000 spectators at Wembley – meant that overall income exceeded expenditure by between £10,000 and £20,000.

Both radio and television transmission were naturally greater in extent than ever before. Although in 1948 the number of television sets in action in Britain was approximately 80,000, the number of viewers probably exceeded half a million.

In track and field events there is almost always at least one competitor whose performances are automatically linked with a particular Games, for example Paavo Nurmi in 1924 and Jesse Owens in 1936. Without doubt thirty-year-old Fanny Blankers-Koen (Netherlands) followed them in 1948. She competed in the 1936 Olympics and during World War II in the occupied Netherlands set world records for the 100 yards, high and long jumps and equalled that for the 80-metres hurdles; in June 1948 she had added the world's 100-metres record to her collection. At Wembley, she broke the tape eleven times (including a heat and final in the sprint relay); her victories in the two sprints being clear, her only struggles were in the 80-metres hurdles and in the relay.

In the former it was Maureen Gardner (Great Britain), who had almost failed to reach the final, who was well away and it was not until the sixth hurdle that Mrs Blankers-Koen caught her gallant rival. Both athletes were credited with a new Olympic record of 11.2 sec. In the relay Mrs Blankers-Koen ran a brilliant 'anchor' stage and brought victory to her country almost literally with her last stride. Had she competed in the long jump, she would almost certainly have won this event, included in the Games for the first time, since the winner, Olga Gyarmati (Hungary) beat a very modest field by four inches, nearly two feet short of Mrs Blankers-Koen's world record.

Emil Zátopek (Czechoslovakia) made his début at the 1948 Games. A few weeks earlier he had run within two seconds of the world 10,000-metres record held by Viljo Heino (Finland). This event was the outstanding competition of the first day and Zátopek took the lead after eight laps from Heino, who retired soon afterwards. Zátopek won by over three-quarters of a minute with a time, which, though almost half a minute slower than the world record, beat the previous Olympic best by more than 10 sec. There was much speculation whether Zátopek would win the 5,000 metres, too, the double having been accomplished only once before, in 1912. In his heat he and Erik Ahldén (Sweden) were well over 100 metres ahead in the last lap and so had qualified but they raced on as if their lives depended on the issue. The struggle was unnecessary and may well have affected Zátopek's running in the final two days later. By half distance the contest was between Zátopek, Gaston Reiff (Belgium), Willem Slijkhuis (Netherlands) and Ahldén. With four laps to go, Reiff broke away from the others, and at the bell, though palpably tiring, was twenty yards ahead of the Dutchman, with Zátopek another thirty yards away. With about 300 yards to go, Zátopek sprinted, caught Slijkhuis and with every stride gained feet on Reiff. With less than ten yards to go, Reiff suddenly sensed danger from the shouting of the crowd and won by about a couple of strides in the new Olympic record time of 14 min 17.6 sec. Twenty years later, Zátopek told me that he was overwhelmed by his 10,000-metres victory, thought the 'double' impossible and, with two laps to go, had felt content to be third. Then he suddenly decided to go after Slijkhuis and with renewed strength all but beat Reiff. His last lap must have been achieved in about sixty seconds – phenomenal running for those days.

It was almost an accepted fact that the United States, with three finalists in both the 100 and 200 metres, should dominate the sprints. Four of the six finalists in the 100 metres were world-record holders and it was ironic that the final winner should be Harrison Dillard, world-record holder for the 120-yards hurdles, who had failed to qualify in the American team for that event, and gained selection for the 100 metres by finishing third behind Barney Ewell and Mel Patton, though Ewell thought he had won. The photo-finish picture (this minutely accurate apparatus was first used at Wembley) left no doubt at all about the result.

Though no male athlete succeeded in being a dual Olympic champion, Arthur Wint (Jamaica) won gold and silver medals, and the American Mal Whitfield from Texas won a gold and a bronze. As in 1932 and 1936, the final of the 400 metres was a contest between Britain, the Empire and the United States. Herbert McKenley (Jamaica) started faster than his opponents and at half-distance was at least five yards ahead of Wint. But, slowly at first and later not so slowly, Wint gained upon his rapidly tiring colleague, caught him twenty yards from the tape and won by two yards, equalling the Olympic record of 46.2 sec. Whitfield, who three days earlier had beaten Wint in the 800 metres, was third.

The men's 110-metres hurdles was a veritable triumph for the United States despite the absence of Dillard. Though William Porter hit three hurdles, his perfect rhythm was not seriously affected and he won in the new Olympic record time of 13.9 sec, ahead of his two compatriots Clyde Scott and Craig Dixon. In the 400 metres, Roy Cochran, who in 1939 had won the United States title in 51.9 sec, did this time at Wembley in his semi-final, a new Olympic record, equalled by the Swede Rune Larsson in the other semi-final. But Cochran was quite supreme in the final, winning from Duncan White (Ceylon) by seven yards in 51.1 sec.

1948. Fanny Blankers-Koen (Netherlands) clearing the last obstacle to win the 80-metres hurdles

The Americans maintained their unbeaten record in the pole vault, the concluding stages of which took place in a downpour, compelling the competitors to shelter in the tunnel between their vaults.

Hungary gained its first victory in men's athletics since 1900 when Imre Németh won the hammer by 1.8 m (5 ft 11 in) with a throw just over one foot (0.42 m) short of the Olympic record; in the discus Italy finished first and second, Adolfo Consolini beating Giuseppe Tosi by exactly one metre, both Italians beating the previous Olympic record.

Perhaps the greatest performance by an American at Wembley came in the decathlon, from Robert Mathias, seventeen and a half and competing in only his third ten-event competition. Mathias, a fine all-round athlete, was a competent football and basketball performer. At the end of the first five events he was third, 49 points behind Enrique Kistenmacher (Argentina) and 32 behind Ignace Heinrich (France). Conditions on the second day could hardly have been worse for the competitors, who started at 10.30 a.m. and finished under floodlight over twelve hours later. The almost incessant downpour caused them to spend most of the day sheltering from the rain except when actually competing. Mathias went into the lead with three events to go, throwing the discus almost 3 metres (10 ft) further than any other opponent. Before the 1,500 metres, the final event, Mathias led by 261 points over Floyd Simmons (United States) and 328 over Heinrich. Hardly able to force his tired body round the 3¾ laps of the stadium, he finished in 5 min 11 sec, the third slowest of the contestants. But his lead after nine events was sufficient to enable him to win by 165 points, to the obvious delight of his mother, father and two brothers who, after travelling 6,000 miles, stayed to the damp, dark end to share in his triumph.

There was plenty of drama on the final day. In the 4 × 100-metres relay, the United States finished a good eight yards ahead of Great Britain, but when it was announced that the American team had been disqualified for passing the baton outside the 20-metre zone, Great Britain's only 'victory' was received almost in silence by a crowd that did not want to win that way. Two days later, after the Jury of Appeal had examined the film of the race, the referee's decision was reversed. The United States also won the 4 × 400-metres relay, but, alas for Jamaica, Arthur Wint suffered from cramp in the third stage and had to retire.

There was, as ever, drama in the marathon. Étienne Gailly, a twenty-one-year-old Belgian paratrooper, led from six to eighteen miles and was five seconds behind Delfo Cabrera of Argentina with a mile to go. By a supreme effort Gailly passed Cabrera 200 yards from the entrance of the stadium, and he entered it hardly able to drag one foot after the other. In the final lap of the track he was overhauled, first by Cabrera, then by Tom Richards (Great Britain).

Most of the vast crowd stayed to watch twenty-eight-year-old Dorothy Tyler (Great Britain) engage in what seemed an endless duel against the black American high jumper Alice Coachman. Twelve years before, as a sixteen-year-old schoolgirl in Berlin, Dorothy had cleared the same height as the winner, but had to be content with second place in the jump off held to decide the contest. Now she and Miss Coachman were the only two left in at 1.66 m (5 ft 5½ in). Both cleared that height. Up went the bar to 1.68 m (5 ft 6¼ in) for a new Olympic record. After taking several minutes to make her attempt, Miss Coachman got over and Mrs Tyler failed. But she got over at her second attempt. Neither could clear 1.70 m (5 ft 7 in) and Miss Coachman was the Olympic champion, having cleared the tying height at her first jump.

This was only the second occasion on which basketball featured in the Games as a competition and, as at Berlin in 1936, the United States won. Twenty-three countries took part in what were regarded as the World Championships, staged at Harringay. The level of play was extremely high and many of the matches very close. Four of the games were won by a single point and no fewer than twenty-seven by six points or less.

After a close match against Argentina in the first round, which the United States won by 59 points to 57, the American team, with several players over 1.98 m (6 ft 6 in) tall and one of 2.0 m (7 ft), met France in the final, winning 65–21. The French were a little lucky to reach the final; the draw in the quarter-finals favoured them since they were in a different half from the Mexicans, who had defeated them in the first round. In the quarter-final they beat Chile by only one point. Throughout the event the United States won all its eight matches and scored 524 goals against 256.

Twenty-seven countries with eighty-six crews provided a record entry for the seven rowing events which took place over the most famous rowing course in the world at Henley. This had been widened to take three crews instead of the usual two. In the single sculls, Jack Kelly Jr (United States), who had won the Diamonds in 1947, was keen to emulate his distinguished father who had won the Olympic title in 1920, although barred from Henley the

same year. Jack Kelly Sr's club, the Vesper Boat Club of Philadelphia, had been banned from Henley in 1905 because its eight were not amateurs according to the Henley rules, and the ban had not been lifted by 1920. Jack Kelly Jr was, however, eliminated in the semi-final by Edouardo Risso (Uruguay) by a narrow margin. The winner was the holder of the Diamonds, Mervyn Wood (Australia), who easily defeated Risso by nearly fourteen seconds in 7 min 24.4 sec.

Great Britain had two victories, in the coxless pairs and double sculls. The United States was also a double victor, in the coxed fours and eights, winning the latter for the sixth Olympics in succession. Denmark gained its first Olympic title ever, beating Italy in the coxed pairs but Italy beat Denmark in the coxless fours.

In the six Olympiads since the modern pentathlon had been introduced into the Games in 1912, Swedish competitors had dominated, having lost the gold medal only once and having gained thirteen medals out of a possible eighteen; 1948 was no exception. The Swedish captain, William Grut, won with a record score of 16 points, the previous being eighteen in 1920 and 1924, when there were fewer competitors than in 1948. Grut won the riding with no faults and followed this, again in first place among forty-five competitors, in the fencing with twenty-eight wins. In the shooting, although he had all twenty shots on target, as did thirty-one competitors, his score of 190 put him in fifth place. He won the swimming (4 sec ahead of the second competitor) and finally had his lowest position of the contest in the cross-country, finishing eighth. No other competitor in this event has ever occupied first position in three of the five events.

The swimming events at Wembley have been described as the greatest swimming tourney in Olympic history. New Olympic records were set in eight events and equalled in another. The United States made a clean sweep in the six men's events, fifteen of its eighteen representatives reaching the finals. The Americans also dominated the diving, winning all four titles for the fifth successive time. Mrs Victoria Draves won the springboard diving with the last dive of the contest, and in the high diving she was third at the end of the compulsory dives but took first place by two magnificent voluntary ones.

There was one world record, in the men's 4 × 200-metres relay, in which a United States team including Walter Ris (winner of the 100-metres freestyle from fellow-American Alan Ford) and the first two in the 400 metres, William Smith and James McLane (the latter also winner of the 1,500 metres), beat the previous record, set by the Japanese in 1936, by over five seconds. Ris beat the Olympic record in the 100-metres freestyle by one-fifth of a second. In the 400-metres freestyle, McLane beat the previous Olympic record in his heat, but in the final lost to fellow American William Smith, who beat him by 2.4 sec and also took 1.2 sec off McLane's recent record. McLane, however, easily proved best in the 1,500 metres, defeating the Australian John Marshall by over twelve seconds.

In the women's swimming, Greta Andersen (Denmark) won the 100-metres freestyle. Ann Curtis (United States) won the 400 metres before producing a remarkable last leg in the 4 × 100-metres relay to give the United States victory; she was timed over her stint at 64.4 sec, one-fifth of a second inside the world record, though this was not recognized as it was made in a relay.

1948. The photo-finish for the 100 metres final shows that Harrison Dillard (United States), bottom, was clearly the winner.

The weightlifting was the most representative ever, with 120 competitors from thirty countries taking part in the six divisions. The United States, which previously had taken only one victory, won four titles, Egypt capturing the other two. The bantamweight, held for the first time, was won by Joseph De Pietro (United States); 1.42 m (4 ft 8 in) tall, he had such short arms that he was only just able to raise the bar above his head in the snatch. The lightweight produced some of the most thrilling lifting of the whole competition. With one attempt in hand, Ibrahim Shams (Egypt) had to lift 147.6 kg ($325\frac{1}{2}$ lb) to win. Actually he achieved 147.4 kg (325 lb), which, with an overall total of 360.0 kg ($793\frac{1}{2}$ lb), meant that he tied with Attia Hamouda, but was awarded the gold because he was 1.36 kg (3 lb) lighter than his fellow Egyptian.

The middleweight winner was Frank Spellman (United States), who beat his fellow American nineteen-year-old Peter George. George, the youngest competitor in the sport, set Olympic records in the snatch and jerk, but just failed with his final attempt in the jerk to exceed his previous best by some 5.5 kg (12 lb). Had he succeeded he would have been Olympic champion.

The United States won both the light heavyweight and the heavyweight classes. The former went to Stan Stanczyk, who easily beat the Olympic records in the press, snatch and jerk and, of course, in the overall total. In the heavyweight John Davis got 452.5 kg ($997\frac{1}{2}$ lb), within 4 lb (1.81 kg) of the 1,000 lb (453.6 kg) total, a mark he was to exceed four years later.

The victories of Turkey in the Greco-Roman wrestling were unexpected, for it is freestyle wrestling which has always been popular in that country and though the skill of Turkish wrestlers in the past had been limited, their strength had always made up for such deficiencies in technique. In the freestyle welterweight, Yaşar Dogu (Turkey) won four of his five contests by falls, while the featherweight Gazanfer Bilge, also of Turkey, the European champion, won five out of his six fights by falls.

In the beautiful setting of Torbay, the opening ceremony for the yachting, which concluded with the arrival of the last of 107 runners who had brought the Olympic torch from Wembley, was a most impressive occasion. The five events, each with six days' racing, produced a great

series of contests of rare excitement. The United States was the only country to win more than one title and nine of the twenty-five countries competing gained medals. Norway, Sweden and Denmark were prominent in the Dragon class, the United States and Cuba in the Star. On the final day's racing, the Norwegian crew had to gain third place to win the Dragon class; this it achieved by only three seconds. In the Swallow, the first time this event had been included, Stewart Morris (Great Britain) had to finish at least fourth to win; this he did with ten seconds to spare. The American crew in the Dragon class included the 1912 dual athletics sprint champion, Ralph Craig.

With 206 competitors from thirty-nine nations, the boxing entry was the biggest since 1924. Argentina, Hungary and South Africa each won two weights, Czechoslovakia and Italy one each. The contests, held at the Empress Hall and at Wembley, were carried out with no serious incident and with exemplary behaviour by the competitors. By contrast, the judging and refereeing was, to say the least, in many cases indifferent, chiefly because of the lack of experienced officials due to World War II.

George Hunter (South Africa), winner of the light heavyweight, was awarded the Val Barker Trophy for the most stylish display in the whole of the Olympic boxing. Never was an honour more richly deserved. He boxed impeccably and correctly, with the knuckle part of the closed glove, and showed a wide variety of punches in his winning bouts.

In at least four of the five cycling events, the forecasts of most of the experts went awry. In the 1,000-metres sprint, twenty-eight-year-old Reg Harris (Great Britain), who had been wounded in the Western Desert but had proved himself to be the outstanding rider in Europe by winning the world title in 1947, succumbed in the final to Mario Ghella (Italy), losing both heats by 3 and $1\frac{1}{2}$ lengths. Harris also had to be content with second place in the 2,000-metres tandem; he and Alan Bannister defeated Ferdinando Terruzi and Renato Perona of Italy in the first race, but lost the next two, the final one by only 15 cm (6 in) in almost complete darkness. The program had fallen badly behind and without floodlights at the Herne Hill track it was only possible to see the white of the British riders' singlets on the back straight in the final race. Journalists had to use matches and torches to send their final reports by telephone for the booths were not equipped with lights. In the 4,000-metre team pursuit, Italy, the favourite, lost to France; in the final, in which both teams appeared jaded after strenuous semi-finals, the four French riders maintained good team formation, while the Italians split up before the end. France won by nearly forty seconds, in 4 min 57.8 sec, some three seconds slower than its time in the semi-final.

Fast times in the 1,000-metres time trial were impossible owing to the heavy and damp weather. The favourite, Jacques Dupont (France) won from Pierre Nihant (Belgium) with one second to spare, but in a time nearly five seconds slower than his previous best.

In the equestrian events, though Sweden was announced as the winner of the team dressage with nearly 100 points more than France, a year later the International Equestrian Federation (FEI) disqualified the Swedish team because one of its members, Gehnäll Persson, was non-commissioned although he had been entered as an officer (at that time the rules of the International

Equestrian Federation limited the competition to officers, a restriction later dropped). The individual dressage was won by Hans Moser (Switzerland), with one of the most remarkable horsemen ever, fifty-four-year-old Captain André Jousseaume (France), second. Captain Jousseaume had already won a gold and silver medal in 1932 and 1936 respectively in the team competition and was to win a bronze in the individual event in 1952. In five Olympics spanning twenty-four years, he finished fifth three times in the individual contest in addition to his silver and bronze medals.

Fencing attracted the largest entry of any Games and the very heavy program necessitated fencing for long hours on most of the thirteen days of the competition. The Games will long be remembered for the severity and intensity of the competition and especially for the atmosphere of good fellowship and good sportsmanship which prevailed throughout.

In the men's individual foil the Frenchman Jehan Buhan, whose brilliant fencing played the leading part in his country's victory in the team event, did not lose a fight in the final. His runner-up was another Frenchman, Christian d'Oriola, who had won the world title the year before at the age of eighteen and who was to win the gold medal in 1952 and 1956.

In the women's foil Ilona Elek (Hungary), in her forty-second year, was to retain the title she had gained in Berlin. Her runner-up, Karen Lachmann (Denmark), who had also competed in Berlin and, like Elek, had won all five qualifying bouts, was defeated 4–2 in the final. Elek's sister Margit finished sixth. Another veteran, thirty-two-year-old Ellen Müller-Preis of Austria, winner in 1932 and third in 1936, again won the bronze medal.

Of the seventeen teams which helped to make the association football competition the most variegated ever held in Britain, the two strongest, Sweden and Yugoslavia, reached the final, in which the Swedes, who throughout the competition scored a total of twenty-two goals to three despite missing many 'sitters' in the early stages, won 3–1. Perhaps the best game in the series was in the semi-final between Sweden and Denmark, when the Danes dominated the match for much of the first half and scored the first goal. In the seventeenth minute Sweden equalized with one of the most extraordinary goals ever seen: except for the Swedish centre forward, Gunnar Nordahl, who had taken refuge there to avoid being offside, the Danish goal was empty and Henry Carlsson, the Swedish inside left, headed the ball into the net, where it was caught by Nordahl after it had crossed the line.

It was originally planned that the gymnastics should be held in Wembley Stadium, but the rainstorms compelled a last-minute transfer to the Empress Hall. The entry of sixteen men's and eleven women's teams made it essential to have many events (both men's and women's) decided simultaneously, so the arena resembled several three-ringed circuses, making the spectators almost cross-eyed as they tried to see as much as they could of everything happening at once. Finland beat Switzerland in the men's team combined exercises and won the individual pommelled horse, Switzerland the rings, parallel and horizontal bars and Hungary the individual floor exercises. In the solitary women's event (combined exercises) Czechoslovakia gained a fine victory despite the fact that one of the team died in London soon after the team's arrival.

XV HELSINKI 1952 Peter Wilson

The 1940 Olympics had been offered to Helsinki after Tokyo had been banned from holding the Games because of the Sino-Japanese War, but World War II delayed Finland's opportunity to be host until 1952. The Games in Helsinki were regarded as the happiest and conducted in the spirit closest to the original Olympic ideals. To competitors from outside Scandinavia, Finland was still very much a land of mystery. All that most visitors to Helsinki knew about the host nation was that it had fought very bravely against the Russians in 1939–40, that in summertime it had a very long day and a very short night, and that in Paavo Nurmi it had produced perhaps the greatest athlete of all time.

There was one blot but this was clearly not the fault of the Finns. The Russians, unexpectedly entering the Games for the first time since 1912, were allowed to set up a separate Olympic Village for their competitors, along with those from Hungary, Poland, Bulgaria, Romania and Czechoslovakia.

This broached the Olympic spirit and it is hard to understand how the International Olympic Committee, which had strained at so many gnats, allowed itself to swallow this particular camel. Probably they were anxious to accommodate the lost sheep which had returned.

Incidentally, one amusing incident was connected with the 'Eastern camp'. At one stage it looked as though the USSR was going to skate home in the unofficial point-scoring system. In fact, so sure of victory were the Russians that they had a large board constructed showing the relative positions of the various competing countries.

But right at the end, the United States came with a rush, winning no fewer than five gold medals in the boxing, and as soon as the Russian officials saw that they were going to be overhauled they began to dismantle the scoreboard. Unfortunately for the Russians, while their 'demolition' job was in progress, a representative of one of the US news agencies came into the camp and sent out the story under the heading, 'Russians caught with points down!'.

There was another 'incident', this time at the opening ceremony. This has become so diverse that spectators are never quite sure what is coming next. And this explains why a rather plump lady, partly veiled and wearing what appeared to be a flowing white nightdress, was able to get onto the track, complete a half circuit of it, and actually ascend the official rostrum and begin a speech with what sounded something like 'Peace'.

But lack of breath, because of her girth and her exertion, and the timely action of the one senior Finnish official who did know that she was not part of the official ceremony stopped her at that point. She was removed by the police, who later announced that she was a mentally deranged German girl who had come to address 'Humanity', as was also an enthusiastic Sunday newspaper journalist who asked so many questions, in English, of the uncomprehending Finnish police that they decided he must, at least, be her accomplice! Fortunately he was released sooner than 'The Angel of Peace'.

But there was one part of the opening ceremony which was truly memorable, when the Olympic flame was borne into the arena on the last lap of its long journey from Greece.

1952. Emil Zátopek (Czechoslovakia), holder of four Olympic gold medals, winning the 5,000 metres

For a moment there was stillness as the crowd looked in silence at the trim but middle-aged figure carrying the torch. Then one mighty roar went up from thousands of throats, from everyone, in fact, except those who were so overcome that they could only weep.

The torch-bearer was Paavo Nurmi, the man who had done as much as any other single athlete to popularize track and field events and, with Sibelius and Field-Marshal Mannerheim, was the most famous of his countrymen.

Although he had been reported as racked with rheumatism, the fifty-five-year-old runner moved as featly as ever until he had completed his lap. Then, after igniting a huge candelabra at the side of the track, Nurmi handed over the torch to his countryman, Hannes Kolehmainen, who had won gold medals for the 5,000 metres, 10,000 metres and the cross country – in the Stockholm Games of 1912. The sixty-two-year-old warrior lit a second flame on top of the stadium tower.

It was rumoured at the time that the International Olympic Committee had not altogether approved of the selection of Nurmi as torchbearer. That was hardly surprising for the International Amateur Athletic Federation, the senior sports federation, had declared the Finn ineligible to compete in the 1932 Los Angeles Games – for alleged breaches of amateurism – where he might well have added to his total of medals. But anyone who knew the stern independence of the Finns would have known that it would take more than an unspoken veto by the IOC to make them abandon their hero.

The Games indicated that the world was recovering strength after the war and finding a new sophistication, for Olympic records were broken on nearly 100 occasions.

There was, of course, only one 'Man of the Games' at Helsinki: the magnificent Czech Emil Zátopek, who triumphed, like some revitalized Nurmi, in the 5,000 metres and 10,000 metres and also in the marathon, a race in which he had never before competed.

The 100-metres final was one of the most exciting – and controversial – that I have ever watched. The first four

men, Lindy Remigino (United States), Herb McKenley (Jamaica), McDonald Bailey (Great Britain) and Dean Smith (United States) were all credited with the same time, 10.4 sec, one-fifth of a second outside the world record.

To this day I am not convinced that the gold medal for this race went to the right man. At the time I wrote: 'From my seat, three yards beyond the finishing tape and about twenty-five feet above, it looked as though McKenley had won by a whisker.' One of my abiding memories is of McKenley remaining behind in a deserted stadium, still studying the photo-finish picture of the race and commenting: 'I feel certain I won. Yes, even after studying the picture of the photo-finish until my eyeballs nearly fell out!' But, to a suggestion that he might protest, he replied: 'No. I don't want to win on a protest – or on a photograph. I want to win on my legs.'

Roger Bannister (Great Britain) had been one of the most confident tips for the 1,500 metres, although he was still nearly two years away from his unforgettable achievement of being the first sub-four-minute miler.

Unfortunately in Helsinki there was such a large entry for the 1,500 metres that an additional round had to be run so that there were races on three successive days – a schedule which Bannister, never the most robust of runners, would certainly not have chosen. He was not particularly impressive in the semi-final, which was won by a virtually unknown runner from Luxembourg, Josef Barthel.

In the final Bannister made his customary 'killing-off burst' some 300 yards from the finish but he could not sustain it and both Robert McMillen (USA) and Werner Lueg (Germany) finished ahead of him.

But ahead of them all, although he was given the same time as the American (since 1500-metres races were timed only to a fifth of a second at that time), was the unconsidered little Barthel, 3.3 seconds faster than his previous best, the only athletics winner from the Grand Duchy in the history of the Olympic Games. Barthel on the winner's pedestal, tears streaming down his face, as his National Anthem was played – after the band had found the music – was one of the memorable sights of the Games.

1952. Paavo Nurmi (Finland) carrying the Olympic torch into the arena

1952. The emotion of an Olympic winner. Josef Barthel (Luxembourg) after the 1,500 metres

And so to Zátopek. No one was particularly surprised when he won the first gold medal of the Games by taking the 10,000 metres. He had after all, won the gold in this event four years earlier in London. In the meantime he had set up a new world record for the distance and although he did not approach this in Helsinki he still won as he liked, by over 90 yards from Alain Mimoun, a French Algerian.

The 5,000 metres was different. In fact Zátopek was beaten in his heat. That needs some explanation – indeed, in those days, whenever Zátopek was beaten it needed more than a bit of explanation!

Zátopek was determined that a Russian competitor, Aleksandr Anufriev, should win this heat. So much so that he kept waving the Soviet athlete on, with a lap to go, and even risked disqualification by actually pushing him home on the last lap.

It was, of course, very different in the final. Then there was no time for playing. The shorter distance was always more of a challenge to Zátopek, and it was not for nearly another two years that he finally beat the world record put up by Gunder Hägg back in 1942.

The final lap of the Helsinki 5,000 metres provided another great athletics memory. With little more than half a furlong to go, Chris Chataway (Great Britain), then a twenty-year-old Oxford undergraduate, was leading. But as they straightened into the last run-in you could see Chataway's face salt-white against his red hair, and working with the effort of keeping going.

All at once Herbert Schade, the German, was past Chataway with Zátopek and Mimoun haring after him – and Chataway, exhausted and possibly brushed by one of them, was lying sprawled half on the track, half on the infield.

Zátopek had to give it everything he had to win in 14 min 06.6 sec, just 0.8 sec ahead of Alain Mimoun; who else? For Mimoun always seemed to be the 'bridesmaid' to Zátopek in those days.

Having already run nearly 12½ competitive miles, in two 5,000- and one 10,000-metres races, Zátopek was now faced with bringing his total up to 62.2 km, slightly over 38⅝ miles in eight days, with his final race, the marathon.

But that was not all. Although he had never run the distance before he was so confident that he was able to joke about it beforehand.

On the same day that Emil had won the 5,000 metres,

his wife, Dana, had won the women's javelin event; Sándor Barcs in his excellent book *The Modern Olympics Story* (1964) relates: 'When he was asked whether he was tired, and if he would enter the marathon race, he said: "At present, the score of the contest in the Zátopek family is 2–1. This result is too close! To restore some prestige I will try to improve on it – in the marathon race."'

It was obvious from the start that this was going to be a personal duel between Britain's Jim Peters, who a few months earlier had set a world's best time of 2 hr 20 min 42 sec (there is no world record in the marathon because of the varying difficulty of the courses) and the apparently irresistible Czech.

At first the cheers came from the Englishman's supporters when, a mile from the stadium, Peters was seen to be leading by about 100 yards; but they were soon hushed as the red singlet of Zátopek was seen licking along after him like some all-consuming flame.

Did Peters set too fast a pace? Probably. The same fault was to crucify him in the agonizing Commonwealth Games marathon at Vancouver two years later. But had he not set such a killing rate Zátopek might have won even more easily. I think the answer was that no runner then competing could have beaten Zátopek on that day.

As it was, Peters led at five, ten and fifteen kilometres but, by the half-way mark, Gustaf Jansson (Sweden) was leading from Zátopek with Peters third. Shortly after that Zátopek took the lead which he was never to surrender. By the 15-mile mark he was 30 yards clear of the Swede with Peters 300 yards adrift. Round about the 20-mile mark Peters was attacked by cramp, sat by the roadside for a time, tried to continue but collapsed again and had to be brought back by car.

In the meantime Zátopek, clearly enjoying the whole 'outing', continued on his way, chatting to cyclists, policemen and enthusiasts lining the route – whether they understood him or not did not matter, his body spoke for him.

It would be idle to say that he showed no signs of strain. If Zátopek had had to run for a bus his face would have been twisted in agony; nevertheless, he ran into the stadium just over 2½ minutes ahead of the second man, Reinaldo Gorno, of Argentina. He had taken 6 min 16 sec off the previous Olympic best for the race and had won by some 750 yards.

I have always believed this to be the greatest Olympic achievement I ever saw in the eight Summer Games which I covered professionally – just marginally eclipsing Jessie Owens' four athletic golds in 1936.

The exploits of Zátopek tended to blur some startling individual performances which were significant breakthroughs in their event. Charles Moore of the United States was expected to win the 400-metres hurdles long before he arrived in Helsinki, so distinctive had been his form in the United States, and he was not to let down the tipsters. He began with a victory in 51.8 sec, then broke the 1948 Olympic record by R. B. Cochran of 51.1 sec by three-tenths of a second and, in the final, where he ran in the difficult outside lane, again recorded 50.8 sec to win by half a second.

Of those who retained their titles in the athletic stadium, Bob Mathias, the decathlon champion, was the most conclusive. He set a world record of 7,887, the largest single increase in points since the 1920s.

Opposite, above The end of an American era. The USSR on its way to victory in the 1972 basketball final. *Below* The USSR's women beat the Japanese at Munich in volleyball, added to the Olympic program in 1964.

In the women's competition there were world records in the 80-metres hurdles, 4 × 100-metres relay and shot, while that for the 100 metres was equalled. There was no single outstanding woman, like Fanny Blankers-Koen of the 1948 Olympics, but the Australian women overcame the difficulty of travelling from their winter to the northern hemisphere summer and finding their best form. Marjorie Jackson took both sprint titles for Australia and Shirley Strickland was the winner of the 80-metres hurdles.

But athletics for once, did not eclipse all the other sports in Helsinki, where some truly remarkable things happened in the boxing ring.

For instance, two of the competitors subsequently won the richest prize in sport, the professional world heavyweight championship. Yet the one who was to win it first, Floyd Patterson (United States), competed in Helsinki as a middleweight; and Ingemar Johansson (Sweden), who was to take the professional title from him, nearly seven years later, was disqualified in the final of the heavyweight competition in Helsinki, and failed so completely to put up any sort of fight that his silver medal was withheld. Patterson made pugilistic history by being the only man to that time to regain the professional title – an achievement made all the more sweet because it was from the Swede that the American black recaptured it.

Yet had it not been for the introduction of two new weights for the Helsinki Games I think it is more than possible that Patterson might never have won an Olympic gold medal – and if he hadn't triumphed in Helsinki his professional future would have probably been much more dubious.

The two new weights which were introduced for the first time were the light middle and the light welter, and the introduction of the light middle meant that László Papp, the Hungarian who had won the middleweight gold medal in London four years previously, was now able to shed several pounds, without the worry of giving weight away.

In one of the preliminary rounds Papp knocked out Ellsworth 'Spider' Webb, an American black who later, after turning professional, stopped future world middleweight champions Joey Giardello and Terry Downes, as well as outpointing future double world champion, Dick Tiger.

Papp was at his peak then, more experienced than he had been in London, not so old as he was in the Melbourne Games of 1956 – although even then he was good enough to beat, in the final José Torres, who was later to win the world professional light-heavyweight title.

In the swimming pool, which had been built for the Games of 1940, the spread of medals was greater than in any previous games. The Hungarian women and the American men left the greatest impact with the former's relay team shattering the world record by nearly three seconds. Within that world record Éva Novák (Hungary) swam her 100-metres leg in 65.1 sec, which was 1.7 sec faster than her countrywoman Katalin Szőke's winning time in the individual 100 metres; Miss Novák was not entered for that event.

Joan Harrison became the first South African Olympic swimming champion when she held off the world-record holder, Geertje Wielema of the Netherlands, a hot favourite to win, in the 100-metres backstroke.

XVI MELBOURNE 1956 Neil Allen

The year of 1956 was not a happy time for much of the world. 'The year of disgrace' is how it has been described in one Olympic book. Whatever one's political views, the 'revolution' or 'rebellion' in Hungary and the 'invasion' or 'action' in the Suez Canal zone left mankind trembling on the brink of a major war with the possibility of atomic weapons being used. Looking back, it seems remarkable that the Melbourne Games were held at all. In 1949 the IOC only had the margin of one vote in favour of Melbourne being the host and it was a nasty shock, much later, when the Australian Government's strict laws on quarantine meant that its country could not organize the Olympic equestrian events.

In violation of the Olympic charter, it was reluctantly decided that the equestrian sports would be held in another country. Between 10 and 17 June, teams from twenty-nine countries rode and jumped in the Stockholm stadium which, forty-four years earlier, had been the scene of the fifth Summer Olympics. Even so there was a worrying moment for the Swedes when a fire broke out near the Olympic stables. Fortunately all the horses were led to safety and Sweden was eventually rewarded for its work as substitute Olympic host by individual and team gold medals in the dressage and individual in the *concours complet*.

The build-up to the Melbourne Olympics proper included a spate of disputes over television and filming of the competitions and so many reports that the main facilities would not be built in time that Avery Brundage, President of the IOC, flew out to investigate. As the opening Olympic day drew nearer, and fighting continued in Hungary, it was astonishing to learn that the Hungarians would be represented at Melbourne, even though many of their competitors had had to shelter in the cellars of their team hotel in Budapest. Then the Dutch Olympic Committee decided unanimously that the Netherlands would not participate because 'events in Hungary had spoiled the festive Olympic atmosphere'. Three days later, on 9 November, the People's Republic of China withdrew from the Games because the Republic of China (Taiwan) had been allowed to compete, saying, 'The Chinese Olympic

1956. The Olympic flag is carried round the stadium in Stockholm at the opening of the equestrian events.

Opposite, above John Akii-Bua (Uganda), winner of the 1972 400-metres hurdles in a world-record time. *Below* Kip Keino (Kenya) leads P. Vasala (Finland) and B. Foster (Gt Britain) in the 1972 1,500 metres.

69

Committee, the All China Athletic Federation, solemnly declares that the Chinese people and the Chinese athletes cannot tolerate this scheme of artificially splitting China.'

The Dutch Olympic officials agreed to donate 100,000 guilders (£10,000 then) to Hungarian sufferers from the fighting in their country and the Spanish Sports Federation decided it was not fitting for Spanish athletes to compete at Melbourne 'while the liberty of peoples is being trampled on'. Egypt withdrew, after demanding that nations 'guilty of cowardly aggression against Egypt' should be expelled from the Games and Lebanon also pulled out in protest against the 'Australian attitude' towards the Middle East crisis. Brundage meanwhile insisted, 'We are dead against any country using the Games for political purposes, whether right or wrong. The Olympics are competitions between individuals and not nations.'

Few Games have been organized under such a cloud of depressing world news as that of 1956 but Australian charm, courtesy and efficiency swept aside the usual minor disagreements and teething problems. No modern Olympic Games has been entirely free from trouble outside the realm of sport and it was a triumph for the people of Melbourne that such an admirable spirit pervaded both the Olympic village at Heidelberg and the city itself.

In spite of the stormy political weather, there was sunshine and blue skies at the Melbourne Cricket Ground when the sixteenth Games of the modern era were opened by HRH the Duke of Edinburgh. For all the talk of withdrawals, sixty-seven countries were represented in the great bowl as spectators shielded themselves with newspapers. One of the biggest cheers, as the parading teams marched in, was for the Hungarians, half dressed in sea-blue suits and half in blazers and flannels because they were short of supplies after their unexpected arrival. On the results board was the statement: 'The Olympic Movement tends to bring together in a radiant union all the qualities which guide mankind to perfection.'

One incident on that opening day which was to be remembered twelve years later, when the Mexico Olympics were almost upon us, was the lighting of the Olympic flame. It was done by a young Australian named Ron Clarke, already holder of the world junior mile record. Clarke suffered burns on his uplifted arm that day as bravely as he was to accept his fate, in the 1960s, of being a multiple world-record breaker who never won an Olympic gold medal.

It was Clarke's speciality, the 10,000 metres, which opened the first act of the 1956 Olympics and it proved to be one of the classic long-distance races. The two giants were Vladimir Kuts, a stocky Soviet ex-marine, and Gordon Pirie, a tall, skinny London bank clerk. In June 1956 Pirie had beaten Kuts over 5,000 m in Norway and set a world record of 13 min 36.8 sec. But two months later, Kuts had shown his great strength by taking more than 12 sec off the 10,000-metres record with 28 min 30.4 sec.

The battle, then, between a bludgeon and a rapier was clearly set down as the two men swiftly detached themselves from the rest of the field and Kuts threw down the gauntlet with 61.4 sec for the first of the twenty-five laps. Head hunched forward, Kuts tried remorselessly to draw the sting from Pirie's finish with a long burst on the fifth lap and, before the end, another six brutal accelerations. Each time Pirie, as if drawn by elastic, went with the Russian, but the British runner's strength ebbed.

It was at the end of the twenty-first lap that Pirie suddenly wilted and gradually slipped back to eighth, as Kuts, now relieved of his persistent shadow, galloped away for a magnificent victory. Years later, the Russian told how the turning point for him in the 10,000 metres was the moment when, on the twentieth lap, he stole a look back at Pirie and saw the British runner's face was glazed with exhaustion.

Kuts gained a magnificent double on the Melbourne Cricket Ground – one which was not destined to be achieved again over 5,000 metres and 10,000 metres until the 1972 Olympics. But for many, the outstanding athletic figure of the 1956 Games was the American sprinter Bobby Joe Morrow. At twenty-one, this 6 ft 1½ in (1.87 m) Texan impressed us most of all by the margin with which he won his titles. Though the timing in the 100 metres gave both Morrow and his runner-up the same time of 10.5 sec, against the wind, the photo-finish timings (not used officially) had Morrow more than 0.1 sec in front. In the 200 metres Morrow was pressed by the 1952 champion, Andy Stanfield (United States), but came through magnificently in the straight to win by more than a yard in 20.6 sec, an Olympic record. Finally Morrow achieved his life ambition of emulating the 1936 hero Jesse Owens with a third gold sprint medal in the 4 × 100 metres relay on the anchor leg. Ironically, the fastest running of the Melbourne Games may well have been that of Leamon King on the second relay leg for the United States. King had twice equalled the then world 100-metres record of 10.1

1956. Vladimir Kuts (USSR) winning the 5,000 metres, Derek Ibbotson and Gordon Pirie (Gt Britain) behind

sec the previous month but in the American 'sudden death' Olympic trials, back in June, he had finished fourth and therefore was selected only for the team event.

Morrow was the spearhead of an American men's athletics team which took fifteen gold medals in twenty-four events – one more gold than at Helsinki in 1952. They had a clean sweep of gold, silver and bronze and gold in the 200 metres, the 110-metres and 400-metres hurdles and the discus, and finished first and second in five other events. In spite of the lack of encouragement for women's track and field in the United States, the Americans also gained a gold medal in the high jump by Mildred McDaniel with a world record leap of 1.76 m (5 ft 9¼ in), a silver medal in the long jump by seventeen-year-old Willye White who was to finish eleventh in the 1972 Games, and bronze awards for a sprint relay team which included a sixteen-year-old named Wilma Rudolph who was to win three golds four years later in Rome.

The only individual men's world athletics record during the Games came in the javelin. A head wind was proving troublesome to the throwers. In the fourth round a Norwegian named Egil Danielsen at first stopped at the end of his approach run without throwing. The next time, however, he came striding through, and his red steel Seefab spear went sailing on and on, with a long, late, low trajectory until I thought it might even strike the pole vaulters at the other end of the ground. The measurement was 85.71 m (281 ft 2½ in) but one did not need the measuring tape to know that this was a major breakthrough in a spectacular event.

The 400 metres was won in only 46.7 sec, thanks to the running of semi-finals on the same day as the final as much as the cold, windy weather. But the 800 metres and 1,500 metres and steeplechase were all memorable for various reasons. The 800 metres was as much of a classic as the 10,000 metres, with a dramatic sight in the home straight as Britain's slightly built Derek Johnson headed the deep-chested American Tom Courtney for about thirty of the last thirty-five metres. Courtney was so exhausted by his eventual narrow victory that he had to receive medical attention.

The 1,500 metres provided an unexpected winner in Ron Delany of Ireland as well as one of the most competitive races at this distance. John Landy (Australia), bitter about being branded as front runner without a finish, lay back during a race marked, in all but its final stages, by a closely packed field. Also 'sitting' was Delany, who was fourth with 200 metres to go as Britain's Brian Hewson made a break. But once Delany did take off, with his high-stepping knee action and shrugging shoulders, he rocketed away unanswerably, covering the last 400 metres in 53.8 sec, the final 100 metres in 12.9 sec and bursting through the tape to fall on his knees in prayer. Running up to him with congratulations, and then checking respectfully for a moment, was the bronze-medal winner Landy who the twenty-one-year-old Delany said later had given him invaluable advice when they met in the United States.

For the British reporters the steeplechase was bound to be a big story when their own little-regarded Chris Brasher, who had only scraped into the team, was a clear winner. Then the rest of the world's press became rather more interested when it was announced that the winner was not Brasher but Hungary's Sándor Rozsnyói who had

1956. Betty Cuthbert (Australia) wins the 200 metres from Christa Stubnick (Germany).

finished 2.4 sec behind. Later came the news that Brasher had been disqualified for impeding Ernst Larsen (Norway) while crossing a hurdle. It was not until 7.5 p.m., three hours after the start of the race, that Brasher's agonized appeal was upheld though he did not have his victory ceremony until the following day. It was Britain's first Olympic athletics gold medal since 1932. But what I remember most warmly is that the three men who stood to gain from Brasher's disqualification, Rozsnyói, Larsen and the fourth finisher Heinz Laufer (Germany), all instantly offered Brasher their support in his protest.

The outstanding woman athlete at Melbourne was an eighteen-year-old Sydney girl named Betty Cuthbert who made up for the lack of any gold by Australian males in winning the 100 metres and 200 metres and producing, characteristically open-mouthed, a tremendous sprint on the last leg of the 4 × 100-metres relay to overhaul a determined British team. Australia also took the 80-metres hurdles through Shirley Strickland (de la Hunty) who, running on the same winning relay team as Betty Cuthbert, ended a unique Olympic career spanning three Games in which she had won three gold, one silver and three bronze medals.

Melbourne's athletics also saw the beginning of a famous sporting romance when the hammer-throwing champion, Harold Connolly of the United States, fell in love with, and later married, Czechoslovakia's discus winner, Olga Fikotová. My most pleasant memory of the athletics is at the end of the marathon, won by Alain Mimoun of France at thirty-six years of age after three silver medals on the track in the Games of 1948 and 1952. The man who had beaten him each time was the great Emil Zátopek (Czechoslovakia) but on that sun-splashed evening of 1 December 1956 it was Mimoun who waited deliberately, waving aside photographers until Zátopek trotted home sixth and Mimoun could embrace his old rival and friend.

For many, the end of the athletics meant the Games were virtually over. But certainly not for the Australian hosts who had purposely arranged the program of sports so that the climax was the sport in which they had the highest hopes. Every one of the 5,500 seats in the swimming and diving complex (costing about £500,000) was booked months before the opening of the Games and the Melbourne public were even ready to queue to pay in order to watch teams in training.

Australian interest and support received a rich reward with eight gold, four silver and two bronze medals in the swimming events, compared with two gold, four silver and five bronze by the Americans who had dominated the previous Games in swimming. For the purists, it was even more impressive that in Melbourne the Australians won every one of the men's and women's freestyle events since they are the most developed races. Such a clean sweep had not been achieved since the Antwerp Olympics of 1920. In both men's and women's 100-metres front crawl Australia won all three medals.

Behind the success of the Australians lay a scheme of preparation so intensive that it included a twelve-week training camp from late July in Townsville where the Australian midwinter temperature was perfect for open-air training. At the same time a revolution in training methods was being advocated by the physiologist Forbes Carlile and refinements in technique suggested by coaches like Frank Guthrie.

With this background it was not surprising that Jon Henricks led his fellow Australians John Devitt and Gary Chapman to the first three places in the 100-metres freestyle and that there was the same national domination in the women's sprint, narrowly won by a young girl named Dawn Fraser who was to win this Olympic crown twice more. Born in England but brought up in Australia was seventeen-year-old Murray Rose, who took the 400-metres freestyle with a burst in the third 100 metres which was too much for Japan's Tsuyoshi Yamanaka. For me the highlight of the swimming was the 1,500 metres in which Rose and Yamanaka also had to face the American George Breen who had achieved a new world record of 17 min 52.9 sec in his heat. In the final Breen set the pace until 850 metres, when Rose made one of his typical mid-race bursts and gradually moved away, only for Yamanaka (Breen now languishing back in third place) to make a remarkable but unsuccessful counter-attack in the final two lengths. Rose had become the first swimmer since Johnny Weissmuller in 1924 to win two freestyle Olympic titles. Britons, meanwhile, were able to rejoice in their first swimming victory since 1924, when Judy Grinham took the 100-metres backstroke by a touch from Carin Cone (United States).

The boxing program, held at the West Melbourne stadium, had neither the glamorous setting nor quite the hyper-efficient organization of the swimming. But the finals had much appeal for the public. Terry Spinks (flyweight) and Dick McTaggart (lightweight) both won gold medals for Britain with McTaggart also taking the Val Barker trophy as the best stylist of the whole competition. Britain's team of seven also won one silver and one bronze medal which is worth noting. The USSR, technically very sound, had three champions and the United States, like Britain, two.

The American boxing team was reduced by mis-calculations about weight limits and their Helsinki triumphs of 1952 were reflected only by James Boyd at light heavyweight and heavyweight Pete Rademacher who took less than a round to beat Lev Mukhin of the USSR. Rademacher's punching drew gasps from the crowd.

The only final decision with which there was serious disagreement was at welterweight in favour of the Romanian southpaw Nicolae Linca over Freddie Tiedt (Ireland). But nothing in the tournament raised the pulse like the light-middleweight final. For sheer emotion, it possibly surpassed any other event in the whole of the 1956 Olympics. The reason was twofold. László Papp was attempting his third successive gold medal in Olympic boxing, having been middleweight champion in London in 1948 and light-middleweight winner in Helsinki in 1952. The second reason was that Papp was Hungarian and the sympathy of many people in Melbourne was with the competitors of the Hungarian team.

Papp's opponent was José Torres, Puerto Rican born but representing the United States and later world professional light-heavyweight champion. I thought that Torres took the first round with left leads against his southpaw opponent. But in the second round the packs of Hungarian supporters nearly lifted the roof off the stadium when Papp exploded a beautifully timed left hook to the jaw which sent Torres skittering across to the ropes. From then on the American was a beaten man though Papp, carrying his thirty years with care, refused to sail in and take unnecessary risks. When the Hungarian, having boxed even better in the third and last round, got the points decision, he was also awarded an ovation and some of his countrymen and women wept tears of joy.

There was a much less happy occasion a few days later in a water-polo match between Hungary, eventually outstanding champions once again in spite of a talented Yugoslav team, and the USSR. As Hungarian spectators booed, Russian players became rough and eventually the Hungarian Ervin Zádor climbed out of the water with a split eyebrow. At one stage it seemed that spectators might intervene but police restored order and Hungary won 4–0.

Looking back over the whole program of sports, I recall India beating Pakistan for the hockey title in a temperature of about 85 °F (29.4 °C); the emergence of a new school of athleticism, rather than pure technique, making some impression in the fencing (though Britain's Gillian Sheen won on classic lines in the foil); and weightlifting having the third biggest entry of all the sports. What I missed because one could not see everything, even in those calmer times, was the heavyweight lifting final in which American Paul Anderson won only by virtue of a lighter body-weight than Humberto Selvetti of Argentina. The next year Anderson lifted more weight than any other human when he raised 6,270 lb (2,844 kg) off trestles with his back.

When we came to the final evening, and discarded newspapers blew round the stadium, the Philistines could claim that the USSR had 'won' the Games with ninety-eight medals, thirty-seven of them gold, to seventy-four (thirty-two gold) by the United States. For my part, I do not think it is nostalgia for the past which makes me choose the following headline as epitomizing the spirit of the 1956 Olympics which had only just escaped cancellation: 'Melbourne's Family Affair. Going to Olympic Games Has Been Great Fun.' So it was.

XVII ROME 1960 Terry O'Connor

Rome, from where the order ending the Ancient Games was sent, became host of the Modern Celebration in 1960. The new and the old were never so closely together in Olympism. Wrestling took place in the Basilica of Maxentius, where two thousand years before similar competitions were held. In the Terme di Caracalla gymnastics were held, thus bridging another sporting canyon between the ancient and modern. The marathon, which started before the Capitol, finished by the Arch of Constantine. But modern Rome indelibly imprinted its image upon the events with athletics, swimming and hockey in the Foro Italico, Mussolini's creation, while within the sporting complex of EUR, the magnificent Sports Palace, for boxing, and the Velodrome, for cycling, were examples of Rome's sporting architecture created specifically for these Games.

Within less than an hour, on 2 September 1960, New Zealand athletes Murray Halberg and Peter Snell captured two of the blue-riband events, the 5,000 metres and the 800 metres, at the seventeenth Olympic Games. During a celebration in which the United States failed to dominate the track and field events as it had for the past half century, it was significant that New Zealand, with a population of less than 3,000,000, should produce two champions. It was a welcome indication of the international spread of world-class talent.

The older of the two runners wearing the famous all-black shorts and singlet emblazoned with a silver fern was twenty-seven-year-old Halberg. He did not look like a champion due to a withered arm which was a legacy of a school Rugby injury, but, as often happens, he compensated with an indomitable spirit. Like so many other Olympic champions, he proved that physical handicaps can be overcome.

Halberg, like his colleague Snell, was coached by Arthur Lydiard, whose ideas had a tremendous impact on athletic training during the period before and after Rome. Like many successful 5,000-metre runners, Halberg had progressed from the shorter distances. Therefore he had the basic speed and the long training runs ordered by Lydiard added to the stamina he was to need on that sweltering September day in Rome.

Kazimierz Zimny, a tenacious little Polish runner, led the twelve runners into the opening stages of the race and in the heat it was obvious that the time would not be exceptionally fast. In fact it was one of only four track events at Rome in which the Olympic record was not improved.

Time was of no concern to Halberg. He was satisfied to be last at 1,000 metres, reached in 2 min 41.2 sec. He had travelled 11,000 miles from a country where losers are not recognized. Before the race he outlined his philosophy when he said:

> I am not concerned about records – only winning. So many men have lost races worrying about the time or opposition. In the Olympic Games you can never be sure who is the most dangerous rival and therefore it is better to concentrate on your own performance. Even if you break a world record it does not last, but you can never take away an Olympic title.

By 2,000 metres Halberg had moved up to fifth position but he was still biding his time while the lead switched between Zimny and the Australian Albert Thomas. With no one capable of breaking up the field as Vladimir Kuts (USSR) had done in Melbourne four years earlier, it was possible for Halberg to settle in. As so often in a 5,000 metres, the early and middle stages were a preliminary to the grand finale.

Coming into the home straight with just over three laps left, Halberg struck. He used the long stretch of track to stun his rivals with an electrifying burst of speed, and by the time he reached the mark indicating that three laps were left had opened a gap of ten yards. This was increased to twenty yards with 800 metres left.

Over the last lap when Halberg's head sagged and he appeared to be in trouble it seemed that he might have attacked too soon. Behind him Hans Grodotzki (Germany), urged on by many of his own supporters, was hacking back the lead. It was fascinating to watch the fast-moving German bearing down on the frail man in black.

The noise of the crowd awakened Halberg to the danger of the situation, and he somehow summoned up the strength to go on to win by eight yards and then collapse as he clutched the tape, which in that moment was his tangible reward as victor. His last lap of 73 sec was the slowest in the race but he would not have cared if his final time had been more than 14 min. It was in fact 13 min 43.4 sec, with Grodotzki second and Zimny third.

Before the Rome athletics began, the twenty-one-year-old barrel-chested Snell was virtually unknown, although he had beaten two well-known Australians Tony Blue and Herb Elliott over 800 metres. Halberg had warned that Snell could well prove himself the strongest man in the two-lap event and this was the case in the final.

The draw for the 800-metres final, from the inside, was Manfred Matuschewski (Germany), Roger Moens, the world-record holder (Belgium), Christian Wägli (Switzerland), George Kerr (Jamaica), Paul Schmidt (Germany); Snell was on the outside. For the first time since 1896 no American runner was in the final. As expected, Wägli, a tall, upright runner, took the lead, going through the first lap in 52.3 sec, but on the final back straight drooped and wilted under the pressure of being chased by such a talented field.

1960. Wrestling was held in the magnificent Basilica of Maxentius.

Impatiently Moens took up the running, followed by the smoothly moving Kerr. Coming aggressively down the final stretch, Moens looked certain to crown a fine career with an Olympic title. In a moment of panic he turned right to see how closely Kerr was placed. It was at that second that Snell, coming through on the inside with a tremendous finish, caught Moens. The Belgian tried to hang on but could not match someone at the beginning of a great athletics career. Snell won in the Olympic record time of 1 min 46.3 sec, with Moens two-tenths of a second behind.

At Rome the 1,500 metres was won by another athlete from the southern hemisphere, Herb Elliott. Every generation produces a sportsman who completely dwarfs his rivals and such a man was the bronzed Australian, who was never beaten over the 1,500 metres or mile. At the age of twenty, in 1958, he had set world records at both distances.

Although work had lured him away from athletics for a long time before Rome, few believed that he could not achieve the dream of winning an Olympic title which he had held since he was a teenaged spectator at the Melbourne Olympic Games four years before. He was coached by Percy Cerutty, who was determined that he should achieve not only victory but a world record to ensure an unforgettable Olympic memory. Concentration and an ability to escape from virtually all human inhibitions were the secrets of Elliott's superiority. Never did he display this in a more ruthless manner than at Rome. As he nursed himself into the race, he was prepared to stay at the back of the field for two-thirds of the course, but then, goaded by the waving of a white towel by Cerutty as a signal that a world record was possible, he took off with a devastating burst and finished with a final 400 metres in 55 sec. Michel Jazy (France) and István Rózsavölgyi (Hungary), second and third respectively, admitted that they felt completely outclassed. Elliott won by an unbelievable margin of 20 yd in a world time of 3 min 35.6 sec. No wonder he was called 'the human deer'.

An indication of how the United States' grip on the Olympic athletic arena had been loosened was seen in the sprints, which were won by two Europeans. Armin Hary captured the 100 metres for Germany's first Olympic track title, and the bespectacled Italian Livio Berruti won a popular local victory over 200 metres. The Latin excitement at this triumph was illustrated when a 280-lb Italian journalist near me collapsed at the end of the race and took an hour to recover.

The Italians made full use of the facilities of their ancient capital to stage the most colourful of Olympic marathons and were rewarded with a dramatic climax. The main stadium was not used and sixty-nine starters began their long haul amid chaotic crowd scenes beneath the Capitol Hill, centre of the ancient Roman Empire, and finished under the moon and torchlights along the Appian Way, almost under the Arch of Constantine.

Such a setting would have been memorable in itself but the race not only produced a world-best time of 2 hr 15 min 16.2 sec but created the first Ethiopian Olympic champion, Abebe Bikila, a barefooted runner who was a member of Emperor Haile Selassie's Personal Guard. It was also the first time that Africans filled the first two places, as behind Bikila was a Moroccan soldier, Rhadi Ben Abdesselam. Bikila's father had fought against the

1960. Abebe Bikila (Ethiopia), barefooted, on his way to win the marathon in a record time

troops of Mussolini in 1935 and it was ironic that Bikila should choose Rome to make his conquest. Another athlete trained by Lydiard, Barry Magee of New Zealand, finished third.

In the 10,000 metres, Pyotr Bolotnikov (USSR) ran a shattering 57.8-sec last lap, breaking Vladimir Kuts' Olympic record to take the title, but he never managed to make the same impression as his countryman who had won two gold medals four years earlier.

This was also a high period for Polish athletics: the very talented Zdzisław Krzyszkowiak won the 3,000-metres steeplechase and the artistic Józef Szmidt took the triple jump, both with Olympic records.

In the 400-metres hurdles, Glenn Davis (United States) was one of the three athletes to retain his Olympic title, but he was disappointed not to be challenged this time by Gert Potgieter (South Africa) who had been eliminated by a serious car accident in Germany two weeks before the Games opened. This was to be the last occasion on which South Africans competed in the Olympic Games because the apartheid policies of their government meant that their National Olympic Committee could not subscribe to the principles of the Olympic Movement. In the 110-metres hurdles, in which the Americans again took the first three positions, Lee Calhoun held his title.

The United States was prevented from winning its traditional gold medal in the 4 × 100-metres relay by a disqualification and the title went to Germany. Britain reached the semi-finals when Nigeria was disqualified in the heat, and then took the bronze medal when the United States was ruled out. Both disqualifications were for exchanging the baton outside the zone limit.

Britain's only athletic gold medal was won by the tiny Don Thompson, called 'little mouse' by the Italians. He won the 50,000-metres walk after training for the Rome temperature in his own bathroom.

In the field events there was a titanic clash in the shot with Bill Neider (United States) taking the title from defending champion Parry O'Brien (United States). Neider was only in Rome as a replacement for the injured Dave Davies. For the first time 7 ft (2.13 m) was cleared in the Olympic high jump and the world-record holder John Thomas (United States) was beaten into third position by two Russians, Robert Shavlakadze and Valeri Brumel. The lead repeatedly changed hands in the decathlon before Rafer Johnson (United States) beat Chuan-Kwang Yang (Republic of China/Taiwan) by a mere 58 points, to set another Olympic record.

In 1960 there were only ten women's events in track and field and the USSR claimed six, but the heroine was the pretty nineteen-year-old black Wilma Rudolph (United States), who won three gold medals in the sprints and relay. As a child, Wilma, a member of a Tennessee family of nineteen, was crippled by polio. There was no trace of any disability as she poured elegantly over the 100-metres stretch in 11.0 sec and the 200 metres in 24.0 sec. Such was the acceleration of this long-legged girl that even her poor starting could not aid her rivals.

In the field events only the 6 ft 2 in (1.88 m) Romanian Iolanda Balaş prevented the Russians winning all the gold medals. There was a double triumph for the Press sisters with Irina winning the 80-metres hurdles and Tamara the shot. Nina Ponomareva, who had won the discus at Helsinki in 1952 under her maiden name of Romashkova, collected her second title.

American swimmers had vowed after winning only five gold medals (two men's and three women's) in Melbourne that it would be different in Rome. It certainly was. They won eleven and broke five world records. This time the Australians suffered disappointment. Bad weather had upset their preparations at home and then most of their young stars suffered from 'Roman tummy' on arrival. It was therefore left to the veterans Dawn Fraser, John Devitt, Murray Rose, John Konrads and David Theile to ensure that they were the second swimming nation.

The only other country among the forty-eight represented that won a swimming gold medal was Great Britain. To achieve this, nineteen-year-old Anita Lonsbrough from Yorkshire had to fight a close battle, in what many considered the race of the tournament, the 200-metres breaststroke against the blonde Wiltrud Urselmann (Germany). At the halfway stage Miss Urselmann was 2 sec ahead but by the last turn the two girls were level. At the beginning of the last 50 metres, the British girl edged ahead and held off a long challenge to break the

world record in 2 min 49.5 sec. Miss Urselmann was timed at 2 min 50.0 sec, also inside the world record.

Ingrid Krämer, a seventeen-year-old German girl, won the springboard and highboard diving events. She was the first non-American to take the springboard title since it was included in the Games in 1920 and the first to win the highboard since 1920.

The floodlit pool provided a perfect setting for the events and it was regrettable that a place of such beauty and friendliness should have been the scene of a bitter controversy over the decision to award the 100-metres freestyle title to John Devitt (Australia). Over the last ten metres the Australian was in the lead but Lance Larson (United States) put in an incredible burst and appeared to touch a hand ahead. This view was confirmed by the timings of 55.0, 55.1 and 55.1 sec but these were calculated to average 55.2 sec like Devitt's. Two of the first-place judges gave Devitt the verdict but two silver-medal judges named him second. Slow-motion television came out in favour of Larson but Devitt kept the gold medal. A tie would have been a fair decision but this was not permitted by FINA laws. It was the last Olympic swimming competition in which electronic timing was not used.

In the women's events the astonishing American squad of teenagers dominated, with Chris Von Saltza, aged sixteen, winning the 400-metres freestyle, Carolyn Schuler, seventeen, the 100-metres butterfly, and Lynn Burke, seventeen, the 100-metres backstroke. They combined with others to win the 4 × 100-metres freestyle and 4 × 100-metres medley relays, both in world-record times.

Boxing took place in the beautiful Palazzo dello Sport, and Italian spectators, burning newspapers to make torches under the magnificent dome, watched six of their countrymen compete for ten of the gold medals. This made the finals night unforgettable. It seemed the stadium would be set alight when heavyweight Franco de Piccoli (Italy), a hard-hitting southpaw, took only 1 min

1960. Livio Berruti (Italy), a popular winner of the 200 metres

30 sec to knock out the portly Russian European champion Andrei Abramov in the quarter-final.

In the light-heavyweight division, Cassius Clay, later Muhammad Ali, was first hailed as a 'world' champion. He was only eighteen but already displayed the showmanship which later became his trademark as a professional. In the final he met the veteran Zbigniew Pietrzykowski (Poland). The Pole succeeded in luring him into indiscretions in the first round but at the end of the second Clay shook off his relaxed mood and lashed Pietrzykowski four times to the head. Then, in the final round, Clay really tightened up, putting his punches together, and it needed all Pietrzykowski's courage to stay on his feet.

Again a regrettable feature of the boxing was the standard of judging. Although judgment in boxing has to be partly a matter of opinion, there were instances where contests were marked 60–57 by one of the five judges and 57–60 by another. This meant that the first judge saw Boxer A as the winner of all three rounds while the other marked the same man as the loser of the same three rounds.

Overshadowing the cycling events was the death of the Danish competitor Knud Jensen in the road race. It was later confirmed that the use of drugs had been a contributory factor. It was in the road race that the USSR prevented Italy achieving a 'grand slam' of victories, but it needed an inches victory by Viktor Kapitonov over Livio Trapè.

Vyacheslav Ivanov (USSR) was the only competitor in the rowing events to retain an Olympic title but his victory in the single sculls was disappointingly easy because the one man who would have provided stern opposition, Stuart Mackenzie of Australia, was missing. Between the Olympic years Mackenzie had gained three major victories over Ivanov but he suffered a relapse after a stomach operation. European oarsmen dominated the other events.

In the association football tournament it looked as if Yugoslavia might fail in its fourth successive Olympic final when its captain Milan Galič was sent off for arguing with the referee after what appeared to be a legitimate goal was disallowed. At that stage Yugoslavia led by 2–0; the Danes, finally beaten 3–1, took second place and Hungary third.

In basketball the United States gained its fifth Olympic win in a row, with the USSR second for the third time, but history changed in the hockey tournament in which India was unthroned after thirty-two years' supremacy by Pakistan.

There were so many competitors in the weightlifting events that competitions sometimes lasted until 4 a.m. The USSR added to its tally of gold medals by winning five titles, while Turkey continued its success in wrestling with seven gold medals.

The Bay of Naples provided a perfect setting for the yachting and it seemed fitting that in such waters Crown Prince Constantine of the Hellenes should be at the helm of *Nirefs* to win the gold medal in the Dragon class.

Of all the memories left after the celebration of the seventeenth Olympiad, none was more beautiful than the closing ceremony – a tribute to the vision and poetry of the Latins. Even when the Olympic flame was extinguished, the torchlights of burning newspapers filled the sky and pointed to the future and Tokyo 1964.

XVIII TOKYO 1964 Vernon Morgan

It is not easy to find the correct epithet to describe the Games of the eighteenth Olympiad, staged in Tokyo in 1964. There is no doubt that at the time these were the greatest modern Olympics. They were also joyous and were named the 'Happy' Games by one veteran reporter. Their success should not be judged by monetary profit or loss; nor by the standard of the performances during the Games. Personally I would say that the success of a Games depends on the feelings of all – organizers, officials, competitors and public at the closing ceremony. Let the opening be joyous and the closing sad. In spite of the frolicking at the closing ceremony at Tokyo – which many interpreted as an expression of thanks – my belief is that the general majority were sad that it was all over, and that they were forced to reconcile themselves with the saying that 'all good things come to an end'.

None was more impressed by the Tokyo Olympics, nor more sad to leave Japan than Avery Brundage, President of the IOC, who has more experience of the Olympic Games than any man alive. He not only said the Games were a success but a phenomenal success. There is little doubt that in spite of their great size, these Games evoked less criticism from every quarter than perhaps any other. Everyone appeared to enjoy themselves; the smiling Japanese did indeed seem to spread a spirit of happiness everywhere. As Brundage declared, 'The entire nation from newsboy to industrial tycoon adopted the Games as his own project and went out of his way to please the visitors.'

One of the highlights of the Games was the consistently large crowd in the main stadium. On one dark wet day, the rain fell steadily from leaden skies as some of the qualifying rounds of field events were taking place; had the terraces been empty one would not have been surprised. But instead they were nearly full; it was unique in Olympic history. Thousands sat huddled under their umbrellas, the rain dripping from them and their raincoats. Such was the enthusiasm and fortitude of the Japanese that they were still there, mostly soaked, for the afternoon's major events. That was the spirit of the 1964 Olympics in Tokyo.

Japan was the first country in the Far East to be given a Games. It had been awarded the 1940 Olympics but withdrew in 1938. Immediately Tokyo had been allocated the 1964 Games, easily defeating its rivals, Detroit, Vienna and Brussels for this honour, the Japanese set about their task to make them the greatest ever, and above all to show the world that though harsh things might have been said about them as a result of World War II, they were at heart human and a friendly nation. It is my belief that it was the latter task that was ever uppermost in the minds of the Japanese hosts.

And how well they succeeded in both their aims. There is no doubt that from a national point of view the Tokyo Olympics could not have been a greater success. But at an enormous financial cost. If one considers every yen spent on Tokyo after it had been given the Games, the cost probably exceeded £1,000 million. Even the £30 million spent on just staging the Games was a staggering figure.

All the efforts of the Japanese to make a success out of the 1964 Olympics looked at one time as if they might be sabotaged – by politics. This was over the GANEFO

(Games of the New Emerging Forces) affair. Indonesia, which had been suspended by the IOC over the question of the admission of competitors from Israel and Taiwan to the fourth Asian Games in 1962 of which it was the host, and was therefore ineligible for the Tokyo Olympics, decided to hold its own GANEFO Games in Jakarta in 1963. And it persuaded the People's Republic of China, no longer a member of the IOC, to take part. Before these Games were held the IOC warned that no persons taking part in these Games were eligible to take part in the Tokyo Olympics. The Indonesians, having had their suspension removed, and North Koreans took no notice of this edict and travelled to Tokyo hoping to take part and banking on the Japanese being able to persuade the IOC to change its mind. The Japanese did not. However much they would have liked the Indonesians and North Koreans to take part, the Japanese realized the dire consequences of fighting the IOC on this matter. Even at this late stage the Games could have been ruined. But though permission to take part was given to both Indonesian and North Korean competitors that had not competed in the GANEFO both teams decided to return home. Tokyo got out of it remarkably well, for the situation was at one time ugly. Sport had triumphed over politics. And it appeared to do so during the competitions.

Just how much their eighteenth Olympiad was appreciated by the members of the IOC was shown by the award to the Tokyo Metropolitan Government of the Olympic Cup 'for their efforts in the successful preparation of the Games'; to the Japanese Olympic Committee the Count Bonacossa Trophy 'for its endeavours over the five years before the Games commenced'; and the Diploma of Merit to Dr Tenzo Kange 'for his creative designing of the National Gymnasium'. The gymnasium contained not only the superb unique swimming pool but the picturesque basketball arena.

Apart from their huge cost the Tokyo Olympics set new records for the Games. No fewer than ninety-four nations took part as against the previous highest figure of eighty-four attained in the previous Olympiad in Rome. Tokyo also beat Rome's record in the number of events, with 163 against 150.

And what of the Games themselves? It is sad to some people, but none the less a fact, that it is no longer true to say that the taking part and not the winning is what matters. Gradually the Olympics have become an arena for the gladiators, and there are those who think the last Olympics staged in the Coubertin spirit were in Helsinki in 1952. Now the aim of all, or at least the majority, is not merely to take part but to win, even if it means cheating. Thus records fall like autumn leaves in each succeeding Olympics and the Tokyo Games were no exception in this respect.

In a galaxy of talent the outstanding man was the Ethiopian marathon runner Abebe Bikila, and the leading woman the Australian 'mermaid' Dawn Fraser. Bikila had surprised the world by winning the marathon in the previous Games in Rome in a time nearly a quarter of an hour faster than the previous Olympic best. He showed this to be no fluke by winning as he liked in Tokyo, beating his Rome time by some three minutes.

The most remarkable aspect of Bikila's victory was the fact that he took part at all. Five weeks before the marathon he had an operation for appendicitis. It was not

1964. Ann Packer (Gt Britain) winning the 800 metres in a new world and Olympic record of 2 min 01.1 sec

thought possible for him to recover sufficiently even to compete, let alone win. But this lean little man was tough. In less than two weeks after the removal of his appendix he had started to train and by the day of the race he was fit again for the 26 miles 385 yards. He let the others do the pacemaking for the early miles but then forged ahead and was virtually unchallenged in winning in the new Olympic time of 2 hr 12 min 11.2 sec. He was more than four minutes ahead of his nearest rival at the finish, Basil Heatley (Great Britain), who took the silver medal by overhauling the Japanese Kokichi Tsuburaya on the final circuit of the track. When Emil Zátopek won the marathon in the 1952 Olympics in Helsinki everyone was astonished to see him so fresh. But in Tokyo he was outdone by Bikila, who jogged onto the grass at the end of the race and provided the crowd with a demonstration of callisthenics. A really great Olympian.

Dawn Fraser, though now at the ripe old age for a sprint swimmer of twenty-seven, won the 100-metres freestyle for the third successive Olympiad, and in doing so set a third successive Olympic record. Eighteen-year-old Don Schollander (United States) set three world and four Olympic records in winning his four gold medals, the 100-metres freestyle, 400-metres freestyle, the 4 × 100-metres relay and 4 × 200-metres relay. His toughest race was the 100 metres, when he beat Bobby McGregor (Gt Britain) by little more than a touch. He could have had a fifth gold had he been picked for the anchor leg of the medley relay but Steve Clark was given the final (freestyle) leg. Schollander, of Swedish extraction, attended to detail in preparation but there were a few eyebrows raised when he shaved not only his body but his fair head to reduce all possible friction and so become as streamlined as possible.

In athletics, Peter Snell of New Zealand, winner of the 800 metres at Rome, retained that title and took the 1,500 metres – the first double in these events since Albert Hill of Britain in 1920; while the New Zealander's victory in the previous Olympiad had been something of a surprise, he was among the favourites at Tokyo, but his head as well as his heart and legs got him the gold. His tactics were superb, and the way he challenged round the final curve took one back to 1936 and the Berlin Games when his similarly black-vested compatriot Jack Lovelock dashed through the field to win the 1,500-metres title. In Rome Snell only just scraped through by two-tenths of a second in the new Olympic time of 1 min 46.3 sec. In Tokyo, in beating his own Olympic record in returning 1 min 45.1 sec he had five-tenths of a second in hand. Snell had fewer problems in getting his double in the 1,500 metres. But once again it was his perfect judgment that helped him to get another gold. His final time was not all that shattering, but he ran the last lap in the remarkable time of 53.2 sec, with 25.4 sec for the final 200 metres to win by some ten metres.

Hardly less remarkable than Bikila's feat was the performance of the American Al Oerter in the discus. He too triumphed over the physical handicaps that looked like preventing him from winning in three consecutive Olympics. In Melbourne in 1956 he had won with an Olympic record of 56.36 m (184 ft 11 in); in Rome in 1960 he had bettered this in winning with a throw of 59.18 m (194 ft 1¾ in). The discus man slipped a disc in 1964 but he looked fit enough to defend his title when he got to Tokyo. But then misfortune struck again. This time, slipping in the wet, he fell heavily and severely damaged his ribs. When it came to the day of competition he was not only heavily strapped but also had to be given a pain-killing injection. In spite of

1964. Peter Snell (New Zealand) elated after taking the 800 metres in an Olympic record of 1 min 45.1 sec

this he actually beat his own Olympic record in qualifying. Yet in the final he had to wait until his penultimate throw of 61.00 m (200 ft 1½ in) to get the gold, snatching victory from his Czechoslovak rival Ludvik Danek by little more than a foot.

In the boxing ring Joe Frazier began his climb to world fame with a gold medal in the heavyweight division; while in the unlimited weight of the judo competition, included in the Olympics for the first time, it was a Dutchman Anton Geesink who brought a cold embarrassing silence to the hall when he became the only overseas winner in the sport that the Japanese really believed was their preserve.

The sport that really developed in Tokyo, largely due to television presentation, was gymnastics. The hall was packed night after night with a pretty blonde Czech, Vera Čáslavská, who won three titles, as the main attraction.

History repeated itself in the equestrian events. In the 1952 Olympic Games in Helsinki Great Britain had begun the final event, the Grand Prix jumping, without a single gold medal. But a faultless last round by Harry Llewellyn on Foxhunter gave Britain the team gold. The individual gold on this occasion was won by a French officer, Pierre Jonquères d'Oriola. In Tokyo, France came to this last final event also without one gold medal. Again it was a horse that came to his country's rescue, for the aptly named Lutteur (Fighter) enabled the same rider, d'Oriola, at forty-four one of the oldest competitors in the Games, to win his second gold, and France's only one in Tokyo.

The men's 100-metres title, which had only three times not been won by someone from the American continent, went back there. From the first round Bob Hayes gave cause for little doubt that he would win, but the connoisseurs of sprinting were bemused by his rolling, lumbering style. It was never more apparent than in the final, where he seemed bent upon the running and overlooked the starting. Enrique Figuerola of Cuba and Harry Jerome of Canada got away best and in most sprinting events had enough advantage at 30 metres to have been fighting for the gold. But then Hayes had got into his stride and thundered past them to equal the world record of 10.0 sec and win by a fifth of a second.

The Americans, having regained this prize, invaded a new province, by taking, for the first time, the 5,000-metres and 10,000-metres titles. Bob Schul, playing a skilful waiting game in the shorter event, outmanoeuvred his more experienced European rivals. After a slowish early pace it looked as though Michel Jazy, France's world-record breaker at a mile would be strong enough to win, but in the final lap he was caught first by Harald Norpoth of Germany and then off the final bend by Schul.

The 10,000 metres left a feeling of some dissatisfaction for so many runners were lapped that those challenging for the medals on the final laps were impeded. It was the last occasion on which this race was run without heats. Ron Clarke of Australia, Billy Mills of the United States and Mohamed Gammoudi of Tunisia were the men in contention. Clarke was slightly impeded by a lapped runner as they swept into the final circuit and Gammoudi dashed to the front. As the Tunisian opened up his stride, Clarke went with him, with Mills on their heels. In the final straight Mills had much the better finish and he streaked past them both to record an unexpected victory.

XIX MEXICO CITY 1968 John Rodda

The Games of the nineteenth Olympiad in Mexico City caused anger in certain areas of the sporting world which led to some useful physiological research, very nearly precipitated a revolution and provided in the end some vivid memories.

When the IOC, at its meeting in Baden-Baden in 1963, awarded the Games to Mexico City, which is situated at a level of over 2,134 m (7,000 ft), very few people understood the significance of competition in the endurance events at this height. It quickly became clear that there would be a disparity between those who lived at altitude and those who came from sea level and whose bodies could not react in the same manner in high-class competition. The disparity was large enough to bring a degree of unfairness. Several countries undertook physiological investigation and the work of the British Olympic Association brought a proposal from the IOC that a period of four weeks in the last three months before the Games could be spent in training at high altitude to acclimatize. It was an unsatisfactory compromise for many countries allowed their athletes to train at altitude for much longer periods.

In Mexico City itself there had been discontent with the régime, particularly from students, many of whom felt that for a country with much poverty it was wasteful and misguided to be spending vast sums on the Olympic Games. The students used the event to draw attention to their cause. Their brushes with authority in the months before the Games produced an alarming-looking situation: three weeks before the Games were due to begin there were tanks on the road outside the University (the source of the trouble) opposite the main Olympic stadium. After several demonstrations and with the protest movement growing in momentum throughout the country and clearly involving far more than student life, the Army crushed the opposition on the night of 2 October – ten days before the Games were due to start. At a demonstration of 10,000 people in the Square of the Three Cultures in Mexico City, the military surrounded the square and opened fire. In the bitter battle which followed, lasting five hours, more than 260 were killed and 1,200 injured. There was no further trouble and the Games went on without interference.

The effects of competition in thin air were soon to be seen. Three of the first four men in the 10,000 metres lived at high altitude and the winning time was almost a minute slower than the Olympic record. In the 5,000 metres the same theme could be traced, with the second-, third- and fourth-placed runners men from the mountains. It blurred the emergence of Africa's talent, Naftali Temu (Kenya) winning the 10,000 metres, Mamo Wolde (Ethiopia) taking the silver and later winning the marathon, Kipchoge Keino (Kenya) winning the 1,500 metres and taking the silver medal in the 5,000 metres and two of his compatriots, Amos Biwott and Ben Kogo, placing first and second in the steeplechase.

There was another side effect of the altitude, seen in its most distorted form in the long jump, which Bob Beamon (United States) won with a prodigious leap of 8.90 m (29 ft 2½ in). The world record was 8.35 m (27 ft 4¾ in). Beamon's jump came in the opening round and destroyed the competitive spirit in the rest, apart from Klaus Beer (German Democratic Republic). Beamon, who only in Mexico had listened to Ralph Boston, his colleague and previous medal-winner, about using a stride pattern in his approach run, bounded down the runway and seemed to run on into the air rather than stamp his foot on the board and lift up. When he cut the sand a world record seemed certain but the moments were long and hanging until the scoreboard flashed out its historic figures 8.90. In addition to Beamon's undoubted talent, there was another factor: 27 per cent less atmospheric pressure and 23 per cent less air density. This assistance means that potential world-record breakers are not going to surpass Beamon's leap without the special circumstances he enjoyed. The triple jump gave another example of help provided by reduced resistance, for the world record was broken nine times during the competition with Viktor Saneev (USSR) winning the event in the final round with a trial of 17.39 m (57 ft 0¾ in).

Most people consider the hero of the Mexico Olympics to be Al Oerter (United States) who won the discus title for the fourth consecutive time. His throwing during the season had been well behind his best and that of Jay Silvester (United States), the world-record holder. The opening throws of the competition had been modest and then rain fell to halt the event; this was a break in concentration and preparedness that the less experienced competitors could not cope with, but on resumption, with the circle wet and the air heavy with dampness, Oerter reached 64.78 m (212 ft 6½ in), a personal best throw. This completely destroyed his opponents, who believed that this sort of distance in these conditions was beyond them. They all faltered but, in the fifth and sixth round, Oerter, with little speed across the circle but whip from his throwing arm again reached distances beyond the mark achieved by the silver medallist Lothar Milde (German Democratic Republic).

Many contests on the track were tinged with doubt because of altitude. Ron Clarke, Australia's multi-world-record holder, exemplified the spirit and hopelessness of the honest lowlanders. He struggled to stay in contention with the leaders in the 10,000 metres run at a pace two minutes slower than his world record but, with two laps remaining and when he was in fourth place, the oxygen debt suddenly became too great and he took 2 min 18 sec to run the last two laps, rather than something close to two minutes, collapsing onto the verge and needing oxygen for revival.

1968. Misuse of the Olympic podium. The US 4 × 400-metres relay team give the black power salute.

1968. Bob Beamon (United States) makes his world-record-shattering leap of 8·90 m (29 ft 2½ in).

The contest for first place evolved into one between Mamo Wolde (Ethiopia), Mohamed Gammoudi (Tunisia) and Naftali Temu (Kenya). These three were in contention two laps from home when Wolde struck and opened a wide gap. Gammoudi tailed off but across the final 250 metres Temu surged back and caught the Ethiopian who had nothing left for a counter-attack. But Wolde was to take a gold medal – in the marathon. At least this event showed that Abebe Bikila (winner in 1960 and 1964) had human frailties after all. A foot injury had made him a doubtful starter and although he ran he dropped out after 17 km. Wolde made his decisive thrust when he still had 10 km to run and it showed the ebbing strength of those around him. On the long climb back to the stadium he took a lead of almost three minutes; many of those behind had found the blazing sun too much.

The most decisive winner in the track and field at Mexico was David Hemery (Great Britain) in the 400-metres hurdles. This was an event in which the thin air helped, for the first seven men in the final broke the previous Olympic record, but Hemery made them look second class as he led from the second hurdle and came into the straight three strides ahead of anyone else. At the last obstacle his leading foot had touched down after the hurdle before those behind were rising on the other side. His time was 48.1 sec, slicing seven-tenths of a second from the record set earlier in the year and beating the previous Olympic mark, set by Glenn Davis (United States) in 1960, by 1.2 sec; it was a performance to put him among the great Olympians.

The search for new techniques or improvements on old ones, particularly in field events, never ceases but there has never been a more dramatic success than the new style of high jumping introduced by Dick Fosbury (United States) and appropriately dubbed the Fosbury Flop. Most Olympic winners either straddled the bar, one foot following the other, or used a western roll in which both feet crossed the bar together. Fosbury revolutionized the event by running in on a curved approach and then at the point of take-off turning to go over the bar backwards, stretching the back and flipping the legs upwards. Fosbury's style was not decisive because Ed Caruthers, using the straddle, matched his fellow American as the bar was raised to each new height until at 2.24 m (7 ft 4¼ in) Fosbury got over on his third attempt; Caruthers failed narrowly.

In the women's competition, Irena Szewińska-Kirszenstein (Poland) added to her Olympic medal collection, which had begun in Tokyo. She finished third, behind the two Americans, Wyomia Tyus and Barbara Ferrell, in the 100 metres. In the 200 metres she won and broke her own world record with 22.5 sec.

The women's 400 metres brought an unexpected gold for France when the long-haired Colette Besson, in the last two strides, overhauled Lillian Board (Great Britain). In the 80-metres hurdles Maureen Caird (Australia) who was only seventeen, beat her more favoured colleague Pam Kilborn and trounced the East Europeans. Another surprise came in the high jump, in which Miroslava Rezková (Czechoslovakia), collecting several failures at the earlier heights, finally achieved the winning height at her third attempt.

The Americans dominated the swimming and diving even more than they had done in Tokyo. They won more medals than the other countries put together, twenty-three gold, fifteen silver and twenty bronze from a total of 102. Perhaps an even greater example of their superiority is shown in the number of finalists, eighty-one out of a possible ninety. Beside this avalanche the few successes of the other countries tend to stand out. Roland Matthes (German Democratic Republic) won both backstroke titles, and the 100 metres by the remarkable margin of 1.5 sec; the Australian Michael Wenden took both free-style sprint titles, setting a world record of 52.22 sec at 100 metres and beating Don Schollander (United States) by three-fifths of a second over 200 metres – a contest where Wenden's rugged power was just sufficient to overcome Schollander's economical style.

Elsewhere in the men's events there was an almost unbroken succession of American victories, often backed up by the silver and bronze medals as well. In the women's events the pattern was much the same even though one of the firmest favourites, Catie Ball, holder of four world records, was well below her best in the 100-metres breaststroke and unable to start in the 200 metres, because of a virus infection. After all the preparation, the daily hours of slogging up and down a pool, such a handicap was a crushing event. In the 100-metres event it brought opportunity for Djurdjica Bjedov (Yugoslavia) who held off Galina Prosumenshchikova (USSR), winner of the 200-metres event in Tokyo. Miss Prosumenshchikova also lost her title; in the longer event she led at the halfway point and seemed safely on her way to victory when suddenly she faded and was overhauled by Sharon Wichman (United States) and Bjedov. Debbie Meyer (United States) won three gold medals, the 200 metres narrowly, the 400 metres comfortably and the 800 metres, a new event in the Games, by the massive margin of 11.7 sec.

The Olympics does not only call together the youth of the world as the equestrian event showed. Bill Steinkraus of the United States, in his forty-fourth year, rode Snowbound to victory in the individual jumping Grand Prix event. He had a clear first round (where there were fourteen obstacles) and had four faults in the second (six obstacles). The three-day event held at Avandro, 100 miles from Mexico City, produced another outstanding performance from a veteran rider. Derek Allhusen (Great Britain), who had previously competed in the 1948 Olympics in London, at fifty-four took the silver medal on Lochinvar, and led his team to victory. He also took the silver medal in the individual event and had a clear round in the final event, the show jumping. In the individual event Jean-Jacques Guyon won with 38.86 penalty points.

Mohammad Nassiri won Iran's first Olympic gold medal in weightlifting, with an Olympic record of 367.5 kg (810 lb) in the bantamweight division; after taking the silver medals in the three previous Olympics, Yugoslavia finally won the water-polo competition; in the boxing the Eastern Europeans were not quite so formidable as had been expected and George Foreman took a crucial step towards becoming world heavyweight boxing champion, when he won the gold medal, beating three of his four opponents.

In gymnastics, held in the magnificent arena with such a dull name, the Municipal Auditorium, its steeply tiered seats turning the audience into a choir which responded to every move on the floor or apparatus, Vera Čáslavská (Czechoslovakia) was the dominating figure. She added four gold medals to the three she won in Tokyo, which made Olympic history, and then, to ensure her place in the Movement's annals, she became, as far as anyone can tell, the first competitor to marry during the period of the Games. Miss Čáslavská went back to Prague as Mrs Odložil, the wife of the man who finished eighth in the athletics 1,500-metres final. Perhaps it was the excitement of approaching this new state of life which lifted Miss Čáslavská but she reached a new peak, winning the horse vault and asymmetrical bars, finishing joint first in the floor exercises and second on the beam. The Japanese men were stronger in gymnastics than in Tokyo, winning eleven individual medals.

At Xochimilco there were also problems for the oarsmen and the canoeists caused by the high altitude but against these were set the magnificence of the course and its facilities; practicality and luxury were superbly combined. In the rowing the United States, for the first time, failed to win a gold medal and the spread of medals was greater than ever before. The West Germans learned more than anyone else that in the thin atmosphere the need is to find the optimum pace and stick with it. Any ideas of surges or bursts at particular points had to be shunned for it was this sort of effort which brought collapse. In this way the West Germans just managed to hold a lead to the faster-finishing Australians. The German Democratic Republic was the only country to win two golds, through Jörg Lucke and Hans-Jürgen Bothe in the coxless pairs and their renowned coxless four.

XX MUNICH 1972 John Rodda

An Olympiad is four years but what name should be given to the span from 6 May 1966 to 6 September 1972? At the beginning there was the elation of a city awarded the task of staging the Games; amid the potted azaleas of the Excelsior Hotel in Rome, Willi Daume, IOC member in Germany, and Karl Heinz Vogel, Mayor of Munich, spoke of their hopes, ambitions of a new vision for the Games. Six years later, on that September morning they joined thousands more in the Olympic stadium in a memorial to the eleven Israeli competitors and officials who died as a result of action by Palestinian terrorists.

The Olympic arena and its periphery has often been abused by cheats and charlatans, but this time the competitors' village was used for the very antithesis of the Olympic spirit by those who trespassed there to commit murder and blackmail.

To draw the blind on this horror and turn to contemplate the riches and successes of the Munich Olympics is difficult but before and after the bloodshed and mourning Munich saw rise many new Olympian peaks. The preparation of the city was one of luxury and lavishness, which had a counter-productive side since, with the news of the final bill of £300 million, others shrank from the idea of being host.

The main complex, with the village alongside the athletic stadium, swimming pool and several other arenas, was like a self-contained town. The steel masts thrusting into the air held a translucent canopy across the main stadium and pool and, as David Lacey, association football correspondent of the *Guardian*, wrote, 'gave the impression that here was a circus that would never leave town'.

Lasse Virén, a gangling Finnish policeman with a wispy beard, achieved a rare, and in the intense competition of modern athletics, an unexpected double victory on the track. He followed Hannes Kolehmainen (1912), Emil Zátopek (1952) and Vladimir Kuts (1956) in winning the 5,000 metres and 10,000 metres at one Games, and moreover, heats were required for the longer distance for the first time. In the final of the 10,000 metres Virén always stayed with the leading group but just before the halfway point Mohamed Gammoudi of Tunisia, running in front of him, fell and Virén went down. The Finn got up and remarkably, shook off the jarring effect which such a fall brings; the rhythm and pace returned and in the final thrust across the last 600 metres he shook off Mariano Haro of Spain and then Emiel Puttemans of Belgium. Virén's enormous stride took him ahead and to the winning line in a faster time by one second than the world record of Ron Clarke (Australia).

To have won, after falling, and to have broken such a world record would have satisfied most champions, but the Finn steeled himself for the following day when he was to qualify for the 5,000-metres final. This contained a vastly experienced field and the weight of conjecture was that one of the fresh men, not someone who had gone through the mill of the 10,000 metres, would win. Virén, though, showed mental and physical depth by the nature of his running. He was, perhaps, fortunate that no one tried to burn off the opposition from the front with a fast pace, but he showed his tactical wit by ignoring some of the early half-hearted breaks but moving up when Steve Prefontaine (United States), the most competent front runner among the finalists, chose to break. This came with four laps remaining and Gammoudi, the titleholder, Ian Stewart (Great Britain) and Puttemans, were all in contention at the bell, when Virén began to make his effort; at that moment champions carry an aura about them and the inferiority becomes manifest in others. Along the final straight Virén was unchallenged; the Finnish flags dotted in the crowd acknowledged his feat and the resurgence of his country's distance running which spanned back to the first occasion when the Games were in Germany – in 1936; Finland had won both titles then.

The men's sprinting had something of a schoolboy magazine touch about it. Three Americans were lounging in one of the rooms at their quarters watching the afternoon athletics on television when suddenly the second round of the 100 metres, in which they were supposed to be taking part, began. They dashed to the stadium but only one arrived in time for his race. It was one of several American disasters at the Munich Games and it deprived the winner of the 100 and 200 metres, Valeri Borzov (USSR), those victories in the perspective they deserved. Borzov has been described as a man-made sprinter; it would be closer to accuracy to say that he is a natural athlete, highly intelligent, capable of understanding the technicalities of sprinting which take him closer to perfection.

The Americans were bruised again in the 1,500 metres, where Jim Ryun, the world-record holder, fell in his heat. In fact he should not have run in that particular race since his best time submitted by the American team management for seeding purposes was that of a mile, not 1,500 metres; that error took him into the same qualifying race as Kipchoge Keino, who beat him in the Mexico final.

Again the blue-and-white flag of Finland came out for the final as Pekka Vasala timed his attack superbly after Keino had tried to surprise the field with a burst, two laps from home. Although the Kenyan's legs were four years older than at Mexico he still managed to hold off all the young bloods with the exception of the Finn, who won in 3 min 36.3 sec, by half a second. In the 800 metres, the Americans were compensated for their mismanagement and ill fortune. Dave Wottle had tantalized the crowd in the heats, with his tactic of staying at the back of the field until late in the race and then swooping to victory. It was almost as much a distinguishing characteristic as the peaked golf cap he wore; that, and the fact that he and his bride chose Munich at Olympic time for their honeymoon, emphasized his casual attitude.

Wottle seemed to have overplayed his waiting game in the final when he was last and did not begin his attack until well inside the last 300 metres. There was a vast amount of running to be done to get to the front and Yevgeni Arzhanov (USSR) was moving powerfully and confidently in the lead. Wottle swept past the strung-out field, closed on the Russian but just did not have sufficient space between him and the finishing line to win, unless – and then in the last two strides Arzhanov was overtaken by disaster as he slipped and, in falling forward, lunged at the line as Wottle came up to him. The two waited in a vacuum of agony for the official verdict; Wottle won by three hundredths of a second.

1972. The second gold for Lasse Virén (Finland), in the 5,000 metres. Ian Stewart (Gt Britain) is 309.

Athletically Africa forged another breakthrough; running is a simple basic expression of athleticism, but the technical events of the sport offer another challenge. That was met and conquered by a man with a smile to match his enormous stride, John Akii-Bua from Uganda, whose technical perfection and power in the 400-metres hurdles not only took the gold medal, but broke David Hemery's world record, set in the 1968 Olympics in Mexico, with 47.82 sec.

The field events in the men's competition provided moments of drama and surprise. The unbroken run of American victories in the pole vault from 1896 was ended through the technical finesse of Wolfgang Nordwig, a slightly built East German, and with a controversy over the type of fibreglass pole permitted. Bob Seagren, the American world-record holder and defending champion, was not allowed to use the type of pole he preferred and at the end of his competition thrust the one he was obliged to use into the hands of an athletic official; an incident which among other things showed how vital the sophistication of equipment is in the struggle.

For the first time since 1956 there was a new champion in the discus. Al Oerter was no longer in the American team and the runner-up to him in 1964 and bronze-medal winner in 1968, Ludvik Danek of Czechoslovakia, duly took over the mantle. But only after a harrowing competition. The Czech went into the circle for the final round lying in fifth position, but his last throw, 64.40 m (211 ft 3 in) took him safely clear.

The javelin provided similar drama and joy for the hosts. Yanis Lusis, the Russian holder of the title, established his presence with two long early throws both beyond 88.40 m (290 ft); but Klaus Wolfermann got close to him in the fourth round and then, to a crescendo of roars, sent the spear 90.48 m (296 ft 10 in). Lusis responded magnificently but his next throw fell 2 cm (1 in) short of the German's.

The organization of athletics in the German Democratic Republic, a country of 17 million people, was well known before the Munich Games and their success in the women's section of the competition was evidence of it. From fourteen events the Germans took twelve medals, including six gold. The powerful limbs of Renate Stecher dominated the sprinting and the slim pale frame of Monika Zehrt provided similar output in both the 400 metres and the 4 × 400-metres relay. If the East Germans' efficient style was admired it was the response to inspiration which drew the greatest applause. Mary Peters, from the troubled city of Belfast in Northern Ireland, exuded joy through every event in the pentathlon, an expression that was quickly caught by the crowd and returned, forging the strongest rapport between competitor and spectator at the athletics. Miss Peters, with a kiss and a hug for everyone, when her two-day competition was over, won the gold medal with a world-record score of 4,801 points.

While for the home crowd there had been the anticipated victory in the long jump of Heide Rosendahl, one of the delights of the athletics came in the triumph of the high jump of Ulrike Meyfarth, a sixteen-year-old schoolgirl. Miss Meyfarth, who is 1.93 m (6 ft 4 in) tall, set a world record of 1.92 m (6 ft 3½ in) which was 11 cm (4½ in) higher than she had ever achieved before, with her flop style of jumping.

The Olympic swimming-pool water bubbled and

1972. Roland Matthes (German Democratic Republic), the champion backstroke swimmer

frothed as thirty world and eighty-four Olympic records were broken or equalled. But out of the bath there was turmoil of a different kind. One winner was disqualified for taking drugs and there were accusations of competitors advertising equipment in the arena, specifically against Mark Spitz of the United States; an IOC investigation led to his exoneration. Spitz took his place in Olympic history by winning seven gold medals, a remarkable achievement but one which did prompt the suggestion (which has been made about gymnastics) that the swimming program might be reduced because of a similarity of events. Spitz won the 100-metres and 200-metres freestyle, the 100-metres and 200-metres butterfly, and helped the United States to win the 4 × 100-metres, 4 × 200-metres, and 4 × 100-metres medley relays; in all his finals a world record was set. The United States was the dominant swimming nation with seventeen gold medals from a possible twenty-nine while only four other nations, Australia, the German Democratic Republic, Japan and Sweden provided champions.

In the eight-day program there were many tense and rich moments, with one of them the victory in the 1,500-metres freestyle of Mike Burton (United States), who at twenty-five was, in swimming terms, a veteran. His superb judgment brought him through to first position with 300 metres remaining and he won in a world-record time of 15 min 52.58 sec, 46.3 sec faster than his winning time four years previously at the Games of Mexico City.

Roland Matthes (GDR) retained his two backstroke titles in a style that looked even more effortless than it was four years earlier. The men's 400-metres final brought a new dimension to this distance and a bitterness afterwards. At the halfway mark only seven-tenths of a second separated the eight finalists and Rick DeMont (USA), fourth at halfway, moved up to second and then began his final attack with 100 metres remaining. He swam that stretch in 58.22 sec, the fastest 100 metres of anyone in the final but Brad Cooper of Australia was with him until the final stroke. DeMont finished ahead of him by one-hundredth of a second but a dope test proved positive and the American was disqualified. He had taken ephedrine which was on the list of banned drugs, because, he said, of asthma. It was a decision which rankled and troubled those who took it because of the apparent lack of vigilance within the American team, but winning by such a narrow margin only stressed the enormity of any advantage which might be obtained.

Olympic history was made at the basketball hall. The United States, winner of every competition hitherto were beaten in the final three seconds by the USSR. There was confusion as the Americans took the lead for the first time in the match at 50–49 and an off-court horn sounded. Finally a FIBA delegate overruled the referee and ordered the final three seconds to be replayed. In that time the Russians hurled the ball from one end of the court to the other where Aleksandr Belov tipped it in for an astounding win. The Americans were so disgusted that they left Munich without accepting their silver medals.

Cuban power and artistry spanned fourteen full days of the boxing competition – with rarely a spare seat at any session. The crowds gave shrill vent to decisions with which they disagreed, but the overriding memory is of the Cubans skilfully punching their way to three gold medals out of eleven to be won; altogether they had five men in the semi-finals and their outstanding champion was the heavyweight Teofilo Stevenson who won his title in less than six rounds of boxing.

The Indian subcontinent's long domination of the hockey was ended by the German Federal Republic. Although there were some exciting and wholesome contests in the early rounds (there were seventy matches altogether) the final provided another of Munich's stained memories. The Pakistan team did not take defeat in the final in the Olympic spirit and, after abuse of officials and assault of a doctor they turned the medal presentation into a mockery. The International Hockey Federation (FIH) took swift action and the players involved were banned from any further Olympic competition. The German tactics throughout the final of close marking certainly taxed the patience of their opponents and spoiled the game from the spectators' point of view but brought the Germans the

1972. Another remarkable contribution to Olympic history was made by New Zealand, in the eights.

results they wanted for they completely suppressed the individual brilliance of the Pakistanis.

Archery returned to the Olympic program for the first time since 1920. At the Englischer Garten, with its sun-shades and gay marquees, there was a gentle and easy atmosphere but there was no doubt about the quality of the sport. One of the youngest competitors, eighteen-year-old John Williams of the United States, won the men's event with a world-record score and established his supremacy by the end of the first day. The women's title was also won by an American, but Doreen Wilber was not such an overwhelming champion as her compatriot.

The British made Olympic history in the equestrian events, where they retained the team title in the three-day event, something not achieved since 1928, when the Netherlands won for the second time in Amsterdam. Britain too provided the individual winner of the three-day event, Richard Meade, riding Laurieston.

Those who are worried by the intensity of nationalistic aid and support towards winning the gold medals were delighted with the outcome of the major event in the rowing, the eights, where New Zealand's crew, who had to raise £20,000 towards their country's Olympic appeal, bound together with a spirit and toughness that was sufficient to overcome the power of both Germanies and the USSR. The New Zealanders staggered their opponents with starting power, for by a quarter of the course they led by two seconds; attacks from behind came over the next 1,200 metres and were resisted, and finally the New Zealanders had power enough to be the fastest eight across the last 500 metres. Another New Zealand crew was involved in a titanic struggle and just lost; the coxless four looked shaped handsomely to take the gold with a solid lead as they reached the final 500 metres but then the crew from the German Democratic Republic, one which had been winning World and Olympic titles since 1966, began the long tantalizing process of overhauling which was accomplished in the last two, or at the most three strokes. That final 500 metres was a great Olympic occasion.

Suddenly, amid the contests, the Games were brought to a juddering halt and suspended for twenty-four hours. In the early hours of 5 September, members of a Palestinian terrorist group climbed over the wire surrounding the village and broke into the quarters of the Israeli team. One Israeli died in the initial attack and another ten were held hostage. Throughout the day there were demands and negotiations. Crowds gathered at the wire perimeter of the village to watch and glimpse the hooded figures; ice-cream and hot-dog vendors came to sustain them; television cameras were positioned so that the anguish of those immediately involved was shared by the hundred million. Finally, after fifteen hours, hostages and captors were hoisted by helicopter to a nearby airfield to be flown to the Middle East. But as the occupants of the helicopters alighted there was shooting, hand grenades were exploded and the helicopters were burned out. Altogether thirteen people died.

The following morning in the Olympic stadium a memorial service to the Israelis began with the Munich Opera House Orchestra playing Beethoven's *Egmont Overture*; in the afternoon sport was resumed. The horror and sadness remained to the end of the Games but with it also a burning in many breasts that whatever happened, Coubertin's conception should be preserved.

Sports on the Olympic Program

ARCHERY S. E. Crisp

Archery has a history going back some ten thousand years, as is revealed by many archaeological findings. Well-preserved yew bows in peat layers have been discovered in England, the Netherlands, Switzerland and Germany; stone arrow heads in a variety of shapes in North Africa, Northwest Europe and North America; and prehistoric paintings in caves in France and Spain show archers as hunters and warriors.

The bow held at full draw, in the shape of the arc from which archery derives its name, is in a state in which the energy is stored in a static form called the potential energy of stress. When the archer releases the arrow the potential energy is able to change to kinetic energy, energy of motion, giving speed to the arrow. Of all the machines invented by man to control energy, the bow must have been one of the earliest.

There has always been much variety, not only in the bows and arrows themselves, but also in their uses. Short bows were used for stalking game in wooded country; special bows and quivers for the chase on horseback; bows with long arrows for shooting fish in shallow water; and bows to shoot arrows with a line attached, to carry baited hooks much further than a fisherman's normal cast.

Some of the most stirring exploits in the history of archery in warfare took place in France in the years 1346, 1356, and 1415, at the battles of Crécy, Poitiers and Agincourt, where the English longbowmen annihilated large forces of heavily armoured French cavalry supported by crossbow mercenaries.

Archery of such quality comes only with regular practice from childhood. In England there were royal decrees, from the fifteenth century to the sixteenth, to ensure that the bulk of the male population should practise archery even in peace time. As happens so often when large numbers are trained in a skill, wide variations in ability came to light, and sporting contests were arranged.

Of all sporting contests today in England, the oldest is an archery tournament: the Antient Scorton Silver Arrow contest in Yorkshire, with written records naming the Captain of the Arrow for every year, except during the two world wars, from 1673.

Tournaments remained local or regional because of deep-rooted regional differences in the shooting. In England, for instance, men took pride in shooting only at the longer distances: the Scorton in 1673 began at 'eight score yards'. On the Continent of Europe the custom was to shoot at shorter distances with smaller targets. In the Netherlands the 'king' of the village would put in much target practice at 25 metres at the back of the inn until he could challenge the 'kings' of the other villages and become 'emperor' of his region. In Belgium shooting at the popinjay, an array of artificial birds at the top of a 30-metre mast, has always flourished. In Switzerland skill with the crossbow was cherished. In Japan archery was part of a ritual, linked with Zen Buddhism. In the United States there arose a desire to combine all that was best in English target archery with the traditions of hunting with the bow of the American Indian.

In spite of these differences there were attempts, in the early 1900s, to find a pattern of shooting that would be generally acceptable for international competition. The fact that archery does not seem to have been considered for inclusion in the first Modern Games may have been due to lack of a strong national feeling in Greece for archery as a sport.

At the second Games in Paris in 1900 there were archery competitions with shooting in Continental style at 50 metres and 33 metres. A competitor would shoot one arrow only before stepping back from the shooting line until each of his target partners had also shot one, as opposed to the English custom, now in general use, of shooting three arrows before stepping back. At the Paris Games there was also popinjay shooting.

At the third Games at St Louis in 1904 the only archery competitors were Americans. The men shot a Double York Round (one York Round followed by another) and a Double American Round. The women shot a Double National Round and a Double Columbia Round. The York Round is 12 dozen arrows; 6 dozen at 100 yd, 4 dozen at 80 yd, and 2 dozen at 60 yd. An American Round is 90 arrows; 30 at each of the distances 60, 50, and 40 yd. A National Round is 6 dozen arrows; 4 dozen at 60 yd, and 2 dozen at 50 yd. The Columbia Round is 6 dozen arrows; 2 dozen at each of the distances 50, 40, and 30 yd. In each case one of the rounds shows its English origins by having fewer arrows at the shorter distances; the other round, with the same number of arrows at each distance, originated in the United States.

In neither of these Games of 1900 and 1904 was archery accorded much more than the status of a demonstration. However, by 1908 it achieved full recognition as an Olympic sport. The maximum number of competitors from each country was laid down as '30 Gentlemen for the

The women's archery teams of (below) 1908, in the National Round, and (bottom) 1972, when the sport returned to the Olympic program

Double York Round, 30 Ladies for the Double National Round, and 30 Gentlemen for the 40 arrows at 50 metres shot singly Continental fashion.' Among other recorded instructions for these Games in London are: 'Gentlemen will not be allowed to smoke at the Ladies' targets', and 'No shooting will be allowed except when competing for the prizes'. France dominated the Continental shooting; the United Kingdom team took all the prizes in the English rounds, except the men's bronze medal, which was won by Henry Richardson of the United States.

Archery was next included in the seventh Games at Antwerp in 1920. Belgium has one of the most royal and ancient archery societies, the Grand Serment Royal de St Sebastien, dating from the fourteenth century. Archers of the rest of the world were not convinced that short-distance shooting and popinjay, the Belgian style, were required and the only archery competitors were Belgians.

It was fifty-two years before archery again became an Olympic sport; but in that period solutions to nearly all of its problems had been found through its own World Championship series. The real advance began in 1931 when an international tournament in target archery took place at Lwów, in Poland; the Fédération Internationale de Tir à l'Arc (FITA) was formed; and the tournament was declared the first World Championship for target archery. Since then FITA has been responsible for organizing World Championships, Continental Championships, and Olympic Games archery. World Championships now take place in alternate years.

Since 1957 the round shot for the World Championship has been the Double FITA Round, shot over four days if weather conditions permit. The FITA Round is 144 arrows: 3 dozen at each of the distances of 90 metres, 70 metres, 50 metres, and 30 metres for the men; and 3 dozen at each of the distances of 70 metres, 60 metres, 50 metres, and 30 metres for the women. This was the pattern of the Munich tournament in which forty women and fifty-five men from twenty-seven countries competed. The two longer distances were shot on the first day and the two shorter distances, on smaller target faces, on the second day. At the end of the first FITA Round John Williams of the United States, aged eighteen, led by 39 points, having set a new World Record score for the Single FITA of 1,268 points. On the third and fourth days the second FITA Round was shot to complete the Double FITA. Williams, who had won the world title the previous year, took the gold medal with a score of 2,528 points, 47 points ahead of Gunnar Jervill of Sweden.

The scores on the women's side were closer. With nine arrows to go before the end of the Ladies' Double FITA, Doreen Wilber of the United States, silver medallist at the 1969 and 1971 World Championships, was only sixteen points ahead of three other competitors, all with the same score. Mrs Wilber took the gold medal with a score of 2,424.

During the last twenty years the technology of new materials has been applied to archery equipment. In 1908 the competitors at the London Games would have used bows made of yew or some other wood, and they would have been troubled with loss of elasticity as the shooting went on. The modern bow is composite, with limbs of laminated wood and fibreglass, with stabilizers to steady the vibrations, a sophisticated bowsight, and a string of some manmade fibre. There would be negligible variation throughout the four days of shooting. Even the arrows, made of tubular aluminium alloy, could be matched so much more closely than the wooden shafts of 1908.

These advances in equipment have made the sport more attractive to many more people, especially those in the younger age-groups who can be successful at an early age. In the 1973 World Championship, a thirteen-year-old girl took tenth place.

Archery has, largely through the dedication of Mrs Inger K. Frith, O.B.E., president of FITA, at last returned to the Olympic program. The success of the competition at the Englischer Garten in Munich in 1972 was not only in the gathering of the world's best archers, but also in the presentation of a highly developed sport, with more than a little glamour, to a very large number of spectators on the field, and, through the media, to even larger numbers who would not normally watch it. Amongst those were many people of influence from Olympic Committees in countries where the sport does not yet flourish, and leaders of other International Sports Federations who came to understand what a high level this sport had reached. This success in the Games in Munich will have been responsible for a great step forward in the progress of archery as a sport.

ASSOCIATION FOOTBALL Sir Stanley Rous and Doug Gardner

There are only two great sporting festivals which bring together competitors from all parts of the world and arouse worldwide interest: the Olympic Games and the World Cup competition.

The World Cup is devoted exclusively to football. It is a competition of the best national teams of professional players from all over the world. The equivalent competition for amateur football players is the association football competition of the Olympic Games. Both football competitions are organized by the Fédération Internationale de Football Association (FIFA), the world governing body of association football, with over 140 nations from every continent affiliated.

The Olympic Games and the World Cup each follow a four-year cycle, with a gap of two years between. The first World Cup competition took place in 1930 and the two competitions have followed in sequence ever since.

Broadly speaking, the Olympic tournament, through the years, has been dominated by three main areas of the playing world, each producing an evolutionary style of play, as well as an approach to competition which in many ways preceded the professional game.

Great Britain, the birthplace of the game, won three of the first four finals to include any teams of repute. Those playing in what is usually called 'the Latin style' took over between 1924 and 1936; since 1952 the Olympic championship has remained within Eastern Europe.

Association football was the first team game admitted to Olympic competition. In 1908 hockey also became an Olympic sport. It was twenty-eight years before a further team game, basketball, was admitted in 1936 (there was a demonstration of it in 1904) and, more recently, volley-ball, in 1964, and handball in 1972. It is not surprising that association football was the pioneer team game in the Olympics: the sound international organization of the sport and its widespread popularity made it the chief financial support of the Olympic Games in the early years of the Movement, before track and field events captured the imagination and interest of the general public. The money earned by the football competition was necessary to subsidize many other less popular sports. Association football remains the sport with the most enthusiastic and widely based following in the world.

The competitions before the London tournament of 1908 were largely an exhibition. In 1896 Smyrna beat Salonika in an elimination game and was then itself beaten 15-0 by Denmark in a final which is usually not considered important enough to be included in the record books. In 1900, in Paris, Great Britain was represented by Upton Park F.C., which beat a team from the Union des Sociétés Françaises de Sports Athlétiques (USFSA) representing France in the final. Two clubs from the United States and one from Canada alone took part in the 1904 tournament; it was not until 1908 that the competition began to assume a reasonably important status – at least in Europe.

But the widely differing standards were reflected in the results. France entered two teams, both of which were beaten by Denmark, 9-0 and 17-1 – the latter score still standing as a record in the final stages of an Olympic tournament. A Danish centre-forward, Sven Nielsen, scored ten goals in one game to set an Olympic record, shared four years later by Gottfried Fuchs, a German who reached the same total in a game against Russia.

But it was the British who dominated, playing a hard, physical but fast game, born in the Universities but bred to a high degree of tough individuality and skilful ball control by consistent play in the country's top amateur clubs – and sometimes among the professionals. Vivian Woodward, a peer among players, epitomized the British team. He had already won sixteen caps playing in 'full' (i.e. professional) England teams as an amateur before collecting his first Olympic gold medal in 1908 and regularly appeared in English League football.

Football was by far the best-organized sport at the end of the nineteenth century and the beginning of the twentieth because of the work done by the Football Associations of the United Kingdom. International competition had been inaugurated in Great Britain by matches played between the four constituent countries of the United Kingdom, England, Ireland, Scotland and Wales.

The modern game can be said to have started with the foundation of the Football Association (of England) in 1863. By 1883 England, Ireland, Scotland and Wales had founded the International Board, which since then has been the sole lawmaker of the game, whose authority is universally accepted. In 1904 FIFA was founded and became the world administrative body for the game, assuming responsibility for organizing the football competition in the Olympic Games.

The British ascendancy in the Olympic tournament died with the birth of football as a truly international sport after World War I. The British left the Olympic scene after a row over 'broken-time' payments but would have almost certainly been unable to retain their superiority in

Kazimierz Deyna scores the winning goal for Poland against Hungary in the 1972 association football final.

the face of developments on the field which ensued. The Olympic tournament at Antwerp in 1920 was not a happy one for football. During the final between Belgium and Czechoslovakia, the entire Czech team walked off the field in protest at one of the decisions of the referee. They were disqualified and the gold medals awarded to the Belgians.

Four years later in Paris, the Latin influence emerged. Uruguay won that tournament and followed it up with victory in Amsterdam in 1928. The latter victory was achieved with virtually the same team which, only two years later, was to prove good enough to win the first professional World Cup tournament.

Between the two world wars there were two events which damaged football in the Olympic Games. After the end of hostilities in Europe in 1919, hatred and ill feeling ran deep for a long time in all spheres of life from which football was not excepted. In Brussels in 1919 a conference was held to consider the relationships with the Central Powers which formed the losing side in the war; Belgium, England, Ireland, Luxembourg, Scotland, and Wales proposed to withdraw from FIFA rather than play matches with teams representing Austria, Germany and Hungary. Meanwhile in Gothenburg the national associations of the Scandinavian countries, which were neutral during the war, affirmed their right to play against any country of their choice. A number of other countries took this view. This conflict within FIFA culminated in the withdrawal of the UK associations. They returned in 1924, only to leave once more in 1928 because of disagreement over broken-time payments. Although the British team was accepted for the Games of 1936 the UK did not rejoin FIFA until 1946.

The other problem that confronted the sport was professionalism. This was particularly difficult for football since it was the first international sport in which professionalism played a significant role from early in the development of the game. The Football Association had known many bitter disputes before the problem was resolved. Its definition, born of long experience, was as follows:

Players are either amateur or professional. Any player registered with his National Association as a professional or receiving remuneration or consideration of any sort above his necessary hotel and travelling expenses actually paid, shall be a professional. Training expenses of amateurs, other than wages paid to a trainer or coach, must be paid by the players themselves. A player competing for any prize money in a football contest shall be a professional.

This was not acceptable to many other countries, where football was not so well organized and where there was not the financial strength behind the game which the British Associations enjoyed.

The differences became acute when at the Rome Congress of FIFA in 1926 a resolution allowing broken-time payments was passed by twelve votes to eight, with two abstentions, in a meeting in which twenty-two national associations were represented.

Belgium had legalized broken-time payments in 1921; France, Norway, Italy and Switzerland permitted various forms of payment or subsidy to players they still recognized as amateur.

By the time the issue came to a head before the Games of 1928, it was clear that through various devices, the grant of leave with pay by benevolent employers, the payment of bonus money or training money, reimbursement by national governing bodies and Olympic Associations, and state subsidies of one sort or another, a new category of player had emerged: this category was regarded by the Football Associations of the United Kingdom as infringing amateur status and offending the spirit of the Olympic competition.

The truth was that the body responsible for the administration of the Olympic association football competition, FIFA, had no clear ruling nor definition of what constituted an amateur. It left the various National Associations to interpret the rules regarding the status of players as they saw fit: 'The National Associations are at liberty to allow compensation for "broken time" or not.' Their indication of the limits of such payments were more an expression of pious hope than firm or clear guidelines at that time. There was evidently a large gap between the pure amateur and the strict professional which left the rules open to much abuse.

The arguments over the use of pseudo-amateurs and making broken-time payments kept football out of the Games of Los Angeles in 1932, and the South American countries, with the exception of Peru, did not appear in Berlin in 1936. Germany, which had trained a team for two years, went out against Norway in the second round – and the players were immediately sent home in disgrace – and Great Britain, which had not even picked a squad until two weeks before the Opening Ceremony, also disappeared, beaten 5–4 by Poland, a skilful and well-prepared combination. Peru accused Austria of making a substitution for an injured player and a large number of spectators invaded the pitch to join in the dispute. The match was abandoned, and Peru disqualified when it refused to take part in a replay. Peru had been leading 4–2 at the time, and earlier had beaten Finland 7–3, so perhaps might have gone on to maintain the South American domination of the final, particularly as Austria went through to the last match and then only lost 1–2 to Italy after extra time. But the Italians, leading European exponents of the Latin style, and current professional World Cup holders, upheld the strength of the short-passing methods.

South America was again absent in 1948 when Sweden became the last 'true' amateur side to win the gold medals for at least twenty-four years, with a trio of forward players, Gunnar Gren, Gunnar Nordahl and Nils Liedholm, who were later to become among the best professional players in Europe.

The rise of Eastern Europe began in 1952 with the victory of a Hungarian team largely composed of army personnel who had lived and trained together for at least two years, supported, of course, by the State. This team went on to give the professionals of England their first home defeat by a foreign side in 1953 and a year later finished second in the World Cup finals. It was only dispersed by the Revolution in Hungary in 1956. Eight years later, Hungary came back with teams good enough to win both the 1964 and 1968 Games and became the first country since Great Britain to win three Olympic soccer titles.

The Hungary of the 1950s injected new thinking into world football, emphasizing the necessity for discipline in coaching and training to acquire ball skills, the need for squads to have constant match preparation to acquire real team spirit and develop new tactics (such as its highly successful deep-lying centre-forward scheme). Its system of recruitment, concentration and continual State support of players also provided the springboard upon which other Eastern European countries launched themselves into Olympic soccer.

Like those of the South Americans of the 1920s, some of the teams have remained virtually unchanged between an Olympic Games and a World Cup tournament final two years later. Ferenc Puskas and Ferenc Bene of Hungary, Lev Yashin of the USSR, Dragan Dzajic of Yugoslavia, Svatopluk Pluskal and Jan Popluhar of Czechoslovakia, Peter Zhekov of Bulgaria and Robert Gadocha of Poland are only a few of the names which have been ranked honourably on both the Olympic and professional Cup rolls.

Some of the toughness of the professional game has also intruded more into Olympic soccer and in 1968 there was a sad climax to the tournament in Mexico City when three Bulgarians and one Hungarian were sent off, turning the final into a mockery of the Olympic spirit. As against that, the discipline and training of both the Poles and Hungarians 'saved' the 1972 final in Munich when they continued to play attractive and skilful football in gale-force winds and torrential rain, conditions which, as one observer noted at the time, 'no true amateur team could have coped with'.

The countries which do not have any professional sport at all have dominated Olympic football since 1952. During the past twenty years only four countries from outside Eastern Europe have placed teams among the medal winners. Eastern Europeans can call upon the whole pool of talent in their countries, whereas in countries where there is a strong professional football competition, the best players turn professional, leaving the amateur sides denuded of talent. This explains the paradox that since World War II many of the countries with the strongest football tradition and the strongest leagues have had no share in Olympic victories.

The position of association football as an Olympic sport has also been challenged. The final competition involves sixteen national teams, with a pool of nineteen players, accompanied by officials, managers, trainers and referees, all requiring accommodation. The final competition also calls for thirty-eight matches at various venues. Many members of the IOC, concerned with the growing 'giganticism' of the modern Olympics, see the elimination of association football as a move that would reduce the numbers of competitors and officials and various organizational problems considerably. But there is also a strongly held view that its popularity throughout the world, because it is basically simple and cheap to organize, should keep football's place on the Olympic program. Some responsible people within the administration of the game believe that association football is now lost and overwhelmed in the Games and that a World Championship, separate and apart from the Olympics, would serve the sport better and focus much wider attention upon the amateur game.

The organization of the preliminary competition to select the sixteen sides which compete at the Games extends through two years. Between seventy and eighty countries enter the competition, and the preliminary rounds take place throughout the world. So the final competition is the climax of a most complex and demanding competition.

Amateur football requires a world competition of this sort and such a competition will continue, whether under the auspices of the Olympic Movement or as a separate Amateur World Championship.

ATHLETICS Tom McNab

Athletics is a series of fantasies bounded by rigid rules. There is little 'natural' about athletics events, for at no time in man's history has he been required to run over hurdles, triple jump or hurl hammers in order to survive. These are challenges he has created for himself, constructs of his own imagination upon which he has imposed strict rules, some of which relate to danger, but most of which are arbitrary. Some of these events are human impingements upon natural objects such as stones (shot and discus), others variations on warlike activities (javelin) or play with work materials (hammer). Hurdles might again be considered as use of work materials (though there is no evidence that shepherds were the first hurdlers) but the even spacing is quite artificial. Basic to all athletics are agreed rules, but it matters little what they are as long as all agree.

It is unlikely that we will ever know with certainty the rules and techniques of the events of the ancient Olympics. The main source of knowledge is of three kinds, literary, sculptural, and ceramic. Unfortunately, none of these disciplines is concerned either with technical accuracy or with rules. For instance, one piece of pottery clearly depicts the range and vitality of the sprinters in the stade (200 yards) and diaulos (400 yards) races, but shows the runners leading with the same arms and legs!

Field events occurred only in the all-round event, the pentathlon, which consisted of stade, long jump, javelin, discus and wrestling. Greek long jumpers used jumping weights (halteres), but there is no evidence that they used them in the same way as nineteenth-century British pro-

Left Robert Dover's seventeenth-century 'Cotswold Olympics'. *Right* Greek competitor in the pentathlon with jumping weights and javelin

fessionals, who released their dumbbells in mid-air to change mass. All Greek pottery shows jumpers retaining their halteres as they swing them backwards on landing to secure a better landing position. Neither is there clear evidence that the Greek long jump was a running jump. Some vases depict a standing jump (though this may have been a training exercise), others show jumpers carrying halteres on the run. The distances cleared – 55 ft (16.81 m) by Phayllus, 52 ft (15.90 m) by Chionis – indicate a series of standing two-footed spring jumps or multiple steps. Pollux talks of 'making the bāter (take-off point) ring', a sound well known to the modern long- or triple-jump coach, again indicating some sort of single-footed running take-off. Harris *(Greek Athletes and Athletics*, 1964) believes that the Greeks used a triple jump 'which caused the introduction into modern athletics of the triple jump', but this ignores the essentially Celtic antecedents of the modern triple jump. The Greek long jump, with its halteres and flute-playing coaches, is likely to remain a tantalizing mystery.

It seems likely that the Greeks threw a discus weighing about 2 kg (4.4 lb), using a running turn with unlimited run. It must be remembered that the imposition of strict limitations upon athletes (i.e. circles of fixed diameter, take-off boards) is a relatively modern phenomenon.

Any modern javelin thrower could easily recognize his event from Greek pottery. The main difference is the Greek use of the amentum, a loop attached to the javelin-grip. The amentum gave great pulling power and possibly also helped the thrower to impart a strong rifling effect to stabilize the javelin. Indeed, in the early nineteenth century, Napoleon instituted a study of the amentum-aided javelin as a possible weapon of war.

Recent studies indicate that the Greeks may have invented the first starting blocks. There seems little doubt that the grooved sills at Olympia were a type of primitive starting block. A major practical problem is created by the 4-in (10-cm) spacing of the grooves, which would not have permitted a standing start with a forward lean, as the sprinter would have found it impossible to maintain balance.

Between the grooves are holes, evenly spaced. Harris puts the view that these holes housed the vertical shaft of the husplex, or starting gate. The husplex was shaped like a railway signal of semaphore type, with the horizontal bar held by a cord running through a staple. From there the cord ran down to another staple at ground level and through a groove to the starter in his pit. When the starter dropped the cords, the horizontal bars fell, allowing the runners to drive forward from the front grooves of their starting blocks. In *Phaedrus* Plato compares a charioteer reining in his horses to a runner rearing back from the husplex, and this description tallies with the writer's view of the mechanics of husplex and starting grooves.

The problems of the diaulos (two-lap) runners were great, as they converged at speed upon a central pillar (the kampter) using a left-hand turn, but the literature contains little advice on how this was resolved.

The events of Greek athletics therefore pose more questions than they answer. No rule books, no statistics, no technical manuals, only a mass of poetic, sculptural and ceramic fragments. However, as we shall soon see, some of the events of the nineteenth-century Scottish Highland Games pose almost as many questions. Greek athletics continued for over a thousand years, so the level of performance must have been high, at least as high as that reached by British professional athletes of the mid-nineteenth century. There is strong evidence of the commanding role of the coach, the aleiptes, from an early period. 'We argue about the navigation of ships more than about the training of athletes, because it has been less well organized as a science,' said Aristotle. There is also good evidence that there was a strong link between the medical practice of the day, based on the humours, and athletic training, and the Greeks can therefore be said to have invented sports medicine.

The Greek Games were corrupt long before they were absorbed by the Romans and the lessons to us are clear. When the prize is more than the struggle, then all is lost, regardless of the quality of the performance. Sport without ethics is not sport, and prizes won by unethical means are but false reward.

Although Coubertin had a direct philosophical link with the ancient Games, the program of the first Athens Games of 1896 was more heavily influenced by Anglo-Saxon and Celtic culture than by that of classical Greece, and this requires explanation. First it must be understood that when the Games died after A.D. 393, an athletics culture died with them, a culture which was never revived in recognizable form.

The rural sports which developed in Great Britain in the twelfth–eighteenth centuries were linked with purely local wakes and fairs, had no agreed program or rules and kept no records. In the seventeenth century, professional foot racing developed in a man-against-man form and this ultimately became the basis for the nineteenth-century pedestrianism, which in turn provided a major stimulus for the development of amateur athletics. The early seventeenth century also saw the institution of Robert Dover's 'Cotswold Olympics'. This was essentially the tacking on of an 'Olympic' label to an already popular rural meeting. The woodcut of the Games shows long jumping and hammer throwing, but no other modern athletic events.

It would be no overstatement to say that the development of sport in the mid-nineteenth-century English public schools and the Highland Games boom of the same period had a more direct influence than did that of the ancient Games upon the program of the 1896 Games. Shot, high, long and triple jumps were all events of Celtic origin. Some of these events, linked with running, formed the program of English public schools and universities when Coubertin visited England in 1889. Immigrant Scots carried to the United States an intact athletics culture, and the first New World highland games were held in Boston in 1853. Thus, when Coubertin visited the United States forty years later, he unwittingly came face to face with a Celtic culture. The final Olympic track-and-field program directly reflected Coubertin's experience in England and the United States.

The first running 'tracks' had been English turnpike roads, the rough grass fields of rural sports meetings and the race tracks used for horse racing. The turnpike roads were replaced by the mid-nineteenth century by natural cinder paths and these were formalized soon after this to become circular cinder tracks. By 1896, when the Englishman Charles Perry (who had laid the Stamford Bridge track) was commissioned to construct the Athens track, England had more running tracks than the whole of Europe put together. Perry was commissioned to create a running track to classic specifications from dry Greek cinders. The result was the loose surface and tight curves of the Averoff Stadium which faced the runners in the 1896 Games. The athletes were hardly representative even of the fledgling national associations of the period. A rabble of untutored but optimistic Greeks, a handful of English university athletes, some skilful East Coast American college athletes and a random collection of Europeans, these were the athletes of the 1896 Games. Nevertheless, the Games were immensely successful.

Distance running had always been the prerogative of the professional athlete and matches in the 10–50 miles range were taking place in the latter part of the eighteenth century. However, amateur athletes of the late nineteenth century rarely competed beyond 10 miles (16 km) and the marathon distance of over 23 miles (37 km) which faced them in Athens was therefore a considerable challenge. The first marathon was a mixture of drama and farce as untrained athletes staggered through dusty Greek villages but the ending, with the Greek Royal Family jogging to the finish with the exhausted Greek, Spiridon Louis, was fitting.

The Paris Games of 1900 produced a much higher level of performance, but represented a step back for the Olympic Movement. It is doubtful for instance, if many of the competitors realized that they were competing in an Olympic Games as the meeting progressed on the bumpy grass track at the Racing Club de France. The Games were dominated by the Americans, whose college system was beginning to produce its first fine fruits. Alvin Kraenzlein won gold in the 60-metres, long jump, 110-metres hurdles, and 200-metres hurdles. Ray Ewry won standing long, high and triple jumps.

As in Paris, the Games of 1904 were linked with an exhibition, in this case the St Louis World Fair, and the Games' three-month duration made them an American inter-club championships rather than an Olympics. Only the French-Canadian, Étienne Desmarteau, broke the sequence of American victories by winning the 56-lb (25.4-kg) weight. The St Louis Games were further prostituted by the inclusion of the 'Anthropological Games', competitions between, among others, Patagonians, Moros, Turks and Sioux. The most entertaining of these competitions were not the 'normal' athletic events (where a Pygmy put the shot 13 ft 7½ in or 4.15 m) but an exhibition of pole climbing by a Filipino and a mud-throwing contest between Pygmies.

The Interim Athens Games of 1906, Games which pro-

Competitors in the 1912 10,000-metres walk being watched closely to ensure that they do not break contact with the ground

vide a significant link in the early development of the Olympic Movement, were held in the same Averoff Stadium that had housed the 1896 Olympic Games, but were a meeting of a much higher calibre. It is noteworthy that Erich Kamper, in his meticulous *Encyclopedia of the Olympic Games* (1972), includes the 1906 Games, observing that their importance is generally underrated; they did, in fact, resuscitate the Olympic Games. The 1906 Games were the first and last to feature a direct copy of the ancient pentathlon, which consisted of standing broad jump, discus (Greek style), javelin, stade (192 metres) run and wrestling (Greco-Roman).

Stone throwing (the throwing of a light 14-lb or 6.35-kg stone using a javelin-type technique) made its first and last appearance at Athens. Rope climbing for speed had featured in the first Games and reappeared in a 10-metre contest won by the Greek Georgios Aliprantis in 11.4 sec.

The 1908 London Games were held in the £40,000 White City Stadium, at that time the most advanced sports stadium in the world. A 660-yd banked concrete cycle track encircled a 586-yd 2-ft (536.5-m) running track, which in turn enclosed an open-air 100-metre swimming tank. The meeting was of outstanding quality. This was the first occasion on which athletes were compelled to be entered in national teams and it was unfortunate that this was to be the occasion of bitter disputes.

A main reason for entry by teams was to ensure some uniformity of status, but even here there were problems. The Americans protested strongly that the Canadian marathon runner Tom Longboat was a professional, but in the end Longboat was allowed to run in a race which marked itself indelibly in Olympic history. The race established the curious distance of 26 miles 385 yd (42,195 m) as the distance of a marathon. The event was to start at Windsor and, because the children of the British Royal Family were eager to see the runners on their long haul, it was decided that the start should be from the private lawns of the Castle. From there over the original course to the Stadium at Shepherd's Bush in London the distance was 26 miles 385 yd (42,195 m).

The 1908 Games were the first Olympics of a truly international character, organized on recognizably modern lines. The 1912 Stockholm Games were to go even further.

It might be worthwhile at this point to describe the position of athletics techniques and technology, factors which are to a great extent interdependent. In 1891 electrical timekeeping was used for the first time at the St Louis AAU Championships. Here the watch was started by the report of the gun, but was stopped by a judge. There was, too, the aid of a photo-finish apparatus.

At a simpler level, high jump and pole vault cross-bars were made on a black/white pattern for better sighting. A safety net was constructed round the cinder circle for hammer throwing. The javelin and all jumps had cinder runways. The 100 metres, 200 metres and 400 metres were run in lanes of chalked rope.

The hammer had evolved from a clumsy wood-shafted implement (East Coast Americans had even experimented with shafts of knotted grape vines!) to a wire shaft with double handles and finally to a single-handed implement. Ash-pole vault poles had been discarded for female bamboos and a take-off box had removed the need for the pole to have a spiked tip. High-jump and pole-vault landing areas were still ground-level sandpits and this severely limited technical developments, particularly in high jump. Hurdles, still recognizable as sheep enclosures, were objects to be cleared rather than skimmed, and this cramped technical development.

The crouch start was now standard practice in sprints, the runners driving from starting holes. In high jump there was an infinity of styles, from a simple 'scissors' to a sophisticated 'Eastern cut-off', through frontal back layouts and primitive side-on hops. However, 1912 did bring an innovation in the shape of the Western roll, demonstrated by the American George Horine; this was a simple, flat lay-out on the side along the bar and was basically only a modification of the crude Irish hop-over style.

In the throws, techniques were still basic. In shot, the side-on hop used by Scottish athletes since the beginning of the nineteenth century still obtained, the hammer consisted of three bent-armed jump turns, and the discus of a side-on jump turn. Only in javelin did technique approximate to modern methods.

The 1912 Games reflected the last primitive innocence of the nineteenth century, for the successful Swedish team had undergone a year's preparation under national coach Ernest Hjertberg. The Americans, while having no national plan, all received coaching at club or college level. Germany appointed the German-American Alvin Kraenzlein to prepare for the 1916 Berlin Games. In 1914 the AAA appointed the Canadian professional athlete W. R. Knox to prepare a British team for Berlin. Thus, even at this early point, the need for coaching was evident.

The United States had taken a different path in the development of coaching. Colleges and universities had found by the late nineteenth century that they could attract large crowds to games of American football. Successful colleges attracted endowments from alumni and the demand for sports success stimulated the employment of the first professional coaches. Although athletics was not a popular spectator sport at college level, it benefited from the sport fever of the late nineteenth century and by the turn of the century Mike Murphy (originator of the crouch start) and Mike Sweeney (the first man to use the Eastern cut-off) had established reputations as coaches.

Intense inter-collegiate competition also resulted in the development of sports scholarships. It was these three factors, inter-collegiate competition, professional coaching and sports scholarships, rather than a broadly based adult club structure, which was to produce some of the greatest athletic performances of the twentieth century.

The 1912 Games were also a watershed for the track-and-field program. In 1913 the newly formed International Amateur Athletic Federation (IAAF) began to organize international programs. Among the events canvassed were all the conventional standing jumps, three standing spring jumps, the 56-lb (25.4-kg) weight for height and distance, Greek-style discus, and the aggregate (left- and right-hand) throws. All of these were rejected and by the 1920s they seemed as dim and distant as those of the ancient Games. This reduction of the athletics program naturally quickened the trend towards specialization.

The 1920 Antwerp Games faced and overcame many difficulties caused by World War I but were notable for the first appearance of the outstanding Finn, Paavo Nurmi. Nurmi returned to the heat of Colombes Stadium, Paris, in 1924 to win the 1,500 metres, 5,000 metres, and the cross-country race. The winner of the high jump, the American Harold Osborn (also winner of decathlon) used a back lay-out version of the Western roll which stimulated a rule change. It was claimed that Osborn pushed the bar back onto the pegs as he jumped (if this was so, then he amply deserved his Olympic medal!) and from then on the rules required that the support-pegs pointed inwards. Paris brought a breakthrough in 400-metre running methods when the Scottish rugby international Eric Liddell blasted through the first 200 metres in 22.2 sec to win in 47.6 sec.

The 1928 Amsterdam Games brought the first impact of a rapidly developing Japanese nationalism when the triple jumper Mikio Oda won with 15.21 m (49 ft 10¾ in) and the pole vaulter Yonataro Nakazawa achieved sixth place. It was, however, the Finns who dominated the Amsterdam Games, winning all track events from 1,500 metres upwards as well as the decathlon. The Americans, whose college system was not particularly sensitive to Olympic needs, had a modest Games. The British, with an Oxbridge and harrier-based system, were unsuccessful.

Amsterdam was significant for the introduction of women's athletics. By a vote of 15–6 the IAAF had agreed to a modest program of 100 metres, high jump, discus, 4 × 100-metres relay and 800 metres. Alas, the memory which remained with many spectators was of ill-trained ladies staggering up the straight in the 800 metres. The event was not to be seen again in the Games until 1960.

The Los Angeles Games of 1932 were probably the finest athletic spectacle staged up till that time. Each day records fell like ninepins on the incredibly fast Colosseum track. Eddie Tolan's 10.3-sec 100 metres, William Carr's 46.2-sec 400 metres, these are times to reckon with even today. The Irishman R. M. N. Tisdall took gold in the 400-metres hurdles from the brilliant American Glenn Hardin in 51.7 sec (officially rounded off to 51.8 sec), only to have the world record denied him because he had toppled the final hurdle, a rule which no longer obtains.

The athlete of the Games was a woman, Mildred 'Babe' Didrikson, who won in 80-metres hurdles and javelin, and placed second in high jump. Under present

Mildred Didrikson (United States) winning the 80-metres hurdles in the 1932 Games in Los Angeles

rules, Miss Didrikson would have won the latter event as she was penalized for 'diving' by leading with head and shoulders over the crossbar, a rule rescinded in 1937.

The success of the German Olympic Committee in at least limiting Nazi pollution of the 1936 Berlin Olympics is one of the least-known successes of the Olympic Movement. The Games, will, however, be remembered for the charismatic quality of one man, the American Negro Jesse Owens. Day after day in the grey Wagnerian stadium Owens was a god among mortals. It was not that Owens won, but rather the manner in which he did so. Here was speed, here was grace, here was beauty.

The Berlin Games was probably the first in which a national team was systematically prepared outside normal working hours. The German team had trained for months in camps in the Black Forest and German athletes in the Civil Service had been given time off for training at government request during a full year before the Games. These preparations were to be a hint of things to come.

In contrast, the 1948 London Games were a return to simpler times. Only the United States, based as it was on college athletics, was able to field a fully representative team. The war-shattered countries of Western Europe produced, in the main, either veteran athletes or those with little international experience. The Dutch athlete Fanny Blankers-Koen had pursued her career through the war period and won four gold medals without competing in long or high jumps, where she held world records. There were some notable exceptions. The grimacing Emil Zátopek demolished the 10,000-metres field and only narrowly failed to win the 5,000 metres. Zátopek transformed distance training, not because of his running style or scientific training methods, but because of the sheer intensity of his preparation. Soon athletes such as the Briton Gordon Pirie and the Russian Vladimir Kuts were vying with the Czech in the severity of their training.

The year 1952 was possibly as significant a turning point in international athletics as the formation of the IAAF in 1913. It marked the entry of the USSR to post-war Games and this resulted in more technical analysis of track and field athletics in the following twenty years than had occurred in the whole of the previous history of the sport put together. This is because the methods behind the Soviet successes of 1952 and 1956 were immediately copied and improved upon by the other Communist-bloc states. Behind this, the central Communist reasoning was that the citizen-athlete reflected the society within which he lived and that his successes were also those of the State. This was not, of course, the general view of the free-enterprise societies of the West, though Finland with its intense nationalism reflected a Western form of this view.

The 1952 Helsinki Games and the 1956 Melbourne

Games were the last 'simple' Olympics, in that they were the last in which television played no major part. The 1960 Games were the last in which no qualifying standards were demanded. Thereafter, though any nation could enter one athlete without his having achieved a qualifying mark, if two or more were entered all had to have qualified.

The most significant victory in the 1960 Games was by a relatively inexperienced New Zealand runner, Peter Snell, in the 800 metres. Snell was the living embodiment of the theories of the great New Zealand coach, Arthur Lydiard. Snell ran up to 100 miles a week as part of his early preparation, a greater distance than most marathon runners up till that time. Until 1960 middle-distance training had been based mainly on interval training (80 per cent effort runs with rests of 1½ minutes, each session being controlled by pulse recovery) and Lydiard's methods were therefore revolutionary. Soon his methods were being copied by runners all over the world and resulted in substantial improvements in distance-running performances.

Snell came back at the Tokyo Olympics of 1964 to win both the 800 and 1,500 metres, the first runner to achieve the 'double' since Albert Hill in 1920. The athlete who captured Japanese hearts was, however, an American, the burly 100-metres winner, Bob Hayes, built more like a heavyweight boxer than a runner. The 1964 Games were full of jewels: Ann Packer strolling through the women's 800-metres field to pluck gold; the great Russian, Valeri Brumel, clearing 2.18 m (7 ft 1⅞ in) to win the high jump; the American, Fred Hansen, slithering over in the vault as midnight approached. It was in the latter event that the first flexible fibreglass poles were used in the Games. The flexibility of a pole dictates the height at which the vaulter can hold on the pole, as a flexible pole creates a shorter quicker-moving lever. The fibreglass pole permitted handholds above 4.57 m (15 ft) and this made vaults of over 5.48 m (18 ft) a possibility.

It is possible that anabolic steroids were being used in athletics as early as 1964. These manmade hormones, which stimulate muscle growth and increase work capacity, were originally used by bodybuilders and weightlifters, but rapidly spread to the heavy throwing events and from there to all events requiring high work levels. It is fairly certain that without steroids large sections of the record book would have to be rewritten. The discovery of tests that will effectively detect steroids at a fair period in time from their ingestion is now close. Alternatively, spot checks during the training period must be instituted. Otherwise, much of international athletics becomes a mockery.

It was difficult at the time, and it is equally difficult now, to see any good reason why the 1968 Games were held in the thin air of Mexico City, although in retrospect they stimulated athletics in Africa. To see the hopes of runners of the calibre of the Australian Ron Clarke die as they sucked desperately at the mean atmosphere was distressing. Nevertheless, Mexico was a magnificent Games. Day after day records tumbled on the rich, red, all-weather track, the first synthetic surface on which the Games had been held. The track – Tartan, a product of the 3M Company – had originally been developed in the United States as a surface for training horses in the bitter winters of the Midwest. Its main advantage was that it

was virtually maintenance-free and this permitted frequent training at all times of day and night. Its stability had meant that running and jumping techniques could be made totally automatic and that all competitions could take place from a completely consistent surface. There is, though, evidence that accidents such as falls are more prevalent on this surface than on cinders, because a bump or knock causes a runner to lose his balance more easily.

Mexico was an athletics hothouse. And what exotic blooms grew there. Tommy Smith (United States), eating up the ground like some black giant in seven-league boots. David Hemery (Great Britain) pouring over the 400-metres hurdles as if they had been spaced for his legs and his alone. Dick Fosbury (United States), arching backwards into high-jump history in a stadium which held its breath each time he began his magic circular run. The Russian, Yanis Lusis, like some god stepped down from Olympus to compete with mortals, unleashing spears which hung suspended as if held in space by his fellow gods. And Beamon! Bob Beamon (United States), running at the take-off board as if lashed by devils, launching himself into space and history like some man from myth.

African success in distance running had begun in 1960 with the marathon victory of the Ethiopian, Abebe Bikila, had been continued by Bikila in 1964, and underlined by the Tokyo medals of Mohamed Gammoudi (Tunisia) and Kipchoge Keino (Kenya). Life at altitude stimulates the oxygen transport system and Mexico City therefore presented few problems to athletes from high-altitude countries. Olympic success stimulated the development of running cultures in central Africa, a simple and inexpensive way of placing a footprint upon the surface of world sport.

Meanwhile in Europe a totally different type of society, East Germany, had begun to take a long, cool look at track and field athletics. Its victories in Mexico had been few. By Munich, East Germany, by integrating sport and medicine and by focusing attention on athletics at all levels, had become, per capita, the world's top athletics nation.

Similarly, in the mid-1960s Finland, its athletics reputation in tatters, employed a management consultant to look at its athletics structure. His recommendations resulted in a reorganization of the Finnish athletics association, and laid the foundation for Finnish victories in Munich.

The period between Helsinki and Munich has seen

Dick Fosbury (United States) winning the high jump at Mexico with his own technique, the Fosbury Flop

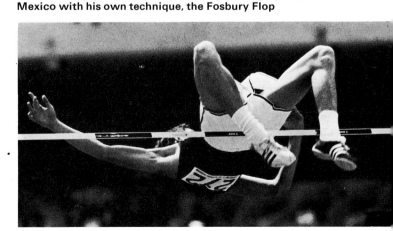

more technical development than the whole of the previous history of the sport. Much of this (the Fosbury Flop, the O'Brien technique in shot) has been the result of experimentation by athletes. Other technical changes such as the highly structured high-jump 'straddle' approach run and modern triple-jump technique has been created by coaches and sport scientists. Little is completely new. The curved Fosbury approach run was used by all Eastern cut-off jumpers and his back lay-out clearance was used by Marshall Jones Brooks of Oxford University, the first man to clear 6 ft (1.83 m) in 1876. The O'Brien technique, which involves applying force to the shot over a greater range, merely extended a technical factor already in existence. The Russian high-jump approach run and triple-jump techniques were, however, completely original, the result of the reassembling of a series of known components.

There were some great moments at Munich in 1972: the silky Russian sprinter, Valeri Borzov, strolling the 100 metres and 200 metres; John Akii-Bua (Uganda) bringing a new dimension to 400-metres hurdles; the hair's-breadth javelin victory of the German, Klaus Wolfermann; and the ruthless last-lap finish of the Finn, Lasse Virén, in the 5,000 metres. The all-rounders reached their peak with world records in decathlon and pentathlon by the Russian Nikolai Avilov and the British girl Mary Peters.

The Munich Olympics reached the ultimate in athletics technology with immediate results to the $\frac{1}{100}$ second in the runs, computerized running result boards in high jump and pole vault and pin-point accuracy in throws measurements. But the internationalism of the Olympics is threatened by high technical demands which few developing nations will ever be able to meet. Developments in pole-vault and high-jump techniques, which in turn have spurred the creation of high-cost landing areas, are tending to price developing nations out of these areas of athletics.

BASKETBALL Paul Zimmerman

Two peach baskets nailed at opposite ends of a gymnasium for goals back in 1891 marked the beginning of a sport that has swept the world and become one of the most popular and exciting events in the modern Olympic Movement.

Its birthplace was the International Young Men's Christian Association (YMCA) Training School at Springfield, Mass. (now Springfield College); the game the brainchild of an instructor, Dr James A. Naismith. It is only natural that the United States, where it was invented and refined, should have displayed its superiority through the first seven Olympiads after the game was introduced. This era of dominance ended abruptly at Munich in 1972 when the USSR scored a sensational 51-50 victory in a championship game with an ending that will be talked about for years.

Quite logically this game is called 'basketball'. Except for a quirk of fate, it might be known today as 'boxball'. The game's unusual beginning and how it finally won its way into the International Olympic arena with the eleventh Games at Berlin in 1936 is fascinating. 'For goals I

The basketball final in 1964, when the United States defeated the USSR

wanted two boxes 18 inches square,' Dr Naismith recalled, 'but Mr Stebbins, the janitor, couldn't find any. He did locate these two peach baskets in the store room.' The inventor settled for them, and the game began.

The original number of players on a side was seven. This fluctuated to nine, then eight, before the rule-makers settled on five.

Dr Naismith's concept was that basketball should be a non-contact sport. At the beginning the ball could be advanced only by passing. To run with the ball was a foul. The dribble, which came later, was not in his original scheme. To further his basic concept of no bodily contact, his original rules decreed there should be 'no shouldering, holding, pushing, tripping nor striking'. Two successive fouls benched a player, without substitute, until the next goal was made. Three successive fouls by a team, providing there was no intervening foul by the opposing team, counted as a goal for their opponents. The centre jump, just as today, started the game and was used again after each basket.

Basketball's popularity in the United States grew to such proportions that the Organizing Committee for the 1904 St Louis Games made it a demonstration sport. Twice thereafter, at Paris in 1924 and at Amsterdam in 1928 it was so designated; an indication of how it was catching on in other parts of the world. But Los Angeles, in staging the tenth Olympics in 1932, ignored basketball. Instead there were demonstrations of lacrosse, of American Indian origin, and college football.

This stung basketball's proponents into action. With the International YMCA, the Amateur Athletic Union and the National Collegiate Athletic Association strongly backing it, a world association, the Fédération Internationale de Basketball Amateur (FIBA) was formed. Rules were translated into thirty languages and enthusiasts claimed that more than ten million were playing the game. Under this pressure, and seeing basketball's growing popularity in Europe, the Berlin organizing committee asked and received permission from the International Olympic Committee to put it in the 1936 program.

In the light of what happened that year in Berlin it is easy to say that the Olympic nations were not yet ready for basketball. The fact remains that twenty-three nations from five continents entered teams: Belgium, Brazil, Canada, Chile, China, Czechoslovakia, Egypt, Estonia, France, Germany, Hungary, Italy, Japan, Latvia, Mexico, Peru, the Philippines, Poland, Spain, Switzerland, Turkey, the United States and Uruguay. Civil war forced Spain to withdraw.

The game's originator, Dr Naismith, then in his mid-sixties, was a special guest of the German committee at the ceremonies inaugurating basketball as an Olympic sport. His enthusiasm at seeing his brainchild reach the pinnacle of Olympic acceptance was somewhat dampened by what transpired. The problem was more than the overwhelming dominance of the team from the United States. Lacking suitable indoor facilities, Berlin relegated basketball to outdoor clay courts. Then the rains came, with disastrous results. This was after the United States clearly established itself as above the class of the other competitors by defeating the European champion, Estonia, 52–28.

'When the rains came the courts were virtually unplayable. It was awful,' said Sam Balter, one of the United States star players.

The day we met Mexico in the semi-finals (25–10), it rained so hard it drove the spectators out of the stands under some nearby trees. The championship game with Canada was moved to the Court of Honour where the permanent stands held several thousand spectators. There was a brick border built around the court. It looked nice but when the rain came all it did was serve to hold water an inch or more deep on the playing surface. This became a kind of swimming pool in which we skidded and slid around. There was no way the ball could be dribbled.

To show you how bad things were, we led 15 to 4 at the half. After that things got worse. Neither team was able to score more than four points in the second half. Unfortunately there was no camera around to record this priceless comedy of errors for posterity.

The United States won 19–8. The bronze medal went to Mexico, showing the dominance of the North American continent.

Basketball was moved indoors at Wembley for the 1948 Games in London and the overpowering United States superiority persisted. Led by Bob Kurland, who towered over the other players, the United States swept France into defeat, 65–21, in the finals. Brazil and Mexico finished third and fourth.

The USSR's appearance at the Olympics after the country's absence of almost half a century served to breathe new life into the basketball program at Helsinki in 1952. For several years the Russian team, built around such stars as Otar Korkiya, Styapas Butautos and Ilmar Kullam, had piled up an unbroken string of impressive victories over European opponents in preparation for the Soviet return to Olympic competition. Inevitably the USSR and United States reached the finals after easy victories, and there was an air of expectancy over the possibility of a Russian upset victory.

It was not to be. United States giants Clyde Lovellette and Kurland controlled the backboards, took the momentum away from the swift Soviet offence with a ball-control game and won handily, 86–58.

Travel distances to Australia helped to reduce the number of teams answering the call to fifteen for the Melbourne Games of 1956. In an attempt to compensate for the superior height of the United States players, the Soviet team had been almost completely rebuilt. Only three members of the 1952 squad remained, Maigonis Valdmanis, Kazis Petkyavichus and Yuri Ozerov. The usual four-year turnover of talent had left the United States with

an even better squad than the one fielded in Helsinki. It was built around 6-ft-10 in (2.083-m) Bill Russell and a fleet player named K. C. Jones. Russell and Jones had been in the same team, that of the University of San Francisco, which won the national collegiate championship in 1955.

The championship game was an even greater mismatch than the one at Helsinki. Russell scored 22 points as the United States beat the USSR 89–55.

Basketball unquestionably came into its own as an Olympic sport in 1960 at Rome. The calibre of the teams was the finest ever and the ancient city of Rome supplied them with an arena of unexcelled beauty, the new Palazzo dello Sport, which had a seating capacity of 16,000.

At a time when world talent had reached a high plateau, the United States was equal to the challenge. Many contend that this squad, which included Jerry West, Jerry Lucas, Oscar Robertson, Walt Bellamy and Terry Dischinger, was the greatest ever assembled, either amateur or professional. It averaged slightly more than 101 points a game. The USSR's greatest asset was experience. Six members of its squad, led by star Viktor Zubkov, had played together for the four years since Melbourne. The United States players had been together as a unit less than a month.

Greater team experience collapsed before superior talent. The United States breezed past the USSR, 81–57, in the semi-final pool. The USSR preserved the silver medal with a wafer-thin 64–62 victory over Brazil. This fast South American quintet, led by Wlamir Marques and Amaury Antônio Pasos, then succumbed to the United States, who won 90–63, in the finals.

Only the setting was changed at Tokyo in 1964, in another imposing arena that had been erected for basketball.

With its usual set of new stars fresh out of college, led by 6-ft 9-in (2.057-m) Lucius Jackson and sharpshooter Bill Bradley, the United States again brushed aside all opposition. Still banking on team experience, the USSR brought back five members of the squad who had played at Rome, including 7-ft (2.134-m) Aleksandr Petrov. It was of no avail. The United States put down this Russian team, 73–59. Brazil, with seven veterans returning, captured the consolation match from Puerto Rico, 76–60.

Mexico City (1968) was the scene of many firsts. To begin with, its domed Palacio de los Deportes seated 25,000 for the largest Olympic crowd ever. For the first time since 1936 the United States was not favoured to win. This was because the USSR and Yugoslavia had twice beaten the Americans in pre-Olympic matches in Europe. And, for the first time, the Americans did not have the tallest team. That edge went to the Russians, who had two 7-ft (2.134-m) players, Sergei Kovalenko and Vladimir Andreev. The United States' biggest man was a little-known junior-college youth, nineteen-year-old Spencer Haywood, who stood 6 ft 9 in (2.057 m).

For the first time, the USSR and the United States failed to meet. Yugoslavia took care of that in dramatic fashion, with a 63–62 semi-final victory over the USSR. With time running out, the Yugoslavs had a 61–60 lead, but the USSR had the ball. Game star Ivo Danev intercepted a USSR pass. Soviet desperation to regain possession led to a foul. Substitute Vladimir Cvetković calmly stepped to the line and made both free throws good. In the four seconds remaining, Yugoslavia let the USSR score unimpeded to avoid a foul, as the final buzzer sounded. •

The untidy Yugoslavs made a game of it during the first half of the championship final, before losing to the United States, 50–65. Haywood, the youngest player ever to represent his country in basketball, led the scoring with 22 points. So, for the first time in sixteen years, the USSR failed to finish second.

Although the results at Mexico City did not reveal it, a chink was beginning to show in the armour of American Olympic basketball. Led by the renowned giant, Lew Alcindor, outstanding collegiate seniors elected to bypass Olympic team tryouts and a summer of preparation. With huge sums being offered to sign professional contracts, they preferred instead to accept the largesse.

This trend continued in 1972. Bill Walton (later a winner of the coveted Sullivan award as top amateur athlete) headed the growing list of graduating seniors who accepted the lure of professionalism in lieu of the opportunity of representing their country at Munich. Even so, the United States almost won in the most controversial championship finish ever seen on any basketball court.

The USSR had played well enough to win and was leading 44–36 with five minutes to play. In a closing surge, the United States had narrowed the gap to 48–49 with three seconds to play when Doug Collins was fouled. He scored both throws. With the Soviet coach frantically trying to get a time-out, the horn sounded and the Americans thought they had a 50–49 victory. But Dr R. William Jones, secretary-general of the International Amateur Basketball Federation, ruled that the clock should be reset, giving the Russians a three-second reprieve. It was all they needed. Ivan Edeshko threw the ball the length of the court to Aleksandr Belov. He did a remarkable job of eluding defenders Kevin Joyce and Jim Forbes to score, making it 51–50. The horn sounded again, this time definitely, finally.

Despite bitter protests from the United States, refusal by the piqued players to accept the silver medals and a fruitless plea before the jury of appeals, the United States' run of victories in international matches had been broken at 63 straight, beginning with Berlin in 1936. The USSR had ended a basketball dominance that spanned 36 years and seven Olympiads. At long last the United States had been beaten at the game of its own invention. A new era in Olympic basketball was born.

BOXING Neil Allen

Boxing, or pugilism, was introduced into the ancient Olympics in 686 B.C. The boxers had headguards and used long leather wrappings to protect their hands and to give increased force to blows. Hard leather gloves, with cutting edges, later replaced thongs and the Romans finally brutalized the sport with the introduction of the *cestus*, an iron-studded gauntlet which sometimes even had metal spikes fixed over the knuckles.

The organizers of the first modern Olympics at Athens in 1896 decided to omit boxing from the program because it was ungentlemanly, dangerous and 'practised by the dregs of the population'. Seventy-six years later, in Munich's Boxhalle, the status of Olympic boxing had changed so much that the West German officials were embarrassed by the public demand for tickets to watch a fourteen-day program involving a record number of 357 boxers in eleven different weight categories.

Boxing made its first appearance in the modern Games at St Louis in 1904 when the program included a demonstration of women boxing. Seven weight categories were decided in St Louis from 21 to 24 September 1904. All the finalists were American. On paper the most remarkable boxer was O. L. Kirk of the Business Men's Gymnasium, St Louis, who won both the bantamweight (115 lb or 52.1 kg) and featherweight (125 lb or 56.7 kg) titles. Kirk had a weight advantage of 10 lb (4.54 kg) over the flyweight winner, George V. Finnegan, in winning the bantamweight final but conceded the same amount to Frank Haller at featherweight. For all the small entry, Kirk is still the only man ever to win two different weights in a single Olympic boxing tournament.

Britain won all five titles at the 1908 Olympic tournament in London but the hosts acknowledged: 'For the most part our visitors were not of sufficiently high class to have a real sporting chance of victory which made their presence all the more meritorious.' The winners included the thirty-eight-year-old Dick Gunn at featherweight and the nineteen-year-old Henry Thomas at bantamweight. But the high point of the tournament was the middleweight final between Britain's Johnny Douglas, an England cricketer and footballer, and the Australian 'Snowy' Baker.

Boxing was not included on the program of the 1912 Olympics in Stockholm because the sport was prohibited by Swedish law. When it returned, in 1920 at Antwerp, there was the first of the many controversial decisions which were to overshadow the sport in several Games. The Americans had grievances about a points decision won by Harry Mallin of Britain over their own representative Sam Lagonia before Mallin went on to win the middleweight title. The US Olympic Report also stated: 'Two Americans (Hartman and Etzell) were awarded decisions but after starting for their dressing rooms the

Teofilo Stevenson (Cuba), 1972 heavyweight champion, (right) defeating Duane Bobick (United States) in a preliminary round

László Papp (Hungary), the holder of three boxing gold medals

hissing of the spectators caused the judges to reverse their decisions.' The American winner at flyweight, Frankie De Genaro, was the first Olympic winner to go on to become a world professional champion.

A total of twenty-nine countries entered 252 boxers for the 1924 Olympics in Paris. The official British report of these Games commented: 'The boxing tournament provided the critics of the Olympic Games with excellent copy for several incidents of a most regrettable nature marred the proceedings and completely destroyed the pleasure of all those who understand the true meaning of the word "sportsmanship".'

Yet the British seem to have gained more than their share of luck from the eventual result of the middleweight bout between Mallin, on his way to a second Olympic title, and Roger Brousse of France. According to the British view, Mallin appeared to be a good winner but the verdict was given to Brousse. Meanwhile, Mallin had been 'attempting to bring to the notice of the referee that he had been bitten on the chest'. A protest launched by a Swedish official succeeded and Brousse was disqualified even though the jury expressed the opinion that the foul was not an intentional one. Altogether the Americans won two gold, two silver and two bronze medals, the British two gold and two silver. The two American winners, Fidel LaBarba (flyweight) and Jackie Fields (featherweight), later won world professional championships. Fields beat another American in his Olympic final but from then on it was decided that a country should be limited to one boxer at each weight.

The number of countries entered at Amsterdam in 1928 remained at twenty-nine but the total number of boxers, 146, was down because of the new restriction. Debatable decisions, however, arose, and those in the finals at featherweight and middleweight caused one team manager to ask, 'Surely really competent officials, officials in whom satisfactory confidence is imposed and maintained, can be appointed?'

To travel to Los Angeles for the 1932 Olympics was such a costly venture for Europeans that it is not surprising that the boxing entry was only eighty-five from eighteen countries. At least the medals won at the Olympic auditorium were divided among twelve teams and the official report of the Games commented: 'No dispute of consequence over decisions arose and the spirit of good sportsmanship prevailed.' The American hosts, South Africa and Argentina, each won two titles. For the first time in Olympic boxing, the referee officiated from the ring.

The efficiency of the 1936 Olympics in Berlin is underlined by a report that 'the boxing timetable was adhered to with scrupulous punctuality. Water pipes were laid direct to the ringside so that the boxers could take refreshment between rounds.' Thirty-two countries and 183 boxers took part. Germany and France each won two titles and the Americans none. There still seemed to be doubts about decisions since one had to be revised officially.

In spite of the ravages of war there was a record entry of thirty-nine countries and 206 individuals for the 1948 Olympic boxing in London. The governing body of the sport, the Association Internationale de Boxe Amateur (AIBA), which had been formed in 1946 to succeed the defunct Fédération Internationale de Boxe Amateur (FIBA), eliminated referees and judges who proved to be below standard during the preliminary rounds and not one of the final verdicts was questioned. The outstanding winner for many was the South African light heavyweight George Hunter. The United States surprisingly provided only one finalist and no winners. The flyweight champion, Pascual Perez of Argentina, won the professional title at this weight eight years later.

The introduction of two new weights, at light welterweight and light middleweight, helped to swell the entry to 240 boxers from forty-four countries for the 1952 Helsinki Olympics. The Americans swept right back to the top with five champions, of which the most talented was Floyd Patterson, a middleweight who was to become the youngest-ever professional world heavyweight champion in 1956. Ironically, the loser in the Helsinki heavyweight final, Ingemar Johansson of Sweden, disqualified for 'not trying', later both beat and lost to Patterson for the world professional title.

The 1956 Olympic boxing in Melbourne will always be remembered for the feat of László Papp of Hungary who, having been middleweight champion in 1948, retained the light middleweight title he won in 1952 for an unprecedented third successive victory in this most demanding sport. The USSR, never having had a winner before, won three weights, and Britain, which had not gained a gold medal since 1924, took the titles at flyweight and lightweight.

The Italians celebrated their role as hosts for the 1960 Olympics in Rome by providing three champions including the welterweight Gino Benvenuti who later won the world professional middleweight title. But the most unforgettable figure was the ebullient young American light heavyweight Cassius Clay who later, both under this name and that of Muhammad Ali, became the best-known heavyweight professional champion of all.

The 1964 tournament in Tokyo provided another future world champion in the American heavyweight Joe Frazier who was the first man to beat Clay-Ali as a professional. The USSR and Poland each won three titles though the Russians had seven finalists in the ten weights.

Earlier in the tournament, a Korean flyweight was so infuriated at his disqualification that he refused to leave the ring for 50 minutes.

For the 1968 Mexico City Olympics an extra division, at light flyweight, was introduced which brought the entry to a record 340, with forty at bantamweight and one less at featherweight. Three titles, one by a walk-over, went to the USSR and two each to the United States and Mexico. The Russian light middleweight Boris Lagutin and the Polish light welterweight Jerzy Kulej both retained their 1964 titles. A new German seamless, soft, leather glove was given credit for the reduction of serious eye injuries to half a dozen from forty-six in 1964. It was estimated that about fourteen referees and judges were asked to stand down for incompetence during a tournament which consequently achieved a reasonably high standard of officiating.

Cuba produced the outstanding team at Munich in 1972, with nine quarter-finalists, and three champions led by a hard-hitting heavyweight, Teofilo Stevenson, who needed fewer than six rounds in his three bouts. Later he emphasized that he would never turn professional, unlike most of his predecessors. The USSR won two titles but Boris Kusnetsov's victory over Philip Waruinge of Kenya at featherweight was hotly disputed. The tournament's efficiency was aided by the use of hooters and buzzers to signal rounds and intervals and only three of the 300 bouts were stopped because of eye damage.

CANOEING J. W. Dudderidge

The canoe was the earliest form of true boat and has been used in all parts of the world since time immemorial. Although no definition can embrace all the variations, the canoe can be described as a boat, usually sharp at both ends and propelled by a crew which faces forward and uses an unsupported paddle (no fixed fulcrum); or sailed under easily dismountable spars and sails.

Canoeing is both a competitive and a recreational ac-

The finish of the 1948 women's 500-metres kayak singles, won by Denmark from the Netherlands

tivity, and the craft used have all been derived from either the decked hunting kayak of the Eskimo, or the open birch-bark canoe of the North American Indian. For racing purposes three types have been developed: from the kayak, singles (K.I), pairs (K.II) and fours (K.IV), for one, two and four paddlers respectively; and from the canoe two important types, the singles (C.I) and the pairs (C.II) for one and two paddlers. The kayaks are paddled from a sitting position using a double-bladed paddle, and the canoe from a kneeling position, with a single-bladed paddle.

The credit for launching canoeing as a modern sport is accorded to John MacGregor, a London Scot who, in 1865, carried out extensive journeys on the rivers and lakes of Europe in a boat, the design of which was inspired by the kayak of the Eskimos, and which he named 'Rob Roy', returning to write a book and to lecture on his experiences. MacGregor's exploits caught the imagination of other young men, who had similar craft built, which all became known as Rob Roy canoes. In 1866 the Canoe Club was formed to foster this new sport, and the Prince of Wales became its first Commodore, an office he was to hold until his accession to the throne (as King Edward VII) in 1901. In 1867 the Canoe Club organized its first regatta and set about establishing rules for competition. By 1868 it had over 300 active members and many of these members, travelling widely in Europe and North America, introduced their new sport wherever they went. This led to the formation in 1871 of the New York Canoe Club, and during the next few years clubs were founded in many parts of Europe, often through the initiative of British students in the universities.

In Canada the native birch-bark canoe had been taken up by European settlers and its shape copied in an all-wood form which became known as the Canadian canoe; this craft was adopted by the canoeing clubs and gradually displaced the Rob Roy canoe. About 1880 canoe builders in Canada began to export their products and Canadian canoes appeared on the rivers of England and France, through their links with Canada, and later spread to Bohemia and Germany.

The rapid growth of the sport in the United States led, in 1880, to the founding of the American Canoe Association, to establish rules and regulations for racing, under paddle and under sail. Seven years later the British Canoe Association was set up, primarily as a nationwide cruising organization and canoeists in Britain continued to race under Royal Canoe Club rules until the British Canoe Union was formed in 1936. In Canada many racing clubs were formed, and in 1900 the Canadian Canoe Association came into being.

During the latter part of the nineteenth century, regattas were held in many Continental cities, including Breslau, Leipzig, Berlin, Cologne, Ghent, Ostend and Paris, often in conjunction with rowing. After 1900 national canoeing associations were set up, in Sweden in 1904, Bohemia in 1913, Germany in 1914, and Austria and Denmark in 1921. In 1924, delegates from Austria, Denmark, Germany and Sweden met in Copenhagen and founded an international authority for the sport, with the name (in Swedish) Internationella Representantskapet för Kanotidrott (IRK); to this body fell responsibility for formulating international competition rules, and also the wider promotion of the sport. The canoeing associations in

Great Britain and across the Atlantic did not accept invitations to collaborate in this work, and they continued their own separate development for another ten years or so.

During the 1920s one of the most valuable contributions to the advancement of the sport in Europe came from the commercial development and promotion of the *Faltboot*, or folding canoe, invented by a German, Alfred Heurich of Munich, in 1907. The folding canoe was in fact a kayak with a skin of canvas and a collapsible framework of wood. When dismantled, the whole kayak could be packed away in a couple of sacks and transported as baggage. This invention widened canoeing's possibilities and a vast new generation of canoeists came into being, first in Germany and Austria, then all over Central Europe and further afield. The folding canoe was taken up to only a minor degree in Scandinavia and North America.

With this growth in interest, canoe racing advanced too, and, following the foundation of the IRK in 1924, a number of international regattas were staged in Europe. Also in 1924 and quite independently of the moves to found the IRK, a demonstration canoe regatta was arranged in Paris to coincide with the Olympic Games being held there, and crews from the United States and Canada took part. From this time onwards the IRK entertained an ambition and determination to see canoe racing accepted by the International Olympic Committee, as one of the sports of the Olympic Games. Efforts were made to gain acceptance for Amsterdam in 1928, then for Los Angeles in 1932, but without success. In 1932 the IRK brought together in Vienna the representatives of Austria, Czechoslovakia, Denmark, Finland, France, Germany, Hungary, Luxembourg, Poland, Sweden and Yugoslavia to consider how it could win acceptance for the sport. It was decided to organize European Championships in Prague the following year, 1933, and at the same time to launch a campaign directly, and through national Olympic committees, for inclusion of canoe racing in the next Olympic Games in Berlin in 1936. It was felt that since the headquarters of the IRK were in Munich, and the German Canoe Association was the largest and strongest association in the federation, there was a reasonable foundation for hope. But again, in 1933, the IOC rejected the application. The IRK appealed to the IOC for further consideration and in Athens in 1934 canoe racing was admitted as one of the sports for 1936 in Berlin.

The effect of this decision on the development of the sport in all the countries where it was practised was immediate: intensive preparations began, with the result that, whereas in Prague in 1933 only ten nations, Austria, Czechoslovakia, Denmark, Germany, Finland, France, the Netherlands, Poland, Sweden and Switzerland, had participated in the European Championships, in 1936, in the first Olympic regatta at Berlin-Grunau, nineteen countries took part, including the United States, Canada, and Great Britain.

The program for the canoe regatta was: 10,000 metres: kayak singles and kayak pairs, folding canoe singles and folding canoe pairs, Canadian canoe pairs; 1,000 metres: kayak singles and kayak pairs, Canadian canoe singles and Canadian canoe pairs.

The regatta was a success in every way, with excellent performances by the competitors and a flawless organization. In canoeing as in rowing, the entries from each

Gert Fredriksson and Sven Sjodelius (Sweden) after their 1,000-metres kayak pairs victory in 1960

nation are restricted to one crew per event, and this has the effect of widening the spread of medals among the nations; the twenty-seven medals were shared between eight nations. The honours went, in the main, to the nations of Central Europe, but in the events for the Canadian canoe, Canada carried off one gold, one silver and one bronze medal. This first Olympic regatta set a high standard and aroused great hopes for the future. In fact, there were no more Olympic regattas for twelve years.

At the end of World War II the international organization was in ruins, literally and metaphorically, for its headquarters in Munich had been bombed and the records destroyed. The German President and Secretary (Dr Eckert and Dr Denk, both of Munich) had been accused by a number of national associations in the lately occupied countries of having been instrumental in bringing about the dissolution and destruction of certain national canoeing associations, instead of using their influence to protect their interests. The German canoeing fraternity was dispersed and, in the prevailing atmosphere, unacceptable to other countries.

In 1946, the prewar Vice-President of the IRK, Jonas Asschier, convened a Congress in Stockholm to reconstruct an international organization. Twelve countries responded to his invitation and formed the International Canoe Federation (ICF), with a new constitution, new competition rules, and new headquarters in Stockholm. Asschier was elected as President and the writer, also from the Board of the IRK, as Vice-President.

In 1948, the regatta was held on the narrow waters of the Thames at Henley, with participants from sixteen countries. There were changes in the program which reflected developments since 1936. The events for the folding canoe classes had been removed, and for men, parity had been established between kayaks and Canadian canoes, with events provided for both singles and pairs in each type and over both 1,000 metres and 10,000 metres. In addition the introduction of an event for women, 500-metres kayak singles, recognized the new place of women in sport. The addition of this event had a stimulating effect in many countries, and ten nations submitted entries.

In the kayak events the Scandinavian canoeists were dominant and the Swedish paddler, Gert Fredriksson, made his Olympic début, winning gold medals for the singles at both 1,000 metres and 10,000 metres. He was to remain a leading contender in this class for twelve years, and won a total of six gold medals, five of them in the singles and his last one, in 1960, in the pairs. In that year, the IOC awarded him the special distinction for an outstanding athlete, the Mohamed Taher Trophy.

Each Olympic regatta brought an increase in the numbers of nations taking part, and a steady rise in standards. In 1952 in Finland, twenty-one nations took part, and there were signs that the Scandinavian dominance might be coming under challenge from the new associations in eastern Europe. Four years later, in Ballarat, Australia, the USSR, Hungary, and Romania, between them, carried off seventeen out of the twenty-seven medals, including six golds, and it was clear that these three nations were making a speciality of the single-blade events.

Four years later in Rome, on the deep waters of Lake Albano, technical problems of laying a course for the 10,000-metres races led to their elimination from the program; in their place were brought in only two events, the 4 × 500-metres kayak singles relay race, and the kayak pairs for women, over a course of 500 metres. A popular innovation was the introduction of the *repêchage* in all the events, allowing each crew a second chance before elimination.

The program was changed again in Tokyo in 1964 by the substitution of the 1,000-metres kayak fours for the relay race introduced in Rome. The 'fours' event is the canoeing equivalent of the 'eights' in rowing, and the IRK had long sought its inclusion. There were entries from fourteen nations and in a magnificent final, the first three crews, from the USSR, Germany and Romania, crossed the line within the space of one second.

The events in Mexico in 1968 brought problems of altitude for the record number of twenty-six nations which appeared in the canoeing events. In spite of the efforts made to achieve a degree of acclimatization, many crews failed to reach their known potential, being overtaken by oxygen starvation in the final stages of their races.

There were no changes in the racing program in Munich and a record number of twenty-eight teams fought it out on the regatta course. In the finals, the team from the USSR were the winners in six out of the seven events, including all the kayak events. However, a new dimension was added in the 1972 Olympic Games through the introduction of the canoe slalom, a competition involving a timed run down a set course on fast turbulent water, with the addition of penalty seconds for faulty negotiation.

'Wild-water' canoeing on mountain torrents has always provided one of the most popular, exciting, and challenging branches of the sport, and, in the 1930s, the canoeists of Austria began to organize 'regattas' on such rivers, timing runs down certain sections of them. Both Austrian and Swiss canoeists were usually members of ski clubs, and were familiar with the downhill and slalom competitions in that sport, and it is not surprising therefore that they sought to complete the parallel by introducing slalom into

canoeing. It took some time to evolve effective methods of marking out slalom courses on mountain torrents, and to establish rules on the negotiation of hazards, but, in due course, a satisfactory system was found, in coloured poles suspended from overhead wires, to hang just clear of the water, forming 'gates' through which the competitor must pass. They also worked out, and revised at various times, a system of penalties for faulty negotiation of the course.

Wild-water racing and canoe slalom soon achieved wide popularity, and this even more when it was realized that a mountain torrent was not a prerequisite, and that a slalom course could be devised on turbulent water below the outflow from a dam. In fact, the first world championship in canoe slalom, in 1949, was on such a course at Geneva, where the water of the lake flows out, through sluicegates to form the River Rhône; the passage through the sluices providing a very challenging hazard on the course. Since that time, world championships have been held biennially, on a variety of courses throughout Europe, in Yugoslavia, Austria, Italy, Germany and France.

In canoe slalom there are classes for kayak singles, for both men and women, and Canadian canoe singles and pairs. The craft used in slalom differ strikingly from the equivalent classes in canoe racing, being shorter and more manoeuvrable. Over the years, canoe slalom has gained a reputation as a sport demanding a high degree of courage and technical skill, and one with a strong spectator appeal.

It was in 1966 that the ICF decided to seek for canoe slalom a place in the program of the Olympic Games, and discussions began with the IOC and later with the Organizing Committee for the Games in Munich in 1972. There were many problems, not the least of which was on the question of a suitable venue near Munich. At last, in Amsterdam, in 1970, the IOC gave approval to the inclusion of canoe slalom on an artificial course to be built at Augsburg. This course, fed from the waters of the River Lech, proved a most challenging one for the competitors. Over 30,000 spectators watched the slalom experts from sixteen countries battle their way down the course, through every form of hazard, and uncounted millions shared the thrills through the medium of television, which gave the racing extensive coverage. The team from the German Democratic Republic, known to be one of the best in the world, distinguished itself by taking the first place in every class.

Despite its successful début in 1972, canoe slalom will not appear in the program for the 1976 Games. This decision is attributed largely to the high cost of providing an artificial course. Nevertheless, increasing numbers are taking up this branch of canoeing, and in a number of countries where suitable natural facilities do not exist, or are inadequate, various forms of artificial, or semi-artificial courses are being planned, often on the outflow from a reservoir.

While withdrawing canoe slalom from the program, the IOC has agreed to the extension of the racing program by the addition of 500-metres events in kayak singles and pairs and Canadian canoe singles and pairs, and these will be in the program for 1976.

Through the emergence of canoeing as an Olympic sport, canoe racing and canoe slalom have become known throughout the world, and this had led to a widening of

A spectacular addition to Olympic events, the canoe slalom on a specially built course at Munich

interest in active participation. This in turn has helped promote the development of the sport on an organized basis, so that the International Canoe Federation now embraces thirty-nine national associations, and during the next few years these are likely to increase in South America, Africa and South East Asia, which are at present rather thinly represented.

CYCLING Włodzimierz Gołębiewski

Three years before the first Olympic Games in Athens the first world cycling championships took place in Chicago and the following year in Antwerp. So it is not surprising that cycling was on the program of the first Olympics and since then has continuously been one of the attractions at each of the successive Games; it is also on the program of all the big regional events such as the Pan-American Games and the Pan-Asian Games. There are also intercontinental cycling championships or championships for geographical regions, such as those for Central America and the Caribbean which are independent of the regular world championships.

Cycling has become a major event on the Olympic program. It is practised in five continents and there are Olympic cycling contests on the track and on the road. Like many other sports it has undergone several changes over the years. Just as there used to be track and field events such as the standing high jump or throwing the javelin with both hands, cyclists, too, used to compete for medals in events which today have long been forgotten; for example, in Athens, in 1896, they attempted a 12-hour race, and in London, in 1908, one of the events was a sprint for 603.49 m (660 yd).

Nobody today could say exactly what form the cycling events took in the first Olympic Games, even many well-known sport historians have serious doubts in this field and differ on many details. One thing is certain, however. From the beginning this sport has been remarkable for its value in basic training, teaching cyclists to fight hard but always fairly and with respect for fellow competitors.

Here is a beautiful incident from the first Olympic Games in Athens in 1896. The 100-km track race was taking place. After 15 laps the Frenchman, Léon Flameng, had lapped his opponents. After 150 laps all the Frenchman's opponents had retired from the contest except the Greek G. (only the first letter of his first name is given in the registration annals) Kolettis, who was far behind. He suffered a further reverse when he had to stop because of some mechanical defect in his machine. Flameng saw his opponent's predicament, stopped and waited until the Greek got a new cycle and was able to continue. At the end the Frenchman won by 11 laps and was warmly applauded not so much for his victory as for his sportsmanship.

The world would not be what it is, however, and people would hardly be human if, even in cycling, there were no episodes to record that are in direct contrast to the event of 1896. It was in 1936, the year of the Olympic Games in Berlin, that a group of cyclists was fighting it out at the end of the individual road race. At the front was the French-

man Guy Lapébie. There were still another 30 metres to the finishing line, Lapébie seemed to slow down for a fraction of a second and another Frenchman, Robert Charpentier, moved in front of him – and received the gold medal.

Several months later, back in France, Lapébie was looking at a photograph of the finish of the Olympic road race. It was then, and in fact not until then, that he began to understand why he had suddenly slowed down 30 metres before the finishing line – it was because his team mate Charpentier had caught hold of his shirt from the back.

Perhaps this unsportsmanlike act was not premeditated; maybe the culprit caught hold of his team mate in the heat of the moment and simply did not think about how very far removed his action was from the spirit of true sportsmanship. The fact, however, remained.

A tragedy happened in 1960 in Rome: the Danish cyclist, Knud Enemark Jensen, a member of the team starting in the 100-km race, fainted on the road and died on the way to hospital. The postmortem indicated that before the start of the race this young man had taken a large overdose of drugs which had been the cause of his death.

No one has ever proved whether he took the overdose himself or whether the drug was administered by someone else without his knowledge. As a result of this tragic accident, the International Cycling Federation (UCI) became the first to bring in doping control. Over the years the fight against drugs has become an important part of the work of the UCI, and it must be realized that in its struggle the Federation has been greatly helped by the International Olympic Committee. Since 1968, testing for drugs, by the International Medical Commission has been obligatory in all sports.

Cycling in the Olympic Games consists of two kinds of road races (the team event and the individual competition) and also four track races (a 1,000-metres sprint, a 100-km time trial, a 4,000-metres individual pursuit and a 4,000-metres team pursuit). Until the 1972 Olympic Games in Munich, a 2,000-metres tandem was also a part of the program. Unfortunately it has been removed as cycling's contribution to cutting events in the Olympic program, which is a pity for this is an interesting speciality: it is appealing to the spectators and teaches the competitor, how to make a cooperative effort, for the two

Robert Charpentier and Guy Lapébie (France) at the finish of the 1936 100-kilometres cycling road race

cyclists must act as one and coordinate all their technical and tactical manoeuvres.

It is curious that cycling, as opposed to many other sports, does not have as yet great contestants who, like Nurmi or Owens in track and field events, Weissmuller or Spitz in swimming, have gained great Olympic fame and have been heroes in their field for many years. Undoubtedly the most famous cyclist of all time is Eddy Merckx, who only once took part in the Olympic Games. This was in the individual road race in Tokyo in 1964 when he was nineteen years old. He rode splendidly and was always out front. Unfortunately, several hundred metres before the finishing line he had an accident and by the time he could continue racing his rivals were quite a long way ahead. He furiously attempted to catch them up and make up for lost ground. At the finishing line he was only 11/100 seconds behind the winner, the Italian Mario Zanin, but placed 12th.

Cycling does not have Olympic stars because the most able competitors turn professional, often at the beginning of their sporting career. Professionalism offers young cyclists, especially those who are struggling with the difficulties of a day-to-day existence, attractive financial rewards. Cycling, especially road cycling, is a tough sport demanding a great deal of effort during races and much time spent training. It also demands of the contestant great physical and psychological stamina. Anybody who knows anything at all about cycling will admit that the famous French saying, *il faut savoir souffrir au vélo* (you must know how to suffer on a bicycle) is quite justified. Boys who take up cycling come for the most part from working-class backgrounds. In becoming cyclists they find social advancement but as the price of equipment increases from year to year, and as in order to win they must train, eat properly and also have time to rest, it is not surprising that when they come across an offer from a professional manager they eagerly take advantage of it. Becoming professional allows them to practise their beloved sport under better conditions than they could by remaining in a small amateur club.

Strangely enough, the fact that the best sportsmen become professionals has had an adverse effect on the standard of cycling in those countries where it is practised. For many years the countries in which cycling as a sport arose and developed, France, Belgium, Italy, Switzerland, the Netherlands, Britain and Luxembourg, have taken great pride in their Olympic success. But in 1960, during the Rome Olympics, cyclists emerged from countries new to the sport: Poland, the German Democratic Republic, Romania and the USSR. One of the Russians, Viktor Kapitonov, even won an Olympic gold medal in the road race, the first gold medal for the USSR in cycling.

In a sense he won it twice. It was the 175.38-km (109-mile) race. In the 85th mile, Kapitonov forged in front of the large group in the lead. Only Trapè (Italy) raced after him, the pair gaining a lead of over two minutes. As they came to the end of the penultimate lap, Kapitonov, who thought it was the final one, sprinted. Trapè did not accelerate but rode on at the normal speed and caught up with Kapitonov just as the latter was about to get off his bicycle. The Russian trainer, Viktor Sheleshniev, managed to put right his competitor's mistake, showing him that it was not yet time for celebrating his victory and that he had to go on for another lap. Would he last out another

Viktor Kapitonov (USSR) narrowly defeats Livio Trapè (Italy) in the 1960 road race.

finish? He did indeed! On the real last lap Kapitonov again sprinted; Trapè matched his speed but lost narrowly.

Over the years the superiority of cyclists from Scandinavia and the East European countries has become increasingly clear, especially in road races. Yet, on the whole, European cyclists are still in a class of their own in comparison with the representatives from other continents. Sometimes their superiority is threatened by the Australians, sometimes the Colombians appear menacing; the standard of cycling is also being raised in Cuba and Japan. Nevertheless, Africa does not have cyclists of the calibre of such athletes as Keino or Akii-Bua; Asia does not have road or track cyclists of the class of the Pakistani or Indian hockey champions.

As always happens in sport, there are never permanently strong competitors nor permanently weak ones. The distribution of strength changes, champions come and go. Thanks to the IOC's support of the idea of helping sport to develop in countries of the third world, the International Federation of Amateur Cycling (FIAC) organizes courses for cycling instructor in Africa and in Asia and cyclists and umpires are trained in all five continents.

EQUESTRIAN SPORTS HRH the Prince Philip, Duke of Edinburgh

The first recorded equestrian event to take place at the ancient Olympic Games was in 680 B.C. in the twenty-fifth Olympiad. It was a race for chariots drawn by four full-grown horses. Chariot racing had been a popular sport for a long time before it was incorporated in the Games, and the winners of races and the breeders of winning horses enjoyed much prestige. In fact, according to Xenophon, the breeding of chariot horses was considered 'the noblest and grandest business in the world.'

Chariot racing in various classes, including teams of four mules and pairs of colts, continued until the Games were abolished by the Romans. The races took place in the Hippodrome at Olympia over distances from two to three miles which involved up to twelve circuits of the 400-metres oblong course. There were complicated arrangements for starting the races so as to compensate the chariots drawn in the outside positions for the extra distance they were required to cover. The same principle is used in foot races up to 800 metres in the present day.

Anything to do with horses is unpredictable and frequently dangerous. It seems that the Hippodrome course was far from smooth and, as the chariots had no springs and the charioteers had their hands full of reins and whip, there must have been some interesting dramas. Furthermore, the course had a hairpin bend at each end which inevitably caused crashes and upsets.

A wall painting of the time shows a chariot being kicked to pieces by infuriated horses and the charioteer sailing through the air. In one type of race a passenger was carried who had to leap out and run with the chariot for the last lap which must have been quite an alarming experience.

Races on horseback were introduced at the thirty-third Olympiad (648 B.C.) and continued till the end. There were classes for various ages and types of horse. The riding races were somewhat less dangerous than the chariot races but as the horses were ridden without saddles or stirrups some nasty falls were only to be expected. In one form of race the rider had to jump off and lead his horse round the last lap – a form of exercise which most present-day riders would not much appreciate.

It appears that two basic types of horses were used in these races. The chariot horses were a strong northern Asiatic type while the ridden-race horses were much lighter and probably of Arabian origin. It seems likely that the Arabians were introduced into Greece between 2000 and 1500 B.C. by the pre-Hellenic people who came from Phoenicia and were famous horsemen and horse breeders. The heavier and stronger Asiatic battle-chariot horses were brought to Greece by the Hellenic people when they crossed the Hellespont from Asia Minor in 1500 B.C.

The art of horsemanship in ancient Greece is clearly described by Xenophon in a treatise written in 365 B.C. and he shows that the main principles of selection and methods of training were similar to those in use today.

The ancient Olympic Games finished in the fourth century A.D., but equestrian competition in various forms continued in all parts of the world where the horse was in use for war, transport and agriculture. Mounted games such as polo were played in different parts of central Asia while jousting tournaments, using heavy horses, were popular in western Europe right through the Middle Ages.

The great change in horsemanship came about at the beginning of the eighteenth century when highly mobile cavalry was recognized in western Europe to be more effective than heavy mounted formations. Frederick the Great's father, Frederick William I of Prussia, first raised and trained regiments of hussars and uhlans, whose names and uniforms were derived from the traditional light horsemen of Hungary and Poland, but it was Frederick who used them with devastating effect.

Also in the early eighteenth century light, fast coaches,

Captain C. F. Pahud de Mortanges (Netherlands), winner of four Olympic equestrian gold medals

originally developed in Hungary, drawn by four horses, transformed the transport system of the western countries from slow-moving carts and pack horses to the fast passenger-carrying coaches of the eighteenth and nineteenth centuries. In their heyday of the early nineteenth century these coaches with regular changes of horses were able to maintain an average speed of 16 km (10 miles) per hour over great distances. With the introduction of lighter and faster horses from Arabia and eastern Europe, all the equestrian sports developed rapidly, particularly racing and hunting.

Dressage, or the schooling of horses in precisely executed movements, has been practised in one form or another ever since men started to ride, but the development of competitive jumping and contests of endurance are relatively recent. Competitive jumping followed naturally from hunting and steeplechasing, while the present three-day event derived from the military requirement of cross-country ability and endurance. In the early days of the twentieth century there was a vogue for long-distance rides, particularly in France and Belgium, but as a number of horses died of exhaustion in these contests, they were eventually abandoned in Europe. In the United States long-distance competitive trail rides still take place.

When Coubertin began the modern series of Olympiads it was, therefore, quite natural that equestrian sports should have been considered from the very beginning. Indeed it was Coubertin himself who called a meeting of the leading people in the horse world to try to persuade them to devise suitable competitions. It was from this initiative that the Fédération Équestre Internationale was eventually formed in 1921.

In spite of the fact that no international governing body or international rules existed, the first equestrian events were included in the second Olympiad in Paris in 1900. Three events – show jumping, high jump and long jump – were contested by twenty-four riders from Belgium, France, Italy and the United States. It was a start but

Above Bridget Parker (Gt Britain) in the 1972 three-day event. *Below* Bill Steinkraus (United States) winning his individual gold medal in 1968

in 1928.) Sixty-two riders from ten nations took part in Stockholm and Swedish competitors took most of the medals. After World War II women began to compete and in 1952 in Helsinki Lis Hartel of Denmark won a silver medal in dressage and Baroness Ida von Nagel was a member of the German team that won the bronze medal.

There is no evidence that polo, or any similar mounted games, were included in the ancient Olympic Games, but in 1924 and 1936 polo found a place in the Olympic program. There is no doubt that it was popular with spectators because it is a marvellous game, but for an international team to play several full-length games within a few days, somewhere between thirty and forty ponies would be required for each team. This was considered to be just a bit too extravagant and polo has not figured in the program since the Berlin Games.

In 1956 the Games were held in Melbourne but owing to quarantine problems the equestrian events were organized on their own in Stockholm. A record number of twenty-nine nations with 164 competitors took part in what many people still believe was the most enjoyable and successful series of equestrian Olympic competitions.

This time the women did even better: the German dressage team – all women – won the silver medal while Lis Hartel of Denmark and Liselott Linsenhoff of Germany carried off the silver and bronze individual medals. The women also invaded the jumping competitions for the first time, when Pat Smythe, as a member of the British team, won a bronze medal in the Nations' Cup. The first woman to win an individual medal for show jumping was Marion Coakes of Britain on Stroller when she won a silver medal in Mexico in 1968. Women took part in the three-day event competition for the first time in Tokyo in 1964, when Lana Dupont was a member of the US team that won a silver medal. Two British women won team gold medals in the three-day event in Munich in 1972, Mary Gordon-Watson on Cornishman V and Bridget Parker on Cornish Gold.

At Rome in 1960 the Australian team won the three-day event title and joined the United States, which won this event in Los Angeles in 1932 and in London in 1948, as the only other nation outside Europe to capture this gold medal.

For many years the places for the individual and team show jumping were decided in the same Nations' Cup competition. In Rome in 1960 separate competitions were held for the first time, but at the following Games in Tokyo there was only one competition for both events. In Mexico a separate competition for individuals was again introduced with three riders from each nation allowed to enter. Forty-two riders from fifteen nations took part. At the same Games separate dressage competitions for teams and individuals were included for the first time.

Although there have been many changes in the details of the rules the same three equestrian competitions have been included in all the Olympic Games since 1912, except for those at Antwerp in 1920, where the team dressage competition was dropped and the competitions in the three-day event were completely changed. Instead of the dressage test on the first day there was a long-distance test over 50 km (31 miles) with eighteen obstacles. On the second day there was another distance test over 20 km (13 miles) followed by a steeplechase course of 4,000 m (4,373 yd). On the third day there was the usual

not a very happy one as the rules were more or less invented as the competitions went along.

It was due to the enthusiasm and persistence of Count Clarence von Rosen, the Master of the Horse to the King of Sweden, that matters improved. He managed to get equestrian events included in the plans for the London Games of 1908 but the organizers of the International Horse Show at Olympia, where the competitions were to be held, eventually decided they could not manage the competitions, so they were cancelled.

Count von Rosen was more successful at the Stockholm Games of 1912 when for the first time the three events of show jumping, three-day event and dressage were included. The dressage competition was for individuals only but medals were awarded for both teams and individuals in the three-day event and in the jumping. (A team competition in dressage was added at the Amsterdam Games jumping test. Sweden won both the team and individual gold medals.

A different type of competition known as 'voltige riding' was tried out at Antwerp but this was the only time it appeared in an Olympic program. It consisted of various vaulting exercises with a horse at the halt and at the canter, both bareback and with a saddle. The team and individual gold medals were both won by Belgium.

The three-day event is usually the first on the equestrian Olympic program. The term 'three-day event' is the English description of what was originally called the *concours militaire* and today the *concours complet* in French. In the early days most of the competitors in this event were army officers, and indeed at one time the event was limited to army officers. Gradually, as the mounted cavalry regiments disappeared from the armies, the proportion of civilian competitors increased.

The three-day event begins with a dressage test on the first day but, owing to the number of competitors and the strain on the three judges, the tests are spread over two days so that the full event really takes four days.

The second competition is the main endurance test which up to 1964 consisted of five phases, since reduced to four. Phases A and C are on roads and tracks over distances of 16–20 km (10–13 miles) at a speed of 240 m (262 yd) per minute. Phase B is a steeplechase course consisting of an average of three fences every 1,000 metres over 3,450–4,140 m (3,773–4,528 yd) at a speed of 690 m (755 yd) per minute. Phase C starts immediately after the steeplechase course, but there is a short rest before the final Phase D, which is a very demanding cross-country obstacle course of 7,410–7,980 m (8,104–8,727 yd) to be ridden at 570 m (623 yd) per minute. (These rather odd distances are necessary so that the time allowed for each phase comes out as a whole number of minutes.) Unlike those in show jumping the obstacles in Phase D are firmly fixed. It is unusual for more than seventy-five per cent of the competitors to complete this competition.

On the morning following the endurance competition all the horses that have completed the course have to be paraded for a veterinary inspection before they are allowed to start in the final jumping competition which is over 10–12 obstacles in 750–900 m (820–984 yd) to be ridden at 350–400 m (383–437 yd) per minute.

Each of the three competitions is marked in penalty points and these are added together to give the final results. Four riders may start for each team but only the scores of the best three are counted.

The Grand Prix dressage competition is usually run over three days. The tests ridden on the first two days, in front of five judges, decide the team placings. A team consists of three competitors. The twenty best individuals in this first round are then entitled to take part in the individual competition which is held on the third day.

The first of the two show-jumping competitions is for individuals and it is decided over a Grand Prix course with 12–15 obstacles over a distance of 1,000 metres. If several riders tie for first place, there is a jump-off with the best time counting.

The climax of the equestrian events, and traditionally the last competition to be staged in the main Olympic arena, is the Nations' Cup team jumping competition. Nations may enter four riders but only the best three scores in each of the two rounds are counted. The competition consists of two rounds over the same Nations' Cup course of 12–15 obstacles over not more than 1,000 metres. Only the eight best teams compete in the second round. Since only the scores of the best three riders are counted, in a team of four, an individual's score may count in one round but not in the other. For instance, at Munich (1972) Kathryn Kusner of the United States scored 20 penalties in the first round but as the other three members of the team did better her score was not counted. However, in the second round she scored 12 faults while Frank Chapot scored 28 so his score in that round was not counted.

Only France and the United States have taken part in all the Games at which equestrian events were included, starting with the Paris Games in 1900. A total of forty nations have taken part at least once and twenty-four nations have gained one or more medals. Germany heads the list with 38 followed by Sweden with 34, France with 27, the United States with 19 and Italy with 18. Since the USSR first appeared in 1952, it has gained seven medals.

Sweden won both the individual dressage title and the Nations' Cup team competitions three times running in 1912, 1920 and 1924, and the individual dressage five times altogether out of a possible thirteen (not counting Paris in 1900). The Netherlands has won the individual three-day event medal three times running in 1924, 1928 and 1932. In 1928 and 1932 it was won by the same man, Lieutenant C. Ferdinand Pahud de Mortanges, on Marcroix, the only nation and the only competitor to have achieved a treble and a double in this event.

Germany is the only nation so far to have won team and individual gold medals in all three competitions. This feat was achieved at Berlin in 1936. Sweden has come nearest by winning four out of five in 1912 and four out of six in 1952. Fifteen nations have won gold medals but only three nations have only won one gold medal, Spain with the team jumping competition in 1928, Czechoslovakia with the individual jumping in the same year and Japan with the individual jumping in 1932.

In 1932 in Los Angeles none of the teams entered in the Nations' Cup competition managed to finish the course and therefore no medals were given for this event. This is the only time such a thing has happened.

Chile was the first South American nation to compete in 1912; Argentina came to the Games for the first time in 1928 and Mexico started in 1952. Australia first competed in 1956; in 1960 it won the team gold medal and the individual gold and silver medals in the three-day event. Canada nearly achieved the same feat. It competed for the first time in 1952 and came third in the three-day event in 1956.

There have been a number of outstanding individual performances. For instance, in 1948 Earl F. Thomson rode Pancraft in the silver medal-winning US dressage team and then rode Reno Rhythm in the gold medal-winning three-day event team. In the same year Humberto Mariles Cortés rode Parral in the bronze medal-winning Mexican three-day event team and, riding Arete, won the individual gold medal for show jumping and was a member of the gold medal-winning show-jumping team.

Liselott Linsenhoff of Germany won an individual bronze medal in 1956 and the gold medal in 1972. Bill Steinkraus first appeared as a member of the US show-jumping team that won the bronze medal in Helsinki in 1952 and twenty years later, after winning an individual gold in 1968, he led his team to a silver medal in Munich with the best individual performance in that competition.

In 1969 the Fédération Équestre Internationale (FEI) introduced rules for a four-in-hand driving competition. Since then European championships have been held in Hungary and Britain and the first world championship took place in Germany. The competition is based on the three-day event for riders and it has stimulated much interest in the ancient art of driving horses. It could well be looked upon as the modern equivalent of the chariot races of the ancient games and although it may not be quite so dangerous it probably requires greater skill and more careful training.

Needless to say the FEI would dearly like to see this competition included in the Olympic program at some future Games. So far, some ten nations have taken part in international competitions and there is every indication that more are becoming interested. If we are to believe some of the gloomy predictions about the world's fuel resources it seems only prudent to keep the art of driving horses alive.

FENCING Sándor Dávid and Dezső Vad

The relief found on the Madinet-Habu temple near Luxor in Egypt is the first noted record of fencing. The temple was built by Rameses III in 1190 B.C. The relief shows the fencers in their masks and earflaps, the weapons with protective knobs at the ends, the umpires and organizers with feathered sticks, and the spectators. Although the value of a sport is not measured by the length of time it can trace back its origins, the traditions of fencing indicate its importance through history and help us to understand why it developed as a competitive sport.

Fencing was one of the earliest sports to be regulated by theoretical and practical rules. The history of fencing runs parallel to the history of fighting, the different weapons requiring various types of combat, so that the weapon shaped the technique of fencing and in turn was shaped by it. Spain, France and Italy vie for the honour of having

Jenő Fuchs (Hungary) and Nedo Nadi (Italy) in the sabre event of 1912

created modern fencing. All three have significant claims and the truth is somewhere 'in the middle' for they have all contributed something to fencing, especially in establishing and cultivating the sport. The first manuscript, written by Filippo dal Serpente, was published in Spain in 1474. Émile Mérignac, the superb nineteenth-century French fencing master, stated that fencing had been introduced to the people of Italy by the Spanish mercenaries of Charles V. The Italian historian Jacopo Gelli, however, states that the Fiore dei Liberi manuscript published in 1410 proves that the Italians were first.

Filippo dal Serpente's manuscript in Spanish is the earliest extant work on the subject. It was followed by several extremely popular Italian books in the sixteenth century.

Fencing's ancient volumes eloquently prove that the techniques and styles used by modern fencers were all precisely described hundreds of years ago. The illustrations from books published in about 1500 clearly resemble the characteristic movements and positions of the body used by the foil's master, the World Champion of 1957, Mihály Fülöp.

The épée was developed at the beginning of the sixteenth century and has been only slightly modified since then. About a hundred years later, in 1635, a new, light weapon called the foil came into use as the épée's practising arm. The word *escrime* (fencing) and its precise meaning first appear in a French encyclopedia of 1735. The Italians and the French were the best masters of the two weapons at that time. Another hundred years passed before the Italian fencing master Giuseppe Radaelli introduced a new theory and a new weapon, the sabre.

Whereas the foil and the épée are thrust weapons, with which hits can be scored only with the point, the sabre is a cut-and-thrust weapon with a light, straight blade. Fencing with the sabre officially began at the Scuola Magistrale, from which young fencing masters started off to conquer the world. In western Europe, where thrust weapons flourished, the new weapon was not successful. In central and eastern Europe it prospered. Today when we trace the roots of Soviet, Polish and Romanian fencing we must take into consideration the influence of the large numbers of Italian and French masters at the beginning of the twentieth century.

Fencing's place in the Olympic Movement can only be understood by its traditions. Since Coubertin was French, he was familiar with this sport. At the time of the first Olympics fencing was an established sport, because the sword was still one of the most important military weapons. The light weapons and helmets used for real fighting had much in common with fencing equipment. The fashion of duelling also helped to maintain the sport's popularity.

It is unique in the history of the Olympics that in the first and second Games, both amateurs and professionals (fencing masters) were allowed to compete. In 1900, in a joint contest for épée and foil the professional Albert Ayat (France) came first, ahead of the Cuban Olympic Champion, Ramón Fonst. At that time there was no international federation, so the Games in Paris (1900) were full of contradictions. Professionals entered as it was natural for masters and pupils to take part in international contests at that time. For instance, Fonst was Ayat's pupil. To a fencer, there was no reason for objecting to the entry

Győző Kulcsár (Hungary) and Grigori Kriss (USSR) in the final of the individual épée event in 1968

of Italo Santelli, the fencing master who had won a historical contest in Budapest and went on to win a silver medal in the Paris Olympics. A generation of Hungarian sabre fencers trained by him began a period of Hungarian supremacy, beginning with the Games in London in 1908, which was to last sixty years.

St Louis was also full of uncertainties, but in the meantime fencing was acquiring an organized framework. In 1901 Dr Béla Nagy of Hungary wrote the first book of rules, which served as a basis of the present ones. The organizers of the London Olympics accepted Nagy's rules and arranged the competition according to them. The International Fencing Association (Fédération Internationale d'Escrime or FIE) was founded on 29 November 1913.

The popularity of the stabbing weapons, the épée and foil, spread after the first three Olympics from Italy and France to the Netherlands. The sabre was not accepted in western Europe for it was considered an insufficiently artistic weapon. However, the sabre was the most popular weapon in Hungary. For almost half a century the Italians, French and Hungarians have dominated the Olympics. They have been followed by a few Belgians, Germans, Dutchmen and Danes, but only the Italians, in an effort to live up to Radaelli, could compare with the Hungarians.

From 1896 until the Games in Rome (1960) the world could see such marvellous fencers as the Italians Saverio Ragno, Edoardo Mangiarotti, Giuseppe Delfino, Giulio Gaudini, Gustavo Marzi, Vincenzo Pinton, Nedo Nadi; the French Lucien Gaudin, Philippe Cattiau, Christian d'Oriola; the Hungarians Jenő Fuchs, György Piller, Pál Kovács, Aladár Gerevich and Rudolf Kárpáti.

The Olympics at Rome marked the end of an era for it was the first time in forty-eight years that neither a French nor an Italian fencer had won the foil event. Viktor Zhdanovich was the first fencer from the USSR to win a gold medal in fencing.

Fencing had had its renaissance after World War II, especially in the socialist countries. State support made it possible for this expensive sport to be practised by the masses. The Hungarians were the first to break the domination of the Latin nations in épée and foil. Soviet, Polish and Romanian fencing also rose to world standard in an unbelievably short period. The systematic and efficient work of these nations brought about a sudden decline in French and Italian achievement.

In the last two decades some rearrangement has taken place in international fencing. Hungarian supremacy in the sabre was broken by the Poles, especially by Jerzy Pawlowski. Then came a time of Soviet success, although today Hungary, Italy and the USSR are roughly equal.

In épée Hungarian fencers took the initiative for fifteen years, winning the team championships in three successive Olympics (Tokyo, Mexico, Munich). In the individual events the last two winners have also been Hungarians; Győző Kulcsár and Dr Csaba Fenyvesi. The most modern and most favoured trend in Hungarian fencing is towards the épée, which has taken the place of the sabre.

Women's fencing took its place on the Olympic program in 1924, though team competitions were introduced only in 1960. Danish, Austrian, German and Hungarian fencers provided the élite at first but today women from Italy and the USSR have joined the Hungarians at the top.

An important innovation in the history of fencing has been the use of electronic scoring equipment, which indicates hits on the target area by a system of lights. That used for the épée was developed in 1933, that for the foil in 1954, the latter being harder to construct because the target is more specific. Electrically registering sabre cuts as well as hits requires more sophisticated equipment. A method invented in Hungary for the sabre was demonstrated at the beginning of 1974. The épée apparatus caused some controversy at first because the wiring added to the weapon was cumbersome and upset the fencer's balance but over the years it has been improved. It is now generally recognized that this equipment does no harm to fencing and in fact its use in competitions has played a decisive part in the sport's continuing prosperity.

From the beginning, the Olympics have taken the place of world championships and the FIE still gives the world title to the winner of the Olympics.

GYMNASTICS Boris Khavin

Gymnastic competitions have occupied a central place in all the Olympic Games of modern times. Gymnastic clubs were formed in Europe towards the end of the nineteenth century. The Germans were particularly well organized and there is a record of Czech clubs having regular competitions in 1877. Four years later the Fédération Internationale de Gymnastique (FIG) was formed, opening the way for international competition, but the first large-scale meeting of gymnasts was in the Olympic Games of Athens in 1896. However, this provided the spur for similar events outside the Olympics and the first world championships in the sport were held in 1903.

Today the Olympic gymnastic competitions (men's and women's) comprise events for individuals and teams; the men do floor exercises, exercises on the rings, pommelled horse, long horse, parallel bars and horizontal bar. The women do floor exercises (which differ from the men's in that they have a musical accompaniment), exercises on the balance beam, asymmetrical bars and the horse.

Obligatory and free exercises are carried out on each piece of apparatus. Besides that, the Olympic Games awards separate titles to the overall champions, taking all the disciplines on the program into consideration, and judging between the six participants who have obtained the most points for the separate disciplines. Each country can be represented by seven men and seven women, six principal competitors and one reserve, with the right to replace one of the principals before the beginning of the competition. The five best results are taken into consideration in the team events. In 1973 the IOC decided to admit in future twelve women's teams and twelve men's teams and to allow only three competitors for the whole program to the individual final events and two to the apparatus events.

The history of Olympic gymnastics began on 9 April 1896, when seventy-five gymnasts from five countries competed at Athens for the first Olympic medals. The competitions at the first Olympics comprised exercises on parallel bars (for individuals and teams), horizontal bar (individuals and teams), pommelled horse, bar, rings, long horse vault and rope climbing. At the end of the nineteenth century gymnastics was particularly widespread in Germany and its representatives did well in the first Olympics. Hermann Weingärtner, a German competitor – who took the horizontal bar, was second on the rings and pommelled horse and third in the individual exercises on the parallel bars – would have become the first all-round Olympic champion in gymnastics. But there was no combined prize in the first Olympics.

The following Games in Paris produced only one champion as one set of medals was given for a combined event, which included horizontal bar, parallel bars, long horse vault, pommelled horse, rings, floor exercises, long jump, rope climbing, combined long and high jump, pole vault and heaving a 50-kg (110-lb) weight. A Frenchman, Gustave Sandras, was thus the first all-round Olympic champion in gymnastics and the five following places in the final classification were shared between his compatriots.

In 1904 at St Louis the champions competed in a combined event, including horizontal bar, parallel bars, long horse vault, side horse vault, 100-yard race and the shot, as well as in (as separate events) team combined exercises, parallel bars, long horse vault, pommelled horse, horizontal bar, rings, rope climbing, club swinging, a nine-event combined competition, triathlon (100-yard race, long jump and shot), and a combined event using seven pieces of apparatus. There were 119 competitors, from five countries, 107 from the United States. Julius Lenhardt, a member of the American team although in fact an Austrian student at the University of Philadelphia, was proclaimed all-round champion. He won the individual combined event, which included horizontal bar, parallel bars, the long horse vault, the pommelled side horse, shot, and a 100-yard dash.

The Games in 1908 and 1912 brought victory to a remarkable Italian gymnast, Alberto Braglia. He was the winner in the individual combined exercises at two Olympic Games, becoming the first gymnast to succeed in winning the title of Olympic all-round champion twice. In the course of the team competitions in 1908 and 1912, it was the Swedes who deserved success and they duly won in 1908. Sweden, at that time, was developing a system of

Larisa Latynina (USSR), winner of nine gold medals, five silver and four bronze, in gymnastics

physical education based on exercises with apparatus. This greatly contributed to the formation of a strong team which achieved success in the years preceding World War I. In 1908 each country was allowed to enter a group of at least sixteen but not more than forty gymnasts in the team combined exercises, which consisted of horizontal bar, parallel bars, flying rings, still rings, long horse vault and rope climbing. Points were awarded to the group as a whole. In 1912 and 1920 the size of the group was restricted to 16–24 men; in 1912, when the team event was won by Italy, the combined exercises included horizontal bar, parallel bars, horse, free exercises and an optional exercise; in 1920 they consisted of horizontal bar, parallel bars and rings, free exercises and a 100-metre obstacle race. In 1920, at Antwerp, Italy retained the first place, not only in the individual exercises, won by Giorgio Zampori, but in the team event as well.

At the Games of 1924 in Paris, real Olympic gymnastics began. The program there formed the basis of present-day Olympic competitions; the athletes began to compete for individual Olympic titles on apparatus, as well as in combined exercises for individuals and for teams. And if the Italian gymnasts held the first place in the team events, those from Yugoslavia, Czechoslovakia, Switzerland, the United States and France took them in the individual events. Leon Štukelj (Yugoslavia) took the title of all-round Olympic champion.

Switzerland took five of the seven gold medals available to the men in 1928. It won the team competition and the Swiss Georges Miez was all-round Olympic champion. In 1928 women gymnasts took part in the Olympics for the first time, in a team competition, won by the Dutch.

The Olympic competitions of 1932 were to have the smallest number of competitors in the history of the Games. Only forty-six athletes from seven countries attended. The women's events were not held because of lack of entries. Italy (with seven competitors), better represented than the other European countries, took the laurels in most of the individual events, of which the winner was Romeo Neri, and in the team event. The rope-climbing and club-swinging events were not held after 1932.

The Swiss gymnasts tried to recover at the 1936 Games in Berlin, but they did not succeed in overtaking the powerful German team. Georges Miez, the hero of the Games, was placed first in the individual floor exercises. Alfred Schwarzmann (Germany) was proclaimed all-round champion. The women's event was won by the German team.

The dominant nation in the 1948 Games was Finland, whose gymnasts had shown their mastery in many international competitions. This time they narrowly defeated the Swiss team, and in the individual events the Finn Veikko Huhtanen beat Walter Lehmann (Switzerland). The Czech women had no equals at the 1948 Games.

The 1952 Games at Helsinki blazed a remarkable trail in the history of Olympic gymnastics. The events achieved a true international level, the women, like the men, participating in combined events and carrying out exercises with apparatus. Soviet athletes made their first appearance and proved to be in the avant-garde of the sport. For the first time the gymnasts from Japan attracted serious attention. The breadth of the competitions was developing, 319 gymnasts came from twenty-nine countries, a huge improvement on former Olympic Games.

The Soviet team achieved a record which they were to repeat in future Olympics: both men and women triumphed in the individual and team events. The Soviet gymnasts, yielding to no one in exercise technique, were way above their rivals in general physical preparation. This was evident especially in the women's events (in the USSR before 1946 women took part in such 'masculine' events with apparatus as the rings and the bar). Besides that, the Soviet teams distinguished themselves in being very homogeneous in composition, which decided the issue in the team events. Viktor Chukarin and Maria Gorokhovskaya were ranked first in the individual events.

The Olympic Games at Melbourne in 1956 brought a repeat of the Soviet success at Helsinki; the USSR won the first place in the individual and team competitions (men and women). However, this time the tension of the struggle in the men's competitions had markedly increased. The Japanese gymnasts, who had worked hard to assimilate the experience of foreign athletes, by, among other methods, filming the major international tournaments, took a very strong team to Australia. In the struggle for the title of all-round champion, Viktor Chukarin defeated the Japanese leader Takashi Ono by only 0.05 point. Chukarin became the second gymnast, forty years after Braglia, to succeed in winning the place of all-round Olympic champion twice. Five Soviet gymnasts and four Japanese were placed among the first ten to finish in the combined event. The Soviet team held its superiority but for the last time. The Soviet women's team, entirely new, led by Larisa Latynina, gave their rivals no chance.

At the 1960 Olympics at Rome, the Japanese achieved a new standard of elegance. They demonstrated the most complicated exercises on apparatus, and in the free exer-

Sawao Kato (Japan), individual and team gold medallist in 1968, a great all-round gymnast

cises showed exceptional grace. The choice of a very homogeneous team had allowed them neither leaders nor followers, each athlete being considered 'a star'. All the Japanese were in the first ten placings, sufficient to decide the team event. Boris Shakhlin (USSR), celebrated for his strength and exceptional endurance, defeated Takashi Ono in the individual competition and, barely credibly, by 0.05 point, the margin by which he had been beaten four years previously. Larisa Latynina took, for the second time, the title of all-round champion, and her team outstripped the Czechs, with their leader Věra Čáslavská, who was not yet ready to confront the Russian girls.

At the 1964 Games at Tokyo, the Japanese triumphed. Yukio Endo, in the team events, added the gold medal to that of all-round champion. The Soviet women's team, led by Larisa Latynina and Polina Astakhova, maintained its superiority, although in the individual events they could not equal Věra Čáslavská (Czechoslovakia). The 1968 Games at Mexico did not bring a change in the balance of power. Again the Japanese were the best in the individual, team and most of the single men's events. This time Sawao Kato was placed first. Now the 0.05 point by which Chukarin and Shakhlin had won allowed Kato to overtake the Soviet leader Mikhail Voronin. In the women's individual events the laurels of all-round champion went to Věra Čáslavská and, in the team competitions, the Soviet women.

The 1972 Olympics again reinforced the position of the Japanese men. Upholding their superiority in the team competitions, they triumphantly took all the individual events on the program except the floor exercises, pommelled horse and long horse vault; the first three places in the combined exercises were shared between Sawao Kato, who became the third gymnast to be all-round Olympic champion twice, Eizo Kenmotsu and Akinori Nakayama. The perfect exhibition by Ludmila Turishcheva, Olga Korbut and their friends took them to the podium for the sixth time! Ludmila Turishcheva also took the title of all-round champion.

During these last Olympics a tendency has shown itself towards the complication of gymnastic combinations, towards acrobatics, and growth in the rhythm of exercises. This is so in women's events as well as men's. The women have borrowed little by little elements which earlier only some men had dared to do. Virtuoso techniques, exhibitions of extreme skill, high mastery bringing sport close to art have distinguished the best gymnasts of recent Olympics.

Among the heroes and heroines we should mention: Viktor Chukarin (USSR), winner of seven gold medals, three silver and one bronze; Boris Shakhlin (USSR), seven gold medals, four silver and two bronze; Akinori Nakayama (Japan), six gold, two silver and two bronze; Sawao Kato (Japan), six gold, two silver and one bronze. Larisa Latynina (USSR) was distinguished in the competitions by taking nine gold medals, five silver and four bronze (no other competitor in any sport in the Games has won so many prizes); Věra Čáslavská (Czechoslovakia), seven gold and four silver.

HANDBALL Andy Mezey

Handball as it is known today is less than half a century old and one of the most recent of the Olympic sports. The history of today's Olympic handball, in which seven players take part in each team, is richly patterned with games involving various numbers of players, in particular eleven-a-side handball which was the original Olympic sport of 1936. Although it is largely the result of transformations of certain popular games, Czech *házená*, German *Torball*, Danish *håndbold*, and others, it also owes much in its development to the game of association football, and more recently also to basketball.

Second-round handball match between Czechoslovakia and the USSR in 1972. Czechoslovakia eventually won the silver medals, Yugoslavia the gold.

As a development of other ball games, it is claimed by some to have originated in Germany; others maintain that it existed at the same time in other countries of Europe. The Slovak *házená*, a game still played today in Czechoslovakia, with many similarities to handball, goes back to 1892, although it was only given formal rules by Professor Vaclov Karas in 1905. In 1898 a Danish teacher, Holger Nielsen (who later became a lieutenant-colonel and invented the Danish method of artificial respiration) introduced a game called *håndbold* (handball) into a Danish school as an alternative to association football. In 1906 Nielsen elaborated the first rules of the present game, organized competitions and recommended the formation of a Danish federation.

In Germany, in about 1915, a gymnastics teacher named Max Heiden combined several popular games (*Raffball*, *Völkerball* and *Korbball*) to create *Torball*, as an indoor activity during the winter months. It was played with a medicine ball or soccer ball stuffed with hair, and many rules were similar to those of association football. But the game did not take hold since the number of players was not specified and there was a lack of other precise rules.

In 1919 Professor Carl Schelenz, of the Physical Education School of Berlin, inspired by *Torball* and other similar games, created a game for which he borrowed the Danish name *håndbold*. This game, played on a soccer field by boys and girls alike, fixed the goal area at 11 metres, the number of players at eleven, and the goal identical to that of association football. The ball formerly used by *Torball* was replaced by a ball used in volleyball or association football, and during play, dribbling while running and physical contact in gaining possession of the ball were now allowed. Gradually other changes were made reducing the size of the ball and increasing the goal area. This game caught on in other European countries and international competitions began, the first taking place in 1925 in Vienna when Austria defeated Germany 6–3. In 1930 the first women's international contest was held in Germany, Austria beating Germany 5–4.

Meanwhile, as this game (now called handball) had not yet been sufficiently widely recognized as a sport in its own right to warrant its own governing body, it came under the jurisdiction of the International Amateur Athletic Association (IAAF), the body responsible for organizing most of the minor sports in Europe at that time. In 1926, to keep pace with the progress of handball the IAAF appointed a special committee representing the countries where handball was played, to look into the possibility of producing a standardized set of rules for the game. From this move handball developed into an internationally recognized autonomous sport, with its own international federation.

In 1928, representatives of eleven handball nations met at the Olympic Games, formed the International Amateur Handball Federation and had the first official international rules printed. Avery Brundage, later a president of the IOC, was a member of that first committee of the new federation.

Demonstration matches of eleven-a-side handball appear to have been played at the Olympic Games of 1928 and 1932, but it was in 1936 at Berlin that it officially became an Olympic sport, with six participants, who finished in the following order: Germany, Austria, Switzerland, Hungary, Romania and the United States.

Because of climatic conditions unfavourable to eleven-a-side, essentially an outdoor form of handball, the Scandinavian countries were developing seven-a-side handball based on the Danish *håndbold*. This game made such progress in Sweden, Denmark and Norway that in 1935 the first international competition took place between Sweden and Denmark. The first world championships of the seven-a-side game as well as eleven-a-side, were held in 1938. In the latter ten countries participated and four, finishing in the order Germany, Austria, Sweden, Denmark, in the seven-a-side tournament.

Although the Fédération Internationale de Handball (IHF) had been reconstituted in 1946, when the Olympic Games were renewed after World War II in 1948, handball was not on the program. The eleven-a-side game declined in popularity and the alternative version progressed throughout Europe and gradually spread to most other continents. As increasing numbers took up the game, so came a greater sophistication in coaching, tactics and strategies. It was at this point that it was influenced by basketball as another indoor team sport where player interaction and limited bodily contact were possible. Thus handball took on characteristics of basketball in tactics, terminology (dribble, pivot, post, man-to-man, etc.) and even minor rules. In spite of these diverse influences which have directed its development, however, handball has maintained its autonomy and has become a discipline with its own character.

In terms of international success, the nations of eastern Europe have increasingly made the best showing, as Romania, Yugoslavia, Hungary, the USSR, Czechoslovakia and the German Democratic Republic have gradually taken over the leadership from the Scandinavian countries between the second world championships in 1954 and the present day.

Although the new handball rose rapidly in popularity in the 1950s and 1960s, it was not until 1972 in Munich that it was restored to the Olympic program. Thus modern handball, played by seven players, became a world-recognized sport. It will again be included in the Games in 1976, when women's teams will have their own Olympic championship.

Today handball is played all over the world. More than sixty countries are affiliated to the International Federation, with 2,600,000 registered players of both sexes.

HOCKEY R. L. Hollands

Hockey in its modern form developed in the favourable social and commercial climate of nineteenth-century England from earlier forms of the game in which the common factors were a curved stick and a ball of sorts. From the more ancient relics, some dating back to pre-Christian times, it is thought that the Egyptians, the Greeks and the Persians were all fairly handy at hockey, though no doubt their game had characteristics peculiar to the time and place.

In the British Isles, Ireland's ancient game of hurling is almost certainly the common stock from which several

The Indian hockey team in 1928. Dhyan Chand is the second on the left in the front row.

closely related games have sprung – shinty in Scotland, bandy in Wales and hockey mainly in England. Of these, the strongest growth proved to be that of hockey.

The oldest hockey club still in existence, Blackheath, has records dating back to 1860 and is thought to have originated twenty years before that. Steady and sustained expansion of the game led to the formation of the Hockey Association in 1886. A rival organization, the National Hockey Union, was disbanded in 1895. Since then the Hockey Association, the oldest national hockey association in the world, has directed the affairs of the game in England.

The Hockey Association also exercised a paternal influence in international affairs for many years, an influence accorded worldwide recognition through the International Hockey Rules Board. The Board was formed by England, Ireland and Wales in 1900 to promote uniformity in the rules of the game.

The constitution of the Board gave the Hockey Association a cogent, if not commanding, position in relation to the rules to which all the world played until 1972, when the Rules Board passed under the aegis of the International Federation.

England won the first Olympic hockey tournament, in 1908, with great ease, scoring 23 goals to 3 in three games. Those were the days for forwards.

An English team, representing Great Britain, also won the 1920 tournament at Antwerp but the game had not then fully recovered from the effects of World War I and only three other countries entered – Belgium, Denmark and France. This time the competition was organized on a league basis instead of by knock-out as in 1908. England headed the results table, winning all its games with an aggregate of 17 goals to 2.

In the British Isles, Ireland's ancient game of hurling tournament at Amsterdam, two important developments occurred which had a profound influence on the course of international hockey. The Hockey Association withdrew from the British Olympic Association in 1921, and in 1924 the International Hockey Federation (Fédération Internationale de Hockey or FIH) was formed – without Britain because the British were opposed to competitions involving medals and prizes. The Hockey Association Council still preserves the right to impose a ban on such competitions. It is therefore not surprising that the Hockey Association, although the senior national association and the strongest numerically, took no part in the formation of the FIH. The founder members were Austria,

The end of India's 32-year domination of hockey in the Olympics, Pakistan winning 1–0 in 1960

Belgium, Czechoslovakia, France, Hungary, Spain and Switzerland. They held their inaugural meeting in Paris on 7 January 1924 and they were successful in getting hockey restored as an Olympic sport at the next Games, held at Amsterdam in 1928. Being the only organization in the game that could speak with international authority, the FIH became responsible for the supervision of the Olympic Games hockey tournament. By then its membership had risen to twelve but still did not include England, Ireland, Scotland and Wales.

Those twenty years saw the rise of India to first place in world ranking. The Indian Hockey Federation, formed in 1925, joined FIH in 1928 and made its first major impact at the Olympic tournament that year in Amsterdam. It was the first of an astonishing sequence of six Olympic victories extending over almost thirty years which not only established the Indians as world champions but won them enduring tribute as 'The Masters'.

India lost first place in the Rome Games (1960) to Pakistan. It was the Indians' first Olympic defeat. They regained the gold medal again in an ill-mannered Olympic final at Tokyo (1964), to lose it once more in Mexico (1968), where they finished third to Pakistan and Australia. India was third again in Munich (1972), behind the German Federal Republic, which won the gold medal, and Pakistan, the runner-up.

The remarkable thing is that, in spite of these fluctuations of fortune, India is still widely regarded as the foremost exponent of the game. It is not just in recollection and admiration of the many years when India was invincible; it is the style, the skills, the elegance its teams brought and still bring to the game that surrounds the name of India with a special aura. The Indian stick, with its thin handle and tight bend, is symbolic of its greatness.

The principal difference between the English stick and the Indian stick lies in that tight bend. The head, or bend, of the English stick, made of native ash, was much more open. Ash could not be successfully compressed to the same degree as the mulberry heads used by Indian manufacturers. The success of Indian teams in international competition, their superb ball control most of all, won them imitators everywhere and the easiest form of imitation was to adopt the Indian stick.

Since 1948, when the Indians won at Wembley (London), the Indian stick has supplanted the English one in England and found favour all over the world.

The factors contributing to the levelling-up process

between India and her rivals have been (1) pace; (2) organization; (3) marking and tackling; (4) the creation of Pakistan in 1947. The enormous advance in physical-training methods, conditioning the body to levels of energy output far in excess of anything previously achieved, has enabled many countries not blessed with a special talent for hockey to raise the pace of their game while maintaining or, perhaps, improving their skills.

Simultaneously team organization has been revised and reorientated with the balance tilted in favour of defence, much as has happened in association football. Instead of five forwards, or strikers, the preference now is for three or four. Instead of two full backs carrying the main weight of defence, there are now as a rule four players committed to defence, one of whom stays inside his own 25-yd area and is appropriately known as a 'sweeper'. The remaining two or three players operate in midfield, exerting, it is hoped, a controlling influence. The theory is that they should support attack or defence as occasion and the fortunes of the game require.

Tight man-to-man marking, accompanied by tough tackling, have had the effect of reinforcing defensive strength. This type of marking had sometimes verged on obstruction of a peculiarly irritating kind, tending to mask a player's sight of the ball. Persistent masking of any player by an opponent leads, almost inevitably, to friction. Modern tackling often aims at striking the ball as the prime target, with the player in possession of the ball as a secondary objective.

The combined effect of these factors has been to shift the balance of power in the game away from attack and this shift has operated against India whose forwards have been its special pride. This explains why that great centre-forward Dhyan Chand is still the first name Indians think of in hockey, though his international career ended a quarter of a century ago.

In 1956 in Melbourne, India won narrow victories in its semi-final and final matches against Germany and Pakistan, the score being 1–0 in each case. Germany won the third-place match against Great Britain 3–1. Four years later in Rome, Pakistan reversed the final placings with India, Spain being third and Great Britain again fourth. Rome provided a majestic setting, especially for the early rounds of the hockey tournament, played in the Stadio dei Marmi, an arena fit for heroes with its glistening terraces and commanding statues. After that, the glass and concrete of the Velodromo seemed commonplace.

The keynote of the Tokyo Games in 1964 was efficiency. Organization, administration and facilities of all kinds won high praise. Australia won the bronze medal, its first Olympic medal for hockey. In other sports Australians have set a standard of physical training that has put them a step or two ahead of their rivals. At Tokyo, they gave opponents in the hockey tournament a taste of what it means to be fit and fast.

Fitness apart, the Australians had a vintage crop of players, including Donald McWatters, a fearsome striker of penalty corner shots, the Pearce brothers Julian and Eric, and Paul Dearing. The full weight of their first onslaught fell upon Great Britain in what was the opening match for both. The result was dramatic, and, for Britain, disastrous. Australia won 7–0.

The final, in which India beat Pakistan 1–0, was fast, brilliant and occasionally bad tempered. At different times Germany and Spain were also involved in gritty incidents. If Tokyo was efficient, the hockey was ruthlessly efficient.

The need for more effective control of fiercely competitive matches was not forgotten and four years later hockey was played in a happier vein at Mexico City in 1968. The Australians were just as fit and fast, the Indians and Pakistanis stylish and skilful as ever, the Germans and Dutch resourceful, determined and consistent.

In general, the approach, though as ambitious and keen as ever, was properly restrained. In a program of sixty-nine hockey matches, I recall only two occasions when tempers became a little frayed and only one serious incident, when Japan left the field by way of protest and refused to play on against India when requested to do so. The Japanese were protesting against the award of a penalty stroke against them. They were given time for second thoughts but declined all appeals to return to the pitch and had to forfeit the match, a score of 5–0 in favour of India being declared. For the first time since 1932, India failed to reach the Olympic final; Pakistan won the gold medal, Australia the silver and India the bronze.

There was much to admire too about the 1972 Olympic hockey tournament at Munich. The gold medal was won by the host country, the German Federal Republic, the first continental European country to become Olympic champion in this sport. Pakistan was second, India again third. In the matter of speed and fitness, the Germans had taken a leaf out of the Australian book. In addition, their teamwork and especially their defensive marking and tackling had been developed to a pitch not previously attained. This suffocating defensive grip had its dangers, as became apparent in and after the final.

Mostly the German Federal Republic commanded a range of movement and turn of speed that was too much for its opponents, but against Pakistan in the final, with the gold and silver medals at stake, it was a different story. The Pakistanis were no less fast, fit and well drilled, just as versatile in the skills of the game. The Germans had to exert their defensive grip as never before in the tournament. Man marked man as close as shadow to substance and the shadow generally took care to be between the opponent and the point of play. This smother-cover frustrated and irritated the Pakistani players.

As time passed without a goal scored, tension grew and friction mounted. When Michael Krause scored for the German Federal Republic from a penalty corner late in the game, there were protests but they were contained. The explosion did not come till afterwards when the teams lined up for the presentation of medals, the gold to the German Federal Republic for its 1–0 win in the final, the silver to Pakistan as runner-up.

Forgetful that defeat, however galling, has to be borne with fortitude, the Pakistanis gave vent to their feelings by gestures of open contempt, accompanied by much jostling and jeering from their supporters. This unruly behaviour led to the suspension of the Pakistan Federation by the International Hockey Federation. This disciplinary action was subsequently modified to suspension for varying periods of those individuals involved in the Munich incident.

Inevitably disagreeable incidents of this kind become a focus of attention, overshadowing much admirable competition between the teams of many countries.

JUDO John Goodbody

Judo had a long and colourful history before it first appeared on the Olympic program at Tokyo in 1964. The international combat sport is derived from medieval Japanese fighting skills, the most famous of which was *ju-jitsu* which the *samurai* (warriors) used when they were unarmed. Many of the principles of these self-defence techniques have survived in the modern sport. A contest is still won immediately a fighter either throws an opponent forcibly on his back, strangles or armlocks him to submission, or holds him immobile on his back for 30 sec; in the *samurai* age any of these would have had a decisive effect in hand-to-hand combat.

The technical principle of *ju* (literally 'soft', with the strong association of 'efficiently economical') is also an essential factor of *judo* (literally 'soft way'). Dr Jigoro Kano, the founder of the sport, studied various different schools of martial arts including *ju-jitsu* before evolving his own style which he called 'Kodokan judo'. For a while after its founding in 1882 the Kodokan was just one of a number of *ju-jitsu* styles. But in a series of matches against other schools the Kodokan became pre-eminent. From then on judo grew in popularity, first in Japan and then internationally, and *ju-jitsu* declined.

Kano realized that the most effective method of defeating an opponent was by using the opponent's own moves to get him off balance in order to throw him. This is the fundamental principle of the sport.

Judo is a sport but it is also a method of physical education and self-defence. Its attraction is that an outstanding fighter has to possess a large number of physical qualities. He needs skill to achieve a decisive throw, the strength to pull an opponent off balance, the speed to execute moves before an opponent can adopt a defensive posture and the stamina to endure a number of contests in one day. Fighting spirit is vital. Dedication to tiring hours of training in *randori* (practice, without the intensity of competition) is also important. Women and children also have competitions but on a less boisterous level than men.

Initially judo developed internationally through the eagerness of the Japanese to spread the sport they had originated. Although they have been principally responsible for the technical development, a number of countries have added special skills from their own native wrestling skills.

Kano first visited Europe in 1899 when Yukio Tani, a leading *ju-jitsu* exponent, made his first appearance in Britain. Another of Kano's leading pupils, Y. Yamashita, began instructing in the United States in 1902. Three years later the Paris police were taught judo and in 1918 the first club in Europe was founded, The Budokwai in London. Another of Kano's pupils, Shinzo Takagaki, took judo to Australia in 1928 and Africa in 1931.

Gunji Koizumi, the founder of The Budokwai, led the development of the sport in Europe, which was to be consistently the most powerful region apart from the Orient. Although international matches were held before World War II and Japan had instituted its single-weight category All-Japan Championships in 1930, competitive judo was rare. Self-defence still played a prominent role in training. It was not until after World War II that the competitive sport really flourished. The European Judo Union was founded in London in 1948 and the first European Championships were held three years later. The International Judo Federation (IJF) was established in 1951 and organized the first world championships in Tokyo in 1956. Japan provided the two finalists but a Dutchman, Anton Geesink, finished third.

Geesink was to revolutionize the sport. Before his arrival it was thought that weight categories were unnecessary in competition because proponents of the sport had always claimed that it was possible for a big skilled fighter to be beaten by an equally skilful smaller man. The trouble with this belief was that Geesink was not only big, he stood 1.98 m (6 ft 6 in) tall and weighed 115 kg (253 lb 8 oz or just over 18 stone), but was tremendously skilful. After a series of successes in European competition he finally beat three Japanese in consecutive rounds to win the world title in Paris in 1961.

Judo was included in the 1964 Olympics under the ruling then in practice that the host country could select a sport of its own choice for the program. For the annual European Championships France had led the move to have weight categories instituted and four divisions were established for the Tokyo Games: lightweight, middleweight, heavyweight and an Open class.

The Japanese were far too dexterous for the rest of the world in the weight divisions. Takehide Nakatani was a convincing winner of the lightweight and Isao Inokuma took the heavyweight division after a desperately boring final with his training partner Doug (A. H.) Rogers (Canada). Japan's most exciting gold medallist was Isao Okano, a squatly built middleweight with a versatile range of throws and the capacity to uproot even the most stable of opponents; he was later to become the lightest man to win the All-Japan Championships by taking the title in 1967 and 1969 in spite of weighing only 85 kg (187 lb or 13 stone). Okano defeated West Germany's Wolfgang Hofmann in the middleweight final after showing a bewildering variety of throws earlier in the competition.

The USSR did remarkably well with four bronze medals. At the 1962 European Championships the Russians had startled exponents with their techniques borrowed from *sambo*, their indigenous form of jacket wrestling. Their facility in applying armlocks and unexpected counter throws made them the most unpredictable of opponents.

In the Open category Geesink was supreme. He twice defeated Akio Kaminaga, three times All-Japan Champion. Kaminaga, 1.79 m (5 ft 10 in) and 98 kg (216 lb or 15 st 6 lb), attacked Geesink determinedly in the final. But after a failed attack Geesink slipped past Kaminaga's defence to clamp on a *kesagatame* (scarf hold-down). With a packed Nippon Budokan Hall silent and with the rest of the Japanese team in tears, Geesink clung on for the required 30 seconds for victory. The Japanese champion had been beaten in his own country and judo had truly become an international sport.

Judo now settled into an established routine of world championships every other year. Brazil staged the 1965 event in which Geesink took the heavyweight title – the Japanese once again having failed to discover someone capable of defeating him. For the 1967 World and European Championships a new system of weight categories was introduced: lightweight, welterweight, middleweight, light heavyweight and heavyweight, plus the

Anton Geesink (Netherlands) defeating Akio Kaminaga (Japan), in Tokyo

traditional Open division. Although Geesink had retired after winning the European title in Rome in May, his eighteenth gold medal in the competition, the Netherlands had produced a new titan, Willem Ruska. He was shorter than Geesink but even more solidly built and was to have only a slightly less illustrious career. He finished first in the heavyweight at the 1967 World Championships but the Japanese picked up the other five titles.

The 1968 Olympics did not include judo in its program but Mexico City staged the World Championships the following year; the Japanese were first and second in three categories and first and third in the other three. The 1971 World Championships were held at Ludwigshafen, West Germany's dress rehearsal for the Olympics the following year. The major upset was the defeat in the heavyweight class of Kaneo Iwatsuri, the reigning All-Japan Champion, by Great Britain's Keith Remfry, who had been a member of the team that won the European title the previous May. But Remfry lost a close decision to Ruska who went on to regain his title.

The Japanese took the other five titles with some memorable performances: middleweight winner Shozo Fujii showing acrobatic suppleness with his superb shoulder throw; light-heavyweight Fumio Sasahara wheeling Nobuyuki Sato to the ground in the final with his *harai-goshi* (hip throw) counter; and Hiroshi Minatoya failing to win the welterweight crown for the third successive time after a furious fight in the final with his countryman Hizashi Tsuzawa.

Judo returned to the Olympic program in Munich as one of the three sports that were added at the 1966 meeting of the IOC in Rome. One competitor from each country was permitted to enter the six categories; in the world championships two had been admitted. This put tremendous pressure on the Japanese who were favourites for most of the divisions. The sequence of classes, with the heavyweight first – the category in which they were weakest – meant that the Japanese were not assured of a title on the opening day. Ruska was in the finest form of his career, immensely powerful and technically precise. He clove his way through to the title, hurling the redoubtable West German Klaus Glahn in the final.

Japan's prestige was severely jolted the following day when Fumio Sasahara, twice world light-heavyweight champion and the firmest of favourites, was unexpectedly thrown by the USSR's Shota Khokhoshvili. Khokhoshvili defeated Great Britain's Dave Starbrook in the final on a decision.

With Japan's supremacy undermined Shinobu Sekine looked anything but the All-Japan Champion in the middleweight class. He showed little sparkle or skill in defeating Great Britain's Brian Jacks in the semi-final and Sang Lip Oh (North Korea) in the final on a split decision. Although lightweight Takao Kawaguchi and welterweight Toyokazu Nomura took gold medals, Japan failed to get even a medal in the Open category. Ruska won the overall title before announcing his retirement; the youngest entry in the class, Great Britain's Angelo Parisi, aged nineteen, did remarkably well to finish third.

The repercussions in Tokyo to what Japan had considered had been a disgrace were harsh. The Olympic trainers were dismissed and Okano, who had founded his own special training group called *seiki-juku* ('true spirit') was given the task of restoring Japan's monopoly. At the 1973 World Championships in Lausanne with Ruska absent and Glahn no longer as formidable as he had been the Japanese were victorious in all six classes. New fighters were blended in with experienced competitors like light-heavyweight Sato, who won the world title for the second time. Okano instilled enormous confidence into the squad and gave them special individual attention which had not always been customary in the past.

Although there were now ninety members of the IJF, Japan, the inventors of the sport, had remained supreme.

MODERN PENTATHLON James Coote

The supreme test of the all-round sportsman, modern pentathlon, fills a unique niche in the annals of Olympic history for it is the only sport to have been administered by the International Olympic Committee. Modern pentathlon was created, nurtured and encouraged by the IOC, which formed a special subcommittee to administer it, to formulate the rules and organize the event's inclusion in each Olympic Games from 1912 in Stockholm to the 1948 Games in London. By then the sport had flourished so well that more international activity between Games was needed and so in August 1948 the Union Internationale de Pentathlon Moderne (UIPM) was founded, taking over the organizational duties for the sport from the IOC. The UIPM immediately introduced World Championships which have been held every non-Olympic year since 1949.

Initially the sport of modern pentathlon was the idea of Coubertin, who wrote in his *Mémoires Olympiques* that after two unsuccessful attempts he finally managed to persuade his colleagues at the 1911 meeting of the IOC in Budapest to have the sport inserted on the Olympic program. Coubertin's reasoning behind the inclusion of this entirely novel and completely artificial sport was that he wished to find the true all-rounder, the athlete *par excellence*, the *Victor Ludorum* who could excel in a number of sports and thus lay claim to be the greatest of all Olympic competitors. The Baron did not accept that those pentathlons and decathlons already on the athletics program were true all-round tests, applying as they did only to the specialists of one particular branch of the Olympic curriculum. The

Victor Ludorum of the ancient Olympics was the winner of the pentathlon, consisting of javelin, discus throwing, jumping, running and wrestling. Thus the 'modern' pentathlon.

The President's struggle to find a place for 'his' event against an initially hostile audience took on a mystical fervour, so apparent throughout his life in the Olympic arena. His own words emphasize his feeling for the event and the importance he attached to the affair.

> I had already submitted twice previously to the IOC a proposal to have the event included but it received an obtuse, almost hostile, reception. I did not press the matter further. This time, thankfully, my colleagues' minds were so enlightened by the Spirit of Sport that they accepted the test to which I attached so much importance: the true communion of the perfect athlete.

Coubertin's intention was that the modern pentathlon should consist of running, riding, swimming, fencing and shooting, although he would initially have preferred to have substituted rowing for shooting had not the additional problems overburdened an already hard-working organizing committee. The thread combining all five events is that of the military messenger who is dispatched with vital orders for the front line: his horse is shot away from under him after clearing certain obstacles, he fights his way through with his sword which in turn breaks and

András Balczó (Hungary), the 1972 champion in modern pentathlon

he is forced to turn to his revolver. Forcing his way to the river bank, he dives in to evade his captors and finally delivers his vital message on foot, like Pheidippides, the original runner, in 190 B.C. from Marathon to Athens.

Even this hard trial was not enough for Coubertin who would have preferred to make the event more difficult by keeping the riding and running courses secret and further by not deciding the order of the five events until the morning of the sport, which would, if he had had his own way, been held not over five days as now, but consecutively with minimal time for recovery. This would have been a real trial – in the Munich Olympics the fencing alone took more than twelve hours to complete.

Although the 1911 meeting of the IOC passed Coubertin's proposal they were not over-enthusiastic. According to the minutes of that discussion, the Rev. R. S. de Courcy Laffan, from Britain, elected to the IOC in 1897, emphasized the difficulties of obtaining a sufficient number of horses of similar standard – still the sport's greatest problem. He also recommended a cross-country race of 3,000 m (later lengthened to 4,000 m), while Colonel (later General) Victor Balck, who became president of the Swedish Organizing Committee for the 1912 Games in Stockholm, mentioned his so far unsuccessful approaches to the government to obtain sufficient horses from the army and suggested that if the horses could not be provided the participants would have to supply their own – a move strongly opposed by the Baron, who felt that the entire concept would be ruined if riders could use horses with which they were familiar.

Although the IOC did not accept the sport until its meeting of 1911, Coubertin had already approached the Swedish Military Sports Federation, a body with a great reputation, suggesting that it should establish a new complex sport that would, like the classic pentathlon, demand multiple abilities from an athlete. This shrewd move by Coubertin at least ensured that a committee had already held discussions and could advise the organizers of the 1912 Games, for in the official report it states specifically that

the first steps for the organization of the competition were taken as early as the autumn of 1910. This was no easy matter, however, for there was nothing to go by as regards the new event as there was in the case of other competitions. In determining the five branches of the sport that were to make up the modern pentathlon, the Swedish Olympic Committee had the following points in view: the events ought to be such as would test the endurance, resolution, presence of mind, integrity, agility and strength of those taking part in the competition, while in drawing up the detailed programme it was necessary to have all the events of equivalent value in order to make the modern pentathlon a competition of really all-round importance.

Thus, extremely efficiently and most effectively, the Swedes took Coubertin's thesis and expanded it without ever losing sight of his ideals. Their final organization of individual events proved remarkably effective since those first days in 1912. It was decided that the shooting should be carried out with pistols, over 25 metres with 20 shots in four series each of five shots, that the swimming would be a 300-metres freestyle, the fencing an épée pool competition, the riding a 5,000-metres cross-country course, and the

running a 3,000-metres cross-country race. Initial suggestions that the order of events should be drawn on the day were discarded for organizational reasons and the order settled down to riding, fencing, shooting, swimming and running. The riding has changed; in recent years it has become a show-jumping test, rather than the first idea of trials, to attract the crowds better. The running has been extended by 1 km to 4,000 metres.

With so much Swedish involvement, followers of the Olympics may be excused for thinking that modern pentathlon had not a French father but a Swedish parentage. This idea has been aggravated by the hold Sweden has kept upon the event, not only because of the almost complete adherence to those original rules formulated by the 1912 organizing committee but also because Sweden won the first five Olympic gold medals (1912–32) and even thereafter have rarely been outside the prize list although in latter years the USSR and Hungary have generally reigned supreme. The only non-Swede in the first six in the 1912 Games was a young American officer called George Smith Patton, who became an outstanding general in World War II. There is the additional Swedish connection in that today the president, secretary-general and treasurer of the International Federation, Brig.-General Sven Thofelt, Lt-Col Wille Grut and Lt-Col Olle Hederen, are themselves Swedish (Thofelt was Olympic champion in 1928 and fourth in 1932 and 1936 and Grut won in London in 1948).

There has always been a military tradition in the event, due naturally to the length of time needed to train and to the great expense of finding and paying for facilities, including the most difficult of all, the riding; indeed there have in recent years been suggestions that the sport should be made more popular by excluding riding in favour of a cyclo-cross event (a combination of cycling and cross-country running), cheaper and perhaps equally exciting for the spectator, though of course robbing the event of much of its charisma, its Beau Geste atmosphere.

Since 1912 the event has always been on the Olympic program but until 1948 only one gold medal was awarded: to the individual winner. Since the Helsinki Games (1952) both individual and team competitions have been held. World Championships for team and individual were held from the start. By 1965 junior World Championships were inaugurated, the first being held in Leipzig with conditions slightly less gruelling than for the senior counterpart.

A winter modern pentathlon competition was held at the 1948 Winter Olympic Games in St Moritz with riding, fencing, shooting, 3,000-m downhill skiing (instead of swimming) and a 10-km cross-country ski event (replacing the cross-country running). Sweden filled the first three places. This competition was not, however, accepted as the basis for future inclusion by the IOC although Avery Brundage and many other leading IOC members felt, like Coubertin, that an Olympic program was not complete without an all-rounder's event, a polyathlon of some sort. Various combinations of shooting, cross-country or downhill skiing, skating and ski jumping were suggested, but in 1954 the UIPM proposed that a biathlon of cross-country skiing and rifle shooting be held; they felt that this combination was the only practical solution in view of the difficulty of finding places convenient for multiple-event training in winter.

Biathlon had its first World Championships in 1958 and first appeared on the Olympic program two years later in Squaw Valley. This new sport has developed almost faster than its elder brother and its interest has been reflected in the change of name from the UIPM to the UIPMB (Union Internationale du Pentathlon Moderne et Biathlon) in 1968 at Mexico City.

The total of countries taking part in the modern pentathlon has been fairly static: ten countries in 1912; this climbed to sixteen in 1936, and a record twenty-three in 1960 (there were nineteen in Munich). It was not until 1952 that more than fifty competitors entered. Rome holds the record for the total of individuals, with sixty, a figure almost approached in Munich with fifty-nine competitors. Of the thirteen Olympics since 1912, Sweden has won nine individual titles, Hungary three and Germany one. The USSR and Hungary have each won three team titles. There are many claimants to the title of the greatest all-rounder of all time, including Lars Hall (Sweden), the only man to have successfully defended his Olympic title, and Igor Novikov (USSR), four times a world champion, twice a member of the gold-medal-winning team and in four successive Games never placed lower than fifth in the individual competition, but the supreme Champion of Champions must be the Hungarian András Balczó. The reigning Olympic individual champion, he was fourth and second respectively in the 1960 and 1968 individual events. At these Games he was a member of the Hungarian winning team. He also won the world title in 1963, 1965, 1966, 1967 and 1969. He is not just a great all-rounder but a competitor who could fill a place in any one of five events in the Olympic teams of most countries – the epitome of Coubertin's ideal.

And of the future? In spite of the increase in riding horses throughout the world of sport, it is still very difficult to obtain them for the pentathlon since owners are unwilling to lend them to riders who are drawn by lot. Once more thoughts are being turned to the idea of canoeing, cyclo-cross or cycling. But it should be noted that, however the sport changes, these competitors, who need a remarkable dedication to achieve the aims of Coubertin, still remain among the friendliest of all sportsmen.

ROWING Richard Burnell

The origins of rowing are lost in prehistory – a funerary inscription, c. 1430 B.C., records that King Amenophis II of Egypt '. . . besides being famous as a warrior was renowned for his feats of oarsmanship'. But competitive rowing, as we know it today, dates from the early years of the nineteenth century. Henley Regatta (founded 1839) was the first amateur event to achieve international fame. The Fédération Internationale des Sociétés d'Aviron (FISA), the international governing body of rowing, was founded in 1892.

The technique of competitive rowing and sculling derives from the professional watermen, who plied their boats for hire, particularly on the Thames tideway, two hundred years ago. Wide, heavy craft dictated a fast, short stroke. Two developments above all led to modern rowing. The first was the invention of the outrigger, by Henry Clasper, of Newcastle upon Tyne, in 1844. By transferring the rowlocks (oarlocks) from the gunwale of the boat to metal rods 'rigged out' from the side of the boat, this divorced the leverage which an oarsman could obtain from the width of the boat which he had to use and made it possible to design long, narrow boats for greater speed.

Longer boats led to wider seats, on which the oarsmen slid backwards and forwards to increase the length of their stroke, and this led to the second great invention, the sliding seat, first developed by J. C. Babcock, of New York, in 1857. The sliding seat not only lengthened the stroke, but shifted the main source of propulsion from the oarsman's back to his legs. All other developments, such as keelless boats, carvel (smooth-skin) construction in place of overlapping planks, swivel rowlocks, and changes in the shape of boats and oars, have been subsidiary to these two basic inventions. Rowing and sculling style has adapted to the development of boats and oars, but, at least over the past fifty years, has been more remarkable for similarity than for change.

An event for coxless pairs was included in the program for the 1896 Athens Olympic Games, but was cancelled due to bad weather. In Paris, in 1900, there were five events, but Britain, then the dominant rowing country, sent only a single sculler, which made the competition somewhat unrepresentative. In St Louis, in 1904, there were no fewer than eleven rowing and sculling events, but none was in a class recognized by FISA.

Britain had long been regarded as the home of amateur rowing, and it was natural to include the sport in the program of the Games in London in 1908. The Henley course was lengthened to give 1½ miles (2,414 m) upstream, the longest distance ever used for an Olympic regatta.

There were two lanes, and each country was allowed two crews for each of the four events, eights, coxless fours, coxless pairs, and single sculls. The countries represented were Britain, Canada, Germany, Belgium, Norway, the Netherlands and Hungary. The racing was hardly eventful, for Britain provided seven of the eight finalists. But the main event – the eights – was no foregone conclusion, as Belgium had won the Henley Grand for the two preceding years. The British selectors nominated Cambridge University as their first string, but, fearing that contemporary British rowing was in eclipse, invited Leander Club to form an eight from the outstanding oarsmen of the past decade. Belgium duly beat Cambridge in the semi-final, but Leander conquered the Belgians in the final.

Jack Beresford (right) and Leslie Southwood (Gt Britain) after their victory in the 1936 double sculls

The second Olympic regatta was held over the modern distance of 2,000 m (1 mile 427 yd), in Stockholm. The course was not altogether satisfactory, as one crew had to 'steer round a bathing shed, and then straighten up for the middle arch of a skew bridge'.

Representation had spread to fourteen countries, but there were only three first-class events. Britain provided both crews in the eights final; Leander, boating seven members of Magdalen College, beat New College by a length. The highlight of the regatta was Leander's narrow victory after trailing by three-quarters of a length at 1,000 metres, over the Australians, who had beaten the club in the Henley Grand two weeks earlier. W. D. Kinnear took the single sculls for Britain without being pressed, and Thames Rowing Club lost to Germany in the final of the coxed fours.

After World War I the United States emerged as a world rowing power at the Olympic regatta on the Vilvoorde Canal, near Brussels. In January 1920, the US Navy picked twenty-five cadets and in due course dispatched its eight to Europe, in a cruiser fitted with practice rowing machines, complete with a second crew for pacing, four spare men, their own doctor, trainer, masseurs, cooks and domestic staff. By contrast the British eight, Leander again, 'devoted five weeks of their holiday' to training. The British did not even discover that the regatta was to be at Vilvoorde, rather than Antwerp, until a week before the first race. The members of the team were accommodated seven miles from the course, and had to carry their boat two miles from the railway station to the boat tents on their shoulders.

However, in the final of the eights Britain led by two-thirds of a length after 1,000 metres, and the Americans only just got through to win by about ten feet, in the record time of 6 min 5 sec. It was a similar story in the single sculls, in which Jack Beresford, at his first appearance, led the American, J. B. Kelly, to within a hundred yards of the line, only to lose by one second. By winning the double sculls with Paul Costello, in which there were only three starters, Kelly became the first rowing double gold medallist.

Of the arrangements for the 1924 Paris Olympic regatta, the *Field* correspondent wrote:

> The arrangements were as faulty as was the case in most of the events outside the stadium itself. All the conditions were bad. The umpire's boat was a punt driven by an aeroplane propeller, which drowned all possibility of hearing anything, and this craft went round the crews at the start, apparently with the object of creating a fine wash in which they might get away.

The United States again took the eights, and, through Kelly and Costello, retained the double sculls. Britain won the coxless fours, and the single sculls gave Beresford his first gold medal.

For a change, all the arrangements for the Olympic regatta on the Sloten Canal, near Amsterdam, were praised in 1928. Seventeen countries competed in the seven events (eights, coxed and coxless fours, coxed and coxless pairs, and single and double sculls) which constituted the Olympic program until 1974, when a new event for quadruple sculls was added, for competition in 1976.

The racing was close, and the eights produced a titanic struggle between the United States, which set a new record of 6 min 2 sec in winning its semi-final against Canada, and Britain's Thames Rowing Club. The Americans led by a length at 1,000 metres, but Britain, though conceding 9 lb (4.08 kg) a man, pulled them back to half a length at the finish. The coxless fours was also an Anglo-American battle, and this time the British crew did overtake the Americans, to win by a bare half length. Terence O'Brien and Archie Nisbet almost achieved the same in the coxless pairs. After trailing Bruno Müller and Kurt Möschter of Germany by two lengths, they fought back to lose by half a length.

The outstanding performer of the regatta, however, was the Australian sculler, Bob (Henry Robert) Pearce. Britain's David Collet was the only man to extend him at all, in a semi-final, which Pearce won by three lengths, having won his first and third round races by ten and twenty lengths respectively.

The Olympic regatta in 1932 at Long Beach Marine Stadium, Los Angeles, was chiefly notable for the achievement of H. R. A. 'Jumbo' Edwards. Picked with Lewis Clive for the coxless pairs, which Britain duly won from New Zealand by one length, Edwards was drafted into the Thames Rowing Club coxless four, when J. H. Tyler fell sick, and won his second medal, over Germany, by $2\frac{1}{2}$ lengths. Bob Pearce (Australia) retained the single sculls, and the United States won its fourth consecutive eights title, from Italy, followed by Canada and Great Britain.

In 1936 the river at Grunau was the site of the Berlin Olympic regatta. Nazi Germany had made superhuman efforts to ensure success, and duly won the first five events. Many thought that it would make a clean sweep of all seven gold medals. It fell to the two Englishmen, Leslie (Dick) Southwood and Jack Beresford, to turn the tide. Having lost to Germany, in a heat of the double sculls, they qualified for the final via the *repêchage*, the draw system which gives all those defeated in the opening heats a second chance to qualify. At 1,000 metres the Germans, Willy Kaidel and Joachim Pirsch, led by a length. Beresford and Southwood then began a sustained spurt. At 1,800 metres they drew level and then inched ahead. Unable to hold them, the Germans stopped short of the

Vyacheslav Ivanov (USSR), at Melbourne in 1956, where he won the first of his three sculling gold medals

finish, and the British couple crossed the line $2\frac{1}{2}$ lengths ahead.

In 1948 Henley-on-Thames became the first, and indeed remains the only town to have the honour of staging two Olympic regattas. Although unable to meet the specifications for a modern course, Henley was granted special dispensation when the 1948 Games were awarded to London. A three-lane course was laid out over a distance of 1,880 metres upstream. A fine University of California eight repeated the familiar pattern of a United States win in the eights, with Britain in second place. The Americans also took the coxed fours. The outstanding performance, however, was that of the Leander veterans, W. G. 'Ran' Laurie and Jack Wilson, who had last raced, and won, in the Henley Regatta pairs ten years earlier. Taking leave from the Sudan, they returned home to repeat their Henley success, and add the Olympic coxless pairs title. Britain took a second gold medal, its last to date, through Bert Bushnell and myself in the double sculls.

The exposed five-lane course at Meilahti, Finland, in 1952, produced a new force in Olympic racing. Yuri Tyukalov (USSR) won the single sculls from the holder, Merv Wood (Australia), and the Russian eight finished second behind the United States.

Racing was open, and seventeen of the thirty competing nations reached the finals. The United States was the only country to take two gold medals, the eights and coxless pairs, the other winners being Czechoslovakia (coxed fours), the USSR (single sculls), France (coxed pairs), Yugoslavia (coxless fours), and the outstanding Argentine double scullers, Tranquilo Cappozzo and Eduardo Guerrero. Britain reached five finals, more than any other country, but finished fourth in every one.

In spite of the distance involved in reaching Australia, teams from twenty-five countries competed in the Ballarat Regatta, on Lake Wendouree, in 1956. This was to be the end of the United States' long domination of the eights, and it went out in a blaze of glory, taking the eights and both pair-oar events, while finishing second in coxless fours and double sculls, and third in the single sculls. Russian influence increased, with gold medals in both sculling events, second place in coxless pairs, and third place in the coxed pairs. For Britain it was the beginning of years of eclipse. For the first time in Olympic history no British crew qualified for the finals. The Ballarat course proved to be excessively exposed, and racing had to be postponed during the *repêchages*.

A new word was coined for the Olympic dictionary in 1960. Because it was impractical to provide overhead steering markers on the Lake Albano course, the six racing lanes were individually buoyed over their entire length, and this 'Albano' system has been used ever since. In the Rome Olympics Germany (then a combined East and West team) emerged as the dominant rowing country, with gold medals in eights, coxed fours and coxed pairs. For the first time in twenty years the United States lost the eight-oar title, finishing fifth, though it had the consolation of winning the coxless fours. The Soviet Union again took the single sculls, through Vyacheslav Ivanov, and also the coxless pairs.

Twenty-eight nations, only five fewer than the record entry in Rome, made the journey to Tokyo in 1964. Sixteen reached the finals, and twelve gained medals,

Gt Britain (R. D. Burnell and B. H. T. Bushnell) winning the 1948 double sculls from Denmark and Uruguay

which indicates that none was really dominant on this occasion. Germany took only the coxed fours, and the Vesper Boat Club regained the eight-oar title for the United States by a margin of five seconds. Britain came near to a gold medal in the coxless fours, but was beaten into second place by Denmark, by 1.1 seconds. The specially constructed Toda course was unfortunately orientated so that the prevailing wind was cross-head. This gave a considerable advantage to the high-numbered lanes, and racing had to be postponed several times.

For the first time in an Olympic regatta the German Democratic Republic and the German Federal Republic competed as separate entities in Mexico in 1968, and between them they took three gold and two silver medals, with the Federal Republic's Ratzburg eight winning the premier trophy, though with only a fraction of a second advantage over Australia. New Zealand finished fourth behind the USSR, and also took the coxed fours title. Another small country which did well was the Netherlands which won the single sculls through Jan Wienese, and finished second in the coxed pairs and double sculls.

The controversy concerning the wisdom of holding an Olympic competition at high altitude was particularly relevant to the rowing events. If a track athlete feels unwell he can slow down, or drop out, albeit at the cost of victory. But for a man in the middle of a crew this is difficult, if not impossible, and certainly dangerous, since he is likely to collide with the man in front, or behind, resulting in someone going overboard. The combination of heat and altitude in Mexico caused much distress, and no fewer than sixteen men had to be resuscitated with oxygen during the *repêchage* heats.

In Munich in 1972 the two Germanies were totally dominant, with the exception of one surprise result. The Democratic Republic won both the pair-oar events and the coxless fours, was second in the coxed fours, and third in the single sculls, double sculls, and eights. The Federal Republic took the coxed fours and was third in the coxless fours. The surprise was not that New Zealand repeated the success it had won in the eights in the previous year's European Championship, which it did handsomely, but that the United States edged the German Democratic

Republic out of second place. New Zealand also split the two Germanies in the coxless fours. It was notable that once again a purpose-built rowing course was criticized for unfairness, this time because the hugely expensive grandstand sheltered one side of the course near the finish.

SHOOTING Karl Heinz Lanz

Shooters all round the world are proud that theirs is one of the traditional Olympic sports. At the Games in Athens in 1896, five shooting events were included among the nine sports on the program. This is the more surprising in view of the fact that the first World Championships for shooting did not take place until the following year at Lyon in France; and it was another eleven years before the governing body of the sport, the Union Internationale de Tir (UIT), was set up in Zürich.

In the strictly chronological sense, the first Olympic Games of 1896 and the second Games at Paris in 1900 were simply a prelude to the emergence and organization of shooting as an international sport (in St Louis, in 1904, only archery events were held). Internationally organized shooting had its official birth on 17 July 1907. At the Swiss

Below Swedish shooters in 1912: left to right, Alfred Swahn, Åke Lundeberg, Oscar Swahn and Olof Arvidsson

Bottom Will Røgeberg (Norway) getting 300 pts out of 300 in the 1936 smallbore rifle

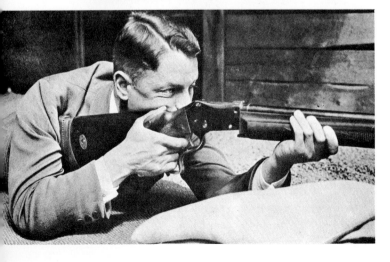

Federal Shooting Festival in Zürich, eight countries established the UIT. The founding nations were Argentina, Austria, Belgium, France, Greece, Italy, the Netherlands and Switzerland. Subsequently Spain responded favourably to an invitation; Great Britain and Germany did not commit themselves at first. Daniel Mérillon, chairman of the French governing body, was elected first president – he had presided over the organizing committee of the 1900 Paris Games.

The aim of the UIT was to provide a coherent framework for the running of international shooting contests. Meetings were to be held in conjunction with the annual World Championships and their agendas were to include discussion of all points of technical interest, competitors' clothing, and the exact definition of firing positions.

From 1897 to 1914 annual World Championships were in fact developed, their programs devoted exclusively to rifle shooting at 300 metres and pistol at 50 metres. The number of nations competing reached a record at Camp Perry, near Port Clinton, Ohio, USA, in 1913: eleven took part, including two teams from South America, those of Argentina and Peru. World War I interrupted these sporting encounters and also resulted in the dissolution of the UIT, which in the meantime had grown to twenty-one member countries. It was not until 1921 that the president declared the union re-established. The World Championships which had last been held at Viborg in Denmark were resumed at Lyon, scene of the first championships in 1897.

Daniel Mérillon, the founding president, died in 1925 after guiding the destiny of the Union for eighteen years. It was not until two years later, after the World Championships had lapsed in 1926 because no country was willing to assume responsibility for them, that the UIT once more had a president: Jean Carnot, also French, and the son-in-law of Mérillon.

From 1931 the representatives of the member nations of the UIT agreed to hold the World Championships in alternate years. By 1937, thirty-five associations from thirty-two countries were affiliated.

Once more the Union had to bow to political circumstances and the world's best shooters were not to meet again until 1947, in Stockholm. In the meantime Jean Carnot had retired and at the delegates' conference on the last day of the Stockholm championship the Swede, Eric Carlsson, vice-president of the UIT, was elected as Carnot's successor. On the occasion of the 1960 Rome Olympics Carlsson, after thirteen years in office, asked to be allowed to step down. From then on Dr Kurt Hasler of Switzerland, the fourth president, has directed the UIT.

A great deal has changed in shooting over the years. The nature of the competitions and their organization have been subject to continual modification. Shooting distances and times have been constantly revised. Preparation, training and the selection of competitors have moved steadily away from the original military aspect and today the emphasis is wholly on shooting as a sport. Keeping up with the world's best requires application to training schedules and practising complementary sports such as swimming, gymnastics, and running. Records, whether in rifle, pistol or clay-pigeon shooting, are not achieved by chance. They are the result of years of preparation, competition experience and dedicated routine.

This truly sporting character of shooting is also apparent in the Olympic Games, in which the sport is represented at present by eight events. From Montreal in 1976, the number will be reduced to seven with the elimination of free rifle at 300 metres. Only two competitors per country are now permitted to qualify. This limitation too denotes a step towards selection wholly according to the criteria of the sport itself: the more so when it is recalled that, for example, in Athens in 1896 no fewer than 111 Greeks competed, 173 Frenchmen took part in Paris in 1900, and in London in 1908 there were still seventy participants from the host country.

There is a general trend towards economy in the practice of the sport of shooting and in its international organization. Although the UIT now counts ninety-four member nations and sixty-nine countries took part in the twentieth Olympiad – a figure exceeded by few sports – efforts are being made to make the sport even more broadly based. Shooting will be on the way to achieving this ambition when events that do not involve large expenditure of money and materials are included at Olympic level: existing examples are the small-bore events (rifle, pistol); air gun and air pistol at 10 metres also fulfil these requirements. They do not need large, elaborate facilities, the equipment and ammunition used is relatively moderate in price and the organization involved calls for considerably less staff.

For some time air gun and air pistol have been compulsory events in championships at world and continental level. A proposal for recognition of 10-metres events has been placed before the IOC. These would be widely welcomed as a substitute for the discontinued 300-metres events and could be organized without any increase in the total number of participants. Furthermore, if 10-metres events could be prescribed as separate women's competitions, this would be a suitable way for them to add Olympic recognition to their other international attainments.

American shooters have at all times played a dominant role at international level. In earlier years the Scandinavian countries, led by Sweden and Norway, always presented a serious challenge. Since 1952 the USSR has come very much to the fore. In spite of this American–Soviet preponderance, there have been opportunities enough for success for other countries. In eight Olympic events at Munich in 1972 shooters from seven countries won eight gold medals: two for the United States and one each for Italy, North Korea, Poland, Sweden, the USSR and the German Federal Republic.

For some time now the World Championships have been held at four-year intervals. In the meantime separate world championships have been held in some events, particularly in trap and skeet shooting, and in running-boar (moving-target) shooting. Since 1955 title contests have also been organized at zone or continental level – for Europe only at first, then for Asia and America. In order to rationalize these title competitions as far as possible they have often been subdivided in recent years. Thus there are separate European championships for air gun and air pistol, for clay-pigeon shooting, for women's and junior events. This is due not least to the enormous expansion of the sport. More and more countries are taking it up so that existing competition facilities will have to be expanded. This is why it is often advantageous to hold title competitions at more than one venue.

This long-established sport undergoes continual renewal. Technical improvements to guns, ammunition and equipment, modern forms of training and the steady increase in the number of participating nations ensure that there is no stagnation in the sport, only continuing modernization.

SWIMMING Monique Berlioux

Seven gold medals – four individual and three in relays – were won by Mark Spitz (United States), the most complete, the most exceptional swimmer of all time. The scene: Munich, 1972. It was the heyday too of Shane Gould, a fifteen-year-old Australian girl; the slightly built American Shirley Babashoff was the rising star. The talented and superlatively trained Roland Matthes of East Germany confirmed his easy victory in Mexico.

As at each Olympics, everyone could take stock: of style, training, the quality of the pool and its water; the morphology of the mermen and mermaids, their physical, mental and respiratory equilibrium. Managers, officials at all levels, coaches, doctors, statisticians, writers thus passed a new examination, acquired fresh knowledge.

Until Munich, the Olympic Games provided the only opportunity for swimmers to compete on the world level. It was the last time, however, that the Games would be in this unique position for a year later the first World Championships were held in Belgrade. These and other national and international championships provided, as in past years, the opportunity to improve upon world records which had been shattered wholesale in the Bavarian capital. By 1974 the names of Shane Gould (Australia), Melissa Belote (United States), Michael Burton (Australia), Novella Calligaris (Italy), Bradford Cooper (Australia) and Mark Spitz (United States) had gradually faded from the lists of world-record holders to be replaced by those of Cornelia Ender (German Democratic Republic), Ulrika Richter (German Democratic Republic), Stephen Holland (Australia) and Tim Shaw (United States), while the 'veteran' Roland Matthes (German Democratic Republic), at the ripe age of twenty-three, was beaten in 1974 by an eighteen-year-old American, John Naber. This was his first defeat in seven years of undisputed supremacy in the backstroke.

Man has always wanted to move around in water without worrying too much about style. However, novices have long been dominated by the instinctive fear of putting their heads in the water. The splashing dog-paddle head-out-of-water style easily developed into the classical breaststroke, known since ancient Egyptian times: a make-up spoon from Egypt in the Louvre Museum depicts a girl swimming breaststroke. But our ancestors probably knew about paddling with their feet; an Egyptian bas-relief shows soldiers crossing a river by this means of propulsion, although supported by goatskins filled with air.

Up to 1800, the breaststroke was considered the fastest and best stroke for man. But at that time endurance was considered more important than speed; Lord Byron's crossing of the Hellespont in 1810 and of the Tagus in 1818, and the first cross-Channel swim by Captain Matthew Webb in 1875 were significant achievements of swimming endurance.

The start of the 1904 100-yd sprint, won by Zoltán von Halmay (Hungary), extreme left

Efficiency in style was sacrificed for the sake of economy. Thus, the sidestroke made its appearance, to be followed by the overarm sidestroke in about 1883. The first association of clubs was created on 7 January 1869 at a meeting at the German Gymnasium in King's Cross, London: this was the Metropolitan Swimming Association, which soon became the London Swimming Association. Disputes over the definition of amateurism led to the creation of the Amateur Swimming Association (ASA) in 1886.

Twenty-two years later, at the request of the ASA, the representatives of a large number of European countries met in London on 19 July 1908, during the Games of the fourth Olympiad, to form a world federation controlling amateur swimming, and thus the Fédération Internationale de Natation Amateur (FINA) came into being.

The introduction of timed speed events quickly led to a profusion of different styles. In 1873 James Trudgen demonstrated a new and faster style with the recovery of both arms over the water. Around 1900, Alec Wickman introduced a stroke in Australia which he had learned from the natives of the Solomon Islands where he was born – each arm clearing the water in time with a deep leg kick. Richard Cavill improved on this stroke and introduced it in 1902 to England, where he took part in competitions. Charles Daniels, an American, saw the stroke, studied it, compared it with the almost identical stroke used by the Hawaiians and returned to Britain in 1906 to win the English 100-yards championship, with a faster and more flexible movement of the feet, in 58.6 sec.

The backstroke is the direct and logical complement to the forward stroke. Although an Egyptian bas-relief shows a swimmer doing the back crawl, this style seems to have been eclipsed by the back breaststroke. It was only in 1912 that the back crawl gained universal acceptance, thanks to Harry Hebner (United States) in particular, who won the Olympic 100 metres in 1 min 21.2 sec in Stockholm.

The butterfly was the result of a loophole in the breaststroke regulations. These did not specify whether the arms were to be thrust forward in or out of the water after

they had been pulled back, so Erich Rademacher (Germany) had the idea in 1926 of lifting them above the surface, while keeping the breaststroke leg scissors movement. Most breaststroke swimmers quickly adopted this new idea to use for part of a race, adding a modification to the leg movement by changing the symmetrical scissors into a vertical dipping movement with the legs together. In 1952, after the Helsinki Games, it was decided to separate the new stroke, called the butterfly, from the classic breaststroke.

On 10 April 1896, in the tiny Bay of Zea, where the small houses of the Piraeus, at that time covered with vines, straggled down to the sea, Crown Prince Constantine and Prince George of Greece gave the signal for the start of the swimming races. Six countries sent eighteen swimmers to compete for the five swimming titles at stake, in the first Olympic Games of modern times.

Alfréd Hajós, a Hungarian, was the first swimmer to win an Olympic title: he won the 100-metres freestyle – the distance must be regarded as approximate – in 1 min 22.2 sec, before going on to win the 1,200 metres too, while the Australian Paul Neumann came first in the 500 metres in 8 min 12.6 sec.

Hajós, in combining both physical and mental qualities, is a shining example of what an Olympic champion should be and typifies the Olympic ideal. At the Olympic Games in Paris twenty-eight years later, he was awarded a silver medal (the gold was not awarded), for architecture this time: for his plan for a stadium. It was he too who designed the famous swimming pool on St Margaret's Island in Budapest where many European and world records have been beaten.

Four years after Athens, a number of rather random races were included in the Paris program, in 1900. The open-air pool at Asnières, which was right in the Seine with boundaries that were far from clear, was not liked at all by the swimmers. The visitors to the Universal Exhibition who crowded along the banks of the river saw hardly anything of the races, and did not really understand what they did see, the events being so confused. A British swimmer, John Jarvis, won the 1,000 metres and the 4,000 metres while the Australian Frederick Lane carried off the 200 metres. A team sport, water polo, was added to the swimming races, and was won by Great Britain, which defeated Belgium in the finals.

Four countries sent fifty-two competitors to St Louis for the 1904 Games. The program was left more or less to the discretion of the organizers. The facilities were scarcely any better than they had been in France. An irregularly shaped pool was marked out in the middle of an artificial lake made for a very large international exhibition, which formed a backcloth to the Games. A Hungarian, Zoltán von Halmay, came first in the sprint, beating the American Charles Daniels, the medium-distance title holder. Philippine swimmers competed with Mexicans, Japanese and even Turks within the framework of 'anthropological days': 'Such an event, so contrary to the Olympic ideal, could hardly have been held anywhere else in the world other than on this frontier of the southern states,' commented Coubertin, horrified but nevertheless happy to see his brainchild, Olympism, conquer the New World.

In 1908, the London Games finally offered the swimmers a specially built pool: 100 metres long, 17 metres wide, it was dug out of the grass of the athletics stadium at

Shepherd's Bush. Its water was neither heated nor filtered, nevertheless Charles Daniels confirmed his worth by beating the Olympic and world records in the 100 metres freestyle.

For the first time, the number of competitors was restricted by regulations, although generous by modern standards: each country was allowed to enter twelve swimmers in the individual events, and three teams in each relay. The program of events, still restricted to men, comprised the 100-metres, 400-metres, 1,500 metres freestyle, 4 × 200-metres freestyle, 100-metres backstroke, 200-metres breaststroke, springboard and high diving (5- and 10-metre platforms) and water polo.

A tall, lanky Australian of seventeen, Frank Beaurepaire, won the silver medal in the 400-metres freestyle and the bronze medal for the 1,500 metres: in this second event, he came third again on two subsequent occasions: at the Antwerp Games in 1920, and in Paris in 1924, a rare achievement!

Women were allowed to compete in Olympic swimming for the first time in 1912 at Stockholm. Three events: 100-metres freestyle, 4 × 100-metres relay and high diving, were open to them. This step towards 'an impractical, uninteresting, unaesthetic and indecorous feminine Olympiad', as he called it, exasperated Coubertin, who never forgave swimming for having opened the breach.

King Gustaf V of Sweden welcomed forty-two girls to his capital, among the 233 swimmers from seventeen countries. The Australian Fanny Durack, clad in a long woollen swimming costume with a skirt, and a rubber cap covered with a cloth bandanna, like a nurse's cap, managed to win the 100-metres freestyle – in the same time, to the nearest tenth of a second, as Hajós in Athens. Duke Kahanamoku and his brother Samuel, descendants of a Hawaiian chief, astonished the spectators not so much by their coppery skin as by their smooth, gliding style. The elder, Duke, became 100-metres Olympic Champion.

Duke Kahanamoku retained his title in the plank-lined pool in the old fortifications at Antwerp in 1920. The diving platforms were also made of wood . . . oh, what spectacular slips! The youngest Olympic competitor, the American Aileen Riggin, barely twelve years old, won the springboard diving, a speciality added, together with the 300-metres freestyle, to the women's program.

In 1924, in Paris, the future Hollywood Tarzan, Johnny Weissmuller, made his first triumphant appearance. Tall, slender, handsome, shy, with a style perfected to the last detail by his trainer, William Bachrach, Weissmuller, just twenty, captured the titles, the spectators and the host of pretty girls who crowded into the Tourelles swimming pool, a concrete pool measuring 50 metres by 18, built for the occasion. The Kahanamoku brothers were also to be seen in Paris again. They came second and third in the 100-metres freestyle.

The 100-metres backstroke and the 200-metres breaststroke were added to the women's events while the 300-metres freestyle was changed to 400 metres and won by Americans, like all the other women's titles with the exception of the breaststroke, in which the British girl Lucy Morton outshone all rivals.

Pete Desjardins (United States) was outstanding on the springboard as well as in the plain high diving. In this second speciality, however, he was beaten by an Australian, Richmond Eve, who became Olympic Champion.

Protecting members of the jury from the weather at the 1928 fancy diving competition

These, together with the victory of the Mexican Joaquin Capilla Pérez in 1956, were the only exceptions to the incomparable American school's monopoly on the diving titles, which continued until 1960. Among these great Americans are the elegant Richard Degener, the blonde Dorothy Poynton, the young and sculptural Marjorie Gestring, only thirteen years old in Berlin, and – more recently – the perfect technician Sammy Lee, the adorable Vicky Draves, the slim Bob Clotworthy and the impeccable Pat McCormick.

Four years later in Amsterdam, in spite of the presence of Weissmuller, six titles escaped the American grasp. The 200-metres breaststroke was won by the Japanese Yoshiyuki Tsuruta; the 400-metres freestyle saw the victory of the Argentinian Alberto Zorilla (the only one from his country ever to win an Olympic title in this sport). The 1,500 metres went to the Swede Arne Borg, already second in this event in 1924, and who, in the space of eight years, broke thirty-two world records! Finally, Germany won the water-polo title from Hungary (which was to recapture the title in 1932 and 1936) and France, which four years earlier, in Paris, had seen its flag flying from the central pole. In the women's events, the 200-metres breaststroke was won by the German Hilde Schrader; the Dutch girl Marie Braun came first in the 100-metres backstroke. Apart from her daughter, Mama Braun trained other champions and her matronly figure coupled with a stentorian voice became a familiar sight in pools all over the world.

In Los Angeles, in 1932, the United States witnessed the sudden end of its supremacy. The Japanese won five of the six men's races and very often the other places of honour too. The American girls, headed by Helene Madison, fortunately saved the day to a certain extent for the home team.

In Berlin, in 1936, while the Japanese captured fewer titles, they nevertheless won the greatest number of medals. Old Europe awoke from its lethargy – the Hungarian Ferenc Csik coming first in the 100-metres freestyle.

The American girls, who had reigned practically supreme – except in breaststroke – since they first took part in the Olympic Games, were often outdone in Berlin by the extraordinary Dutch team, followed closely by the German swimmers and a few Danes, including Ragnhild Hveger, only fifteen and a half. An incomparable style, a strong determination to win, combined with a magnificent physique and perfect health, were the invaluable assets of the Dutch girl Rie Mastenbroek, who came first in the 100- and 400-metres freestyle in the capital of the Reich. The runner-up at the time, Miss Hveger, later beat all the freestyle records, except the 100 metres, held by Willy den Ouden, crowned Olympic Champion with the Dutch team in Berlin. Altogether, between 1936 and 1942, Hveger was to shatter forty-two world records.

The Berlin Games drew much attention: thirty-six countries sent 455 competitors, including 122 women, and the pool held 20,000 spectators at each event – a new record, never equalled.

Almost all the Olympic records were broken, and several world records too for the men's events in 1948 at London, where there were 456 competitors including 111 women. Yet none of the Wembley record holders, in these first post-World War II Games, came anywhere near the times of the young winners in Munich.

In the providential absence of the Japanese and with a Europe torn by six years of war, the Americans carried all before them in London. On the other hand, in Helsinki in 1952 and Melbourne in 1956, their success was mitigated: the Old World was recovering and the titles were more evenly distributed. To such an extent, in fact, that in 1952 the American girls could hardly manage to achieve places. The Hungarian women carried off all the titles, except the 100-metres backstroke which was won by a South African, Joan Harrison. An Australian, John Davies, won the 200-metres breaststroke; a Frenchman, Jean Boiteux, the 400-metres freestyle.

Four years later, in Melbourne, before its own public, the Australian team made off with a tremendous number of medals, winning all the men's and women's freestyle events, as well as the backstroke, thanks to David Theile. The champions with their kangaroo badge were Jon Henricks, John Devitt, Murray Rose, Kevin O'Halloran. Their feminine team mates were Lorraine Crapp and Dawn Fraser. In the speciality swimming races, the Japanese Masaru Furukawa and the German girl Ursula Happe in the breaststroke, the English girl Judy Grinham in the backstroke, the American Shelley Mann and her compatriot William Yorzyk in the butterfly, won gold medals. Frank Guthrie, the Australian coach, was exultant; one of his innovations was to make his swimmers

Dawn Fraser being congratulated by her parents after winning the 100-metres event in 1956

practise weightlifting, neglecting gymnastics, one of the classical training exercises of the Americans. His compatriot, Gallagher, stated at the time: 'The whole effort must be concentrated in the arms, even at the expense of the legs.' This is the training method he used with the powerful, determined Dawn Fraser, who always put on a tremendous spurt at the end of her races. Together they formed a close-knit, triumphant pair.

Coming rather late – for a swimmer – to big international competitions, Dawn Fraser was nineteen years old in 1956. She dominated the sprints until 1964, when she decided to retire from competition, having been the first woman – and the only one for several years – to swim 100 metres in less than a minute.

The Melbourne Games started in December 1956, just before the Russian army marched into Budapest and on the eve of Egypt's takeover of the Suez Canal. Certain countries, as a result, did not let their teams take part. The Netherlands was one. As fate would have it, a Hungarian and a Russian team met in a final round of the water-polo event. The team from Budapest, electrified by the encouragement of the crowd, won 4–0. They hardly heard the final whistle, so violent was the fighting in and even under the water.

In 1960 at Rome the Stadio del Nuoto was the arena for the competition, the Piscina delle Rose for training, in the heart of the Foro Italico conceived by Mussolini, where 602 swimmers from eighty-five countries competed in games as keen and impassioned, but so much less dangerous, than those of the ancient circus.

The men's and women's titles were shared between the United States and Australia with only four exceptions: the 200-metres breaststroke was won by the strong and beautiful stylist, Anita Lonsbrough (Great Britain), who broke both the Olympic and world record; the women's diving titles, springboard and high diving, were awarded to a young German girl, Ingrid Krämer, who put an end to the long American reign; in water polo, Italy triumphed before a wildly enthusiastic public. Murray Rose repeated his 1956 victory in the 400-metres freestyle, while the crowds raved about the 'wonder kids' John and Ilsa Konrads, born Lithuanian and now Australian, who had broken record after record during the previous two years. John won the 1,500 metres; his sister, deprived of her 400-metres world record before the Games by the future winner of this distance, the American Chris Von Saltza, obtained only a silver medal, in the 4 × 100-metres freestyle, won by the United States.

The American swimmers, shaped and trained by Bob Kiputh, who was ending his career as a coach which began with Bachrach and Weissmuller forty years earlier, snapped up the first places, also winning the 4 × 200-metres freestyle and the 4 × 100-metres medley, the latter having just been added to the Olympic program.

John Devitt (Australia), second in Melbourne, this time won the 100-metres freestyle, thanks to the judges at the finish. Credited with a time longer by one-tenth of a second than that of the American Lance Larson, he was nevertheless awarded the gold medal. No protests were able to change the jury's decision but they did succeed in changing the system: it was the last time the Olympic Games were to be timed by hand. In Tokyo in 1964, Japan introduced electronic timekeeping which enabled times to be taken to the nearest thousandth of a second, thus

Ingrid Engel-Krämer (Germany) diving to take her second
gold medal for the springboard in 1964

putting an end to any possibility of dispute. Such equipment was needed for there were many close decisions.

The United States, with Don Schollander, gold medallist in the 100- and 400-metres freestyle, 4 × 200-metres and 4 × 100-metres freestyle relays, and Australia, with Dawn Fraser, still going strong, dominated world swimming. For the first time, a Russian girl, Galina Prosumenshchikova, won a gold medal in a swimming event. The French Christine Caron, in the backstroke, and the Dutch Ada Kok, in the butterfly, were the only European girls to succeed in squeezing into second place.

An innovation before Tokyo: the somersault turn. Already used for quite a while in the backstroke, the half-somersault gradually gained acceptance in freestyle too. The swimmer now twists completely round on himself, going into his somersault a yard or more from the end of the pool, which he touches only with his feet as he pushes off. This turn, which was prohibited at Tokyo, was accepted a year later by FINA and made new progress possible for the swimmers who came to Mexico in 1968.

Mexico, at a height of 2,278 m (7,500 ft), was the occasion for grave fears as to the effects of the altitude, especially for the long-distance specialists. Seven hundred and eleven competitors met in the Alberca pool where a Mexican victory in the 200-metres breaststroke came as Felipe Muñoz was swept along on a wave of cheers from 14,000 wildly enthusiastic compatriots.

Don Schollander (United States) no longer had his youthful energy and Mark Spitz had not yet gained the experience of an adult. Both failed to strike gold in Mexico. A first title was won by East Germany, now recognized separately from West Germany: it was the tall, long-limbed Roland Matthes who had the honour of causing his country's flag to be hoisted. Klaus Dibiasi, a handsome fair-haired Italian, reigned supreme in the high diving. He repeated his victory at the Munich Games, in 1972, where the Russian Vladimir Vasin, winner of the springboard, put an end to the series of American victories uninterrupted since 1920. Munich was also the occasion for the Russian team to gain its revenge and beat Hungary in the water-polo final; the United States came third.

In 1948 the indoor, heated Wembley pool showed that swimming was after all not only an open-air sport. The glass-and-steel Melbourne pool of 1956, with its water

heated to 22 °C (72 °F) – a temperature considered far too cool by contemporary stars – sounded the knell of open-air pools. A few sighs of regret . . . on remembering the Helsinki swimming pool bordered by clumps of conifers, in that never-fading northern light, and the sumptuous facilities in Rome in 1960: the Stadio del Nuoto, with its series of pools. In 1964 came the 'cathedral' swimming pool of Tokyo with its suspended shell-shaped roof, its ideal water temperature: 25 °C (77 °F), and the absence of any steam. Nothing impeded the view of even the most distant spectator. Mexico offered a practical aquarium. In Munich, the public felt crowded on the grandstands made to resemble waves.

In Mexico, as in Munich, as well as at any other international meeting today, swimming pools no longer hold any surprises for swimmers, for strict rules govern their construction. The racing pool, 50 metres long, 21 metres wide, 1.80 metres deep from one end to the other, has eight lanes. The diving pool, 15 metres by 10.5 metres, is 5 metres deep. Completing this aquatic complex, for the big international competitions, are separate pools, also of regulation length, in which divers, swimmers and water-polo players warm up. Everywhere the water is heated to a constant temperature of 25 °C (77 °F). The waves cut by small gutters, the lines of big plastic floats separating the lanes so as to stop the wash from other competitors, the water artificially stirred for the divers who do not like reflections and the lift taking divers effortlessly up to the 10-metres platform are just a few examples of the improvements now taken for granted by the super-athletes. The 2,000 to 3,000 yards a day covered by Allen Stack, the 100-metre backstroke gold medallist in London in 1948, would be just a light warming up today, for the daily stint of the East German or Australian schools ranges, for the moment, between 13 and 16 miles.

Just a word about the program. Enriched, since the Melbourne Games, with the butterfly event (200 metres for men, 100 metres for women), in Rome it was further widened with the 4 × 100-metres medley for both men and women, and in Tokyo with the 200-metres backstroke and the 4 × 100-metres freestyle for men, the 400-metres individual medley for both men and women. In Mexico, the program became so overcrowded with the addition of the 100-metres butterfly, 100-metres breaststroke, 200-metres freestyle, 200-metres individual medley, for men, and 200- and 800-metres freestyle, 200-metres backstroke, 100-metres breaststroke, 200-metres butterfly, 200-metres individual medley for women that criticism flew fast and furious. FINA, at the request of the International Olympic Committee, has agreed to cut out in Montreal the 200-metres medley in both categories and the men's 4 × 100-metres freestyle.

There have always been Doctor Fausts trying, more or less, to force nature, to transform talented subjects into monsters, to metamorphose middling or undertrained athletes into champions. They have, on occasion, obtained results, but these have always been short-lived. There is no doubt at all that, especially in swimming, human limits have not yet been reached. And, at the same time, training methods keep on improving. During and after the 1976 Games we can expect many more records to be smashed, in this basic sport, which is so important for the balanced development of individuals, and which is now beginning to be so popular throughout the world.

VOLLEYBALL Don Anthony

Joseph Strutt, in *The Sports and Pastimes of the People of England* (1801), records a volleyball-like game played by yeomen in the Middle Ages, five a side, but it was not until 1895 that the Director of the Holyoke Young Men's Christian Association (YMCA) Gymnasium, in Massachusetts, USA, William G. Morgan, invented the game of 'minonette', soon to become known as volleyball.

Morgan invented his game as a diversion for middle-aged businessmen who found basketball too strenuous. The game had a very ordinary beginning; a basketball bladder was inflated and presented to a group for 'batting about with the hands'. The activity proved enjoyable; a rope was stretched between the group to make opposing sides, and another world game was born.

The YMCA physical directors saw the potential of the game; it provided enjoyable activity for all ages, both sexes, indoors and out. It did not need expensive equipment; the rules were simple; the skills few. On the wings of the international YMCA movement, volleyball – together with its older brother, basketball – was taken to many countries. In some it gained an extraordinary foothold: eastern Europe and Japan, for example; in others, like Britain, it did not penetrate beyond 'recreational activity' until the 1950s, despite the fact that eight-a-side volleyball appeared in the 1933 *Syllabus of Physical Training for Schools*.

By 1896 volleyball was played by five players on each team, up to 21 points a game, and over a net 2.1 m (6 ft 10½ in) high. In its worldwide spread there were many interpretations of the rules; in Japan it was played nine-a-side; in the United States some local rules allowed for a kick to keep the ball off the ground; for women an 'assisted serve' was allowed, i.e. a second person on the same side could 'assist' the ball over the net. By 1918, however, the six-a-side game was established; at this time the 'rotation', moving one place clockwise on winning service, was introduced. Three years later the games were decided by fifteen points.

By 1923 the game was becoming structured on a competitive basis. The All-USA Championship was held in that year; the USSR national federation was established in 1925, the Japanese two years later, and the French in 1938. In these years before World War II there was a move to form an international federation but it was not until 1948 that the Fédération Internationale de Volleyball (FIVB) was born with headquarters in Paris. One year later the first World Championships were held in Prague.

The 1950s began with an attempt to bring the international regulations into force everywhere. The game had also experienced tactical changes. To avoid 'feeding' the tallest players who merely stood near the net, leaped upwards, and 'spiked' (smashed) the ball incessantly, attack by back players was forbidden as early as 1924. A 'spike line' 10 ft (3.048 m) from the net appeared on the court markings; players behind this line at service could not take part in an offensive spike. The rules were kept simple: no invasion of the space on the opponent's side; no touching of the net; no stepping on the halfway line. With increasing sophistication of the game, tactical maturation, and the skilled expertise of the players, however, even these simple rules have been changed at the highest level

of play. In the 1970s there are occasions when one can reach over the net – but not touch it – for example, when taking part in a block (when one or more players in the front jump to make a 'wall of hands' to block the opposition's attack); and one can step on the midway line and still not foul (a foul is given when one steps completely over this line).

During World War II volleyball was played extensively in military camps, by prisoners of war, and in refugee camps. It was a game which could be played over a rope by peasants in villages, by miners outside coal mines, by sailors on aircraft carriers, by women factory workers, by naturists. It could be set up easily on a bomb site, in a field, in a church hall. It was also attractive as a training game for athletes and other sportsmen. For these and other reasons there was a tremendous leap in participation, and the FIVB began a campaign for Olympic entry almost as soon as it was formed. In 1957 volleyball was added to the list of sports recognized by the International Olympic Committee. In 1961 the men's event was included in the 1964 Tokyo Olympic program, and two years later a women's competition was added. Meanwhile, World Championships for men and women had been held in Moscow (1952) and Paris (1956). In Moscow crowds up to 60,000 had watched outdoor volleyball in the World Championships. The world of sport and the Olympic Movement were forced to take notice. Furthermore, there had been the growth of regional championships; European Cups for men and women were in force by 1959; the game played a major part in university sports championships.

In the developing countries volleyball had demonstrated its unique appeal. They wanted a game which could be played outdoors, which required little organization, cheap equipment and simple rules. In all the developing countries therefore, volleyball has met a real need and it appears ubiquitously in the games curricula. In many countries of western Europe, outside France, the Netherlands, and Belgium, and in Scandinavia, the game has had a struggle to gain total acceptance. There are several reasons for this: most of these countries boasted a long tradition of schools' physical education, the curriculum was already 'full', and where the emphasis was on gymnastics as the core of the work, the indoor facilities were not designed for games. The centres for the training of physical-education teachers were also heavily bound by tradition and this did not encourage the adoption of a 'new' game, no matter what the advantages. In the United Kingdom all these factors were in evidence when the Amateur Volleyball Association was formally constituted in 1955. Today, however, almost all colleges of physical education and an enormous number of schools play the game. With financial support from the state organizations, especially with regard to equipment, facilities, teachers and coaches, the voluntary organizations controlling volleyball have been enabled to flower. A game like volleyball must find its roots in the schools; even with poor after-school provision for the sport there will be adequate 'spin-off' from a good physical education program to promote the vitality of the game in the community.

After World War II a further factor helped to spread the popularity of volleyball in new environments: the movement of displaced persons. In Britain and Canada, for example, the east European groups, especially the Poles, demonstrated to their hosts that volleyball was a game of great entertainment, that it aided group cohesiveness, that it could be played by all age groups, and that it lent itself to the disciplines of school physical education. In the United Kingdom there had been special problems. Owing to the shortage of indoor halls, and the fact that there seemed to be no need for another 'ball-handling' game in a society which had apparently reached saturation point with association football, the two codes of Rugby, cricket and basketball, volleyball had cantered along as a YMCA sport and an amusing recreative pastime. Nevertheless the FIVB wanted the game to flower in the United Kingdom. Since 1960 volleyball in Britain has demonstrated a capacity for growth. Problems at national level illustrate the general questions which must be understood if the game is to grow still further in the world. A coaching scheme was essential; it is now thriving and is a model for many other sports. The schools section has branched off as a separate Schools Sports Association. In 1974 there was hardly a school or college in the country which did not 'know' volleyball. The armed services play with enthusiasm; for the Fire Service volleyball has been adopted as *the* game. The Amateur Volleyball Association of Great Britain and Northern Ireland has now divided into English and Scottish autonomous associations, both affiliated to the FIVB. For Olympic purposes they are linked through a small committee, the British Volleyball Federation.

The game was ideally suitable for the climates and personalities of Africa and South America, as well as for the countries of Asia. In Japan the game started again in 1945 under the slogan of 'Volleyball for a Million People'. As early as 1925 the Soviet Communist Party Central Committee was calling for 'the encouragement of volleyball for farmers and the working class . . . it should be brought to the level of the people at large, not only the youth, but the aged also.'

Different countries have imposed their distinctive styles. The Russians introduced very tall and heavy men (6 ft 5 in or 1.956 m; and as much as 120 kg, 242 lb or 17 stone, for example) and are adept at the power game which eventually wears down any block. The Poles and Czechs blend the Slav power with surprise and cunning. The Japanese have introduced incredible skill, imaginative court movement, and new variations on old techniques. These are broad generalizations but they *do* appear. It is interesting to notice, also, how these styles are yet again matured when exported by coaches to developing countries. The Cubans have given their original twist to Russian and German coaching methods; the Brazilians, Peruvians, Mexicans, Tunisians, Finns, Dutch and others, have all added unique 'stamps' to the modern game. There is enormous growth of international competition at 'sub-élite' level. Club and college teams move about the world for tournaments and festivals. The mass media have recognized the appeal of the game. In Japan a national league is sponsored by a television company.

Despite all this, it was the wedding of volleyball to the Olympic Movement that significantly developed the world game. When the famous Japanese women's team played the Soviet team in the final of the 1964 Tokyo Olympics, it was reported that 'the people clung to their television sets to watch the game, leaving the public bath-

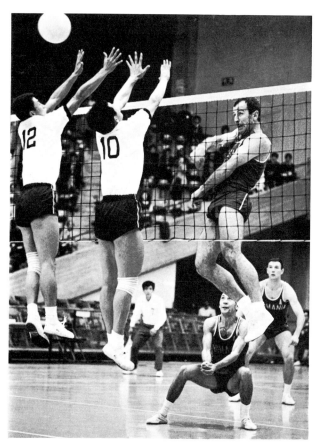

The Koreans go up for the ball during the volleyball match between Korea and Romania in 1964.

houses nearly empty, the Ginza Street nearly deserted, and the toll switchboard out of action' (Report of the First Asian Volleyball Coaching Course, 1971). The report goes on: 'anyway, each of Japan's television networks enjoyed the first, and probably the last, record audience ratings of 90% for that game'. The live presentation and the films of these Olympic matches were sold all over the world. The films of the Japanese girls, *in training alone*, gained astonishing audience ratings. It was the same story in Mexico and again in Munich. Wherever the Olympic Games are staged the sports in the program enjoy an unequalled opportunity for rapid growth. Since the host country participates by right in its Games, it can avoid the complicated and difficult routes via regional qualification. Canada would most definitely not have qualified 'normally' in volleyball. However, the fact that it will be competing in 1976 has caused the organizers of volleyball in Canada to develop their highest levels of ability. This in turn has a spin-off value to develop 'volleyball for all'. The Olympic matches will be an added bonus for Canadian volleyball. It is this Olympic 'charisma', the 'wedding of mind to muscle' of which Coubertin wrote, the obvious 'more than just sport' which the Olympics has in abundance, which ensures success for any sport which falls into its orbit.

Volleyball continues to develop technically – as it must if it is to continue to attract each generation – but it retains its fundamental simplicity. The 'dig' (in which the ball is played by both forearms) was *out* and is now very much *in* again; the 'block' has become an *offensive* skill; as many as four players on the same side can be off the ground during the execution of a 'spike'. Research studies in Belgium show that while the ball size is probably right for men it is wrong for women. We might also see new variations in the height of the net. The 'antennae' on the net are relatively new. There was talk at one time of the need for a 'fourth touch' (at present each team can play or 'touch' the ball a maximum of three times before sending it back to the other court) but this was outvoted since the best players would doubtlessly spike the fourth touch with complete success. With the traditional three-touch game (receive of service – set up – spike), the second touch is often badly placed, thus allowing the opposing defence to block the spike.

Among women as well as men the game is enjoying immense growth. In 1970 an Olympic survey of sports showed volleyball second to basketball in the classification list; 110 federations organized volleyball for sixty-five million players (compared with twenty-six million players of association football, twenty million athletes, and eleven million swimmers, for example). The most recent new development has been 'mini volley', a simple variation of the major game designed for children between nine and twelve years old.

Already we have had three volleyball tournaments in the Olympic Games. In all three we have witnessed the true Olympic spirit, we have seen expertise, drama and passion of the highest order, we have seen capacity spectator attendances. We have begun to appreciate the personalities in the game; Inna Ryskal and Ludmila Buldakova (USSR), for example, who both played in Tokyo, Mexico and Munich; Katsutoshi Nekoda (Japan) is another player known throughout the world. There is no doubt that, even within the confines of the simple skills and tactics of basic volleyball, we will be astonished by new variations and permutations at future Games. The Japanese have already shown the world how *training* for volleyball can be an art in itself. Right along the continuum from simple play to high-level Olympic competition, volleyball has now measured up to world criticism. It will remain an integral part of Olympism.

WEIGHTLIFTING Jenő Boscovics and Dezső Vad

The ancient weightlifter Atlas, according to Greek mythology, held the heavens on his shoulders as a punishment for fighting with the Titans against the Gods. Superheavyweight Vasili Alekseev (USSR), who weighs 150 kg (330 lb 11 oz or 23 stone 8 lb 11 oz), lifts incredible weights above his head, not as a punishment but from love of the sport and the desire to achieve new records.

The legendary Biblical hero Samson's remarkable strength was attributed to never having cut his hair. He buried the Philistines in rubble by tearing down the two pillars that supported their temple to Dagon. Mohammad Nassiri (Iran), who weighs 52 kg (114 lb 7 oz or 8 stone 2 lb 7 oz), shaved his head but lifted fantastic weights. He has won five world titles, the Olympic bantamweight championship of 1968 and holds three world records.

The combination of strength with virtue has always created unforgettable ideals. The legends also show that

Mohammad Nassiri (Iran) lifts 367.5 kg (810 lb) in the bantamweight class of the 1968 weightlifting

competitions between strong men go back for thousands of years, even if the sport was not called weightlifting then. Traces of competition and of comparisons of power can be found in legends and traditions all over the world.

As a branch of competitive sport weightlifting began in Germany and spread quickly to Austria, Switzerland and then to the whole of Europe. Athletic clubs for strong men were first formed in the 1860s.

The competitions of a hundred years ago were quite different from those of today. The weights were simple and they could not be adjusted. So the order of ranking had to be determined by lifting a certain weight several times. A metal bar with a ball of 40–50 cm (approximately $15\frac{3}{4}$–$19\frac{1}{2}$ in) in diameter at each end was the first form of weight. The balls were either solid iron filled with sand, pebbles, lead shot or pieces of metal. Before 1920 when the International Weightlifting Federation (IWF) was established, weightlifting was governed by the International Gymnastics Federation (FIG) and played the part of the poor relation.

It took its place as an important and respected sport in the Olympic program in 1896. Unofficial European and World Championships were held before 1900 but these were rather chaotic.

The first winner of the World Championships held in Vienna from 31 July to 1 August 1898 was Wilhelm Türk (Austria), who achieved the following: snatching 76.5 kg ($168\frac{1}{2}$ lb) with one hand, pressing 60.7 kg ($133\frac{3}{4}$ lb) with right and 60.5 kg ($133\frac{3}{4}$ lb) with left hand, 73.4 kg ($161\frac{3}{4}$ lb) and 72.0 kg ($158\frac{1}{2}$ lb) in right and left hand jerk, pressing 52.0 kg ($114\frac{1}{2}$ lb) with one hand, 3 × 50 kg (110 lb) in pressing with both hands, 127.5 kg (281 lb) pressing with two hands, jerking 150.8 kg ($332\frac{1}{4}$ lb) using two hands, 9 × 100 kg ($220\frac{1}{4}$ lb) pressing, 110.2 kg ($242\frac{3}{4}$ lb) in jerking with one hand and 19 × 50.0 kg (110 lb) pressing – thirty placings in all.

Weightlifting took its present-day form in 1928. It was then that the exercises done with one hand were abolished and disc barbells appeared. The program of the Amsterdam Olympics in 1928 included the press, the snatch and the jerk, all with two hands. In the two hands snatch the bar is placed horizontally in front of the lifter's legs. He must grip the bar, palms down, and pull it in a single movement from the ground to the full extent of both arms above his head, while bending the legs. In the jerk the bar is lifted first to the shoulders, then the legs are bent and then the arms and legs are extended to raise the bar overhead. In the press the bar was lifted first to the shoulders, then, at a signal from the chief referee, was pressed to arms' length overhead without any impetus from the legs or trunk. This proved inceasingly difficult to adjudicate and was abolished at the IWF Congress in 1972.

The Olympic Games followed the same system until Munich (1972). Controversy over pressing began to be acute in 1950. A certain deviation started to show between the valid lay-back style and the 'Military Press'. Finally the IWF, at a meeting in Melbourne in 1956, deleted from the Rules the part that prescribed for the body and the head to be straight.

Except for the Games at Paris (1900), London (1908) and Stockholm (1912), weightlifting has always been on the program of the Olympics. In the lightweight event of 1928 two gold medals were awarded to Hans Haas (Austria) and Kurt Helbig (Germany). In 1936 in the same event Mohammed Mesbah (Egypt) and Robert Fein (Austria) were both similarly awarded gold medals. They both lifted the same weight; the rule determining the winner of a tie by placing the lighter competitor first had not been introduced. The eighty-one first places were shared between seventy-three competitors from twenty countries: USSR twenty-one; United States fifteen; France nine; Egypt five; Germany, Italy and Poland four each; Austria and Bulgaria three each; Czechoslovakia and Japan two each; Belgium, Denmark, Estonia, Finland, Great Britain, Greece, Hungary, Iran and Norway one each.

There have been only eight weightlifters in eighty years who have won twice: Waldemar Baszanowski (Poland), lightweight, 1964 and 1968; John Davis (United States), heavyweight, 1948 and 1952; Louis Hostin (France), light heavyweight, 1932 and 1936; Thomas Kono (United States) lightweight, 1952, and light heavyweight, 1956; Yoshinobu Miyake (Japan), featherweight, 1964 and 1968; Charles Vinci (United States), bantamweight, 1956 and 1960; Arkadi Vorobev (USSR), middle heavyweight, 1956 and 1960; Leonid Zhabotinski (USSR), heavyweight, 1964 and 1968.

Weightlifting has become increasingly popular as the results have become more dramatic. Even the experts have given up judging the records of the future and trying to estimate the ability of man, for year after year new records are broken.

The great development between 1928 and 1972 is shown by the Olympic records. For example, compare the record of Josef Strassberger (Germany) in 1928 with that of Imre Földi (Hungary) in 1972: Strassberger, the 1928 heavyweight champion, lifted 372.5 kg (821 lb) – 122.5 kg (270 lb) in the press, 107.5 kg (236¾ lb) in the snatch, and 142.5 kg (314 lb) in the jerk; Földi, the 1972 *bantamweight* champion, surpassed him with 377.5 kg (832 lb) – 127.5 kg (281 lb), 107.5 kg (236¾ lb) and 142.5 kg (314 lb).

Between the Munich Olympics in 1972 and 1 August 1974 no fewer than eighty world records were broken (without the press, since it has been discontinued): an indication that the heroes of modern times have not yet reached their limit.

WRESTLING Jacques M. Caryotakis and John Goodbody

Statues, reliefs and paintings found in archaeological excavations prove that wrestling was known for thousands of years B.C. in Japan, China, India, Babylon, Persia, Egypt, Crete and other ancient civilizations. The first written description of wrestling extant is that given by Homer in the *Iliad* (c. 850 B.C.). The fight he was describing took place between Ajax, son of King Telamon of Salamis, and Odysseus (Ulysses) during the siege of Troy.

However, wrestling as a competition sport first appeared in ancient Greece. Events between men were introduced in the 18th Olympic Games (708 B.C.), when the Spartan Evryalos won, and events for boys up to eighteen years of age *(ephebes)* in the 37th Olympic Games (632 B.C.), won by the Spartan Hipposthenes. The latter also won the Olympic wreath in the men's event five times.

The three forms of wrestling practised by the ancient Greeks were *orthopali, alindissis* or *kylissis* and *acrochirismos,* In orthopali the athlete had to throw his opponent to the ground three times or make him touch the ground three times with any part of his body other than his feet. Alindissis, in which the athlete had to force his opponent to submit completely, was used principally for training; it could take such a long time that it was not included in the big Games. In acrochirismos the wrestlers used only their fingers, which called for strength and a particular technique. This style was used (with boxing) in the *pancrace* event. Wrestling also formed the last and most important event of the pentathlon.

Wrestling, which held such an esteemed position in the ancient Games, was naturally included in the sports of the first modern Olympics. But it took time before the present program of ten weight categories, ranging from light flyweight to super-heavyweight in both freestyle and Greco-Roman, began to take shape. Many countries had

Mithat Bayrak (Turkey) defeating René Schiermeyer (France) in the 1960 welterweight wrestling, Greco-Roman style

developed their indigenous styles of wrestling over the years, such as *sumo* in Japan, *yagli* in Turkey, *glima* in Iceland, *sambo* in the USSR and the style of Cumberland and Westmorland in England. Gradually these largely regional styles were superseded by the truly international freestyle and Greco-Roman. Neither insisted on any particular hold being fixed before the start of a bout and no special clothes or harness had to be worn. Although training for both styles is similar, freestyle tends to attract more agile wrestlers than Greco-Roman, in which the use of the legs in either attack or defence is forbidden.

When the modern Olympic Movement began the outstanding wrestlers were professionals. But gradually the professionals became purely entertainers and the Olympic Movement can be credited with keeping the genuine sport alive until the International Amateur Wrestling Federation (Fédération Internationale des Luttes Amateurs; FILA) was founded in 1912. Until then the only worthwhile international wrestling events were at the Games. Even so, they were not comprehensive. Only one category, heavyweight, was contested in 1896 and the sport was not even included in the program four years later.

The three remaining celebrations before World War I saw the sport grow in importance. Freestyle (in seven weight categories) was a part of the 1904 Games, inevitably dominated by the American hosts, and the 1908 Games (in five weight categories). Greco-Roman (in four weight categories) was introduced at the London Games. This style, in fact, which had survived two thousand years since the Romans had adapted classical Greek methods, formed the whole of the wrestling program at Stockholm in 1912. The absence of freestyle in favour of the less universally popular Greco-Roman was an indication of the popularity of the classical style in Scandinavia, a tradition which was to bring Sweden and Finland many successes in international competition.

During the 1912 Games there was the longest final ever to be staged in a combat sport. The light-heavyweight bout between Anders Ahlgren (Sweden) and Ivar Böhling (Finland) remained drawn after nine hours' fighting. Changes had to be made to the rules to make the sport better suited for competition. So during the 1920s wrestling became increasingly regulated: international rules were established and eventually World and European Championships staged, at first on a haphazard system but eventually on an annual basis. The period between the two world wars was dominated by the struggle between the Scandinavian countries and the United States which shared most of the titles between them. Sweden produced two wrestlers, Carl Westergren and Ivar Johansson, who won three Olympic gold medals each, and Finland's Kalle Anttila showed his versatility by winning the lightweight freestyle title in 1920 and the Greco-Roman featherweight gold medal four years later.

Wrestling expanded after World War II. In London, in 1948, 266 competitors from twenty-seven nations entered – the largest number of wrestlers in any Olympics until then. Turkey led overall, taking six gold medals in the two styles. But Sweden was still formidable in Greco-Roman, winning five titles. In the 1952 Games the Turkish entry forms arrived too late and four of their most talented wrestlers were not allowed to compete. This allowed the USSR, competing for the first time, to have a less hazar-

Mustafa Dagistanli (Turkey) beating Erkki Penttilä (Finland) in an elimination round of the featherweight freestyle wrestling in 1960

dous début in international competition than it might have expected, for the Russian wrestlers took most of the medals. The Russians maintained their grip at Melbourne in spite of entering a team from which Olympic and World champions were deliberately omitted. Despite this unusual policy they collected six gold, two silver and five bronze medals, and in only one event did their representative fail to finish in the first three.

Turkey regained its leadership of the sport at the 1960 Games, winning seven gold medals. In many of the divisions, its struggle with the USSR produced some memorable contests. In the Greco-Roman welterweight class Turkey's Mithat Bayrak drew with Grigori Garmarnik after an enthralling bout and went on to retain his title. Another Turk to win a second gold medal was Mustafa Dagistanli, who took the freestyle bantamweight in Melbourne and the featherweight in Rome.

But probably the leading individual was the West German heavyweight Wilfried Dietrich, first in the freestyle and second in the Greco-Roman. His performance in both styles was remarkable; increased competition had caused most wrestlers to concentrate on one or the other.

Japan's traditional devotion to the allied combat sport of judo enabled it to become prominent in the lighter classes, and at the 1964 Games in Tokyo it was the most successful nation. Osamu Watanabe, the freestyle featherweight champion, was particularly impressive with his dexterity in standing wrestling and his ruggedness in the moves requiring sheer force on the mat. He was one of five Japanese gold medallists – three in freestyle and two in Greco-Roman.

Although the USSR and to a lesser extent Turkey were still dominant, the other medals were more widely distributed. The other Communist countries regularly challenged for places. In 1968 the Hungarian 'Pici' ('Tiny') Kozma superbly retained his Greco-Roman heavyweight crown; two years later he was killed in a car crash. Japan had three outstanding champions, of whom the best was Shigero Nakata, at flyweight in the freestyle, who repeated his World Championship victory over Dick Sanders (United States).

In 1972 two categories were added to the program:

light flyweight (under 48 kg or 105 lb 13 oz) and super-heavyweight (over 100 kg or 220 lb 7¼ oz). The USSR increased its supremacy by taking nine titles. Its distinguished super-heavyweight Aleksandr Medved took the freestyle title to become the first man to win wrestling gold medals in three successive Games.

Equally impressive was his heavyweight compatriot Ivan Yarygin, who completed the unusual feat of pinning (holding an opponent's shoulder to the mat for a count of one) all his opponents. Although Turkey had faded from its former position, the United States re-emerged to take three titles. In the Greco-Roman Wilfried Dietrich (German Federal Republic) attempted to set an all-time record of winning a medal in five different Olympics. But after pinning Chris Taylor (United States) with the finest throw of the Games, he was disqualified in a subsequent bout and withdrew from the competition.

The increasingly high standard and the growth of the sport throughout the world has been reflected in the large number of countries achieving places in the first six – thirty-eight in 1972 as against eighteen in 1936.

YACHTING Hugh Somerville

King Charles II of England has been credited as being the father of British yachting, having been presented with a 20-ton yacht by the East India Company in 1660. He raced against his brother, the Duke of York, in 1662, from Greenwich to Gravesend. The stake, which the King won, was £100. Samuel Pepys, in his *Diaries*, records this early yachting scene.

The Royal Cork Yacht Club is believed to have been the world's first yacht club, although it started as the Water Club of the Harbour of Cork, in 1720, and cannot claim continuous existence. It was mainly concerned with yachts manoeuvring in company.

In 1775 the Cumberland Society was formed by a number of men who raced on the Thames, under the patronage of the Duke of Cumberland. Most of the racing took place between Blackfriars and Putney, and the Royal Thames Yacht Club, which was formed by a number of members of the original Cumberland Society in 1823, possesses some of its original cups and flags. The date of the formation of the Cumberland Fleet, or the yachts of the Society, coincided approximately with the running of the first of the horseracing 'classics' (the St Leger in 1776, the Oaks in 1779, the Derby in 1780).

It is known that yachting was a sport in the Netherlands before 1660, if only because Charles II's first yacht was built there. The Royal Swedish Yacht Club (KSSS) was founded in 1830, the New York Yacht Club in 1844, the Royal Yacht Club of Ostend in 1847, the Royal Netherlands Yacht Club in 1850, and the Cercle de la Voile de Paris in 1858.

Yachting has been an Olympic sport, with only one break, ever since the Games at Athens in 1896. The Olympic regattas of 1900 were held at Meulan and Le Havre, with six nations taking part. The racing was in six classes and there was also an 'Open' class.

The various authorities differ as to exactly what rating or tonnage rules governed the Olympic classes in 1896 and

The start of the 8-metre class race on the second day of the yachting at Kiel in 1936

1900 because each yachting country had its own rules. It was not until 1904 that Great Britain and France agreed to producing what has become known as the International Rule of rating, which applies, slightly modified, to the International 12-metre class used for the America's Cup and also the other metre classes such as 8-metre and 6-metre, which were long part of the Olympic yachting scene.

There was no yachting in the St Louis Games of 1904, probably for the simple reason of the distance involved and also because in those days there was no agreement between yachtsmen on the two sides of the Atlantic over rules of measurement. However, in 1906 a conference held in London united the yachting countries of Europe by forming the International Yacht Racing Union. The original members were Britain, France, Germany, Norway, Sweden, Denmark, the Netherlands, Belgium, Italy, Switzerland, Austria-Hungary, Finland and Spain. The United States did not become a member, nor did it have any national authority and in yachting matters the voice of America was usually that of the New York Yacht Club. The IYRU at that first meeting agreed upon what was to become known as the 'International Rule of 1906'. This was a formula which included length, girth and sail area to rate the yachts in metres, e.g. 6-, 7-, 8-, 10- and 12-metres, and it was under this that the yachts were rated for the 1908 Games; the yachting regatta was held off Ryde, Isle of Wight, while the 12-metre class raced on the Clyde. Only five nations competed and the winners in each class, the 6-, 7-, 8- and 12-metres, were all British. In those days there was no limit to the numbers of boats from each country in each class. While the British boat had a sail-over in the 7-metres, the two 12-metres concerned were both British, and one magazine of the time commented that the international element in the class was introduced

The winning Greek Dragon team in 1960: left to right Georgios Zaimis, Crown Prince Constantine, Odysseus Eskidjoglou

by the fact that one crew came from the Clyde and the other from the Mersey. The Clyde yacht won. There were no entries for the 15-metre class, no doubt because of the difficulty of finding enough amateurs to man such a craft, of 75 ft (22.86 m) in length or more.

In the 12-metres event that year, the winning owner received a gold medal and his crew silver, while the owner of the second boat was awarded a silver and his crew bronze. It was in 1908 also that motor boating appeared for the first and last time as an Olympic sport.

The year of 1919 was an important one for international racing for the 1906 rule was revised and a new formula, to which the United States was a party, came into operation in 1920. The Antwerp Games of 1920, with yachting held off Ostend, had fourteen classes. For the first time there were races for two dinghy classes, the International 12-ft dinghy, which had been adopted by the International Yacht Racing Union, at its 1919 meeting, and the 18-ft dinghy. There were also the 30-sq-m and 40-sq-m classes, with one, which appeared only in these Olympics, for Scandinavian skerry cruiser-type boats.

Sweden took both the 30- and 40-sq-m classes, the crew of the winner of the latter including Swedish designer Tore Holm. For the rest of the classes, the Belgian yacht took the old (1906) type 6-metre and Norway the new (1920); the Netherlands won the new 6.5-metre and Great Britain the old-type 7-metre class. Norway also made a clean sweep in the remaining classes, both the old and the new 8-, 10- and 12-metres.

The 1924 Paris Games regattas were held at Meulan and Le Havre. This seems to have been the first time that entries in each class were restricted to one boat per class per country. There were nineteen countries taking part, with seventeen boats in the 12-ft dinghy, nine in the 6-metres and five in the 8-metres.

Belgium won the dinghy class, while Norway took the two metre classes. Sailing the Norwegian 6-metre was Eugen Lunde, whose son and grandson were to win medals in the Games of 1952 and 1960. Peder the son won the silver medal at Helsinki in the 5.5-metre class in 1952, and Peder the grandson won the gold in the Flying Dutchman in 1960 and silver in the Star in 1968. The younger Peder's mother also won a silver medal, crewing for her husband in 1952.

In 1924 the two August Ringvolds, senior and junior, of Norway, were in the winning 8-metre crew. That Games also brought the first South American entry, a yacht from Argentina, in the 8-metre event.

The 1928 Olympic regatta was held on the Zuider Zee (now called the IJsselmeer), twenty-three countries taking part in the same three classes. The Crown Prince, later King Olav V, of Norway won his gold medal in the 6-metre *Norna*, while that famous French yachtswoman, Madame Virginie Hériot, owned and sailed in the 8-metre *L'Ailée VI*, one of the many yachts of that name which she owned. In the 12-ft dinghy Henrik Robert of Norway, who, with King Olav, has served the IYRU for many years, won his second silver medal.

In 1932 at Los Angeles only eleven countries entered. The Snowbird was the single-handed dinghy, instead of the 12-ft, virtually unknown in the United States, while the Star boat appeared for the first time. These two classes were won by France and the United States respectively. In the 6-metre Tore Holm won his second gold medal for Sweden, and the United States won the 8-metre.

For the Berlin Games in 1936, Kiel was the venue, the racing taking place in the mouth of Kieler Förde. The number of competing countries was twenty-six, with the specially designed Olympiajolle being the most popular class with twenty-five boats. The Netherlands won this event, Germany the Star, Great Britain the 6-metre and Italy the 8-metre.

After World War II the regatta for the 1948 Games was held at Torbay on England's south coast. Twenty-three countries took part, with two classes appearing for the first and last time, the Firefly and the Swallow. The Dragon was in the Olympics for the first time, too, with the evergreen Star and 6-metre. A total of seventy-five boats sailed on three courses of Olympic type (explained below) laid in Torbay.

Before 1948 the course for the Olympic regattas tended to be set using the existing navigation marks. At Torbay, Helsinki, Melbourne, Naples and Acapulco a circle of eight buoys was permanently laid and the start was made at the leeward mark to give a beat to windward. Two reaches were sailed, followed by a beat and run and a final beat. At Kiel in 1972 the course was laid each day, just before the start, and it has become established practice to lay the marks just before the start to ensure that the first leg of the course is into the wind.

Before the Torbay regatta a purely linear point-scoring system had been used, with the highest score winning. In 1948 a new, logarithmic system was adopted, which after 1964 was replaced by a revised points rule. The 1948–64 points system was thought to give too great a bonus to the leading boats. The system in force for 1968 and 1972 gave 0 points for first place; 3 for second; 5.7 for third; 8 for fourth; 10 for fifth; 11.7 for sixth; and for seventh place and below the place number plus 6 points.

The Firefly was a new 12-ft dinghy built by Fairey of Hamble, England, which was designed by Uffa Fox of Great Britain. It resembled a National 12-ft dinghy, but was of hot-moulded plywood construction. It was really designed for two light people to sail, and as it had two sails, main and jib, was not liked by sailors from other countries, who were accustomed to a more sedate type of single hander which had only one sail. However, it was in this class at Torbay that Paul Elvstrøm of Denmark won the

Vera Čáslavská (Czechoslovakia), whose grace and power in gymnastics in 1964 ended Russian domination

first of his four successive Olympic gold medals in the single-handed dinghy class.

For the Helsinki Games in 1952, the regatta was held at Harmaja, in the approaches to Helsinki. Knowing the general dislike of the Firefly as a single-hander, the Finns held a competition to find one suitable for Olympic sailing. The winner was Rickard Sarby's Finn, which has remained the Olympic single-hander ever since. Sarby, a Swedish hairdresser, had been fourth in 1948 in the Firefly and won the bronze in this event at Helsinki.

Italy's Agostino Straulino won the gold in the Star, and Thor Thorvaldsen (Norway) won his second gold in the Dragon. Herman Whiton (United States) took his second gold in the 6-metres, while Dr Britton Chance won the gold in the 5.5-metres, in the only example of this class under American ownership at the time. The 5.5-metres had been introduced a year or two before by the IYRU as a possible replacement for the 6-metres, under a new and slightly different formula to that governing the 'six'. In its place the Australians had asked for the International 12-sq-metre to be used for the Melbourne Regatta, which was sailed in Port Phillip Bay. A total of twenty-eight countries, one fewer than at Helsinki, took part with seventy-one boats in competition. Paul Elvstrøm (Denmark) won the Finn for his third gold medal, New Zealand the 12-sq-metres, the United States the Star, Sweden the Dragon and the 5.5-metres. The Dragon result was decided on a tie-break between Folke Bohlin (Sweden) and Ole Berntsen (Denmark); the Royal Dragon *Bluebottle*, owned by HRH Queen Elizabeth II and HRH the Prince Philip, Duke of Edinburgh, skippered by Cdr Graham Mann, RN, taking the bronze.

At Naples, in 1960, Paul Elvstrøm duly won his fourth gold in the single-handed dinghy (Finn), while Peder Lunde, Jr (Norway) took the Flying Dutchman, being very much an 'outsider' in this new Olympic class. The Flying Dutchman was originally conceived as a European lake boat, about 20 ft long, but proved so good that it had been adopted as a two-man centreboard class for all conditions by the IYRU. It was designed by U. van Essen, as a result of much research by Conrad Gülcher, both of the Netherlands. The Russians took the Star class to win their first yachting gold medal, although sailing in an American-built boat with American sails. At the other end of the political scale, the Dragon gold medal was won by Crown Prince Constantine of the Hellenes, and the 5.5-metres gold went to the United States.

The Italian organizers had spent a great amount of money for the 1960 regatta but the Japanese spent even more on the facilities at Enoshima, the base for the 1964 regatta. There the same classes were held as at Naples, although there were forty countries involved, in contrast to forty-six in Italy. Germany won the Finn, New Zealand the Flying Dutchman and the Bahamas the Star. In the Dragon the gold, which had so narrowly eluded him at Melbourne, went to Denmark's Ole Berntsen, and Bill Northam (Australia), who was then sixty-five, took the honours in the 5.5 metres.

The classes were unchanged at Acapulco in 1968, forty-one countries competing with 123 boats. The Finn gold medal went to Valentin Mankin (USSR) and Rodney Pattisson (Great Britain) in the Flying Dutchman *Super . . . docious* finished first in every race except the last, in which he was second. He was disqualified after a protest

Rodney Pattisson and Chris Davies (Gt Britain) in Super-doso, on the way to win the 1972 Flying Dutchman

by Canada for an incident at the start of the first race, but his placings still constituted an Olympic record.

The United States took the Star and the Dragon classes; Sweden, with the Sunderlin brothers, won the last of the 5.5-metres championships.

The capital costs at Enoshima and Acapulco were capped by the Germans at Kiel for the 1972 regatta. The lavishness of the facilities was unbelievable – two years after the Games, the accommodation which was built with shop and restaurant facilities had proved too expensive for the normal German yachtsman. Forty-two countries competed, with 165 boats in six classes. Two new classes had been added, the Soling, a 27-ft Norwegian-designed three-man keelboat replacing the 5.5-metre, and the Tempest. The latter was a British boat, also a keel craft, of about 22 ft overall length, manned by two.

Serge Maury (France) took the gold medal in the Finn, while Rodney Pattisson (Great Britain) in *Superdoso* won his second gold running in the Flying Dutchman. Valentin Mankin (USSR) won a second gold, in the Tempest class, after a battle with Britain's Alan Warren, who had made the running early in the series. Australia won the Star and the Dragon, with Dave Forbes and John Cuneo as the respective helmsmen, and 'Buddy' Melges (United States) took the Soling title.

For the 1976 regatta sailing will be in the following categories: Finn, 470 and Flying Dutchman dinghies, Tornado catamaran, Tempest and Soling. This is a better proportion of centreboard to keelboats and should attract more competitors with a lower average age, even though costs have soared, making even a Finn or 470 dinghy prohibitive for the average youngster of any country.

Many sailors famous in their own countries have taken part in the fifteen Olympic regattas sailed so far. Some have succeeded, while some have been overwhelmed by the occasion, the tension being far greater than in a national, continental or world championship. Pressures on the men at the top, such as Mankin and Pattisson, who have each won two golds, are far greater nowadays than they were for the old and bold Tore Holm, 'Swede' Whiton and Thor Thorvaldsen, who also won two golds (Holm had a bronze too). Whether anyone will equal Paul Elvstrøm's four golds in a row remains to be seen.

Wolfgang Nordwig (German Democratic Republic), the first pole vaulter to beat the Americans in the Games

The Background to the Olympics

THE FOUNDER OF THE MODERN GAMES Marie-Thérèse Eyquem

Baron Pierre de Coubertin was born in Paris on 1 January 1863. His father, Charles Louis Baron Frédy de Coubertin, was a well-known painter; his works, in an academic style and generally of a religious nature, were widely admired. His ancestor Pierre de Frédy was given his title by Louis XI. In 1577 the Coubertin estate near Paris was acquired and the Frédy family took its name from then on. Through his mother, Agathe Gabrielle de Crisenoy, Pierre de Coubertin belonged to a Normandy family, descended from companions of William the Conqueror; it was for this reason that the estate of Mirville in Normandy was so dear to Coubertin. A branch of the family was descended from a son of King Louis VI of France. Faithful to tradition, Pierre de Coubertin's relations were monarchists and devout Catholics. Their family had given to the Church monks, to France officers, to the State loyal servants.

Eight years after Coubertin's birth in 1871, France had suffered a serious defeat in the Franco–Prussian War. The humiliation which Coubertin felt from this was bitter and without it the modern Olympic Games would possibly not have seen the light of day.

It was Coubertin's sensitivity rather than his intelligence that gave birth to the Games. This sensitivity which came from love of his humiliated fatherland. How could he best serve France? Politics had little attraction for him – too many compromises. Neither did the army – he was a peacemaker. The greatness of France lay elsewhere – it was in the openness of spirit, the character and the soul of all her children. A generous and free sould. He would therefore apply himself to what he called the *rebronzage* (burnishing) of France:

> I shall burnish a flabby and cramped youth, its body and its character, by sport, its risks and even its excesses. I shall enlarge its vision and its hearing by showing it with wide horizons, heavenly, planetary, historical, horizons of universal history which, in engendering mutual respect, will bring about a ferment of international peace. All this is to be for everyone, with no discrimination on account of birth, caste, wealth, situation or occupation.

Coubertin's main objectives are contained in that resolution; the practice of sport would help to fight physical and moral decadence; a new, broader approach to teaching would counteract, according to Coubertin, the harmful effects of specialization; the teaching of history would have to be fundamentally transformed in order to allay the threat of nationalism and for nations to be looked upon as part of one humanity; the masses must be provided with the means to participate in the culture which the middle classes had denied them.

Coubertin's creative imagination sometimes gave him the appearance of a visionary:

> Nothing in ancient history had given me more food for thought than Olympia. This dream city . . . loomed with its colonnades and porticoes unceasingly before my adolescent mind . . . my imagination had been occupied in rebuilding it . . . (*Une Campagne de vingt-et-un ans*, Paris, 1908).

The time will come for deciding whether history must continue to be used as a material for war or whether it will be allowed to play the peacemaking role of which it is capable. . . . Ceaselessly distorted by nationalist appetites and imperialist passions, history has been called upon to feed these same appetites and passions . . . (*Histoire Universelle*, 1926–7).

His four-volume *Histoire Universelle* also includes these astounding predictions: Communism would spread to China; colonialism would end; the African countries would recover their independence; the world would witness the brilliant reawakening of the Arabs to their great past.

> Ever since I achieved manhood, I have listened to that deep murmur coming from the mass of disinherited people . . . it was an article of faith that the worker on whose job society depends cannot be, without harm to that society, turned away from his path towards self-improvement. . . . . The division of functions is going! And so is the division of knowledge! The gates of the Temple remain closed . . . this Bastille must be demolished! Open the gates of the Temple! It is time. The future of humanity demands it.

If I have emphasized his 'illuminations', it is primarily to demonstrate the importance of inspiration in Coubertin's thought. He was an artist, poet, musician, a disciple of Ruskin. But such inspiration did not prevent him from also being a pragmatist, a man of action.

Through the visions which he had almost in spite of himself, and which corresponded to his passionate and altruistic nature and to his humanism, stand out the three essentials of his plan for the reform of education: the first was sport to which the Olympic Movement was to give its seal of nobility; the second was a new kind of teaching in which world history, in creating international understanding, would bring about peace; the third was access to culture for the underprivileged.

The whole of Coubertin's life would be dedicated to the realization of these three objectives.

He had discovered the virtue of sport himself. As a boy he practised rowing, fencing and boxing. But the role of sport in education had been revealed to him by the experience of Dr Thomas Arnold, the headmaster of Rugby School in England, whose principles he came to understand by reading *Tom Brown's Schooldays* and the French philosopher Taine's *Notes sur l'Angleterre*. After a pilgrimage to Rugby to Thomas Arnold's tomb, he decided to attempt in his own country a reform of education in which sport would hold an important place. He was to apply himself to this with a tenacity that deserved a better outcome.

How did he come to think of re-establishing the Olympic Games? It was in 1887 (he was then twenty-four) that, during a conference on English Education, he made a first allusion to the Games in linking them with educational priorities:

> It is not easy, if indeed easiness is a good thing, to get children enthusiastic about Alexander or Caesar. They need something more alive, more real. Olympic dust is what excites their emulation best and most naturally.

In 1890 he visited an English doctor at Much Wenlock,

Pierre and Marie de Coubertin, photographed in 1890, just after their marriage

Shropshire, Dr W. P. Brooke, who had made that village a centre of popular sports by founding the Much Wenlock Olympian Society. 'Dr Brooke also had the sense of internationalism,' Coubertin wrote in *Une Campagne de vingt-et-un ans*. 'At the time of King Otho and Queen Amelia [1833–62], he had sent to Athens a fine cup destined to be offered to the winners of the footraces which were adorned with the name "Olympic".'

In 1891 Coubertin told the young men of the (French) Christian Union: 'The rebirth of sport within our societies, which have been transformed by scientific discoveries, will perhaps assure it of an international role which no one can yet fully envisage.'

On 25 November 1892, at the jubilee of the Union des Sports Athlétiques, held at the Sorbonne, he finished a conference on physical exercises in the modern world by this phrase which, at the time, evoked no response:

Let us export rowers, runners and fencers; there is the free trade of the future . . . your servant hopes that . . . with you he will be able to continue and complete, on a basis suited to the conditions of modern life, this grandiose and salutary task, the restoration of the Olympic Games.

If no one else understood his intentions, he himself knew what he wanted and where he was going. An International Congress to study the principles of amateurism was held, again at the Sorbonne, in June 1894. He had added to the seven items on the agenda relating to amateurism, another: 'On the possibility of restoring the Olympic Games. Under what conditions could they be restored?' This would ensure that the meeting would become the 'Congress for the restoring of the Olympic Games'.

Meanwhile he tried, with varying success, to persuade people from other countries to adopt his views, since France remained indifferent. Even the Union of French Athletic Associations (USFSA), of which he became secretary-general in 1890, rejected his ideas. The

Committee reproached him for his 'English ideas on education'. When he turned to America, the response was half-hearted. When he went to England, the response was nil. Adherents came to him from Sweden, from New Zealand and Jamaica.

On 23 June he realized his dream. He must have known how to cast a spell over the seventy-nine delegates from twelve countries. There were poems, music and songs. And after every delegate had heard the hymn to Apollo, discovered at Delphi in 1893, set to music by Gabriel Fauré and sung by Jeanne Remacle from the Paris Opéra, the assembly, unanimously and by acclaim, decided to restore the Olympic Games.

It is ironic today to realize that Coubertin was not primarily concerned with furthering the Olympic Games. His objective was to use the Games as a platform to popularize the educational role of sport – the moral as well as the physical development of the athlete. He believed that it was essential to internationalize sport in order to popularize it, but it had to be internationalized in such a way that young people everywhere could benefit from it. To achieve this it was necessary to have a noble and beautiful spectacle which would take the event beyond competition, creating an aura like that of the Olympic Games of antiquity.

Why have I restored the Olympic Games? In order to ennoble and strengthen sports, in order to assure their independence and duration and thus to set them better to fill the *educational* role which devolves upon them in the modern world. To exalt the individual athlete, whose very existence is necessary for the involvement of the community in athletic sports, and whose achievements provide an example to be emulated.

The Games would only be uplifting and really educational if they touched the spirit and if athletes set an example.

Having wished to renew not so much the form as the principle of this thousand-year institution because I saw in it for my country and for humanity an educational orientation which had become necessary, I had to seek to restore the powerful fibre which had strengthened it in the past; intellectual and moral fibre.

Like all human activity, sport could indeed be the best or the worst of things:

Athleticism can occasion the most noble passions or the most vile; it can develop impartiality and the feeling of honour as can love of winning; it can be chivalrous or corrupt, vile, bestial; one can use it to consolidate peace or to prepare for war.

That is why for him an ideal, whether based on religious conviction or not, had to be presented to sportsmen. Coubertin explained his ideas in a work called *L'Éducation des Adolescents de XXe Siècle* (The Education of Twentieth-Century Adolescents), in three parts, concerning physical, intellectual and moral education. He planned to include in the Games 'the pentathlon of the Muses': competitions in architecture, sculpture, music, painting and literature. He designed the intellectual and moral symbols of the Games himself: the torch lighted at Olympia as homage to those who had given birth to the idea; the pigeons carrying their message of peace between all nations to the heights;

the raising of the national flags of the winners and of the Olympic flag; exaltation of an ideal, the podium for the best, whatever his origins, social position, race, religion, country – egalitarian aristocracy – and the athlete's oath.

This ceremonial illustrated the doctrine that Coubertin called 'Olympism' and which was in his eyes 'cultivation of effort, contempt of danger, love of one's country, generosity and a chivalrous spirit, contact with arts and letters'.

It was to help the athlete to show his nobleness of soul, his independence, that the IOC defined the rules on amateurism. Coubertin would never agree with the narrow character of these rules, established by the majority of the IOC against his advice. He wrote in 1934:

The actual rules are wicked. Their terms are indefensible as much from the point of view of logic which they offend as that of human liberty which they cheapen.

And he wanted the rules on amateurism to be completely rewritten.

By the Olympic oath I ask only one thing: loyalty to sport. . . . . It is the sportsman's spirit that interests me and not respect of that ridiculous English concept that allows only lone millionaires to dedicate themselves to sport without being tied to an out-of-date dogma (*L'Auto*, 4 September 1936, a year before his death).

Certainly for Coubertin, independence was the ideal towards which the Olympic athlete should tend, but, as he wrote as early as 1894, he made a distinction 'between profit and expenses'. Financial help for athletes, above all the underprivileged, would not make them professionals but rather would give them an equal standing, reducing what 'a man of feeling cannot tolerate – social inequality'.

The life of the Olympic Movement was inseparable from that of the founder of the Modern Games until 1924. He played a crucial part in the success of the first Olympic Games (Athens, 1896), where he suffered opposition from the Greek government and scepticism from the competing countries. In 1897, at the Olympic Congress at The Hague, he declared as an article of faith the independence of the IOC, and, four years later, when the Olympic Games at Paris were mixed up with the World Fair, he affirmed that their autonomy was essential.

At the end of 1900, the IOC came under violent attack from certain countries and individuals, specifically James Sullivan (United States), who wanted to take over the Olympic Movement and planned to stage the third Games at Buffalo in 1901 in connection with a Pan-American exhibition with which he was associated. Some International Federations reproached Coubertin for his authoritarianism. But he yielded to none. In 1904, in St Louis, the Olympic Games were a kind of fair where people played around, cheated and exhibited monsters. Coubertin, who did not attend, drew from this Games lessons from which the next Games were to benefit, for the IOC then passed a rule that the games must not be staged in association with any exhibition with a commercial purpose.

In 1906 new attacks on the IOC came at Athens from within as well as from a world beginning to realize the unbounded power and influence which the organization

The Château de Mirville in Normandy, drawn by Pierre de Coubertin in 1890

might develop. About ten members of the IOC met in Athens without Coubertin in order to study how the IOC might be reorganized. Although Coubertin had asked that they make no decisions without him, they offered the honorary presidency of the IOC to the Crown Prince of Greece, thus Hellenizing an organization which ought to have remained beyond the influence of any particular country. This step did not seem unrelated to another move in which Germany and Sweden wanted to turn the Athens committee organizing the 1906 Games into an Inter-National Olympic Committee composed of government representatives. In addition, the first evidence of anti-Semitism loomed when Count Andrassy of Hungary made it known to Coubertin that another Hungarian member, Ferenc Kemény, who was a personal friend of Coubertin, was undesirable because he was Jewish.

'I disassociated myself from all of it,' wrote Coubertin, 'including the honour intended for the royal prince. Shortly afterwards, in Paris, the prince and I had a long talk on this subject. It was not pleasant, neither for him nor me. I took it upon myself to express my thoughts quite freely and frankly and the meeting preserved this character right until the end.'

In 1908, in London, the Games took a somewhat definitive form. Shocked by the partiality of the British judges, Coubertin called for international officials in future.

The fourth Games at Stockholm showed further improvement and were closer to the Olympic ideal. Coubertin was personally involved in these Games since (under a pseudonym) he was awarded a gold medal for his *Ode to Sport*. This was also the year that his sporting creation, the modern pentathlon, was introduced to the program.

During all this time and later, he never stopped fighting against chauvinism, racism, the attempts to take over by certain international organizations and the influence of politics and money.

The rejection of a military career early in Coubertin's life had been interpreted by some people as meaning that he was a pacifist; that clearly was not so for in 1915 he attempted to enlist for military service and was turned down. At the end of the year he tried again and wrote to his friend the Baron de Blonay:

There are difficulties because men over fifty years of age are not admitted to active service and for my part I do not want to be in auxiliary service . . . What has made me decide on this is that it appears that the cataclysm unleashed by Germany cannot be ended for a number of years; there is nothing anyone can do except fight on for a peace which will not come in the near future . . .

He became an interpreter early in 1916 in a ministerial propaganda department. He was employed on the promise of going to the front after six weeks' training. 'The promise was denied with the coolest impudence,' he wrote.

Attacks on the IOC multiplied during World War I. Some of his friends had doubts. Bertier de Sauvigny, a relation, wrote in May 1917 to Baron de Blonay:

I have no more confidence in Olympism. I admire Pierre who is deceiving himself and seeking to salvage the fragments of his work . . . and I am happy that he has enough moral strength not to be broken by the destruction visited upon his work.

The nations of Europe, submerged by war, barely thought of the Games. But events showed that the Olympic Movement was not confined to Europe; it was universal. Coubertin was convinced that if Europe's youth was going to let the Olympic torch temporarily slip from its hands, others would be found to maintain the ideal. He was right.

In 1914, the Olympic flag flew over Alexandria on the occasion of the Pan-Egyptian Games; in 1915 it waved at San Francisco over an exhibition dedicated to the Olympic Movement. The following year the Olympic ideal reached South America, thanks to Coubertin's personal action.

The Games of the Far East asked for the IOC's patronage and Coubertin regretted that the Asian countries that were French colonies were prevented from taking part independently in the new sporting movement.

At the bottom of things, there was the essential conflict, the struggle of the colonial mind against movement towards emancipation of the native peoples, a tendency full of perils from the point of view of the metropolitan powers. . . . I remain convinced that before long sporting Africa will organize itself in spite of everything.

He commented on the Games at Antwerp (1920) in a brochure, *About the VIIth Olympiad*, in which he particularly praised the gymnastics and deplored the public's lack of interest:

When fashion has swung back to these young men and when their just right to sporting existence has been recognized, the public will realize that it has been deprived for a long time, by snobbery, of a spectacle which is singularly attractive for its strength and beauty.

One of the most positive changes in Coubertin's thinking in relation to the Olympic Movement was that in his attitude towards women. At one point in the early days he seemed totally opposed to their participation in the Games but he gradually changed his mind.

In his report on the 1920 Games he referred to the participation of women in the swimming events: 'they have excelled, beating their previous records'.

From 1900 he had protested against the differences between educational programs for girls and boys and deplored that 'certain careers which they would willingly take up are barred to women'. He was no less conscious of the importance, in women as in men, of the qualities of force, endurance, skill, objectivity, fair play and will, which sport developed. He was therefore very quickly a supporter of women's participation in gymnastics, dancing, games, then sporting competitions, but on certain conditions.

When he wrote on the subject in the *Olympic Review* of July 1912, he admitted that time, psychological and social factors would ensure the eventual admission of women.

In 1920 the Executive Committee of the IOC voted by a majority to admit women to the Olympic Games. But Coubertin was not happy.

Should women be allowed access to all Olympic sports? No. Then why allow them to take part in some and prohibit others? And, above all, upon what is the barrier between permitted and forbidden sports to be based?

By the latter days of his life, however, his only reservations were about the presence of the public at women's competitions, which was curious since he accepted women's presence in other forms of public life. He always opposed the injustices of which women were victims. Writing on *La Crise de Mariage et la Femme Nouvelle aux États-Unis* (The Crisis of Marriage and the New Woman in the United States) in 1920, he noted stages of women's evolution. Women were restricted for different reasons, he wrote, by war, economic conditions, the industrial revolution. When they worked at the same jobs as men, they claimed equality of rights, and, having proved that they possessed the same qualities they demanded access to the same careers. Women, he claimed, had exercised the right to vote in France since the first assembly of the États-Généraux and he admired the 'progressive boldness' that led Christine de Prisan to become a writer and avant-garde feminist in the fourteenth century.

In 1937 he said: 'Let women practise all the sports if they wish, but let them not show off.'

In the end, Coubertin's reservations only prompted the counter-propaganda brought about by sportswomen who were inadequately prepared or struggled in events that required mainly strength and violent effort, those that risked shocking the public and provoking its hostility against sportswomen in general.

So, in writing about the 1920 Games, after praising the women swimmers and tennis players, he commented, referring to certain athletic specialities and to football: 'Which sports practised by women would constitute therefore a *spectacle* suitable for the crowds that assemble for an Olympiad? We do not think that one can be claimed.'

He was worried by the possible reactions of the public to sportswomen and especially athletes – that possibility shocked him more than the reality of sporting women which he considered normal and even necessary.

At the Congress in Lausanne in 1921, France proposed to add to the Olympic Games a 'Week of Winter Sports' which would be organized the same year as the Games. This proposition aroused lively opposition, notably from the Scandinavians, who 'wanted no prizes' (*Mémoires Olympiques*), fearing that these events, if they were considered to be Olympic, would jeopardize their annual Nordic competitions.

Coubertin supported the Winter Games for reasons which seem ironic today:

Left Pierre de Coubertin during World War I. *Right* The memorial at Olympia, in Greece, containing the heart of the Founder of the Modern Games

In these twenty-five years, winter sports have been not only taken up in a number of other countries [other than Sweden], but they have demonstrated a quality of amateurism, of sporting dignity, so frank and pure that their total exclusion from the Olympic program would take away much of strength and value. (*Mémoires Olympiques*)

In the end, since Sigfrid Edström (of Sweden; later President of the IOC) did not oppose the IOC's giving its patronage to the 'Week of Winter Sports' which would be held in Chamonix in 1924, the Congress adopted this solution, while ruling that the events would not be considered as part of the Olympic Games. At the Congress in Prague in 1925, the IOC adopted a Charter for the Winter Games which gave them the name of 'Winter Olympic Games . . . subject to all the rules of the Olympic protocol'. The integration was therefore realized, and the Games at Chamonix were christened 'Olympic' retroactively at the IOC meeting in Lisbon in May 1926.

After the Games in 1924, Coubertin, considering himself too old (he was sixty-one), resigned the Presidency of the IOC with the intention of dedicating himself entirely to the reform of education and the popularization of culture. From time to time, however, he was to offer his experience and knowledge to sportsmen.

In 1927, speaking at Olympia, he said:

. . . My friends and I have not laboured to restore the Olympic Games to you in order to make them an object fit for a museum or a cinema; nor is it our wish that mercantile or electoral interest should seize upon them. Our object in reviving an institution twenty-five centuries old was that you should become new adepts of the religion of sport, as our great ancestors conceived it.

Coubertin defined 'religion' as a search for perfection. The Olympic athlete would not therefore regard sport as an end but as a means of acquiring a higher value in order to better serve his ideal of man.

Coubertin saw the transformation of education as an essential part of man's development. It should be the 'intellectual and moral fibre' which would enable the physical potential of the individual to be fully expressed. He advocated this ideal by writing articles and books,

and founding an association for the reform of teaching, the *Union Pédagogique Universelle* (Universal Pedagogical Union).

'The over-riding ideal of this system is that of a culture conceived as a principle of universal integration, or, if it is preferred, as a frame of reference within which will organize themselves all the knowledge and the experience of the adult,' wrote Professor Louis Meylan in *The Integral Humanism of Pierre de Coubertin*, in which he compared Coubertin's views with those expressed by Aldous Huxley in *Ends and Means*.

Naturally, the new system of teaching was also to be distinguished by the place of physical and sporting activities, the responsibility exercised by the pupils, their freedom of judgment and of expression.

It was essential, according to Coubertin, that the underprivileged should benefit in this reform of education. While he wanted 'industrial service' for everyone – an obligatory period in a workshop, factory, or on a building site – he called for permanent education and 'Workers' Universities'. He outlined his thoughts in a pamphlet published in 1921, *Les Universités Ouvrières:*

They ought to be the instruments of equalizing culture and free from all constraint . . . They will develop freely or else they will not survive. The direction must be left to the students. They are not children nor adolescents. They are adults who have jobs and are already in contact with the hard realities of existence. Moreover, they are sceptical and it is natural that they should be. This is a point of view which penetrates with great difficulty into the heads of the privileged. The latter imagine in all good faith that it is only necessary for them to approach the proletariat and hold out a hand for that hand to be seized with alacrity, gratitude and trust. That's a bit naïve. Even if alacrity and gratitude show themselves, it takes time for trust to be built up and for the memory of all the accumulated social injustices to fade away.

Inequality in the realm of teaching, Coubertin claimed, was one of the worst injustices for it created other forms of inequality. No aspects of culture should be refused to the working class.

'What,' it will be said to me, 'you want to teach all this to manual workers? What foolishness! They haven't the time nor the taste for such studies!' 'I know. I am familiar with this scorn and unbelief. When I wanted to restore the Olympic Games, I was considered mad!'

To reject convention, to propose other ideas which had not yet been tried out, to attempt to apply them, was to risk being taken for a madman – because Coubertin was actually a revolutionary.

He was really a revolutionary when, in order to force on his country educational changes which it did not want, he encouraged pupils to free themselves from authority and to demand reform from within. He was a revolutionary when he declared at the banquet at the end of the historic day of 23 June 1894:

The adherents of the old school were appalled when they saw us holding our meetings in the heart of the Sorbonne; they realized that we were rebels and that we would finish by casting down the edifice of their worm-eaten philosophy. It is true, gentlemen; we are rebels . . .

He was a revolutionary when he wanted to change fundamentally the teaching in schools and to create permanent education for all: 'It is a revolution that we are proposing,' he wrote, 'and one which cannot but cause the most vehement objections.'

He was a revolutionary, but precisely in order to avoid the revolution.

I have always loved and admired in history decisive and even rapid evolution: that is life. And been repelled by revolution: that is anger and most often thoughtlessness . . .

Still, there was 'revolution and revolution, according to whether it is concerned with satisfying needs or appetites'.

'If France had applied Pierre de Coubertin's ideas,' wrote Abbé Jean Toulat, 'she would have avoided the revolutionary outburst of 1968.'

The end of Coubertin's life was clouded by numerous dramas.

There were financial dramas: having spent most of his fortune in the service of sport, and having lost the rest in bad investments, he was to be seen, at the age of seventy-two, vainly attempting to obtain a salaried position; the family home of Mirville in Normandy, the maternal inheritance to which he was so deeply attached, was sold by his brother, and did not come back into his family until twenty-five years after his death.

There were family dramas: he had married, on 12 March 1895, Marie Rothan, of Alsatian origin. Charles de Coubertin was a close friend of Marie's father, who was a lover of art, a historian and diplomat. She gave him two children, a son who died young, and an artistic daughter, intelligent, but of fragile mental health.

Marie de Coubertin was to die at Lausanne on 6 May 1963, in her 102nd year. In spite of a difficult character, she remained faithfully and deeply attached to Pierre, whom she admired, accompanied him in his moves and tenderly sustained him in his dark hours. He loved her and could not do without her but suffered from her behaviour and from her unstable disposition.

And there was the drama of being misunderstood: if, in sport, his work has had results, his work for the reform of teaching left his contemporaries indifferent, as did his views on workers' education.

His country ignored or forgot him. But his stoic philosophy kept him from despair and so did his faith in youth that he retained until the end.

On 2 September 1937 he went for a walk in the Lagrange park in Geneva and collapsed and died from a heart attack. A few days before his death he had written:

Effort is the supreme joy. Success is not a goal, but a means to aim still higher. The individual has worth only in relation to humanity. He is created to act without giving up and to die with resignation.

His heart, which had beaten so much for others, rests at Olympia.

Olympia . . . that ground belongs to me, to the one who has made its soul and deep consciousness live again . . .

ELIGIBILITY AND AMATEURISM
Lord Killanin

The question who should be able to compete in the Olympic Games has not just been a subject of recent debate. It was one of the principal subjects at the Sorbonne Conference of 1894 which revived the Games, and across eighty years it has been a continual source of discussion for the International Olympic Committee.

At the IOC Session in Vienna in 1974 the new rule for Eligibility was introduced. This is the climax of the history traced here. Basically, the rule is short. It reads:

To be eligible for participation in the Olympic Games, a competitor must:

1. Observe and abide by the Rules and Regulations of the IOC and in addition the Rules and Regulations of his or her International Federation, as approved by the IOC, even if the Federation rules are more strict than those of the IOC.

2. Not have received any financial rewards or material benefit in connection with his or her sports participation, except as permitted in the bye-laws to this rule.

The Bye-Laws, which can be altered by a simple majority of the IOC, detail what an Olympic Competitor may and may not do.

1. *A Competitor may:*
a) Be a physical education or sports teacher who gives elementary instruction.
b) Accept, during the period of preparation and actual competition which shall be limited by the rules of each International Federation:

   i) Assistance administered through his or her National Olympic Committee or National Federation for:
Food and lodging
Cost of transport
Pocket money to cover incidental expenses
Insurance cover in respect of accidents, illness, personal property and disability
Personal sports equipment and clothing
Cost of medical treatment, physiotherapy and authorized coaches
   ii) Compensation, authorised by his or her National Olympic Committee or National Federation, in case of necessity, to cover financial loss resulting from his or her absence from work or basic occupation, on account of preparation for, or participation in, the Olympic Games and international sports competitions. In no circumstances shall payment made under this provision exceed the sum which the competitor would have earned in the same periods. The compensation may be paid with the approval of the national federations or the National Olympic Committees at their discretion.
c) Accept prizes won in competition within the limits of the rules established by the respective International Federations.
d) Accept academic and technical scholarships.

2. *A Competitor must not:*
a) Be or have been a professional athlete in any sport, or contracted to be so before the official closing of the Games.

b) Have allowed his person, name, picture or sports performance to be used for advertising, except when his or her International Federation, National Olympic Committee or National Federation enters into a contract for sponsorship or equipment. All payments must be made to the International Federation, National Olympic Committee or National Federation concerned, and not to the individual.

c) Carry advertising material on his person or clothing in the Olympic Games, World or Continental Championships and Games under patronage of the IOC, other than trade marks on technical equipment or clothing as agreed by the IOC with the International Federations.

d) Have acted as a professional coach or trainer in any sport.

3. *Eligibility Commission*

A commission may be appointed to enforce Rule 26 and these Bye-Laws, together with Rules 1 and 3 (fundamental principles), 7 (citizenship), 27 (special conditions), 33 (affiliation), 48 (reporting).

The word 'amateur', except under the heading of 'Fundamental Principles' and in relation to the controlling sports authorities, is not used in the current Olympic Rules. This reflects the positive effort to modernize the terms under which one person may compete in the Olympic Games, yet another making his living from sport should be barred. There were two main points of discussion in Vienna concerning this Rule and the Bye-Laws.

The first related to competitors carrying advertising material on their clothing or equipment. Normal trademarks are permitted but in certain sports, notably skiing and track and field, there is a recent tradition which permits competitors to carry advertising material on running numbers or bibs. This can be an embarrassment to the individual, who may find such advertising repugnant to his conscience (e.g. having to carry an advertisement for alcohol); he must therefore be offered protection.

The second problem was whether a sportsman who was a professional in one sport could be regarded as an amateur in another. Some Federations accept this under their own rules for non-Olympic competition. To my mind, in not agreeing to this, the IOC may have erred. In the past, for example, a professional jockey has boxed in Olympic competitions and a professional fencer has thrown the discus. This is no longer permissible.

In examining the origins of the modern Olympics and of these problems, one must be aware of the social climate and its divergent aspects at the time. At the end of the nineteenth century there were sports which were popular, such as football and cycling, and sports which were, by their nature, eclectic or expensive, such as equestrianism and yachting. Most of those competing in the sports that flourished in the early years of the twentieth century did so for enjoyment and recreation and not financial gain.

The response to the Olympic motto *Citius, Altius, Fortius* ('faster, higher, stronger') has not just come from the individual; at the opening Games in Athens there were thirteen competing countries; in 1972 there were 121 National Olympic Committees represented at the Games of Munich; in 1896 there were nine sports on the program and in 1972 twenty-one. In 1939 there were forty-seven

NOCs recognized by the IOC, while in the decades after World War II, the numbers increased from sixty-three in 1950 to ninety-five in 1960 and 127 in 1970, with the total in 1974 of 132. This increase was due partly to the increase in the number of sovereign nations in the gaining of independence by countries such as Ireland and the breaking up of the Austro-Hungarian Empire. After World War II many countries in Africa and Asia obtained their independence. The first step taken by many newly independent countries has been to develop the sports facilities which previously were restricted to the colonial powers.

At the same time, communications have improved. Perhaps the most important innovation has been the development of air transport, reducing the travelling time from London to Melbourne, for instance, from five weeks by steamer to twenty-four hours by plane; from Sydney to New York from five weeks through the Panama Canal by ship to less than thirty hours by air. This has increased international competition in many sports, and this competition in turn has increased the standard of performance.

Another aspect of communication – that provided by the media – has played a crucial part. At the turn of the century the exploits of the Olympic competitor were communicated by the Press only and photographs were transmitted to newspapers by wire, relatively slowly. Today people throughout the world are able to watch on television at home sporting events as they happen, from all the continents. This has led to a greater interest in and knowledge of all sports in many countries. The enormous growth and development of some sports since World War II can be directly related to their suitability for television.

All these influences must be borne in mind when the eligibility of the Olympic competitor is considered.

The first amateur ruling appears in Bulletin No. 1 of the IOC dated July 1894:

I An amateur in athletics is to be considered as any person who has never participated in a competition open to all comers, or competed for a cash prize or a sum of money from whatever source, in particular entry to the grounds – or with professionals – and who has never at any time of his life been a paid teacher or instructor of physical education.

II Whoever has been disqualified may only be requalified if the Union, Federation or Society upon which he depends in the last instance decides that the disqualification was caused by error, ignorance or good faith.

III A person who procures money through the prizes he has won loses even his amateur status on this account. The value of works of art is not necessarily limited but is not in general to reach too high a figure.

IV Money obtained from entry to the grounds may be divided among the Societies taking part as a travel indemnity, but never among the competitors themselves.

V Public betting being incompatible with amateurism, the Societies are to stop or restrain it by every means within their power and especially by opposing its official organization in the competition areas.

VI The tendency of every sport without exception must be towards pure amateurism, with no permanent motive existing in any sport to justify cash prizes; but as far as horse racing, shooting and yachting are concerned, the general definition of an amateur must not be applied to them temporarily.

VII A competitor may not be an amateur in one sport and a professional in another.

The first review of these original Rules began with a questionnaire sent out in 1901. The London paper *Sporting Life* in 1908 followed up the enquiry with one of its own to all the various interested groups. Not surprisingly, widely divergent views were expressed, and these were reflected by the various countries and sporting groups competing in the Games of 1908 in London. There was a desire for reform but no agreement on the solution.

The value of the IOC's independence was made evident at this point and particularly at its Berlin Session in 1909, as it was a body of individuals endeavouring to look at the problem objectively and independently, not a committee representing nations nor a grouping of international federations.

By that year, the 'Shamateur' or false amateur (a person who received money or other reward outside the rules allowed by his competition) had already surfaced; while he was despised, it was fully admitted by the IOC as a whole that most professionals were excellent sportsmen.

At the beginning of the century the problems were much as they are now. They included payments from money which might be part of the gate takings, or betting, or the free issue of clothes and equipment. Athletes were giving testimonials for equipment but any reward had to be in kind and not cash. However, some athletes accepted money and, when they were discovered, lost their amateur status.

The reimbursement of normal expenses had become accepted by most of the International Federations but 'broken time' (compensation for loss of wages or salary during competition) does not appear to have been raised. When the world had cavalries, it was considered justifiable for an officer – but not a soldier of lower rank – to be an amateur. This situation continued until after World War II. Sweden indeed lost a gold medal which its team had won for dressage in 1948. Twelve months after the Games the International Equestrian Federation (FEI) disqualified the team after discovering that one member, Gehnäll Persson, was not a commissioned officer.

In the replies to the *Sporting Life* questions, the large majority considered that an amateur who had competitive contact with a professional immediately lost his amateur status. It appears that by 1900 the rules laid down in 1894 had been modified, since at the Paris Games special regulations were made for professionals.

It is a possibility, and indeed a likelihood, that an amateur world champion or Olympic medallist may turn professional as a result of his success. My personal view has always been that this is in order outside the Games and I am not against open competition outside the Games if the International Federations agree.

The question of whether coaches and physical training instructors should be considered professionals was also raised. For over sixty years this problem of instructors and coaches has worried International Federations and the IOC.

All these points were discussed at the Berlin Session in

The design of Olympic medals has not always been standard. In 1896 only the first and second places were recognized, the winner had a silver medal, the second a bronze, designed by Jules Chaplain of France. Gold medals were first awarded to winners in 1908.

1936

1948

1952

1956

1956
Equestrian Games

1960

1964

1968

1972

1909 but no policy was agreed. The Americans, whose development of sport, particularly at colleges and universities, was much more sophisticated than in most countries, urgently required to know the dividing line between amateur and professional. Professor William M. Sloane (United States) was instructed to consult both the university and non-university associations in the United States on these questions. Among the conclusions were: that an athlete should not profit directly in money or money's worth and remain an amateur; that no limit should be put on the expenses of a competitor; that an amateur should not compete with a professional, except in teams; that a competitor should not be professional in one sport and amateur in another. There was complete division on whether there was a difference between a professor of sport (i.e. a coach) and a professional. There was again division on whether an international or national federation should disqualify a competitor believed to be a professional or whether he automatically disqualified himself. The United States appears to have been more flexible in trying to produce a rule to embrace all sports than the British. Theodore Cook, IOC member in Britain, discovered that each sport had made its own regulations and he reported that he had found it difficult to write a rule for all sports. He pointed out that members of the Royal Yacht Squadron and the Jockey Club were not above receiving large prizes in kind and paying professionals to help them win their competitions and races. He drew attention to the fact that if this applied to track and field, lawn tennis and swimming, the people involved would be rapidly excluded from competition because this was against the amateur rules in those sports. Cook felt that the IOC should persuade the large international sports associations to agree upon a rule, which the smaller federations would then follow.

In the meantime, Jules de Muzsa (Hungary) had discovered that the Europeans had not shown the same enthusiasm as the United States or the British for views expressed by various national federations. The Italian Athletic Federation did not believe that one could be professional in one sport and amateur in another but fully agreed to the reimbursement of all expenses. The Italians also felt that there was no danger in contact between a professional and an amateur, a view expressed more strongly by the Netherlands Amateur Fencing Association but opposed by the Netherlands Gymnastic Association. The Belgian Gymnastic Federation considered professionals to be those who appeared in public to earn a direct financial reward.

These discussions were brought to a head at the IOC Session in Budapest in 1911 when R. S. de Courcy Laffan (Great Britain) presented a new definition of an amateur which he hoped would be adopted for the Olympic Games:

Any person is entitled to compete in the Olympic Games as an amateur as long as he has never:
A a) competed in an athletic meeting for a cash prize, money, or any kind of wager;
b) been rewarded by money or any kind of pecuniary

From 1928 the design for both sides of the medals by Prof. Giuseppe Cassioli (Italy) depicting victory, fraternity and universality became the standard. The reverse side was changed in 1972.

benefit for having participated in an athletic competition, exhibition or representation;

(NB: The repayment to a competitor, by the Society which selected him to represent it, of the travel and hotel expenses he thus incurred does not entail the loss of his amateur status.)

c) received either directly or indirectly any kind of payment or premium to make up for the time he may have lost by competing or training to compete in athletic competition;

d) sold or pawned a prize won in an athletic competition;

B a) received pecuniary benefit from the teaching of any athletic exercise or from services he may have given;

b) accepted paid employment on the formal or tacit condition that he must encourage, teach or take part in any athletic exercise, the practice, encouragement or teaching of which do not form part of the normal functions of this employment;

C a) competed in an athletic meeting open to persons other than amateurs;

b) competed in an athletic meeting against a professional whether for a prize or not;

c) been recognized as a professional or disqualified forever as an amateur in any other sport whatever.

This text was adopted and it was hoped that after the 1912 Games it would become the basic rule for all amateur sports. Four years of war followed the Games of 1912 and the question did not arise again until the 1920 Session of the IOC in Antwerp. From this period onwards the definition of amateurism became a matter of increasing concern for the IOC because of the growth of professional sport. The outcome of the Antwerp meeting was that each International Federation would write its own rule but that the IOC must maintain its ultimate authority. At this point, too, in the life of the IOC, there were other important developments – women were formally admitted to the Games and Count Clarence von Rosen (Sweden) asked if a staff consisting of a secretary and shorthand typist could be made available to the IOC. This is the first reference to IOC headquarters staff.

The IOC appreciated that National Olympic Committees carried out different functions: some were concerned only in the preparation of their team for the Games (and were not necessarily permanent), others had a much wider brief of sport in their country, both in physical education and on the organizational side. It was therefore at this Session in 1920 that the first rules intended to coordinate and organize all NOCs along similar lines were introduced.

One important point now arose which had not been mentioned previously – pocket money for athletes. It was raised by the President (Coubertin), who pointed out that there were rich and poor athletes. It was decided that the qualifications for an Olympic competitor at the Games of 1920 should include that only a person born with or having acquired the nationality of a country, or the sovereign state of which this country was a constituent part, should be eligible to represent that country at the Olympic Games. A person who had already competed in the Olympic Games could not compete in the Games of the following Olympiad for another country, even after acquiring its nationality by naturalization, except in the case of conquest or the creation of a new state. There was to be no age limit for competitors. Women were to be admitted to the Games.

In 1921, the IOC met at Lausanne, where Courcy Laffan said that the Olympic Games must not become a 'nursery for professionals'. In the discussion that followed, M. Gautier-Vignal (Monaco) suggested that the names of winners who turned professional should be marked in some way in the Olympic records. A new set of rules was introduced:

1. *Definition of an amateur*

The amateur rule drawn up by the International Sports Federations is respected for the admission of athletes taking part in the Olympic Games.

If there is no international federation governing a sport, the definition will be drawn up by the Organising Committee in agreement with the IOC. The national federation, governing a particular sport in each country, must certify on the entry form that each competitor is an amateur in accordance with the rules of the International Federation governing this sport.

This declaration must be countersigned by the National Olympic Committee of this country. This Committee must also declare that it considers the competitor an amateur according to the definition of the International Federation concerned.

All was not to go smoothly. In 1922 in rowing, which was in every sense a truly amateur sport then as it is now, there was a conflict between the Amateur Rowing Association (of England), which was recognized by the International Federation (FISA) but not by the British Olympic Association, and the National Amateur Rowing Association. The ARA rule, which prevented manual labourers from competing, deprived people eligible under the IOC rule from competing in the Games. The President of the IOC (Coubertin) rightly said that this was in complete defiance of democracy but that he could not interfere in internal International Federation disputes unless invited to do so.

In 1923 the IOC was back again on the question of broken time, which was raised by Sigfrid Edström (Sweden), later President of the IOC during World War II. He was concerned with compensation for loss of earnings caused by an athlete's participation in international competition. Laffan said that before condemning this practice completely it should be remembered that this was a period of general democratization, in which the amateur point of view was evolving like every other:

> Would we have accepted twenty-five years ago that an athlete whose travel expenses were paid could continue to be considered an amateur? But if we do accept the indemnity principle, it must never on any account exceed the equivalent of the daily salary.

Count von Rosen wondered why the trade unions could not support this type of expense. Count Henri de Baillet-Latour (Belgium), later also to be IOC President, said that in Chile a public subscription had been raised for an athlete from which he obtained advantages which were competely incompatible with his theoretical status as an amateur.

General Kentish (Great Britain) took a conservative

1928

1924 1932 1936 1948

For the Winter Games cities have not been required to maintain a continuing design.

view, saying that if a workman wanted to compete he must do so during his holiday time. He did not appear to realize that there might be a difference between a workman with a week's holiday a year and a student with perhaps four or five months in the summer or an officer who could get extra leave.

Once again the IOC kicked for touch and referred the matter of broken time to its Congress, to be held in Prague in 1925. It had progressed further in 1924 in Paris, where the Olympic oath, which was to be signed by the individual, was not considered sufficient proof of his amateur status. Baillet-Latour took up the following recommendations of the Executive:

Without going into the details of a definition which is still difficult to establish, the International Olympic Committee considers it would be suitable to understand by 'amateur' a person who obtains no appreciable material benefit from sport and is prepared to declare this in writing upon his honour, and by 'professional' a person who directly or indirectly receives material benefit from the personal practice of sport.

At Prague the following year the outcome of the Congress was:

1. *Amateurism*
The Amateur Status drawn up by the International Sports Federations is respected for the eligibility of athletes taking part in the Olympic Games.

However the athletes taking part in the Olympic Games must satisfy the following minimum obligations, i.e.
1. A person who is or has been wittingly a professional in his sport or in another sport, or
2. a person who has received payments in compensation for loss of salary
may not be qualified to take part in the Games.

The International Federations and NOCs were asked to study the suggestions contained in the fourth and seventh principles of the Congress Report of the Amateurism Commission, which were:

4th principle: Trainers, monitors, instructors and coaches teaching competition sport for direct or indirect financial gain may neither compete nor be judges or jurymen in the Olympic Games. Teachers who do not in particular teach or instruct sport and competition exercises may compete and be jurymen at the Olympic Games.

7th principle: Prolonged sports competitions which take place in a country far from a competitor's own country are to be condemned and it is recommended as a general rule that no competitor remains away from his home to take part in sports competitions more than two weeks in any one year. It is appreciated that for important international competitions such as the Olympic Games and for national competitions in countries with a large surface area, distances make certain exceptions necessary. These exceptions should be rare and brought under strict regulation.

The declaration of honour necessary for qualification to the Olympic Games shall be as follows, as the IOC has decided:

'I, the undersigned, declare on my honour that I am an amateur in accordance with the Olympic rules on amateurism.'

This oath, signed by each competitor, is considered sufficient and no other method of control, apart from that foreseen in the GENERAL RULES, is recommended.

After the Congress the International Federations, some being more active than others, continued their discussions which included not only the definition of an amateur but also the whole question of the length of time for international competitions both at home and abroad. The International Amateur Athletic Federation (IAAF) decided on 27 August 1926:

No amateur shall have the right to receive payment for his travelling and other expenses, to enable him to take part in competitions abroad for a longer sojourn than twenty-one days in all per calendar year spent in foreign countries. Accumulation of these twenty-one days in two consecutive years cannot be allowed. An extension can be given the athlete by the Association of his country, if he is selected by said Association to take part in Olympic Games or represent his country in matches against another country. The Council of the IAAF is entitled to make extensions also in other cases if it deems proper. The National Associations are responsible for the faithful observance of the above rule and shall keep a complete record of time spent abroad and expenses incurred by their athletes, the record to be laid before the IAAF if called for.

Edström, President of the IAAF and one of the IOC members in Sweden, subsequently requested that this decision should be communicated to all the International Federations and that the IOC itself should take no immediate steps. Neither the discussions with the International Federations nor the IOC Congress at Budapest had resulted in any firm decisions, and at the 1929 Lausanne IOC Session the most important point was to find clear definitions of payment for lost time and leave with salary, since the former was prohibited and the latter approved in the Olympic regulations. The President said that apart from the situation in England, almost every athlete in every sport received indemnities. If he was not well off it would be impossible for him to take part in international competitions. Was it better to close one's eyes to the situation or to draw up a broader rule which could be applied?

Once again, the IOC kicked for touch, after studying a definition of the Amateur Rule provided by the International Association Football Federation (FIFA) for the 1930 Olympic Congress at Berlin. The IOC believed that it held the exclusive right to decide who should compete in the Olympic Games. On no account would it admit the principle of broken time.

At the Barcelona Session in 1931 Baillet-Latour said:

> . . . You will be pleased to learn that the unanimous agreement reached [at a meeting of the Council of Delegates of the International Federations and the Executive Board in 1930] is in complete conformity with the Amateurism Commission's proposal made at Berlin, and which was adopted by the Congress with a large majority.

> Paid leave is only authorized as long as the employer does not claim reimbursement from a federation or an official body for the salary he pays his employee during the length of his leave to participate in a sports tournament. We can therefore consider this question of qualifications for the Olympic Games, from the theoretic point of view, settled to everybody's satisfaction.

So the Olympic Movement proceeded to the 1932 Games in Los Angeles, where the question of semi-professionalism (small irregular payments) was raised at the request of the IAAF and a special committee set up to discuss the matter. This committee proposed the following for the Executive to discuss at Vienna in 1933:

I National Federations and National Olympic Committees must refuse to countersign the Amateur's declaration when there is the slightest doubt about the Amateur status of a competitor without regard to national or individual interest.

II It is necessary to impress on athletes the importance of the oath and to make them understand that they offend the codes of honour by signing a false declaration.

III It is necessary to improve by every available means Physical Education in Schools, Colleges and Universities of the countries where it has hitherto been neglected with the idea of making it possible to recruit Olympic competitors amongst the young.

IV It is necessary to limit very strictly the number of International matches.

V It is necessary to recommend as a general rule that no competitor should spend more than *two weeks* of any year away from home competing in any one sport except when longer leave of absence is necessary in order to compete in the Olympic Games or in the Championships of Europe.

VI It is necessary to recommend that for every sport a Professional section should be inaugurated to enable those who wish to turn Professional to do so.

VII It is necessary to get the leaders of University sports to use their own Championships as trials for the Olympic Games.

VIII It is advisable to recommend International Federations to come to an agreement on the following questions:

   1. Contamination [amateurs competing with or against professionals]

   2. Professionals incompatible with Amateurism

   3. Compulsory classification of coaches, trainers and instructors as professionals.

IX It is necessary to consider before solving these problems the Charter of Sporting Reforms drafted by Baron P. de Coubertin [a document written by Coubertin in 1930].

The Vienna Session was also to hear a report from Paul Rousseau, a member of the French Olympic Committee and National Committee of Sports, which raised for the first time the question of doping in relation to eligibility. This arose from the Games at Los Angeles where some Japanese swimmers were said to have been given oxygen by their doctors between races. Muscular injections were also included in Rousseau's report.

At a meeting of the International Federations in 1934 it was resolved to confirm that all correspondence and negotiations about competitions and tours of sportsmen in foreign countries should be supervised and sanctioned by the national association of the competitor's country and the national association of the visited country. This was decided because some clubs had asked for 'appearance money' for prominent athletes. All payments of the competitor's actual expenses were to be sent to the association in future and not to the competitor. It was decided that the duration of competition in foreign countries should not exceed twenty-one days in any calendar year with the exception of the time taken for the Olympic Games, official championships and international meetings arranged officially through the Federations. International Federations, NOCs and National Sporting Associations were implored to keep the Olympic ideal and not permit any transgression in the smallest way of the amateur rule. The emphasis on the importance of the part played by schools and colleges to produce Olympic championships indicates that the IOC was still mainly involved with those from higher education levels rather than with the less privileged. There was a liberalization, however, in that the IOC realized that amateurs could become professionals and further did not disqualify from Olympic participation those involved in competition with professionals.

The following year, 1935, the IOC was faced with another sport with 'professional problems', ice skating. It was rumoured that skaters were signing contracts before the 1936 Olympics and a secret minute of the Session requested that information should be given to the President of the suggested breaches.

The highly political Games of 1936 passed but in 1937 the question of long training periods caused by nationalism in sport and the introduction of training camps arose. There had been wide criticism of Germany's policy of camps for both Games of 1936.

1952

1956

Changes in the medals of the Winter Games reflect the attitude that they are only lately members of the Olympic family.

It was also at Warsaw in 1937 that Lord Burghley (now the Marquess of Exeter) gave a report on doping and the first doping commission was set up.

The IOC Session of 1938 at Cairo produced another hazard: the question of competitors writing for newspapers was discussed again; it had first appeared on an IOC agenda in 1924. It was ruled that athletes who used their sporting prowess to exploit it for journalism, theatre, cinema or radio were in breach of the Olympic spirit. It did also rule that competitors could be paid by their employers, provided the amount was not above the competitors' normal wages or salary and that in further exceptional cases, payment could be made to a family which might suffer due to the athlete's absence. This progress came to an abrupt stop with World War II.

It was not until 1946 that, under the presidency of Sigfrid Edström, amateurism was once more discussed. Bo Ekelund (Sweden) proposed that the difference between amateurs and professionals should be abolished, or at least that the word 'amateur' should be. This brought an objection from Avery Brundage (United States), who said for the first recorded time that he had never heard of an athlete who was prevented from taking part in the Olympic Games for financial reasons. He strongly attacked materialism and the excesses of sport, which to him was purely a *divertissement*. This approach, which was to be Brundage's basic philosophy, received rapturous applause.

An Amateur Commission was set up under the presidency of Brundage, including R. W. Seeldrayers (Belgium), Bo Ekelund (Sweden) and Billy Holt, not a member of the IOC but a representative of the IAAF (he was the Hon. Secretary of that organization). The commission reported at the Session in Stockholm on 17 June 1947 as follows:

Definition of an Amateur
An amateur is one whose connection with sport is and always has been solely for pleasure and for the physical, mental or social benefits he derives therefrom and to whom sport is nothing more than recreation without material gain of any kind, direct or indirect. As a condition precedent to taking part in the Olympic Games a competitor must be an amateur and a member of an organization affiliated with the International Federation recognized by the International Olympic Committee as governing the sport in which he is to participate. The National Association, which in each country governs each particular sport, must certify on a special form provided by the Organizing Committee that each competitor is an amateur in accordance with the rules of the International Federation governing that sport. This declaration must be countersigned by the National Olympic Committee, which shall verify that the competitors are amateurs according to the rules of the International Federation concerned and of the IOC. Finally, each competitor must sign the following statement:

'I, the undersigned, declare on my honour that I am an amateur according to the rules of the International Federation governing my sport, that I have never knowingly transgressed such rules and that I have participated in sport solely for pleasure and for the physical, mental or social benefits I derive therefrom: that sport to me is nothing more than a recreation without material gain of any kind, direct or indirect, and that I am eligible in all respects for participation in the Olympic Games.'

With these rules the Games of Helsinki took place in 1952 but at the Session in Mexico in 1953 Brundage, elected President the year before, mentioned that during the conference of the Executive and the NOCs, several delegates had expressed their indignation when they heard that some professional players, parading as amateurs, had been participating in the Helsinki Games. The permission given in 1938 for the payment of compensation had become one of broken time which had therefore been tacitly approved. It came up for discussion again the following year.

The Sessions of the IOC in Paris in 1955 and Tokyo in 1958 brought reminders from the President of the importance of sticking to the 1947 Stockholm rule. In the meantime, several cases of commercial advertising containing photographs of well-known Olympic athletes had been reported to the IOC office. In some instances the benefit had gone to the national sports federations but it was impossible to be sure that athletes had not received direct payment. Meanwhile another Amateur Commission, consisting of the members of the Executive Board with Albert Meyer (Switzerland), François Piétri (France), Mohammed Taher (Egypt) and Ivar Vind (Denmark) continued to study the rules and at the Athens Session on 21 June 1961 a new text was submitted for consideration the following year:

Amateurism Rule 26
An amateur is one who participates and always has participated in sport without material gain. To qualify as an amateur, it is necessary to comply with the following conditions:

a) Have a normal occupation destined to ensure his present and future livelihood.
b) Never have received any payment for taking part in any sports competitions.
c) Comply with the rules of the International Federation concerned.
d) Comply with the official interpretation of this regulation.

This rule was approved in Moscow in 1962. There were problems with this brief rule, for at the Baden-Baden Session in 1963 Lord Exeter proposed an amendment to it under the heading 'Official Interpretations'. This was accepted as follows:

1960 1964 1968 1972

The figures on the Squaw Valley (1960) medal represent American youth; Grenoble (1968) carried its own Olympic symbol of a snowflake and three roses.

The IOC reserves to itself the right to make exceptions to these rules in the case of sports or individuals, provided that the basic principle that an athlete does not make a profit or livelihood out of his sport is not infringed.

The rule was also discussed very fully with the NOCs at a meeting with the Executive Board at Baden-Baden. There was, for the first time, specific reference to state amateurs, soldiers taken off military duties and placed in training camps where they received intensive coaching, and other 'amateurs' holding scholarships at school or university given purely on athletic prowess. There was also at this time a conflict within the IOC, headed by Brundage, over manufacturers' advertising on skis which started at the 1964 Winter Games and culminated with the problems of the International Ski Federation at the Innsbruck Session and went on to Sapporo in 1972.

Also, the IOC suggested to FIFA and the International Cycling Union (UCI) that an independent amateur federation should be created within a year. This, in my view, was a mistake. It was barely implemented other than that each set up a separate committee but both were administered by the same staff. I have always felt that it is often easier for one body to control amateur and professional sport as its members are the people who know who is paid and who is not paid. The professional is the first to endeavour to prevent the amateur taking his money.

At this 1964 Session no change was made in the amateur rule except that the duration of training camps, which had become general in the 1950s, was extended from three weeks to four in any one year.

In 1965 in Madrid a new Eligibility Commission was set up under the chairmanship of Hugh Weir (Australia), who reported to the Rome Session in the following year. The Commission regarded amateurism as an ideal, finding it difficult to produce a simple definition to meet the rules, which demanded that participation in the Olympic Games should be confined to amateurs:

The subject is one which all realize requires constant and intensive study and, even though it has caused concern for many years, should not now be approached with haste.

The Commission took the view that the most effective method to ensure that the Games were confined to amateurs was the establishment of a code enumerating infringements rendering a competitor ineligible.

Hugh Weir was to continue as President of the Eligibility Commission and took a most active part in keeping the Olympic Games and amateurism free from professionalism up to his death in 1975.

At the IOC Session at Teheran in 1967 Constantin Andrianov (USSR) said:

The unsuccessful discussion concerning amateurism in sport has been lasting for many years. Over fifty years the IOC has been endeavouring to find a way out of the deadlock created to a certain extent due to the IOC itself. The IOC endeavours to prove to the world its own point of view without taking into account the requirements of life and conditions in which the modern sport is developing. This is one of the most knotty questions, and it seems necessary to find out a new approach to this problem, renouncing the antiquated formulas of the amateur status, formulated at the end of the nineteenth century. What significance has, for example, the fact that some champions leave amateur sport for a professional one? They are few in all and this should not call sanctions against the sports discipline as a whole.

We should be able to muster sufficient courage and, in the face of the modern requirements, to determine the new rules of amateur status, and not to cling to the former ones, which . . . are very often violated. We should make our choice in this question too. It is proposed that the IOC should work out new eligibility rules for the Olympic Games.

This summed up the situation and shifted the IOC's position to a more modern one. The Commission reported the following year at the full Session in Grenoble, asking for more time, but raised the important point that it would be wrong for the IOC to have rules less strict than those of some of the International Federations. There was still no report from the Mexico City Session, although by then various suggestions had been made by members to alter the rule.

A number of IOC/NOC joint commissions had been set up at Mexico and at the Warsaw Session in 1969 a full report on amateurism was received. Alexandru Siperco (Romania), who had presided over a joint commission, recognized that political and social changes had taken place in sport. It was as a result of this commission's report, together with that of Hugh Weir, that the three Vice-Presidents (Count Jean de Beaumont, Jonkheer Herman van Karnebeek and myself) were given the task in October 1970 of discussing eligibility with all the International Federations. It was discovered that there were many different views on eligibility. Popularity for competitor and spectator, television appeal, potential professional attraction and cost of equipment were all factors examined by the Vice-Presidents.

After some exhaustive interviewing and research, the three Vice-Presidents drafted a rule which did away with the restrictions about the number of days a competitor could go away to a training camp in any one year. But the President (Brundage) considered this, and other items, too liberal and made some drastic alterations. The result was the following:

Eligibility Code Rule 26

I To be eligible for participation in the Olympic Games, a competitor must observe the traditional Olympic spirit and ethic and have always participated in sport as an avocation without having received any remuneration for his participation.

His livelihood must not be derived from or be dependent upon income from sport and he must be engaged in a basic occupation to provide for his present and future.

He must not be, or have been, a professional, semi-professional or so-called 'non-amateur' in any sport. He must not have coached, taught or trained sports competitors for personal gain. Physical education teachers who instruct beginners are eligible.

II A competitor must observe and abide by the Rules of the International Federation that controls the sport in which he participates, even if these Rules should be stricter than those imposed by the International Olympic Committee.

He must comply with his Federation's directives and those issued by the International Olympic Committee.*

*The International Olympic Committee's directives are:
a) He must not have directly or indirectly allowed his name, his photograph or his sports performance to be used individually for advertising purposes.
b) He may not write or sign any publication or allow any to be signed on his behalf, nor may he appear on radio or television during the Olympic Games in which he is participating without the permission of his chef de mission.
c) Advertising resulting from any equipment contracts by National Federations shall be strictly controlled by the International Federations, and copies of such contracts shall be lodged with and approved by the International Olympic Committee.

III A competitor is permitted to accept:

1. Assistance via his National Olympic Committee or National Sports Federation during the recognised periods for training and participation in competitions including the Olympic Games. Such assistance shall include only: lodging in training, food, transport, sports equipment and installations, coaching, medical care, as well as pocket money to cover incidental expenses within the limits agreed by his respective International Sports Federation or by his National Olympic Committee.

The recognised period for full time training, where agreed by the International Federations or National Olympic Committees must not normally exceed an aggregate of 30 days and in no case exceed 60 in one calendar year.

2. Insurance coverage in respect of accidents or illness in connection with training or competition.

3. Scholarships granted in accordance with academic and technical standards, dependent upon the fulfillment of scholastic obligations and not on athletic prowess.

4. Prizes won in competition within the limits of the Rules established by the respective International Federations and approved by the International Olympic Committee.

5. The International Olympic Committee is opposed to payment for broken time, except that compensation in deserving cases may be authorised by National Olympic Committees or International Federations to cover only the loss of salary or wages resulting from the competitor's absence from work on account of participation in the Olympic Games and important international sports meetings approved by the International Federations. Under no circumstances may payment made under this provision exceed the sum which the competitor would have earned in his occupation over the same period.

IV It is intended to eliminate those who are interested in sport for financial reasons and to confine the Olympic Games to those eligible according to this rule and a Committee will be established to consult and cooperate with International Federations and National Olympic Committees in its enforcement.

Doping

Any athlete refusing to take a doping test or who is found guilty of doping shall be eliminated from the Olympic Games by the International Federation concerned, following the proposal of the IOC Medical Commission.

If the athlete belongs to a team, the game or competition in question shall be forfeited by that team.

After the explanations of the team have been considered and the case discussed with the International Federation concerned, a team in which one or more members have been found guilty of doping may be disqualified from the Olympic Games.

In certain sports, in which a team may no longer compete after a member has been disqualified, the remaining members may compete on an individual basis.

A medal shall be withdrawn by decision of the IOC Executive Board, following the proposal of the IOC Medical Commission.

The above regulations shall in no way affect further sanctions by the International Federations.

Non-amateurs and semi-professionals

Individuals subsidized by governments, educational institutions, or business concerns because of their athletic ability are not amateurs. Business and industrial concerns sometimes employ athletes for their advertising value. The athletes are given paid employment with little work to do and are free to practise and compete at all times. For national aggrandizement, governments occasionally adopt the same methods and give athletes positions in the Army, on the police force or in a government office. They also operate training camps for extended periods. Some colleges and universities offer outstanding athletes scholarships and inducements of various kinds. Recipients of these special favours which are granted only because of athletic ability are not eligible to compete in the Olympic Games.

The IOC reserves to itself the right to make exceptions to these rules in the case of sports or individuals, provided that the basic principles that a competitor does not make a profit or livelihood out of his sport is not infringed, and that this right should be vested in the Executive Board.

Every time I read this rule, accepted in 1971 and used for the Games held the following year in Sapporo and Munich, I realized that it was full of anomalies and was not laid out in the manner one would expect to find. If there can be any excuse, it was that the Eligibility Commission and the Vice-Presidents had been working intensively in one or two areas and had not achieved the right sort of balance.

By the beginning of 1972 the Eligibility Commission had become an enforcement/fact-finding commission. Their task was to question the eligibility of competitors, and their work soon brought uproar throughout the sporting world. At Sapporo they recommended that Karl Schranz (Austria) be disqualified and, after examining the evidence, the Executive Board and then the IOC supported their action. The outcry was largely because it was well known that if Schranz was ineligible then so were other skiers. But the case against Schranz was proven. While others may have been guilty of receiving payments for skiing and inducements to wear certain clothing and use particular equipment, Schranz, having signed the Olympic entry form, did not deny newspaper reports that he was earning between $40,000 and $50,000 a year from skiing when interviewed in the Olympic Village by Will Grimsley of Associated Press. That, as far as many IOC members were concerned, was the final impertinence.

I had always been worried about implementing the Amateur Rule because there were three people responsible: the participant (who must know whether he is eligible or not), the National Federation, which certainly should know about the competitor's eligibility, and the NOC, which may not necessarily know whether the competitor is eligible. One of my first duties as President of the IOC was to preside over the Congress at Varna in 1973 where the subject of eligibility arose frequently. There the International Federations made it clear that a short rule would suffice and submitted the following:

> A competitor to take part in the Olympic Games must be eligible in accordance with the rules and regulations of his International Federation, as approved by the IOC.
>
> He shall be eligible provided he has not derived any personal profit from competing in his sport.

Having listened to the divergent views of the International Federations and the NOCs, I decided that with the three Vice-Presidents (Count Jean de Beaumont, Jonkheer Herman van Karnebeek and Willi Daume) and under my chairmanship, we would go back again and interview all the Federations separately. The reports on these interviews and discussions are voluminous and at times contradictory. As a result of the discussions, initially with the Federations and then with the Executive Board, keeping the IOC and NOCs fully informed, the new draft rule, quoted at the beginning of this article, on page 143, was instituted in 1974 in an effort to bring the Olympic Movement up to date.

ORGANIZING THE GAMES
Dr H. C. Willi Daume

The responsibility of the Olympic Games is borne by the International Olympic Committee. To some extent, it holds all the idealistic and material rights to this event, the greatest in the world. The organizers of the Games can be either a National Olympic Committee (NOC) or a committee formed especially for this purpose. But this body acts only by order of the IOC.

Candidates for organizing the Olympic Games and the Winter Olympics can only be cities, not sporting organizations or a region or a country. The reason for cities rather than countries being candidates is that originally Coubertin wanted to eliminate the possibility of governmental influence. When the Olympics were revived, sporting organizations were not strong enough to bear the financial risks involved in the Games. Coubertin attached great importance to the 'unity of place and time'. This fundamental conception has remained unchanged and the special function of the city for the celebration of an Olympiad is expressed in the IOC's rules time and again. For example, it is laid down in the rules that the Mayor of the previous Olympic City must have the official flag of the IOC kept in the principal municipal building during the four years until the next Games in order to hand it over to the Mayor of the new Olympic City at the official Opening Ceremony. Application by cities to stage the Games is normally made six months before the Session of the IOC which takes place six years before the respective year of the Games. The Games of the twenty-second Olympiad in 1980, for example, were allocated to Moscow at the IOC Session in Vienna in 1974.

If more than one city in a country wishes to invite the IOC to celebrate the Olympics there, it is the responsibility of that country's NOC to decide which city should be the candidate. The NOC must then also ensure that the town is suitable for staging the Games and support its candidature at the IOC. The government of the country also plays a responsible part in the application; it must submit to the IOC a written authorization that it guarantees adherence to the IOC's rules, which specify unhindered entry of all those involved in the Games – competitors, officials and journalists – the avoidance of racial or ideological discrimination, and so on. The candidate city must also fill in a detailed questionnaire drawn up by the IOC, asking for information on the nature and size of the competition and training sites offered, hotel facilities, plans for the Olympic Village, ideas for the Fine Arts program, whether adherence to all the IOC's rules and regulations can be guaranteed, and so on.

When a city has been chosen to stage the Games, it sets up, under the guidance and influence of the National Olympic Committee, an Organizing Committee, which throughout the six years grows, first through the planning stages, then through the building of stadia and other installations; it finally ensures that the thousands of employees needed during the period just before, during and immediately after the Games are available. The Organization thus grows from a small advisory group to one responsible for the work of several thousands of people, who in turn ensure that competitors, officials and spectators have all the facilities necessary during the Games.

Organizing an Olympic Games generally requires the building of large structures for sports areas, access roads, car parks, the Olympic Village to house the competitors, living quarters for the Press, a working area for the international news media, and a youth camp to enable young people from different countries to live together reasonably cheaply while attending the Games. The organizing committee is free to decide whether it will carry out the building on its own responsibility or leave it to be done by public bodies. Munich formed the Olympia Building Association, with limited liability. Members of the association were again representatives of sports and the public bodies mentioned above.

Under this organizational structure, the necessary administrative bodies must be formed step by step to proceed with all aspects of preparation. A general secretariat is set up which before the Games will have a staff of several hundred people and during the Games will be reinforced by several thousand salaried members. Apart from this several thousand soldiers and members of the police force are also required to take over security. I think it is no longer possible to organize a good Olympic Games without the active assistance of the military services. They can offer valuable help not only with security but with transport, news communications, air services, the Olympic Village and the Press quarters, and in furnishing and equipping several thousand temporary lodgings, and can therefore decisively decrease the cost of the Games. In many countries the necessary work force would not be available without using the army. Moreover, because of their training and discipline, army personnel are able to enhance the good name of the country which they serve by their unselfish and friendly assistance during the Games.

Planning is the most important task connected with the Olympic Games. This begins, years before the Games themselves, with building. There is one absolutely fundamental principle: the requirements for the Games themselves are obviously important in planning but the use of the facilities after the Games is crucial. Olympic Games today require such a high investment that it is not justifiable to provide the facilities only for the sixteen days of the Games themselves. The building and subsequent use of accommodation for competitors and spectators is still relatively uncomplicated. The Olympic youth camp has become a well-established component of the Games as temporary facilities, tents, for example, can usually be provided for it. On the other hand, the living quarters in the Olympic Village, for the athletes and their coaches (about 10,000 people), and those for the journalists and the enormous staffs of technicians for radio and television (also about 10,000), are a huge enterprise. Therefore it must also be considered carefully how these residential quarters can later be integrated into the city or locality. In Munich the Press town was built by local construction companies which rented the living quarters to the Organizing Committee. After their use by journalists they became homes for families with many children or low incomes or for old people. This future use was taken into account when the Organizing Committee was given a sizeable subsidy by the city of Munich for the building of the homes.

The Olympic Village was divided into living quarters for men and women. The women's section is used today as a hall of residence for students; the accommodation in the men's section has been sold as homes or rented. As well as

The Gymnasium Annexe at Shibuya under construction for the 1964 Games

The Organizing Committee is responsible only to the IOC but it must have a majority of NOC members in its voting structure. The IOC representative in the host city's country must also have a vote on the Organizing Committee and on its executive board. The members of the committee, apart from those representing individual sports, should represent public bodies and large social organizations in the country concerned. The Organizing Committee should also be legally independent. For the Games of the twentieth Olympiad in Munich (1972), for example, the Organizing Committee was, according to German law, a 'registered company'. Its members were representatives of sports and of the governments of the German Federal Republic, the Bavarian Free State, the region, and Munich, the regional capital. There were also private members. On one subcommittee, political parties, trade unions, trade associations, the major religious denominations and various youth organizations were represented.

living accommodation, recreational and service facilities must be provided for the athletes in an Olympic Village. These usually include a cinema, a theatre for daily musical and other performances, shops for personal requirements, a hospital for the treatment of simple ailments, rooms for social meetings, dancing and so on. In Munich there was also a church, used for religious services of all denominations. There was also a Village paper, reporting the main political events all over the world and naturally the events of the Games themselves, and also television rooms.

There is no great difficulty over providing the infrastructure, that is to say the roads, public transport, electricity and water, sewage, etc., for this is the result of close cooperation with the appropriate authorities in the host city. But the construction of sports facilities is intrinsically more complex. For the training areas for the Olympic sports (twenty-one for the Summer Games or six for the Winter) which concern all the member nations of the IOC, the host city can usually confine itself to the available sports facilities of the sports organizations, clubs, high schools and primary schools.

But when a city has to build a new large stadium or reconstruct an existing one into an Olympic stadium, and also provide halls for indoor sports, a large swimming pool, a regatta course for rowing and canoeing or facilities for winter sports, then the question of their use after the Games becomes of paramount importance if one is to retain the good will and enthusiasm of those involved in the Games – from the Organizing Committee chairman down to the taxpayer. It becomes complicated because the international sports federations usually have diametrically opposed interests. The Organizing Committee has to come to an understanding with the Federations about the technical problems of staging the Games. The Federations are naturally interested in having the biggest and as perfect as possible sports areas for the Games. That is quite legitimate from their point of view. But the priority for an Olympic host city should be to provide the basic requirements of a 'celebration' of the world's young sporting elite. It is expensive and utopian to demand that the Organizing Committee should provide ultimate perfection for every sport, but the facilities offered must be good enough to guarantee fair competition and adequate provision for spectators. When the size of the facilities is considered, their subsequent use is an important factor here, too. Something temporary can usually be built for spectators' grandstands. But technical equipment, especially electronic, must be limited because of its high cost.

In most instances the building costs for each Olympic Games will be higher than those for the organization as such. As an example, Munich spent DM 1,350 million on building. Most of this expenditure was for sports facilities but it also covered certain infrastructures.

When such figures are discussed, world public opinion speaks glibly of 'gigantism', saying that only the rich, industrial nations could be Olympic hosts. But what does 'gigantism' mean? In Berlin (1936) 49 nations took part, London (1948) 59, Helsinki (1952) 69, Melbourne (1956) 67, Rome (1960) 83, Tokyo (1964) 93, Mexico City (1968) 112 and Munich (1972) 122; in Montreal (1976) there will be over 130 and in Moscow (1980) maybe even more. Naturally the Olympic Games will tend to keep increasing in size but new participating nations can-

The new harbour at Kiel, where building costs were DM 95 million in 1972

not be turned away. Quite the reverse, they must all be encouraged. Restricting the sports program is also difficult, particularly as new sports become popular and many sports have separate competitions for women.

It is difficult to compare the costs of and benefits from holding a Games. The ratios are different in every country and city. Munich gained about fifteen years in its development specifically in the improvement of traffic conditions and the building of its underground system. I maintain that the Olympic cities usually gain a great deal from the Games, in idealism of course, but also materially. Munich certainly did so, as DM 711,250,000 was spent on the reconstruction of roads, bridges, public transport, parking places and schools, in other words the greatest part of the building costs. Thus the city of Munich acquired exemplary sports facilities for a direct expenditure of only DM 170,900,000. Kiel profited proportionately even more. It put in DM 6,400,000 for the Olympics but the structures there are worth DM 95 million and after the Games these became the city's.

There was an agreement between the Organizing Committee and the three area authorities, that the Federal Government should assume fifty per cent of the cost deficit, the Bavarian Republic and the City of Munich twenty-five per cent each. All in all, the building costs amounted to DM 1,350 million in Munich and DM 95 million in Kiel. For the organization in Munich and Kiel DM 527 million was spent.

To avoid misunderstanding, it should be stressed that these figures ought not to be compared with those of other Olympic cities, for each has a different set of social circumstances, creating totally different requirements. Munich raised about two-thirds of the Olympic costs on its own initiative, through various ventures – altogether DM 1,286 million. Included in this were the 100 million 10-DM commemorative coins, produced by the Federal Bank and sold to collectors all over the world; and DM 420 million was raised from two different lotteries. A large part of the proceeds came from television rights, the sale of entrance tickets, the rights to use emblems from the Games, commemorative medals, posters, etc. The Munich Olympics therefore not only financed themselves but also made a huge profit.

In calculating the benefits and costs of large undertakings, the incomes from taxes must also be considered. A sum of at least DM 25 million was returned to the state through economic activity concerned with the preparation and duration of the Games. The Olympics always inspire much private commercial initiative, which benefits public services as well. When the deficit assumed by the public bodies is reduced by this DM 25 million, a deficit of DM 436 million is left. These 1971 prices can be compared with the new facilities in Munich and Kiel, which cost a total of DM 1,445 million. These rough calculations show what the Olympics can mean in terms of economics.

It would be quite wrong, however, for one Olympic city to set out to imitate another, in whatever respect. Each city must stage its own Games and their quality is not guaranteed by expenditure alone. The differences are seen particularly in the cultural program; after all, art cannot simply be regimented. There is an equally worthy place for science, and I feel that a scientific congress should always be incorporated into the structure of the Olympic Games. Each Games should make a contribution to the development of international sport, which is in constant need of informed and discerning guidance. Scientific advice is most necessary as sport depends so much upon help from doctors, educationalists, anthropologists, psychologists, sociologists, biochemists, philosophers and experts in other disciplines. And of course the results of such conferences must be accurately written up and published. In my opinion, in spite of Rule 54, it is in this distanced view of the Games that the great value of science lies.

The special meaning of the Olympics for the future lies in its coverage through Press, radio and television. The exploitation of television rights contributes considerably, through royalties, towards the financing of the Games. But publicity for the Olympic Movement is even more important. It was established, for example, that the Olympic opening ceremony in Munich alone was watched by over a thousand million television viewers throughout the world. The expenses incurred by the Organizing Committee over equipment and accommodation for the media is enormous. At Munich over 9,000 people from all over the world were involved in the dissemination of news, by Press, radio and television. For all these the Organizing Committee provides a heavy subsidy for facilities and accommodation and from the television rights receives a percentage of the fees paid to the IOC.

It is only natural that the Olympic Games should draw heavily on tradition: after all the Olympic idea was still potent enough after almost two and a half thousand years for revival to be possible. It is therefore all the more necessary that the form and image the Games are given should be genuinely modern. A very suitable way of doing this, apart from in the arts program, lies in the total visual presentation of the Games. The danger here is that the Games have an inbuilt tendency to pathos and exalted heroics which all too readily finds expression in the formal, heraldic imagery of flags and insignia. The contest in the Olympic stadium is taken so seriously, and in a sense must be so taken, that it is vital to keep the true basis of the Games in view. To this end it is important that the Games

should, if at all possible, be set in a festive interplay of architecture and landscape. And with this must go a comprehensive system of visual communication, one effect of which will be the building up of a world language of ideographs from the signs and images of sport – its dress, its presentation of information, its symbols and colours. All of which must proceed from painstaking attention to a thousand and one details.

The visitor naturally is also part of the celebrations of the Games. He is not just a passive spectator. There is also open space around the Games which the organizers ought to take just as seriously as any other aspect. It is an area of communication, too. Munich tried, successfully, I think, to create an area of understanding, of really supranational communication, of solidarity. At the least, Munich succeeded to the point where the crowd behaviour that usually evokes so much criticism from opponents of sport was hardly noticeable. People simply mingled and met as fellow inhabitants of one world.

Since Coubertin's time, the host of the Olympic Games has been obliged to renounce nationalist propaganda. For example, in the Olympic stadium the flag of the host country must not be flown more often than those of all the other participating countries. The Organizing Committee must represent not the host country but Olympic sport.

Other detailed questions which play a part in the preparation and carrying out of the Games have to be seriously considered. They include ceremony and protocol, the variety of tickets and passes required, uniforms and schooling for hostesses and attendants, the compiling, printing and distribution of all the schedules and programs, service facilities for the spectators, the computerized results service, transport facilities for competitors, officials and journalists between all the sites, the Olympic Village and Press quarters, recreational facilities for the athletes in the Olympic Village, etc., etc. Naturally the sporting events, *Citius, Altius, Fortius*, have priority. Connected with them is the extremely difficult and responsible area of drug control and femininity tests.

With all the prominence given to the competitions between the world's sporting elite, the Games would have no future if they consisted merely of dramatic feats of speed, strength and endurance and world records. In my opinion the prime task of the Olympic Games lies just round the corner. Over the years it has come nearer to its main function, the participation of the youth of the world in a world peace festival. The Olympic ideal brings with it many preconditions, not least the vast and unparalleled acclamation which the Games have found throughout the world. This worldwide understanding of the Olympic Games will increase through world longing for peace, which is perhaps the subconscious reason for the passion for the Games. I see two reasons why the Games appear more suitable than any other institution for accomplishing peace. Sporting competitions have no language barriers, and they have no age or class barrier: they are for young and old, and for educated and uneducated. They are a means within reach of not only the rich or those from particular geographic regions but quite simply of the whole world. They are not perfect but perfection will never be achieved. Peace depends on harmony between nations. For this reason I think the world would be poorer and unhappier if it did not have this peace festival of youth. And I believe in the future of the Olympic Games.

OLYMPIC CEREMONIAL Nadjeda Lekarska

Olympic ceremonies have become a controversial issue. Are those who wish to maintain the traditional ceremonial outdated conservatives and those who want to change certain elements progressive innovators?

Coubertin wanted the Olympic Games to outshine in substance and aspect all other sporting events. They were to bring into harmony physical and mental effort, the strife for perfection and moral stamina, the endeavour for friendship and the conditions for its manifestation, the link between personal glory, national pride and international understanding. The Olympic Games were not only to encourage peace. They were to embody it. Speeches and competitions seemed insufficient – for words often tend to degenerate into sermons and competitions to become self-centred, even to lapse into animosity.

Coubertin well understood the impact of audio-visual display and the need for distinguished solemnity to stimulate thorough understanding of the Olympic principles. But he was also aware of the danger of cheap glamour. He therefore planned carefully. The ceremonies were to be three: the official opening of the Games, the distribution of medals and the closing of the Games. He emphasized, to start with, several basic elements, the athlete's oath, the victory ceremony and the opening of the Games.

The proclamation of the opening of the Games by the head of state of the organizing country was the only act of solemnity until 1920. 'It was, however, not enough to give the occasion the full impressiveness of which it was capable,' says Coubertin in *The Olympic Idea*. Symbols were needed to stir the imagination and stimulate ambition. And they were found! It took, however, considerable time for the Olympic ceremonies to mature and gain body.

The Olympic Flag, with the five interlaced rings symbolizing the five continents in the colours of all participating nations, most eloquently reflects the Olympic spirit of friendship and equality among sportsmen the

The opening ceremony in 1912, before the Olympic flag and flame were introduced

world over. The model, designed by Coubertin himself from a symbol of ancient Greece, was ready as far back as 1913 and presented for adoption at the Olympic Congress in 1914. The flag was hoisted for the first time at the Olympic Games in 1920 at Antwerp.

The Olympic flame, symbolizing the endeavour for perfection and the struggle for victory, was introduced to the Olympic ceremonies in 1928 at the Games of the ninth Olympiad. The International Olympic Committee had adopted a suggestion from Theodore Lewald, IOC member in Germany, for its lighting in Olympia and transportation by a torch relay through various countries on its way to the Olympic stadium. This scheme was not implemented immediately, although the flame burned for the first time at the Amsterdam Olympics in 1928. In 1936 for the Games of the eleventh Olympiad the IOC's plan was carried out. The torch relay started in Olympia and was carried by runners across Europe to the main stadium in Berlin. Ever since the torch relay has become part of the ceremonial for the Games and for the Winter Games since 1964.

The flight of doves was officially introduced at the opening ceremony of the Games in 1920 although this classical symbol of peace was not new to Olympism. At the Games of 1896 in Athens a flight of doves accompanied the proclamation of the opening of the Games, but this was due to the initiative of the organizers rather than a deliberate decision by the IOC.

The Olympic hymn, which has always been part of the Olympic ceremonial, is still a problem issue. After the song composed by Spyros Samaras from Greece for the Games of the first Olympiad in Athens, the musical background of the Olympics was unstable. Various attempts were made to find a new hymn but they were all short-lived. The fact that Samaras' hymn was adopted in 1958 as the official Olympic hymn confirms this inadequacy. What the Olympic ceremonies still need is a popular tune capable of inspiring sportsmen of the world, a tune that lives up to the five circles, the burning flame and the flight of doves.

The oath is a component of the opening ceremony which Coubertin adopted directly from the dawn of Olympic history and placed within a modern international frame. 'Before the opening of the Games', he said, 'those athletes who had been admitted as competitors went to the temple of Zeus and vowed to observe in every particular the law of the Games. They declared themselves without taint and worthy to appear in the stadium. If the image of God were replaced for each athlete by the flag of his country, the grandeur of the ceremony could surely not fail to be enhanced and the appropriateness of this "modernization" is so obvious that there is no need to insist upon it' (*The Olympic Idea, Discourses and Essays*, 1966).

The oath was first pronounced by Victor Boin, a Belgian fencer, at the opening ceremony of the Games of the seventh Olympiad at Antwerp in 1920.

The victory ceremony was elaborated by Coubertin with a deep sense of significance and beauty. Olympic victory merited the highest moral reward. The act of presenting medals had therefore to become an unforgettable moment for the winners, for all participants and spectators. What Coubertin and his colleagues probably did not foresee at the beginning was that it was this ceremony, imbued with so much emotion, that would provoke such opposing views during the second half of the century.

Some people are against the hoisting of national flags and playing of anthems, others have nothing against flags but object to the anthems, and still others favour the traditional ceremony of both flags and anthems. The main argument against national emblems is that the Games are supposed to be competitions between individuals only and that the hoisting of flags and playing of national anthems enhance exaggerated nationalism. Today it is difficult to defend the individual character of the Games, considering that team sports are based on national representation. National emblems no doubt stimulate patriotic pride but this need have nothing in common with narrow-minded nationalism. If the victory ceremony were shorn of national emblems it would hardly differ from the distribution of medals at national competitions.

The most widely seen Olympic ceremonies are those opening and closing each Games. Each Organizing Committee can provide its own spectacular interpretation and, with colour television pictures now available in many parts of the world, imagination and artistry are given new resources. But the IOC has laid down the theme which the ceremonies will maintain.

After the arrival of the Sovereign Head of State, the parade of teams follows. Each contingent, dressed in an official uniform, is preceded by a shield bearing its name and the national flag. Greece, as the home of the ancient Games, leads the parade and the host country is the last to enter the stadium. Once all the teams are lined up in the middle of the arena, the President of the Organizing Committee introduces the President of the IOC, who then calls upon the sovereign or head of state to open the Games, with the words 'I declare open the Olympic Games of . . . celebrating the . . . Olympiad of the modern era'.

The Olympic flag is brought into the arena, usually by a military detachment, and after a fanfare of trumpets, is raised to the music of the Olympic anthem. The Mayor of

Victor Boin (Belgium) taking the first oath on behalf of all competitors in 1920

the host city then joins the IOC President on the rostrum, and representatives of the previous Olympic city deliver a special embroidered satin flag presented by the Belgian Olympic Committee in 1920. The president receives it and hands it to the mayor for safe keeping in the principal municipal hall until the next Games.

Then comes a salute of three guns and the release of pigeons, as a symbol of peace. The Olympic flame, which has been carried by a relay of runners from Olympia in Greece, arrives; the last runner circles the track and lights the sacred flame, which burns throughout the duration of the Games.

The solemn Olympic oath is then taken, on behalf of the competitors, by an athlete of the country where the Games are being staged. All the flag bearers move forward in a semicircle around the rostrum and the athlete holds a corner of his national flag in one hand as he takes the oath. A judge takes a similar oath on behalf of the judges.

Once the athletes have marched out of the arena, the Organizing Committee has freedom to put on a demonstration or display.

The closing ceremony is normally shorter and simpler. The flag bearers march into the arena, taking the places they held at the opening ceremony but are followed by six representatives of each nation, intermingled in a column eight or ten abreast. With the President of the IOC at the rostrum, the flags of Greece, the country organizing the Games and the next host country, are hoisted in turn to the strains of each national anthem. The President then closes the Games, calling upon the youth of the countries taking part to assemble again in four years' time. A fanfare is sounded, the Olympic flame extinguished, the flag is slowly lowered from the pole and carried from the arena, and, after a salute of five guns, the competitors march from the arena.

Are the Olympic Games tiresome because the ceremonies are repeated? I do not think so, because the atmosphere of the Games differs as a result of the temperament of the peoples and the creative imagination of the organizers. This involves a certain danger of a spasmodic and unfitting intervention of doubtful taste. On the other hand, preservation of simple and distinguished ceremonies should be complemented by care not to fetter any creative initiative. In fact each opening and closing ceremony is unique.

Here are some examples, drawn from personal observation. At the closing ceremony of the 1956 Games in Melbourne, the ranks of the athletes were broken when girls and boys from all over the world merged and formed one united international group. This spontaneous move was a remarkable demonstration of international understanding through sport.

Walt Disney's scenario for the opening ceremony in Squaw Valley (1960) was a masterpiece of creative imagination. The athletes stood under a roof with an open view to the mountain tops across the valley. One of the long walls of the roofed stadium parted, sliding sideways like an open two-winged door. The Olympic flame, carried by the former Olympic champion Andrea Mead Lawrence and escorted by sixteen more burning torches, appeared on top of Mount Papoose. The steep down-hill resembled an unwinding crimson ribbon – a flaming message of good will which had crossed the globe from Morgedal in Norway, the home of Sondre Norheim, the founder of modern Nordic skiing, to the snowy peaks of Sierra Nevada.

At the closing ceremony in Mexico (1968), exactly at the moment when interest was likely to degenerate into boredom, a song known to every Mexican came like one mighty voice from the centre of the ground. Hundreds of folk musicians sang to the tune of violins and guitars 'Guadalajara, Guadalajara'. 'Viva, Viva!' came the answer from the stands. A sombrero went into the air and thousands followed. The Olympic flame was extinguished among song and bubbling enthusiasm. The requiem of farewell turned into a Mexican hymn of joy.

In Grenoble (1968) the torch bearer started his ascent to the top of the flight of 300 steps that led to the bowl. An unusual sound, remote and voiceless, resounded from all parts. It was like the beats of a human heart, but nobody could tell for sure, it was so unusual. The higher the athlete climbed, the clearer the sound. It was no vain imagination. The athlete's heart was in fact connected to a stereo loudspeaker device. It was beating strongly, evenly, like any heart of a young person – that of an athlete filled with Olympic enthusiasm. These beats were contagious!

In Munich (1972) it was the music that made the difference. It did not act like a background but rather played a leading part. The traditional military band was supplanted by a modern orchestra, the usual march melodies by a variety of national rhythms, changing to match and introduce the nationality of each team entering the stadium. It sounded like a repeated welcome to all. Modern, national and international!

The same and yet always different! Such are the Olympic Games, with ceremonies strict and unchanging in substance, flexible and varied in form – a vast panorama which broadens the mind and spirit of those who contemplate it.

THE INTERNATIONAL OLYMPIC ACADEMY Sandy Duncan

The International Olympic Academy is a mixture of idealism and realism – conceived by Coubertin, nourished by the Germans and now enthusiastically organized by the Hellenic Olympic Committee under the patronage of the IOC.

The Academy, situated just outside the site of the Ancient Games at Olympia, holds an annual session/seminar of students nominated by their National Olympic Committees. It was Coubertin's belief that there was a need for collective study and investigation in order for sport to develop. Every aspect, from anatomy and psychology to the theory of human development through physical exercise, he believed, should be examined. There could be no better place for young people to find inspiration than the site of the Ancient Games, raped by vandals and ravaged by flood and earthquake, but beginning to yield to the archaeologists' tools from 1875 onwards. Excavations resumed in 1936, financed by the surplus funds of the Berlin Olympic Games, continued until 1941 and started again in 1952. Nearly a quarter of a million cubic yards of soil had to be removed to reveal the Stadium.

The IOC at its Session in Rome in April 1949 agreed to the foundation of the International Olympic Academy in Greece. But it was twelve years before the first Session was held in Ancient Olympia with thirty-one students from twenty-four countries present, and coinciding with the ceremonial handing over of the newly revealed Stadium. Initially there were few permanent buildings and the participants slept in tents, as did the competitors at the Ancient Games, and lectures were given out of doors. Now, at the cost of more than US $2 million, the Academy has excellent buildings able to house 150 participants, thirty lecturers, a large dining room, a lecture hall with simultaneous translation facilities, a museum, a library containing more than 3,000 books in different languages, and sports facilities.

The workings of the Academy are controlled by a Council elected for a four-year period by the Hellenic Olympic Committee. Prince George of Hanover, an IOC member, was its President for many years and did much to ensure that the early improvisations were satisfactory. He was succeeded by Epaminondas Petralias and later by Athanasios Tzartzanos, both of Greece. The IOC also has a small commission to supervise its work.

The Academy is financed by the Hellenic Olympic Committee at an annual cost of about US $100,000 and all National Olympic Committees are asked to send students, generally under thirty-five years old, one or more students from each country at each Session being given free board and lodging.

Certain basic subjects are dealt with at all Sessions – the history of the Ancient and Modern Olympic Games; the philosophy of 'Olympism'; archaeology; psychology; sports medicine; the roles of the IOC, International Federations and National Olympic Committees; techniques of modern sport and the fine arts.

Each Session has its distinctive theme. For example, in 1967 the theme was the athlete, the human being; in 1971, the prospects of the Olympic Movement and sport in general; in 1973, the contribution of the intellectual world to the Olympic Movement.

Inauguration of an Olympic Academy Session on the Hill of the Pnyx at the Acropolis, Athens

Lecturers come from all over the world and, after the 1973 Session, 2,150 students from seventy-three countries and 108 lecturers from thirty countries had been present at the thirteen annual Sessions, which each last two weeks.

The Session assembles in Athens on a Friday. The next day all participants are shown the archaeological sites in Athens, including the Parthenon and Acropolis. In the evening the opening ceremony is performed on the Hill of the Pnyx where democracy is said to have been born, since it was here that the male citizens of Athens met together to decide on matters of importance affecting Athens.

On Sunday students and lecturers leave by the coast road via Corinth and Patras. After lunch at the Academy there are conducted tours of the archaeological museum and of the sacred Altis of Olympia. The students are accommodated in large rooms containing four comfortable double bunks and excellent and ample ablution arrangements.

The working hours are in the morning and late afternoon when the heat of the day has subsided. Normally each lecturer will give points to be discussed by the students who, for this purpose, split into language group seminars – English, French, German and Greek. Later all groups meet and group leaders give their group's findings which are then open to general discussion. After dinner in the evening there may be a film show or participants may walk into the town of Olympia and sit and chat together in one of the numerous outdoor cafés.

There is the Academy's museum to visit, the library in which to research. Sport, too, is not forgotten since there is a running track, swimming pool, basketball courts, and so on. The students themselves organize competitions in these sports. There is also one free day when the whole Academy personnel goes to the sea or visits a Greek island. One will also see groups from each country practising for their turn at the student's concert held towards the end of the Session, which closes with the presentation of diplomas.

The return to Athens is via the Delphi Games sites. These did not suffer the same destruction as Olympia and, even now, are wonderfully imposing.

What have the organizers hoped to achieve at the Session? Firstly, it is to maintain and explain the high ideals and workings of the Olympic Movement so that the students will disseminate their knowledge to others in many different countries. Secondly, the Academy is a link between the establishment, controlled by those of an older age group, and the younger element, often active in physical education. The opinions of youth are sought and it is hoped that, after the discussions, they will leave with renewed enthusiasm. Finally, it is hard to imagine a better way to bring some measure of understanding and friendship between the youth of many countries than for them to live and work in peace and harmony together in such a wonderful setting, united in the love of sport.

ART AND THE OLYMPICS Henri Pouret

The marriage of the Olympic Games and the Fine Arts occurs at each celebration of the Games. Even though there are no longer any artistic events officially included in the Olympic program, each Olympic event is a powerful source of inspiration for the Arts. This makes it possible to say that Olympism, consisting of a spiritualization of muscular movement, leads sport to become one with thought, creating, or rather rediscovering, Platonic humanism, in which the body is the source of inspiration for the mind and where the mind commands the movements of the body.

Competitive art within the framework of the Olympics declined almost from its beginning, mainly because of the tremendous problems of transporting exhibits, mustering large orchestras to play new works and the fact that prospective competitors who already enjoyed a certain reputation preferred to be judges rather than to be judged. Yet if the competitive aspect declined, man's response to the Olympics through art forms developed and has enriched society. First through the building of stadia, with such outstanding examples as the swimming pool in Tokyo; through writing, from the basic reportage of Olympic events to the many volumes inspired by Olympic feats; through photographs and the media of film; through broadcasting, the vividness of the spoken word, and finally the medium of television through which the Olympic Stadium became a sort of universal theatre in which the sports drama unfolded and could be watched, by millions, as it took place, in their own homes. Avery Brundage described the Olympic Movement as one of the greatest social forces in the world today, even before the Games became the largest single event to be shown throughout the world on television, as it is today.

When Coubertin thought of reviving the Olympic Games, he had no intention of limiting this revival to sports events alone. He saw Olympism as a philosophy helping to create the complete man; that is why, in addition to the sports contests to be held every four years, a new educational method was to be introduced comprising the study of a series of intellectual and artistic subjects.

On 23 May 1906, Coubertin organized a consultative conference in Paris on the arts, literature and sport. His idea was for this conference to study to what extent and in what form the arts and literature might be incorporated in the celebration of the modern Olympiads and be combined with the practice of sport so as to benefit from it and at the same time ennoble it. The conference proposed: 'the creation of five contests in architecture, sculpture, painting, music, and literature with prizes being awarded every four years for new works of art directly inspired by sport'. At the same time, he issued to those attending the congress the following program for discussion:

ARCHITECTURE: Conditions and characteristics of the modern gymnasium. Open-air clubs and athletic centres, swimming pools, rifle ranges, riding schools, yacht clubs, fencing schools, architectural materials, motifs, costs and quotations.
DRAMATIC ART: Open-air performances. Main principles: sport on the stage.
CHOREOGRAPHY: Processions, parades, grouped and coordinated movements, rhythmic dances.

DECORATION: Stands and premises, flagpoles, shields, garlands, hangings, spotlights, night festivals, torchlight sports.
LITERATURE: Literary contests, conditions governing these contests, the emotional side of sport, source of inspiration for the man of letters.
MUSIC: Open-air orchestras and choirs, repertoire, rhythms, fanfares, conditions governing an Olympic music contest.
PAINTING: Individual figures and groups. Possibilities and conditions governing an Olympic painting contest, help given to the artist by photography.
SCULPTURE: Athletic attitudes and movements in relation to art. Interpretation of effort, objects given as prizes, statuettes and medals.

Thus from 1906 on, there was a trend towards artistic events organized on the occasion of the Olympic Games. But it was not until the Stockholm Games in 1912 that artistic events were actually included in the Olympic program, although these were organized directly by the IOC and not by the Organizing Committee, since the latter did not wish to shoulder their responsibility. They were held during every Olympiad from the fifth (1912) to the fourteenth (1948). The competitions were divided as follows:

ARCHITECTURE: The architectural contests covered plans for sports constructions, plans for stadia and town planning. The contests held in 1936 at the Berlin Games were particularly interesting: Werner March (Germany) won the gold medal for town planning for his *Main Berlin Stadium*, followed in this category by Charles Downing Lay (United States), who competed with a plan for *A Marina Park in Brooklyn.*
SCULPTURE: In 1924 the first prize was won by a Greek, Konstantinos Dimitriadis, for a fine statue entitled *The Finnish Discus Thrower*; in 1936 the German sculptor Arno Brecker with his statue, *The Decathlon Athlete*, came second to the Italian artist Farpi Vignoli, who had entered a statue called *Biga* (Chariot).

From 1928 to 1948, bas reliefs and medals were added to the sculpture category and from 1936 to 1948, i.e. during two Olympic Games, there were contests for plaques.
PAINTING: From 1912 to 1924 all kinds of painting came under one heading. In 1912 the Italian Giovanni Pellegrini won with three friezes entitled *Winter Sports*. After 1928, four subdivisions were created in the painting contests: oil paintings in classical style; watercolours and drawings; applied graphics (posters, diplomas, stamps, seals); other graphic works (wood engravings, copper etchings, lithographs).

In this last group, in 1928, William Nicholson (Great Britain) won with coloured wood engravings of twelve sports; in 1936, Alex Walter Diggelmann (Switzerland) won the first prize for applied graphics with a poster entitled *Arosa*. In 1948, the French engraver Albert Decaris won a gold medal with a copper engraving, *Swimming Pool*.
MUSIC: Music contests were held though prizes were seldom awarded partly because composers of standing preferred to be on the jury rather than compete, and partly for economic reasons: paying for an orchestra to perform a new work is always expensive and the organizers of the Games did not have the finances to allocate to

the performance of works which might never be played again. In 1924 and 1928 no prize at all was awarded, and in 1932 only a silver medal, to Josef Suk (Czechoslovakia) for his march *Into a New Life*. The first to win a prize in a musical contest was an Italian, Ricardo Barthelemy, in 1912, who had composed a *Triumphal Olympic March*. From 1936 on, musical works were divided into works for orchestras, instrumental works and songs. The first prize for instrumental works was never awarded: a second prize was awarded in 1948 to Jean Weinzweig (Canada) for *Divertimenti for solo flute and string orchestra*. There was also a song contest under the music heading and, in 1936, the German Paul Höffer won first prize with his choral work, *The Olympic Oath*; his two compatriots, Kurt Thomas, with *Cantata for the 1936 Olympiad*, and Harald Genzmer, with *The Runner*, were second and third. The first two prizes for songs were not awarded in London in 1948, only the third prize, which was won by the Italian Gabriele Bianchi for his *Olympic Hymn*.
LITERATURE: At Stockholm in 1912 the prize for literature was awarded for an *Ode to Sport*, whose authors were officially Georg Hohrod and Martin Eschbach (Germany); in fact, behind the two pseudonyms, the real author was Coubertin himself. He wrote it originally in French but presented it in German to maintain the ruse behind the pseudonyms. The text follows:

Ode to Sport
I. O Sport, delight of the Gods, distillation of life! In the grey dingle of modern existence, restless with barren toil, you suddenly appeared like the shining messenger of vanished ages, those ages when humanity could smile. And to the mountain tops came dawn's first glimmer, and sunbeams dappled the forest's gloomy floor.
II. O Sport, you are Beauty! You – the architect of this house, the human body, which may become abject or sublime according as to whether it is defiled by base passions or cherished with wholesome endeavour. There can be no beauty without poise and proportion, and you are the incomparable master of both, for you create harmony, you fill movement with rhythm, you make strength gracious, and you lend power to supple things.
III. O Sport, you are Justice! The perfect fairness which men seek in vain in their social institutions rises around you of its own accord. No man can surpass by one centimetre the height he can jump or the time for which he can run. His combined strength of body and mind alone set the bounds to his success.
IV. O Sport, you are Daring! The whole meaning of muscular effort lies in one word – to dare. What good are muscles, what good is it to feel nimble and strong and to train one's nimbleness and strength if not to dare? But the daring you inspire is far from the rashness which impels the gambler to stake his all on a throw. It is a prudent and considered daring.
V. O Sport, you are Honour! The titles you bestow are worthless save if won in absolute fairness and perfect unselfishness. Whoever succeeds in deceiving his fellows by some ignoble trick, suffers the shame of it in the depths of himself and dreads the dishonourable epithet which will be coupled with his name if the fraud from which he prospers should come to light.

VI. O Sport, you are Joy! At your call the flesh makes holiday and the eyes smile; the blood flows free and strong in the arteries. Thought's horizon grows lighter and more clear. Even to the griefstricken you can bring a healing distraction from their sorrows, while you enable the happy to taste the joy of living to the full.

VII. O Sport, you are Fecundity! You tend by straight and noble paths towards a more perfect race, blasting the seeds of sickness and righting the flaws which threaten its needful soundness. And you quicken within the athlete the wish to see growing about him brisk and sturdy sons to follow him in the arena and in their turn bear off joyful laurels.

VIII. O Sport, you are Progress! To serve you well, man must better himself in body and in soul. You enjoin him to observe a loftier hygiene; you require him refrain from all excess. You teach him wise rules which will give his effort the maximum intensity without impairing the balance of his health.

IX. O Sport, you are Peace! You forge happy bonds between the peoples by drawing them together in reverence for strength which is controlled, organized and self-disciplined. Through you the young of all the world learn to respect one another, and thus the diversity of national traits becomes a source of generous and peaceful emulation.

Before 1928 there was no subdivision in the literature contests, three prizes being awarded for all kinds of literature. From 1928 literary works were divided into three categories: lyric, dramatic and epic. Although prizes were always awarded for lyric works right up until 1948, no prize was given for any dramatic work from 1928 to 1948 except for *Icarus*, by Lauro De Bossis (Italy), which won the second prize in 1928. Epic works (novels, romances, tales and other writings) were honoured with three prizes in Amsterdam, Berlin and London. No prize, however, was awarded at Los Angeles in 1932.

After 1948 the art contests were discontinued. Not only were there the problems mentioned above but it must be admitted that both participants and spectators at the Games were only interested in the sports events and had no desire to go to admire art contests. Consequently, since 1948, the Games Organizing Committees, in particular at Helsinki (1952) and Melbourne (1956), have contented themselves with arranging exhibitions of art and ballet performances.

In 1960, in Rome, it was very easy for the Italians to lend a cultural note to the Games by holding some of the sports events in the architectural setting of the city's monuments: the thermal baths of Caracalla were used as a setting for the gymnastics, the Maxentius Basilica for wrestling, the square at Siena and the Borghese Villa for equestrian events, while Constantine's Arch provided the finish of the marathon, and hockey was played in the magnificent marble stadium. An original experiment, however, was tried out in Rome, one that succeeded perfectly within the framework of the relations between art and sport: the halls of the EUR Main Sports Palace were used to hold an exhibition of photographs of sport, in which thirty-three National Olympic Committees were represented.

In Tokyo, in 1964, all the sports facilities built for the Games gave competitors and spectators a fine lesson in architectural aesthetics, especially the Olympic swimming pool, which Avery Brundage enthusiastically described as a real sports cathedral.

In Mexico, in 1968, the organizers added to the cultural events a huge exhibition of children's drawings, but here, too, it was the setting for the Games that really set the aesthetic note, in particular the Aztec Stadium and the University City Stadium, as well as the outstanding performances of the National Ballet of Mexico with the mural paintings of Diégo Rivéra, the Fine Arts Palace, with the Mexican paintings of Orozzo, Tamayo and, above all, the National Museum of Anthropology with the famous Aztec calendar in a single block of stone weighing some twenty tons, which was used as an Olympic emblem.

If the art contests desired by Coubertin were not in themselves a success, they were fruitful in many other ways for the Olympic Games has continued to inspire writers and artists. I emphasized this in the papers I read to the Olympic Academy in 1964, 1965 and 1968. However, even though the divorce between athletic contests and art contests became final and absolute in 1948, it is still true that the Olympic Games have provided an important source of inspiration in the different spheres of art. Journalists and writers always find abundant copy in the celebration of the Games, and in a great many countries, during the year of the Olympics, the public has the opportunity of reading much excellent reporting, vivid live commentaries on what is happening in the stadium or, a few weeks later, brilliant accounts reliving and glorifying the highlights of the Games.

Sometimes we even have the opportunity of reading an exceptional work of thought and reflection which places the Olympic Games within the context of the cultural or philosophical concerns of mankind. In connection with the Olympic Games, men feel the need to write or listen to stories of everything relating to the great deeds performed, they need to create a heightened awareness and exploit the significance of these friendly contests; in this way sport enters the world of culture. Literature helps to compensate for and perpetuate the fleeting quality of the sporting act and confers, as Coubertin wished, 'letters patent of nobility' in the real sense of the words, on muscular action.

Sculpture is essentially athletic; its language is that of a man's muscles and the genius of the artist consists of capturing in stone or metal the movements of the human body. Watching athletes in the stadium enables the sculptor to use the form of man to express an idea. The Olympic Games, with their growing number of athletes, enable us to discover men of perfection; many sculptors come to the stadia with their notebooks and sketch pads to seize the grace of movement and the beauty of the human form.

The first and inescapable concern of any city that takes on the heavy burden of organizing the Olympic Games is to take stock of the grounds at its disposal in which to create sports facilities; for all sport is movement in a given space. To provide the setting for Olympic events, the organizers must not only build; they also have to create a total environment for the Games. They must deal with the conflicting problems inherent in planning the buildings, parks, roads and transport facilities; each of these problems is almost always handled not only from the practical but from the aesthetic point of view. When we look at the town planning achieved in Tokyo in 1964, and, for ex-

Top, left **The Fehse quartet playing in the 1936 Art competition.** *Right* **The first transmission of the Games on television, 1936.** *Above Diana*, **a drawing which won third prize for W. Skoczylas (Poland), 1928**

ample, the swimming pool designed by Kenzo Tange, or at the work done in Mexico by Pedro Ramírez Vázquez (now a member of the IOC) for the celebration of the 1968 Games, or at the sports facilities in Munich for the 1972 Games created by Günter Behnisch and his colleagues, we are speechless with admiration. This major art of moving soil and building, so that the four-yearly festival of youth may be held in a setting of beauty, is an expression of a particular country at a particular time.

In every country taking part in the Games sport serves as a theme for many artists. Paintings and reliefs flourish on the walls of halls and sports buildings; medals, posters, programs, signs, newspapers and stamps are created for the Games.

Sport and Olympism have also been inspiring composers for many years. This is particularly true of the music composed for the films devoted to each Games. There is a very direct link here between musical creation and the holding of the Games, since the most important moments of each Olympiad are emphasized by an original musical score. Perhaps the most successful in this area has been Toshiro Mayuzumi's soundtrack for *Tokyo Olympiad* (1964). Many consider film to be an art in its own right and those who have seen *Olympische Spiele 1936* by Leni Riefenstahl or Kon Ichikawa's *Tokyo Olympiad* will agree. It is worth recalling what Kon Ichikawa has said about the latter:

> In this documentary film about the Olympic Games, I tried to capture the solemnity of the moment when man exceeds his limits and to express the loneliness of the athlete who, in order to win, struggles to surpass himself; I tried to penetrate the heart of human nature, not through fiction but through the fact of the Games. We attempt to become one with what in the Olympic spirit denotes the wish for peace, the love of man, the courage of a shining ideal, all aspirations dear to the heart of

man but which the daily pace of life often makes us forget. My friends, this film aims to make you feel the splendour of man and his destiny.

The 'splendour of man and his destiny' was also the wish of Coubertin and of those who, today, are responsible for the Olympic Movement.

The steadily growing importance of broadcasting suggests that this should also be considered as an art in its own right. Television makes it possible not only to widen the framework of the Olympic stadia but to show the whole world what is happening at the instant that it is taking place. Television is perhaps the art best suited to the Olympic Games and their spirit, since it enables men all over the world to participate directly. What better way has there been of achieving the wishes of the founder of the Modern Games than to make them available to all men? While the cinema brought the Olympic Movement to a much wider audience than ever before, television has, from the point of view of communication, social and financial influence, had the greatest magnetic effect of any medium.

The first television pictures of an Olympic Games were made at the Berlin Celebration, where cameras were set up in the main arena and the swimming pool and shown to audiences in leading German cities in halls and other large buildings on a closed circuit. That was the beginning; for the Games of 1976 107 electronic colour cameras, part of equipment costing over $100 million, will be used to relay events to an audience of over 800 million people.

From 1936 to 1964 the development of television as a medium for the Olympic Games was slow, but the event was one of those which gave impetus to the development of relaying pictures from continent to continent round the curve of the earth by means of satellites in space. There are few events which command worldwide attention, transcending political, social and religious boundaries, but the Olympic Games is one of them.

After World War I it was a happy coincidence that the Games should be celebrated in London, where television had been developed in the 1930s. Nine cameras, relaying black-and-white pictures from the main events at Wembley, mostly to a radius of fifty miles around London, provided a significant advance in television which not only enhanced the British experience but was then used, if meagrely to begin with, elsewhere in the wider development of the medium.

The first use of television as a financial lever came in the 1956 Games at Melbourne. Here the Organizing Committee wanted complete control of the resources and as a result several countries boycotted the film and television facilities the Games offered.

Four years later, another important step was taken

when at Rome pictures were relayed through the European Broadcasting Union to many countries throughout Western Europe and also to Poland, Hungary, Czechoslovakia and the German Democratic Republic. They were also relayed to North America by CBS, working with the Italian and French television companies.

In 1964, for the first time live television pictures of the Olympics (at Innsbruck) were transmitted to the United States via Early Bird satellite, by ABC, working with ORTF and the BBC and Austrian television. Since Early Bird was a moving satellite, live pictures could be seen in North America for only 10–12 minutes a day but it was a beginning. The Games of Tokyo were also relayed by Early Bird and thirty-nine countries were involved. Europe and North America (this time through NBC) were also able to take video recordings of events and show them much more quickly than by the air transportation of film. It was from these Games that the IOC first benefited financially, from the Japanese television organization NHK, who were the first to produce colour television pictures – these were confined to Japan.

In 1968 there was live colour coverage of the Games at Grenoble in North America (through ABC and CBC); Mexico City's operation was far more sophisticated than that of any previous Games, with many broadcasting companies and corporations, including the EBU, NHK, Telesystema Mexicano, ABC and CBC networks, co-operating to provide instant pictures throughout the world. There were last-minute problems with the satellite sending the pictures back to Europe but these were solved and the colour of the Opening Ceremony was seen clearly in Rome, Paris, London, and other cities all over western and eastern Europe as well as in America and Asia. It was, though, not a happy Games for the IOC, as far as television was concerned, since the Organizing Committee had made the television contract, worth over $10 million, with the various agencies, and the IOC received only a small sum.

This led to the IOC introducing new rules relating to television and from the fees of the 1972 Games, it, the International Federations and the NOCs benefited.

The 1972 Olympics were again covered by live transmissions in colour, pictures of Sapporo being relayed to North America by NBC and of Munich by ABC, the latter providing three hours of continuous transmission every day. In Munich, too, the technical equipment enabled people watching television at home to see events relayed again and again, in slow motion. The slightest wrinkled eyebrow could be repeated and its significance analysed.

No other event in the world draws such a large television audience as the Olympic Games and there can be no doubt that the Movement and the sports within it gain their greatest publicity from this medium.

Today, in the months and years during which the competitors are engrossed in their preparation for the Games, the huge staffs of television authorities throughout the world work together to ensure that technical efficiency is achieved for the period of the Games; pictures flashed instantly round the world to a vast number of countries present an example of Olympic cooperation which even the Founder could not have foreseen. It has undoubtedly led to a great strengthening of international bonds through communication.

THE OLYMPICS ON FILM Ken Wlaschin

Most of the Olympic Games have been filmed, though not always as well as they might have been. Indeed the cinema and the modern Olympics were born at the same time though unfortunately the Lumière Brothers in Paris, who made their first films in 1895, did not think it worthwhile recording the first Olympics in Athens in 1896 or even, for that matter, the Games in Paris in 1900. But by 1906 the newsreel cameramen were aware of the interpolated Games in Athens, though the prime interest seems to have been the Kings and Queens of Great Britain and Greece.

In truth, all of the Olympic films until 1936 were essentially newsreels, or, at best, documentary records filmed in a flat and relatively dull manner. The German Leni Riefenstahl was the first to believe that the greatest sporting event could also be great cinema and her achievement in filming the Berlin and Garmisch-Partenkirchen Games had an enormous worldwide influence on Olympic film making. Her masterpiece has never been surpassed and, with the exception of Kon Ichikawa's delightful picture of the 1964 Olympics in Japan, has rarely been approached.

The difficulty with Olympic films, as with all sports films, is simply in what they are meant to be. Are they intended as matter-of-fact reportage giving a documentary record of what happened, or are they to be artistic achievements which give up comprehensiveness and objectivity in order to gain power and beauty through editing and other subjective techniques? If pure records are wanted, as for use as training film loops, the interest must remain limited. But if the purpose of the Olympics is also to promote international interest in sport, then the high quality films are of real importance. The opposition between the prosaic and the poetic or the informational and artistic is somewhat false in that finally the best films are both.

This is nowhere better shown than in Leni Riefenstahl's *Olympische Spiele 1936*, probably the finest film ever made about sport of any kind. It is much more than a factual diary of the Games, it is a hymn to physical health, to the human body and to the glory of youth. Although she tried to make the film appear classic in its opening sequences, it ultimately becomes high German romanticism, as exhilarating as it is beautiful. Miss Riefenstahl was already a film maker of high reputation when she shot the events

Kon Ichikawa, right, directing the shooting of his film of the 1964 Games in Tokyo

Aryan beauty and strength, a theme which Leni Riefenstahl propounded through part of her *Olympische Spiele 1936,* which was not only a brilliant sporting film but remains an outstanding contribution to the art of cinema

at Berlin and Garmisch-Partenkirchen, having earlier attracted Hitler's attention and created the evil but impressive *Triumph of the Will*. For this reason she was provided with greater technical facilities than any other Olympic film maker in the past. She used thirty cameramen, shot over a million feet of film (seventy per cent of which was not usable) and had much special equipment. But her greatest asset was her own skill in editing, an ability to create rhythms and patterns rarely equalled in world cinema and she spent two years cutting her miles of film into a cohesive four-hour masterpiece. She has stated that the strength of the film comes from the music and sound which heighten the impact of the images (the sound was not live, but post-synchronized).

The structure is brilliant. There are two natural parts. The first, 'Festival of the People', begins with a symbolic paeon to the human body and concentrates on track and field events culminating in the marathon. The second part, 'Festival of Beauty', emphasizes the more poetic sports; it begins with a dawn march past the stadium and mass gymnastic exercises and includes yacht racing, riding and diving. Each event has been superbly photographed and the individual shots have then been combined in the editing with a particular rhythm. The high jump, filmed at dusk, is presented in slow motion. The pole vaulters are shown competing into the night, silhouetted against the moon. The discus and javelin throwers are as graceful as they are competitive. In the riding competition, each national entrant is shown succeeding or failing at the same difficult jump. The divers

become a poem of slow and reverse motion. Miss Riefenstahl insists that the film is apolitical though German critics of the left have argued about the ethos of the work. It is worth noting, however, that the star of the film is the black American athlete Jesse Owens, winner of four gold medals, not Hitler (an ironic comment on the Nazi theories of 'Aryan' superiority).

While Riefenstahl's film could be described as an epic hymn to sporting achievement, Kon Ichikawa's celebration of the 1964 Olympics in Japan is a lyrical ode to the human spirit. Rather than concentrating on the beauty and romance of sport (though the film is exceedingly beautiful), Ichikawa shows us the human being under the sportsman, the man struggling to conquer the limitations of his own body. The dedication, desperation, anguish and grief of the competitors is depicted with technological aides that Riefenstahl did not have, notably the telephoto lens and colour film. Ichikawa also achieves moments of pure elegance and lyrical splendour with diving, jumping, running bodies seeming to defy gravity as they appear suspended in space. With his 164 cameramen, the Japanese director is able to give us a more intimate portrait of the meaning of athleticism; instead of viewing impassive figures from a distance, we are able to observe the tiniest flicker of emotion in close-up. There is a nicely balanced use of humour, as in the marathon race, and superb all-over structure. Lesser known but almost as impressive is the film of the Winter Olympics in Japan, Masahiro Shinoda's *Sapporo Winter Olympics*. Shinoda used a crew of 275 with fifty-two cameras to shoot eighty-seven hours of film in Fujicolor and 'scope. He edited this material into 108 delightful minutes about flight and motion in the snow which also emphasizes the anxiety and rapture of the competitors.

The film poems of Riefenstahl, Ichikawa and Shinoda bear little resemblance to the earliest Olympic films. The newsreel of the interpolated Games at Athens in 1906 shows the participants marching past the Kings and Queens of Greece and England. Newsreel material of the 1912 Games at Stockholm shot by Pathé shows lawn tennis, association football, wrestling , the high jump, hammer throw and marathon and Charles Reidpath (United States) winning the 400 metres. There is film of the Olympic skating trials in Switzerland in 1915 and full newsreel coverage of the Antwerp Games. The first feature-length film was made in 1925 by Rapid Films of France. Their *Jeux Olympiques, Paris 1924*, was made to be screened in six two-reel sections; the star of the film is the great Paavo Nurmi winning his five gold medals. There was no attempt to make an important film of the 1932 Olympics.

Modern Olympic film making began in 1936 but the German example was not a popular model for the next Games in London in 1948. Castleton Knight's *XIVth Olympiad: The Glory of Sport* is simply a 130-minute glorified newsreel, shot with sixteen cameramen and 400,000 feet of Technicolor film and completed in three weeks. The Finnish film of the 1952 Games in Helsinki was again very much of the straightforward newsreel type while the record of the Melbourne Olympics in 1956 was a marvel of speed with art sacrificed for immediacy: Ian K. Barner used thirty teams of cameramen and presented the results in London nine days after the end of the Games.

For the 1960 Olympics in Rome, director Romolo Marcellini attempted to pick up the torch from Riefenstahl. He used a crew of 120 with forty cameras, gave the film structure, accented the faces of the athletes rather than their muscles and generally succeeded in presenting the excitement and highlights of the Games, notably the winning performances by the Ethiopian Abebe Bikila in the marathon and the American Wilma Rudolph in the sprints. Again in 1964 Kon Ichikawa brought the highest cinematic skills to the filming of the Games in Japan and in Mexico in 1968 another film maker of reputation tried his hand at the competition. Alberto Isaac used seventy-nine cameramen to make a rather fine and stunningly photographed movie somewhat marred by a dull narration but full of outstanding technical innovations such as cutting off crowd noises so that record-breaking swimmer Debby Meyer's strokes are counterpointed by the ticking of the computer clock. In Grenoble two other notable film directors, Claude Lelouch and François Reichenbach, created an impressionistic view of the Winter Olympics with a dazzling display of camera virtuosity which sometimes made the athletes performers rather than competitors. For the 1972 Games in Munich David Wolper signed ten major directors to make a $1½ million epic. Unhappily the team did not blend and *Visions of Eight* is an uneven if fascinating look at the psychology of the directors rather than the competitors. Mai Zetterling's strenuous portrayal of weightlifting is the highlight.

There are of course, many other films about various aspects of the Olympics, including Henri Champetier's documentary about Coubertin and some outstanding short films from the National Film Board of Canada. There is even a compilation film of all the film records of the Olympics, the German-made *Olympia, Olympia*, which shows many of the highlights of the existing material.

THE WORK OF THE IOC MEDICAL COMMISSION A. H. Beckett, DSc, PhD FRIC, FPS

The IOC Medical Commission was originally established in Athens in 1961 with Sir Arthur Porritt (now Lord Porritt) as President, and with three additional members. On the resignation of Sir Arthur, Prince Alexandre de Mérode of Belgium, a member of the IOC, became President in 1967 and the Commission was re-established. At present there are nine other permanent members from Austria, Belgium, Great Britain, Italy, Japan, Mexico, Senegal, the United States and the USSR. For a particular Games, a representative of the host country serves on the Commission. The members cover a broad range of medical and scientific interests linked with the Olympic Games, including general medical aspects, sports medicine, pharmacy, medicinal chemistry, physiology, pharmacology and gynaecology.

The Commission has three main responsibilities as far as the Olympic Games are concerned. It gives guidance and approval to the host country on medical and paramedical installations, organization and facilities at the Olympic Village and at the various sports sites. It is responsible for doping control at the Games, classifying the chemicals considered to be doping substances and proposing courses of action to the IOC Executive Board when the doping rules have been contravened. It is also responsible for femininity control for women's sporting events at the Games and issues certificates to those who have passed this control.

The Commission functions as the medical counsellor of the IOC and as a contact organization for the 'Olympic Solidarity' movement. It also works closely with the International Sports Federations.

Doping Control

In the past few decades, there has been increasing pressure on athletes to achieve success at all costs. This has resulted from national and social esteem and the financial or other rewards which accompany success.

In society as a whole, during the same period, the belief has grown that drugs cure many ills and diseases, shield the individual from the problems of his environment, and protect him from the consequences of his failure to adopt a correct life style and from the excesses to which he subjects his body and mind. Many people expect the scientist and physician to provide pills for all ills and problems. It is therefore not surprising that some athletes and their trainers and sports physicians seek to short-circuit or supplement the rigours of extensive and very demanding training programs by using drugs with the intention of improving performance.

The success of the pharmaceutical industry in making available effective drugs which have brought benefit to mankind *when used correctly*, provides sportsmen with a whole range of chemical substances which have profound actions on all aspects of bodily and mental functions.

Doping in sport is not in itself a recent phenomenon. It is believed that athletes in the Olympic Games at the end of the third century B.C. tried to improve performance by any means possible. In 1865, canal swimmers in Amsterdam were using drugs. Fourteen years later, in the first six-day cycle races, some riders were suspected of using doping agents; nitroglycerine, caffeine, ether, heroin and cocaine were among them. In 1886 the first doping fatality in sport was reported. At the turn of the century association football players and boxers were said to be using strychnine, alcohol and cocaine.

The first scientific proof of doping was reported from Austria in 1910 when a Russian chemist brought to Austria by the Austrian jockey club demonstrated the presence of alkaloids in the saliva of horses. By 1933 the word 'doping' was included in some dictionaries but it was not until 1950 that there was real alarm about doping in sport. Used ampoules and syringes were found in some changing rooms at the 1952 Winter Olympics in Oslo. In the 1955 Tour de France cycle race, one of the riders was accused of doping; in another cycle race that year, five urine samples out of twenty-five were classed as positive for doping agents. A number of cyclists in the following year were shown to be taking amphetamines. The American College of Sports Medicine reported in 1958 that out of 441 trainers, coaches and assistants, thirty-five per cent had personal experience with amphetamines or at least knew how to use them, while only seven per cent knew nothing about their use. A survey by the Italian association football organization in 1961 showed that seventeen per cent of all players took psychotonics and ninety-four per cent of the A-league clubs used some sort of drug. Reports of drug misuse have been increasing in the last two decades.

A few statements from sportsmen and others closely connected with sport indicate the escalating problems although some may be exaggerated. Jacques Anquetil, a French cyclist, has said that 'everyone in cycling dopes himself' and 'those who claim they don't are liars'. Harold Connolly (United States), former Olympic hammer champion, said in 1973,

For eight years prior to 1972 I would have to refer to myself as a hooked athlete. Like all my competitors I was using anabolic steroids as an integral part of my training in the hammer throw.

He also wrote:

Just prior to the 1964 Olympic Games in Tokyo, all around me it seemed that more and more athletes were using steroids for athletic preparation and one began to feel that he was placing himself in a decided disadvantage if he did not also get on the sports medicine bandwagon. . . .

His most frightening statement to the subcommittee of the US Senate Committee on the Judiciary in 1973 was:

I knew any number of athletes in the 1968 Olympic team who had so much scar tissue and so many puncture holes on their backsides that it was difficult to find a fresh spot to give them a new shot. I relate these incidents to emphasize my contention that the overwhelming majority of the international track and field athletes I know would take anything and do anything short of killing themselves to improve their athletic performance.

The words of certain sports physicians who warned against the misuse of drugs in sports were ignored by sports officials and the Press for many years. However, the deaths which occurred because of doping, for example those of the Danish cyclist Knud Enemark Jensen in the 1960 Olympic Games, and the British cyclist Tommy Simpson in the 1967 Tour de France, as well as those of lesser-known sportsmen (Dr Albert Dirix of Belgium, a member of the IOC Medical Commission, states that doping to improve performance has accounted for at least thirty deaths in sport) gave impetus to those who were pressing for action against doping in sport.

In 1959, in France, a doping commission was formed by the Association Nationale d'Éducation Physique, and in the same year the International Sports Medicine Congresses in Paris and Évian were devoted mainly to the problem of doping. In 1962, the Italian Sport Doctors' Association organized a doping inquiry and in Moscow in the same year the IOC passed a resolution against doping. The anti-doping law passed by the French Senate became effective in 1965, and in the same year Belgium introduced an anti-doping act.

At about the same time, some of the International Sports Federations were including in their rules a ban on certain drugs and introducing doping tests.

The establishment in 1967 of the present IOC Medical Commission, with dope control as one of its terms of reference, was a significant step forward in the recognition that the fight against dope in sport was an international problem requiring international action.

The question used to be frequently asked, 'Why should not the right of choice be allowed to any competitor to use any method of training or even any drug in spite of possible danger to health or life? If he dies in the attempt to excel, is that not his responsibility?'

One answer is that the use of drugs contravenes the basic characteristics of sport which should involve the matching of skill and strength based upon the natural capabilities of the participants, and therefore sporting morality is contravened by doping.

However, there are equally telling reasons not based upon subjective moral or ethical arguments.

Some physicians and coaches do not always put competitors' welfare first. They have given drugs to competitors without the latter being aware of their effects or dangers. If competition in sport were to become competition between pharmacologists and physicians, with competitors being used as guinea pigs and receiving potent drugs, the name of sport would suffer and the countries with sophisticated and ruthless physicians would have an unfair advantage over less pharmacologically developed countries.

Some drugs, e.g. amphetamines, can cause aggression and loss of judgment; so drug taking by a competitor, either on his own initiative or on that of his physician or coach, can cause hazards to other competitors or spectators or officials – crashes in cycling, dangerous tactics in team sports, carelessness in track and field events.

Some young people in many countries today take drugs for thrills, to escape boredom or because of pressures within their group, and thus drug abuse is increasing in many societies. For many young people, sportsmen and sportswomen constitute heroes and heroines whose actions have a great influence. If these leading figures were known to be allowed drugs in competitions and in training, the misuse of drugs in society would be likely to escalate.

The continued use of some drugs may cause psychological or physical harm to those who take them, e.g.

amphetamines can produce psychosis and psychological dependence and narcotics can produce physical dependence.

In recent years the need to attempt to control doping in sport has been generally accepted.

A commission of experts convened by the Council of Europe in 1963 gave the following definition of doping:

> Doping is defined as the administering or use of substances in any form alien to the body or of physiological substances in abnormal amounts and with abnormal methods by healthy persons with the exclusive aim of attaining an artificial and unfair increase of performance in competitions. Furthermore, various psychological measures to increase performance in sport must be regarded as doping.

This definition emphasizes the intent of the drug misuser. However, problems arise in the assessment of intent and in drawing the line between the therapeutic use and the use of drugs as doping agents. Some International Sports Federations, e.g. the International Amateur Cycling Federation (FIAC), therefore drew up lists of banned drugs; the proof of the use of any of these drugs by a competitor then constituted the proof that a doping agent had been used. A definitive list, however, does not necessarily lead to the desired results, because chemicals not on the list but with actions similar to those brought about by those on the list may be used. The pharmacologically sophisticated countries could gain in circumventing the listed compounds and competitors would perhaps be placed in even greater danger than by using some of the listed drugs.

The IOC Medical Commission defined its policy as the attempt to prevent the use of those drugs in sport which constituted dangers when used as doping agents, but with the minimum of interference with therapeutic use of drugs. Nevertheless, a clear line had to be drawn. Certain classes of drugs could not be accepted even for therapeutic use without destroying the whole of the doping control system. The Commission also decided to ban only those compounds for which suitable analytical methods could be devised to detect the compounds unequivocally in urine (or blood) samples, i.e. contravention of the rules would be considered as established only if a drug belonging to one of the banned classes of drugs could be demonstrated in a urine sample obtained from the competitor under controlled conditions (see below). Therefore, although the banning of anabolic steroids was considered necessary as early as 1967, this class of compounds was not included in the list of doping agents banned for the 1968 and 1972 Olympic Games because suitable tests to determine the presence of all the drugs of this class had not been developed at that time.

While the Commission had drawn up its list of classes of doping agents to be banned at the Olympics, certain sports had also faced their own particular problems of drug misuse – for example, the use of alcohol in pistol shooting in the modern pentathlon. It was therefore agreed that International Sports Federations could request the addition but not the deletion of types of drugs to the Commission's list.

The Commission approved the following list of banned classes of doping agents for the 1972 Olympics. It should be noted that 'and related compounds' are included.

a) psychomotor stimulant drugs, e.g. amphetamine; benzphetamine; cocaine; diethylpropion; dimethylamphetamine; ethylamphetamine; fencamfamin; methylamphetamine; methylphenidate; norpseudoephedrine; phendimetrazine; phenmetrazine; prolintane; and related compounds;

b) sympathomimetic amines, e.g. ephedrine; methylephedrine; methoxyphenamine; and related compounds;

c) miscellaneous central nervous system stimulants, e.g. amiphenazole; bemigride; leptazol; nikethamide; strychnine; and related compounds;

d) narcotic analgesics, e.g. heroin; morphine; methadone; dextromoramide; dipipanone; pethidine; and related compounds.

In April 1975 an additional banned class of doping agents was included, namely:

e) anabolic steroids, e.g. methandienone; stanozolol; oxymetholone; nandrolone decanoate; nandrolone phenylpropionate; and related compounds.

The banning of the psychomotor stimulant drugs presented no problems since there is no medical justification for using such drugs in sport and their abuse constitutes a potential danger to the user and to other competitors and spectators. Similarly, the use of narcotic analgesics for therapeutic reasons could not be accepted; the danger of addiction to the use of such compounds is well recognized.

The sympathomimetic amines represent a special problem, however, because some of these compounds are used to treat colds, allergies and asthma. However, to exclude compounds like ephedrine from any ban would have undermined the whole system of doping control because much use was made of these compounds in doping in sport after the amphetamines had been controlled. To allow their medical use would lead only to spurious statements of ailments by physicians, coaches or competitors. Some drugs have been developed to deal with these medical problems which have negligible stimulant effects on the central nervous system and are therefore not on the banned list. The Commission receives applications from team physicians at the Olympic Games for the use of particular medicines and decides whether or not the drug concerned comes within the class of 'related compound' to the sympathomimetic amines. Thus the principle of ensuring an effective doping ban while recognizing the need for therapeutic treatment is maintained.

Consideration has been given to the inclusion of tranquillizing agents in the ban and, in fact, the phenothiazines were so included for the 1968 Games. However, as competitors sometimes need to use sedatives and nonnarcotic analgesics because of problems occurring after travelling and in new environments, these compounds were taken off the list for 1972; in any case they would not improve performance in most sports.

Attempts to find suitable analytical methods to determine the presence of anabolic steroids continued; by 1974 sufficient progress had been made for the Commission to include them in the list of prohibited drugs at the Olympic Games. Anabolic steroids are compounds which represent chemical modifications of the male hormone testosterone in which the anabolic (muscle-building) actions are enhanced and the 'maleness' actions of the hormone are decreased. Their use does not only contravene sporting ethics but constitutes a danger to women and to the growth of young people of both sexes; the use of some anabolic steroids in large doses may cause liver damage, gastric ulcers, personality changes, fluid retention, and may affect spermatogenesis; there are also reports that their use may lead to cancer.

Many International Federations have cooperated very closely with the Commission in adopting in their own rules the general principles and classes of compounds banned by the Commission, but modified to deal with their own separate problems. Some Federations have also set up their own Medical Commissions or Advisory Boards. In general, athletes are selected at random for testing; usually the first three or four in finals are also selected. At the Olympic Games, the number of athletes to be checked is agreed between the Commission and the Federation concerned. Urine is the most convenient sample to use for analysis because higher concentrations of the drugs are found in it than in blood, and urine constituents give less interference in the tests.

At the Olympic Games, immediately after a contest, the selected athlete is told to report at a doping control station within a stated time. He may be accompanied by a team official, coach or doctor. At the control station, his identity is checked. He is asked to select two bottles bearing codes and pass urine into one of them. It is determined that the urine comes from the designated competitor because there have been instances in international competitions when cyclists have attached other persons' urine in plastic bags in their armpits and provided this sample for their test. After its pH (acidity) has been measured, the urine sample is subdivided by pouring a portion into the second bottle. The samples are then sealed securely; the competitor and his attendant witness this and sign records which are then countersigned by appropriate officials. The samples and records are transmitted in sealed containers to the laboratory, which acknowledges that they have been received in a sealed condition. The laboratory is not aware of the identity of the samples except by the code. The results of the tests on the coded samples are made known directly to the Chairman of the Commission or his appointee, who are the only people who can identify the result with a competitor's name.

At the same time, on some days, samples coded in the same way, but taken from volunteers among the members of the IOC Medical Commission who have taken one of the banned drugs, are submitted for analysis. The identification of the drug in these samples checks the method of analysis.

Each sample is analysed as soon as possible after receipt. A portion of one of each pair is analysed after suitable records have been made and containers and bottles checked to ensure that tampering with the samples could not have occurred. The sample is extracted with an organic solvent under controlled conditions and then portions of the extract are examined by techniques such as thin-layer chromatography and gas-liquid chromatography to identify the compounds present. Confirmation of the substances present depends upon more sophisticated and expensive techniques such as mass spectrometry, in which the molecules are shattered into fragment ions, some of which are diagnostic for the particular molecule. The presence or absence of the banned drug is thus established in an objective and unequivocal manner.

The duplicate sample is reserved for a repeat analysis. This test, as far as the Olympic Games are concerned, is carried out in the same laboratory as the first analysis but by different personnel. This second test is supervised by a member of the Commission and the delegation of the country whose competitor is showing a positive result is allowed to send an observer.

The tests for anabolic steroids depend upon the use of radio-immune assays which distinguish the steroids from natural hormones found in the body. Some of the anabolic steroids can be determined also by mass spectrometry, which establishes which steroid is present. At present, establishing the misuse of a drug in the banned classes, other than that of the anabolic steroids, necessitates the unequivocal identification of the particular compound. For anabolic steroids, a positive result is defined as 'failure to pass a test for the absence of anabolic steroids in urine as measured by a radio-immune assay based upon the use of a number of antisera with selectivity for structures in anabolic steroid molecules'.

In April 1975, the IOC Medical Commission designated the radio-immune assay as a screening test only and required gas-liquid chromatography/mass spectrometry evidence to identify the particular anabolic steroid being used and/or its metabolite(s) before the declaration of a positive result in the banned class of anabolic steroids. This decision brings this class into line with the other classes of banned drugs.

There are some problems. Doping control requires well-equipped laboratories and highly skilled staff. A laboratory without the necessary experience can report a negative result when doping has occurred, and therefore it is important that authorities in sport only use laboratories which have been approved for this specific purpose. Problems have occurred in international events when non-approved laboratories have been used for the repeat analysis on the duplicate sample.

Stimulant drugs taken just before competition will show a positive result in a urine sample immediately after the sporting event. However, a competitor may take anabolic steroids during training, discontinue their use a week or two before a particular event, and still have an advantage, at least in weight, from the drug misuse; a urine sample collected at the event does not show a positive result. If International Sports Federations decide to introduce random testing at various events throughout the year, thereby making it difficult to establish a continuous anabolic steroid schedule, this should constitute a deterrent.

The introduction of doping controls by the International Sports Federations as well as by the Commission has led to a great reduction in the misuse of those drugs included in the banned classes since 1968. Although some drug misuse was detected in the 1972 Olympic Games, the positive results represented less than 0.5 per cent of the large number of competitors tested. It is significant that the International Federations that have routine tests, for example the IAAF, have virtually eliminated drug misuse in their sport. Unfortunately not all sports have introduced tests and reports indicate that drug misuse is still occurring.

The control of doping has probably saved lives and has certainly improved the image of sport. The deterrent effect of dope controls rather than the punitive aspect has been recognized and commands support from all concerned. On the other hand, the misuse of anabolic steroids has greatly increased since 1968 because of the lack of suitable tests.

It will be important to preserve doping control as a deterrent. Any relaxation would have serious consequences because the pressures to succeed in sport will not lessen. Attempts will continually be made by some to use compounds which they hope will defeat the analytical skills involved in the present successful testing procedures. However, detection methods, including those for anabolic steroids, are continuing to improve rapidly, both in sensitivity and specificity.

There are problems, however, concerned with the treatment during competitions of certain medical complaints. No doubt continuing research will indicate those drugs which can be used for these complaints without undermining the basis of doping control.

Femininity Control

Not all humans can be classified physically as completely male or completely female. Those individuals who are in outlook, in lifestyle and in many physical characteristics considered as women but who are, because of chromosome abnormalities, not truly female, while very few in number, represent a higher proportion of the competitors in women's sports than they do in society as a whole. This is because they have physical advantages, for example, in muscle development, over the true female.

Before the establishment of the Commission, reports had been circulating for many years that not completely female individuals were competing in women's sports and that some world records in women's sports were held by such persons. Sporadic action had been taken in some international events when the female character of some individuals had been challenged and, in fact, certain persons had been banned from some competitions with much attendant publicity. The countries concerned were probably aware of the doubts about the female characteristics of some of their competitors but such was the pressure in competitions that firm international action was required.

Thus the Commission had to attempt to safeguard the right to fair competition for women by barring these very few persons but to do so in as delicate and sensitive a manner as possible and without publicity which would affect banned individuals. It was decided that physical examination of all those who wished to compete in women's sports at the Olympic Games would not be acceptable and therefore other methods were sought. The announcement that femininity control of intending competitors in women's events would be mandatory did much in itself to solve the problem at international level because most countries immediately took greater care in their own selection of competitors for women's events.

The question arises of apparent discrimination between women's events, in which there is femininity control, and men's events, in which there is no such control. However, the purpose of the control is to protect women against unfair competition. In men's sports, individuals who are not truly male do not have an advantage over the truly male in competition, and therefore those who are not truly either male or female are not barred from competing in men's events.

Competitors who wish to take part in women's sports at the Olympics must in general take a femininity-control examination within a few days of entering the Olympic Village. However, those who have been tested in past competitions and can present a valid certificate issued either by the IOC Medical Commission or by an International Federation during a world or continental championships are exempt. The examination room is located in the Olympic Village; a member of the Commission is present during the examination.

A member of the Commission identifies the competitor. Biological samples for testing are collected by scraping the buccal mucous membrane (inside the cheek) of the competitor and smearing the samples on glass slides, or some hairs from the head are plucked out for a similar examination of the roots.

In females, organelles called Barr bodies are present in a large proportion of nuclei of cells, whereas they are absent from cell nuclei in males. These Barr bodies, which stain intensely with nuclear dyes, for example red with a dye called Biebrich Scarlet, are small and well defined. After staining, the slide is examined under a microscope; a few hundred nuclei are usually examined and the appearance of Barr bodies in more than twenty-five per cent of them is considered to be indicative of cells from a female. On the other hand, Y-chromatin is found in more than thirty-five per cent of cell nuclei from males but in less than three per cent of nuclei from females. In testing for Y-chromatin, the cells are examined by a fluorescent microscope and the bodies containing Y-chromatin are seen to be fluorescent. In general, the presence of Y-chromatin in more than thirty-five per cent of the nuclei is considered to indicate cells from males. Thus cells from a female will give a positive result for Barr bodies and a negative result in the Y-chromatin test.

A failure to indicate female in these two tests leads to a re-examination of the competitor by the taking of a blood sample for a karyotype test, a chromosome mapping test, in which the distribution of chromosomes in terms of length, area and volume is examined; female and male give different results.

If all these tests indicate doubt as to the female character of the competitor, a meeting is called between the Commission, the physician of the team concerned and a representative of the appropriate International Federation. The competitor is then invited to undergo a detailed physical examination by one or more gynaecologists before the final decision of whether or not to bar from competition is taken.

All these tests and examinations are carried out in secret. Every attempt is made to ensure that any irregularity resulting in a competitor's not participating in the Olympic Games does not attract the attention of the Press.

It is important to stress that, as with dope-control tests, the emphasis of the Commission in dealing with femininity control, is on preventing problems in sport rather than taking punitive measures. Now that femininity-control testing is routine procedure at the Olympic Games, the right of women to compete fairly as women has been safeguarded. Furthermore, the realization by all countries that tests will be carried out at the Games has resulted in relatively few problems for the Commission at the Games themselves. A measure of the success of the control is that actions taken have not received publicity; thus the rights of individuals in this delicate area have been protected.

SPORTS NO LONGER ON THE OLYMPIC PROGRAM Erich Kamper

During the eighty years of the modern Games the Olympic program has undergone considerable change, and not until 1924 did any degree of standardization begin to develop. At Athens in 1896 there were forty-three events; in Munich in 1972 the total was 198. Only four sports – athletics, fencing, gymnastics and swimming – have been represented at all the Games. Rowing was included for 1896 in the program but was a casualty of the stormy weather, and at St Louis in 1904 professional competitions were included in the cycling events so these have not been given official status.

As late as 1920 the distribution and scope of the Olympic program still left much to be desired: there were no fewer than twenty-one shooting events – World War I continued with nonbelligerent arms – and fourteen sailing events of which seven were such curiosities that only one boat started in each of them.

In compiling their program the organizers of the Games obtained considerable concessions from the IOC, particularly before 1924. This was due in no small part to the fact that the IOC wanted to develop and diversify the program. So it was that typical national sports were brought into the program. In this way it was hoped to increase recognition and popularity for sports of less than worldwide appeal. Cricket, croquet, golf, lacrosse, motor boating, polo, paume (real tennis), rackets, roque (a form of croquet played on a court with a hard raised edge used as a cushion in bank shots) and rugby football were among such sports. Participation in, and response to, these sports was limited and only a few of them appeared for a second time on the Olympic program. They did not become permanent because the organizers of the following Games would lose interest in them and look on their continuation as a needless burden. An exception among these transient items on the program was lawn tennis, which retained its Olympic status from 1896 to 1924, enabling such famous players as Vincent Richards, Henri Cochet, Suzanne Lenglen and Helen Wills to compete and inspire great crowds of spectators. The most remarkable achievement of all the Olympic tennis players, however, was undoubtedly that of the Frenchman Max Decugis, who won the men's singles at the Interpolated or Extraordinary Olympic Games in Athens in 1906, and the mixed doubles with Suzanne Lenglen at Antwerp in 1920 when he was thirty-eight: proof of tremendous competitive capacity over a decade and a half.

There were many who regretted the removal from the program of the Arts competitions. These were introduced in 1912 at the particular wish of Coubertin and up to 1948 they put many notable works of architecture, sculpture, painting, graphics, literature and music before a wider public and, particularly in the field of sports architecture, provided many stimuli to development. These Olympic contests in the arts were intended to bring about a synthesis of athletic and intellectual talents on the ancient Greek model. How far Coubertin's own interest went in this direction is best shown by the fact that in Stockholm in 1912 he entered for the literature competition under the pseudonyms Georg Hohrod and Martin Eschbach and won the gold medal for his *Ode to Sport*.

There have also been changes over the years within the various sports. Thus there used to be (from 1900 to 1912) standing jumps events: these enabled the American Ray Ewry to rank among the most successful of all Olympic competitors. He won no fewer than ten Olympic gold medals from 1900 to 1908, two of them in the Extraordinary Games of 1906: ten Olympic victories from ten entries is a record that is unique for the modern Games and not likely to be broken. Ewry was twenty-seven when he won his first three Olympic victories in Paris in 1900. He had suffered from polio for many years as a child and a successful career in athletics seemed an unrealizable dream then. His 1904 world's best performance for the standing long jump at St Louis (3.476 m; 11ft $4\frac{7}{8}$ in) stood until after World War II.

A special event on the Olympic program (from 1900 to 1920) was the tug-of-war, which proved particularly popular in 1908 (London) and 1912 (Stockholm), and led to keen if not bitter rivalry between British and Swedish police teams. Although the 1908 event was dominated by British teams (the City of London police won), their specially designed shoes giving them a clear advantage over their opponents, the splendidly trained Stockholm Police gained their longed-for and jubilantly received revenge over the Londoners four years later.

One of the greatest curiosities of the Olympics was undoubtedly the underwater swimming event, held once only at Paris in 1900, and won by the Frenchman Charles de Vendeville from his countryman A. Six and the Dane Peder Lykkeberg. In this unusual competition two points were scored for every metre swum and one point for every second under water. De Vendeville and Six both swam sixty metres (196 ft 10 in), but de Vendeville stayed under for 1 min 8.4 sec, his compatriot for 1 min 5.4 sec.

Another swimming event with a certain curiosity value at the 1900 Paris Games was the 200-metres swimming obstacle race, for which agility as well as swimming talent was required: competitors had to climb over a pole and scramble over and swim under a row of boats. The winner was the Australian Frederick Lane (2 min 38.4 sec), followed by the Austrian Otto Wahle (2 min 40.0 sec) and the Briton Peter Kemp (2 min 47.4 sec). The amazingly good times are explained by the fact that the event was swum in the Seine, with the current.

Great Britain beating the United States in tug-of-war at the 1920 Games

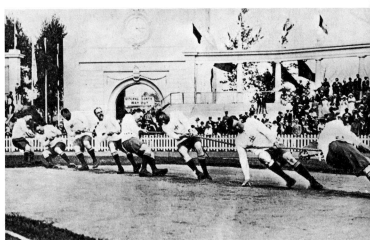

Sports No Longer on the Olympic Program ★ Competition ● Demonstration

	1896	1900	1904	1908	1912	1920	1924	1928	1932	1936	1948	1952	1956	1960	1964	1968
American Football									●							
Australian Football													●			
Baseball					●					●		●	●		●	
Budo															●	
Cricket		★														
Croquet		★														
Gliding										●						
Golf		★	★													
Jeu de Paume (Real Tennis)				★												
Lacrosse			★	★				●	●		●					
Lawn Tennis: men's singles	★	★	★	★	★	★	★									
women's singles		★		★	★	★	★									
men's doubles	★	★	★	★	★	★	★									
women's doubles						★	★									
mixed doubles		★			★	★	★									
Motor Boating				★												
Pelota							●									●
Polo		★		★		★	★			★						
Rackets: men's singles and men's doubles				★												
Roque			★													
Rugby Football		★		★		★	★									

In 1908 and 1912 there were indoor as well as outdoor competitions in lawn tennis.

Athletics

	1896	1900	1904	1908	1912	1920	1924	1928	1932	1936	1948	1952	1956	1960	1964	1968
60 m		★	★													
5 miles				★												
200-m hurdles		★	★													
4,000-m steeplechase		★														
3,000 m, team					★	★	★									
3 miles, team				★												
5,000 m, team		★														
cross-country, individual					★	★	★									
cross-country, team			★		★	★	★									
pentathlon					★	★	★									
standing high jump		★	★	★	★											
standing long jump		★	★	★	★											
standing triple jump		★	★													
56-lb weight			★			★										
discus, ancient style				★												
javelin, free style				★												
shot, both hands					★											
discus, both hands					★											
javelin, both hands					★											
tug-of-war		★	★	★	★	★										
3,000-m walk						★										
3,500-m walk				★												
10,000-m walk					★	★	★				★	★				
10-miles walk				★												

Canoeing

	1896	1900	1904	1908	1912	1920	1924	1928	1932	1936	1948	1952	1956	1960	1964	1968
10,000-m kayak singles										★	★	★	★			
10,000-m kayak pairs										★	★	★	★			
4 x 500-m kayak singles relay														★		
10,000-m Canadian singles											★	★	★			
10,000-m Canadian pairs										★	★	★	★			
10,000-m folding kayak singles										★						
10,000-m folding kayak pairs										★						
800-m: kayak singles							●									
kayak pairs							●									
kayak fours							●									
Canadian singles							●									
Canadian pairs							●									
Canadian fours							●									

	1896	1900	1904	1908	1912	1920	1924	1928	1932	1936	1948	1952	1956	1960	1964	1968
Cycling																
road race, team					★	★	★	★	★	★	★	★	★			
one-lap race (660 yd)				★												
5,000-m track race				★												
10,000-m track race	★															
20-km track race				★												
50-km track race						★	★									
100-km track race	★			★												
12-hour race	★															
Equestrian Sports																
high jump		★														
long jump		★														
figure riding						★										
Fencing																
foil for fencing masters		★														
épée for fencing masters		★														
épée for amateurs and fencing masters		★														
sabre for fencing masters		★														
single sticks			★													
Gymnastics																
parallel bars, team, men	★															
horizontal bar, team, men	★															
rope climbing, men	★		★				★		★							
club swinging, men			★													
combined competition, 9 events, men				★												
triathlon, men			★													
combined competition, 7 kinds of apparatus, men			★													
sidehorse vault, men							★									
tumbling, men									★							
Swedish exercises, team, men					★	★										
free exercises, team, men					★	★										
team exercises with portable apparatus, women												★	★			
Rowing																
coxed fours, inriggers					★											
Shooting																
free rifle: individual	★			★												
team				★	★	★	★									
military rifle: individual		★			★	★										
team		★		★	★	★										
smallbore rifle: individual				★	★											
team				★	★	★										
live pigeon shooting		★														
clay pigeon shooting, team				★	★	★	★									
running deer shooting: single																
shot, individual				★	★	★	★									
single shot, team				★	★	★	★									
double shot, individual				★	★	★	★									
double shot, team						★	★									
single and double shot												★	★			
military revolver: individual	★															
team		★		★	★	★										

	1896	1900	1904	1908	1912	1920	1924	1928	1932	1936	1948	1952	1956	1960	1964	1968
Swimming																
50-yd freestyle			★													
100-m freestyle for sailors	★															
200-m obstacle race		★														
400-m breaststroke			★		★	★										
880-yd freestyle			★													
4,000-m freestyle		★														
underwater		★														
plunge for distance			★													
plain high diving					★	★	★									
200-m team swimming		★														
4 x 50-yd relay			★													
Yachting																
5.5 m												★	★	★	★	★
6 m				★	★	★	★	★	★	★	★	★				
6 m, 1907 rating						★										
6.5 m, 1919 rating						★										
7 m				★		★										
8 m				★	★	★	★	★	★	★						
8 m, 1907 rating						★										
10 m					★											
10 m, 1907 rating						★										
10 m, 1919 rating						★										
12 m				★	★											
12 m, 1907 rating						★										
12 m, 1919 rating						★										
sharpie													★			
30 sq m						★										
40 sq m						★										
swallow											★					
open class		★														
0.5 ton		★														
0.5–1.0 ton		★														
1–2 ton		★														
2–3 ton		★														
3–10 ton		★														
10–20 ton		★														
The Arts																
designs for town planning					★	★	★	★	★	★	★					
architectural designs								★	★	★	★					
sculptures					★	★	★	★	★	★	★					
medals and badges								★	★	★	★					
reliefs										★	★					
paintings					★	★	★	★	★	★	★					
drawings and watercolours								★	★	★						
applied graphics (posters, diplomas, stamps, seals)										★	★					
other graphic art (wood engravings, copperplate engravings, etchings, lithographs)								★	★	★	★					
literature (all kinds)					★	★	★		★							
lyric works (hymns, cantatas)								★		★	★					
compositions for one instrument								★		★	★					
orchestral works (all kinds)								★		★	★					

In 1912, 1920 and 1924 all architecture was judged in one group; sculptures, medals, badges and reliefs were judged in one group; paintings and all graphic art were judged in one group. In 1928 and 1932 medals, badges and reliefs were judged in one group.

Discontinued Olympic Awards   Merit for Alpinism awarded in 1924, 1932, 1936
Merit for Aeronautics awarded in 1936

The Winter Olympics

INTRODUCTION John Rodda

Winter sport is the black sheep of the Olympic family. The relationship between the Summer and Winter Games has at the best been uneasy, at the worst barely tolerable.

The popular version of the root of this trouble is that Coubertin was opposed to a separate Games for winter events because they would bring about disunity within the Olympic Movement. That was a contributory factor to the discord, which was more closely related, however, to the strength of winter sports.

Snow sports in the first quarter of the twentieth century were really confined to the Scandinavian countries. The Nordic Games had been organized every four years from 1901 to 1917, then in 1922 and 1926. The main events were Nordic skiing (cross-country events), ski jumping and bandy, a Nordic variety of ice hockey. With these and other smaller competitions and the annual Holmenkollen Week in Norway winter sports as the Scandinavian nations understood them were organized in a style similar to the Summer Olympics.

Holmenkollen was as much a cult as a sporting event; competing there was as much a pilgrimage as anything else. Sir Arnold Lunn, the creator of downhill ski racing and the most influential figure in the sport, was contributing a chapter to this book when he died in 1974. He wrote of Holmenkollen from personal experience:

> I myself felt that there was something which, for want of a more accurate description, could be described as a mystique about Holmenkollen and which recalled the mystique of the classic Olympics, restricted as Herodotus wrote, 'to those who had common temples and sacrifices and like ways of life'.

It was then not surprising that if Coubertin and his colleagues were suspicious of what effect winter sports might have on the Games, the Nordic sportsmen believed that only at Holmenkollen could the 'immortal garland' be won. The Norwegian attitude had, too, the unfortunate effect of delaying the formation of the International Ski Federation, largely because the Norwegians felt that no world championship could replace their events.

The opposition to the Scandinavian countries' containment of winter events grew, however, particularly after the invention of Alpine skiing in 1911 by an Englishman, Henry Lunn, father of Sir Arnold Lunn, who pioneered downhill racing and the slalom. These quickly became popular and by 1914 at the Olympic Congress in Paris (after figure skating had been included in the 1908 London Games) there was a much stronger demand for separate Winter Games, with support coming this time from Norway. The first Games after World War I, at Antwerp in 1920, conceded ground with the inclusion of skating and ice hockey.

The year of 1924 was the most significant in winter sports; an International Winter Sports Week at Chamonix, France, first given patronage by the International Olympic Committee, was two years later accorded the title of 'First Winter Games'. In 1924 also, after the events of Chamonix, the International Ski Federation (FIS) was founded.

As Coubertin had foreseen, winter sports and specifically downhill skiing were to bring the Olympic Movement continuing trouble.

Winter sports at Holmenkollen, near Oslo, in 1892, twenty-two years before the first Winter Olympics

The first confrontation came in 1935 when the IOC told FIS that ski teachers would be excluded from the Games in 1936. Under FIS rules, teachers were not professionals and since the IOC rules took the Federations' rulings on amateurism this was the sort of contradiction in attitude that undermined the standing of the IOC. Many members of FIS were not so much angry at the IOC's contradiction of its own rules as by the exclusion of teachers and the inclusion of the German team which had been training together for months and was far more professional than the teachers from other countries. After the Games at Garmisch-Partenkirchen, FIS resolved to withdraw from future Games unless ski teachers were allowed to compete, a decision that was confirmed two years later. But whether that decision would have been put into effect was never tested because of World War II.

From 1952 onwards the Winter Games had a more dangerous and consistent opponent – Avery Brundage, the President of the IOC. Never was his dislike for the Games concealed; never did he miss an opportunity to point out the commercial overtones of skiing which, with the Games as a valuable advertising source, was developing throughout the world as a vast new leisure activity.

The dialogue between FIS and the IOC, about advertising and about the amount of time skiers spent in training (particularly those from the lowland countries), seemed to lurch through the 1960s from one explosion to another. In 1968 at Grenoble Brundage felt that the betrayal by FIS was ultimate, when, in the belief that skiers would not carry advertising material, he discovered at the eleventh hour that they were to do so – on their skis – and no changes to the equipment were made.

Four years later, Brundage was instrumental in disqualifying Karl Schranz of Austria, at Sapporo, when Schranz, in the Olympic Village, said that he was making thousands of dollars from skiing.

Sir Arnold Lunn succinctly summed up, in one of his last writings, the problems which the IOC had faced for forty years in skiing and to a lesser degree in other sports over a longer period:

> The greater the prestige of the event and the greater the financial rewards to the victorious amateurs, the

greater the risk of unpleasant incidents and unfriendly relations between rival teams. The importance of the Olympic Games is so manifest that their supporters can afford to be realistic. Those who remember the nature of man will realize that Coubertin's dream is far less likely to be fulfilled in the Olympic Games than in less important events.

While skiing caused the IOC much concern, the Olympic skating rinks were used by some individuals to raise their contractual price for ice shows, once they had won their Olympic medal; and the expensive installation of bob runs at Winter Games sites, for what is a little-practised sport, was criticized for being against the Olympic rule that a sport must be widely engaged in if it is to be maintained on the Olympic program. And then in 1971 the Winter Games image suffered another blow when Denver, which was chosen in 1970 to stage the Winter Games, withdrew from its commitment because of opposition from environmentalists and conservationists and because the State of Colorado would not guarantee full financial support.

But against all these troubles can be set the growing number of people who in winter turn to the snows and ice for their sport and leisure. It would be a denial of a basic Olympic principle if the Movement was to close its door upon them.

THE CELEBRATIONS OF THE WINTER GAMES John Samuel

The Winter Olympic Games came into being amid some muddle and acrimony. The first Games, at Chamonix in 1924, were only accorded their status retrospectively, officially at the IOC meeting at Lisbon in May 1926. The previous year at its meeting in Prague, the IOC acknowledged the success of the 'Chamonix International Winter Sports Week', as it was termed at the time, and a charter worked out by the Executive Commission was formally submitted to the IOC by the Marquis de Polignac on 27 May 1925 and accepted. At the same meeting St Moritz successfully canvassed for the next Winter Games. Thus, a rather difficult infant came into the world.

The charter read:

The International Olympic Committee will carry out a special cycle of the Olympic Winter Games, which have to take place in the same years as the Summer Games. They will be called the first, second, third Winter Games etc., and are subject to all rules of the Olympic protocol. The prizes, medals and diplomas must be different from those of the Olympic Summer Games, and the term 'Olympiad' shall not be used in this connection. The IOC will select the place for the Olympic Winter Games and will reserve priority to the country arranging the Summer Games of that particular Olympiad provided that the latter can furnish sufficient guarantee of its ability to organize the Winter Games in their entirety.

The pairing of Summer and Winter Games in the same

country was a pleasing notion which was not long sustained. Amsterdam, which staged the 1928 Summer Games, might provide ice rinks in abundance, but not mountains, and St Moritz in Switzerland was chosen for the first time. The United States was able to stage both Games in 1932, at Los Angeles and Lake Placid, and Germany did the same in 1936, at Berlin and Garmisch-Partenkirchen. But already the options were running out. World War II interfered with plans for twin events in Japan, the Summer Games in Tokyo and the Winter in Sapporo, and although London was able to stage the 1948 Summer Games, the winter events went to St Moritz again. No single country has since held both events in the same year, not least because of the problems of costs. Only a wealthy community has been able to stage the Winter Games since the war. Grenoble's overall budget in 1968 was $200 million, although this included major civic improvements, such as road, airport and housing works, which benefited the Olympic events but were truly long-term investments for the entire area. Sapporo's overall budget in 1972 was higher than Grenoble's, but the true figure for the thirteen Olympic sites was more like $50 million than the more frequently quoted $250 million.

Nevertheless, by the 1970s, the element of gigantism in Winter Games costing was embarrassing for the Olympic movement, and hard to reconcile with the philosophy of amateur sport. The staging of all Games had become a matter of high professionalism, with the world's press and television following every move in the game, and inventing a few of their own.

The Winter Games have tended to highlight the problems of wealthier countries. Recreations on mountainsides at 5,000 to 10,000 feet, or on artificial ice which has to be frozen layer by layer on artfully constructed concrete beds, tend to be costly of time, place and equipment. Minor industries grow up round them, merging into the major industry of tourism. Avery Brundage, president of the IOC from 1952 to 1972, believed the Winter Games had no place in the Olympic movement because of these physical characteristics which in their turn encouraged commercialism and professionalism. When Denver, having successfully canvassed for the 1976 Games, withdrew in late 1972 because a Colorado state referendum refused further funds, many believed that the Winter Games were on their deathbed. But Innsbruck, Lake Placid, the Mont Blanc region and Tampere (Finland) were all prepared to take over the Games at short notice.

The instinct to slide on snow and ice is basic to mankind, and to develop skill and pleasure in doing so is a legitimate aspect of recreation. Winter sports are primarily for the participant rather than the spectator, television audiences notwithstanding, and all these factors tend to balance the argument whether or not the Winter Games truly comply with Olympic concepts. The limited number of countries with adequate mountains and snow cover for Nordic and Alpine skiing has bothered some critics. But easier transport, increasing leisure time and natural growth have meant that after 294 competitors (13 women) and 16 countries at Chamonix in 1924 the Games drew 1,128 (217 women) and 35 nations at Sapporo in 1972. Events themselves had diversified from 14 at Chamonix to 35 in Japan and these were figures achieved in spite of the long journeys involved for most of the competitors.

Top Sonja Henie (Norway) competing in her first Olympics at Chamonix, 1924. *Above* Anna Hübler and Heinrich Burger (Germany), 1908 pairs skating winners

One of the stronger arguments for winter sports is that there is a long history of participation by both sexes. Ice skating, especially, has led in this respect. In the eighteenth century Marie-Antoinette skated with the Chevalier de St Georges, one of the greatest skaters of his time, and in the Netherlands in the winter of 1768-9 Casanova related how he donned skates to pursue a high society maiden. The first skating club as such was founded in Edinburgh, some say as early as 1642. Skating was included in the list of desirable Olympic contests at the 1894 Paris congress, partly because the sport had been the first to institute World and European Championships.

Although combining athletic and aesthetic qualities to a degree unmatched until gymnastics made its mark in the Summer program, ice skating has rarely been less than controversial because of the subjective nature of its judging. The great majority of sports have an objective outcome in terms of time or points or goals scored. Ice skating is marked according to personal opinion but an element of the partisan, whether of style or country, is rarely missing – it would be less than human if it was, judgments so often being based on familiarity.

Alpine skiing, which after World War II took over the centre stage in Winter Olympic Games, in fact was only introduced into Olympic competition as late as 1936.

In June 1914, immediately before the outbreak of World War I, pleas were raised on all sides for a Winter Games at the congress of National Olympic Committees in Paris. A representative of the Norwegian Skiing Federation, in a remarkable departure from previous Norwegian attitudes, proposed the inclusion of skiing in the Olympic program. Germany, Austria, Switzerland and Canada also pushed for the inclusion of ice and snow sports. Antwerp, in 1920, not only included figure skating in the Summer Games program, but also ice hockey, won by Canada, represented by a club team, the Winnipeg Falcons. A bitter fight was still to come, however. At the Lausanne meeting of the IOC in 1921 an advisory committee report showed Norway and Sweden totally opposed to the introduction of the Winter Games advocated by France, Switzerland and Canada. The Scandinavian representatives went so far as to deny all other countries the right to deal with questions of winter sport.

Mr Sigfrid Edström, the Swedish member of the IOC and later President of the Committee, somewhat embarrassed, said he had no objections to the IOC granting its patronage to the winter sports week at Chamonix. The Marquis de Polignac emphatically rejected the idea that the Scandinavian countries alone cultivated winter sports, and quoted Switzerland, Canada and France in particular. He then put a motion which read:

> The Congress suggests to the International Olympic Committee that in all countries where Olympic Games are held and where it is also possible to organize winter sports competitions, such competitions should be put under the patronage of the IOC and arranged in accordance with the rules of the international sports associations concerned.

A lively discussion followed, at the end of which Coubertin startled the proponents of winter sports by stating that the Marquis de Polignac's motion could not be put to the vote as it was contrary to an earlier decision by the IOC. He proposed a winter sports congress in 1922, arranged by the International Skating Union, to investigate the Marquis's suggestion. The winter sports protagonists immediately recognized this as a delaying procedure, and Polignac's motion was eventually put to the vote and carried. The way was opened for the first Winter Games. At the French Olympic Committee meeting in Paris in June 1922, international associations and commissions were represented. An International Ski Commission, predecessor of the International Ski Federation, came into being in 1911. Chamonix was chosen from among other French resorts and on 20 February 1923 a contract was signed. The municipality of Chamonix

Thorleif Haug (Norway), winner of three Nordic skiing gold medals in 1924

undertook to complete the necessary installations by 1 November 1923, to keep them in shape for at least thirty years, and in that time to let them to the Olympic Committee or French sports associations for a maximum ten per cent of the gross takings from events taking place. In exchange, the French Olympic committee undertook to pay to Chamonix forty per cent of the gross takings from the International Sports Week, with a guaranteed minimum of half a million francs.

I Chamonix 1924

Most Winter Games have had to survive actual or threatened disruption by the weather, and Chamonix in 1924 was no exception. On 23 December there was not a flake of snow anywhere in the resort. The next morning there was a layer 1.10 m (3 ft 8 in) deep, and 36,000 sq m (43,000 sq yd) had to be cleared from the skating rink, mostly by the shovel load, for efficient snow ploughs did not then exist. A week before the start, rain turned the ice stadium into a lake. But, on the eve of the Games, a hard frost set in and the opening ceremony was held without hitch.

The 294 competitors from sixteen countries (Estonia was represented in the procession but no Estonian competed) took part in fourteen events, the sixteen pioneers being: Austria, Belgium, Canada, Czechoslovakia, Finland, France, Great Britain, Hungary, Italy, Latvia, Norway, Poland, Sweden, Switzerland, the United States and Yugoslavia.

The first Winter Games skiing hero was the twenty-nine-year-old Norwegian, Thorleif Haug, who won three gold medals in the 18-km and 50-km Nordic skiing and the Nordic combination. He also won a bronze medal in the special jumping, a success still unrivalled, though Toni Sailer (Austria), in the Alpine skiing at Cortina in 1956, and Jean-Claude Killy (France), again in Alpine skiing at Grenoble in 1968, each gained three gold medals.

The Finn, Clas Thunberg, had an even greater haul than Haug in the speed skating, with three gold medals, one silver and one bronze.

II St Moritz 1928

Winter sports came of age during the 1920s, and St Moritz in 1928 reflected this with 494 competitors from twenty-five countries. Once again the organizers were reminded of the uncertainties of winter weather when a warm wind from the south set in to disrupt events, or, in the case of the 10,000-metres speed skating, cause their cancellation. On the morning of the 50-km cross-country skiing race the temperature was around −17.8 °C (0 °F) when the skiers made their first wax tests. By the afternoon, and in spite of St Moritz's high altitude (1,850 m, or 6,066 ft, above sea level) the thermometer rose to 25 °C (77 °F). The skill and luck that goes into waxing now became all important, and Sweden emerged best, Per Erik Hedlund, Gustav Jonsson and Volger Andersson winning all three medals. It was an indication of the gruelling nature of the race that a quarter of the skiers had to give up, and Hedlund's winning time was almost 70 minutes slower than Haug's in winning the same race at Chamonix. The weather was unremitting, and it rained all the following day and night – a phenomenon rarely known in the Engadine at this time of year – so that every competition on 15 February had to be postponed. Suddenly the weather changed, hard frost set into the watery snow, and the Games were saved.

They were outstanding Games for figure skating. The Swede, Gillis Grafström, achieved his third and last Olympic gold medal, but it was now that the Norwegian girl, Sonja Henie, not yet sixteen, who had already won a World Championship in 1927, confirmed her domination with her first Olympic gold. The United States won both the five-man bob and the tobogganing on the Cresta Run.

It was during the Games of St Moritz that Sir Arnold Lunn, of Great Britain, persuaded the International Skiing Federation (FIS) to include downhill and slalom competitions experimentally in international competition. The way was open for Alpine skiing to take over its important role, although eight years elapsed before the first Olympic competitions in this style were held.

III Lake Placid 1932

Lake Placid, New York, a newly established resort close to the Canadian border, was only 568 m (1,862 ft) high and subject to changeable snow conditions. In fact snow had to be brought by the truckload from Canada to help repair the cross-country tracks, a circumstance derided by some Europeans at the time, although winter-sport resorts throughout the world came to respect the need for artificial snow-making and other devices to defeat variable weather. For the first time figure skating was held at an indoor arena, but another revolution, massed starts in speed skating, was less successful. The Americans and Canadians, encouraged by the spectators, enjoyed the free-for-all of the massed starts and took 10 of the 12 available medals. The Europeans, accustomed to starting in pairs and the best times counting, were eclipsed. They insisted on the traditional starts being restored for the World Championships which took place on the same rink immediately after the Games, and the Norwegian, Ivar Ballangrud, won the 1,500, 5,000 and 10,000 metres to prove the European point.

The bobsleigh brought the innovation of two-man sleds, but there were a number of accidents on the course. When Deutschland II became unserviceable it was replaced by an American bob and its team recruited from Germans living in the USA who were untrained as serious bob competitors. The special ski jump also provided diversions. Sudden cold followed rain to save the event, but

Horse sled park at the bottom of the ski jump at St Moritz in 1928, notable for bad skiing weather

Birger Ruud (Norway), outstanding Olympic Champion in ski jumping, seen here in 1932

Speed skating, Garmisch-Partenkirchen, 1936. Ivar Ballangrud (Norway), inside, won three gold medals that year.

in the outrun of the jump hill a small pool remained which many competitors could not avoid and so they took an involuntary bath. Soaked competitors complained bitterly as they waited for their second jump on the tower open to the merciless winds. Hans Beck of Norway caused a surprise by jumping five metres farther than his fellow countryman, Birger Ruud, the FIS champion the year before, on the first jump, but Ruud, with a mighty effort, outjumped Beck by 5.50 metres on the second to take the first of his gold medals in a remarkable Olympic career.

IV Garmisch-Partenkirchen 1936

The staging of a Winter Games close to a big population area, the support given by the Nazi regime anxious to assert itself, and the introduction of Alpine skiing all combined to make the fourth Winter Games the first with a truly mass following. There were 755 competitors from twenty-eight countries, and half a million paying spectators. The special ski jump, the concluding event, was watched by 150,000 people. Trains had left Munich at intervals of ten minutes from 11 p.m. until 10 a.m., and many thousands more came from Innsbruck. The weather was favourable to a remarkable degree. Rain fell regularly until the eve of the Games. Then there was providential snow and frost, which ensured good conditions for all the events, with the rain returning as soon as the Games were finished.

Although Sir Arnold Lunn and his supporters had by now won their fight for the inclusion of Alpine skiing, medals were awarded only for the combined positions in men's and women's events, and not for the individual races in slalom and downhill. The irony was that Norway, the principle opponents to Alpine skiing in the committee meetings, should at once succeed on the slopes, for Birger Ruud, the ski-jumping king, won the men's downhill and Laila Schou Nilsen, an outstanding speed skater and tennis player, the women's downhill. Ruud, who had raced frequently in Germany, Austria and Switzerland from 1935 to 1937 while on business there, had benefited

from the fact that ski instructors had been ruled out of the Games, but it was still an extraordinary feat. He was pushed into fourth place overall, the winner being Franz Pfnür (Germany), but Miss Nilsen finished with the bronze medal.

In the speed skating, Ballangrud made amends for the disappointments at Lake Placid with three gold medals and a silver, and in figure skating Karl Schäfer, from Vienna, and Sonja Henie again demonstrated their superb talent. But Miss Henie's ten-year domination was coming to an end. The English skater, Cecilia Colledge, who had competed at Lake Placid at the age of eleven, was close behind her now, and soon afterwards Miss Henie turned professional, leaving Miss Colledge to go on and take the World Championship in 1937. Another remarkable run ended when Canada, victor in each of the previous Olympic ice-hockey competitions, was beaten by Britain 2–1. Although Britain, with a team primarily of British-born Canadians, only drew 0–0 against the United States, the Americans lost 0–1 to Canada. Britain thus gained one of the most extraordinary gold medals in Winter Games history.

The IOC meeting in Berlin in 1936 adopted Sapporo, on Japan's most northerly island of Hokkaido, as the Winter Games centre for 1940, but because of the Sino-Japanese war and World War II, Sapporo had to wait until 1972 before it staged the Games. Both Oslo and St Moritz offered and then withdrew candidature for 1940 after Japan officially waived its claim in July 1938. The position was complicated by the first of many disputes between FIS and the IOC over amateur rules, with the FIS refusing to compete in Alpine skiing because the IOC deemed instructors inadmissible. Garmisch offered to stage the Games again, and, although the war clouds were gathering, the IOC, meeting in London in June 1939, agreed. In spite of the outbreak of war on 1 September, German preparations went on until 22 November 1939, when the assignment for Games due to take place on 2–11 February of the following year was formally relinquished.

V St Moritz 1948

The separation of Summer and Winter Games as distinct organizational entities proved to be the postwar pattern. London staged the Summer Games and St Moritz the Winter. Although Germany and Japan were not admitted, twenty-eight countries competed at St Moritz, the same number as at Garmisch-Partenkirchen, with 636 men and seventy-seven women competitors. Alpine skiing had grown considerably since 1936. At Garmisch-Partenkirchen the 18 kilometres had been contested by racers from twenty-two countries, and the men's Alpine event from twenty-one nations. At St Moritz the figures were fifteen and twenty-five respectively. Furthermore gold medals were now being awarded for downhill and slalom, so there were six Alpine contests – three each for men and women – as opposed to the five traditional Nordic events.

The almost inevitable disputes and problems with the weather flawed but did not spoil an otherwise joyful winter sports reunion. Once again the *Föhn* (warm wind) set in after the Games had begun in excellent weather, and ice-hockey matches and the 10,000-metres race suffered postponements because of poor ice. But it was not as severe as in 1928 and the program was successfully completed with Henri Oreiller (France) gaining the most medals with victories in the men's downhill and combination, and a bronze in the special slalom. Oreiller was both a well-known skier and motor-rally and racing driver, and tragically met his death in a race at Montlhéry, France, on 7 October 1962. Ski racing in 1948 still had much simplicity, and one of the spectacles of the Games was the American girl, Gretchen Fraser, winning the special slalom with twin plaits flying. She was then twenty-nine, an age at which most racing skiers of the 1970s would have retired.

There was sentiment to other performances. John R. Heaton won the silver medal on the Cresta Run twenty years after gaining second place to his brother, Jennison. Birger Ruud took the silver in the ski jump sixteen years after his first Olympic victory and twelve years after his

Stein Eriksen (Norway), winner of the giant slalom at Oslo in 1953

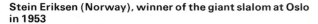

Nino Bibbia (Italy), an outstanding exponent of the Cresta Run, winning his 1948 gold medal

second. The Norwegians took all three medals in the ski jump chiefly due to their style, for the winner, Petter Hugsted, was outjumped by both the Finn, Matti Pietikäinen, later World Champion, and the American, Gordon Wren. The principal dispute was in ice hockey, to which the United States sent two teams. The American Hockey Association team was admitted in spite of the protests of the US Olympic Committee, the AHA team being affiliated not to the Olympic Committee but to the International Ice Hockey Association. The AHA team finished fourth, but was subsequently disqualified because of the lack of affiliation. Canada took the gold medal again, but only on a better goal average compared with Czechoslovakia. The European challenge in ice hockey had begun. Sweden dominated the cross-country skiing, and in the men's figure skating, the eighteen-year-old American Richard Button, with his fine jumping, set a new athletic standard.

VI Oslo 1952

Norway, the homeland of skiing, at last was host to a Winter Games and a sense of occasion pervaded events from beginning to end. The Olympic flame was brought not from Greece but from the hearth of the house in Morgedal, southern Norway, where Sondre Norheim (1825–97), the outstanding pioneer of modern skiing, was born. Norheim's introduction of primitive heel bindings and a shaped ski meant a giant leap forward in ski jumping and turning technique. At the end of a relay run over the 220 kilometres from Morgedal to Oslo, Eigil Nansen, a grandson of the explorer Fridtjof Nansen, whose book, *The First Crossing of Greenland* (1890), had given modern skiing its most important intellectual impetus, lit the Olympic flame in the Bislet Stadium.

For the first time, a capital city in which winter sports

held an outstanding place was playing host, and 561,407 spectators watched a record number of thirty nations competing. The weather was excellent, and the climax was undoubtedly the Holmenkollen ski jump, which Arnfinn Bergmann won for Norway before 130,000 highly critical and knowledgeable spectators. Almost equalling this, however, was the giant slalom victory of another Norwegian, Stein Eriksen, who also took the silver in the special slalom. There was considerable irony in this after Norway's early opposition both to the Winter Games concept and the adoption of Alpine skiing. Hjalmar Andersen added to the Norwegian delight by winning the 1,500-metres, 5,000-metres and 10,000-metres speed-skating events. Richard Button, with the first triple rotation jump, again won the men's figure skating, and Jeanette Altwegg (Great Britain), having won the women's, unlike many of her predecessors, gave up not to become a professional but to help run the Pestalozzi Children's Village in Switzerland. Germany won both the two-man and four-man bob, but with competitors so large that the International Bobsleigh Federation had to change its rules to limit the weight of teams and try to create equal conditions.

VII Cortina d'Ampezzo 1956

Cortina set some important landmarks in the history of Olympic winter sport. It was the first televised Winter Games, and a whole new world was introduced to the colour and pageantry of the 'five-ring circus' and to the ice and snow heroes of the mountain countries. The firework display which ended the Games seemed to set the magical peaks of the Dolomites aflame, though, alas, black-and-white television hardly did it justice. Anton (Toni) Sailer, the twenty-year-old Austrian Alpine skier, dominated the Games beyond compare. Indeed to many people these were Sailer's Games. The beauty, skill, speed and daring of Alpine skiing were personified in the young Kitzbüheler, who won all three Alpine events by extraordinary margins – the giant slalom by 6.2 sec, the special slalom by 4.00 sec and the downhill by 3.5 sec. He was only the fifth winter sportsman to win three gold medals at a single games – the others were the Scandinavian athletes Thorleif Haug, Clas Thunberg, Ivar Ballangrud and Hjalmar Andersen – and the impetus he gave to the ski holiday industry is incalculable.

The USSR was represented for the first time, and at once caused a surprise by taking the ice-hockey tournament, with Canada a disconsolate third. It was to be the start of a long period of Russian domination. Russians also excelled in the speed skating, in which Norway failed to gain a gold medal for the first time since 1932. Norway was also eclipsed in the ski jumping; the Finns, arms held back in the new, aerodynamic 'drop' style, instead of forward in front of their heads, took both gold and silver medals. The best Norwegian was ninth. Franz Kapus (Switzerland) became the oldest gold medal winner at forty-six in piloting his four-man bob to victory, and the United States had two men on the medals rostrum when Hayes Alan Jenkins, first, and his brother David, third, were honoured after the men's figure-skating championship. Another American, Ronald Robertson, took the silver, and to round off the American triumph, Tenley Albright and Carol Heiss were first and second in the women's figure-skating competition.

VIII Squaw Valley 1960

Squaw Valley set another Winter Olympic precedent by being the first purpose-built centre for the Games, and a monument to the extraordinary entrepreneurial skill of Alexander Cushing, an American who persuaded the IOC to choose Squaw Valley – by thirty-two votes to thirty for Innsbruck – when all that existed there was a tourist hostel. Even many IOC members were hazy on the whereabouts of Squaw Valley, at an altitude of 1,900 m (6,230 ft) on the east side of the Sierra Nevada, about 200 miles (320 km) from San Francisco. It was attacked variously after the choice. Artificial obstacles were added to make the downhill course more of a test, which was against FIS rules, and the Scandinavians complained that an altitude of 2,000 m (6,650 ft) was too high for the cross-country skiers. The organizers refused to build a bob run because only nine countries were interested in competing. In spite of the attacks, the Games were a great success, the best example after World War II of a 'village' event, with the competitors in close touch and not overborne by transport and communication problems in a big-city complex.

There were two innovations to set against the loss of the

Below Cortina, 1956. The start of the 4 × 10-kilometres ski relay. *Bottom* Lidia Skoblikova (USSR) winning the first of her six gold medals, in 1960

bob: biathlon, a 20-km cross-country ski run interspersed by four series of rifle-shooting tests, and women's speed-skating events, which had not been held since demonstrations in 1932. Lidia Skoblikova won the 1,500 metres and 3,000 metres (she was to go on to Innsbruck in 1964 to win four gold medals in four successive days). The Nordic skiing events were dominated by Sixten Jernberg (Sweden) and Veikko Hakulinen (Finland); Jernberg won the 30 kilometres and came second in the 15 kilometres, and Hakulinen, now over thirty-five, took a bronze and silver and in the last leg of the 4 × 10-kilometres relay made up a lag of 22 seconds to win by a ski length from Haakon Brusveen, the Norwegian winner of the 15 kilometres.

All the figure-skating gold medals went to North America, and the United States won the ice-hockey championship for the first time – an indication, perhaps, of the psychological and physical advantages of 'playing at home', certainly in sports that draw the spectators. The Alpine skiing medals were shared around, in contrast to those at Cortina, but one of the chief surprises was in the Nordic combination (15-km cross-country running and 70-metres jumping) where Georg Thoma (Germany) became the first non-Scandinavian to take the gold medal.

IX Innsbruck 1964

Innsbruck, as the first of a series of big-city Winter Games, set several new fashions. A number of events, including the slaloms and giant slaloms at Axamer-Lizum, the Nordic cross-country at Seefeld, and the bob and toboganing at Igls, were at satellite centres up to 25 km ($15\frac{1}{2}$ miles) from the city centre. Because of its convenience geographically, Innsbruck could welcome a record number of 1,186 competitors, and over a million spectators. Transport and communications problems were posed and answered with considerable effort and enterprise. These were the first fully computerized Games, and where for example at Cortina the figure-skating results had taken eight hours to compile, here it was done in seconds by IBM machines. The operation cost IBM £500,000, but the total budget for the Austrian authorities was nearer £12 million. At the very last moment the one missing link was the most elementary of all – snow! The Austrian army had to haul nearly 20,000 cubic metres of snow from bowls and slopes far up 2,500-m (8,200-ft) mountains so that Nordic and Alpine ski trails could be adequately packed. On the other hand, the Austrian economy, so heavily dependent on tourist income, benefited incalculably from the publicity. Opponents of the Winter Games, among them the President of the IOC, Avery Brundage, were quick to point out the commercial factors affecting individual competitors. In particular Brundage objected to those Alpine skiers who displayed their skis, all of them carrying brand names prominently, for newspaper photographers. Never before had the Winter Games received such publicity. Newspaper and radio men outnumbered competitors, and thirty-four television networks were represented.

Women took a prominent part in these Games. The Goitschel sisters of France had an extraordinary family duel in the Alpine skiing. Marielle won the giant slalom with Christine second. She then won the first leg of the slalom, also ahead of her sister, but Christine won the second leg and the competition overall. Austrian women

Christine Goitschel (France), winner of one of the family's two gold medals in Alpine skiing in 1964

recovered their self-respect by taking all three medals in the downhill, won by Christl Haas. Other outstanding women competitors were Lidia Skoblikova, the Russian speed skater, with gold medals in the 500, 1,000, 1,500 and 3,000 metres, and her fellow countrywoman, Klaudia Boyarskikh, first in the 5- and 10-km Nordic skiing. Sixten Jernberg, of Sweden, at thirty-five, was the man of the Games, gaining his ninth medal in three Olympics as a member of the victorious Swedish 4 × 10-km team. He had earlier won the skiing marathon, the 50 km. The USSR took the largest number of medals, including the ice hockey, in which Sweden and Czechoslovakia gained the silver and bronze respectively, with the United States and Canada trailing. The Russian pairs skaters, Oleg Protopopov and Ludmila Belousova, took their country's first figure-skating medal. Brundage, for all his opposition to the principle of Winter Games, was impressed enough to remark at the closing ceremony: 'The Innsbruck Games have shown how much the human will is capable of achieving.'

If reminder were needed that modern man was well capable of honouring Olympic codes, then there was no better example than in the two-man bob. Eugenio Monti (Italy), many times world champion but never, at that point, an Olympic champion, effectively destroyed his own chances when he whipped out a bolt from his own bobsleigh at the completion of his run and got it up to the start for Tony Nash (Great Britain), whose own bolt had sheered. Nash went on to win the gold medal. Less happily two men were killed during training, an Australian skier, Ross Milne, and a Polish-born tobogganist in the British team, Kay Skrzypecki.

X Grenoble 1968

No amount of controversy – and Grenoble had more than its share – could hide the personal accomplishments of athletes such as Jean-Claude Killy (France), who, like Sailer in 1956, won all three Alpine gold medals; Nancy Greene (Canada), who took the giant slalom gold and special slalom silver; and Eugenio Monti (Italy), nine times world bob champion, and finally, at the age of forty, possessor of an Olympic gold.

Grenoble, with 1,560 competitors from thirty-seven nations, and hosts of journalists, cameramen, TV and radio personnel, was an operation of its time – politicized, computerized and, to the chagrin of Brundage, commercialized. Its budget was $200 million, but more than half of this went into permanent facilities such as housing and motorways. But the scale of building directly linked with the Games was still formidable, especially the Olympic indoor ice stadium, a superb modern arena, designed to seat nearly 12,000, no pillars to obstruct the view, and, unlike the bob run at Alpe d'Huez, available to a large community for countless years ahead. Grenoble suffered, as did Innsbruck, problems of transport with satellite sites up to 40 km (25 miles) away, and the bobbers were forced to live in Alpe d'Huez hotels, far from the Olympic village, awaiting pre-dawn calls. The run proved highly unsatisfactory, sited on the open mountainside without shade from the sun, and safe bobbing was only possible in the hour or so before dawn.

In the committee rooms there was further trouble. The IOC tried to curb advertising and commercial exploitation by banning the use of trade names on skis and other equipment. But many leading skiers, and their national teams, were heavily reliant on sponsorship from the equipment manufacturers, and after threats of revolt against

Jean-Claude Killy (France), who won all three Alpine gold medals in 1968

this ruling a compromise was reached whereby skiers removed their equipment before being photographed or televised.

Finally, Killy won his third gold medal in the special slalom amid bitter controversy, for it involved the outstanding skiers of the two leading Alpine countries, Austria and France, and the reverberations were to affect the Games of Sapporo four years later. In the first instance Killy was involved in a revolt by leading skiers against the principle of an elimination slalom, introduced by FIS only for Olympic Games and World Championships. The eliminations were intended to reduce the field – special slalom, being over a shorter course, can be practised in more parts of the world than downhill or giant slalom, thus attracting a bigger entry – and starting positions in the competition proper. Top skiers argued that handicap points gained over a whole season ought to be the only criterion, but this ignored the disadvantages to skiers not able to ski regularly on the FIS circuit. The problem, which was close to the heart of the amateur–professional conflict, was side-stepped by the cancellation of the eliminating contests because of bad weather. If anything the fog was even thicker on the following day, and in all normal circumstances the race would have been postponed, but this was the last-but-one day of the Games and no one wanted a conflict on the last day between the 90-metre jumping and the special slalom. So, with the procrastinations unfortunately compounding problems, the slalom took place, with the skiers taking off as and when the mist momentarily cleared. Killy had the fastest first run, but after going first in the second run his overall time still looked vulnerable. In the German-speaking countries there was considerable popular support for Karl Schranz,

Irina Rodnina and Aleksei Ulanov (USSR) winning the pairs skating gold medal in 1972

Austria's veteran skier, who had gained every honour except an Olympic gold medal. Schranz began his second run, but missed gates 18 and 19 of the course of 69 gates and gave up. He claimed he had been distracted by a shadow a few gates below him, and after three witnesses had said that a course policeman had crossed the track at Gate 21 (about 50–60 ft or 15–18 m farther down) Schranz was allowed another run. His time for this would have given him the gold medal, but the French protested that Schranz could not have seen interference at such a range. The jury, which had to decide whether Schranz missed the gate because of interference or whether he did so before the interference was apparent, voted 3–1 to accept the protest, with one abstention.

There was another major incident when three East Germans, including Ortrun Enderlein, the 1964 Olympic women's champion, were disqualified from the single-seater tobogganing for heating the runners of their sleds over an open fire in an effort to obtain greater speed. More happily, Franco Nones (Italy), in winning the 30-km cross-country skiing race, became the first *Langlauf* medal holder from a country outside Scandinavia and the USSR. The Protopopovs, at thirty-five and thirty-two respectively, took their second Olympic gold medal on one of the few sentimental occasions of a Games which posed rather too many of the problems of the times.

XI Sapporo 1972

If Grenoble was big, then Sapporo financially was bigger. If Grenoble was controversial, then Sapporo produced major confrontation. It ended with the expulsion of Karl Schranz, Austria's leading skier, whose early ticket home brought him a hero's welcome from a crowd in Vienna estimated at over 200,000. The Austrian team was withdrawn in protest, then re-entered, after Schranz had pleaded that he did not wish to be responsible for his team mates missing their chance of Olympic competition and medals after so much striving.

Schranz was expelled by the IOC by twenty-eight votes to fourteen for permitting the use of his name and pictures in commercial advertising. He was one among many – Brundage said he had a 'black list' of forty names – but he

was singled out, according to the president, because he was 'the most blatant and the most verbose we could find'. On the eve of the Games, in the Olympic village, Schranz gave an interview to Will Grimsley, sports editor of the American agency, Associated Press, which appeared in the English language newspaper, the *Japan Times*. In it Schranz said that if Brundage's ideas were followed to their true conclusion then the Olympics would only be for the very rich. 'This thing of amateur purity is something that dates back to the nineteenth century when amateur sportsmen were regarded as gentlemen and everyone else was an outcast. The Olympics should be a competition of skill and strength and speed – and no more.' This appeared one day before the IOC executive met to consider the recommendation of Hugh Weir's eligibility committee. The timing could not have been more unfortunate, but Brundage had to face much hostile press and television questioning for the decision to make an example of one man. Schranz, he said, was not allowed to state his case because the IOC dealt with groups and not individuals. In this instance, however, it was an individual who was punished.

Sapporo, while highlighting many of the problems of a modern Olympic Games, at the same time provided a memorable setting and a gracious welcome. Situated on Hokkaido, the most northerly island of Japan, it had grown from a sparse settlement to a city of a million and more in only a hundred years, and was anxious now to establish itself in world eyes, and also to millions of Japanese, looking for new ways to enjoy their increasing money and leisure, as a ski centre. The outlay of $555,556,000 from 1967 to 1972 on the Olympic Games thus had long-term implications over and above ten days of snow and ice sport. The fact that 3,000 press, television and radio personnel outnumbered competitors by more than two to one was a matter of high significance. The data-processing centre alone cost £365,000, the broadcasting facilities £121,000 – thirteen different programs with sixty commentaries could be sent out simultaneously. The Japanese electronics industry undoubtedly benefited directly or indirectly. Sapporo, too, is famous for its Snow Sculpture Festival at Otaru Park, with creatures of legend sculpted in snow and ice, and beautiful flowers preserved in showcases of diamond-like ice – all there and gone in a few days. Thus Mount Eniwa, a virgin mountain of 4,000 ft (1,220 m) glittering with silver birches could be manipulated by 15,000 men, 850 bulldozers and six tons of explosives for two downhill races, the men's and women's, adorned with two cable cars capable of transporting 330 people an hour, and a chairlift, and then returned to its beautiful pristine state, as required by the conservation laws, within weeks of the Games being over. The cost of this operation alone was about £2 million. The bob run on Mount Teine, which also staged the slalom and giant slalom races but was never to be used again, cost another £2 million.

Mount Teine set another record. Overlooking the Sea of Japan, which divides Hokkaido from the Siberian mainland, it was the first Winter Games site with an ocean view. In theory the climate should have been temperate. In fact, with the juxtaposition of the Siberian high- and the Pacific low-pressure weather systems, Sapporo was subject to violent changes of weather. Waxing of skis, always a tricky art, became a matter of almost neurotic

Opposite Vasili Alekseev (USSR), super-heavyweight champion in the 1972 weightlifting competitions.
Overleaf Gustav Thoeni (Italy), gold and silver medal winner in the slalom events at Sapporo in 1972

Sports on the Winter Program

concern. Undoubtedly Swiss research and organization in this area contributed to their domination of Alpine skiing – six medals, including three golds, of the eighteen available. Austria suffered bitter disappointment with Anne-marie Pröll, the outstanding favourite for the downhill and giant slalom, bearing a considerable psychological burden after Schranz's expulsion, and coming second in both events to Marie-Thérèse Nadig (Switzerland), who had never before won a major race. Bernhard Russi, the Swiss World Champion, won the men's downhill, and Gustav Thoeni (Italy), another great world figure, the giant slalom, but the special slalom again proved an outsider's race, Francisco Fernández Ochoa providing Spain with its first Winter Olympic gold medal. It represented, too, the increasing geographical spread of winter sports, although Alpine skiing's popularity was scarcely represented in its six events as against Nordic skiing's ten.

The USSR took eight medals in cross-country events, including four in the women's, and Norway seven, but the outstanding surprise was the success of the Japanese in ski jumping. In the 70 metres they took all three medals, and another Japanese skier won the jumping section of the combined jumping and cross-country competition. Wojciech Fortuna gave Poland an unexpected gold medal in the 90-metre jump, his longest jump being 111 metres (365 feet).

In spite of his first fall in a major competition for four years, Ondrej Nepela (Czechoslovakia) won the men's figure skating. Trixi Schuba (Austria), an immaculate tracer of figure eights, won the women's competition on possibly the last occasion a skater of her style could do so. After 1972 the rules were changed which accorded the free-skating section of the individual competition a higher proportion of the marks. Irina Rodnina and Aleksei Ulanov, from Moscow, won the pairs competition, but this also was in the nature of a farewell. The Western press was much intrigued by a romantic involvement between Ulanov and Ludmila Smirnova, who partnered Andrei Suraikin to the silver medal. Russian skating officials denied that it was of any consequence, but Ulanov later married Miss Smirnova and became her partner in international competition. The USSR took the ice-hockey gold medal for the third successive Games, but the competition was the worse for Canada's refusal to participate because of amateur–professional arguments. Ard Schenk (Netherlands) became only the third speed skater in Olympic history to take three titles when he won the 10,000 kilometres to add to the 5,000 and 1,500. The Chicago suburb of Northbrook provided two gold medallists in the women's speed skating, Anne Henning in the 500 metres and Dianne Holum in the 1,500 metres, which meant all three gold medals gained by the United States were won by girls – Barbara Ann Cochran's gold in the Alpine skiing special slalom was won by the smallest margin in Olympic history, two-hundredths of a second. Japan's *sayonora*, or goodbye, was expressed touchingly and warmly at the closing ceremony, but the last word was with its weather, which closed in so violently with gale, snow, rain and thaw on the day afterwards that many competitors were marooned in the Olympic village or waited many hours at Sapporo airport with planes unable to take off. A few days earlier and the Games, which had survived a few minor ups and downs with the weather, would have been ruined.

BOBSLEIGHING AND TOBOGGANING
John Hennessy

There has been a tendency to regard tobogganing as a poor relation of bobsleighing, since it was introduced into the Olympic Games, in its present form, only in 1964. Yet the aristocratic bobsleigh owes its crude origin to the toboggan, more properly the Cresta skeleton, at St Moritz in 1888, and it may now owe its survival as an Olympic sport to its small, more democratic, brother.

With the background of three successive white elephants expensively constructed for the Olympic bobsleigh events in 1964 (Innsbruck), 1968 (Grenoble) and 1972 (Sapporo), all now long since defunct, the International Olympic Committee readily agreed with the suggestion of the organizing committee for the twelfth Winter Games at Innsbruck in 1976 that there was no justification for erecting another.

Thus the idea emerged that the same run at Igls, near Innsbruck, should be used for both toboggan and bob. It will measure only 1,200 metres, about three-quarters the usual bobsleigh length. At first the Fédération Internationale de Bobsleigh et de Tobogganing (FIBT; founded in 1924 but today concerned only with the bob) was resentful, but commonsense supervened at last and it swallowed its pride. The 1976 Winter Games therefore offer the novelty of five events on the same run, two for bobsleigh and three for toboggan, the latter organized by the Fédération Internationale de Luge de Course (FIL; founded in 1957).

Ordinarily a bob run should be 1,500 metres long, with an average gradient of at least 8 per cent. It should have at least fifteen curves, some daunting enough to require a wall six metres high. A toboggan run may be 1,000–1,500 metres long and should have an average gradient of between 9 and 10 per cent. The compromise Innsbruck run for 1976, embracing fourteen curves, has a gradient of $8\frac{1}{2}$ per cent with a unique feature called a *Kreisel* (spinning top), in which the track whirls back under itself through 270 degrees. It is best visualized as a right turn, except that to achieve it the course swings left to describe a tight three-quarter circle.

Modern runs are artificially constructed, of course, and such is the work of precision engineering in concrete that abstruse calculations of gradient, radii, speed and centrifugal force have to be exactly correlated if human disaster is to be avoided at speeds of up to 125 kph (84 mph). With artificial refrigeration added to combat the uncertainties of the weather, they are extremely expensive undertakings. In both sports four descents are required of each rider, two on successive days.

The bob is much the older in Olympic terms – bobsleigh was included in the first Winter Games at Chamonix in 1924 – but it has not always had its present form, in which it resembles an open sports car with an aerodynamic front cowl and has the riders seated. In the early days the style of the Cresta was often followed, with a number of riders (as many as six, or as few as two or three in the 'boblet') lying on the stomach and plunging down the hill head first.

This is still the position on the Cresta, but tobogganing, in the Olympic Games since 1964, has followed, with refinements, the conventional form seen on any hill covered with snow, except that the riders lie back and look along the length of their bodies as they career feet

Erhard Keller (German Federal Republic) winning the gold medal in the 1972 500-metres speed skating

first through the gulley of ice. Whereas the bob is steered by ropes or wheel the toboggan now used in the Olympic Games (*luge* in French, *Rodel* in German) is steered by changing the weight and pressure of the feet on the front runners, as well as by a rope.

In the early days the bob was dominated by the Americans and the Swiss, but the United States drew a total blank at the first Winter Games, for the Swiss second crew (the first having been involved in a serious accident) was followed home by a quartet from Britain and another from Belgium. (The two-man event was not held until 1932.) It was the United States' turn in 1928, when William Fiske, who was later to become a famous pilot of military aircraft, won the first of his two gold medals at St Moritz, adopting the *ventre-à-terre* position. The competition, for crews of five men, was decided on two runs because of a catastrophic thaw.

Since St Moritz had been the birthplace not only of the bobsleigh but also the home of the Cresta Run (first used in 1884), the temptation to include toboggan races in the second Winter Games could not be resisted, in spite of the fact that only ten entries were assembled from only six countries, which hardly met the Olympic requirement of a sport generally practised throughout the world. By comparison there were twenty-three bob crews from fourteen countries.

Yet 1928 had a number of outstanding features: a victory for the United States on both bob and Cresta, two brothers sharing the same victory podium (Jennison and John Heaton, first and second on the Cresta), and a double medal winner in Jennison Heaton, who piloted the second-placed bob.

The Americans gathered a rich harvest at Lake Placid in 1932, with first and second in the four-man bob (crews of only four from now onwards) and first and third in the two-man, John Heaton this time piloting the third-placed bob. By now the present practice of sitting in the bob had been made compulsory. Fiske again showed the courage and daring that led to his death on active service in 1941.

The fourth Winter Games bob events, held at Garmisch-Partenkirchen in 1936, lack any great historical interest. Overlaid with a strong atmosphere of nationalism, they were a severe disappointment to Germany, whose best position was the fifth place in the two-man event of Hanns Kilian, who had previously won the four-man bronze medal at both St Moritz and Lake Placid.

After World War II the Winter Games returned to St Moritz in 1948 with a program now swollen to two events on the bob run and one on the Cresta. There was a marginally better turn-out on the Cresta, fifteen from six countries, among them a man who was to inscribe his name on almost every trophy the Cresta has to offer for more than two decades. He was Nino Bibbia, an Italian now living at St Moritz, who was held to a tie over the first three runs by John Heaton (reappearing in his fortieth year), and roared away on the second day.

The United States won its fifth and last (to date) gold medal on the bob run through Francis Tyler (four-man) in 1948. That year, then, was the end of an era on the bob run as well as on the Cresta. The Swiss, on the other hand, not only won the two-man event (Felix Endrich) but have since maintained their place among the élite. Belgium gained its best placing so far when the first and second American two-man bobs, though in reverse order, were

split by Max Houben, later to be killed in an accident at Lake Placid.

Something of a watershed in bob racing came in 1952. Germany won both gold medals at Oslo, a result not entirely divorced from the fact that Andreas Ostler and Lorenz Nieberl put up a net weight of 236.6 kg (521 lb 9 oz) in the two-man event and, with equally sturdy compatriots, 472.5 kg (1,041 lb 10 oz) in the four-man. Since that year a maximum combined weight of 375 kg (826 lb 12 oz) and 630 kg (1,388 lb 14 oz) for the two events has been in force and ballast may be bolted to the machines within these limitations.

The Cortina Games of 1956 brought the appearance of the greatest figure in the history of the sport, the little Italian, Eugenio Monti, the bobsleigh counterpart of Nino Bibbia. Armed with the new Podar bobs and a number of partners, he was to win eleven World Championships from 1957 to 1968, but not until that last year could he achieve an Olympic gold medal. A week or two after his twenty-eighth birthday he won both silver medals at Cortina, but twelve further years of frustration lay ahead. There were no bobsleigh events in 1960, because the Squaw Valley organizing committee sensibly refused to breed another white elephant, and the 1964 Games at Innsbruck were to salute two new countries with gold medals – Britain in the two-man event (Tony Nash) and Canada in the four-man (Victor Emery). But all came right in the end, for Monti took both titles at Grenoble.

The toboggan as we know it, unlike the bob a source of fun for young people of all ages and incomes, made its entry in 1964 on a note of tragedy, for a Briton of Polish

Avery Brundage (left), about to begin his reign as IOC President, with Andreas Ostler and Lorenze Nieberl (Germany), weighty winners of the bob

British winners in the 1964 two-man bob, Tony Nash and Robin Dixon (obscured)

ICE HOCKEY Doug Gilbert

There has long been a debate in ice-hockey circles as to whether the game evolved Darwinian fashion from earlier antecedents including France's hoquet, Britain's field hockey, shinty, bandy, and perhaps even football and rugby, or was created with a thunderclap by a man who sweated over the rules for six days and rested on the seventh.

There is a long history of stick games on ice. At the end of the twelfth century a monk named Stephen, who wrote the life of St Thomas à Becket for King Henry II, described a pond near the walls of the city of London:

> When it is frozen, many young men run over the ice. Some of them have bones tied to their feet and use a stick with a sharp end. They slide as quickly as a bird flying in the air or the arrow from a bow. Sometimes from two opposite points, at a long distance, two young men race towards each other and one of them, or perhaps both, falls to the ground after beating each other with their sticks. Many of them incur head wounds, and most of them break an arm or a leg; but in our day and age youth is forever seeking glory and these mock fights make them more courageous when it comes to real fighting.

'Shinny' games on river ice in Canada are reported in military diaries as early as 1855 in Halifax, Nova Scotia, and Kingston, Ontario, where groups of up to fifty a side would gather in the harbour and go at each other all afternoon.

However, the game as it is known today was born on 3 March 1875 in Montreal's Victoria Skating Rink, and the first normal rules are credited to John George Alwyn Creighton, an engineer from Halifax who was working in Montreal under Sir Sanford Fleming in the building of the Grand Trunk Railroad.

Creighton was one of the better all-round athletes of his day and a superior rugby player. His thought for hockey apparently came while he and his friends in rugby and lacrosse were searching for a new game that would allow them to practise their skills and maintain their fitness throughout the long Canadian winters. With this in mind it is perhaps not surprising that a group of eighteen appeared at the Victoria rink that day with bandy sticks, skates and a lacrosse ball.

Early Olympic ice hockey winners, the Canadian team of 1924

extraction, Kay Skrzypecki, was killed during practice at Igls. That apart, the tobogganing was a big success. Although the medals were shared by only three countries, four other nations were represented in the first six of the three results lists, which points to cosmopolitan participation. There were thirty-eight entries from twelve countries in the men's single-seater, thirty-two from eight in the double and seventeen from seven in the women's (single-seater only). Germany took a lion's share of the medals, five in all, leaving Italy with a bronze in the men's two-seater and Austria with gold and silver in the two-seater and bronze in the women's event.

Scandal, alas, touched the 1968 Games at Grenoble, more exactly Villard de Lans, for the three girls from the German Democratic Republic (by now the two Germanies were recognized separately) were disqualified for heating their runners, among them Ortrun Enderlein, the winner in 1964 and arguably one of the most attractive Olympic champions of them all. The way was open then for Italy's first gold medal (Ericha Lechner). In the other events Austria and the German Democratic Republic changed places, with Manfred Schmid (Austria) the single-seater champion, and Thomas Köhler surrendering one title for another, in company with Klaus Bonsack.

At Sapporo in 1972 the German Democratic Republic made almost a clean sweep, being denied only one of the nine medals in *luge*, the two-seater gold shared with Italy. But the IOC (if not the FIL) ought to be concerned about competitors, however courageous, gaining cheap Olympic blazers in these formative days of Olympic tobogganing. Competitors in other sports, perfecting their skills after many years of trial and travail, cannot be expected to view kindly a situation whereby a man can progress from complete innocence to an Olympic team in six weeks, as was the case with some entrants in 1972. It stretches Coubertin's doctrine just a little too far.

Two Russian ice hockey victories. *Top* **USSR beating Sweden in the final in 1964.** *Above* **USSR defeating the United States at Sapporo in 1972**

The Victoria rink was 200 ft (60.96 m) long and 85 ft (25.91 m) wide, dimensions that even today are taken as standard for an ice-hockey rink. The initial 'puck' was a lacrosse ball that quickly had the rounded edges cut away to stop its infernal bouncing all over the ice.

'There is absolutely no doubt this was the first game of hockey as we know it,' says Canadian sports historian (amateur) and political pundit (professional) Doug Fisher, 'but the shame was Creighton was steeped in rugby rather than lacrosse. He was obsessed with the need for everyone to stay onside and thanks to that the forward pass wasn't brought into hockey for another fifty years.'

From Montreal Creighton eventually drifted off to the capital city of Ottawa, leaving Fleming and railroading on the eve of the great Canadian Pacific project to become the law clerk of the Senate. From this position he came in direct contact with Lord Stanley of Preston, the sixth Governor-General of Canada, and more important, with Lord Stanley's sons, who took up the new game.

On his retirement from Canada the Governor-General left behind a perpetual challenge trophy for the hockey champion of the Dominion and he directed the first cup to the Montreal Hockey Club in 1893.

The Stanley Cup today is the most storied and treasured trophy in all of North American professional sport, even if a tipsy group of Ottawa Senators returning home from a victory party did once leave it by the roadside when they had stopped to change a flat tyre. A sober search party found it where they left it at noon the next day. In 1893 the cup was a modest silver bowl worth $50, but today it is a skyscraper among trophies with additional silver bases constantly being added to make room for the names of the players of every team that has ever won it.

In its first fifteen years the Stanley Cup was awarded to amateur teams, there being no professionals at that time, and these were the days when the new game caught on with students in the Canadian universities. Through them it moved across the border into the United States colleges where it was an instant hit, eventually forming the base for the strong American representations in the Winter Games.

Lord Stanley's sons were among the first to bring the sport to England in 1893, but it really caught on in 1902 and 1903 when Canadian students went to the Prince's Skating Club in London. The first hockey league was the Amateur Hockey Association of Canada formed in 1887 with the Amateur Hockey Association of the United States following in 1894. Europeans became interested about ten years later as new Alpine resorts searched for games to complement skiing in their winter schedule.

The International Ice Hockey Federation (IIHF) was formed in London in 1908; Great Britain, France, Belgium, Switzerland, and Bohemia were founder members.

But, while Europe was taking these baby steps, Canada, ignorant of the international scene, was moving forward with seven-league strides. Within twenty years hockey had easily become Canada's national game and once towns started to make financial offers to their neighbours' stars it was only a matter of time before professionalism took command. In 1908 the Ontario Professional Hockey League was organized and their challenge for the Stanley Cup was accepted. Since 1910 all teams competing for the Stanley Cup have been professional.

Even as early as 1920 it would have been difficult for Canada to send a strong amateur team to the Olympics from either the east coast or the west where the professional leagues flourished. Thus, when ice hockey was given a trial in the Games at Antwerp, it was the Winnipeg Falcons, an amateur club from the central prairie region, who were nominated to play. Seven countries took part and the competition reflected the sport's early history with Canada much the strongest and the United States college players putting up the lone fight. The Falcons defeated the Czechs 15–0 in their first game, the United States 2–0 in the second, and turned back Sweden easily in the final, 12–1.

The competition assured ice hockey of a place in the first formal Winter Olympic Games in Chamonix four years later. This time the Toronto Granite club was sent to represent Canada and if anything, the competition was even more one-sided than in 1920. Eight nations showed up and were drawn into two divisions of four, to play round-robin style.

The Canadians proceeded to pile up the most one-sided victory in Olympic history as they rolled over Sweden, 22–0, Czechoslovakia, 30–0, and Switzerland, 33–0. Canada and Sweden advanced to the semi-finals against Great Britain and the United States, but there was no suspense here with Canada dismissing Britain 19–2, while the Americans beat Sweden 22–0. In the gold-medal final Canada easily disposed of the United States, 6–1. The winners then took the boat home, completing a fifty-eight-day journey with the words that 'the Europeans are learning fast'.

What they were learning, it seems, was that hockey games against Canada were not much fun. In 1928 at St Moritz Canada got an unexpected free pass to the final because the organizers could not work out a competition between eleven teams. Ten nations fought it out for three places with Great Britain, Switzerland, and Sweden advancing, all to little avail as far as the gold medal was concerned. The Canadians beat Switzerland 13–0, Sweden 11–0, and Great Britain 14–0 to win once again for fun.

Travel to Lake Placid proved impossible for most European teams in 1932, and only Germany and Poland joined Canada and the United States for a double round-robin tournament. Thanks to the United States, though, the gold-medal competition was for the first time truly competitive.

Largely through the efforts of Boston millionaire Ralph Windsor, all the hockey areas in the country were scoured with the result that fourteen players were brought to Boston and honed under Art Ross, Eddie Powers, and the entire Boston Bruin professional team.

The first time the teams met the Americans led 1–0 and looked like winners until a goal at the five-minute mark was decisive. Still, the Americans did better than Canada against the Germans and Poles and if they could have won the second game the United States could still have won the gold. This time Canada's Romeo Rivers bounced a long shot off the American goalie's knee and into the net with thirty-three seconds left to keep the Canadian gold-medal record intact.

It was broken four years later in Garmisch-Partenkirchen, not by the United States as might have been expected, but by Great Britain. The tournament began on an acrimonious note with Canada charging that fourteen of its players had moved from Canada to Great Britain for the purposes of playing hockey without seeking releases from the Canadian Amateur Hockey Association. Since they had all been suspended by the CAHA the Canadians asked the International Federation to respect the suspensions, an act that would have barred two of the fourteen from the British team.

The IIHF, at its meetings in Berlin, upheld the Canadian position, but, since the players were already at the Games site and the point had been established, the Canadians withdrew their objection and the pair played after all.

Canada finally got its Olympic hockey come-uppance in the semi-final round when the British team pulled off a 2–1 victory upset leading to another outburst of acrimony with the announcement that this result would be carried forward into the finals with no chance for a replay. Thus, in the finals, Canada beat Czechoslovakia 7–0 and the United States 1–0, while Great Britain beat Czechoslovakia 5–0 and tied with the United States 0–0. The Canadians claimed they had never heard of the innovation of carrying scores from one round through to the next, which says something about Canadian team management, Federation communications, or both. In any event Britain had won the gold and there were now three strong teams in Olympic hockey with the Czechs not far behind. It was also becoming more and more apparent that there were two distinct schools of hockey developing in the world – Canadian and European.

Canadian hockey was evolving into an extremely hard-hitting physical game where fist fights were not only accepted, but often anticipated. Canadians have never been particularly concerned about hockey fighting since it is difficult to do much damage with a punch if you cannot set your feet on something firm. The rest of the world did not follow suit, however; for more than three decades Canadian teams have often not been well received in Europe.

Official squabbling overshadowed a fine Czech performance in St Moritz in 1948. This time the United States could not manage its own affairs and two teams from two rival associations (the Amateur Athletic Union and the American Amateur Hockey Association) turned up, both claiming to represent the United States. The team finally admitted finished fourth and then was disqualified by the IOC. In the tournament itself the Canadians and Czechs played to a 0–0 tie with Canada winning the gold on a 69–5 goal ratio against 80–16 for Czechoslovakia.

This 1948 showing by the Czechs offered perhaps the first sign of the coming shift of world hockey supremacy from Canada to eastern Europe. Two years earlier the USSR had drafted its national bandy team into a new ice-hockey program as a part of its long-range plans to enter the Olympic Games. This is where the role of the Olympic Movement in the development of ice hockey cannot be overemphasized. Although hockey is just as natural a game in the rugged Russian climate as it is in the equally forbidding Canadian winter, it is doubtful if the Russians would have financed an all-out hockey program had the game not been on the Olympic calendar. In fact it has taken less than twenty years for hockey to come from nowhere in the USSR to its position as the country's second most popular team game behind football.

The Games of Oslo, in 1952, went according to tradition, with Canada winning the gold medal, the United States the silver and Sweden the bronze but two years later the USSR made its first impact on the sport when the Dynamo Club appeared at the 1954 World Championships in Stockholm and beat Canada 7–2 in the final game. Suddenly Western hockey fans had new names to deal with like Alexandrov and Starshinov.

After hopeless performances by the early bandy players in 1946 the Russians had brought in Czech teachers to get them started, but by the time of the 1956 Olympics in Cortina, the Russians themselves were already making innovations. In less than ten years the USSR coaches were bringing superior condition, play planning, and the scientific approach to sport to bear on a game Canadians had always approached as mostly a matter of individual action and reaction. Armed with this they won the gold medal in Cortina, beating Canada 2–0 in the final. When the medals were distributed Canada had slipped to the bronze, having lost 1–4 to the United States as well.

The 1960 Games in Squaw Valley proved an aberration

as far as the general development of the sport was concerned, with the United States rising delightfully to the occasion on home ground to prove that the best team does not always win. Jack McCartan was simply sensational in the American goal as the United States defeated Canada 2–1 and the USSR 3–2 to win big games in which they were basically outplayed. Canada even upset the USSR 8–5 to win the silver medal. McCartan, strange to say, went on to become a very mediocre professional goaltender.

Canada had still been able to win World Championships through these years with teams made up of a mixture of old pros reinstated as amateurs and young up-and-comers, but after 1961 that, too, proved insufficient. In an effort to overcome frustration at not being able to send its best to the Games it tried to develop a national team concept for 1964 and 1968.

Under this scheme promising youngsters were packed into the same university to develop together. Canada finished without medals in 1964, with USSR, Sweden, and Czechoslovakia mounting the dais, but in 1968 came close by beating the United States 3–2, the Czechs 3–2 and the Swedes 3–0 after being upset early by Finland 5–2. Once again the Canadians met the Russians in the final and lost 0–5. The Canadian professionals never fully supported this scheme out of self-interest, however, and with continued failure it was dropped; Canada fell out of international amateur hockey, to the dismay of both amateur hockey and the Canadian Olympic Association.

In 1972, while the Summer Games were in progress in Munich, the Soviet gold medallists challenged the Canadian professionals and the two met in a historic eight-game confrontation in Canada and the USSR. The USSR astounded Canada by winning game one 7–3 in Montreal, but the professionals struggled back in Moscow to finish the series with four wins, three defeats and a draw.

With that series the Soviet team proved that they, the Czechs and the Swedes all played the game just as proficiently as the leading professionals; and the Finns, Germans, Poles, and Americans were not far behind. There were even some signs that Canadians were becoming interested in turning their backs on the more violent aspects of their game and adopting European coaching and training methods.

The Olympic Movement can take some pride in that.

FIGURE SKATING John Hennessy

Figure skating is an Olympic curiosity, a winter sport that made its début in association with the Summer Games of 1908. Skating, indeed, was a pioneer in the whole world of sport (the first to organize World Championships) and its honourable antiquity was recognized on that historic day in 1894 when Coubertin set the modern Olympics in motion.

Until the inauguration of separate Games for winter sports at Chamonix in 1924, however, skating could join in the Olympics only when there happened to be an artificial rink handy. It was on the original program for the Paris Games of 1900, but in fact had to wait eight more years before the old Prince's Club, at Knightsbridge, offered a suitable setting during the London Games of 1908.

In spite of a moderate number of entries, the skating events were an immediate hit and the official report for the Games records that they aroused 'great interest', especially on the afternoon of 29 October when the men's and women's free programs were held.

The roll of honour down the years is headed by a legendary figure of the sport, Ulrich Salchow (Sweden), who gave his name to a jump that is now a compulsory requirement, allied to two or, in these demanding times, preferably three rotations in the air. Already seven times World Champion, Salchow was an easy winner from two other Swedes, though the Russian champion, Nikolai Panin, would probably have taken the silver had he not had to withdraw through illness. As it is, Panin has a unique niche in the records as the holder in perpetuity of the special figures title, an event requiring elaborate patterns cut in the ice that has never been held since. He faced, however, only modest competition from two challengers.

Britain, dominating the sport with Sweden in those early days, provided three of the five entries in the women's event and the first women's champion in Madge Syers, who had finished second to Salchow in the 1902 World Championships, then open to both sexes. The first gold medal for pairs went to Heinrich Burger and Anna Hübler (Germany). The four competitions had only twenty-three entrants.

By 1920 in Antwerp there was a strong lobby in favour of a separate Winter Games, but there was equally strong opposition from the Nordic countries: they felt that their skiing events would thereby be devalued. Since they had powerful friends at court, including Sigfrid Edström, later to become President of the IOC, the eloquent advocacy of the French Marquis de Polignac was to some extent frustrated.

Salchow, defying the years, defended his title but, at forty-three, he could not defy the advance of three fellow Scandinavians. Sweden retained the championship through Gillis Grafström, an idiosyncratic character who could rarely be bothered to compete in the World Championships. An exceptionally elegant skater, he was among the first to appreciate the advantage of interpreting music on the ice. Sweden won a second title through Magda Julin and Finland its first skating gold medal through Walter Jakobsson and his German-born wife, Ludovika.

The first Winter Games were a historic landmark in 1924, of course, but for skating they held a special significance, for it was at Chamonix that another legend was born. In last place among the eight women solo skaters was a tiny Norwegian of only eleven, a girl who was to win fame on the ice, fortune on the cinema screen and admiration everywhere. She was Sonja Henie, precociously stepping out of the pages of Hans Andersen to parade, even at this tender age, her burgeoning skill and winning smile.

The fairy tale was to have a proper ending. For the moment, though, Herma Plank-Szabo, an outstanding representative of the Viennese school of skating, won the unanimous approval of the 1924 judges and another

Dick Button, a superlative jumper, winner of the figure-skating titles at the Games of 1948 and 1952

Austrian, Willy Böckl, narrowly failed to depose Grafström. It was indeed Austria's year, for a Viennese pair, Alfred Berger and Helene Engelmann, relegated the Jakobssons to second place.

Sonja Henie, now an old-stager of fifteen and already World Champion, won the first of her three gold medals at St Moritz in 1928 with a display that carried women's skating into new areas of athleticism. Throughout three Olympics only once did any judge fail to place her clear of the field: in 1936, when one official placed Cecilia Colledge (Great Britain), then fifteen, on the same exalted pedestal. There are some who think that the threat from Miss Colledge, eight years the younger, gave Miss Henie the final nudge towards professionalism.

As Miss Henie rose from the launching pad in 1928, so another illustrious skater, Grafström, prepared for his touchdown. He won at St Moritz only by a majority decision, since three of the seven judges chose otherwise, a clear indication of waning supremacy. Another medal was to come his way at Lake Placid, New York, in 1932, but, handicapped by a heavy fall, he had no hope of withstanding the advance of a rising young Austrian, Karl Schäfer. Schäfer was champion again in 1936 (Garmisch-Partenkirchen). Ernst Baier (Germany), second to Schäfer in the individual event and first in the pairs with Maxi Herber, who was later to become his wife, has the distinction of being the only figure-skating competitor to have won gold and silver in two different events, thus surpassing Madge Syer's gold and bronze in the pioneering days of 1908.

When the Games were resumed after World War II the skating bore a strong British accent for four successive Olympiads, the eight individual titles being shared by the United States, Canada and Britain. The lion's share, however, belonged to the Americans, with all four men's titles (two won by Richard Button, a superlative jumper) and the women's titles of 1956 (Cortina) and 1960 (Squaw Valley). By contrast, in the pairs event the winners came from continental Europe – Belgium, Germany and Austria except for 1960, when Robert Paul and Barbara Wagner (Canada) completed a North American clean sweep at Squaw Valley.

Jeanette Altwegg, the winner for Britain at Oslo in 1952, struck a new and hearteningly altruistic note by retiring not to the show arenas but to the austere life of the Pestalozzi Children's Village at Trogen, Switzerland. Admittedly, she won on the strength of her school figures and was clearly outshone in the free by Jacqueline du Bief (France), among others, but an Olympic gold medal can always be exploited by a skater minded to do so. She chose otherwise – and won new admirers.

The Cortina Games of 1956 were notable for the fact that two brothers occupied the medal winners' podium for the first time in skating (there had been a precedent in tobogganing when Jennison and John Heaton had come first and second on the Cresta). They were Hayes and David Jenkins (United States), first and third respectively, the latter to become a spectacular winner in 1960 with a program that included triple jumps and elicited a maximum mark of 6.0 from the French judge.

The pattern has changed sharply since, partly because of the increasingly predatory activities of American show promoters and partly because of the air tragedy of 1961 that destroyed the flower of American skating talent. The accident occurred at Brussels, where a charter flight carrying the whole of the American team for the World Championships in Czechoslovakia, together with trainers and families and friends, crashed with total loss of life.

The most distinguished skaters to emerge during this period, at least in terms of public recognition, were the Russian pair, Oleg Protopopov and his wife, Ludmila Belousova. Theirs was something of a love affair on ice; each, apparently oblivious of the thousands of spectators and millions of distant television viewers, communed only with the other and the ice. They almost made spectators feel guilty of intrusion into their private life. If others were able to achieve greater technical deeds of derring-do (pair skating has its special hazards), the Protopopovs brought new meaning to the expression 'poetry of motion'.

They brought, too, disaster to an apparently enterprising gentleman at Innsbruck in 1964. So convinced was he of a victory for the European champions, Hans-Jürgen Bäumler and Marika Kilius, that he stood outside the stadium that cold, dark night armed to the teeth with postcards commemorating the Olympic victory of the Germans. History, alas, does not record his reaction when the perfidy of the judges percolated through to him.

The 'death spiral', part of the outstanding performance by Oleg and Ludmila Protopopov (USSR)

Nor could the result have done a great deal to promote the sale of a pop record by the alluring Miss Kilius, fetchingly clad in American Western style on the record's sleeve. Later the German pair suffered a further disappointment when they were held to have infringed Olympic rules by signing a professional contract before the Games and the silver medals were withdrawn in favour of Guy Revell and Debbie Wilkes (Canada).

The Protopopovs left behind not only a trail of commercial upheaval, but also a fitting memorial to their art, the haunting 'death spiral' on the back inside edge. This was the beginning of a period of Russian domination in the pairs which continues to this day.

The Protopopovs were not the only ones to upset the form book in Innsbruck's Olympic Stadium, for Manfred Schnelldörfer, a twenty-year-old West German, turned the tables, too, on a European champion, Alain Calmat (France), whose nerve broke during the free skating. Calmat, indeed, only just managed to take the silver medal in the face of an almost outrageously extrovert performance by a fifteen-year-old American, Scot Allen. Sjoukje Dijkstra (Netherlands), on the other hand, was an utterly convincing winner of the women's event, with a superb presentation of both figures and free.

In spite of the new trend towards giving greater reward for the free skating, the two individual winners at Sapporo in 1972 were disappointing, living, as they did, on the cold, clinical mastery of the compulsory figures before a scattering of spectators rather than charming the many thousands who attend the free-skating finals. Both Ondrej Nepela (Czechoslovakia) and Beatrix Schuba (Austria) were heavily outpointed on their big night, which tended to produce something of an anti-climax. As the move away from the compulsory figures gathers momentum we may find that nobody will be able to win a gold medal who has not evolved a commanding free-skating program. Then we shall probably see the North Americans regain their former Olympic stature, the show promoters notwithstanding.

SPEED SKATING Jean Grenier

Although skating as a recreation was popular in most countries of central and northern Europe up to the end of the nineteenth century, competition was mainly local. Speed skating became international during the general growth of international sport at the end of the nineteenth century. The first World Championship, held at the Amsterdam Ice Club in the Netherlands, was decided on the results at three distances, half a mile, one mile and two miles, but the title was only to be awarded to a man who won all three. Aleksandr von Panschin, of Russia, took the half mile and mile but finished second in the longer distance and so no champion was declared. The following year, again in Amsterdam, races were held over four distances but again no champion emerged, but in 1891 an American, Joseph Donoghue, won over four distances – five miles having been added – and was thus regarded as the first World Champion.

The natural step forward was the formation of an international body, the International Skating Union (ISU), which took place in 1892 in Scheveningen, the Netherlands, with representatives from five countries taking part. The rules governing the World Championship were altered so that the skater who won three out of four races became champion. The distances were changed to the metric measure and in 1893 Jaap Eden (Netherlands), winning three races (and falling in the fourth), became the titleholder.

Speed skating was included in the list of sports considered desirable for the Olympic Games at the first Olympic Congress in 1894. However, although demonstration races were included at the 1908 and 1920 Olympics in London and Antwerp, it was only when the Winter Olympic Games were first held in 1924 at Chamonix that speed-skating competitions appeared on the program.

The supremacy of Scandinavia was almost unchallenged for the first six Games, from 1924 to 1952, except for 1932, when the Americans, on home ground at Lake Placid, won most of the medals. The use of the mass start, instead of starting in pairs and racing in lanes against the clock, utterly confused the Europeans and led to the IOC ruling that in future the sport must be conducted under the rules of the ISU.

The changes in climate in the first half of the twentieth century had an adverse effect in the countries from which the sport had originated, Great Britain, the Netherlands and Scandinavia, and where the first competitions had been held. Great Britain and the Netherlands now had generally mild winters; the temperature did not allow natural ice to form and consequently the training of skaters suffered. It was not until after World War II that, with the large-scale building of artificial rinks, the Dutch were at last capable of making a good show in the Olympic Games. Other nations, including the Japanese, followed this development.

Since 1924 the standard distances skated in the Olympics have been 500 metres, 1,500 metres, 5,000 metres and

Hjalmar Andersen (Norway), winner of three speed-skating gold medals at the Games of Oslo

10,000 metres for men. Women's events were not included until 1960, although there had been a demonstration of women's races in 1932 at Lake Placid. The women's distances are 500 metres, 1,000 metres, 1,500 metres and 3,000 metres. In 1924 Charles Jewtraw (United States) won the 500 metres in 44.0 sec; today this distance is skated in less than 38 sec. The great hero of the first Olympics in speed skating, Clas Thunberg (Finland), who took the 1,500 metres and 5,000 metres and was second in the 10,000 metres, won the 1,500 metres in 2 min 20.8 sec. Today it is accomplished in close to two minutes.

In 1928 in St Moritz, Thunberg was challenged by the Norwegian Ivar Ballangrud. In 1936 at Garmisch-Partenkirchen the Norwegians maintained their supremacy, with Ballangrud winning the 500 metres, 5,000 metres and 10,000 metres and coming second to his countryman Charles Mathiesen in the 1,500 metres.

At St Moritz in 1948, the Norwegian team was still the most successful and it was only at the Games of 1952 and 1956 in Oslo and Cortina d'Ampezzo respectively that other medal winners appeared, particularly Americans and Russians, although the Norwegians were still supreme, thanks to Hjalmar Andersen, triple gold medallist. The very strong sprinter Yevgeni Grishin (USSR) was outstanding in 1956 and 1960, winning gold medals in the 500 metres and 1,500 metres in both years. From this period Scandinavians faced growing competition from the Russians, Americans and Japanese but maintained their hold in the long-distance events. Over the shorter distances, the Dutch appeared among the medal winners, followed by the Germans and Japanese: Erhard Keller (German Federal Republic) won the 500 metres in 1968 at Grenoble while Cornelis (Kees) Verkerk (Netherlands) took the 1,500 metres.

Speed skating received a rare Olympic award after the Games of 1968, when the Tokyo Trophy was awarded to David Bodington, a twenty-two-year-old from Birmingham, England. The trophy awarded at each Olympiad for noble and outstanding qualities of sportsmanship was given for Bodington's exemplary example of unselfishness during the 400-metres event. Drawn against Jan Bols (Netherlands), the Englishman, somewhat surprisingly, gained an edge in the first part of the race and the Dutchman, pressing to close the gap, lost his balance on a bend and went over, sliding into Bodington's lane, just ahead of the Briton. Bodington could have risked jumping across his opponent and cutting him with his sharp blades. But to avoid such an accident he threw himself down and skidded into the side boarding, suffering cuts and bruises which not only put him out of this particular race but effectively put him last of the fifty-three competitors in the 1,500-metres event.

The domination of Olympic speed skating by less than a dozen nations is unlikely to continue. The building of artificial tracks will produce a much broader base to the sport in a large number of countries, including those where the climate does not allow the formation of natural ice or even of outdoor artificial ice.

Speed skating was at first practised on natural ice surfaces which were straight, as on the canals of the Netherlands and in the fen country of England. However, international competitions are now held on outdoor oval tracks on which the official distances skated per lap are 333 or 400 metres.

According to the rules originally established by the ISU, skaters take part, two at a time, changing lanes at every turn according to a well-defined procedure; the starting lines and the lanes are set up so that each racer skates the same distance in equivalent conditions. The only time this system has not been used in the Olympic Games was in 1932, when, following American practice, the starts were made in heats ('mass start'), the racers not being restricted to a lane but, as in long-distance running, the first skater racing close to the inner edge of the track with overtaking allowed on the outside.

Outdoor speed skating can be practised only in a climate cold enough to permit natural or artificial ice to form. Sportsmen living in countries where this is not possible or where economic factors do not permit the investment necessary for an artificial track (at least £1,500,000 today) are denied the opportunity of speed skating.

Indoor speed skating varies according to location; in Europe there are oval tracks of 100–125 metres, in North America tracks obliquely laid, and double-radius tracks in Australia and New Zealand. In indoor speed skating, the starts in races are in heats of four competitors, except for events of 1,500 metres or longer, in which the heats are for eight, in two lines of four. The rules for competitions are sanctioned by the ISU but in the United States and Canada skaters race under the rules of the American Skating Union, which is not recognized by the ISU or the other indoor-skating countries.

Speed and figure skating and ice dancing are closely related and all are governed by the ISU. Figure skating is practised both indoors and out like ice hockey and curling, and the arenas used for these sports now also serve for a shortened version of speed skating. This variant makes

Ard Schenk (Netherlands) who took three speed-skating titles in 1972, all in Olympic record times

speed skating accessible to more countries and is playing a crucial part in its development. Hundreds of towns across the world already have artificial indoor hockey rinks; in North America alone there are over a thousand. The Europeans, particularly the Scandinavians and Dutch, aware of the vast cost of the large rinks, are also turning to the use of smaller ones. This new style of racing may one day appear on the Olympic program.

SKIING Peter Lunn

The oldest sports are those that have their roots in man's most natural needs: running and swimming, various forms of combat, boating and equestrianism. And also skiing, which has been an essential form of locomotion in Scandinavia since the earliest times. A number of prehistoric skis have been discovered, and the oldest of them, the Hoting Ski, belongs to the third millennium before Christ.

Though the ancient Scandinavian sagas record the exploits of gods and men on skis – Ullur was the god and Ondurrdis the goddess of skiing – the first recorded ski race took place in 1767. But this was an isolated event which had no effect on the later history of the sport.

The father of modern cross-country racing and jumping was Sondre Norheim, an impecunious peasant from the Telemark district of Norway. In 1870 a number of Telemark skiers gave an exhibition near Christiania, as Oslo was then called. It was this exhibition of what could be achieved on skis that led to the foundation of the Christiania Ski Club and thus, indirectly, to the foundation of the Holmenkollen events in 1892. These cross-country and jumping events are the oldest international ski competitions with a continuous history.

In 1892 the Holmenkollen events consisted of a 17-kilometre cross-country race, won by S. Sollid, and a jumping competition, won by Arne Ustvedt. The King's

Tormod Knutsen (Norway), winner of the Nordic combined event at Innsbruck in 1964

Toni Sailer (Austria), winner of all three Olympic Alpine skiing medals in 1956

Cup, which for a long time was to have far more prestige than either of the individual events, was awarded to the competitor who had the best combined result in the cross-country race and the jumping competition. In the first year of competition it was won by Sollid.

A long-distance race was introduced for the first time in 1900, and was held over a distance of 30 kilometres. In 1902 this was lengthened to 50 kilometres, which has remained the classic distance for the really long event.

From their foundation in 1892 till the first Winter Olympics in 1924, a period of thirty-two years, the Holmenkollen events were accepted without question as outstandingly the most important competitions in the skiing world. Merely to have competed at Holmenkollen was a title to recognition, but to state this still gives no idea just what has been the position of the Holmenkollen events in Norway, a position with which Wimbledon in lawn tennis, Henley in rowing and Bisley in shooting cannot compare. The Holmenkollen jump was only used on one day of the year, Holmenkollen Day. During 1940 to 1945, while Norway was occupied by the Germans, the jump was never used. Anyone who was present at the first Holmenkollen Day after the war, and could feel the charged emotion of the vast crowd as King Haakon made his traditional appearance, will know beyond doubt that the position of Holmenkollen in Norwegian national feeling is something unique. No other sporting event can compare with Holmenkollen as a symbol of national identity.

At the 1924 Olympics, medals were awarded for the 18-kilometre and the 50-kilometre cross-country races, for the jumping competition, and for the best combined performance in the 18-kilometre and the jumping. Thorleif Haug of Norway won both the 18-kilometre and the 50-kilometre races and the combined 18-kilometre/jumping event. So he won three out of the four gold medals available, and his compatriot, Jacob Tullin Thams, won the jumping and got the fourth. In 1928 Norway won three out of the four gold medals.

In the modern Olympics there are cross-country

races for men over 15 kilometres, 30 kilometres and 50 kilometres; for women over 5 and 10 kilometres; the 15-kilometre/jumping combined, biathlon events (cross-country racing and shooting) and jumping competitions on both big and small hills, which are specially constructed. (Jumping and biathlon are for men only.) At the 1972 Olympics the winning jump on the small hill was 84 metres (276 ft) and the winning jump on the large hill was 111 metres (364 ft).

In 1933 the world record for jumping was 87 metres (285 ft). In 1934, 92 metres (302 ft) was achieved on the Planica jump in Yugoslavia, the first jump that made much longer performances possible. 120 metres (394 ft) was jumped at Planica in 1948. In 1950, 135 metres (443 ft) was jumped on the new and even bigger Oberstdorf jump in Bavaria. In March 1973, Heinz Wosipiwo of the German Democratic Republic jumped 169 metres (554 ft) on the Oberstdorf jump. The Norwegians were for a time resolutely opposed to jumping hills that made such long jumps possible and discouraged their competitors from using them. They regarded monster jumping, or ski flying, as it later came to be called, as the product of a sensationalism which would damage the healthy development of the sport.

On these very long jumps the skier has time in the air to experiment with his aerodynamic position till he suddenly gets the feeling that he is gliding. It is this aerodynamic position, rather than the force and timing of the skier's jump as he leaves the platform, that is decisive in achieving distance.

Although this correct aerodynamic position can only be properly learned on the very large jumps, it is also of great importance on jumps of normal size. Because the Norwegians discouraged jumping on these very large hills, skiers from other countries surpassed them in acquiring the correct aerodynamic position, so that the Norwegians lost their superiority even on normal hills. In the Olympics from 1924 to 1952, the Norwegians won all six gold medals for jumping, five of the silver medals, and four of the bronze. In 1956 and 1960 they did not win any medals at all for jumping.

In 1964, for the first time, there were Olympic jumping events on both large and small hills. Some time before this the Norwegians had become reconciled to the use of large hills, and in 1964 Toralf Engan of Norway won the gold medal on the big hill and the silver medal on the small hill. His compatriot Torgeir Brandtzäg won the bronze medal on both hills. Since then the Norwegians have won no medals for jumping.

By 1892, the year when the Holmenkollen events started, skis had been used, not only for sport, but also for serious exploration. In 1888 Fridtjof Nansen used skis to cross Greenland from East to West. It was his book *Paa Ski over Grønland* (1890), translated into English as *The First Crossing of Greenland*, and into several other languages, that spread enthusiasm for skiing from Scandinavia to the Alps. Among those who read it was Mathias Zdarsky, an Austrian eccentric, who had retired to a mountain hermitage near Lilienfeld in order, as he put it, to develop undisturbed his scientific and artistic ideas. Inspired by Nansen's book, he bought a pair of skis from Norway and proceeded, alone and unaided to work out a technique for their use. At a time when skiing was dominated by reverence for the Scandinavian fathers of the sport, Zdarsky

Japan's first skiing medal. Yukio Kasaya taking the 70-metre jump at Sapporo

realized that technique developed in the undulating terrain of the north simply did not work on the steep Alpine slopes. He was the first person to realize that there was such a thing as downhill skiing, and his book, *Lilienfeld Skilauf-Technik* (1896), was the first serious attempt to work out a technique for downhill, as opposed to cross-country, skiing. Before then ideas were crude. 'The runners', to quote from a contemporary account, 'let the ski carry them where it will until the air acts as a natural brake and brings them to rest.'

Zdarsky was an indomitable character. In an avalanche accident in later life he received between seventy and eighty fractures and dislocations, but he managed to take up skiing again. And he needed to be indomitable because the opposition he encountered was fierce. Downhill skiing seems to have inspired a number of quasi-mystical controversies, and Zdarsky was eminently fitted to be the prophet of the new sport. 'It is the most primitive rule of conduct,' he wrote, 'that of two people who have dealings with each other, one must be the speaker, the other the listener.'

Zdarsky is the father of downhill skiing, but he was uninterested in racing. Downhill ski racing really had its origins when a Methodist missionary, invalided home from India, decided in 1892 to organize a conference to reunite a divided Christendom. This man, Henry Lunn, my grandfather, had never been to Switzerland in his life, but he decided to organize the conference in the mountain valley of Grindelwald for the reason, which seemed sufficient to him, that St Bernard of Clairvaux had once made a retreat there. 'At the end of the conference,' he wrote, in the tone of one reporting a lamentable mishap, 'I found myself £500 in pocket.' He came to found a travel business, only to discover that the English upper classes regarded it as 'not done', to holiday under the auspices of a travel agent. So my grandfather founded the Public Schools Alpine Sports Club, in the name of which he would book whole hotels, so that his clientele could practise winter sports abroad in the serene confidence that they would find among their fellow guests no foreigners and no Englishmen who were not of the right class. It was this Club that opened for the first time in winter no fewer than ten centres, including such now-famous resorts as Adelboden, Klosters, Montana, Wengen and Mürren. Indeed, in Mürren every hotel except one was booked during the winter months by the Public Schools Alpine

Sports Club. The oddest thing about this display of class-conscious chauvinism is that it does not seem to have struck people as in the least strange. Though I do remember there was one Swiss visitor, who was at first bewildered, and then enraged, to find he could not get a room in a Mürren hotel on the grounds, which seemed inadequate to him, that he had not been to a British public school. Assuming, wrongly as it happened, that the manager of this outfit must himself be English, he cried out in anger, 'You bloody boy. Here I stand on Swiss bottom and cannot get a bed.'

In 1903, to amuse his guests, my grandfather organized the Public Schools Alpine Sports Club Challenge Cup on the combined results of skiing, skating, and tobogganing events. The ski race was not very arduous. The Swiss course setter stuck a flag in each corner of a field and asked the competitors to walk round them. In 1911 the idea of one championship for all three winter sports was abandoned, and three separate competitions were established. My grandfather persuaded Lord Roberts of Kandahar (a Vice-President of the Public Schools Alpine Sports Club, though he never figured as a skier) to give his name to the ski event, and the first competition for the Roberts of Kandahar Challenge Cup was organized at Montana in 1911. Arnold Lunn, my father, was present, a young man of twenty-two, his leg badly smashed by a recent mountaineering accident. The competition was, as it has been ever since, a downhill race. It is the oldest downhill ski race in the world, and it was from this race that my father took the name Kandahar for the club he founded in Mürren to campaign for the recognition of downhill and slalom racing.

The Alpine skiers had slavishly followed Scandinavian precedent in awarding their national ski championships on the combined results of cross-country races and jumping competitions. My father's book, *Skiing* (1913), contains the first advocacy of downhill racing. After World War I he drew up the first rules for downhill racing and invented the modern slalom. Although downhill racing as a sport seems obvious today, my father encountered fierce opposition in trying to put his ideas into practice.

In 1921 the British broke with Scandinavian precedent and awarded national championships on the combined result of a downhill race and a style competition. (The next country to award a national championship for a downhill event was Austria in 1929.)

The style competition was derived from a Norwegian event and bore the Norwegian name of slalom. Each competitor had to descend a given slope in front of judges and perform certain turns; he was then awarded marks according to his style. It proved, however, impossible to devise any system of marking for style which was not arbitrary, and these style competitions tended, in any case, to encourage pretty, rather than fast and accurate, skiing.

My father, therefore, came to regard the style competition as unsatisfactory but remained convinced that, while downhill racing was a fine test of nerve and rapid judgment, it must be complemented by some other form of competition which would test technique and skill. He therefore invented the idea of racing through pairs of flags, known as gates, placed on the hillside in various figures so as to test so far as possible the skier's ability to turn fast and accurately. Each competitor went down the course

in turn, the winner being the one to complete it in the shortest time; no marks were awarded for style. To this entirely new form of race my father gave the name of the old-style competition which it was designed to replace; he called it a slalom. But his slalom had nothing in common with the old-style competition except the name and the fact that both were designed to test technique rather than dash.

My father set the first slalom on the practice slope at Mürren on 21 January 1922, the most significant single date in the history of skiing. Before this he had drawn up in Mürren the first rules for downhill racing ever published. It was only fitting that, in 1931, he should organize, also in Mürren, the first World Championships in downhill racing, and that later he should referee the slalom at the 1952 Olympics. His was the unique achievement of refereeing an Olympic sport which he had himself invented.

It was in 1936 that downhill and slalom racing were included in the Olympic program. The sport, whose seeds lay in the Public Schools Alpine Sports Club, had arrived.

Downhill racing has changed out of all recognition in fifty years. 'John Joannides', to quote a contemporary account of an international race in the 1920s, 'spoiled his chances by getting stuck under a bridge'. Progress has not simply been in the improving skills of competitors. Fundamental changes came with the preparation of downhill courses from 1936 and the development of the stiff ski.

The acceptance of skiing in the Winter Olympics gave a new impetus to the sport. Newspapers began to take it seriously. Centres appreciated the publicity from staging downhill races; far more money became available for the preparation of courses.

Before 1936 the only rule about the preparation of courses, apart from controls to avoid danger, related to heavy snowfalls: two skiers must go down before the first racer, to prepare firm tracks. The skis used were flexible and suitable for soft snow. Racers chose their own routes which could be half a mile apart on the hillside. There was no difference between racing and ordinary skiing.

Then it came to be realized that a stiff ski holds far better on hard and icy snow. The problem with stiff skis is that they dig in and can cause a dangerous fall in soft snow. Even before courses were prepared, hard snow was commoner than soft, so racers took to stiff skis. They then became terrified of running off the hard snow into soft and called for safety measures. As a result downhill races came to be held on specially prepared courses which ran like ribbons down the mountain side. Racing and ordinary skiing thus separated, for the former required increasingly specialized equipment.

As standards improved, more and more specialized training became necessary for the different events. This in turn was reflected in the organization of the Games. In 1936, two gold medals (one for men and one for women) were awarded for the combined event of downhill and slalom. Today there are six gold medals for downhill skiing. In 1936, seven gold medals were awarded for skiing events. In 1972 there were eighteen gold medals for ski events, including biathlon. Specialization has moved a long way since my grandfather organized one winter-sports championship for combined performance in skiing, skating and tobogganing. The performance of Birger Ruud, who won both the downhill and the jumping in 1936, would be virtually impossible today.

Who's Who in the Olympic Games

The editors would have liked to include in this section a biography of every Olympian who has mounted the middle position of the prizewinners' podium; regrettably we did not have space for so many entries. Instead we have had to be selective, choosing those champions who have reached some higher distinction. Some qualifiers do not appear only because all our research proved fruitless.

The editors are grateful to Neil Allen, Richard Burnell, James Coote, Brian Crowther, Alan Gayfer, John Goodbody, John Hennessy, Richard Hollands, John Kerr, Gaston Meyer and Jakob Vaage for providing much of the information; we should also like to thank the staffs of many National Olympic Committees, International Federations and National Federations, and in some instances relatives of competitors for their help.

The abbreviations for names of countries are the official ones used by the International Olympic Committee and listed on page 229. A name appearing in SMALL CAPITALS within an entry indicates that a separate biography of that person will be found in this section of the book. Olympic medals are listed at the end of each entry.

Anderson, Gary L. (USA)
B. Holdrege, Neb., 8 Oct. 1939. He won eleven individual and ten team gold medals in international competition during the 1960s. A rare left-handed shooter, Anderson taught himself to shoot. He was the first American in over forty years to win the free rifle event in two consecutive Olympic Games.
Gold free rifle 1964, 1968

Astakhova, Polina (URS)
B. Donetsk, Ukraine, 30 Oct. 1936. This seemingly fragile Russian gymnast would have won even more honours if she had not been a contemporary of Larisa LATYNINA. At Tokyo (1964) she finished only 0.033 pt behind Latynina in an event won by Vera ČÁSLAVSKÁ (TCH). On the asymmetrical bars Čáslavská seemed likely to finish first but missed a pirouette off the top bar and fell, thus allowing Astakhova to take the title.
Gold asymmetrical bars 1960, 1964; combined exercises (team) 1956, 1960, 1964
Silver floor exercises 1960, 1964
Bronze combined exercises (individual) 1960, 1964

Baillet-Latour, Comte Henri de (BEL)
B. 1 Mar. 1876; d. Brussels, 6 Jan. 1942. Became an IOC Member in 1903; responsible for organizing the Games in Antwerp (1920) for which there was only one year to make preparations. It was largely his energy in the management of this task that led his colleagues to elect him to the Presidency of the IOC, succeeding COUBER-

TIN in 1925. He tried to keep commercialism and politics out of the Olympic Movement, the latter notably in Berlin, in 1936. He was President of the IOC until his death.

Balaş, Iolanda (ROM)
B. Timisoara, 12 Dec. 1936. World's outstanding woman high jumper from 1958 to 1966, she set the first of her fourteen world records in this event in July 1956. At the 1956 Olympics she finished fifth but was European Champion in 1958 and 1962 and won the Olympic title with 1.85 m (6 ft 0¾ in) in 1960 and with 1.90 m (6 ft 2¾ in) in 1964. She was 1.85 m (6ft 0¾ in) tall but found it impossible to use any style but a version of the old-fashioned 'scissors'. Otherwise she might well have raised the record higher than her 1.91 m (6 ft 3¼ in) in 1961.
Gold high jump 1960, 1964

Iolanda Balaş (ROM), 1964

Balczó, András (HUN)
B. Kondoros, 16 Aug. 1939. Probably the greatest all-rounder in the history of modern pentathlon. He first competed in the 1960 Olympics, where he placed fourth, only 15 pts behind the silver medallist, and won a gold in the team event. In spite of being the reigning World Champion, he was not in the Hungarian team in Tokyo. As well as his Olympic achievements, he won the world title in 1963, 1965, 1966, 1967 and 1969.
Gold modern pentathlon (individual) 1972; (team) 1960, 1968
Silver modern pentathlon (individual) 1968, (team) 1972

Ballangrud, Ivar (NOR)
B. Lunner, Hadeland, 7 Mar. 1904; d. Trondheim, 6 June 1969. In his first years in competitive speed skating his best distances were 5,000 metres and 10,000 metres. Later he was also an excellent sprinter. As well as his Olympic successes, he won the World Championship four times, the

European Championship four times, was Norwegian Champion five times, and set five world records in the 1,500 metres, 5,000 metres (three times) and 10,000 metres.
Gold 500 metres 1936; 5,000 metres 1928, 1936; 10,000 metres 1936
Silver 1,500 metres 1936; 10,000 metres 1932
Bronze 1,500 metres 1928

Beamon, Robert (USA)
B. Jamaica, N.Y., 29 Aug. 1946. Achieved possibly the outstanding single Olympic athletics performance with his long jump of 8.90 m (29 ft 2½ in), which added 55 cm (21½ in) to the world record at Mexico City on 18 October 1968. Beamon was a sometimes unpredictable but undoubtedly talented jumper who could run 100 yd in 9.5 sec and, before the 1968 Games, had cleared 8.33 m (27 ft 4 in). On his greatest day he had speed, spring and height; the following wind was right on the limit, for record ratification, of 2 metres per second (4.47 mph) and at the altitude of 2,260 m (7,415 ft), resistance is some 20 per cent less than at sea level. Even so, he was staggered at his accomplishment and never again did better than 8.20 m (26 ft 11 in). He turned professional in 1973.
Gold long jump 1968

Belote, Melissa (USA)
B. Washington, D.C., 16 Oct. 1956. Miss Belote was only fifteen when she won three swimming gold medals at Munich. She had broken the world record for 200-metres backstroke at Chicago a month before the Games and had won both backstroke finals in the US Olympic trials. In Munich she twice broke the world record for 200-metres backstroke, with 2 min 20.58 sec in her heat and 2 min 19.19 sec in the final – the first woman to beat 2 min 20 sec for the event. She also won the 100-metres backstroke in the Olympic record time of 1 min 5.78 sec and shared in another world record as a member of the medley relay winning team; her time on the backstroke stage was 1 min 6.24 sec.
Gold 100-metres backstroke 1972; 200-metres backstroke 1972; 4 × 100-metres medley relay 1972

Belousova, Ludmila (URS) see
PROTOPOPOV

Beresford, Jack (GBR)
B. Chiswick, 1 Jan. 1899. Although weighing only some 72½ kg (160 lb) Beresford was the most successful Olympic oarsman and sculler of all time, competing in five consecutive Games; in 1939 he was preparing for a sixth appearance in the 1940 Games, when war intervened. In 1949 he was awarded the Olympic Diploma of Merit by the IOC.
Gold single sculls 1924; coxless fours 1932; double sculls 1936
Silver single sculls 1920; eights 1928

Bianchetto, Sergio (ITA)

B. Torre (Padova), 16 Feb. 1939. From his first cycling race in 1955 his talent was recognized and at seventeen he was selected as first reserve for the 1956 Italian Olympic team. Although twice world sprint champion, in 1961 and 1962, his Olympic gold medals were won on a tandem. In both instances it was his rare aggression and exceptional skill in handling a cycle that gave him the medal. In 1960 he was partnered by an old school friend Giuseppe Beghetto; in 1964 he rode with Andrea Damiano.

Gold 2,000-metres tandem 1960, 1964
Silver individual 1,000-metres sprint 1964

Bikila, Abebe (ETH)

B. Mout, Ethiopia, 7 Aug. 1932; d. 25 Oct. 1973. Celebrated as the first man to win the Olympic marathon twice, Bikila should also be remembered as the first athletics gold medal winner from black Africa. In 1960 he was completely unknown outside his own country though he had just run a marathon in 2 hr 21 min 23 sec in the high altitude of Ethiopia which may, through its process of lung ventilation, have played a considerable part in his successes. Running barefoot through the floodlit streets of Rome, Bikila pulled away from his only real challenger, Rhadi Ben Abdesselam (MAR), in a world's best time of 2 hr 15 min 16.2 sec. The bemused press then discovered that this was only the third marathon run by this member of the Imperial Guard of Emperor Haile Selassie.

Four years later, this time wearing shoes, Bikila ran in the 1964 marathon on 21 October, although on 16 September he had had his appendix removed and had not been able to resume training until 27 September.

Sadly, in 1968 Bikila had to drop out after ten miles with an injured leg. Tragically, he received such severe injuries in a car accident in 1969 that he was unable to walk again. He bravely took up competitive paraplegic sport, including archery, but what had become a bitter struggle ended with his death at only forty-one years of age.

Gold marathon 1960, 1964

Blankers-Koen, Francina (HOL)

B. Amsterdam, 26 Apr. 1918. Most famous woman athlete of all, between 1938 and 1951 she set world records in seven different events: 100 yards and 100 metres, 220 yards, 80-metres hurdles, high jump, long jump and pentathlon. She was sixth equal in the 1936 Olympic high jump. Because of World War II she was thirty by her next Games in 1948. She made the most of her chance with four gold medals, in spite of increasing emotional fatigue – just thirteen years after starting athletics as an 800-metres runner. In the European Championships of 1938, 1946 and 1950 she won eight medals and five titles.

Gold 100 metres 1948; 200 metres 1948; 80-metres hurdles 1948; 4 × 100-metres relay 1948

Bleibtrey, Ethelda (USA)

B. Waterford, N.Y., 27 Feb. 1902. It was possible to win only three gold medals in the women's swimming events at the 1920 Olympics, which Miss Bleibtrey achieved. She was the first woman to win three Olympic titles in any sport and she would probably have won four if there had been a backstroke event in the Games at that time, for she was the holder of a world record in that event in 1920. She set world records in the 100-metres freestyle (1 min 13.6 sec) and the now defunct 300-metres freestyle (4 min 34.0 sec). She set seven world records in her career.

Gold 100-metres freestyle 1920; 300-metres freestyle 1920; 4 × 100-metres freestyle relay 1920

Bogdanov, Anatoli (URS)

B. Leningrad, 1 Jan. 1931. One of the best shooters in free and smallbore rifle events in the 1950s, he was the first Soviet Olympic Champion, won twenty-five gold medals at the Olympic Games, World and European Championships and held the world record 1954–9. He took up shooting in 1950 and two years later won the free rifle event at the Olympic Games at Helsinki.

Gold free rifle 1952; smallbore rifle three positions 1956

Borzov, Valeri (URS)

B. near Lvov, 20 Oct. 1949. The only European to have won both the Olympic 100- and 200-metres titles, which he did almost effortlessly in 1972. A remarkably polished runner, Borzov was said to be a sprinter made rather than born, by a group of Kiev physiologists and coaches. This does less than justice to his coolness under pressure which gave him a perfect competitive record in major championships from 1968, when he won both European junior titles. Only a year later he equalled the European senior record for the 100-metres event of 10 sec.

At Munich Borzov was deprived of the chance of racing against the two fastest Americans, Eddie Hart and Reynaud Robinson, because they failed to turn up on time for their quarter-final races. But even so Borzov looked unbeatable in the final which he won with both hands held high as he crossed the line. Over 200 metres, again with hands raised, he set a European record time of 20 sec.

After the Olympic Games of 1972 Borzov suffered both a psychological reaction and a muscle injury but in 1974 in Rome he retained his European 100-metres title.

Gold 100 metres 1972; 200 metres 1972
Silver 4 × 100-metres relay 1972

Boyarskikh, Klaudia (URS)

B. Verkhnyaya Pyshma, Sverdlovsk, 11 Nov. 1939. Teacher of physical education and the best woman skier of the mid-1960s. While a student she took part in athletics and then skiing. She won a prize at the international skiing competitions in Kavgolovo in 1963, three gold medals at the Winter Olympic Games in 1964 and two at the World Championships in 1966. She also won the women's Holmenkollen events in 1965 and 1967.

Gold 5 kilometres 1964; 10 kilometres 1964; 3 × 5-kilometres relay 1964

Braglia, Alberto (ITA)

B. Campogalliano, Modena, 23 Mar. 1883; d. 5 Feb. 1954. Regarded as Italy's first Olympic gold medal winner but this was at the Interim Games in Athens in 1906 where, in gymnastics, he was joint champion in pentathlon and hexathlon. His reputation as one of the greatest gymnastics technicians grew and was confirmed in 1908 in London and maintained to 1912 in Stockholm, where he took the individual prize and helped Italy to win the team event. He achieved equal success in coaching; as the chief coach to the 1932 Italian Olympic team, he played a part in Italy's greatest triumph in the sport, winning four gold medals at one Games.

Gold combined exercises (individual) 1908, 1912, (team) 1912

Brenden, Hallgeir (NOR)

B. Trysil, 10 Feb. 1929. In the Oslo Olympics he won the gold medal for the 18-km cross-country skiing and repeated the victory in 1956. He was Norwegian champion in the 30-km cross-country three times, and in the 15-km six times. He was also a good track-and-field athlete, holding the Norwegian record for the 3,000-metres steeplechase.

Gold 18-kilometres cross-country 1952; 15-kilometres cross-country 1956
Silver 4 × 10-kilometres relay 1952, 1960

Brundage, Avery (USA)

B. Detroit, Mich., 28 Sept. 1887; d. Garmisch-Partenkirchen, 7 May 1975. Orphaned by the age of eleven, he was brought up by an uncle and aunt. He graduated from the University of Illinois in engineering with a first-class degree. He was also an outstanding athlete, a member of the University basketball team and intercollegiate discus champion. He competed in the Games at Stockholm in 1912 and was three times US all-round champion. He formed the Avery Brundage Company in 1915, which constructed a number of skyscrapers and other big buildings around Chicago. He was active in sports administration from an early age, holding the position of President of the Amateur Athletic Union of the United States for seven terms and the Presidency of the US Olympic Committee for twenty-five years. He became a member of the IOC in 1936, Vice-president in 1945 and President in 1952; he resigned in 1972. He gathered one of the finest Asiatic art collections in the world, estimated to be worth $50 million, and presented it to the city of San Francisco, which built a museum to house it.

Brunet, Pierre and Andrée (Joly) (FRA)

Pierre B. Paris, 28 June 1902; Andrée B. Paris, 16 Sept. 1901. Pierre Brunet competed in singles and pairs figure-skating events before World War II. He was eighth in the Winter Games men's championship at Chamonix (1924), seventh in the 1928 Winter Games at St Moritz, and ninth in the World Championship in 1931. It was, however, as a pair skater, in association with Andrée Joly, that he achieved most renown. In addition to their Olympic achievements they were European Champions in 1932 and won the world title four times in alternate years, 1926, 1928, 1930 and 1932. They then turned professional and went to the United States, where Pierre Brunet has coached such distinguished figure skaters as Carol Heiss (1960 Olympic Champion), Donald Jackson (1962 World Champion), and Janet Lynn.

Their son, Jean-Pierre, was one of the only two skaters to beat Richard BUTTON.
Gold figure skating (pairs) 1928, 1932
Bronze figure skating (pairs) 1924

Burton, Michael (USA)

B. Des Moines, Iowa, 3 July 1947. Only swimmer to have won the 1,500-metres freestyle at two successive Games, in 1968 he set Olympic records by substantial margins in the 1,500-metres and 400-metres freestyle, even though the altitude of Mexico City was said to be against fast times at 400 metres and greater distances. He made his reputation as a swimmer capable of prodigious feats of self-punishment as a member of Sherman Chavoor's squad at Arden Hills, Calif., where he was a contemporary of Mark SPITZ and Debbie MEYER. At the age of thirteen, Burton, whose sporting activity up till then had been largely cross-country running, was involved while cycling in an accident with a truck. He severed tendons under his right knee and the ball joint of his hip was forced into his rib cage. Doctors said that he would never be able to compete in sports again, but advised him to do a little swimming to strengthen his leg muscles.

The first of Burton's seven world records was his 16 min 41.6 sec for 1,500-metres freestyle in 1966. The last of his five world records in that event brought him the Olympic title in 1972 (15 min 52.58 sec).

Burton, who also set two world records for 800-metres freestyle, became a club coach and a member of the US Olympic Committee.

Gold 400-metres freestyle 1968; 1,500-metres freestyle 1968, 1972

Button, Richard Totten (USA)

B. Englewood, N.J., 18 July 1929. A graduate of Harvard Law School, Button was US Figure Skating Champion 1946–52, winner of the European title in 1948 (then an Open championship), runner-up in his first World Championship in 1947, five times World Champion, 1948–52, and twice an Olympic champion. In his entire championship career, from the 1943 US Mid-Atlantic novice event (his first title) to the 1952 Winter Games, he was beaten only twice – by Jean-Pierre Brunet in the 1943 US Eastern States novice championship, and by Hans Gerschwiler (Switzerland) in the 1947 World Championship in Stockholm.

Button brought a new, dynamic style to free skating and pioneered the multi-rotation jumps. He performed the first triple jump (a triple loop) in a championship in the 1952 Winter Games. He turned professional in 1952 and later became a television skating commentator. His other interests include lawn tennis, sailing, music and drama. On 10 March 1973 he married Slavka Kohout, a pupil of Pierre BRUNET and trainer of Janet Lynn, a distinguished fellow American.

Gold figure skating 1948, 1952

Calhoun, Lee Q. (USA)

B. Laurel, Miss., 23 Feb. 1933. Only man to win the Olympic 110-metres hurdles twice, he tied with Jack Davis for first place in the 1956 US Olympic trials and then at Melbourne had an almost equally close battle, with Davis, both men being level from the eighth hurdle, before inspection of the official photo-finish gave victory to Calhoun in 13.5 sec. In 1958 he was suspended by the Amateur Athletic Union for appearing with his bride on a television 'give away' show and receiving nearly £1,000 worth of gifts. After missing a season he returned to the track to set a world high-hurdles record of 13.2 sec and at Rome won a second gold medal, again in a photo-finish, with a spectacular body lean.

Gold 110-metres hurdles 1956, 1960

Capilla Pérez, Joaquin (MEX)

B. Mexico, D.F., 23 Dec. 1928. The first Mexican to win an Olympic diving title, in 1956, eight years after his first Olympic medal. In 1948 and 1952 he was fourth in the springboard event. His brother Alberto was also in the Mexican diving team at the 1952 and 1956 Games. Joaquin was the Pan-American Games springboard and highboard champion in both 1951 and 1955.
Gold highboard diving 1956
Silver highboard diving 1952
Bronze highboard diving 1948; springboard diving 1956

Čáslavská, Vera (TCH)

B. Prague, 3 May 1942. Miss Čáslavská, one of the most glamorous and successful women gymnasts, won eleven Olympic medals. In all she collected twenty-two titles in Olympics, World and European Championships between 1959 and 1968. Initially an ice skater, 1.60 m (5 ft 3 in) tall, she displayed remarkable dexterity in nationwide gymnastic trials at the age of fifteen. Miss Čáslavská made her international début at the 1958 World Championships, taking a silver medal in the team competition. It took her six years of steady progress before she finally defeated Larisa LATYNINA (URS) in the combined exercises competition in 1964. The pair shared in many memorable events, in which Miss Čáslavská's sparkling personality was offset by the marginally superior technical precision of her Russian rival. But at the 1964 Games Miss Čáslavská was a clear winner overall. In 1968 she retained her title in spite of the determined opposition of Zinaida Voronina (URS) and the nineteen-year-old Natasha Kuchinskaya (URS), who had threatened Miss Čáslavská's supremacy at the 1966 World Championships. Her floor exercises routine to the tune of the 'Mexican Hat Dance' entranced the spectators and was one of the most memorable moments of those Games. She announced her retirement after the victory ceremony and married Josef Odložil, the 1964 Olympic 1,500-metres silver medallist, in a ceremony in Mexico City, during the Games, that attracted enormous crowds and publicity.
Gold combined exercises (individual) 1964, 1968; beam 1964; horse vault 1964, 1968; asymmetrical bars 1968; floor exercises 1968
Silver beam 1968; combined exercises (team) 1960, 1964, 1968

Cerar, Miroslav (YUG)

B. Ljubljana, 28 Oct. 1939. A gymnast from the age of ten. He studied law in Ljubljana. At the Moscow World Championships in 1958, he was third in the pommelled horse; and until 1970 he was unbeaten in that discipline, winning the event and the parallel bars at the 1962 World Championships. In 1966 he was again World Champion on the pommelled horse and third on the parallel bars; in 1970 he took the pommelled horse title again. He was the Yugoslav Champion for thirteen successive years.
Gold pommelled horse 1964, 1968
Bronze horizontal bar 1964

Chand, Capt. Dhyan (IND)

B. Allahabad, 28 Aug. 1905. The greatest of all hockey players, he learned the game in the Indian Army and had a dazzling international career between 1926 and 1936, days when Indian hockey was incomparably the best in the world. Chand

played centre forward in the teams which won the Olympic gold medal in 1928 and 1932, and captained India to win a third successive Olympic title in 1936. In those three tournaments, India scored an aggregate of 102 goals to three. During a tour of New Zealand in 1935, Chand scored 201 goals out of an aggregate of 584. In 1947–8 he made his parting appearance at international level as captain of the team which India sent on a goodwill demonstration tour of East Africa. The magic touch of Chand was all his own, a gift of nature.
Gold hockey 1928, 1932, 1936

Chukarin, Viktor (URS)

B. Mariupol (now Zhdanov), 9 Nov. 1921. Chukarin established his country in the forefront of gymnastics by winning a total of seven Olympic gold medals. He was especially gifted on the parallel bars, winning the 1954 world title on this apparatus as well as an Olympic gold medal. He led the first USSR Olympic gymnastics team in 1952. He tied for the world title with his compatriot Valentin Muratov two years later but finished first in 1956.
Gold combined exercises (individual) 1952, 1956; pommelled horse 1952; long horse vault 1952; parallel bars 1956; combined exercises (team) 1952, 1956
Silver parallel bars 1952; rings 1952; floor exercises 1956
Bronze pommelled horse 1956

Costello, Paul V. (USA)

B. Philadelphia, Pa., 27 Dec. 1899. The first man to win three consecutive Olympic sculling titles. In 1920 and 1924 he partnered Jack KELLY, Sr; in 1928 Costello was partnered by Charles McIlvaine.
Gold double sculls 1920, 1924, 1928

Coubertin, Baron Pierre de (FRA)

B. Paris, 1 Jan. 1863; d. Geneva, 2 Sept. 1937. Coubertin showed a profound interest in literature, history, education and sociology. He gave up a career in the Army, which broke a family tradition and, declining a career in politics, launched a campaign for broadening and restructuring education when he was twenty-four. The revival of the Olympic Games was but a small part of this work. He was President of the International Olympic Committee 1896–1925 and on his retirement was given the title of Honorary President. In 1912 at Stockholm, under the pseudonym Georg Hohrod and Martin Eschbach, he won an Olympic gold medal for literature with his *Ode to Sport*.

In addition to teaching sport and the development of its techniques, he was the author of several historical works. He is buried in Lausanne, where he lived, but his heart was interred at Olympia in a marble monument commemorating the revival of the Games. See The Founder of the Modern Games by Marie-Thérèse Eyquem, pages 138–43.

Craig, Ralph C. (USA)

B. Detroit, Mich., 21 June 1889; d. Alexandria, Va., 24 July 1972. In 1912 Craig won gold medals in the 100 and 200 metres with times of 10.8 sec and 21.7 sec respectively. He equalled the world 220-yards record in 1910 and 1912, and also won three American intercollegiate sprint titles. At Stockholm (1912) there were eight attempts at getting the field away for the 100-metres final before Craig pulled away in the last half of the race ahead of Alvah Meyer. In the 200 metres, Meyer, the American champion, was eliminated in the semi-finals and it was left to Craig to take the title. Craig was also a member of the US Olympic yachting team in 1948.
Gold 100 metres 1912; 200 metres 1912

Cuthbert, Betty (AUS)

B. Merrylands, near Sydney, 20 Apr. 1938. Rare example of a teenage athletics champion re-establishing herself as an Olympic winner, she was undoubtedly the heroine of the 1956 Olympics. She was injured during the 1960 Olympics. But at Tokyo she successfully moved up a distance to 400 metres and won her fourth gold medal in 52.0 sec. She broke sixteen world records including performances at 100 yards, 200 metres, 220 yards and 440 yards between 1956 and 1963 and will be remembered for her slim build, sunny temperament and great determination.
Gold 100 metres 1956; 200 metres 1956; 4 × 100-metres relay 1956; 400 metres 1964

Daniels, Charles M. (USA)

B. 12 July 1884; d. 9 Aug. 1973. Daniels won six swimming medals in 1904 and 1908. A colourful personality inside the sport and out, he set seven world records in various events between 1907 and 1911.

In the 1904 Games, aged nineteen, he won the freestyle events over 220 yards and 440 yards, was runner-up in the 100 yards, and third in the 50 yards, which was in the Olympic program for the first and last time. His performances were regarded in his day with almost as much reverence as were Mark SPITZ's sixty-eight years later. At the Interim Games in Athens in 1906 he won the 100-metres freestyle.

Perhaps his greatest contribution to the sport was the way he influenced swimmers with his use of the crawl.
Gold 100-metres freestyle 1908; 220-yards freestyle 1904; 440-yards freestyle 1904; 4 × 50-yards relay 1904
Silver 100-yards freestyle 1904
Bronze 4 × 200-metres freestyle relay 1908; 50-yards freestyle 1904

Davis, Glenn A. (USA)

B. Wellsburg, W. Va., 12 Sept. 1934. The only man to win the Olympic 400-metres hurdles twice, in 1956 and 1960. Davis, a talented all-rounder in high school, did not turn to the 400-metres hurdles until April 1956 but in just two months he had cut the

world record by 0.9 sec down to 49.5 sec. At Melbourne he won his gold medal in 50.1 sec with a strong finish and in Rome his winning time was 49.3 sec, just 0.1 sec slower than the world record he had set in 1958, when he also set new world records for 440 yards flat (45.7 sec) and 440-yards hurdles (49.9 sec). He showed astonishing versatility and stamina in two-day meetings at Oslo (21.1 sec for 200 metres, 400-metres hurdles in 49.8 sec, 10.3 sec for 100 metres, 45.6 sec for flat 400 metres) and Warsaw (45.5 sec for 400 metres, 49.8 sec for 400-metres hurdles and 45.1 sec for 400-metres relay leg). His last race was the third stage for the American 4 × 400-metres relay team in Rome which he ran in 45.4 sec – a vital contribution as his team set a world record of 3 min 02.2 sec. He later became a professional American footballer.
Gold 400-metres hurdles 1956, 1960; 4 × 400-metres relay 1960

De La Hunty (Strickland), Shirley (AUS)

B. Guildford, Western Australia, 18 July 1925. She won more Olympic medals than any other woman in athletics: three gold, one silver and three bronze. She was the first woman to beat 11 sec for the 80-metres hurdles and also had a world record in the flat 100 metres at 11.3 sec. As late as 1960 she ran 100 yards in 10.9 sec.
Gold 80-metres hurdles 1952, 1956; 4 × 100-metres relay 1956
Silver 4 × 100-metres relay 1948
Bronze 100 metres 1948, 1952; 80-metres hurdles 1948

Desjardins, Pete (USA)

B. St. Pierre, Canada, 10 Apr. 1907. He became an American citizen after moving to Miami Beach, Fla. with his family as a child. He was an economics graduate of Stanford University, which had the finest diving instruction facilities in the early 1920s in the United States, following two other Olympic champions from that school, Clarence Pinkston and Albert

Shirley De La Hunty (AUS), 1956

WHITE. Only 1.60 m (5 ft 3 in) tall, Desjardins was runner-up to White in the 1924 Olympic springboard event. In winning the same event four years later he became the only Olympic competitor to get the maximum ten points.

Gold springboard diving 1928, highboard diving 1928
Silver springboard diving 1924

Dibiasi, Klaus (ITA)

B. Solbad Hall, Austria, 6 Oct. 1947. In Dibiasi's childhood his family moved from Austria to Bolzano, Italy; both his parents were Italian. At seventeen he won the Olympic silver medal for highboard, an achievement which moved the inhabitants of Bolzano to build an indoor diving tank for him. Four years later he became the first Italian to win an Olympic diving title. He was coached by his father, a former Italian springboard champion. In the 1966 and 1974 European Championships he won three titles.

Gold highboard diving 1968, 1972
Silver highboard diving 1964, springboard diving 1968

Didrikson, Mildred (USA)

B. Port Arthur, Tex., 26 June 1914; d. 27 Sept. 1956. In the 1932 Olympics she won the 80-metres hurdles, with a world record. In the high jump, she and fellow American Jean Shiley both cleared 1.65 m (5 ft 5¼ in) for a new world record but a judge decided that Didrikson, who went over 1.67 m (5 ft 5¾ in), had been jumping all afternoon with an illegal diving style and she was placed second. It was not until 1939 that the rules which had led to this peremptory ruling were changed. 'Babe' Didrikson later became famous under her married name of Zaharias as a golfer and won seventeen international titles between 1934 and 1950.

Gold 80-metres hurdles 1932; javelin 1932
Silver high jump 1932

Diem, Carl (GER)

B. Würzburg, 24 June 1882; d. Cologne, 17 Dec. 1962. His enthusiasm for the Olympic idea, which he first encountered at the Interim Games in Athens in 1906, and his friendship with COUBERTIN provided Olympism with some fertile thinking and ensured that Germany played a continuing part in the Olympic Movement.

Diem was able to fulfil many of Coubertin's ideas through Germany, where they were received, unlike Coubertin's experience in France. Diem was the outstanding administrator and organizer of sport in Germany during the first half of the century. He was leader of Germany's Olympic team for the Games of 1912, 1928 and 1932; he ordered the construction of the stadium in Berlin intended for the Games of 1916 which were cancelled. He was General Secretary of the organization for the Games from 1931 and

among many aspects provided the artistic direction; among his innovations was the torch relay from Olympia which he organized with his friend Jean Ketseas. He lost influence in Germany with the rise of the Nazis but after Coubertin's death continued to produce the *Olympic Review* and was a prolific writer, producing over 2,000 works, essays, articles and books, on the Olympic Movement. Olympic youth tours and the founding of the International Olympic Academy were largely the result of his vision. He never lost vitality for new ideas, for in 1955 he began the Golden Plan in Germany which ensured that outstanding athletes there had every opportunity to fulfil Olympic ambition.

Dillard, Harrison W. (USA)

B. Cleveland, Ohio, 8 July 1923. Inspired by the sight of the victory celebration for Jesse OWENS following the 1936 Olympics, Dillard became a specialist high hurdler and, between May 1947 and June 1948, had eighty-two sprint and hurdles races without a defeat. In the 1948 US Olympic trials he fell in the hurdles and failed to finish, though he did qualify as third string in the 100-metres flat; in an extraordinary upset he won the final in London in 10.3 sec to equal Owens' Olympic record – particularly fitting since Owens had presented him with his 1936 Olympic shoes. In 1952, Dillard returned to his first love to win the high hurdles. At only 1.78 m (5 ft 10 in) Dillard was short for a high hurdler but had great speed between the fences. He won five US outdoor titles and set world records for both the 120- and 220-yards hurdles.

Gold 100 metres 1948; 4 × 100-metres relay 1948, 1952; 110-metres hurdles 1952

Edström, J. Sigfrid (SWE)

B. Gothenburg, 21 Nov. 1870; d. Stockholm, 18 Mar. 1964. Was an outstanding administrator in Scandinavian sport, and a good sprinter, running the 100 metres in 11 sec. After studying and working in technology in Zürich, he helped to combine the various branches of sport in Sweden under one administration. He was one of the organizers of the 1912 Games in Stockholm and took the lead in founding the International Amateur Athletic Federation, of which he was President 1912–46. He was elected member of the IOC in 1920 and held a number of offices in it before becoming President 1946–52.

Elek, Ilona (HUN)

B. Budapest, 17 May 1907. Her domination of women's fencing, in the foil, straddled the period of World War II. She won a world title in 1933 in Budapest and took a winning team medal in the World Championships of Rome in 1955, finishing fifth in the individual event. Her style was sometimes described as dull but she had a compelling desire to win. In

addition to her Olympic medals which, spanning twelve years, indicate her extraordinary powers of strength and resilience, she won eleven gold medals in World Championships, five silver and one bronze.
Gold foil (individual) 1936, 1948
Silver foil (individual) 1952

Elliott, Herb (AUS)

B. Perth, 25 Feb. 1938. From the age of sixteen until his retirement from athletics this Australian prodigy was never beaten over one mile or 1,500 metres. Elliott first made his mark in 1957 with world junior track records. Inspired by the coaching of Percy Cerutty, he ran his first mile in under 4 min before he was twenty, in 1958. The same year he lowered the world records in the mile to 3 min 54.5 sec and the 1,500 metres to 3 min 36.0 sec and won the British Commonwealth Games titles over 880 yards and the mile; he rejected an offer to turn professional. At the 1960 Olympics he crushed the opposition in the 1,500 metres and won in a world-record time of 3 min 35.6 sec. It was among the most sweeping of all modern Olympic victories.
Gold 1,500 metres 1960

Elvstrøm, Paul (DEN)

B. Copenhagen, 25 Feb. 1928. His approach to small-boat sailing, a belief that fitness from land training was a way to win, revolutionized competitive sailing. The first of his four gold medals was won at Torbay in 1948 and at Acapulco in 1968 he was fourth in the Star class.

He realized that hanging over the side of the boat for a longer period than his opponents gave him an advantage and the only way to achieve this was through physical fitness. He was also a student of weather lore and relished the idea of going out on stormy days to learn more about his craft and how to handle it. He won eleven

Herb Elliott (AUS), 1960

World Championships in seven different classes between 1957 and 1974. He wrote several books and in 1954 started a company, Elvstrøm Sails, with branches throughout the world; he also built pleasure boats. It was these activities which brought him under scrutiny by the IOC Eligibility Commission in 1972.

Gold yachting Firefly 1948; Finn 1952, 1956, 1960

Engel-Krämer, Ingrid (GDR)

B. Dresden, 29 July 1943. She competed in the diving events at three Olympic Games; as Miss Krämer in 1960 she became the first non-American winner of the springboard diving title and completed the double on highboard; as Mrs Engel she retained the springboard title in 1964 and was runner-up on highboard; and in 1968 (divorced and remarried) as Mrs Gulbin she finished fifth in the springboard.

In her first major international competition, the 1958 European Championships in Budapest, the 15-year-old Miss Krämer was on the point of victory in the springboard, but failed with her last dive and finished fourth. She won both springboard and highboard in the 1962 European Championships. She carried the flag for the united German team at the opening ceremony of the 1964 Olympic Games. She became the first woman gold medallist of those Games when she retained the springboard title, in spite of complaining that the water was too cold; she took a hot shower between each dive.

Gold springboard diving 1960, 1964; highboard diving 1960

Silver highboard diving 1964

Ewry, Ray C. (USA)

B. Lafayette, Ind., 14 Oct. 1873 or 1874; d. 29 Sept. 1937. Ewry won ten Olympic gold medals (including two in 1906) in the now-abandoned standing high, long and triple jump events. He was paralysed as a boy but dedicated exercising developed unusual strength in his legs. His standing long jump record of 3.47 m (11 ft 4⅞ in) remained on the official world record list until the event was discarded in 1938. He was fifteen times an American athletics champion.

Gold standing high jump 1900, 1904, 1908; standing long jump 1900, 1904, 1908; standing triple jump 1900, 1904

Faggin, Leandro (ITA)

B. Padova, 18 July 1933; d. 5 Dec. 1970. A natural track cyclist, Faggin dominated world pursuit cycling for a dozen years. He set new records three times for riding 5,000 metres unpaced, as an amateur and as a professional. His great stamina enabled him to set an Olympic record for 1,000 metres at Melbourne and then lead his colleagues to gold medals in the 4,000-metres team pursuit. Between the World Championships in 1954 and his bronze medal as a professional in 1968, he col-

Ray C. Ewry (USA), 1908

lected twelve medals, including those for three world professional championships.

Gold 1,000-metres time trial 1956; 4,000-metres team pursuit 1956

Fisher, Morris (USA)

B. 4 May 1892; d. Honolulu, 23 May 1963. Fisher began serious competitive shooting in 1911, his first year in the US Marine Corps. During the 1920s, the United States entered twelve teams in international competition, nine in ISU World Championship competitions, two in Olympic Games and one in Pan-American matches; Fisher was a member of every one of these teams. He shot a military rifle in winning the gold medal in the free rifle event in 1920.

Gold free rifle (individual) 1920, 1924, (team) 1920, 1924; military rifle, prone (team) 1924

Flack, Edwin (AUS)

B. 1874. Australia's first great middle-distance runner, he had travelled from Australia, where he was mile champion, to work as an accountant in England and decided, in the casual atmosphere of those early days, to take his month's holiday competing in the Olympics. Lightheartedly, he rented a flat in Athens with two British competitors and they cooked for themselves. The day after his 800-metres victory, Flack ran in the marathon and was in the lead but dropped out at 35 kilometres.

Gold 800 metres 1896; 1,500 metres 1896

Flanagan, John J. (USA)

B. Limerick, Ireland, 9 Jan. 1868; d. Ireland, 1938. The father of modern hammer throwing, Flanagan raised the world record in sixteen instalments from 44.47 m (145 ft 10½ in) in Ireland in 1895 to 56.20 m (184 ft 4 in) in 1909 after emigrating to the United States. His best Olympic record (1908) was 51.92 m (170 ft 4¼ in). He was fourth in the discus at St Louis in 1904 and second in throwing the 56-lb weight. Until the advent of Al OERTER, Flanagan was the only Olympic athlete to win three successive gold medals in a standard event.

Gold hammer 1900, 1904, 1908

Silver 56-lb weight 1904

Forberger, Frank (GDR)

B. Meissen, 5 Mar. 1943. Member of the

Einheit Dresden coxless four, with Dieter Grahn, Frank Rühle and Dieter Schubert, the most successful rowing crew of the post-World-War-II period. They were World Champions in 1966 and 1970, and European Champions in 1967 and 1971. They were, in fact, never beaten in an Olympic, World, or European Championship regatta.

Gold coxless fours 1968, 1972

Fraser, Dawn (AUS)

B. Balmain, N.S.W., 4 Sept. 1937. The only swimmer to have won an Olympic title in the same event at three successive Games. Although she had the advantage of a lean, boylike figure, not everything in Miss Fraser's physical make-up was in her favour when, aged fourteen she first came to the attention of her coach Harry Gallagher. Throughout her swimming life she suffered from bronchial asthma.

Miss Fraser's name appears on the world record lists thirty-nine times. She beat a twenty-year-old world record when she returned 1 min 4.5 sec for 100-metres freestyle in February 1956. Her progress after that was remarkable and eight years later she brought the time down to 58.9 sec, which stood for eight years as the world record though Shane GOULD (AUS) equalled it in 1971. Her best world records for 200-metres and 220-yards freestyle were achieved in the same swim – 2 min 11.6 sec at Sydney, 1960. She was an all-rounder of considerable ability and won Australian titles in butterfly and individual medley.

In all three of her Olympics she reached the final of the 400-metres freestyle, her best placing being second in 1956 and her fastest time 4 min 47.6 sec in 1964.

Gold 100-metres freestyle 1956, 1960, 1964; 4 × 100-metres freestyle relay 1956

Silver 400-metres freestyle 1956; 4 × 100-metres freestyle relay 1960, 1964; 4 × 100-metres medley relay 1960

Fredriksson, Gert (SWE)

B. Nyköping, 21 Nov. 1919. Besides his Olympic achievements he also won seven gold medals in World Canoeing Championships, over 500, 1,000 and 10,000 metres. Seventeen years old when he began canoeing, his best competition years were stunted because of World War II.

No other canoeist has struck such fear into his opponents and none has been at the top so long. He had the remarkable capacity, rare in canoeing, of being able to attack at any point in the race, and his acceleration was phenomenal. Although in nineteen years there were defeats, he always sought an opportunity to meet the conqueror and none of these return matches was lost.

Gold kayak singles 1,000 metres 1948, 1952, 1956; 10,000 metres 1948, 1956; kayak pairs 1,000 metres 1960

Silver kayak singles 10,000 metres 1952

Bronze kayak singles 1,000 metres 1960

Gaiardoni, Sante (ITA)

B. Villafranca, 29 June 1939. Short and immensely muscled, he was one of a school of Italian cycling sprinters. At twenty-one he reached his athletic peak for the Games in Rome, where he beat the world professional record in establishing a new time for the standing-start 1,000-metres time trial of 1 min 7.27 sec. He was also the outstanding sprint cyclist of these Games. As a professional, he was only able to win one world title, a sprint championship in 1963 at Liège. He married an opera singer and retired in 1971.
Gold 1,000-metres time trial 1960; individual 1,000-metres sprint 1960

Gaudin, Lucien (FRA)

B. Arras, Pas-de-Calais, 27 Sept. 1886; d. 23 Sept. 1934. Gaudin had an extraordinary fencing career from 1904 to 1929; he was French foil champion from 1906 to 1914, World Champion in foil in 1904 and European Champion in épée in 1928. He won his two individual Olympic gold medals at the age of forty-two.
Gold foil (individual) 1928, (team) 1924; épée (individual) 1928, (team) 1924
Silver foil (team) 1920, 1928

Gaudini, Giulio (ITA)

B. Rome, 28 Sept. 1904; d. Rome, 6 Jan. 1948. This great fencer competed at four Olympic Games, from 1924 to 1936. At Paris (1924) he was a member of the Italian foil team which came fourth. Besides his Olympic victories, he was also World Champion in individual foil in 1929 and 1934 and a member of the winning foil teams of 1929, 1930, 1931, 1934 and 1935 as well as of the team that won the sabre in 1938.
Gold foil (individual) 1936, (team) 1928, 1936
Silver foil (team) 1932; sabre (individual) 1932, (team) 1932, 1936
Bronze foil (individual) 1928, 1932

Geesink, Anton (HOL)

B. Utrecht, 6 Apr. 1934. The first to defeat the Japanese at the sport they invented. Geesink, 1.98 m (6 ft 6 in) and 121 kg (266 lb or 19 stone) dominated judo from 1961, when he took his first world title, until his retirement in 1967. Ability to combine skill and speed in spite of his huge size also brought him eighteen European individual titles between 1952 and 1967. He was particularly gifted at ankle techniques which require exact timing, was versatile on the ground and was also a determined trainer. Geesink finished third in the first World Championships in Tokyo in 1956 but five years later defeated the three Japanese entrants to take the title. The Japanese were determined to get their revenge when the sport appeared on the Olympic program for the first time in Tokyo. Geesink twice defeated Akio Kaminaga, whom he had

Shane Gould (AUS), 1972

beaten in the quarter-final of the World Championship in 1961, to win the Open gold medal. It was a significant moment in sporting history because it ended Japanese invincibility. After his retirement in 1967 Geesink devoted himself to teaching.
Gold judo open (unlimited weight) 1964

Gillan, James Angus (GBR)

B. Aberdeen, 11 Oct. 1885. Gillan was the first man to gain two Olympic gold medals for rowing. He was a member of the Magdalen College, Oxford, coxless four, which, in 1908, won both the Visitors' and Stewards' Challenge Cups at Henley Royal Regatta, and proceeded, a month later, to win the Olympic title. In Stockholm he won his second gold medal, rowing for the Great Britain eight.
Gold coxless fours 1908; eights 1912

Goitschel, Marielle (FRA)

B. Ste Maxime, 28 Sept. 1945. Marielle, the younger of two sisters, both Olympic ski champions, matured at an early age, winning the overall World Championship at Chamonix in 1962 at sixteen. Her strongest discipline was the slalom and when she finished second to her sister, Christine, at Innsbruck she said she had sacrificed her chance of gold as it already belonged in the family, settling for a steady second run that brought a silver medal. She duly won the giant slalom, with her sister this time in second place. Four years later, with her sister no longer in competition, she won the Olympic gold medal for slalom at Grenoble, but her six-year-old reign as World Champion ended there.
Gold giant slalom 1964; slalom 1968
Silver slalom 1964

Golubnichi, Vladimir (URS)

B. Sumy, 2 June 1936. He had a remarkable career in Olympic walking. A Ukraine school teacher, he set his first world track record in 1955 at only nineteen and first entered the Soviet team in 1959. He became European Champion in 1974 after being third in 1972 and second in 1966.
Gold 20-kilometres walk 1960, 1968
Silver 20-kilometres walk 1972
Bronze 20-kilometres walk 1964

Gould, Shane (AUS)

B. Brisbane, 4 Sept. 1956. Probably the greatest woman swimmer ever, Miss Gould

is certainly the only woman to have won three Olympic swimming gold medals in individual events in world-record times at one Games.

She first got her name on the world-record lists at the age of fourteen in 1971 when she equalled Dawn FRASER's long-standing mark for 100-metres freestyle with 58.9 sec. On the following day she took the world record for 200-metres freestyle for herself with 2 min 6.5 sec. By 12 December 1971, she became the first woman ever to hold every world freestyle record from 100 metres to 1,500 metres. She completed her set in Sydney with 17 min 00.6 sec for 1,500 metres, more than 18 sec faster than the previous best.

By the 1972 Olympic Games, Miss Gould was regarded with such awe by the American swimmers that they wore tee-shirts at Munich bearing the motto 'All that glitters is not Gould' in an attempt to boost their own morale. It was claimed on her behalf that she might win all five individual events in which she entered. Though she failed narrowly in this, she still dominated the women's events, winning the 200-metres freestyle (2 min 3.56 sec), 400-metres freestyle (4 min 19.04 sec), and 200-metres individual medley (2 min 23.07 sec), all in world-record time. She could not cope with the American Sandy Neilson's fast start in the 100-metres freestyle and finished third in 59.06 sec and another American, Keena Rothhammer, beat her in the 800-metres freestyle.

Miss Gould was a contemporary of another Australian Olympic champion, Gail Neall, at Turramurra High School, Sydney. She was the first Olympic champion of the outstanding Australian coach Forbes Carlile.
Gold 200-metres freestyle 1972; 400-metres freestyle 1972; 200-metres individual medley 1972
Silver 800-metres freestyle 1972
Bronze 100-metres freestyle 1972

Grafström, Gillis (SWE)

B. Stockholm, 7 June 1893; d. Potsdam, 14 Apr. 1938. An architect, professionally (and a poet, painter and etcher), Grafström was noted for the elegance and musical feeling of his free figure skating. He originated the Grafström spin (on the back outside edge of the skate) and the flying sitspin, and was the first to make the 'Axel Paulsen' a controlled jump. He won three Olympic gold medals, the first at Antwerp, where he broke a skate and, being unable to get a replacement, went into the town and bought an old-fashioned curly-toed one. At Lake Placid, aged thirty-eight, he took the silver medal after an accident in which he collided with a photographer on the ice. Grafström was a highly individualistic character who skated for his own aesthetic satisfaction and could never be bothered much with competitive skating outside the Olympic Games. He never

deigned to enter the European Championships and skated only three times for the world title, in 1922, 1924 and 1929, winning every time.
Gold figure skating 1920, 1924, 1928
Silver figure skating 1932

Grahn, Dieter (GDR)
B. Zobten, 20 Mar. 1944. Member of the unbeaten Einheit Dresden coxless four. See FORBERGER, Frank
Gold coxless fours 1968, 1972

Grishin, Yevgeni (URS)
B. Tula, 23 Mar. 1931. The best sprinter in speed skating in the 1950s and early 1960s. A member of the USSR national cycling team in 1952, he was in the USSR national speed-skating team 1952–68 and held the world record at 500 metres and 1,500 metres 1955–8. European Champion in 1956, he won the bronze medals at the 1954 and 1955 World Championships, the USSR Champion title ten times over different distances 1956–65, and was the first skater to cover 500 metres in less than 40 sec. He is the present coach to the sprinters of the USSR national team.
Gold 500 metres 1956, 1960; 1,500 metres 1956, 1960
Silver 500 metres 1964

Grønningen, Harald (NOR)
B. Lensvik, 9 Oct. 1934. In 1968, aged thirty-three, he won the 15-kilometres cross-country skiing race in Grenoble and also the 4 × 10-kilometres relay. For twenty years he was among the leading cross-country skiers. He won the 15-kilometres race at Holmenkollen twice, in 1960 and 1961.
Gold 15-kilometres cross-country 1968; 4 × 10-kilometres relay 1968
Silver 15-kilometres cross-country 1964; 30-kilometres cross-country 1964; 4 × 10-kilometres relay 1960

Grøttumsbraaten, Johan (NOR)
B. Sørkedalen, Oslo, 24 Feb. 1899. He took part in skiing events in three Winter Games, winning medals each time. For fifteen years among the best skiers in the world in the combined and 18-kilometres cross-country events, he won the Holmenkollen combined event (the King's Cup) five times. In all he won ten King's Cups in Norway. He was also World Champion twice in the combined event (1926 and 1931) and once in the 18-kilometres cross-country, in 1926.
Gold combined event 1928, 1932; 18-kilometres cross-country 1928
Silver 18-kilometres cross-country 1924
Bronze 50-kilometres cross-country 1924; combined event 1924

Gulbin, Ingrid (GDR) see ENGEL-KRÄMER, Ingrid

Hahn, Archie (USA)
B. Dodgeville, Wis., 14 Sept. 1880; d. 21 Jan. 1955. Winner of three sprint titles at the St Louis Olympics of 1904. His 200-metres time of 21.6 sec was an Olympic record until 1932, though he was fortunate in his final in that his three rivals were all penalized one yard for making a false start after he had been somewhat restive on his marks. He also won the 100 metres in 1906 at the Interim Games in Athens.
Gold 60 metres 1904; 100 metres 1904; 200 metres 1904

Hall, Lars (SWE)
B. Karlskrona, 30 Apr. 1927. Individual winner of the modern pentathlon in 1952 and 1956, the only person to win successive individual gold medals. He won the World Championship in 1950 and 1951.
Gold modern pentathlon (individual) 1952, 1956
Silver modern pentathlon (team) 1952

Haug, Thorleif (NOR)
B. Årkvisla, near Drammen, 28 Sept. 1894; d. Drammen, 12 Dec. 1934. An outstanding skier, not until he was almost thirty years old did he have the opportunity to take part in Olympics, since they were not held until 1924. In Chamonix Haug won three gold medals and in the jumping event took the bronze. Fifty years after this first Olympic Winter Games, in 1974, in Oslo, it was discovered that in the official results there had been a miscalculation in the special jumping: Haug had 18.00 points and his fellow Norwegian Anders Haugen, who had emigrated to the United States and represented that country, had 17.91. Haug's points should have been 17.81 and so the bronze medal was presented to the eighty-six-year-old Haugen by Haug's daughter. Haug won the famous 50-kilometres race at Holmenkollen six times and the King's Cup there (for the combined event) three times. His memory was honoured in Drammen with a lifesize stone statue erected in 1946.
Gold 18-kilometres cross-country, 50-kilometres cross-country and combined event 1924

Henie, Sonja (NOR)
B. Oslo, 8 Apr. 1912; d. 12 Oct. 1969. The outstanding figure in the history of skating, for she later turned her skills to good professional account and won a host of new admirers throughout the world by way of films. She became Norwegian Champion in 1924. Competing in the Winter Olympics at Chamonix (1924), before her twelfth birthday, she was last of eight competitors, but she won the title at her second attempt, at St Moritz (1928). After twice retaining her title, she turned professional and was given a contract by the Hollywood company, 20th Century Fox. In the World Championships she was fifth in 1924 and in 1926 she was runner-up in the women's event and fifth in the pairs with Arne Lie. She was never beaten again.

She won ten World titles, 1927–36 (a record equalled only by Ulrich Salchow of Sweden), six European (1931–6) and three Olympic titles.

She made eleven films between 1938 and 1960. With her third husband, Niels Onstad, a fellow Norwegian, she founded the Henie-Onstad collection of modern paintings which they presented to Norway. Miss Henie developed leukaemia in 1969 and died in an aircraft which was carrying her from Paris to Oslo for medical treatment.
Gold figure skating 1928, 1932, 1936

Hickcox, Charles (USA)
B. Phoenix, Ariz., 6 Feb. 1947. The most successful male swimmer of the 1968 Games, Hickcox scored a double in the individual medley events, was runner-up in the 100-metres backstroke, and won another gold medal as a member of the US medley relay team. Hickcox, 1.90 m (6 ft 3 in) tall, was a backstroke stylist who, as he became stronger physically, developed as the world's best individual medley swimmer. While at Indiana University, he set world records in the 200-metres and 400-metres individual medley during the US Olympic trials of 1968 at Long Beach. With the problems created by the altitude of Mexico City, his individual medley double there was the more meritorious. The fact that the bronze medallist in the 200-metres medley, John Ferris, collapsed at the medal ceremony and was given oxygen illustrated the physical effort required from a lowlander for events of 200 metres and longer.

Hickcox also had a good year in 1967, winning gold medals at the World Student Games in Tokyo in the 100-metres and 200-metres backstroke and as a member of the US team in the medley relay with world records in each. In his career he set five world records in individual events and shared in two in medley relays.
Gold 400-metres individual medley 1968; 200-metres individual medley 1968; 4 × 100-metres medley relay 1968
Silver 100-metres backstroke 1968

Hill, Albert George (GBR)
B. Tooting, London, 24 Mar. 1889; d. Canada, 8 Jan. 1969. He gained the extraordinary double, at thirty-one, of the 800 and 1,500 metres in the Antwerp Olympics with a program of five races in four days, ten years after winning his first British title. His winning times were 1 min 53.4 sec and 4 min 01.8 sec. He was helped considerably by his British colleague, Philip Noel-Baker, who was pacemaker in the longer race.
Gold 800 metres 1920; 1,500 metres 1920
Silver 3,000 metres (team) 1920

Houser, Clarence (USA)
B. 25 Sept. 1901. The first discus thrower to demonstrate the value of rotating speed in

the circle. In 1926 he set a world discus record of 48.20 m (158 ft 1¾ in). He was the last man to win both shot and discus in the Olympics.
Gold discus 1924, 1928; shot 1924

Iso-Hollo, Volmari (FIN)

B. Ylöjärvi, 1 May 1907; d. Heinola, 23 June 1969. The only man who twice won the Olympic steeplechase, at Los Angeles and Berlin. At Los Angeles he set an Olympic record of 9 min 14.6 sec in his heat so it was puzzling when his winning time in the final was announced as 10 min 33.4 sec. In fact the official scoring the laps had been taken ill, his substitute missed a lap and the field ran 460 extra metres. Four years later he set a world's best ever time of 9 min 3.8 sec. An outstanding 10,000-metres runner who gave Janusz Kusociński (POL) a tough battle in the 1932 Olympic event before losing by just 1.2 sec, he was third in the 1936 race when Finland took all three Olympic medals. His Olympic steeplechase record was not beaten until 1952.
Gold 3,000-metres steeplechase 1932, 1936
Silver 10,000 metres 1932
Bronze 10,000 metres 1936

Ivanov, Vyacheslav (URS)

B. Moscow, 30 July 1938. The outstanding single sculler post World War II. After winning both the European Championship and Olympic single sculls in 1956, he had to be content with European bronze medals in the next two seasons. But in 1959 he took the European title, in 1960 a second Olympic gold medal, in 1961 the European, and 1962 the first World Championship sculling title. In 1963 he dropped to fourth place in the European Championships, but returned, in 1964, to regain his European title, and to win his third consecutive Olympic gold medal in Tokyo.
Gold single sculls 1956, 1960, 1964

Janz, Karin (GDR)

B. Hartmannsdorf, 17 Feb. 1952. Although lacking the balletic grace of such Russian contemporaries as Ludmila Turishcheva or Olga Korbut, this gifted East German gymnast possessed such technical expertise that she challenged Miss Turishcheva strongly for the Olympic combined exercises title at Munich. At the Mexico Games (1968) she was a member of the East German team placed third. She improved steadily over the following four years and in Munich, together with her compatriot Erika Zuchold, pressed the USSR for the team title.
Gold horse vault 1972; asymmetrical bars 1972
Silver asymmetrical bars 1968; combined exercises (individual) 1972, (team) 1972
Bronze combined exercises (team) 1968; beam 1972

Jernberg, Sixten (SWE)

B. Limedsforsen, 6 Feb. 1929. His total of four gold medals, three silver and two bronze is the largest ever won by a skier in the Olympic Winter Games. He also won the World Championships in 1958 and 1962 in the 50-kilometres cross-country event and in the 4 × 10-kilometres relay.
Gold 50-kilometres cross-country 1956, 1964; 30-kilometres cross-country 1960; 4 × 10-kilometres relay 1964
Silver 15-kilometres cross-country 1956, 1960; 30-kilometres 1956
Bronze 15-kilometres cross-country 1964; 4 × 10-kilometres relay 1956

Johansson, Ivar (SWE)

B. Norrköping, 31 Jan. 1903. As well as his Olympic achievements, he was European Champion at middleweight in Greco-Roman wrestling in 1934, 1935 and 1937–9, and in freestyle in 1934–5 and 1937. In 1932 he was nominated as Sweden's best athlete.
Gold wrestling Greco-Roman welterweight 1932, middleweight 1936; freestyle middleweight 1932

Jousseaume, André (FRA)

B. Yvré l'Évêque, Sarthe, 27 July 1894; d. Paris, 26 May 1960. One of the greatest French riders, from the famous Cadre Noir at Saumur, he had a military career, becoming a colonel in 1952. He took part in four Olympic Games over a span of twenty years and won five medals; he was twelfth in the three-day event in 1948.
Gold dressage (team) 1932, 1948
Silver dressage (team) 1936, (individual) 1948
Bronze dressage (individual) 1952

Kahanamoku, Duke Paoa (USA)

B. Honolulu, Hawaii, 24 Aug. 1890; d. Honolulu, 22 Jan. 1968. He and Johnny WEISSMULLER, whose swimming careers overlapped, shared the distinction of being the only men to win the 100-metres freestyle at two successive Olympic Games.

There are at least two versions of how Kahanamoku got his Christian name of Duke. One is that he acquired the name because he was born in Princess Ruth's palace in Honolulu during a visit by HRH Prince Alfred, Duke of Edinburgh, the second son of Queen Victoria. Another is that he was named after the Duke of Wellington. He became Sheriff of Honolulu.

When he retained the Olympic title in the 100-metres freestyle in 1920 it was in a re-swim after the Australians protested that their competitor William Herald had been boxed in by an American the first time (this was before lane ropes were used). Kahanamoku's winning time in the original swim, 1 min 0.4 sec, was the third and last of his world records in that event. Weissmuller prevented him from gaining a hat-trick of gold medals in the 100-metres freestyle when he beat him by 2.4 sec in the 1924 final with a time of 59 sec. Like his conqueror, Kahanamoku became a film actor. An expert at surfing, he introduced that sport to many parts of the world.
Gold 100-metres freestyle 1912, 1920; 4 × 200-metres freestyle relay 1920
Silver 100-metres freestyle 1924; 4 × 200-metres freestyle relay 1912

Kárpáti, Rudolf (HUN)

B. Budapest, 17 July 1920. Sabre champion of Hungary in 1948 and 1955, he won two individual world titles, in 1954 and 1959, and was also a member of the World Champion sabre team of 1953, 1954, 1955, 1957 and 1958. Kárpáti is leader of the Hungarian People's Army Central Artistic Ensemble.
Gold sabre (individual) 1956, 1960, (team) 1948, 1952, 1956, 1960

Kato, Sawao (JPN)

B. Niigata Prefecture, 11 Oct. 1946. In Mexico, although trailing behind Mikhail Voronin (URS) and Akinori NAKAYAMA (JPN) after the compulsory exercises, this diminutive gymnast, 1.62 m (5 ft 4 in) tall and 53.5 kg (118 lb or 8 stone 6 lb), produced an inspiring 9.9 mark on the floor exercises to give him the overall title. Kato was an all-rounder, not a specialist; in fact he won only two medals (a gold on the floor exercises and a bronze on the rings) in individual items. He was an easier winner in Munich, where he also collected separate awards on the parallel bars, pommelled horse and horizontal bar. His original routine and perfection of movement brought him victory by 0.075 pt from Eizo Kenmotsu in a clean sweep by the Japanese of the combined exercises medals.
Gold combined exercises (individual) 1968, 1972, (team) 1968, 1972; floor exercises 1968; parallel bars 1972
Silver pommelled horse 1972; horizontal bar 1972
Bronze rings 1968

Kealoha, Warren Paoa (USA)

B. Honolulu, Hawaii, 3 Mar. 1903; d. 8 Sept. 1972. One of several famous swimmers from Hawaii. He was the first to retain an Olympic backstroke title, doing so in 1924. When he broke the world record for 100-metres backstroke in 1920 he began a period of US domination in that event that continued until Gilbert Bozon (FRA) became the holder in 1952. Kealoha broke the record four times in six years, bringing it down from 1 min 15.6 sec to 1 min 11.4 sec, a remarkable improvement. In 1923 he set another world record, for the now-discontinued 150-yards backstroke. The man he succeeded on this record list was Johnny WEISSMULLER. The backstroke styles of these two swimmers were the subject of much technical discussion. Weissmuller used a bent-arm recovery, and Kealoha, straight-arm.

Kealoha, who twice won the US freestyle sprint championship, had victories over Johnny Weissmuller and Duke KAHANAMOKU on front crawl. He returned 1 min 15.2 sec in winning the Olympic 100-metres backstroke title in 1920 when, aged sixteen, he was the youngest member of the US team.

Gold 100-metres backstroke 1920, 1924

Keino, Kipchoge (KEN)

B. Kipsano, 17 Jan. 1940. Black Africa's first Olympic track champion showed remarkable range as a runner for ten years from 1962 when he first competed internationally. At the Tokyo Olympics he ran in both the 1,500 and 5,000 metres and finished fifth in the longer event. The following season he made an exciting breakthrough with 3,000 and 5,000 metres world records and ran a 3-min 54.2-sec mile. By 1968, when the Olympics went to Mexico City, it was obvious that his ability, together with the fact that he lived at a high altitude similar to that of Mexico, would bring him medals. He amazed everyone by running in the 10,000 metres (dropping out before the finish), heat and final of the 5,000 metres, in which he finished second, and two preliminary rounds of the 1,500 metres before he crushed Jim Ryun (USA) in the final with an extraordinary time, in oxygen-thin air, of 3 min 34.9 sec. At Munich Keino had lost a little of his speed, and so finished second in the 1,500 metres. But he still had his canniness and won the steeplechase, which he had never taken seriously before, in a fast time of 8 min 23.6 sec, after deliberately slowing the early pace in order not to be dropped by better hurdlers. In 1973 he turned to professional athletics in the United States.

Gold 1,500 metres 1968; 3,000-metres steeplechase 1972

Silver 5,000 metres 1968; 1,500 metres 1972

Keleti, Ágnes (HUN)

B. Budapest, 9 June 1921. Only a weakness on the vault prevented Miss Keleti from winning more gymnastic honours during the 1950s. In particular, a lapse on the vault at the Melbourne Olympics probably led to her losing the gold medal to Larisa LATYNINA (URS). Mrs Latynina's steadiness brought her the title by 0.30 pt. Although lacking the skill of many of her successors, Miss Keleti, with her compatriot Margit Korondi, was the chief opponent to the USSR's domination of the sport. She was one of several Hungarians who chose not to return to Hungary after the 1956 Games and during the 1960s was coach to the Israeli national team.

Gold floor exercises 1952, 1956; beam 1956; asymmetrical bars 1956; exercise with portable apparatus (team) 1956

Silver combined exercises (individual) 1956, (team) 1952, 1956

Bronze asymmetrical bars 1952; exercise with portable apparatus (team) 1952

Keller, Erhard (GER)

B. Günzburg, 24 Dec. 1944. The most famous German speed skater, he won his first Olympic race at Grenoble. In 1971 he was World Champion in the sprint event (500 metres and 1,000 metres) and from 1967 to 1972 set five world records in the 500 metres (39.5 sec, 39.2 sec, 38.42 sec, 38.30 sec and 38.00 sec). He was also one of the best 1,000-metres skaters. In the summer of 1972 he became a professional and is a successful television commentator.

Gold 500-metres speed skating 1968, 1972

Kelly, John B. (USA)

B. Philadelphia, Pa., 4 Oct. 1890; d. Philadelphia, 20 June 1960. Kelly is the only man to have won two Olympic sculling titles on the same day – at the Antwerp Games, where he narrowly beat Jack BERESFORD (GBR) in the single sculls, and, in partnership with Paul COSTELLO, won the double sculls. The latter success he repeated in Paris.

In 1920 Kelly was the centre of controversy, when Henley Royal Regatta refused his entry for the Diamond Sculls. This was not, as was subsequently sometimes claimed, because he was a manual labourer (bricklayer), but because Henley, at that time, had a standing resolution not to accept any entries from the Vesper Boat Club of Philadelphia, due to a previous infringement of their amateur status rules. However, the Henley Stewards did indicate that they thought it doubtful, quite apart from his membership of Vesper, whether Kelly would be eligible under their rules, which, unlike the Olympic rules, did classify all manual labourers as non-amateur.

Gold single sculls 1920; double sculls 1920, 1924

Killanin, 3rd Baron; Michael Morris, Bt (IRL)

B. 30 July 1914. He was educated at Eton, the Sorbonne, Paris and Magdalene College, Cambridge (MA). At school he boxed and rowed. On leaving Cambridge, he joined the London *Daily Express* and subsequently transferred to the *Daily Mail*. In 1937–8 he was War Correspondent in the Sino-Japanese War; on returning to Europe, he became Assistant Political and Diplomatic Correspondent to the *Daily Mail* and wrote the political column in the *Sunday Dispatch*. In 1938 he volunteered and served throughout World War II in the King's Royal Rifle Corps, being Brigade Major 30th Armoured Brigade; he took part in the invasion of Normandy, for which he was made a Member of the Order of the British Empire (Military Division).

In 1952 he was associated with John Ford, making *The Quiet Man*, and subsequently produced a number of other films, including *The Rising of the Moon, The Playboy of the Western World* and *Gideon's Day*. He was also associated with the pro-

John B. Kelly (USA), 1920

duction of *Young Cassidy* and *Alfred the Great*. He edited and contributed to *Four Days*, a book on the Munich crisis; he is also the author of *Sir Godfrey Kneller*, a life of the eighteenth-century painter, and, with Professor Michael Duignan, edited *Shell Guide to Ireland*, besides contributing to European and United States newspapers. He joined the Board of Irish Shell & BP Limited in 1947 and is a Director of a number of other companies.

Killanin was elected President of the Olympic Council of Ireland in 1950 and a Member of the International Olympic Committee in 1952, becoming a Member of the Executive Board in 1967, Vice-President in 1968 and President in 1972.

Killanin is a member of the Irish Turf Club (Steward 1973–5) and a member of the Irish National Hunt Steeplechase Committee. He was elected a Member of the Royal Irish Academy in 1952 and made LL.D. by the National University of Ireland, 1975. His decorations include: Grand Officer of the Order of Merit of the Italian Republic; Order of the Sacred Treasure (2nd class), Japan; Commander of the German Grand Cross of Merit; Officer of the French Legion of Honour; Commander of the Order of Gimaldi (Monaco); Knight of Honour and Devotion of the Order of Malta; Commander of the Finnish Order of Merit; Star of Solidarity (Italy); he has also received awards from Austria, Brazil, Czechoslovakia, Colombia, the Dominican Republic and the USSR.

In 1945 he married Sheila Mary Dunlop, MBE, and has four children.

Killy, Jean-Claude (FRA)

B. St Cloud, 30 Aug. 1943. Killy emulated at Chamrousse (near Grenoble) the Olympic skiing triple gold medal triumph of Toni SAILER at Cortina (1956), but with much less conviction than the Austrian, winning the slalom and giant slalom by less than a tenth of a second. The slalom, furthermore, followed the disqualification of another famous Austrian, Karl Schranz, and led to much acrimony. Schranz, given a second chance on his second run (he claimed to have been baulked first time), finished with a better time but many hours later a jury ruled that his claim to a second chance was invalid.

Killy promptly turned professional to exploit his triple triumph, mostly by way of endorsements. He has since dabbled in films, motor racing and professional ski racing but without any great distinction. He competed at Innsbruck (1964) and was third in the World Championship based on the three Olympic results. He won the World Championship in 1966, but was first in only one event, the downhill. He retained the World Championship two years later with three first places. Although, like that of the Goitschel sisters, his name is closely associated with Val d'Isère, his early life was spent in Alsace. He derives his name from Irish mercenaries in the Napoleonic wars, Killy being a corruption of Kelly.

Gold downhill, slalom and giant slalom 1968

Kirszenstein, Irena (POL)

see SZEWIŃSKA, Irena

Kokkinen, Väinö (FIN)

B. Hollola, 25 Nov. 1899; d. Kuusankoski, 27 Aug. 1967. His wrestling expertise came from his push-overs while standing and merciless nelsons. He won the European Championship of 1930 and was silver medallist in 1925, 1929, 1931 and 1933 (the latter in the middle-heavyweight division).

Gold wrestling Greco-Roman middleweight 1928, 1932

Kolb, Claudia (USA)

B. Hayward, Calif., 19 Dec. 1949. Associated with the swimming centre of Santa Clara throughout her career, it was as a member of its team that she achieved the first of her eleven world records, swimming the breaststroke stage in a medley relay at Los Altos in July 1964. A few days later she set her first world record in an individual event (1 min 17.9 sec for 100-metres breaststroke). In 1966 she became the first holder of the world record for 200-metres individual medley (2 min 27.8 sec). She broke that record four times in the course of the next two years, finishing with 2 min 23.5 sec, which was still a world-class time in 1974 as was the last of her four world records for 400-metres individual medley (5 min 4.7 sec).

Gold 200-metres individual medley 1968, 400-metres individual medley 1968
Silver 200-metres breaststroke 1964

Kolehmainen, Johannes Petteri ('Hannes') (FIN)

B. Kuopio, 9 Dec. 1889; d. Helsinki, 11 Nov. 1966. The first outstanding Finnish Olympic champion runner, he set a world record of 14 min 36.6 sec in winning the 5,000 metres in Stockholm, after a memorable race with Jean Bouin (FRA), as well as the 10,000 metres in 31 min 20.8 sec. At Antwerp he won the marathon over 42,750 m (26½ miles) in 2 hr 32 min 35.8 sec. In 1912 he also won the now abandoned 8,000-

metres cross-country event for the Finnish team and set a world record for 3,000 metres of 8 min 36.8 sec in a heat of the team 3,000-metres event. If World War I had not prevented the 1916 Olympics from being held, he would surely have more Olympic medals to his credit.

Gold 5,000 metres 1912; 10,000 metres 1912; marathon 1920; 8,000-metres cross-country (individual) 1912
Silver 8,000-metres cross-country (team) 1912

Kraenzlein, Alvin (USA)

B. 12 Dec. 1876; d. 6 Jan. 1928. He set world records in the high and low hurdles and the long jump, and at the 1900 Olympics in Paris gained victories in the 60-metres, 110-metres and 200-metres hurdles and then the long jump, in which he beat the qualifying mark of Myer PRINSTEIN by a bare centimetre. Kraenzlein's world records included 23.6 sec for the low hurdles, unbeaten for twenty-five years, 15.2 sec for the high hurdles and a long jump of 7.43 m (24 ft 4½ in).

Gold 60 metres 1900; 110-metres hurdles 1900; 200-metres hurdles 1900; long jump 1900

Krämer, Ingrid (GDR) see ENGEL-KRÄMER, Ingrid

Kulakova, Galina (URS)

B. Logachi, Udmurt, 29 April 1942. A teacher of physical education and one of the best women skiers in the history of the sport, she was USSR Champion in 1967 and won silver and bronze medals at the Winter Olympic Games in Grenoble in 1968. Since then she has won eight World Championship and Olympic titles. At the 1972 Olympics and 1974 World Championships she was overall champion, winning three gold medals in each competition.

Gold 5 kilometres 1972; 10 kilometres 1972; 3 × 5-kilometres relay 1972
Silver 5 kilometres 1968
Bronze 3 × 5-kilometres relay 1968

Kulej, Jerzy (POL)

B. Częstochowa, 19 Oct. 1940. Began by being more interested in swimming and football but at nineteen represented Poland in the European boxing championships and later became European Champion at light welterweight in 1963 and 1965. At Mexico City this policeman's victory was a split-points decision over Enrique Regueiferos (CUB) who started strongly before Kulej's experience and determination allowed the Pole to weather the storm.

Gold boxing light welterweight 1964, 1968

Kuts, Vladimir (URS)

B. Aleksino, Ukraine, 7 Feb. 1927. The outstanding distance runner at the 1956 Melbourne Olympics. In the 10,000

metres he had a classic battle with Gordon Pirie (GBR) controlling the pace from the front until the last five laps when Kuts went away. Strongly built for a distance runner, Kuts showed the aggression of a former amateur boxer in his tactics from the day in 1954 when he ran away from the rest of Europe over 5,000 metres. In four attempts he lowered the world record for this event from 13 min 57.2 sec to 13 min 0.35 sec and set the 10,000-metres time of 28 min 30.4 sec.

Gold 5,000 metres 1956; 10,000 metres 1956

Lagutin, Boris (URS)

B. Moscow, 24 June 1938. He started boxing in 1955 and was European light-middleweight champion in 1961 and 1963. He won his first international in 1960. At Tokyo he won his first Olympic title in a ferocious clash with Joseph Gonzales (FRA). Four years later the thirty-year-old Lagutin won a unanimous points decision over Rolando Garbey (CUB) after Garbey had been down twice in the first round.

Gold boxing light middleweight 1964, 1968
Bronze light middleweight 1960

Lane, Alfred P. (USA)

B. 26 Sept. 1891. Achieved remarkable success in the 1912 Olympics when, at the age of twenty and after only two years of competitive experience, he won three gold medals, more than any other competitor in shooting. In the 1912 team 50 metres he scored 509 pts, 34 more than the second best.

Gold rapid-fire pistol 1912; free pistol 1912; team pistol (50 metres) 1912, 1920, (30 metres) 1920
Bronze free pistol 1920

Larsson, Gunnar (SWE)

B. Malmö, 12 May 1951. A swimmer with great competitive flair, but it took coaching in the United States to enable him to fulfil his potential. This he did so well that he scored a double in the taxing individual medley events at the 1972 Olympic Games in Munich.

At the European Championships of 1970 Larsson broke two world records and won three gold medals and a silver.

Larsson's victory in the 1972 Olympic 400-metres individual medley caused a change in the swimming rules. A remarkable breaststroke leg in 1 min 18.1 sec put him well in the race. After a breathtaking finish to the final leg, the freestyle, Larsson and Tim McKee (USA) were shown as equal first in 4 min 31.98 sec. Further reference to the electronic timekeeper showed that Larsson had won by 0.002 sec. Or had he? Some argued that the slight variation in length of the lanes made it unreasonable to divide by such fine margins. Now times are taken only to hundredths of a second. Larsson added the title for 200-metres individual medley in the world-record time of 2 min 07.17 sec, again beating the favourite Gary Hall (USA).

Gold 200-metres individual medley 1972; 400-metres individual medley 1972

Latynina, Larisa (URS)

B. Kherson, Ukraine, 27 Dec. 1934. This spectacular gymnast took nine Olympic titles (a total equalled by Mark SPITZ and only exceeded by Ray EWRY), five silver and four bronze medals. Her complete record in all major events shows her domination of the sport between her début in 1954 and her retirement twelve years later. In Olympics, World and European Championships she took twenty-four gold medals, fifteen silver and five bronze. What makes this feat even more astonishing is that her career was interrupted by her giving birth to two children.

Mrs Latynina was renowned for her technical proficiency. Her ease in moving from one intricate position to another gave the sport a new concept. Moreover her desire for perfection meant that she kept on improving, forcing her contemporaries to raise their standard as well. Her best event, the floor exercises, in which she won three Olympic gold medals, emphasized this grace of movement. Her efforts and example firmly established the USSR's prominence in the women's branch of the sport.

Gold combined exercises (individual) 1956, 1960, (team) 1956, 1960, 1964; horse vault 1956; floor exercises 1956, 1960, 1964
Silver asymmetrical bars 1956, 1960; beam 1960; combined exercises (individual) 1964; horse vault 1964
Bronze exercise with portable apparatus (team) 1956; horse vault 1960; beam 1964; asymmetrical bars 1964

Lee, Sammy (USA)

B. Fresno, Calif., 1 Aug. 1920. His parents were Korean. The first male diver to retain an Olympic highboard diving title, Lee had the satisfaction of seeing one of his pupils, Bob Webster (USA) also complete an Olympic double on highboard (1960 and 1964). Lee won his first US titles in 1942. In 1948 he won the Olympic highboard event by more than seven points from Bruce Harlan (USA), who took the springboard event with Lee in third place. In 1952 Lee was an even more convincing winner of the highboard from Joaquin CAPILLA PÉREZ (MEX), who succeeded him as champion. In 1953 Lee received the Sullivan Award as the United States' outstanding amateur athlete. He is a doctor of medicine and has been honoured by the US Swimming Hall of Fame.

Gold highboard diving 1948, 1952
Bronze springboard diving 1948

Lemming, Erik (SWE)

B. Gothenburg, 22 Feb. 1880; d. 5 June 1930. At nineteen he set a world javelin record of 49.31 m (161 ft 9¾ in) in 1899, then broke it nine times, pushing it up to 62.32 m (204 ft 5½ in) in 1912. He was fourth equal in the pole vault and fifth in the high jump in the Paris Olympics (1900), and in London (1908) he won both the orthodox javelin event with 54.83 m (179 ft 10½ in) and the javelin freestyle (he held the spear in the middle) with 54.44 m (178 ft 7½ in). In 1912 he retained his standard title with 60.64 m (198 ft 11½ in) and in the aggregate (two-handed) javelin event finished fourth.

Gold javelin 1908, 1912; freestyle javelin 1908

Lightbody, James D. (USA)

B. Pittsburgh, Pa., 17 Mar. 1882; d. Charleston, S.C., 2 Mar. 1953. In St Louis, on an oval-shaped 1½-lap track he won the 800 metres in 1 min 56.0 sec and 1,500 metres in the then world-record time of 4 min 05.4 sec. In the shorter event it is said he watched the field as a hawk does a chicken before running wide round the others over the second lap and finally taking the lead in the last 30 metres. At the same Games he won the 2,500-metres steeplechase and was second in the 6,437-metres (4-miles) team race for Chicago AA. At the 1908 Games in London he was eliminated in the 1,500-metres heats.

Gold 800 metres 1904; 1,500 metres 1904; 2,500-metres steeplechase 1904
Silver 4 miles (team)

James D. Lightbody (USA), 1904

Linsenhoff, Liselott (GER)

B. Frankfurt, 27 Aug. 1927. One of Germany's great dressage riders, she won both her Olympic gold medals riding the famous Swedish stallion Piaff. She was individual European Champion in 1969 and 1971 and a member of the winning team in 1973; in World Championships she was placed second in the individual event in 1970 and 1974 and was a member of the winning team in 1974.

Gold dressage (individual) 1972, (team) 1968
Silver dressage (team) 1956, 1972
Bronze dressage (individual) 1956

Lowe, Douglas (GBR)

B. Manchester, 7 Aug. 1902. One of the outstanding middle-distance tacticians of the 1920s. He was a schoolboy champion over 880 yards but while at Cambridge University matured so swiftly that he was able to win his first Olympic Gold medal before he had ever won a British title. His win in Paris in 1 min 52.4 sec came after a prolonged battle in the final straight with Paul Martin (SUI). In 1926, in the British championships, Lowe lost a thrilling race over 880 yards to Otto Peltzer (GER), who set a new world record of 1 min 51.6 sec. Just before the Amsterdam Olympics the world 800-metres record was lowered to 1 min 50.6 sec by Sera Martin (FRA) and the Americans had a strong contender for Lowe's title in Lloyd Hahn. One Olympic semi-final was won by Hahn in 1 min 52.6 sec but Lowe cannily qualified nearly five seconds slower. In the final Hahn set the pace but Lowe launched an irresistible attack on the last backstraight and won in 1 min 51.8 sec, a personal and Olympic record.

Gold 800 metres 1924, 1928

McCormick (Keller), Patricia (USA)

B. Seal Beach, Calif., 12 May 1930. The only diver, man or woman, who has scored a double at two Olympic Games. In 1952 she succeeded Vicky Draves (USA) as double Olympic champion, winning both titles by substantial margins, and repeated her success at the Melbourne Games five months after the birth of her son. She was one of the first to be honoured by the US Swimming Hall of Fame.

Gold springboard diving 1952, 1956; highboard 1952, 1956

Mallin, Harry (GBR)

B. London, 1 June 1892; d. Lewisham, 8 Nov. 1969. Mallin never lost an amateur contest and was British champion for five years (1919–23).

In the Paris Games he figured in one of the most unusual boxing controversies. In a contest with Roger Brousse (FRA) the British boxer seemed to have done enough to have won on points. But as soon as the last round was ended, Mallin tried to complain to the referee that he had been bitten on the chest. Before he could make himself understood the bout was awarded on points to Brousse. A protest launched by a Swedish official brought forward medical evidence that Mallin had been bitten, and Brousse was disqualified though the jury declared the foul had not been intentional. In the final Mallin narrowly outpointed John Elliott (GBR).

Gold boxing middleweight 1920, 1924

Mangiarotti, Edoardo (ITA)

B. Renate Veduggio (Milan), 7 Apr. 1919. The passion which some Italians show towards fencing is shown through Mangiarotti; his father already having one son who showed the skills which were to make him a World Champion, changed Edoardo to a left-handed fencer in order that he would be the best ever left-handed fencer. The ploy worked; Edoardo began winning world titles in Paris in 1937 and, in spite of the interruption of World War II, was still in winning teams until the Games of 1960.
Gold épée (individual) 1952, (team) 1936, 1952, 1956, 1960; foil (team) 1956
Silver foil (individual) 1952, (team) 1948, 1952, 1960; épée (team) 1948
Bronze épée (individual) 1948, 1956

Mankin, Valentin (URS)

B. Belokorovichi, Zhitomir area of the Ukraine, 19 Aug. 1938. A military man and one of the best sailors in the Finn and Tempest classes in the 1960s–70s, he won the USSR Championships for the first time in 1959 and held his title in 1961, 1962, 1963, 1967 (Finn), 1970, 1972, 1974 (Tempest). He was the first Soviet sailor to win a World Championship, in the Tempest class in 1973.
Gold yachting Finn 1968; Tempest 1972

Mäntyranta, Eero (FIN)

B. Pello, Finnish Lapland, 20 Nov. 1937. The outstanding cross-country skier in the 1960s, he took part in the competitions at Sapporo (1972) and was placed nineteenth in the 30 kilometres. He won the World Championship at 30 kilometres in 1962 and 1966 and World Championship silver medal at 50 kilometres in 1966. In the Holmenkollen Games in Norway he won the 15-kilometres race in 1962, 1964 and 1968. In the Salpausselkä Games in Finland he won the 15-kilometres race in 1964. Mäntyranta was a splendid technician on the ski tracks and a sound competitor who knew how to prepare himself for major races.
Gold 15-kilometres cross-country 1964; 30-kilometres cross-country 1964; 4 × 10-kilometres relay 1960
Silver 15-kilometres cross-country 1968; 4 × 10-kilometres relay 1964
Bronze 30-kilometres cross-country 1968; 4 × 10-kilometres relay 1968

Mastenbroek, Hendrika ('Rie') (HOL)

B. Rotterdam, 26 Feb. 1919. Dutch competitors won four of the five swimming gold medals open to women in the 1936 Games, Miss Mastenbroek taking two individual titles and swimming in the freestyle relay. In her first international season, she won the 400-metres freestyle (5 min 27.4 sec) and the 100-metres backstroke (1 min 20.3 sec) at the 1934 European Championships; she was also a member of the winning Dutch freestyle relay squad. Later that year she set the first of her seven world records in individual events, returning 1 min 16.8 sec for 100-metres backstroke at Düsseldorf. She also held world records for 440-yards freestyle, 200-metres backstroke, and 400-metres backstroke (5 min 48.8 sec in this event, records for which ceased to be recognized in 1948). She twice swam in Dutch quartets that broke the world record for the 4 × 100-metres freestyle relay.
Gold 100-metres freestyle 1936; 400-metres freestyle 1936; 4 × 100-metres freestyle relay 1936
Silver 100-metres backstroke 1936

Mathias, Robert B. (USA)

B. Tulare, Calif., 17 Nov. 1930. In winning the Olympic decathlon at London, Mathias, aged seventeen and a half, became the youngest ever athletics gold-medal winner. It was astonishing that someone so young should win this exhausting ten-events test over two days. At the end of the competition Mathias told his father 'never again, never again'. But he beat the world decathlon record in 1950 before doing so again in retaining his Olympic title (the first athlete ever to do this in the decathlon) at Helsinki. His performances there were 10.9 sec (100 metres), 6.98 m or 22 ft 11 in (long jump), 15.30 m or 50 ft 2½ in (shot), 1.90 m or 6 ft 3 in (high jump), 50.2 sec (400 metres), 14.7 sec (110-metres hurdles), 46.89 m or 153 ft 9¾ in (discus), 4.00 m or 13 ft 1½ in (pole vault), 59.21 m or 194 ft 2½ in (javelin), 4 min 50.8 sec (1,500 metres).

A boyhood victim of anaemia, Mathias was never beaten in the ten decathlons he contested from 1948 until 1956. In a post-Olympic meeting in 1952, he ran the high hurdles in 13.8 sec, at that time a mark beaten by only nine men. In 1953 he forfeited his amateur status by appearing in a film about his career. In 1972 he was re-elected to the United States Congress but defeated for re-election in 1974.
Gold decathlon 1948, 1952

Matthes, Roland (GDR)

B. Pössneck, 17 Nov. 1950. From April 1967, when he was beaten by Joachim Rother (GDR), until 31 August 1974, when he lost to John Naber (USA) in a match between the United States and the German Democratic Republic, at Concord, Calif., Matthes was undefeated in backstroke events. Thus, for nearly seven and a half years, during which he scored backstroke doubles at two Olympic Games and at the first ever World Championships, Matthes dominated world swimming in that stroke and influenced its development.

He has a reputation for ekeing out energy evenly to win a race in individual events. His approach to swimming relays is different – his world records for 100-metres backstroke have been achieved when swimming the first stage of the medley relay for his country. He has beaten the 100-metres backstroke record six times and equalled it once and has lowered the 200-metres backstroke record from 2 min 9.04 sec to 2 min 1.87 sec.

A highly versatile swimmer, Matthes also set the European record for 100-metres butterfly (55.7 sec). In 1970 he was European record holder for the 200-metres individual medley (2 min 12.8 sec) and has been one of the world's leading front-crawl swimmers. Matthes's coach at the Turbine Club of Erfurt is a woman, Marlies Grohe, who first noted his ability in backstroke.
Gold 100-metres backstroke 1968, 1972; 200-metres backstroke 1968, 1972
Silver 4 × 100-metres medley relay 1968, 1972
Bronze 4 × 100-metres freestyle relay 1972

Meade, Richard (GBR)

B. Chepstow, 4 Dec. 1938. Britain's first individual equestrian gold medallist when he triumphed on Laurieston at Munich, contributing greatly to his team's victory in the process. It was his third Olympics. At Tokyo (1964), on Barberry, he was leading at the end of the second stage of the three-day event but dropped back to eighth after the show-jumping test. In Mexico (1968) he finished fourth on Cornishman V and was one of the gold-medal winning team.

With one exception he has been in the British team each year since 1964 and has participated in five victories – two Olympic gold medals, one world and two European titles. He was individual runner-up in two World Championships, on Barberry (1966) and The Poacher (1970). In 1974, riding Wayfarer, he was in the team which finished second in the World Championships at Burghley, placing individual seventh.
Gold three-day event (individual) 1972, (team) 1968, 1972

Richard Meade (GBR), 1972

Medved, Aleksandr (URS)

B. Belaya Tserkov, Ukraine, 16 Sept. 1937. His performance in becoming the first man to win wrestling gold medals at three successive Olympics makes him one of the greatest wrestlers in history. Between 1962 and his retirement after the Munich Games (1972) he lost the Olympic or World title on only one occasion – the 1965 World Championships when he drew with Ahmer Ayik (TUR) and conceded the gold medal on fewer bad marks.

What made his career even more remarkable was that he rarely weighed more than 105 kg (231 lb or 16½ stone) and sometimes fought competitors more than 63.5 kg (140 lb or 10 stone) heavier than himself. Yet his deft armoury of attacks and sudden evasions enabled him to outmanoeuvre more burly opponents.

He was initially a light-heavyweight, taking the gold medal at the Tokyo Games (1964). Two years later he moved up to heavyweight. At Mexico (1968) he was helped by an injury to his leading rival, Wilfried Dietrich (GER). In Munich (1972) he had to use all his experience to keep clear of the formidable strength of Chris Taylor (USA), who weighed 190.5 kg (420 lb or 30 stone). Although the second lightest man in the class he retained his title.

Gold wrestling freestyle light heavyweight 1964; heavyweight 1968; super heavyweight 1972

Meyer, Deborah (USA)

B. Annapolis, Md., 14 Aug. 1952. Miss Meyer was the first swimmer, man or woman, to win three gold medals for individual events in one Olympic Games. The freestyle events over 200 metres and 800 metres were added to the Olympic women's program for the 1968 Games in Mexico and Miss Meyer won them both as well as the 400-metres freestyle. Her Olympic treble was the more meritorious since she went down with a stomach upset on the morning of her second final, that for 200 metres.

She set sixteen world freestyle records during her career; three of them came in the 1968 US Olympic trials at the Los Angeles Coliseum: 2 min 06.7 sec for 200 metres; 4 min 24.5 sec for 400 metres; and 9 min 10.4 sec for 800 metres. In 1970, shortly before her retirement, she improved the record for 400 metres to 4 min 24.3 sec. Her career at the top merely spanned three years from 1967.

She was coached by Sherman Chavoor at the Arden Hills Club. In addition to her achievements at Olympic distances, she made the 1,500-metres freestyle her preserve, breaking the world record four times and having a best performance of 17 min 19.9 sec in a long-course pool.

Gold 200-metres freestyle 1968; 400-metres freestyle 1968; 800-metres freestyle 1968

Miez, Georges (SUI)

B. Töss, Zürich, 2 Oct. 1904. His life has been devoted to gymnastics, beginning at the age of thirteen and becoming an international competitor at eighteen. From then onwards he was a competitor, instructor, propagandist for his sport and even a designer of gymnastic apparatus and trousers, as well as a writer on apparatus. He won more world and Olympic medals than any other Swiss sportsman. He competed in the World Championships of 1931, winning the free exercises, defended that title in 1934, winning also the horizontal bar title and a team prize.

Gold combined exercises (individual) 1928, (team) 1928; horizontal bar 1928; floor exercises 1936

Silver pommelled horse 1928; floor exercises 1932; combined exercises (team) 1936

Bronze combined exercises (team) 1924

Mockridge, Russell (AUS)

B. Melbourne, 18 July 1930; d. Melbourne, 13 Sept. 1958. A quiet man who had studied for the church, Mockridge had the heart of an amateur long after he had become a professional cyclist, and was an outstanding all-rounder.

Beginning as a sprinter, he was the first amateur to win the Open Grand Prix of Paris (1951). He went to the other end of competitive cycling to complete the Tour de France (2,600 miles or 4,184 km) in 1955. He raced in the London Olympics (1948), but did not win medals until 1952 in Helsinki, where he set a new record for the 1,000-metres time trial and won the tandem sprint with Lionel Cox. He was killed in a car crash.

Gold 1,000-metres time trial 1952; 2,000-metres tandem 1952

Morelon, Daniel (FRA)

B. Bourg en Bresse, 28 July 1944. Generally considered the most outstanding Olympic cyclist. In amateur sprint cycling he won medals at eight out of ten World Championships, including six world titles. He has always had the knack of winning by a narrow margin, thus making his opponents look better than they were. He is also the fastest unpaced cyclist, with a time of 10.72 sec (42 mph or 67.6 kph) for a 200-metres flying start, set in Zürich in 1966.

Gold 1,000-metres individual sprint 1968, 1972; 2,000-metres tandem 1968

Bronze 1,000-metres individual sprint 1964

Morrow, Bobby (USA)

B. Harlingen, Tex., 15 Oct. 1935. The outstanding sprinter at the Melbourne Olympics, Morrow is considered as one of the supreme competitors over 100 and 200 metres. Between 1955 and 1958 he lost only one championship race. He held individual world records for the 100 yards (9.3 sec) and 200 metres turn (20.6 sec) and as late as 1960 narrowly missed being selec-

ted for the US team. In 1956, as a student at Abilene Christian College, he won the US Olympic sprint trials in 10.3 sec and 20.6 sec. At Melbourne he proved as great a sprinter as any yet seen in the Games. He went through four rounds of the 100 metres undefeated and won the final, against a wind of 5 metres per second, in 10.5 sec. In the 200 metres he ran with a bandaged thigh but unleashed an unanswerable burst of power to win in the Olympic record time of 20.6 sec. In the 4 × 100-metres relay he gained his third gold medal with a fine last stage which made up for two indifferent baton exchanges. The following year Morrow equalled the then world 100-yards record of 9.3 sec three times and lost only one race all season.

Gold 100 metres 1956; 200 metres 1956; 4 × 100-metres relay 1956

Mortanges, Charles Ferdinand Pahud de (HOL)

B. The Hague, 13 May 1896; d. 8 April 1971. As a winner of two consecutive individual gold medals in Olympic three-day events, General (as he became) de Mortanges held an equestrian record which still stands after forty years. As a Lieutenant in the Dutch Hussars, he rode in four Olympic events, making his début at Paris where he finished fourth on Johnny Walker as one of his country's gold-medal winning team. At Amsterdam, where the Dutch team was again successful, he won his first individual medal, riding Marcroix. At Los Angeles he triumphed again with the same horse, the Dutch team then taking the silver medal. He also rode Marcroix, then seventeen years old, at Berlin (1936), but was unplaced although completing the course. Marcroix, an Anglo-Norman palomino, is believed to be the only horse to have competed in three successive Olympic three-day events.

Gold three-day event (individual) 1928, 1932, (team) 1924, 1928

Silver three-day event (team) 1932

Myyrä, Jonni (FIN)

B. Savitaipale, 13 July 1892; d. 22 Jan. 1955. A pioneer in the Finnish school of javelin throwing, he achieved a world record of 62.57 m (205 ft 3½ in) in 1915 and eventually raised it to 66.10 m (216 ft 10½ in) in 1919 before winning the Olympic titles in 1920 and 1924 with 65.78 m (215 ft 9½ in) and 62.96 m (206 ft 6½ in). Myyrä, who started his Olympic career by finishing eighth in the 1912 Games, had an unofficial throw of 67.96 m (222 ft 11 in) in 1925, at the age of thirty-three.

Gold javelin 1920, 1924

Nadi, Nedo (ITA)

B. Livorno, 9 June 1893; d. Rome, 29 Jan. 1940. The greatest and most versatile fencer of the century, he won more international success in this sport than anyone. He was initially taught foil in his father's gymnasium at an extremely young age, but at fifteen he was skilful in the other weapons. He started international competition in 1911 and in 1912 at Stockholm won the gold medal in foil without suffering a single defeat in the course of the final. This victory in an event which usually requires many years of preparation and international experience was considered one of the outstanding achievements in the history of fencing. At Antwerp (1920) Nadi accomplished the biggest feat of his career, winning five gold medals – still one of the most outstanding feats in the history of the modern Games. After becoming a professional and teaching in Buenos Aires, he returned to Europe and, against all precedent, was reinstated as an amateur so that from 1935 until his death he was President of the Italian Fencing Federation.

Gold foil (individual) 1912, 1920, (team) 1920; épée (team) 1920; sabre (individual) 1920, (team) 1920

Nadig, Marie-Thérèse (SUI)

B. Tannenboden, 8 Mar. 1954. In 1972 Miss Nadig sprang almost from nowhere to win two Olympic skiing gold medals at Sapporo. Although Swiss junior champion in 1970, she accomplished little of international significance in 1971, yet her results in the winter of 1971–2 progressively improved and she reached her peak just in time for the Sapporo Games. Annemarie Pröll (AUT) was the favourite for both downhill and giant slalom, but Miss Nadig confounded her both times. She had the stocky build that characterizes the downhill specialists, 1.63 m (5 ft 4¼ in) tall and weighing 65 kg (143 lb 7 oz).

Gold downhill and giant slalom 1972

Nakayama, Akinori (JPN)

B. Aichi Prefecture, 1 Mar. 1943. One of the most successful Japanese gymnasts of the late 1960s. He finished first in the parallel bars and floor exercises in his World Championships début in 1966. Although twenty-nine by the Munich Games (1972), unusually old for a leading competitor, he

Akinori Nakayama (JPN), 1972

showed that he was still a superb all-round athlete.

Gold rings 1968, 1972; parallel bars 1968; horizontal bar 1968; combined exercises (team) 1968, 1972
Silver floor exercises 1968, 1972
Bronze combined exercises (individual) 1968, 1972

Neckermann, Josef (GER)

B. Würzburg, 5 June 1912. Owner of one of Europe's largest department stores and President of the Stiftung Deutsche Sporthilfe (a foundation to aid high-performance sportsmen) and a member of the West German National Olympic Committee and Sports Federation. He became World Dressage Champion in 1966 (individual and team).

Gold dressage (team) 1964, 1968
Silver dressage (individual) 1968, (team) 1972
Bronze dressage (individual) 1960, 1972

Norelius, Martha (USA)

B. Stockholm, Sweden, 20 Jan. 1908; d. 1955. Her father represented Sweden in the Interim Games in Athens (1906), but Miss Norelius was brought up in the United States, where she was first coached by her father and then by Louis de B. Handley, who, as coach to the New York Women's Swimming Association, also trained other US Olympic gold medallists in Ethelda BLEIBTREY and Aileen Riggin. Miss Norelius was the first woman to win an Olympic gold medal for the same event at successive Games: in the 400-metres freestyle in 1924 in 6 min 02.2 sec and in 1928 in 5 min 42.8 sec (a world record). She won sixteen US titles and had nineteen world amateur records ratified. After the 1928 Games she became a professional. Her world records were all in freestyle events from 200 metres to a mile. She married Joseph Wright, a Canadian oarsman who won the 1928 Olympic silver medal for double sculls.

Gold 400-metres freestyle 1924, 1928; 4 × 100-metres freestyle relay 1928

Nurmi, Paavo Johannes (FIN)

B. Turku, 13 June 1897; d. Helsinki, 2 Oct. 1973. Nurmi set, altogether, twenty-two world records in athletics from distances between 1,500 metres and 20 kilometres and those feats together with his Olympic performances and his style of training brought a fundamental change in attitude towards middle- and long-distance running.

Nurmi began running when he was about nine years old and at fifteen he was fired with the exploits of Hannes KOLEHMAINEN (FIN). Running from then onwards became Nurmi's overriding passion and he set out to emulate Kolehmainen. In 1920 he began holding a stopwatch as he ran, both in training and competition, and this played a crucial part in his develop-

ment. It helped judgment of pace, which eluded many other runners, it conserved energy and gave him greater confidence.

At the 1924 Olympics he won all four of his races, two of them, the 1,500 metres and 5,000 metres within an hour and a half; a few weeks previously he set world records for those distances within the space of an hour.

He was upset at being left out of the 10,000 metres in the 1924 Games, and while a fellow countryman, Ville Ritola, was winning the event in a world-record time of 30 min 23.2 sec, Nurmi was said to have been on a training run over the same distance, which he completed in 29 min 58 sec. Four years later, he won the 10,000 metres again and he would probably have taken a medal in the marathon at Los Angeles in 1932 had he not been disqualified from athletics for alleged professionalism. That decision embittered him, although it was rescinded for domestic competition, until his death. There is a bronze statue of him outside the Olympic stadium in Helsinki and he carried the torch into that arena at the Games of 1952.

Gold 1,500 metres 1924; 5,000 metres 1924; 10,000 metres 1920, 1928; 3,000 metres (team) 1924; cross-country (individual) 1920, 1924, (team) 1920, 1924
Silver 5,000 metres 1920, 1928; 3,000-metres steeplechase 1928

O'Brien, William Parry (USA)

B. Santa Monica, Calif., 28 Jan. 1932. Will be remembered by close students of athletics as the man who pioneered the step-back style of shot putting in which the competitor starts with his back towards the direction of the throw and gains more time to apply force. O'Brien was Olympic champion at only twenty, retained the title and was fourth in 1964. Between 1953 and 1955 he beat the world record fourteen times and became the first man to beat 60 ft, 18 m and 19 m. It was in 1966, still competing at thirty-four, that he achieved the greatest putt of his life 19.7 m (64 ft 7½ in). He was eighteen times US national or collegiate champion and between 1952 and 1956 had 116 consecutive victories.

Gold shot 1952, 1956
Silver shot 1960

O'Callaghan, Patrick (IRL)

B. Kanturk, Co. Cork, 28 Jan. 1906. A year after he began specializing in the hammer throw, O'Callaghan astonished the experts by winning the gold medal in Amsterdam (1928) with a throw of 51.39 m (168 ft 7 in). He defended the title in 1932 but only won the gold medal with his last throw, 53.92 m (176 ft 11 in). He was an all-round athlete and probably one of his finest performances was never recognized officially; in 1937 from a circle six inches too small and with a hammer six ounces overweight he achieved a throw of 59.56 m (195 ft 5 in), six feet further than the world record set twenty-four years earlier by the Irish-American Patrick Ryan.

Gold hammer 1928, 1932

Oerter, Alfred A. (USA)

B. Astoria, N.Y., 19 Sept. 1936. Often cited as the supreme Olympic athletics competitor on his four successive gold discus medals. He was American high-school discus record holder in 1954 and two years later surprised many, at only twenty, by winning his first Olympic title with a record throw of 56.36 m (184 ft 11 in). In spite of all the pressure he again had a personal record, this time of 59.18 m (194 ft 1¾ in) in taking his second gold medal at Rome. For his third Olympics, at Tokyo, he was seriously handicapped by torn cartilages in his lower rib cage. He came out for the final with his ribs heavily taped and his right side packed in ice to prevent internal haemorrhage. Yet he still won. Four years later, at Mexico City, the rain swamped the throwing circle but Oerter, now thirty-two, adjusted his technique by leaving out preliminary swings and had the best three throws of his whole career, including a winning 64.78 m (212 ft 6½ in). Four times the world-record holder in the discus, Oerter strongly condemned the use of illegal anabolic steroids, saying, 'The Olympics are unique. There is no job, no amount of power, no money to approach the meaning of the Olympic experience.'

Gold discus 1956, 1960, 1964, 1968

Alfred A. Oerter (USA), 1968

Okano, Isao (JPN)

B. Ibaragi Prefecture, 20 Jan. 1944. A graduate of the Chuo University, Tokyo, he started judo while attending middle school. After winning the middleweight class at the Tokyo Games (1964), while at university, he also won the World title in Rio de Janeiro the following year in the middleweight class. He belongs to the or-

thodox school of judo with its principle based on faith that 'softness can subdue wrath'. He established a private judo school, the *Shoki-Jiku* ('school of righteous mind') in 1969 and succeeded in gathering disciples not only in Japan but from Europe, the United States and South America.

Gold judo middleweight 1964

Ono, Takashi (JPN)

B. Akita Prefecture, 26 July 1931. The first of the outstanding Japanese gymnasts, Ono led his country's assault on the USSR's male domination of the sport. In 1956 he finished only 0.05 point behind Viktor CHUKARIN (URS) in the combined exercises competition and produced a splendid performance on the horizontal bar where he obtained 19.60 out of a possible 20 pts for victory. His control and suppleness earned him widespread appreciation.

Four years later Ono again failed to take the gold medal by 0.05 pt – from another Russian, Boris SHAKHLIN. However, Ono had considerable compensation in winning the gold medal in the horizontal bar and vault and bronze on the rings and parallel bars. He also led Japan to its first team triumph, a title it has not lost since in either Olympics or World Championships. By 1964 he had been surpassed but still took a gold medal in the team event.

Gold horizontal bar 1956, 1960; long-horse vault 1960; combined exercises (team) 1960, 1964

Silver combined exercises (individual) 1956, 1960; pommelled horse 1956; combined exercises (team) 1956

Bronze long-horse vault 1952; parallel bars 1956, 1960; rings 1960

Oriola, Christian d' (FRA)

B. Perpignan, Eastern Pyrenees, 3 Oct. 1928. With Lucien GAUDIN, the greatest French fencer of all time. Four times World Champion in foil, in 1947, 1949, 1953 and 1954, he took four team World titles, in 1947, 1951, 1953 and 1958. He allowed his comrade Jehan Buhan, sixteen years older, to take the gold medal in the 1948 Games. He rebelled against the introduction of the electric foil but took up competition again in 1958 and at Rome (1960) was seventh. He carried the flag for the French delegation. Ten times Champion of France, from 1952 to 1970, he was awarded the Legion of Honour in 1971. He is first cousin of Pierre Jonquères d'ORIOLA.

Gold foil (individual) 1952, 1956, (team) 1948, 1952

Silver foil (individual) 1948, (team) 1956

Oriola, Pierre Jonquères d' (FRA)

B. Corneilla del Vercol, Eastern Pyrenees, 1 Feb. 1920. The only rider to have won two individual gold medals for show jumping, the first riding Ali Baba at Helsinki (1952) and the other on Lutteur B at

Tokyo (1964) when the French took the team silver. After World War II, he was one of the first French riders to move into a hitherto military preserve and make an international reputation: his early successes included the Zürich Grand Prix in 1946 and the first postwar King George V Gold Cup in London in 1947. He won the men's World Championship on Pomone at Buenos Aires in 1966 after finishing second in 1953 and third in 1954.

Gold show jumping (individual) 1952, 1964

Silver show jumping (team) 1964, 1968

Osborn, Harold (USA)

B. Butler, Ill., 13 Apr. 1899; d. Los Angeles, 5 April 1975. Remarkable both for his versatility and long career. In Paris he set a world high-jump record of 2.04 m (6 ft 8¼ in) and won the Olympic title with a Games record of 1.98 m (6 ft 6 in). Then he became the first athlete to win the Olympic decathlon with a world-record score. He is still the only man to combine an individual victory with one in the decathlon. In the Amsterdam Olympics (1928) he finished only fifth in the high jump but his Olympic record in this event was not beaten until 1936. In the same year he finished his career with a world indoor best of 1.68 m (5 ft 6 in) for the standing high jump. Altogether he won eighteen US titles in six different events.

Gold high jump 1924; decathlon 1924

Ostermeyer, Micheline (FRA)

B. Rang de Fliers, 23 Dec. 1922. Third in the French discus championship of 1948, she was a most unexpected winner of the Olympic title in London that year; she was only entered as an afterthought following her initial selection for the shot, which she also won at Wembley, and the high jump, in which she was third. Winner of a Paris Conservatoire piano prize, she celebrated her Olympic victories with an impromptu recital of Beethoven at France's team headquarters.

Gold shot 1948; discus 1948

Bronze high jump 1948

Owens, James Cleveland ('Jesse') (USA)

B. Danville, Ala., 12 Sept. 1913. One of the greatest of all track and field athletes, certainly in the first half of the twentieth century. His combination of grace, speed, spring and power has been captured forever on film. He is also remembered for his record breaking and especially his feat on 25 May 1935 at Ann Arbor, Michigan, when he beat or equalled six world records within forty-five minutes. Apart from 100 yards in 9.4 sec and 220 yards in 20.3 sec, his records that day included his single long jump of 8.13 m (26 ft 8¼ in) which was to last for twenty-five years.

Possessing great natural ability, Owens says he was motivated towards winning an Olympic title by meeting American sprinter Charley Paddock in 1928, just as eight years later the success of Owens drove Harrison DILLARD (USA) towards victory. At Ohio State University Owens had his technique polished by coach Larry Snyder as he approached the peak of a career which was to bring him nine world records in seven events and an unbeaten run over 200 metres.

At Berlin, on 2 August 1936, Owens opened his marvellous golden chapter in the Olympic book with a 100-metres heat in 10.3 sec, which, because it was wind-assisted, could not be a Games record. Before the week was over he had won the 100 metres in 10.3 sec, the 200 metres in 20.7 sec, the fastest ever at that time round a full turn, the long jump in 8.06 m (26 ft 5¼ in), an Olympic record, and anchored the American 4 × 100-metres relay team to a new world record of 39.8 sec. His only serious challenge came in the long jump where he was level with Luz Long (GER) until the fifth round. Owens turned professional soon after the Olympics.

Gold 100 metres 1936; 200 metres 1936; long jump 1936; 4 × 100-metres relay 1936

Papp, László (HUN)
B. Budapest, 25 Mar. 1926. The outstanding champion in Olympic boxing history. Papp said once that his hardest bout in the Olympics was in 1948 against Johnny Wright (GBR). But his peak may well have been his third victory in 1956 against José Torres (USA) who later became world professional light-heavyweight champion. Papp won the European professional middleweight title in 1962 and was unbeaten until he finally retired. He combined both technical skill and a powerful punch and successfully coached the Hungarian teams.
Gold boxing middleweight 1948; light middleweight 1952, 1956

Pattisson, Rodney Stuart (GBR)
B. Cambeltown, Scotland, 5 Aug. 1943. The first Briton to win two consecutive gold medals for yachting. At Acapulco (1968) he helmed his Flying Dutchman *Super . . . docious* and was crewed by Iain Macdonald Smith; they had five firsts and one second, incurring only three penalty points, the lowest number of points by the winner in any class in an Olympic regatta. This was the first yachting gold medal for Britain for twenty years. At Kiel (1972), Pattisson helmed his Flying Dutchman *Superdoso*, with Chris Davies as crew. From 1968 to 1972, Pattisson held the Flying Dutchman World and European Championships. His success has been based on the belief that racing sailors should be physically fit. He began each day with a long training run. His boat is always immaculate and he pays much attention to detail and to the meticulous tuning of his boat.

Gold yachting Flying Dutchman 1968, 1972

Pearce, Henry Robert (AUS)
B. 30 Sept. 1905. Son of a professional waterman at Hammersmith, London, who later emigrated to Australia. He completely dominated single sculling, and so confident was he that, on occasions, he would scull with, and coach his opponents. It was probably this confidence, rather than any real threat from any contemporary scullers, which accounted for the fact that he did not always win by large margins. Besides his Olympic successes, he won the British Empire title, against Jack BERESFORD (GBR), in 1930 at Hamilton, Ontario, and then became a Canadian citizen. The following year he won the Diamond Sculls at Henley Royal Regatta. He retained his qualification as an Australian for Olympic purposes. He turned professional in 1933, and took the world professional sculling title.
Gold single sculls 1928, 1932

Pihlajamäki, Kustaa (FIN)
B. Nurmo, 7 Apr. 1902; d. Helsinki, 10 Feb. 1944. From an outstanding family of wrestlers, he was very tough, quick and versatile. He was equally competent in freestyle and Greco-Roman. Many wrestling experts regard him as the best lightweight wrestler of all time. He competed in four Olympics and won the European Championship in Greco-Roman style in 1930, 1931, 1933, 1934, 1937, 1938, 1939, and in freestyle in 1931 and 1937. He represented Finland in forty-one international matches, of which he won thirty-eight. There is a monument to him in Helsinki. His brothers, Arvi (b. 1904; d. 1940) and Paavo (b. 1911) were Finnish freestyle champions many times. A cousin, Hermanni Pihlajamäki (b. 1903) won an Olympic gold medal in the freestyle featherweight division in 1932 and a bronze in 1936 in the lightweight class.
Gold wrestling freestyle bantamweight 1924, featherweight 1932, 1936
Silver featherweight 1928

Poynton-Hill, Dorothy (USA)
B. Salt Lake City, Utah, 17 July 1915. Miss Poynton was barely thirteen when she competed in her first Olympic Games at Amsterdam, yet won the silver medal for springboard diving. As Mrs Hill, she won the springboard bronze medal in 1936, but her real talent was seen from the highboard. An attractive blonde, she opened her own aquatic club in Los Angeles, where she had learned her diving.
Gold highboard diving 1932, 1936
Silver springboard diving 1928
Bronze springboard diving 1936

Press, Irina (URS)
B. Kharkov, 10 Mar. 1939. She started athletics in 1955 and entered the Russian team in 1958. Her Olympic pentathlon

Tamara Press (URS), 1960

victory brought with a world-record score (her eighth record in this event), and she finished fourth in the 80-metres hurdles and sixth in the shot, won by her sister Tamara. She retired before the 1966 European Championships.
Gold 80-metres hurdles 1960; pentathlon 1964

Press, Tamara (URS)
B. Kharkov, 10 May 1937. Six times world-record holder in both the shot and discus and also winner of three European titles. She retired before the 1966 European Championships.
Gold shot 1960, 1964; discus 1964
Silver discus 1960

Prinstein, Myer (USA)
B. 1878; d. 10 Mar. 1928. The only man to win the Olympic long jump and triple jump on the same day (1904). In 1900 he had been first in the triple jump, too, but having competed in the qualifying round of the long jump, was prevented by his college, Syracuse, from taking part in the final because it was on a Sunday. He finished second in that event with his qualifying mark of 7.175 m (23 ft 6½ in) to 7.185 m (23 ft 6⅞ in) by Alvin KRAENZLEIN (USA). In 1904 Prinstein was also fifth in the 400 metres and the 60 metres. His best

long jump was 7.50 m (24 ft 7¼ in) in 1900. He also won the long jump at the 1906 Interim Games in Athens.

Gold long jump 1904; triple jump 1900, 1904
Silver long jump 1900

Protopopov, Oleg and Ludmila (Belousova) (URS)

Oleg, B. Leningrad, 16 July 1932; Ludmila, B. Ulyanovsk, 22 Nov. 1935. After serving in the Soviet Navy from 1951 to 1953, Oleg Protopopov took third place in the 1953 Russian pair championship with Margarita Bogoyavlenskaya. Until 1957 Ludmila Belousova's partner was Yuri Nevski. The Protopopovs began skating as a pair in 1957, and were married in the same year. They were runners-up for both World and European titles in 1962, 1963 and 1964, and were European and World Champions four times, from 1965 to 1968. In the Olympic Games they were ninth at Squaw Valley (1960) and champions at Innsbruck (1964) and Grenoble (1968). By 1969 they were beyond their peak at thirty-six and thirty-three respectively and lost their European and World titles to Aleksei Ulanov and Irina Rodnina (URS). They turned professional and won a lucrative competition promoted by Richard BUT-TON in Tokyo in 1973.
Gold figure skating (pairs) 1964, 1968

Richards, Robert E. (USA)

B. Champaign, Ill., 20 Feb. 1926. A remarkably consistent pole vaulter although only 1.76 m (5 ft 9½ in) tall, Richards was nine times American champion. In 1956 Richards, a preacher nicknamed 'The Vaulting Vicar', only qualified for the Olympic final on his third and last attempt. He was three times American decathlon champion and represented the United States in that event at Melbourne in 1956.
Gold pole vault 1952, 1956
Bronze pole vault 1948

Richthoff, Johan (SWE)

B. Limhamn, near Malmö, 1898. He began as a cooper and became a minister in the Swedish free church and a campaigner against alcohol. He weighed 112 kg (17 stone 9 lb or 247 lb) and was an excellent technician. He was a professional catch-wrestler in the United States 1932–3.
Gold wrestling freestyle heavyweight 1928, 1932

Rose, Iain Murray (AUS)

B. Nairn, Scotland, 6 Jan. 1939. The Rose family emigrated to Sydney, Australia, when Murray was a baby. At the time of his greatest success, 1956, when he won his first three Olympic gold medals, he was acclaimed as the best Australian swimmer ever. In individual events and relays, Rose's contribution always being on front crawl, his name appears on the world-record lists fifteen times. His first world record was 9 min 34.3 sec for 880-yards freestyle at Sydney in January 1956; more than eight and a half years later he set his last, returning 8 min 55.5 sec in the same event at Vancouver.

At Melbourne Rose won the 400-metres freestyle and the 1,500-metres freestyle as well as being a member of the winning Australian team in the 4 × 200-metres freestyle relay to become the youngest triple gold medal winner up to that time. In 1960 he retained the 400-metres title, the only man ever to have done so. Curiously in each of these victories he beat Tsuyoshi Yamanaka (JPN) by 3.1 sec.
Gold 400-metres freestyle 1956, 1960; 1,500-metres freestyle 1956; 4 × 200-metres freestyle relay 1956
Silver 1,500-metres freestyle 1960
Bronze 4 × 200-metres freestyle relay 1960

Rose, Ralph W. (USA)

B. Louisville, Ky., 17 Mar. 1884; d. 16 Oct. 1913. Literally a giant by the standards of the early Olympics, Rose was 1.96 m (6 ft 5 in) and 106.6 kg (235 lb). Only twenty when he won his first Olympic shot title in St Louis with 14.81 m (48 ft 7 in), between 1907 and 1909 he beat the world record four more times, eventually reaching 15.56 m (51 ft 0¾ in), and was unbeaten for nineteen years. He also had an unratified mark of 16.56 m (54 ft 4 in) in 1909, as well as another unofficial world record of 54.38 m (178 ft 5 in) for the hammer event.
Gold shot 1904, 1908; two-handed shot 1912
Silver discus 1904; shot 1912
Bronze hammer 1904

Rosendahl, Heide (GER)

B. Hückeswagen, 14 Feb. 1947. The victim of ill fortune in the 1968 Olympics, when illness and injury deprived her of any medals, she became the darling of the West German crowd at Munich by winning the long jump, finishing second in the pentathlon and then anchoring the German sprint relay team to victory in world-record-equalling time. The daughter of a national discus champion, she set a world long-jump record of 6.84 m (22 ft 5½ in) in 1970.
Gold long jump 1972; 4 × 100-metres relay 1972
Silver pentathlon 1972

Rudolph, Wilma (USA)

B. Clarksville, Tenn., 23 June 1940. Outstanding athletics champion of the 1960 Olympics, with victories in the 100 and 200 metres and the 4 × 100-metres relay. She was the seventeenth of nineteen children and once said that she learned to run fast because she wanted to get to the dining table first. At only four she became paralysed and did not learn to walk normally until she was seven. Yet at sixteen she won a bronze Olympic medal as a member of the US 4 × 100-metres relay team at Melbourne. She came to Rome as holder of the world 200-metres record but even so she amazed spectators by the wide margins with which she won both sprints. In the 100 metres her time of 11.0 sec was ineligible for world-record ratification because the following wind was just over the permissible limit. In 1961 she lowered her 100-metres record to 11.2 sec.
Gold 100 metres 1960; 200 metres 1960; 4 × 100-metres relay 1960
Bronze 4 × 100-metres relay 1956

Rühle, Frank (GDR)

B. Dehna, 5 Mar. 1944. Member of the unbeaten Einheit Dresden coxless four. See FORBERGER, Frank
Gold coxless fours 1968, 1972

Ruska, Willem (HOL)

B. Amsterdam, 29 Aug. 1940. Twice World Champion between 1967 and 1971, he won European titles from 1965 to 1972 and is the only *judoka* to have won two Olympic titles in one Olympic Games. He started in the sport when he was twenty and after training for seven years won his first world title in Salt Lake City, Utah. He participates in a variety of other sports and although he has a body weight of 110 kg (242 lb or 17 stone 4 lb) he ran 100 metres in 11 sec. He is now coach of the Dutch judo team.
Gold judo heavyweight 1972, open 1972

Ruud, Birger (NOR)

B. Kongsberg, 23 Aug. 1911. He took part in three Olympic Winter Games, the first time in 1932 and the third time sixteen

Ralph W. Rose (USA), 1904

years later in 1948, when he was the coach to the Norwegian ski-jumping team. During training in the days before the competition he was added to the team and justified this late selection by winning the silver medal in special jumping; he was thirty-six. Ruud is perhaps the most famous ski jumper in the world. In addition to his Olympic medals, he took the gold medal in the World Championships in 1931, 1935 and 1937 and was US champion in 1938. Twice he held the world record in ski jumping, in 1926 in Ødnesbakken, Norway, achieving 76.5 m (251 ft), and in 1934 in Planica, Yugoslavia, with 92.0 m (301 ft 10 in).
Gold special ski jumping 1932, 1936
Silver special ski jumping 1948

Sailer, Anton ('Toni') (AUT)

B. Kitzbühel, 17 Nov. 1935. Sailer is the outstanding Alpine skier in Olympic history and still a national hero. His feat of winning all three gold medals in one Games has since been emulated by Jean-Claude KILLY (FRA) but Sailer's record is much the more impressive, since he triumphed by substantial margins – 3.5 sec in the downhill, 4.0 sec in the slalom and 6.2 sec in the giant slalom. These results placed him in a class apart from his contemporaries. He was World Champion on the strength of his Cortina performances, a title he retained two years later, though on that occasion he won only two races, being second in the slalom, not his strongest discipline.

Sailer's was a brief, meteoric career spanning only four seasons at international level. His first big success was the Lauberhorn Cup at Wengen (downhill and combined) in 1955 and his last the World Championships in 1958. Handsome as well as athletic, he later moved into the world of motion pictures, but with only moderate success, and he came back to ski racing in 1972 as director of the Austrian Alpine teams.
Gold downhill, slalom and giant slalom 1956

Donald Schollander (USA), 1968

St Cyr, Major Henri (SWE)

B. Stockholm, 15 Mar. 1902. The only rider to win two individual gold medals for dressage, on Master Rufus at Helsinki (1952) and on Juli at Stockholm (1956). Each performance contributed to the Swedish team victory. He came close to winning a bronze at London in 1948 and at Rome in 1960. He competed at Berlin in 1936 when he was one of the Swedish three-day-event team. In this sphere he was three times Swedish National Champion, in 1935, 1937 and 1939. Following his triumph at Helsinki, he won the World Championship in dressage at Wiesbaden in 1953. In 1956 he took the Olympic oath on behalf of all riders at the Equestrian events, which because of Australian quarantine rules, were held in Stockholm.
Gold dressage (individual) 1952, 1956, (team) 1952, 1956

Saneev, Viktor (URS)

B. Sukhumi, 3 Oct. 1945. Initially a long jumper, he switched to the triple jump in 1967 and in 1968 won the Olympic gold medal with an extraordinary world record of 17.39 m (57 ft 0¾ in). He won the European title in 1969 and though he lost it to Jörg Drehmel (GDR) in 1971, he retained his Olympic title in 1972. Later that year he regained the world record he had lost to Pedro Pérez (CUB) with an effort of 17.44 m (57 ft 2¾ in). He was European Champion again in 1974. He high jumped 1.90 m (6 ft 2¾ in) when aged seventeen.
Gold triple jump 1968, 1972

Schäfer, Karl (AUT)

B. Vienna, 17 May 1909. A brilliant figure skater who ended the Olympic supremacy in 1932 of the legendary Gillis GRAFSTRÖM (SWE), Schäfer had the generosity to say afterwards: 'Yes, I beat him, but he is still the world's greatest skater.' Schäfer was a rare all-rounder who competed in both Winter and Summer Games, for he was a good enough swimmer to be chosen for Austria in 1928 and 1932, finishing fourth in the 1928 breaststroke.

Schäfer first broke through to the top of ice skating with third place in both the European and World Championships of 1927. In 1928 he moved up a place in both events and was fourth in the Winter Games of 1928. After finishing second again in the World Championship of 1929, he went on to win that title from 1929 to 1936. He was known as 'the man who never fell'.
Gold figure skating 1932, 1936

Schenk, Ard (HOL)

B. Anna Paulowna, 16 Sept. 1944. The most advanced speed skater in the world, from 1970 until he became professional in 1972 he was unbeaten.

In 1972 he won the World Championship, the European Championship and the three longest distances in the Olympic Games in Sapporo, beating his opponents

decisively. In the 500 metres he fell. He won the European and World Championships three times, set nineteen world records and created a class of his own through his remarkable physique, outstanding technique and strength.
Gold 1,500 metres, 5,000 metres and 10,000 metres 1972
Silver 1,500 metres 1968

Schollander, Donald Arthur (USA)

B. Charlotte, N.C., 30 Apr. 1946. His technique on front crawl was considered the best ever developed. It helped him to win five Olympic gold medals, three titles in the 1967 Pan-American Games and eleven titles in individual events at the US championships. Always swimming front crawl, he set thirteen world records in individual events and eight in relays when representing either the Santa Clara Club or the United States. His best long-course times were: 100 metres 52.9 sec; 200 metres 1 min 54.3 sec and 400 metres 4 min 11.6 sec. He was particularly associated with the 200-metres freestyle, nine of his world records being set in that event, the first (1 min 58.8 sec) in Los Angeles in 1963 and the last (1 min 54.3 sec) at Long Beach in 1968.

The 1964 Olympic Games in Tokyo brought Schollander to the attention of a wider public. He was the first swimmer to win four gold medals at one Games.

Though he never held the world record for 100-metres freestyle and claimed not to be a sprinter, Schollander won the Olympic title in 1964 by a tenth of a second after a magnificent race with Bobby McGregor (GBR). His win in the 400-metres freestyle set a world record of 4 min 12.2 sec and helped the United States to win both the freestyle relays in world-record times.
Gold 100-metres freestyle 1964; 400-metres freestyle 1964; 4 × 100-metres freestyle relay 1964; 4 × 200-metres freestyle relay 1964, 1968
Silver 200-metres freestyle 1968

Schubert, Dieter (GDR)

B. Pirna, 11 Sept. 1943. Member of the unbeaten Einheit Dresden coxless four. See FORBERGER, Frank
Gold coxless fours 1968, 1972

Schwarzmann, Alfred (GER)

B. Fürth, 23 Mar. 1912. The most successful gymnast of the 1936 Olympic Games in Berlin. Sixteen years later when forty years old he won a silver medal at the Olympics in the horizontal bar competition.
Gold combined exercises (individual) 1936, (team) 1936; long-horse vault 1936
Silver horizontal bar 1952
Bronze horizontal bar 1936, parallel bars 1936

Shakhlin, Boris (URS)

B. Ishim, Kazakhstan, 27 Jan. 1932. Although rather large for a competitive gym-

Opposite **Takehide Nakatani, one of the three Japanese winners in judo at the Games of Tokyo in 1964.**
Overleaf **Mark Spitz (United States), winner of more gold medals at one Games (1972) than any other competitor.**

nast, 1.71 m (5 ft 7½ in) tall and weighing 70 kg (154 lb or 11 stone), Shakhlin's strength and precision brought him ten individual and team titles in Olympics and World Championships between 1954 and 1964.

Shakhlin's height and reach made him particularly successful on the horizontal bar. He was second in this event at the 1954 World Championships and after numerous honours in the following ten years won the gold medal on this apparatus at the Tokyo Games. His powerful forearms and long legs also helped him to win two Olympic gold medals and a world title on the pommelled horse. But his ability in these comparatively rugged movements meant that he was less adaptable for the floor exercises and in his long career he failed to finish in the first three of this event at Olympics or World Championships. His outstanding moment came in the 1960 Olympics when a determined display prevented the Japanese from capturing the combined exercises title for the individual event.

Gold pommelled horse 1956, 1960; combined exercises (individual) 1960; long-horse vault 1960; parallel bars 1960; horizontal bar 1964; combined exercises (team) 1956
Silver combined exercises (individual) 1964, (team) 1960, 1964; rings 1960
Bronze horizontal bar 1960; rings 1964

Sheppard, Melvin W. (USA)

B. Almonesson, N.J., 5 Sept. 1883; d. 1942. Sheppard was an important catalyst in middle-distance racing because of his readiness to set a fast pace. In London (1908) Sheppard went through the first 400 metres of the 800 metres in 53 sec and held on to win in the world-record time of 1 min 52.8 sec. Four years later, at Stockholm, he took the field through the opening lap in 52.4 sec but was overhauled by nineteen-year-old James ('Ted') Meredith (USA) who set world records both at 800 metres (1 min 51.9 sec) and 880 yards (1 min 52.5 sec).

Gold 800 metres 1908; 1,500 metres 1908; 4 × 400-metres relay 1908, 1912
Silver 800 metres 1912

Silva, Adhemar Ferreira da (BRA)

B. São Paulo, 29 Sept. 1927. The outstanding Olympic athlete from the South American continent. He was world-record holder for the triple jump 1950–3 and 1955–8, with a personal best distance of 16.56 m (54 ft 4 in). He finished fourteenth at Rome (1960), at the age of thirty-two, having made his biggest Olympic impact in Helsinki where he four times beat his own world record in the final.

Gold triple jump 1952, 1956

Skoblikova, Lidia (URS)

B. Zlatoust, Chelyabinsk, 8 Mar. 1939. She was reaching her peak when ice speed-skating events for women were introduced to the Olympic program at Squaw Valley (1960). Four years later she took every gold medal at Innsbruck, a unique achievement. In 1963–4 she was also placed first in every World Championship event.

Gold 500 metres 1964; 1,000 metres 1964; 1,500 metres 1960, 1964; 3,000 metres 1960, 1964

Snell, Peter (NZL)

B. Opunake, 17 Dec. 1938. The only middle-distance runner to win three Olympic individual gold medals, Snell was an unexpected winner of the 800 metres at Rome (1960) and then achieved the incredible double of both 800 and 1,500 metres, after qualifying heats in both events, at Tokyo (1964).

A good lawn-tennis player, Snell did not take up running seriously until he was eighteen and came under the guidance of the New Zealand coach Arthur Lydiard. Long-distance training greatly increased Snell's strength though he was seriously handicapped by a stress fracture of a foot in the months before the Rome Olympics.

In the post-Olympic season of 1960, Snell ran a remarkable 880-yards relay leg in 1 min 44.8 sec. The following summer he combined, in just one hour, an 880 yards in 1 min 47.2 sec with a mile relay leg in 4 min 1.2 sec. Early in 1962 he set a world mile record of 3 min 54.4 sec and a week later also ran records for 880 yards (1 min 45.1 sec) and 800 metres (1 min 44.3 sec). He was the first man for twenty-five years to hold both half-mile and mile records.

By 1964 Snell was an experienced racer but still not sure whether he would be capable of doubling up in the Olympic 800 and 1,500 metres. But when he won his 800-metres semi-final at Tokyo in 1 min 46.1 sec his confidence returned. He took the final in 1 min 45.1 sec, and five days later the 1,500 metres in 3 min 38.1 sec after a powerful last lap in 52.7 sec. In November 1964 Snell lowered his mile record to 3 min 54.1 sec. He retired in 1965, the epitome of the strong, silent hero.

Gold 800 metres 1960, 1964; 1,500 metres 1964

Solberg, Magnar (NOR)

B. Sokndal, 4 Feb. 1937. The only man to win two gold medals in biathlon (20-kilometres cross-country and shooting).
Gold biathlon (individual) 1968, 1972
Silver 4 × 10-kilometres biathlon relay 1968

Spitz, Mark (USA)

B. Modesto, Calif., 10 Feb. 1950. At Munich, Spitz won seven gold medals in the swimming events, a record number in any sport at a single Games. The previous best was the five golds won by the Italian fencer, Nedo NADI, at the 1920 Games in Antwerp. The previous highest tally in swimming was Don SCHOLLANDER's four

in 1964. Schollander and Spitz were great rivals, for their careers overlapped, and until the 1972 Games, Schollander had been considered the better competitor.

Spitz's comparative failure in the 1968 Games – two relay gold medals – brought him almost as much publicity as did his vindication as a competitor four years later. Sherman Chavoor, the coach at Arden Hills Club with whom Spitz achieved his best results, has claimed that Spitz had to contend with anti-Semitism during his career even from fellow members of US teams. This and his nervous disposition may have contributed to his early setbacks.

Spitz broke or equalled world records thirty-two times in his career. Best known for his performances at 100- and 200-metres freestyle and butterfly, he had considerable potential at longer distances, setting three world records for 400-metres freestyle and even coming within four-tenths of a second of breaking the world record for 1,500-metres freestyle in 1966. His best world records were 51.22 sec for 100 metres freestyle; 1 min 52.78 sec for 200-metres freestyle; 54.27 sec for 100-metres butterfly; and 2 min 00.70 sec for 200-metres butterfly. During the 1972 Olympic Games he set six world records.

A poster of Spitz, on which he is standing in his swimming suit and wearing his Olympic medals, brought him $10,000 and royalties of 15¢ on every one sold. He thus became a professional and later a reputed dollar millionaire through various commercial ventures.

Gold 100-metres freestyle 1972; 200-metres freestyle 1972; 100-metres butterfly 1972; 200-metres butterfly 1972; 4 × 100-metres freestyle relay 1968, 1972; 4 × 200-metres freestyle relay 1968, 1972; 4 × 100-metres medley relay 1972
Silver 100-metres butterfly 1968
Bronze 100-metres freestyle 1968

Stecher (Meissner), Renate (GDR)

B. Süptitz, 12 May 1950. She was double Olympic sprint champion at the 1972 Munich Olympics with remarkable times of 11.07 sec (100 metres) and 22.40 sec (200 metres), the latter equalling the world record. 1971 European double champion, she set world records of 10.8 sec (100 metres) and 22.1 sec (200 metres), both hand timed, during the 1973 season. Noted for strength and unusually powerful build, she was remarkably consistent as a racer as well as a record breaker.

Gold 100 metres 1972; 200 metres 1972
Silver 4 × 100-metres relay 1972

Steinkraus, William C. (USA)

B. Cleveland, Ohio, 12 Oct. 1925. He won the United States' first show-jumping gold medal riding Snowbound at Mexico in 1968, his fourth Olympic ride. His début was at Helsinki in 1952, when his team took a bronze medal. A silver team medal

The outstanding woman sprinter of the 1972 Games, Renate Stecher (German Democratic Republic)

followed eight years later at Rome but at Tokyo he was unfortunate when his intended partner, the highly rated Sinjon, was a last-minute withdrawal through lameness. He captained the US equestrian team from 1955 until his retirement at the end of 1972, leading the squad to two successes (1966 and 1968) in the President's Cup, the season's team championship. Grand Prix in London and New York and two King George V Gold Cups in London were among many individual triumphs.

Gold show jumping (individual) 1968
Silver show jumping (team) 1960, 1972
Bronze show jumping (team) 1952

Strickland, Shirley (AUS)

SEE DE LA HUNTY

Štukelj, Leon (YUG)

B. Maribor, 12 Nov. 1898. Studied law and took part in gymnastic events for fourteen consecutive years, ending with his last competition in Berlin (1936) at the age of thirty-eight. He won five gold, two silver and four bronze medals in World Championships 1922–31. In the Olympics he was also fourth in the long horse vault and rings in 1924.

Gold combined exercises (individual) 1924; horizontal bar 1924; rings 1928
Silver rings 1936
Bronze combined exercises (individual) 1928, (team) 1928

Swahn, Alfred Gomer Albert (SWE)

B. Uddevalla, 20 Aug. 1879; d. Stockholm, 16 Mar. 1931. Son of Oscar SWAHN. Not surprisingly, after the dedication of his father, he began shooting at twelve and was brought up on running-deer shooting; for twenty years he was the best Swede in the event. He competed in the Games of 1908, 1912, 1920 and 1924, winning three gold, three silver and three bronze medals.

Gold running-deer single shot (individual) 1912, (team) 1908, 1912
Silver running-deer single shot (individual) 1920, (team) 1924, double shot (team) 1920
Bronze clay pigeon (team) 1920; running-deer double shot (individual) 1924, (team) 1924

Swahn, Oscar Gomer (SWE)

B. Tanum, Bohuslän, 20 Oct. 1847; d. Stockholm, 1 May 1927. Legendary rifleman with sixty-five years of competition, he started shooting in 1863 in Uddevalla. He competed in the Olympic Games in 1908, 1912 and 1920, winning three gold, one silver and two bronze medals, all in his speciality, running deer. He qualified for the Games of 1924 at the age of seventy-seven but had to remain at home because of ill health. He won more than 500 first prizes in competitions, all of which he donated to the Army Museum in Stockholm.

Gold running-deer single shot (individual) 1908, (team) 1908, 1912
Silver running-deer double shot (team) 1920
Bronze running-deer double shot (individual) 1908, 1912

Szewinska (Kirszenstein), Irena (POL)

B. Leningrad, 24 May 1946. She has achieved a wide range of records. When only eighteen, at the Tokyo Olympics, she finished second in both the long jump and 200 metres and was a member of Poland's victorious sprint relay team. At Mexico City she won the 200 metres in a world-record time of 22.5 sec and was third in the 100 metres. She dropped the baton in the relay. At Munich, although not quite back to full racing fitness after the birth of a son, she was third over 200 metres. An intelligent and modest champion, she had a further remarkable season in 1974 when she won the European 100 and 200 metres ahead of the formidable Renate STECHER and became the first woman to beat 50 sec for 400 metres.

Gold 4 × 100 metres relay 1964; 200 metres 1968
Silver long jump 1964; 200 metres 1964
Bronze 100 metres 1968; 200 metres 1972

Szmidt, Józef (POL)

B. Michałkowice, 28 Mar. 1935. The first triple jumper to surpass the barriers of 55 ft and 17 metres with 17.03 m (55 ft 10½ in) in 1960, which remained unbeaten for eight years. In spite of suffering several leg injuries, he ran 100 metres in 10.4 sec, long jumped 7.84 m (25 ft 8¾ in), was seventh in the triple jump at Mexico City (1968) with a remarkable 16.89 m (55 ft 5 in) and continued to compete internationally until 1972. He was European Champion in 1958 and 1962.

Gold triple jump 1960, 1964

Takács, Károly (HUN)

B. Budapest, 21 Jan. 1910. Between 1929 and 1938 he shot right-handed; he was a member of the Hungarian national team which won the world title in Lucerne in 1939, having a year earlier lost his right hand in a hand-grenade explosion and having learned to shoot with his left.

Gold rapid-fire pistol 1948, 1952

Tewksbury, John Walter (USA)

B. Ashley, Pa., 21 Mar. 1876; d. Tunkhannock, Pa., 25 Apr. 1968. Brought the ability of a top-class sprinter to the rather underdeveloped 400-metres hurdles, previously thought of as a European speciality, beating the French favourite, Henri Tauzin, in 57.6 sec at the Paris Olympics of 1900. Seven days later Tewksbury won the 200-metres flat by 5 metres in 22.2 sec.

Gold 200 metres 1900; 400-metres hurdles 1900
Silver 60 metres 1900; 100 metres 1900

Károly Takács (HUN), 1956

Bronze 200-metres hurdles 1900

Theile, David (AUS)

B. Maryborough, Queensland, 17 Jan. 1938. Theile won the first of his two Olympic titles for 100-metres backstroke in a world-record time of 1 min 02.2 sec; his margin of victory, 3.0 sec over another Australian, John Monckton, was the greatest in this event in the history of the Games. Theile retained the Olympic title in 1 min 01.9 sec in 1960. After winning the Australian 110-yards backstroke title in 1955 and 1956 he studied medicine at the University of Queensland for two years, missing the British Commonwealth Games of 1958. He regained the national title from Monckton in 1959 and held it in 1960. He never had much success at distances over 100 metres.

Gold 100-metres backstroke 1956, 1960
Silver 4 × 100-metres medley relay 1960

Thorpe, Jim (USA)

B. Shawnee, Okla., 28 May 1888; d. Carlisle, Pa., 28 Mar. 1953. An Olympic legend, not only because of his prowess as an all-rounder, but also because he was disqualified from his 1912 Olympic decathlon and pentathlon victories when it was revealed that he had accepted small sums of money for playing holiday baseball three years before. An extraordinarily talented athlete, Thorpe was also fourth in the Olympic high jump and seventh in the long jump. His best individual performances included under 49 sec for 440 yards, the high hurdles in 15 sec, equalling the world record, and a high jump of 1.96 m (6 ft 5 in), only 1.6 cm (⅝ in) lower than the world record. Thorpe's total points score in the 1912 Stockholm Olympic decathlon, held over three days rather than the now compulsory two days, was not beaten for fifteen years.

Thunberg, Clas Arnold Robert (FIN)

B. Helsinki, 5 Apr. 1893; d. 28 Apr. 1973.

The world's outstanding speed skater of the 1920s. He would probably have won more than five Olympic medals had he decided to compete in 1932 but the Americans used the mass start style of racing, with which he and many other Europeans did not agree, so he did not go to the United States. In addition to many World and European Championships, he broke four world records, the first 42.8 sec for 500 metres in 1929 when he was thirty-five; the others were 42.6 sec for 500 metres, 1 min 28.4 sec for 1,000 metres and 5 min 19.2 sec for 3,000 metres. He adopted Paavo NURMI's attitude to his sport, training throughout the year. He was a man of tremendous will-power.

Gold 500 metres 1928, 1,500 metres 1924, 1928; 5,000 metres 1924; best all four distances 1924
Silver 10,000 metres 1924
Bronze 500 metres 1924

Timoshinin, Aleksandr (URS)

B. Moscow, 20 May, 1948. Timoshinin has had an unusual rowing career, encompassing two gold medals, yet apparently with only limited success in other events. In 1968 he was partnered by Anatoli Sass. Dropped from the Soviet team in 1969, he reappeared, with Edward Zhdanovich, to finish fourth in the 1970 World Championships. He was absent again in 1971, but in 1972 won the Diamond Sculls at Henley Royal Regatta, and then teamed up with Gennadi Korshikov, to win his second Olympic gold medal. In 1973 Timoshinin and Korshikov finished second in the European Championships. In 1974 they won the double sculls at Henley.

Gold double sculls 1968, 1972

Tolan, Eddie (USA)

B. Denver, Col., 29 Sept. 1908; d. Detroit, Mich., 31 Jan. 1967. He was the first man to be officially credited with a time of 9.5 sec for 100 yards – on 25 May 1929. Known as 'The Midnight Express', Tolan was short and stocky but had remarkably fast leg speed. In the 1932 American Olympic trials he was twice beaten by Ralph Metcalfe but two weeks later, when it really mattered, Tolan was the man in form. Film of the race indicates that Tolan won by 2.5 cm (an inch). In the 200-metres final Tolan set an Olympic record of 21.2 sec.

Gold 100 metres 1932; 200 metres 1932

Trentin, Pierre (FRA)

B. Créteil, 15 May 1944. A big, burly man, Trentin is a leather craftsman and found time between setting up and running his own business to become one of the world's leading cyclists. He began competing when he was fourteen. Three years later he was the French junior champion and then entered the track championships, more or less on a whim. He was a sprint finalist that year, twelve months later he won the bronze medal in the World Championship and again in 1963. Fighting to keep his weight down he nevertheless won three World cycling Championships in the following three years, reaching his peak in the rarefied atmosphere at Mexico (1968). There he set a world amateur record for the kilometre, 1 min 3.91 sec and was also successful on a tandem with Daniel MORELON.

Gold 1,000-metres time trial 1968; 2,000-metres tandem 1968
Bronze 1,000-metres time trial 1964; 1,000-metres sprint 1968

Tsuruta, Yoshiyuki (JPN)

B. Kagoshima Prefecture, 1 Oct. 1903. The only swimmer ever to have scored a double victory in Olympic breaststroke events. His time in 1928 was 2 min 48.8 sec which beat the Olympic record by the substantial margin of 7.8 sec and compared favourably with the world record of 2 min 48 sec set by the German Erich Rademacher in a 25-yard pool.

The following year Tsuruta set his only world record, 2 min 45 sec for 200-metres breaststroke in the 25-metre pool at Kyoto. His victory in the Los Angeles Games (1932) was part of the greatest Olympic performance by Japanese competitors.

Gold 200-metres breaststroke 1928, 1932

Tyus, Wyomia (USA)

B. Griffin, Ga., 29 Aug. 1945. The only athlete, male or female, to win an Olympic sprint title twice. At the 1964 Olympics she cut her personal record for 100 metres down by 0.3 sec in her heat when equalling the world record of 11.2 sec by Wilma RUDOLPH. In the 4 × 100-metres relay she ran the second stage for the US team which won the silver medals. She was still only twenty-three when she defended her title in 1968 and had meanwhile set an 11.1-sec world record for 100 metres. In the final she again lowered the world record, to 11 sec. In the 4 × 100-metres relay she anchored the US team for her third gold medal plus a world-record time of 42.8 sec. During her career she beat or equalled world records twice at 100 yards and four times at 100 metres.

Gold 100 metres 1964, 1968; 4 × 100-metres relay 1968
Silver 4 × 100-metres relay 1964

Väre, Eemeli Ernesti (FIN)

B. Kärkölä, 28 Sept. 1885; d. Kärkölä, 31 Jan. 1974. He became interested in wrestling at the beginning of the century in St Petersburg (now Leningrad), Russia, as he saw the performances of the world's best wrestlers in the local circuses. Training hard and developing new wrestling holds, he soon turned out to be one of the best of his period on the mat. In the middleweight class he won the World Championship in 1911 and a European Championship in 1912.

Gold wrestling Greco-Roman lightweight 1912, 1920

Virén, Lasse (FIN)

B. Myrskyla, 22 July 1949. With the 1,500-metres winner, Pekka Vasala, Virén revived the Finnish Olympic running supremacy at the Munich Games of 1972 by taking both the 5,000 metres (13 min 26.4 sec) and 10,000 metres (27 min 38.4 sec). In the longer race he survived a fall just before halfway and yet recovered to cover the final 800 metres in 1 min 56.2 sec, and beat the world record by one sec. He became only the fourth man in the history of the modern Olympics to win both these titles in one Games. This rather shy village policeman followed up his Olympic medals with a world record of 13 min 16.4 sec for 5,000 metres in 1972 to add just the right footnote to his racing style and zest.

Gold 5,000 metres 1972; 10,000 metres 1972

Walasiewicz, Stanisława (POL)

B. Wierzchownia, 11 Apr. 1911. Later known as Stella Walsh in the United States, where she was taken at the age of two, she held the world 200-metres record in athletics at 23.6 sec for sixteen years after starting competition in 1926. She was sixth in the 1932 Olympic discus event. She represented Poland in the 1946 European Championships, after winning over forty US titles, and ran 400 metres in 61.3 sec as late as 1960.

Gold 100 metres 1932
Silver 100 metres 1936

Weissmuller, Johnny (USA)

B. Windber, Pa., 2 June 1904. Until Mark SPITZ, Weissmuller was always the winner of ballots for 'the greatest swimmer ever'. The issue is still arguable. Weissmuller won three Olympic gold medals in 1924 and two more four years later. Five of Spitz's events were not on the Olympic program in those days and so Weissmuller might have a case for equal ranking with Spitz.

He was the physical prototype of the modern swimmer – 1.90 m (6 ft 3 in) with a strong, tapering frame. Weissmuller and his coach at the Illinois Athletic Club, William Bachrach, strove scientifically for the perfection of the American crawl. He rode higher in the water than any other swimmer of his day and his breathing pattern was unusual in its day, turning to either side and watching his opponents without interfering with his stroke, the main strength of which was the pull-in under the body.

Weissmuller swam about 500 yards a day in training, which would be derisory today. He won fifty-two US titles, had twenty-eight world records ratified, holding them from 100 yards to 880 yards freestyle inclusive and also for 150 yards backstroke.

His records were notable for their longevity. He began breaking world records at the age of seventeen. Perhaps his most celebrated one was 51 sec for the 100 yards which stood for seventeen years (at the age of thirty-six, as a professional, he covered the same distance in 48.5 sec). He was the first man to swim 100 metres in under a minute (58.6 sec in 1922); the first to beat five minutes for 440-yards freestyle (4 min 57 sec in 1923).

Weissmuller became the best-known of the screen Tarzans. Because of the reshowing of his best films on television Weissmuller is probably better known today than he was at the height of his swimming career.

Gold 100-metres freestyle 1924, 1928; 400-metres freestyle 1924; 4 × 200-metres freestyle relay 1924, 1928
Bronze water polo 1924

Johnny Weissmuller (USA), 1924

Wenden, Michael Vincent (AUS)

B. Liverpool, N.S.W., 17 Nov. 1949. Wenden's international career lasted from the British Commonwealth Games of 1966 to those of 1974. In all that time he was among the world's best front-crawl sprinters.

He broke his right leg in 1963 when jumping a fence and, unable to play football, turned to swimming, building up his right leg by use of isometric exercises. This aspect of his preparation for swimming developed and he became an apostle of land conditioning. His coach Vic Arneil shaped his frame by isometrics, Wenden's body being tapered from powerful shoulders to unusually slim legs. Though light in weight he had remarkable strength, a necessary attribute because of the 'windmill' stroke he employed.

He had six world records in his career, the highlight of which came at the Olympic Games of 1968. Wenden was reputed to have trained up to 15,000 metres a day before the Games and such unprecedented work for a sprinter paid off in the defeat of the Americans. He won the 100-metres freestyle in a world record of 52.2 sec and the 200-metres freestyle in 1 min 55.2 sec defeating the holder of the world record, the remarkable Don SCHOLLANDER.

Gold 100-metres freestyle 1968; 200-metres freestyle 1968
Silver 4 × 200-metres freestyle relay 1968
Bronze 4 × 100-metres freestyle relay 1968

Westergren, Carl (SWE)

B. Malmö, 13 Oct. 1895; d. 5 Aug. 1958. He began wrestling in 1911 and was World Champion in middleweight A in 1922, European Champion in middleweight B in 1925 and in heavyweight in 1930–1. He took part in the Olympic Games in 1920, 1924, 1928 and 1932; his speciality was the backhammer and he invented the 'Westergren roll'.

Gold wrestling Greco-Roman middleweight A 1920; middleweight B (light heavyweight) 1924; heavyweight 1932

White, Albert C. (USA)

B. Oakland, Calif., 14 May 1895. White was the first diver to win springboard and highboard titles at the same Olympic Games, 1924. A member of Stanford University school, whose students took all the men's diving medals at the 1924 Games, he has been honoured by the Swimming Hall of Fame at Fort Lauderdale, Fla. He never lost a lowboard diving contest in the United States.

Gold springboard diving 1924, highboard diving 1924

Whitfield, Malvin G. (USA)

B. Bay City, Tex., 11 Oct. 1924. With beautiful style – his favourite burst in the third 200 metres of two-lap races made him look as though he was running downhill – and his brilliant competitive record, Whitfield was the world's best over 800 metres for six years. Between June 1948 and June 1954 he suffered only two defeats, both in early season. Though he set world records for both 880 yards (1 min 48.6 sec) and 1,000 metres (2 min 20.8 sec), he was much more concerned about winning than times. Only one hour after his kilometre world record he set an American record of 46.2 sec for 440 yards. His range, greater than that of any other runner of his time, covered 10.7 sec for 100 metres to 4 min 12.6 sec for the mile. In 1948 he won the American Olympic trials at both 400 and 800 metres on the same day. In the Wembley 800-metres final he set an Olympic record of 1 min 49.2 sec. He retired in 1956 after failing to qualify for the US team for Melbourne.

Gold 800 metres 1948, 1952; 4 × 400-metres relay 1948
Silver 4 × 400-metres relay 1952
Bronze 400 metres 1948

Wigger, Lones W., Jr (USA)

B. Great Falls, Mont., 25 Aug. 1937. A major in the US Army, Wigger is the only American to win Olympic gold medals in the 50-metre three-position smallbore rifle and in the 300-metre free rifle. He began

shooting on his family's Montana ranch.

Gold smallbore rifle, three positions 1964; free rifle 1972
Silver smallbore rifle, prone 1964

Williams, Percy (CAN)

B. Vancouver, 19 May 1908. His double sprint victory at Amsterdam, when he was only twenty, was surprising to those who did not appreciate that he had won the Canadian trials in 10.6 sec. In the Olympic 100-metres final there were three false starts before Williams was away fastest and kept the lead to win in 10.8 sec; in the 200 metres he pulled away in the last 30 metres to win in 21.8 sec. On 9 August 1930 he set an official time of 10.3 sec for the 100 metres.

Gold 100 metres 1928; 200 metres 1928

Winkler, Hans Günter (GER)

B. Wuppertal-Barmen, 24 July 1926. He won more gold medals for show jumping than any other rider. His individual triumph and first team medal was at Stockholm in 1956, riding his famous mare Halla, only four years after his international début. He wrenched a riding muscle in the first round and rode the second, without fault, in considerable pain.

He won the World Championship in 1954 and retained it the next year, each time on Halla. In European Championship contests he has won once, been second once and third three times.

Gold show jumping (individual) 1956, (team) 1956, 1960, 1964, 1972
Bronze show jumping (team) 1968

Zátopek, Emil (TCH)

B. Koprivnice, Moravia, 19 Sept. 1922. Zátopek will always be remembered in Olympic history for his three victories in the 5,000 metres (14 min 06.6 sec), 10,000 metres (29 min 17.0 sec) and marathon (2 hr 23 min 03.2 sec) at Helsinki (1952). It was his first marathon. Zátopek was the father of the rugged school of modern interval training, the logical successor to NURMI but a man who relied on shattering mid-race surges rather than level-pace running to beat the opposition. He caught the imagination with facial grimaces and contorted upper body and was capable of a withering final burst as he showed with a last lap of 58.1 sec in the Helsinki 5,000 metres. He was unbeaten over 10,000 metres between 1948 and 1954, a total of thirty-eight consecutive victories, and broke all world records between 5,000 and 30,000 metres. He was the first man to beat 29 min for the 10,000 metres and to run more than 20,000 metres in one hour. He loved the Olympics and his fellow men and in return was one of the most popular of all Olympic champions. His wife Dana was Olympic javelin champion in 1952.

Gold 10,000 metres 1948, 1952; 5,000 metres 1952; marathon 1952
Silver 5,000 metres 1948

The following statistics relate to events currently in the Olympic program. For these records we have drawn on many sources including the Official Reports, the records of the International Sports Federations and of many National Olympic Committees. In the early Games, the times and distances were not always recorded. There was no Official Report of the Paris Games in 1900 and there is controversy over the records of many of the events. No Official Report of the Antwerp Games in 1920 was produced immediately after the Games. The Belgian Olympic Committee compiled one in 1959 from its archives.

The following official Olympic abbreviations have been used for the names of countries in this section:

AFG	Afghanistan	GER	German Federal
AHO	Netherlands		Republic (Germany
	Antilles		until 1968)
ALB	Albania	GHA	Ghana
ALG	Algeria	GRE	Greece
ARG	Argentina	GUA	Guatemala
ARS	Saudi Arabia	GUI	Guinea
AUS	Australia	GUY	Guyana
	(or Australasia,	HAI	Haiti
	representing a	HBR	British Honduras
	combined team	HKG	Hong Kong
	from Australia	HOL	Netherlands
	and New Zealand,	HON	Honduras
	in the years up to	HUN	Hungary
	and including 1912)	INA	Indonesia
AUT	Austria	IND	India
BAH	Bahamas	IRL	Ireland
BAR	Barbados	IRN	Iran
BEL	Belgium	IRQ	Iraq
BER	Bermuda	ISL	Iceland
BIR	Burma	ISR	Israel
BOL	Bolivia	ITA	Italy
BRA	Brazil	ISV	Virgin Islands
BUL	Bulgaria	JAM	Jamaica
CAF	Central Africa	JOR	Jordan
CAN	Canada	JPN	Japan
CEY	Ceylon	KEN	Kenya
	(up to 1972)	KHM	Cambodia
CGO	Congo Republic	KOR	South Korea
CHA	Chad	KUW	Kuwait
CHI	Chile	LBA	Libya
CIV	Ivory Coast	LBR	Liberia
CMR	Cameroon Republic	LES	Lesotho
COK	Congo Kinshasa	LIB	Lebanon
COL	Colombia	LIE	Liechtenstein
CRC	Costa Rica	LUX	Luxembourg
CUB	Cuba	MAD	Madagascar
DAH	Dahomey	MAL	Malaysia
DEN	Denmark	MAR	Morocco
DOM	Dominican Republic	MAW	Malawi
ECU	Ecuador	MEX	Mexico
EGY	Egypt (or United	MGL	Mongolia
	Arab Republic)	MLI	Mali
ESP	Spain	MLT	Malta
ETH	Ethiopia	MON	Monaco
FIJ	Fiji	MRI	Mauritius
FIN	Finland	NCA	Nicaragua
FRA	France	NEP	Nepal
GAB	Gabon	NGR	Nigeria
GBR	Great Britain	NIG	Niger
GDR	German Democratic	NOR	Norway
	Republic 1968 on	NZL	New Zealand

PAK	Pakistan	SWE	Sweden
PAN	Panama	SWZ	Swaziland
PAR	Paraguay	SYR	Syria
PER	Peru	TAN	Tanzania
PHI	Philippines	TCH	Czechoslovákia
POL	Poland	THA	Thailand
POR	Portugal	TOG	Togoland
PRK	North Korea	TRI	Trinidad and
PUR	Puerto Rica		Tobago
RHO	Rhodesia	TUN	Tunisia
ROM	Romania	TUR	Turkey
SAL	El Salvador	UGA	Uganda
SEN	Senegal	URS	USSR
SIN	Singapore	URU	Uruguay
SLE	Sierra Leone	USA	United States of
SMR	San Marino		America
SOM	Somali Republic	VEN	Venezuela
SRI	Sri Lanka	VNM	Viet Nam
	(formerly Ceylon)	VOL	Upper Volta
SUD	Sudan	YUG	Yugoslavia
SUI	Switzerland	ZAI	Zaire
SUR	Surinam	ZAM	Zambia

Other abbreviations for countries used in this section are:

ANT	Antilles	LIT	Lithuania
	(West Indies)	RUS	(Tsarist) Russia
BOH	Bohemia	SAF	South Africa
ENG	England	SCO	Scotland
EST	Estonia	WAL	Wales
LAT	Latvia		

A few other usages need elucidation. We spell all personal names as the owner would himself, complete with accents. Transliteration from Cyrillic follows recommended current Anglo-American practice. We have not been consistent in the presentation of married women's names, generally preferring to follow the system used in the competitor's country of origin since her name is generally known in that form. (This may be married name only, maiden name followed by married name, with or without a hyphen, or married name followed by maiden name, with or without a hyphen. Another convention adopted here is to show the maiden name in parentheses.) The official results of the Olympic Games are today recorded using the metric system, although in the early years some events were first recorded in feet and inches and pounds. As far as possible, we have gone back to the results as originally recorded. For the conversion of metric measurements into feet and inches and pounds (and *vice versa*) we have used the *Metric Conversion Tables* compiled by Bob Sparks and Charles Elliott (Arena Publications Ltd), officially approved by the International Amateur Athletic Federation, and *Cassell's Concise Conversion Tables* by Stephen Naft and Ralph de Sola, revised by P. H. Bigg. Conversion factors: 1 inch = 0.0254 metre; 1 pound avoirdupois = 0.45359 kilogram (British Standard 350).

The abbreviations used in measurements follow British Standard 350. Other abbreviations used are: flts faults; pts points; nda no data available.

	Gold	Silver	Bronze

Approximate Metric Guide

1 metre (m)	3ft 3½in
100m	109yd 1ft 1in
200m	218yd 2ft 2in
400m	437yd 1ft 4in
800m	874yd 2ft 8in
1,000m	1,093yd 1ft 10in
1,500m	1,640yd 1ft 3in
1609.3m	1 mile
3,000m	1 mile 1,520yd 2ft 6in
5,000m	3 miles 188yd 0ft 2in
10,000m (10km)	6 miles 376yd 0ft 4in
15km	9 miles 564yd 0ft 9in
20km	12 miles 752yd 0ft 8in
30km	18 miles 1,130yd 1ft 0in
50km	31 miles 119yd 2ft 10in

Archery *Men*

Double Men's International Round (36 arrows each at 90, 70, 50 and 30 metres). Not held before 1972.

	Gold	Silver	Bronze
1972	J. Williams *USA* 2,528 pts	G. Jervill *SWE* 2,481 pts	K. Laasonen *FIN* 2,467 pts

Archery *Women*

Double Women's International Round (36 arrows each at 70, 60, 50 and 30 metres). Not held before 1972.

	Gold	Silver	Bronze
1972	D. Wilber *USA* 2,424 pts	I. Szydłowska *POL* 2,407 pts	E. Gapchenko *URS* 2,403 pts

Association Football

Not held before 1900.

	Gold	Silver	Bronze
1900	GBR	FRA	BEL
1904	CAN	USA	USA
1908	GBR	DEN	HOL
1912	GBR	DEN	HOL
1920	BEL	ESP	HOL
1924	URU	SUI	SWE
1928	URU	ARG	ITA
1932	*Not held*		
1936	ITA	AUT	NOR
1948	SWE	YUG	DEN
1952	HUN	YUG	SWE
1956	URS	YUG	BUL
1960	YUG	DEN	HUN
1964	HUN	TCH	GER
1968	HUN	BUL	JPN
1972	POL	HUN	GDR & URS

Athletics *Men*

100 Metres

	Gold	Silver	Bronze
1896	T. Burke *USA* 12.0sec	F. Hofmann *GER* 12.2sec	A. Szokolyi *HUN* 12.6sec
1900	F. Jarvis *USA* 11.0sec	J. W. Tewksbury *USA* 11.1sec	S. Rowley *AUS* 11.2sec
1904	A. Hahn *USA* 11.0sec	N. Cartmell *USA* 11.2sec	W. Hogenson *USA* 11.2sec
1908	R. Walker *SAF* 10.8sec	J. Rector *USA* 10.9sec	R. Kerr *CAN* 11.0sec
1912	R. Craig *USA* 10.8sec	A. Meyer *USA* 10.9sec	D. Lippincott *USA* 10.9sec
1920	C. Paddock *USA* 10.8sec	M. Kirksey *USA* 10.8sec	H. Edward *GBR* 11.9sec
1924	H. Abrahams *GBR* 10.6sec	J. Scholz *USA* 10.7sec	A. Porritt *NZL* 10.8sec
1928	P. Williams *CAN* 10.8sec	J. London *GBR* 10.9sec	G. Lammers *GER* 10.9sec
1932	E. Tolan *USA* 10.3sec	R. Metcalfe *USA* 10.3sec	A. Jonath *GER* 10.4sec
1936	J. Owens *USA* 10.3sec	R. Metcalfe *USA* 10.4sec	M. Osendarp *HOL* 10.5sec
1948	H. Dillard *USA* 10.3sec	H. N. Ewell *USA* 10.4sec	L. La Beach *PAN* 10.4sec
1952	L. Remigino *USA* 10.4sec	H. McKenley *JAM* 10.4sec	E. M. Bailey *GBR* 10.4sec
1956	B. Morrow *USA* 10.5sec	W. T. Baker *USA* 10.5sec	H. Hogan *AUS* 10.6sec
1960	A. Hary *GER* 10.2sec	D. Sime *USA* 10.2sec	P. Radford *GBR* 10.3sec
1964	R. Hayes *USA* 10.0sec	E. Figuerola *CUB* 10.2sec	H. Jerome *CAN* 10.2sec
1968	J. Hines *USA* 9.9sec	L. Miller *JAM* 10.0sec	C. Greene *USA* 10.0sec
1972	V. Borzov *URS* 10.14sec	R. Taylor *USA* 10.24sec	L. Miller *JAM* 10.33sec

200 Metres

Not held before 1900.

	Gold	Silver	Bronze
1900	J. W. Tewksbury *USA* 22.2sec	N. Pritchard *IND* 22.8sec	S. Rowley *AUS* 22.9sec
1904	A. Hahn *USA* 21.6sec	N. Cartmell *USA* 21.9sec	W. Hogenson *USA* nda
1908	R. Kerr *CAN* 22.6sec	R. Cloughen *USA* 22.6sec	N. Cartmell *USA* 22.7sec
1912	R. Craig *USA* 21.7sec	D. Lippincott *USA* 21.8sec	W. Applegarth *GBR* 22.0sec
1920	A. Woodring *USA* 22.0sec	C. Paddock *USA* 22.1sec	H. Edward *GBR* 22.2sec
1924	J. Scholz *USA* 21.6sec	C. Paddock *USA* 21.7sec	E. Liddell *GBR* 21.9sec

	Gold	Silver	Bronze
1928	P. Williams *CAN* 21.8sec	W. Rangeley *GBR* 21.9sec	H. Körnig *GER* 21.9sec
1932	E. Tolan *USA* 21.2sec	G. Simpson *USA* 21.4sec	R. Metcalfe *USA* 21.5sec
1936	J. Owens *USA* 20.7sec	M. Robinson *USA* 21.1sec	M. Osendarp *HOL* 21.3sec
1948	M. Patton *USA* 21.1sec	H. N. Ewell *USA* 21.1sec	L. La Beach *PAN* 21.2sec
1952	A. Stanfield *USA* 20.7sec	W. T. Baker *USA* 20.8sec	J. Gathers *USA* 20.8sec
1956	B. Morrow *USA* 20.6sec	A. Stanfield *USA* 20.7sec	W. T. Baker *USA* 20.9sec
1960	L. Berutti *ITA* 20.5sec	L. Carney *USA* 20.6sec	A. Seye *FRA* 20.7sec
1964	H. Carr *USA* 20.3sec	P. Drayton *USA* 20.5sec	E. Roberts *TRI* 20.6sec
1968	T. Smith *USA* 19.8sec	P. Norman *AUS* 20.0sec	J. Carlos *USA* 20.0sec
1972	V. Borzov *URS* 20.00sec	L. Black *USA* 20.19sec	P. Mennea *ITA* 20.30sec

400 Metres

In 1908 a re-run was ordered after J. C. Carpenter USA was disqualified in the final. Halswelle was the only competitor.

	Gold	Silver	Bronze
1896	T. Burke *USA* 54.2sec	H. Jamison *USA* 55.2sec	F. Hofmann *GER* nda
1900	M. Long *USA* 49.4sec	W. Holland *USA* 49.6sec	E. Schultz *DEN* 15yd behind
1904	H. Hillman *USA* 49.2sec	F. Waller *USA* 49.9sec	H. Groman *USA* 50.0sec
1908	W. Halswelle *GBR* 50.0sec		
1912	C. Reidpath *USA* 48.2sec	H. Braun *GER* 48.3sec	E. Lindberg *USA* 48.4sec
1920	B. Rudd *SAF* 49.6sec	G. Butler *GBR* 49.9sec	N. Engdahl *SWE* 50.0sec
1924	E. Liddell *GBR* 47.6sec	H. Fitch *USA* 48.4sec	G. Butler *GBR* 48.6sec
1928	R. Barbuti *USA* 47.8sec	J. Ball *CAN* 48.0sec	J. Büchner *GER* 48.2sec
1932	W. Carr *USA* 46.2sec	B. Eastman *USA* 46.4sec	A. Wilson *CAN* 47.4sec
1936	A. Williams *USA* 46.5sec	A. G. Brown *GBR* 46.7sec	J. LuValle *USA* 46.8sec
1948	A. Wint *JAM* 46.2sec	H. McKenley *JAM* 46.4sec	M. Whitfield *USA* 46.9sec
1952	G. Rhoden *JAM* 45.9sec	H. McKenley *JAM* 45.9sec	O. Matson *USA* 46.8sec
1956	C. Jenkins *USA* 46.7sec	K. F. Haas *GER* 46.8sec	V. Hellsten *FIN* & A. Ignatiev *URS* 47.0sec
1960	O. Davis *USA* 44.9sec	C. Kaufmann *GER* 44.9sec	M. Spence *SAF* 45.5sec
1964	M. Larrabee *USA* 45.1sec	W. Mottley *TRI* 45.2sec	A. Badeński *POL* 45.6sec
1968	L. Evans *USA* 43.8sec	L. James *USA* 43.9sec	R. Freeman *USA* 44.4sec
1972	V. Matthews *USA* 44.66sec	W. Collett *USA* 44.80sec	J. Sang *KEN* 44.92sec

800 Metres

	Gold	Silver	Bronze
1896	E. Flack *AUS* 2min 11.0sec	N. Dáni *HUN* 2min 11.8sec	D. Golemis *GRE* nda
1900	A. Tysoe *GBR* 2min 01.2sec	J. Cregan *USA* 2min 03.0sec	D. Hall *USA* nda
1904	J. Lightbody *USA* 1min 56.0sec	H. Valentine *USA* 1min 56.3sec	E. Breitkreutz *USA* 1min 56.4sec
1908	M. Sheppard *USA* 1min 52.8sec	E. Lunghi *ITA* 1min 54.2sec	H. Braun *GER* 1min 55.2sec
1912	J. Meredith *USA* 1min 51.9sec	M. Sheppard *USA* 1min 52.0sec	I. Davenport *USA* 1min 52.0sec
1920	A. Hill *GBR* 1min 53.4sec	E. Eby *USA* 1min 53.6sec	B. Rudd *SAF* 1min 54.0sec
1924	D. Lowe *GBR* 1min 52.4sec	P. Martin *SUI* 1min 52.6sec	S. Enck *USA* 1min 53.0sec
1928	D. Lowe *GBR* 1min 51.8sec	E. Byléhn *SWE* 1min 52.8sec	H. Engelhard *GER* 1min 53.2sec
1932	T. Hampson *GBR* 1min 49.7sec	A. Wilson *CAN* 1min 49.9sec	P. Edwards *CAN* 1min 51.5sec
1936	J. Woodruff *USA* 1min 52.9sec	M. Lanzi *ITA* 1min 53.3sec	P. Edwards *CAN* 1min 53.6sec
1948	M. Whitfield *USA* 1min 49.2sec	A. Wint *JAM* 1min 49.5sec	M. Hansenne *FRA* 1min 49.8sec
1952	M. Whitfield *USA* 1min 49.2sec	A. Wint *JAM* 1min 49.4sec	H. Ulzheimer *GER* 1min 49.7sec
1956	T. Courtney *USA* 1min 47.7sec	D. Johnson *GBR* 1min 47.8sec	A. Boysen *NOR* 1min 48.1sec
1960	P. Snell *NZL* 1min 46.3sec	R. Moens *BEL* 1min 46.5sec	G. Kerr *JAM* 1min 47.1sec

	Gold	Silver	Bronze
1964	P. Snell *NZL* 1min 45.1sec	W. Crothers *CAN* 1min 45.6sec	W. Kiprugut *KEN* 1min 45.9sec
1968	R. Doubell *AUS* 1min 44.3sec	W. Kiprugut *KEN* 1min 44.5sec	T. Farrell *USA* 1min 45.4sec
1972	D. Wottle *USA* 1min 45.9sec	Y. Arzhanov *URS* 1min 45.9sec	M. Boit *KEN* 1min 46.0sec

1,500 Metres

	Gold	Silver	Bronze
1896	E. Flack *AUS* 4min 33.2sec	A. Blake *USA* 4min 35.4sec	A. Lermusiaux *FRA* 4min 36.0sec
1900	C. Bennett *GBR* 4min 06.2sec	H. Deloge *FRA* 4min 06.6sec	J. Bray *USA* 4min 07.2sec
1904	J. Lightbody *USA* 4min 05.4sec	F. Verner *USA* 4min 06.8sec	L. Hearn *USA* nda
1908	M. Sheppard *USA* 4min 03.4sec	H. Wilson *GBR* 4min 03.6sec	N. Hallows *GBR* 4min 04.0sec
1912	A. Jackson *GBR* 3min 56.8sec	A. Kiviat *USA* 3min 56.9sec	N. Taber *USA* 3min 56.9sec
1920	A. Hill *GBR* 4min 01.8sec	P. Baker *GBR* 4min 02.4sec	L. Shields *USA* 4min 03.1sec
1924	P. Nurmi *FIN* 3min 53.6sec	W. Schärer *SUI* 3min 55.0sec	H. Stallard *GBR* 3min 55.6sec
1928	H. Larva *FIN* 3min 53.2sec	J. Ladoumègue *FRA* 3min 53.8sec	E. Purje *FIN* 3min 56.4sec
1932	L. Beccali *ITA* 3min 51.2sec	J. Cornes *GBR* 3min 52.6sec	P. Edwards *CAN* 3min 52.8sec
1936	J. Lovelock *NZL* 3min 47.8sec	G. Cunningham *USA* 3min 48.4sec	L. Beccali *ITA* 3min 49.2sec
1948	H. Eriksson *SWE* 3min 49.8sec	L. Strand *SWE* 3min 50.4sec	W. Slijkhuis *HOL* 3min 50.4sec
1952	J. Barthel *LUX* 3min 45.1sec	R. McMillen *USA* 3min 45.2sec	W. Lueg *GER* 3min 45.4sec
1956	R. Delany *IRL* 3min 41.2sec	K. Richtzenhain *GER* 3min 42.0sec	J. Landy *AUS* 3min 42.0sec
1960	H. Elliott *AUS* 3min 35.6sec	M. Jazy *FRA* 3min 38.4sec	I. Rózsavölgyi *HUN* 3min 39.2sec
1964	P. Snell *NZL* 3min 38.1sec	J. Odložil *TCH* 3min 39.6sec	J. Davies *NZL* 3min 39.6sec
1968	K. Keino *KEN* 3min 34.9sec	J. Ryun *USA* 3min 37.8sec	B. Tümmler *GER* 3min 39.0sec
1972	P. Vasala *FIN* 3min 36.3sec	K. Keino *KEN* 3min 36.8sec	R. Dixon *NZL* 3min 37.5sec

5,000 Metres

Not held before 1912.

	Gold	Silver	Bronze
1912	H. Kolehmainen *FIN* 14min 36.6sec	J. Bouin *FRA* 14min 36.7sec	G. Hutson *GBR* 15min 07.6sec
1920	J. Guillemot *FRA* 14min 55.6sec	P. Nurmi *FIN* 15min 00.0sec	E. Backman *SWE* 15min 13.0sec
1924	P. Nurmi *FIN* 14min 31.2sec	V. Ritola *FIN* 14min 31.4sec	E. Wide *SWE* 15min 01.8sec
1928	V. Ritola *FIN* 14min 38.0sec	P. Nurmi *FIN* 14min 40.0sec	E. Wide *SWE* 14min 41.2sec
1932	L. Lehtinen *FIN* 14min 30.0sec	R. Hill *USA* 14min 30.0sec	L. Virtanen *FIN* 14min 44.0sec
1936	G. Höckert *FIN* 14min 22.2sec	L. Lehtinen *FIN* 14min 25.8sec	H. Jonsson *SWE* 14min 29.0sec
1948	G. Rieff *BEL* 14min 17.6sec	E. Zátopek *TCH* 14min 17.8sec	W. Slijkhuis *HOL* 14min 26.8sec
1952	E. Zátopek *TCH* 14min 06.6sec	A. Mimoun *FRA* 14min 07.4sec	H. Schade *GER* 14min 08.6sec
1956	V. Kuts *URS* 13min 39.6sec	G. Pirie *GBR* 13min 50.6sec	D. Ibbotson *GBR* 13min 54.4sec
1960	M. Halberg *NZL* 13min 43.4sec	H. Grodotzki *GER* 13min 44.6sec	K. Zimny *POL* 13min 44.8sec
1964	R. Schul *USA* 13min 48.8sec	H. Norpoth *GER* 13min 49.6sec	W. Dellinger *USA* 13min 49.8sec
1968	M. Gammoudi *TUN* 14min 05.0sec	K. Keino *KEN* 14min 05.2sec	N. Temu *KEN* 14min 06.4sec
1972	L. Virén *FIN* 13min 26.4sec	M. Gammoudi *TUN* 13min 27.4sec	I. Stewart *GBR* 13min 27.6sec

10,000 Metres

Not held before 1912.

	Gold	Silver	Bronze
1912	H. Kolehmainen *FIN* 31min 20.8sec	L. Tewanima *USA* 32min 06.6sec	A. Stenroos *FIN* 32min 21.8sec
1920	P. Nurmi *FIN* 31min 45.8sec	J. Guillemot *FRA* 31min 47.2sec	J. Wilson *GBR* 31min 50.8sec
1924	V. Ritola *FIN* 30min 23.2sec	E. Wide *SWE* 30min 55.2sec	E. Berg *FIN* 31min 43.0sec
1928	P. Nurmi *FIN* 30min 18.8sec	V. Ritola *FIN* 30min 19.4sec	E. Wide *SWE* 31min 00.8sec
1932	J. Kusociński *POL* 30min 11.4sec	V. Iso-Hollo *FIN* 30min 12.6sec	L. Virtanen *FIN* 30min 35.0sec
1936	I. Salminen *FIN* 30min 15.4sec	A. Askola *FIN* 30min 15.6sec	V. Iso-Hollo *FIN* 30min 20.2sec
1948	E. Zátopek *TCH* 29min 59.6sec	A. Mimoun *FRA* 30min 47.4sec	B. Albertsson *SWE* 30min 53.6sec
1952	E. Zátopek *TCH* 29min 17.0sec	A. Mimoun *FRA* 29min 32.8sec	A. Anufriev *URS* 29min 48.2sec

	Gold	Silver	Bronze
1956	V. Kuts *URS* 28min 45.6sec	J. Kovács *HUN* 28min 52.4sec	A. Lawrence *AUS* 28min 53.6sec
1960	P. Bolotnikov *URS* 28min 32.2sec	H. Grodotzki *GER* 28min 37.0sec	D. Power *AUS* 28min 38.2sec
1964	B. Mills *USA* 28min 24.4sec	M. Gammoudi *TUN* 28min 24.8sec	R. Clarke *AUS* 28min 25.8sec
1968	N. Temu *KEN* 29min 27.4sec	M. Wolde *ETH* 29min 28.0sec	M. Gammoudi *TUN* 29min 34.2sec
1972	L. Virén *FIN* 27min 38.4sec	E. Puttemans *BEL* 27min 39.6sec	M. Yifter *ETH* 27min 41.0sec

Marathon

The standard distance of 42,195m (26 miles 385yd) was established in 1908 and has been retained since 1924. In other years the distance has varied.

	Gold	Silver	Bronze
1896	S. Louis *GRE* 2hr 58min 50.0sec	C. Vasilakos *GRE* 3hr 06min 03.0sec	G. Kellner *HUN* 3hr 06min 35.0sec
1900	M. Theato *FRA* 2hr 59min 45.0sec	E. Champion *FRA* 3hr 04min 17.0sec	E. Fast *SWE* 3hr 37min 14.0sec
1904	T. Hicks *USA* 3hr 28min 53.0sec	A. Corey *USA* 3hr 34min 52.0sec	A. Newton *USA* 3hr 47min 33.0sec
1908	J. Hayes *USA* 2hr 55min 18.4sec	C. Hefferon *SAF* 2hr 56min 06.0sec	J. Forshaw *USA* 2hr 57min 10.4sec
1912	K. McArthur *SAF* 2hr 36min 54.8sec	C. Gitsham *SAF* 2hr 37min 52.0sec	G. Strobino *USA* 2hr 38min 42.4sec
1920	H. Kolehmainen *FIN* 2hr 32min 35.8sec	Y. Lossman *EST* 2hr 32min 48.6sec	V. Arri *ITA* 2hr 36min 32.8sec
1924	A. Stenroos *FIN* 2hr 41min 22.6sec	R. Bertini *ITA* 2hr 47min 19.6sec	C. DeMar *USA* 2hr 48min 14.0sec
1928	M. El Ouafi *FRA* 2hr 32min 57.0sec	M. Plaza *CHI* 2hr 33min 23.0sec	M. Marttelin *FIN* 2hr 35min 02.0sec
1932	J. Zabala *ARG* 2hr 31min 36.0sec	S. Ferris *GBR* 2hr 31min 55.0sec	A. Toivonen *FIN* 2hr 32min 12.0sec
1936	K. Son *JPN* 2hr 29min 19.2sec	E. Harper *GBR* 2hr 31min 23.2sec	S. Nan *JPN* 2hr 31min 42.0sec
1948	D. Cabrera *ARG* 2hr 34min 51.6sec	T. Richards *GBR* 2hr 35min 07.6sec	E. Gailly *BEL* 2hr 35min 33.6sec
1952	E. Zátopek *TCH* 2hr 23min 03.2sec	R. Gorno *ARG* 2hr 25min 35.0sec	G. Jansson *SWE* 2hr 26min 07.0sec
1956	A. Mimoun *FRA* 2hr 25min 00.0sec	F. Mihalič *YUG* 2hr 26min 32.0sec	V. Karvonen *FIN* 2hr 27min 47.0sec
1960	A. Bikila *ETH* 2hr 15min 16.2sec	R. Ben Abdesselem *MAR* 2hr 15min 41.6sec	B. Magee *NZL* 2hr 17min 18.2sec
1964	A. Bikila *ETH* 2hr 12min 11.2sec	B. Heatley *GBR* 2hr 16min 19.2sec	K. Tsuburaya *JPN* 2hr 16min 22.8sec
1968	M. Wolde *ETH* 2hr 20min 26.4sec	K. Kimihara *JPN* 2hr 23min 31.0sec	M. Ryan *NZL* 2hr 23min 45.0sec
1972	F. Shorter *USA* 2hr 12min 19.8sec	K. Lismont *BEL* 2hr 14min 31.8sec	M. Wolde *ETH* 2hr 15min 08.4sec

110 Metres Hurdles

In 1896 the distance was 100m (100yd 28ft).

	Gold	Silver	Bronze
1896	T. Curtis *USA* 17.6sec	G. Goulding *GBR* 17.7sec	
1900	A. Kraenzlein *USA* 15.4sec	J. McLean *USA* 15.5sec	F. Moloney *USA* nda
1904	F. Schule *USA* 16.0sec	T. Shideler *USA* 16.3sec	L. Ashburner *USA* 16.4sec
1908	F. Smithson *USA* 15.0sec	J. Garrels *USA* 5yd	A. Shaw *USA* nda
1912	F. Kelly *USA* 15.1sec	J. Wendell *USA* 15.2sec	M. Hawkins *USA* 15.3sec
1920	E. Thomson *CAN* 14.8sec	H. Barron *USA* 15.1sec	F. Murray *USA* 15.2sec
1924	D. Kinsey *USA* 15.0sec	S. Atkinson *SAF* 15.0sec	S. Pettersson *SWE* 15.4sec
1928	S. Atkinson *SAF* 14.8sec	S. Anderson *USA* 14.8sec	J. Collier *USA* 14.9sec
1932	G. Saling *USA* 14.6sec	P. Beard *USA* 14.7sec	D. Finlay *GBR* 14.8sec
1936	F. Towns *USA* 14.2sec	D. Finlay *GBR* 14.4sec	F. Pollard *USA* 14.4sec
1948	W. Porter *USA* 13.9sec	C. Scott *USA* 14.1sec	C. Dixon *USA* 14.1sec
1952	W. H. Dillard *USA* 13.7sec	J. Davis *USA* 13.7sec	A. Barnard *USA* 14.1sec
1956	L. Calhoun *USA* 13.5sec	J. Davis *USA* 13.5sec	J. Shankle *USA* 14.1sec
1960	L. Calhoun *USA* 13.8sec	W. May *USA* 13.8sec	H. Jones *USA* 14.0sec
1964	H. Jones *USA* 13.6sec	H. B. Lindgren *USA* 13.7sec	A. Mikhailov *URS* 13.7sec
1968	W. Davenport *USA* 13.3sec	E. Hall *USA* 13.4sec	E. Ottoz *ITA* 13.4sec
1972	R. Milburn *USA* 13.24sec	G. Drut *FRA* 13.34sec	T. Hill *USA* 13.48sec

400 Metres Hurdles

Not held before 1900.

	Gold	Silver	Bronze
1900	J. W. Tewksbury *USA* 57.6sec	H. Tausin *FRA* 58.3sec	G. Orton *CAN* nda
1904	H. Hillman *USA* 53.0sec	F. Waller *USA* 53.2sec	G. Poage *USA* nda
1908	C. Bacon *USA* 55.0sec	H. Hillman *USA* 55.3sec	L. Tremeer *GBR* 57.0sec
1912	*Not held*		
1920	F. Loomis *USA* 54.0sec	J. Norton *USA* 54.3sec	A. Desch *USA* 54.5sec
1924	F. M. Taylor *USA* 52.6sec	E. Vilén *FIN* 53.8sec	I. Riley *USA* 54.2sec
1928	Lord Burghley *GBR* 53.4sec	F. Cuhel *USA* 53.6sec	F. M. Taylor *USA* 53.6sec
1932	R. Tisdall *IRL* 51.7sec	G. Hardin *USA* 51.9sec	F. M. Taylor *USA* 52.0sec
1936	G. Hardin *USA* 52.4sec	J. Loaring *CAN* 52.7sec	M. White *PHI* 52.8sec
1948	R. Cochran *USA* 51.1sec	D. White *CEY* 51.8sec	R. Larsson *SWE* 52.2sec
1952	C. Moore *USA* 50.8sec	Y. Lituyev *URS* 51.3sec	J. Holland *NZL* 52.2sec
1956	G. Davis *USA* 50.1sec	E. Southern *USA* 50.8sec	J. Culbreath *USA* 51.6sec
1960	G. Davis *USA* 49.3sec	C. Cushman *USA* 49.6sec	R. Howard *USA* 49.7sec
1964	R. W. Cawley *USA* 49.6sec	J. Cooper *GBR* 50.1sec	S. Morale *ITA* 50.1sec
1968	D. Hemery *GBR* 48.1sec	G. Hennige *GER* 49.0sec	J. Sherwood *GBR* 49.0sec
1972	J. Akii-Bua *UGA* 47.82sec	R. Mann *USA* 48.51sec	D. Hemery *GBR* 48.52sec

3,000 Metres Steeplechase

Not held before 1900. In 1900 and 1904 the distance was 2,500m; in 1908 it was 3,200m. In 1932 the distance in the final was 3,460m due to an error on the part of an official.

	Gold	Silver	Bronze
1900	G. Orton *CAN* 7min 34.4sec	S. Robinson *GBR* 7min 38.0sec	J. Chastanié *FRA* nda
1904	J. Lightbody *USA* 7min 39.6sec	J. Daly *GBR/IRL* 7min 40.6sec	A. Newton *USA* 30yd
1908	A. Russell *GBR* 10min 47.8sec	A. Robertson *GBR* 10min 48.4sec	J. L. Eisele *USA* 11min 00.8sec
1912	*Not held*		
1920	P. Hodge *GBR* 10min 00.4sec	P. Flynn *USA* 100yd	E. Ambrosini *ITA* 130yd
1924	V. Ritola *FIN* 9min 33.6sec	E. Katz *FIN* 9min 44.0sec	P. Bontemps *FRA* 9min 45.2sec
1928	T. Loukola *FIN* 9min 21.8sec	P. Nurmi *FIN* 9min 31.2sec	O. Andersen *FIN* 9min 35.6sec
1932	V. Iso-Hollo *FIN* 10min 33.4sec	T. Evenson *GBR* 10min 46.0sec	J. McCluskey *USA* 10min 46.2sec
1936	V. Iso-Hollo *FIN* 9min 03.8sec	K. Tuominen *FIN* 9min 06.8sec	A. Dompert *GER* 9min 07.2sec
1948	T. Sjöstrand *SWE* 9min 04.6sec	E. Elmsäter *SWE* 9min 08.2sec	G. Hagström *SWE* 9min 11.8sec
1952	H. Ashenfelter *USA* 8min 45.4sec	V. Kazantsev *URS* 8min 51.6sec	J. Disley *GBR* 8min 51.8sec
1956	C. Brasher *GBR* 8min 41.2sec	S. Rozsnyói *HUN* 8min 43.6sec	E. Larsen *NOR* 8min 44.0sec
1960	Z. Krzyszkowiak *POL* 8min 34.2sec	N. Sokolov *URS* 8min 36.4sec	S. Rzhishchin *URS* 8min 42.2sec
1964	G. Roelants *BEL* 8min 30.8sec	M. Herriott *GBR* 8min 32.4sec	I. Belyaiev *URS* 8min 33.8sec
1968	A. Biwott *KEN* 8min 51.0sec	B. Kogo *KEN* 8min 51.6sec	G. Young *USA* 8min 51.8sec
1972	K. Keino *KEN* 8min 23.6sec	B. Jipcho *KEN* 8min 24.6sec	T. Kantanen *FIN* 8min 24.8sec

4 × 100 Metres Relay

Not held before 1912.

	Gold	Silver	Bronze
1912	GBR 42.4sec	SWE 42.6sec	
1920	USA 42.2sec	FRA 42.6sec	SWE 42.9sec
1924	USA 41.0sec	GBR 41.2sec	HOL 41.8sec
1928	USA 41.0sec	GER 41.2sec	GBR 41.8sec
1932	USA 40.0sec	GER 40.9sec	ITA 41.2sec
1936	USA 39.8sec	ITA 41.1sec	GER 41.2sec
1948	USA 40.6sec	GBR 41.3sec	ITA 41.5sec
1952	USA 40.1sec	URS 40.3sec	HUN 40.5sec
1956	USA 39.5sec	URS 39.8sec	GER 40.3sec
1960	GER 39.5sec	URS 40.1sec	GBR 40.2sec
1964	USA 39.0sec	POL 39.3sec	FRA 39.3sec
1968	USA 38.2sec	CUB 38.3sec	FRA 38.4sec
1972	USA 38.19sec	URS 38.50sec	GER 38.79sec

4 × 400 Metres Relay

Not held before 1912.

Year	Gold	Silver	Bronze
1912	USA 3min 16.6sec	FRA 3min 20.7sec	GBR 3min 23.2sec
1920	GBR 3min 22.2sec	SAF 3min 24.2sec	FRA 3min 24.8sec
1924	USA 3min 16.0sec	SWE 3min 17.0sec	GBR 3min 17.4sec
1928	USA 3min 14.2sec	GER 3min 14.8sec	CAN 3min 15.4sec
1932	USA 3min 08.2sec	GBR 3min 11.2sec	CAN 3min 12.8sec
1936	GBR 3min 09.0sec	USA 3min 11.2sec	GER 3min 11.8sec
1948	USA 3min 10.4sec	FRA 3min 14.8sec	SWE 3min 16.0sec
1952	JAM 3min 03.9sec	USA 3min 04.0sec	GER 3min 06.6sec
1956	USA 3min 04.8sec	AUS 3min 06.2sec	GBR 3min 07.2sec
1960	USA 3min 02.2sec	GER 3min 02.7sec	ANT 3min 04.0sec
1964	USA 3min 00.7sec	GBR 3min 01.6sec	TRI 3min 01.7sec
1968	USA 2min 56.1sec	KEN 2min 59.6sec	GER 3min 00.5sec
1972	KEN 2min 59.8sec	GBR 3min 00.5sec	FRA 3min 00.7sec

20 Kilometres Walk

Not held before 1956.

Year	Gold	Silver	Bronze
1956	L. Spirin *URS* 1hr 31min 27.4sec	A. Mikenas *URS* 1hr 32min 03.0sec	B. Yunk *URS* 1hr 32min 12.0sec
1960	V. Golubnichi *URS* 1hr 34min 07.2sec	N. Freeman *AUS* 1hr 34min 16.4sec	S. Vickers *GBR* 1hr 34min 56.4sec
1964	K. Matthews *GBR* 1hr 29min 34.0sec	D. Linder *GER* 1hr 31min 13.2sec	V. Golubnichi *URS* 1hr 31min 59.4sec
1968	V. Golubnichi *URS* 1hr 33min 58.4sec	J. Pedraza *MEX* 1hr 34min 00.0sec	N. Smaga *URS* 1hr 34min 03.4sec
1972	P. Frenkel *GDR* 1hr 26min 42.4sec	V. Golubnichi *URS* 1hr 26min 55.2sec	H. Reimann *GDR* 1hr 27min 16.6sec

50 Kilometres Walk

Not held before 1932.

Year	Gold	Silver	Bronze
1932	T. Green *GBR* 4hr 50min 10.0sec	J. Dalinsh *LAT* 4hr 57min 20.0sec	U. Frigerio *ITA* 4hr 59min 06.0sec
1936	H. Whitlock *GBR* 4hr 30min 41.1sec	A. Schwab *SUI* 4hr 32min 09.2sec	A. Bubenko *LAT* 4hr 32min 42.2sec
1948	J. Ljunggren *SWE* 4hr 41min 52.0sec	G. Godel *SUI* 4hr 48min 17.0sec	T. Johnson *GBR* 4hr 48min 31.0sec
1952	G. Dordoni *ITA* 4hr 28min 07.8sec	J. Doležal *TCH* 4hr 30min 17.8sec	A. Róka *HUN* 4hr 31min 27.2sec
1956	N. Read *NZL* 4hr 30min 42.8sec	Y. Maskinskov *URS* 4hr 32min 57.0sec	J. Ljunggren *SWE* 4hr 35min 02.0sec
1960	D. Thompson *GBR* 4hr 25min 30.0sec	J. Ljunggren *SWE* 4hr 25min 47.0sec	A. Pamich *ITA* 4hr 27min 55.4sec
1964	A. Pamich *ITA* 4hr 11min 12.4sec	P. Nihill *GBR* 4hr 11min 31.2sec	I. Pettersson *SWE* 4hr 14min 17.4sec
1968	C. Höhne *GDR* 4hr 20min 13.6sec	A. Kiss *HUN* 4hr 30min 17.0sec	L. Young *USA* 4hr 31min 55.4sec
1972	B. Kannenberg *GER* 3hr 56min 11.6sec	V. Soldatenko *URS* 3hr 58min 24.0sec	L. Young *USA* 4hr 00min 46.0sec

High Jump

Year	Gold	Silver	Bronze
1896	E. Clark *USA* 1.81m (5ft 11¼in)	J. Connolly *USA* 1.65m (5ft 5in)	R. Garrett *USA* 1.65m (5ft 5in)
1900	I. Baxter *USA* 1.90m (6ft 2¾in)	P. Leahy *GBR/IRL* 1.78m (5ft 10⅛in)	L. Gönczy *HUN* 1.75m (5ft 8⅞in)
1904	S. Jones *USA* 1.80m (5ft 11in)	G. P. Serviss *USA* 1.78m (5ft 10in)	P. Weinstein *GER* 1.78m (5ft 10in)
1908	H. Porter *USA* 1.90m (6ft 3in)	C. Leahy *GBR/IRL*, I. Somodi *HUN* & G. André *FRA* 1.88m (6ft 2in)	
1912	A. Richards *USA* 1.93m (6ft 4in)	H. Leische *GER* 1.91m (6ft 3¼in)	G. Horine *USA* 1.89m (6ft 2⅜in)
1920	R. Landon *USA* 1.94m (6ft 4⅜in)	H. Muller *USA* 1.90m (6ft 2¾in)	B. Ekelund *SWE* 1.90m (6ft 2¾in)
1924	H. Osborn *USA* 1.98m (6ft 6in)	L. Brown *USA* 1.95in (6ft 4¾in)	P. Lewden *FRA* 1.92m (6ft 3⅝in)
1928	R. King *USA* 1.94m (6ft 4⅜in)	B. Hedges *USA* 1.91m (6ft 3¼in)	C. Ménard *FRA* 1.91m (6ft 3¼in)
1932	D. McNaughton *CAN* 1.97m (6ft 5½in)	R. Van Osdel *USA* 1.97m (6ft 5½in)	S. Toribio *PHI* 1.97m (6ft 5½in)
1936	C. Johnson *USA* 2.03m (6ft 7⅞in)	D. Albritton *USA* 2.00m (6ft 6¾in)	D. Thurber *USA* 2.00m (6ft 6¾in)
1948	J. Winter *AUS* 1.98m (6ft 6in)	B. Paulsen *NOR* 1.95m (6ft 4¾in)	G. Stanich *USA* 1.95m (6ft 4¾in)
1952	W. Davis *USA* 2.04m (6ft 8⅜in)	K. Wiesner *USA* 2.01m (6ft 7⅛in)	J. Telles da Conceição *BRA* 1.98m (6ft 6in)
1956	C. Dumas *USA* 2.12m (6ft 11½in)	C. Porter *AUS* 2.10m (6ft 10⅝in)	I. Kashkarov *USA* 2.08m (6ft 9⅞in)
1960	R. Shavlakadze *URS* 2.16m (7ft 1⅛in)	V. Brumel *URS* 2.16m (7ft 1⅛in)	J. Thomas *USA* 2.14m (7ft 0¼in)
1964	V. Brumel *URS* 2.18m (7ft 1¾in)	J. Thomas *USA* 2.18m (7ft 1¾in)	J. Rambo *USA* 2.16m (7ft 1in)
1968	R. Fosbury *USA* 2.24m (7ft 4¼in)	E. Caruthers *USA* 2.22m (7ft 3½in)	V. Gavrilov *URS* 2.20m (7ft 2⅝in)
1972	Y. Tarmak *URS* 2.23m (7ft 3¾in)	S. Junge *GDR* 2.21m (7ft 3in)	D. Stones *USA* 2.21m (7ft 3in)

Long Jump

Year	Gold	Silver	Bronze
1896	E. Clark *USA* 6.35m (20ft 10in)	R. Garrett *USA* 6.18m (20ft 3¼in)	J. Connolly *USA* 6.11m (20ft 0½in)
1900	A. Kraenzlein *USA* 7.185m (23ft 6¾in)	M. Prinstein *USA* 7.17m (23ft 6½in)	P. Leahy *GBR* 6.95m (22ft 9½in)
1904	M. Prinstein *USA* 7.34m (24ft 1in)	D. Frank *USA* 6.89m (22ft 7¼in)	R. Stangland *USA* 6.88m (22ft 7in)
1908	F. Irons *USA* 7.48m (24ft 6½in)	D. Kelly *USA* 7.09m (23ft 3¼in)	C. Bricker *CAN* 7.08m (23ft 3in)
1912	A. Gutterson *USA* 7.60m (24ft 11¼in)	C. Bricker *CAN* 7.21m (23ft 7¾in)	G. Åberg *SWE* 7.18m (23ft 6¾in)
1920	W. Pettersson *SWE* 7.15m (23ft 5½in)	C. Johnson *USA* 7.09m (23ft 3¼in)	E. Abrahamsson *SWE* 7.08m (23ft 2¾in)
1924	W. D. H. Hubbard *USA* 7.44m (24ft 5in)	E. Gourdin *USA* 7.28m (23ft 10½in)	S. Hansen *NOR* 7.26m (23ft 9¾in)
1928	E. Hamm *USA* 7.73m (25ft 4½in)	S. Cator *HAI* 7.58m (24ft 10½in)	A. Bates *USA* 7.40m (24ft 3¼in)
1932	E. Gordon *USA* 7.64m (25ft 0¾in)	C. L. Redd *USA* 7.60m (24ft 11¼in)	C. Nambu *JPN* 7.45m (24ft 5¼in)
1936	J. Owens *USA* 8.06m (26ft 5¼in)	L. Long *GER* 7.87m (25ft 9¾in)	N. Tajima *JPN* 7.74m (25ft 4¾in)
1948	W. Steele *USA* 7.82m (25ft 8in)	T. Bruce *AUS* 7.55m (24ft 9¼in)	H. Douglas *USA* 7.54m (24ft 9in)
1952	J. Biffle *USA* 7.57m (24ft 10in)	M. Gourdine *USA* 7.53m (24ft 8½in)	O. Földessy *HUN* 7.30m (23ft 11½in)
1956	G. Bell *USA* 7.83m (25ft 8¼in)	J. Bennett *USA* 7.68m (25ft 2¼in)	J. Valkama *FIN* 7.48m (24ft 6½in)
1960	R. Boston *USA* 8.12m (26ft 7¾in)	I. Roberson *USA* 8.11m (26ft 7¼in)	I. Ter-Ovanesyan *URS* 8.04m (26ft 4½in)
1964	L. Davies *GBR* 8.07m (26ft 5¾in)	R. Boston *USA* 8.03m (26ft 4¼in)	I. Ter-Ovanesyan *URS* 7.99m (26ft 2¾in)
1968	R. Beamon *USA* 8.90m (29ft 2½in)	K. Beer *GDR* 8.19m (26ft 10½in)	R. Boston *USA* 8.16m (26ft 9¼in)
1972	R. Williams *USA* 8.24m (27ft 0½in)	H. Baumgärtner *GER* 8.18m (26ft 10in)	A. Robinson *USA* 8.03m (26ft 4¼in)

Triple Jump

Year	Gold	Silver	Bronze
1896	J. Connolly *USA* 13.71m (44ft 11¾in)	A. Tuffère *FRA* 12.70m (41ft 8in)	I. Persakis *GRE* 12.52m (41ft 1in)
1900	M. Prinstein *USA* 14.47m (47ft 5¾in)	J. Connolly *USA* 13.97m (45ft 10in)	L. P. Sheldon *USA* 13.64m (44ft 9in)
1904	M. Prinstein *USA* 14.35m (47ft 1in)	F. Englehardt *USA* 13.90m (45ft 7¼in)	R. Stangland *USA* 13.36m (43ft 10¼in)
1908	T. Ahearne *GBR/IRL* 14.91m (48ft 11¼in)	J. G. MacDonald *CAN* 14.76m (48ft 5¼in)	E. Larsen *NOR* 14.39m (47ft 2¾in)
1912	G. Lindblom *SWE* 14.76m (48ft 5in)	G. Åberg *SWE* 14.51m (47ft 7¼in)	E. Almlöf *SWE* 14.17m (46ft 5¾in)
1920	V. Tuulos *FIN* 14.50m (47ft 7in)	F. Jansson *SWE* 14.48m (47ft 6in)	E. Almlöf *SWE* 14.27m (46ft 10in)
1924	A. Winter *AUS* 15.52m (50ft 11¼in)	L. Bruneto *ARG* 15.42m (50ft 7¼in)	V. Tuulos *FIN* 15.37m (50ft 5in)
1928	M. Oda *JPN* 15.21m (49ft 10¾in)	L. Casey *USA* 15.17m (49ft 9¼in)	V. Tuulos *FIN* 15.11m (49ft 7in)
1932	C. Nambu *JPN* 15.72m (51ft 7in)	E. Svensson *SWE* 15.32m (50ft 3¼in)	K. Oshima *JPN* 15.12m (49ft 7¼in)
1936	N. Tajima *JPN* 16.00m (52ft 6in)	M. Harada *JPN* 15.66m (51ft 4½in)	J. P. Metcalfe *AUS* 15.50m (50ft 10¼in)
1948	A. Åhman *SWE* 15.40m (50ft 6¼in)	G. Avery *AUS* 15.37m (50ft 5in)	R. Sarialp *TUR* 15.02m (49ft 3½in)
1952	A. F. da Silva *BRA* 16.22m (53ft 2½in)	L. Shcherbakov *URS* 15.98m (52ft 5¼in)	A. Devonish *VEN* 15.52m (50ft 11in)
1956	A. F. da Silva *BRA* 16.35m (53ft 7¾in)	V. Einarsson *ISL* 16.26m (53ft 4¼in)	V. Kreyer *URS* 16.02m (52ft 6¾in)
1960	J. Szmidt *POL* 16.81m (55ft 1¾in)	V. Goryayev *URS* 16.63m (54ft 6¾in)	V. Kreyer *URS* 16.43m (53ft 10¾in)
1964	J. Szmidt *POL* 16.85m (55ft 3½in)	O. Fedoseyev *URS* 16.58m (54ft 4¾in)	V. Kravchenko *URS* 16.57m (54ft 4¼in)
1968	V. Saneev *URS* 17.39m (57ft 0¾in)	N. Prudencio *BRA* 17.27m (56ft 8in)	G. Gentile *ITA* 17.22m (56ft 6in)
1972	V. Saneev *URS* 17.35m (56ft 11¼in)	J. Drehmel *GDR* 17.31m (56ft 9½in)	N. Prudencio *BRA* 17.05m (55ft 11¼in)

Pole Vault

Year	Gold	Silver	Bronze
1896	W. Hoyt *USA* 3.30m (10ft 10in)	A. Tyler *USA* 3.25m (10ft 8in)	E. Damaskos *GRE* 2.85m (9ft 4¼in)
1900	I. Baxter *USA* 3.30m (10ft 10in)	M. B. Colkett *USA* 3.25m (10ft 8in)	C. A. Andersen *NOR* 3.20m (10ft 6in)
1904	C. Dvorak *USA* 3.50m (11ft 6in)	L. Samse *USA* 3.43m (11ft 3in)	L. Wilkins *USA* 3.43m (11ft 3in)
1908	A. Gilbert *USA* & E. Cooke *USA* 3.71m (12ft 2in)		E. Archibald *CAN* 3.58m (11ft 9in)
1912	H. Babcock *USA* 3.95m (12ft 11½in)	F. Nelson *USA* & M. Wright *USA* 3.85m (12ft 7½in)	
1920	F. Foss *USA* 4.09m (13ft 5in)	H. Petersen *DEN* 3.70m (12ft 1¾in)	E. Myers *USA* 3.60m (11ft 9¾in)

	Gold	Silver	Bronze
1924	L. Barnes *USA* 3.95m (12ft 11½in)	G. Graham *USA* 3.95m (12ft 11½in)	J. Brooker *USA* 3.90m (12ft 9½in)
1928	S. Carr *USA* 4.20m (13ft 9½in)	W. Droegemuller *USA* 4.10m (13ft 5½in)	C. McGinnis *USA* 3.95m (12ft 11½in)
1932	W. Miller *USA* 4.32m (14ft 1⅞in)	S. Nishida *JPN* 4.30m (14ft 1¼in)	G. Jefferson *USA* 4.20m (13ft 9½in)
1936	E. Meadows *USA* 4.35m (14ft 3¼in)	S. Nishida *JPN* 4.25m (13ft 11¼in)	S. Oe *JPN* 4.25m (13ft 11¼in)
1948	O. G. Smith *USA* 4.30m (14ft 1¼in)	E. Kataja *FIN* 4.20m (13ft 9½in)	R. Richards *USA* 4.20m (13ft 9½in)
1952	R. Richards *USA* 4.55m (14ft 11¼in)	D. Laz *USA* 4.50m (14ft 9¼in)	R. Lundberg *SWE* 4.40m (14ft 5¼in)
1956	R. Richards *USA* 4.56m (14ft 11½in)	R. Gutowski *USA* 4.53m (14ft 10¼in)	G. Roubanis *GRE* 4.50m (14ft 9¼in)
1960	D. Bragg *USA* 4.70m (15ft 5in)	R. Morris *USA* 4.60m (15ft 1¼in)	E. Landström *FIN* 4.55m (14ft 11¼in)
1964	F. Hansen *USA* 5.10m (16ft 8¾in)	W. Reinhardt *GER* 5.05m (16ft 6¾in)	K. Lehnertz *GER* 5.00m (16ft 5in)
1968	R. Seagren *USA* 5.40m (17ft 8½in)	C. Schiprowski *GER* 5.40m (17ft 8½in)	W. Nordwig *GDR* 5.40m (17ft 8½in)
1972	W. Nordwig *GDR* 5.50m (18ft 0½in)	R. Seagren *USA* 5.40m (17ft 8½in)	J. Johnson *USA* 5.35m (17ft 6½in)

Shot

Weight 7.257kg (16lb) from a circle of 2.135m (7ft); in 1896 and 1900 a square of 2.135m (7ft).

	Gold	Silver	Bronze
1896	R. Garrett *USA* 11.22m (36ft 9¾in)	M. Gouscos *GRE* 11.20m (36ft 9in)	G. Papasideris *GRE* 10.36m (34ft 0in)
1900	R. Sheldon *USA* 14.10m (46ft 3in)	J. McCracken *USA* 12.85m (42ft 2in)	R. Garrett *USA* 12.37m (40ft 7in)
1904	R. Rose *USA* 14.81m (48ft 7in)	W. Coe *USA* 14.40m (47ft 3in)	L. Feuerbach *USA* 13.37m (43ft 10½in)
1908	R. Rose *USA* 14.21m (46ft 7½in)	D. Horgan *GBR* 13.62m (44ft 8¼in)	J. Garrels *USA* 13.18m (43ft 3in)
1912	P. McDonald *USA* 15.34m (50ft 4in)	R. Rose *USA* 15.25m (50ft 0½in)	L. Whitney *USA* 13.93m (45ft 8½in)
1920	V. Pörhölä *FIN* 14.81m (48ft 7in)	E. Niklander *FIN* 14.15m (46ft 5¼in)	H. Liversedge *USA* 14.15m (46ft 5in)
1924	C. Houser *USA* 14.99m (49ft 2½in)	G. Hartranft *USA* 14.90m (48ft 10½in)	R. Hills *USA* 14.64m (48ft 0½in)
1928	J. Kuck *USA* 15.87m (52ft 0¾in)	H. Brix *USA* 15.75m (51ft 8in)	E. Hirschfeld *GER* 15.72m (51ft 7in)
1932	L. Sexton *USA* 16.01m (52ft 6⅛in)	H. Rothert *USA* 15.67m (51ft 5in)	F. Douda *TCH* 15.61m (51ft 2½in)
1936	H. Wöllke *GER* 16.20m (53ft 1¾in)	S. Bärlund *FIN* 16.12m (52ft 10¾in)	G. Stöck *GER* 15.66m (51ft 4½in)
1948	W. Thompson *USA* 17.12m (56ft 2in)	J. Delaney *USA* 16.68m (54ft 8¾in)	J. Fuchs *USA* 16.42m (53ft 10½in)
1952	P. O'Brien *USA* 17.41m (57ft 1½in)	D. Hooper *USA* 17.39m (57ft 0¾in)	J. Fuchs *USA* 17.06m (55ft 11¾in)
1956	P. O'Brien *USA* 18.57m (60ft 11¼in)	W. Nieder *USA* 18.18m (59ft 7¾in)	J. Skobla *TCH* 17.65m (57ft 11in)
1960	W. Nieder *USA* 19.68m (64ft 6¾in)	P. O'Brien *USA* 19.11m (62ft 8¼in)	D. Long *USA* 19.01m (62ft 4¼in)
1964	D. Long *USA* 20.33m (66ft 8½in)	R. Matson *USA* 20.20m (66ft 3¼in)	V. Varju *HUN* 19.39m (63ft 7½in)
1968	R. Matson *USA* 20.54m (67ft 4¾in)	G. Woods *USA* 20.12m (66ft 0¼in)	E. Gushchin *URS* 20.09m (65ft 11in)
1972	W. Komar *POL* 21.18m (69ft 6in)	G. Woods *USA* 21.17m (69ft 5½in)	H. Briesenick *GDR* 21.14m (69ft 4¼in)

Discus

Weight 2kg (4lb 6.547oz) from a circle of 2.50m (8ft 2½in).

	Gold	Silver	Bronze
1896	R. Garrett *USA* 29.15m (95ft 7¾in)	P. Paraskevopoulos *GRE* 28.96m (95ft 0in)	S. Versis *GRE* 28.78m (94ft 5in)
1900	R. Bauer *HUN* 36.04m (118ft 3in)	F. Janda-Suk *BOH* 35.25m (115ft 7¾in)	R. Sheldon *USA* 34.60m (113ft 6in)
1904	M. Sheridan *USA* 39.28m (128ft 10½in)	R. Rose *USA* 39.28m (128ft 10½in)	N. Georgantos *GRE* 37.68m (123ft 7½in)
1908	M. Sheridan *USA* 40.89m (134ft 2in)	M. H. Giffin *USA* 40.70m (133ft 6½in)	M. Horr *USA* 39.45m (129ft 5¼in)
1912	A. Taipale *FIN* 45.21m (148ft 4in)	R. Byrd *USA* 42.32m (138ft 10in)	J. Duncan *USA* 42.28m (138ft 8½in)
1920	E. Niklander *FIN* 44.69m (146ft 7½in)	A. Taipale *FIN* 44.19m (144ft 11½in)	A. Pope *USA* 42.13m (138ft 2½in)
1924	C. Houser *USA* 46.16m (151ft 5in)	V. Niittymaa *FIN* 44.95m (147ft 5½in)	T. Lieb *USA* 44.83m (147ft 1in)
1928	C. Houser *USA* 47.32m (155ft 3in)	A. Kivi *FIN* 47.23m (154ft 11½in)	J. Corson *USA* 47.10m (154ft 6½in)
1932	J. Anderson *USA* 49.49m (162ft 4½in)	H. J. Laborde *FRA* 48.47m (159ft 0½in)	P. Winter *FRA* 47.85m (157ft 0in)
1936	K. Carpenter *USA* 50.48m (165ft 7½in)	G. Dunn *USA* 49.36m (161ft 11in)	G. Oberweger *ITA* 49.23m (161ft 6in)
1948	A. Consolini *ITA* 52.78m (172ft 2in)	G. Tosi *ITA* 51.78m (169ft 10½in)	F. Gordien *USA* 50.77m (166ft 7in)
1952	S. Iness *USA* 55.03m (180ft 6½in)	A. Consolini *ITA* 53.78m (176ft 5in)	J. Dillion *USA* 53.28m (174ft 9½in)
1956	A. Oerter *USA* 56.36m (184ft 11in)	F. Gordien *USA* 54.81m (179ft 9in)	D. Koch *USA* 54.40m (178ft 5½in)
1960	A. Oerter *USA* 59.18m (194ft 1¾in)	R. Babka *USA* 58.01m (190ft 4¼in)	R. Cochran *USA* 57.16m (187ft 6¼in)
1964	A. Oerter *USA* 61.00m (200ft 1½in)	L. Danek *TCH* 60.52m (198ft 6½in)	D. Weill *USA* 59.49m (195ft 2in)
1968	A. Oerter *USA* 64.78m (212ft 6½in)	L. Milde *GDR* 63.08m (206ft 11½in)	L. Danek *TCH* 62.92m (206ft 5in)
1972	L. Danek *TCH* 64.40m (211ft 3in)	L. J. Silvester *USA* 63.50m (208ft 4in)	R. Bruch *SWE* 63.40m (208ft 0in)

Hammer

Weight 7.257kg (16lb) from a circle of 2.135m (7ft); in 1900 from a 9ft circle. Not held before 1900.

	Gold	Silver	Bronze
1900	J. Flanagan *USA* 49.73m (163ft 2in)	T. Hare *USA* 49.13m (161ft 2in)	J. McCracken *USA* 42.46m (139ft 3½in)
1904	J. Flanagan *USA* 51.23m (168ft 1in)	J. DeWitt *USA* 50.26m (164ft 11in)	R. Rose *USA* 45.73m (150ft 0½in)
1908	J. Flanagan *USA* 51.92m (170ft 4¼in)	M. McGrath *USA* 51.18m (167ft 11in)	C. Walsh *USA* 48.50m (159ft 1½in)
1912	M. McGrath *USA* 54.74m (179ft 7in)	D. Gillis *CAN* 48.39m (158ft 9in)	C. Childs *USA* 48.17m (158ft 0½in)
1920	P. Ryan *USA* 52.88m (173ft 5½in)	C. H. Lind *SWE* 48.43m (158ft 10½in)	B. Bennett *USA* 48.25m (158ft 3½in)
1924	F. Tootell *USA* 53.30m (174ft)	M. McGrath *USA* 50.84m (166ft 9½in)	M. Nokes *GBR* 48.88m (160ft 4in)
1928	P. O'Callaghan *IRL* 51.39m (168ft 7in)	O. Skiöld *SWE* 51.29m (168ft 3in)	E. Black *USA* 49.03m (160ft 10in)
1932	P. O'Callaghan *IRL* 53.92m (176ft 11in)	V. Pörhölä *FIN* 52.27m (171ft 6in)	P. Zaremba *USA* 50.33m (165ft 1½in)
1936	K. Hein *GER* 56.49m (185ft 4in)	E. Blask *GER* 55.04m (180ft 7in)	F. Warngård *SWE* 54.83m (179ft 10½in)
1948	I. Németh *HUN* 56.07m (183ft 11½in)	I. Gubijan *YUG* 54.27m (178ft 0½in)	R. Bennett *USA* 53.73m (176ft 3½in)
1952	J. Csermák *HUN* 60.34m (197ft 11½in)	K. Storch *GER* 58.86m (193ft 1in)	I. Németh *HUN* 57.74m (189ft 5in)
1956	H. Connolly *USA* 63.19m (207ft 3½in)	M. Krivonosov *URS* 63.03m (206ft 9½in)	A. Samotsvetov *URS* 62.56m (205ft 3in)
1960	V. Rudenkov *URS* 67.10m (220ft 1¾in)	G. Zsivótzky *HUN* 65.79m (215ft 10in)	T. Rut *POL* 65.64m (215ft 4½in)
1964	R. Klim *URS* 69.74m (228ft 10in)	G. Zsivótzky *HUN* 69.09m (226ft 8in)	U. Beyer *GER* 68.09m (223ft 4½in)
1968	G. Zsivótzky *HUN* 73.36m (240ft 8in)	R. Klim *URS* 73.28m (240ft 5in)	L. Lovász *HUN* 69.78m (228ft 11in)
1972	A. Bondarchuk *URS* 75.50m (247ft 8in)	J. Sachse *GDR* 74.96m (245ft 11in)	V. Khmelevski *URS* 74.04m (242ft 11in)

Javelin

Not held before 1908.

	Gold	Silver	Bronze
1908	E. Lemming *SWE* 54.83m (179ft 10½in)	A. Halse *NOR* 50.57m (165ft 11in)	O. Nilsson *SWE* 47.10m (154ft 6¼in)
1912	E. Lemming *SWE* 60.64m (198ft 11½in)	J. Saaristo *FIN* 58.66m (192ft 5½in)	M. Koczán *HUN* 55.50m (182ft 1in)
1920	J. Myyrä *FIN* 65.78m (215ft 9½in)	U. Peltonen *FIN* 63.50m (208ft 4in)	P. Johansson *FIN* 63.10m (207ft 0in)
1924	J. Myyrä *FIN* 62.96m (206ft 6½in)	G. Lindström *SWE* 60.92m (199ft 10½in)	E. Oberst *USA* 58.35m (191ft 5in)
1928	E. Lundkvist *SWE* 66.60m (218ft 6in)	B. Szepes *HUN* 65.26m (214ft 1in)	O. Sunde *NOR* 63.97m (209ft 10½in)
1932	M. Järvinen *FIN* 72.71m (238ft 6½in)	M. Sippala *FIN* 69.80m (229ft 0in)	E. Penttilä *FIN* 68.70m (225ft 4½in)
1936	G. Stöck *GER* 71.84m (235ft 8½in)	Y. Nikkanen *FIN* 70.77m (232ft 2in)	K. Toivonen *FIN* 70.72m (232ft 0in)
1948	T. Rautavaara *FIN* 69.77m (228ft 11in)	S. Seymour *USA* 67.56m (221ft 8in)	J. Várszegi *HUN* 67.03m (219ft 11in)
1952	C. Young *USA* 73.78m (242ft 0½in)	W. Miller *USA* 72.46m (237ft 8½in)	T. Hyytiäinen *FIN* 71.89m (235ft 10½in)
1956	E. Danielsen *NOR* 85.71m (281ft 2½in)	J. Sidlo *POL* 79.98m (262ft 4½in)	V. Tsibulenko *URS* 79.50m (260ft 10in)
1960	V. Tsibulenko *URS* 84.64m (277ft 8in)	W. Krüger *GER* 79.36m (260ft 4½in)	G. Kulcsár *HUN* 78.57m (257ft 9¼in)
1964	P. Nevala *FIN* 82.66m (271ft 2in)	G. Kulcsár *HUN* 82.32m (270ft 0½in)	Y. Lusis *URS* 80.57m (264ft 4½in)
1968	Y. Lusis *URS* 90.10m (295ft 7in)	J. Kinnunen *FIN* 88.58m (290ft 7½in)	G. Kulcsár *HUN* 87.06m (285ft 7½in)
1972	K. Wolfermann *GER* 90.48m (296ft 10in)	Y. Lusis *URS* 90.46m (296ft 9in)	W. Schmidt *USA* 84.42m (276ft 11in)

Decathlon

Consists of ten events on two consecutive days; 100 metres, long jump, shot, high jump, 400 metres, on the first day; 110-metres hurdles, discus, pole vault, javelin, 1,500 metres, on the second day. Not held in its present form before 1912.

	Gold	Silver	Bronze
1912	H. Wieslander *SWE* 7,724.495 pts	C. Lomberg *SWE* 7,413.510 pts	G. Holmér *SWE* 7,347.855 pts
1920	H. Lövland *NOR* 6,803.355 pts	B. Hamilton *USA* 6,771.085 pts	B. Ohlson *SWE* 6,580.030 pts
1924	H. Osborn *USA* 7,710.775 pts	E. Norton *USA* 7,350.895 pts	A. Klumberg *EST* 7,329.360 pts

	Gold	Silver	Bronze
1928	P. Yrjölä *FIN* 8,053.290 pts	A. Järvinen *FIN* 7,931.500 pts	J. K. Doherty *USA* 7,706.650 pts
1932	J. Bausch *USA* 8,462.230 pts	A. Järvinen *FIN* 8,292.480 pts	W. Eberle *GER* 8,030.800 pts
1936	G. Morris *USA* 7,900 pts	R. Clark *USA* 7,601 pts	J. Parker *USA* 7,275 pts
1948	R. Mathias *USA* 7,139 pts	I. Heinrich *FRA* 6,974 pts	F. Simmons *USA* 6,950 pts
1952	R. Mathias *USA* 7,887 pts	M. Campbell *USA* 6,975 pts	F. Simmons *USA* 6,788 pts
1956	M. Campbell *USA* 7,937 pts	R. Johnson *USA* 7,587 pts	V. Kuznetsov *URS* 7,465 pts
1960	R. Johnson *USA* 8,392 pts	C. K. Yang *ROC* 8,334 pts	V. Kuznetsov *URS* 7,809 pts
1964	W. Holdorf *GER* 7,887 pts	R. Aun *URS* 7,842 pts	H. J. Walde *GER* 7,809 pts
1968	B. Toomey *USA* 8,193 pts	H. J. Walde *GER* 8,111 pts	K. Bendlin *GER* 8,064 pts
1972	N. Avilov *URS* 8,454 pts	L. Litvinenko *URS* 8,035 pts	R. Katus *POL* 7,984 pts

Athletics *Women*

100 Metres
Not held before 1928.

	Gold	Silver	Bronze
1928	E. Robinson *USA* 12.2sec	F. Rosenfeld *CAN* 12.3sec	E. Smith *CAN* 12.3sec
1932	S. Walasiewicz *POL* 11.9sec	H. Strike *CAN* 11.9sec	W. von Bremen *USA* 12.0sec
1936	H. Stephens *USA* 11.5sec	S. Walasiewicz *POL* 11.7sec	K. Krauss *GER* 11.9sec
1948	F. Blankers-Koen *HOL* 11.9sec	D. Manley *GBR* 12.2sec	S. Strickland *AUS* 12.2sec
1952	M. Jackson *AUS* 11.5sec	D. Hasenjager *SAF* 11.8sec	S. Strickland *AUS* 11.9sec
1956	B. Cuthbert *AUS* 11.5sec	C. Stubnick *GER* 11.7sec	M. Matthews *AUS* 11.7sec
1960	W. Rudolph *USA* 11.0sec	D. Hyman *GBR* 11.3sec	G. Leone *ITA* 11.3sec
1964	W. Tyus *USA* 11.4sec	E. Maguire *USA* 11.6sec	E. Kłobukowska *POL* 11.6sec
1968	W. Tyus *USA* 11.0sec	B. Ferrell *USA* 11.1sec	I. Szewińska-Kirszenstein *POL* 11.1sec
1972	R. Stecher *GDR* 11.07sec	R. Boyle *AUS* 11.23sec	S. Chivas *CUB* 11.24sec

200 Metres
Not held before 1948.

	Gold	Silver	Bronze
1948	F. Blankers-Koen *HOL* 24.4sec	A. Williamson *GBR* 25.1sec	A. Patterson *USA* 25.2sec
1952	M. Jackson *AUS* 23.7sec	B. Brouwer *HOL* 24.2sec	N. Khnykina *URS* 24.2sec
1956	B. Cuthbert *AUS* 23.4sec	C. Stubnick *GER* 23.7sec	M. Matthews *AUS* 23.8sec
1960	W. Rudolph *USA* 24.0sec	J. Heine *GER* 24.4sec	D. Hyman *GBR* 24.7sec
1964	E. Maguire *USA* 23.0sec	I. Kirszenstein *POL* 23.1sec	M. Black *AUS* 23.1sec
1968	I. Szewińska-Kirszenstein *POL* 22.5sec	R. Boyle *AUS* 22.7sec	J. Lamy *AUS* 22.8sec
1972	R. Stecher *GDR* 22.40sec	R. Boyle *AUS* 22.45sec	I. Szewińska-Kirszenstein *POL* 22.74sec

400 Metres
Not held before 1964.

	Gold	Silver	Bronze
1964	B. Cuthbert *AUS* 52.0sec	A. Packer *GBR* 52.2sec	J. Amoore *AUS* 53.4sec
1968	C. Besson *FRA* 52.0sec	L. Board *GBR* 52.1sec	N. Pechenkina *URS* 52.2sec
1972	M. Zehrt *GDR* 51.08sec	R. Wilden *GER* 51.21sec	K. Hammond *USA* 51.64sec

800 Metres
Not held before 1928.

	Gold	Silver	Bronze
1928	L. Radke *GER* 2min 16.8sec	K. Hitomi *JPN* 2min 17.6sec	I. Gentzel *SWE* 2min 17.8sec
1932-1956	Not held		
1960	L. Shevtsova *URS* 2min 04.3sec	B. Jones *AUS* 2min 04.4sec	U. Donath *GER* 2min 05.6sec
1964	A. Packer *GBR* 2min 01.1sec	M. Dupureur *FRA* 2min 01.9sec	A. Chamberlain *NZL* 2min 02.8sec
1968	M. Manning *USA* 2min 00.9sec	I. Silai *ROM* 2min 02.5sec	M. Gommers *HOL* 2min 02.6sec
1972	H. Falck *GER* 1min 58.6sec	N. Sabaite *URS* 1min 58.7sec	G. Hoffmeister *GDR* 1min 59.2sec

80 Metres Hurdles
Not held before 1932.

	Gold	Silver	Bronze
1932	M. Didrikson *USA* 11.7sec	E. Hall *USA* 11.7sec	M. Clark *SAF* 11.8sec
1936	T. Valla *ITA* 11.7sec	A. Steuer *GER* 11.7sec	E. Taylor *CAN* 11.7sec
1948	F. Blankers-Koen *HOL* 11.2sec	M. Gardner *GBR* 11.2sec	S. Strickland *AUS* 11.4sec
1952	S. Strickland *AUS* 10.9sec	M. Golubnichaya *URS* 11.1sec	M. Sander *GER* 11.1sec
1956	S. (Strickland) de la Hunty *AUS* 10.7sec	G. Köhler *GER* 10.9sec	N. Thrower *AUS* 11.0sec
1960	I. Press *URS* 10.8sec	C. Quinton *GBR* 10.9sec	G. (Köhler) Birkemeyer *GER* 11.0sec
1964	K. Balzer *GER* 10.5sec	T. Ciepła *POL* 10.5sec	P. Kilborn *AUS* 10.5sec
1968	M. Caird *AUS* 10.3sec	P. Kilborn *AUS* 10.4sec	C. Cheng *ROC* 10.4sec

In 1972 this event was changed to 100 Metres Hurdles.

100 Metres Hurdles
Not held before 1972.

	Gold	Silver	Bronze
1972	A. Ehrhardt *GDR* 12.59sec	V. Bufanu *ROM* 12.84sec	K. Balzer *GDR* 12.90sec

4 × 100 Metres Relay
Not held before 1928.

	Gold	Silver	Bronze
1928	CAN 48.4sec	USA 48.8sec	GER 49.0sec
1932	USA 47.0sec	CAN 47.0sec	GBR 47.6sec
1936	USA 46.9sec	GBR 47.6sec	CAN 47.8sec
1948	HOL 47.5sec	AUS 47.6sec	CAN 47.8sec
1952	USA 45.9sec	GER 45.9sec	GBR 46.2sec
1956	AUS 44.5sec	GBR 44.7sec	USA 44.9sec
1960	USA 44.5sec	GER 44.8sec	POL 45.0sec
1964	POL 43.6sec	USA 43.9sec	GBR 44.0sec
1968	USA 42.8sec	CUB 43.3sec	URS 43.4sec
1972	GER 42.81sec	GDR 42.95sec	CUB 43.36sec

4 × 400 Metres Relay
Not held before 1972.

	Gold	Silver	Bronze
1972	GDR 3min 23.0sec	USA 3min 25.2sec	GER 3min 26.5sec

1,500 Metres
Not held before 1972.

	Gold	Silver	Bronze
1972	L. Bragina *URS* 4min 01.4sec	G. Hoffmeister *GDR* 4min 02.8sec	P. Cacchi *ITA* 4min 02.9sec

Pentathlon
Consists of five events on two consecutive days: 80-metres hurdles (100-metres hurdles after 1968), shot, high jump, on the first day; long jump and 200 metres on the second. Not held before 1964.

	Gold	Silver	Bronze
1964	I. Press *URS* 5,246 pts	M. Rand *GBR* 5,035 pts	G. Bystrova *URS* 4,956 pts
1968	I. Becker *GER* 5,098 pts	L. Prokop *AUT* 4,966 pts	A. T. Kovács *HUN* 4,959 pts
1972	M. Peters *GBR* 4,801 pts	H. Rosendahl *GER* 4,791 pts	B. Pollak *GDR* 4,768 pts

High Jump
Not held before 1928.

	Gold	Silver	Bronze
1928	E. Catherwood *CAN* 1.59m (5ft 2¼in)	C. Gisolf *HOL* 1.56m (5ft 1½in)	M. Wiley *USA* 1.56m (5ft 1½in)
1932	J. Shiley *USA* 1.65m (5ft 5¼in)	M. Didrikson *USA* 1.65m (5ft 5¼in)	E. Dawes *CAN* 1.60m (5ft 3in)
1936	I. Csák *HUN* 1.60m (5ft 3in)	D. Odam *GBR* 1.60m (5ft 3in)	E. Kaun *GER* 1.60m (5ft 3in)
1948	A. Coachman *USA* 1.68m (5ft 6¼in)	D. (Odam) Tyler *GBR* 1.68m (5ft 6¼in)	M. Ostermeyer *FRA* 1.61m (5ft 3¼in)
1952	E. Brand *SAF* 1.67m (5ft 5¾in)	S. Lerwill *GBR* 1.65m (5ft 5¼in)	A. Chudina *URS* 1.63m (5ft 4in)
1956	M. McDaniel *USA* 1.76m (5ft 9¼in)	T. Hopkins *GBR* & M. Pisaryeva *URS* 1.67m (5ft 5¾in)	
1960	I. Balaş *ROM* 1.85m (6ft 0¾in)	J. Józwiakowska *POL* & D. Shirley *GBR* 1.71m (5ft 7¼in)	
1964	I. Balaş *ROM* 1.90m (6ft 2¾in)	M. Brown *AUS* 1.80m (5ft 11in)	T. Chenchik *URS* 1.78m (5ft 10in)
1968	M. Rezková *TCH* 1.82m (5ft 11¾in)	A. Okorokova *URS* 1.80m (5ft 10¾in)	V. Kozyr *URS* 1.80m (5ft 10¾in)
1972	U. Meyfarth *GER* 1.92m (6ft 3½in)	Y. Blagoyeva *BUL* 1.88m (6ft 2in)	I. Gusenbauer *AUT* 1.88m (6ft 2in)

Long Jump
Not held before 1948.

	Gold	Silver	Bronze
1948	O. Gyarmati *HUN* 5.70m (18ft 8¼in)	N. S. de Portela *ARG* 5.60m (18ft 4½in)	A. B. Leyman *SWE* 5.58m (18ft 3¾in)

	Gold	Silver	Bronze
1952	Y. Williams *NZL* 6.24m (20ft 5½in)	A. Chudina *URS* 6.14m (20ft 1¾in)	S. Cawley *GBR* 5.92m (19ft 5in)
1956	E. Krzesinska *POL* 6.35m (20ft 10in)	W. White *USA* 6.09m (19ft 11¾in)	N. (Khnykina) Dvalishvili *URS* 6.07m (19ft 11in)
1960	V. Krepkina *URS* 6.37m (20ft 10¾in)	E. Krzesinska *POL* 6.27m (20ft 6¾in)	H. Claus *GER* 6.21m (20ft 4½in)
1964	M. Rand *GBR* 6.76m (22ft 2¼in)	I. Kirszenstein *POL* 6.60m (21ft 7¾in)	T. Shchelkanova *URS* 6.42m (21ft 0¾in)
1968	V. Viscopoleanu *ROM* 6.82m (22ft 4½in)	S. Sherwood *GBR* 6.68m (21ft 11in)	T. Talysheva *URS* 6.66m (21ft 10¼in)
1972	H. Rosendahl *GER* 6.78m (22ft 3in)	D. Yorgova *BUL* 6.77m (22ft 2½in)	E. Suranová *TCH* 6.67m (21ft 10¾in)

Shot

Weight 4kg (8lb 13oz) from a circle of 2.135m (7ft). Not held before 1948.

	Gold	Silver	Bronze
1948	M. Ostermeyer *FRA* 13.75m (45ft 1½in)	A. Piccinini *ITA* 13.10m (42ft 11¼in)	I. Schäffer *AUT* 13.08m (42ft 10¾in)
1952	G. Zybina *URS* 15.28m (50ft 1½in)	M. Werner *GER* 14.57m (47ft 9½in)	K. Tochenova *URS* 14.50m (47ft 6¾in)
1956	T. Tyshkevich *URS* 16.59m (54ft 5in)	G. Zybina *URS* 16.53m (54ft 2¾in)	M. Werner *GER* 15.61m (51ft 2½in)
1960	T. Press *URS* 17.32m (56ft 10in)	J. Lüttge *GER* 16.61m (54ft 6in)	E. Brown *USA* 16.42m (53ft 10½in)
1964	T. Press *URS* 18.14m (59ft 6in)	R. Garisch *GER* 17.61m (57ft 9¼in)	G. Zybina *URS* 17.45m (57ft 3in)
1968	M. Gummel *GDR* 19.61m (64ft 4in)	M. Lange *GDR* 18.78m (61ft 7½in)	N. Chizhova *URS* 18.19m (59ft 8¼in)
1972	N. Chizhova *URS* 21.03m (69ft 0in)	M. Gummel *GDR* 20.22m (66ft 4¼in)	I. Khristova *BUL* 19.35m (63ft 6in)

Discus

Weight 1kg (2lb 3.274oz) from a circle of 2.50m (8ft 2½in). Not held before 1928.

	Gold	Silver	Bronze
1928	H. Konopacka *POL* 39.62m (129ft 11¾in)	L. Copeland *USA* 37.08m (121ft 7⅞in)	R. Svedberg *SWE* 35.92m (117ft 10¼in)
1932	L. Copeland *USA* 40.58m (133ft 1¾in)	R. Osburn *USA* 40.12m (131ft 7½in)	J. Wajsówna *POL* 38.74m (127ft 1¼in)
1936	G. Mauermayer *GER* 47.63m (156ft 3¼in)	J. Wajsówna *POL* 46.22m (151ft 7¾in)	P. Mollenhauer *GER* 39.80m (130ft 6⅞in)
1948	M. Ostermeyer *FRA* 41.92m (137ft 6⅛in)	E. Gentile Cordiale *ITA* 41.17m (135ft 0⅞in)	J. Mazeas *FRA* 40.47m (132ft 9½in)
1952	N. Romashkova *URS* 51.42m (168ft 8½in)	Y. Bagryantseva *URS* 47.08m (154ft 5⅝in)	N. Dumbadze *URS* 46.29m (151ft 10½in)
1956	O. Fikotová *TCH* 53.69m (176ft 1½in)	I. Beglyakova *URS* 52.54m (172ft 4½in)	N. (Romashkova) Ponomareva *URS* 52.02m (170ft 8in)
1960	N. Ponomareva *URS* 55.10m (180ft 9¼in)	T. Press *URS* 52.59m (172ft 6½in)	L. Manoliu *ROM* 52.36m (171ft 9½in)
1964	T. Press *URS* 57.27m (187ft 10½in)	I. Lotz *GER* 57.21m (187ft 8½in)	L. Manoliu *ROM* 56.97m (186ft 11in)
1968	L. Manoliu *ROM* 58.28m (191ft 2½in)	L. Westermann *GER* 57.76m (189ft 6in)	J. Kleiber *HUN* 54.90m (180ft 1½in)
1972	F. Melnik *URS* 66.62m (218ft 7in)	A. Menis *ROM* 65.06m (213ft 5in)	V. Stoeva *BUL* 64.34m (211ft 1in)

Javelin

Not held before 1932.

	Gold	Silver	Bronze
1932	M. Didrikson *USA* 43.68m (143ft 4in)	E. Braumüller *GER* 43.49m (142ft 8⅝in)	T. Fleischer *GER* 43.00m (141ft 1½in)
1936	T. Fleischer *GER* 45.18m (148ft 2¾in)	L. Krüger *GER* 43.29m (142ft 0⅜in)	M. Kwasniewska *POL* 41.80m (137ft 1¼in)
1948	H. Bauma *AUT* 45.57m (149ft 6in)	K. Parviänen *FIN* 43.79m (143ft 8⅛in)	L. Carlstedt *DEN* 42.80m (140ft 5⅛in)
1952	D. Zátopková *TCH* 50.47m (165ft 7in)	A. Chudina *URS* 50.01m (164ft 0⅞in)	Y. Gorchakova *URS* 49.76m (163ft 3⅛in)
1956	I. Yaunzeme *URS* 53.86m (176ft 8½in)	M. Ahrens *CHI* 50.38m (165ft 3½in)	N. Konyaeva *URS* 50.28m (164ft 11½in)
1960	E. Ozolina *URS* 55.98m (183ft 8in)	D. Zátopková *TCH* 53.78m (176ft 5¼in)	B. Kalediene *URS* 53.45m (175ft 4½in)
1964	M. Peneş *ROM* 60.54m (198ft 7½in)	M. Rudas *HUN* 58.27m (191ft 2in)	Y. Gorchakova *URS* 57.06m (187ft 2½in)
1968	A. Németh *HUN* 60.36m (198ft 0½in)	M. Peneş *ROM* 59.92m (196ft 7in)	E. Janko *AUT* 58.04m (190ft 5in)
1972	R. Fuchs *GDR* 63.88m (209ft 7in)	J. Todten *GDR* 62.54m (205ft 2in)	K. Schmidt *USA* 59.94m (196ft 8in)

Basketball

Not held as a competition before 1936.

	Gold	Silver	Bronze
1936	USA	CAN	MEX
1948	USA	FRA	BRA
1952	USA	URS	URU
1956	USA	URS	URU
1960	USA	URS	BRA
1964	USA	URS	BRA
1968	USA	YUG	URS
1972	URS	USA	CUB

Boxing

From 1952 both losing semi-finalists have been awarded bronze medals.

Light Flyweight

Not held before 1968. Weight limit 48kg (105lb 13oz).

	Gold	Silver	Bronze
1968	F. Rodríguez *VEN*	Y. J. Jee *KOR*	H. Marbley *USA* & H. Skrzypczak *POL*
1972	G. Gedo *HUN*	U.G. Kim *PRK*	R. Evans *GBR* & E. Rodríguez *ESP*

Flyweight

Not held before 1904. In 1904 weight limit 47.6kg (105lb); 1920-36 50.8kg (112lb); from 1948 51kg (112lb 6oz).

	Gold	Silver	Bronze
1904	G. Finnegan *USA*	M. Burke *USA*	
1908–1912	*Not held*		
1920	F. De Genaro *USA*	A. Petersen *DEN*	W. Cuthbertson *GBR*
1924	F. LaBarba *USA*	J. Mackenzie *GBR*	R. Fee *USA*
1928	A. Kocsis *HUN*	A. Appel *FRA*	C. Cavagnoli *ITA*
1932	I. Énekes *HUN*	F. Cabañas *MEX*	L. Salica *USA*
1936	W. Kaiser *GER*	G. Matta *ITA*	L. Laurie *USA*
1948	P. Perez *ARG*	S. Bandinelli *ITA*	S. A. Han *KOR*
1952	N. Brooks *USA*	E. Basel *GER*	A. Bulakov *URS* & W. Toweel *SAF*
1956	T. Spinks *GBR*	M. Dobrescu *ROM*	J. Caldwell *IRL* & R. Libeer *FRA*
1960	G. Török *HUN*	S. Sivko *URS*	K. Tanabe *JPN* & A. Elgvindi *UAR*
1964	F. Atzori *ITA*	A. Olech *POL*	S. Sorokin *URS* & R. Carmody *USA*
1968	R. Delgado *MEX*	A. Olech *POL*	S. de Oliveira *BRA* & L. Rwabwogo *UGA*
1972	G. Kostadinov *BUL*	L. Rwabwogo *UGA*	I. Błażyński *POL* & D. Rodríguez *CUB*

Bantamweight

Not held before 1904. In 1904 weight limit 52.1kg (115lb); 1908 52.6kg (116lb); 1920 53.6kg (118lb 2oz); 1924-36 53.5kg (118lb); from 1948 54kg (119lb).

	Gold	Silver	Bronze
1904	O. L. Kirk *USA*	G. Finnegan *USA*	
1908	H. Thomas *GBR*	J. Condon *GBR*	W. Webb *GBR*
1912	*Not held*		
1920	C. Walker *SAF*	C. J. Graham *CAN*	J. McKenzie *GBR*
1924	W. Smith *SAF*	S. Tripoli *USA*	J. Ces *FRA*
1928	V. Tamagnini *ITA*	J. Daley *USA*	H. Isaacs *SAF*
1932	H. Gwynne *CAN*	H. Ziglarski *GER*	J. Villanueva *PHI*
1936	U. Sergo *ITA*	J. Wilson *USA*	F. Ortiz *MEX*
1948	T. Csik *HUN*	G. Zuddas *ITA*	J. Venegas *PUR*
1952	P. Hämäläinen *FIN*	J. McNally *IRL*	G. Garbuzov *URS* & J. H. Kang *KOR*
1956	W. Behrendt *GER*	S. C. Song *KOR*	F. Gilroy *IRL* & C. Barrientos *CHI*
1960	O. Grigoriev *URS*	P. Zamparini *ITA*	O. Taylor *AUS* & B. Bendig *POL*
1964	T. Sakurai *JPN*	S. C. Chung *KOR*	B. J. Fabila *MEX* & W. Rodríguez *URU*
1968	V. Sokolov *URS*	E. Mukwanga *UGA*	E. Morioka *JPN* & K. C. Chang *KOR*
1972	O. Martínez *CUB*	A. Zamora *MEX*	G. Turpin *GBR* & R. Carreras *USA*

Featherweight

Not held before 1904. In 1904 weight limit 56.7kg (125lb); 1908–36 57.15kg (126lb); 1948 58kg (127lb 14oz); from 1952 57kg (125lb 10½oz).

	Gold	Silver	Bronze
1904	O. L. Kirk *USA*	F. Haller *USA*	
1908	R. Gunn *GBR*	C. W. Morris *GBR*	H. Roddin *GBR*
1912	*Not held*		
1920	P. Fritsch *FRA*	J. Gachet *FRA*	E. Garzena *ITA*
1924	J. Fields *USA*	J. Salas *USA*	P. Quartucci *ARG*
1928	L. van Klaveren *HOL*	V. Peralta *ARG*	H. Devine *USA*
1932	C. Robledo *ARG*	J. Schleinkofer *GER*	C. Carlsson *SWE*
1936	O. Casanovas *ARG*	C. Catterall *SAF*	J. Miner *GER*
1948	E. Formenti *ITA*	D. Shepherd *SAF*	A. Antkiewicz *POL*
1952	J. Zachara *TCH*	S. Caprari *ITA*	L. Leisching *SAF* & J. Ventaja *FRA*
1956	V. Safronov *URS*	T. Nicholls *GBR*	H. Niedźwiedzki *POL* & P. Hämäläinen *FIN*
1960	F. Musso *ITA*	J. Adamski *POL*	W. Meyers *SAF* & J. Limmonen *FIN*
1964	S. Stepashkin *URS*	A. Villaneuva *PHI*	C. Brown *USA* & H. Schulz *GER*
1968	A. Roldan *MEX*	A. Robinson *USA*	P. Waruinge *KEN* & I. Mikhailov *BUL*
1972	B. Kusnetsov *URS*	P. Waruinge *KEN*	C. Rojas *COL* & A. Botos *HUN*

Gold	Silver	Bronze

Lightweight

Not held before 1904. In 1904 weight limit 61.2kg (135lb); 1908 63.5kg (140lb); 1920–36 61.24kg (135lb); 1948 62kg (136lb 11oz); from 1952 60kg (132lb 4½oz).

Gold	Silver	Bronze
1904 H. Spanger *USA*	J. Eagan *USA*	R. Van Horn *USA*
1908 F. Grace *GBR*	F. Spiller *GBR*	H. H. Johnson *GBR*
1912 *Not held*		
1920 S. Mosberg *USA*	G. Johanssen *DEN*	C. Newton *CAN*
1924 H. Nielsen *DEN*	A. Copello *ARG*	F. Boylstein *USA*
1928 C. Orlandi *ITA*	S. Halaiko *USA*	G. Berggren *SWE*
1932 L. Stevens *SAF*	T. Ahlqvist *SWE*	N. Bor *USA*
1936 I. Harangi *HUN*	N. Stepulov *EST*	E. Ågren *SWE*
1948 G. Dreyer *SAF*	J. Vissers *BEL*	S. Wad *DEN*
1952 A. Bolognesi *ITA*	A. Antkiewicz *POL*	G. Fiat *ROM* & E. Pakkanen *FIN*
1956 R. McTaggart *GBR*	H. Kurschat *GER*	A. Byrne *IRL* & A. Lagetko *URS*
1960 K. Paździor *POL*	S. Lopopolo *ITA*	R. McTaggart *GBR* & A. Laudonio *ARG*
1964 J. Grudzień *POL*	V. Baranikov *URS*	R. Harris *USA* & J. McCourt *IRL*
1968 R. Harris *USA*	J. Grudzień *POL*	C. Cutov *ROM* & Z. Vujin *YUG*
1972 J. Szczepanski *POL*	L. Orban *HUN*	S. Mbugua *KEN* & A. Pérez *COL*

Light Welterweight

Not held before 1952. Weight limit 63.5kg (140lb).

Gold	Silver	Bronze
1952 C. Adkins *USA*	V. Mednov *URS*	E. Mallenius *FIN* & B. Visintin *ITA*
1956 V. Yengibaryan *URS*	F. Nenci *ITA*	H. Loubscher *SAF* & C. Dumitrescu *ROM*
1960 B. Nemeček *TCH*	C. Quartey *GHA*	Q. Daniels *USA* & M. Kasprzyk *POL*
1964 J. Kulej *POL*	Y. Frolov *URS*	E. Blay *GHA* & H. Galhia *TUN*
1968 J. Kulej *POL*	E. Regueiferos *CUB*	A. Nilsson *FIN* & J. Wallington *USA*
1972 R. Seales *USA*	A. Anghelov *BUL*	Z. Vujin *YUG* & I. Daborg *NIG*

Welterweight

Not held before 1904. In 1904 weight limit 65.27kg (144lb); 1920–36 66.68kg (147lb); from 1968 67kg (147lb 11½oz). In 1924 this weight category was called 'Light Middleweight'.

Gold	Silver	Bronze
1904 A. Young *USA*	H. Spanger *USA*	J. Lydon *USA*
1908–1912 *Not held*		
1920 J. Schneider *CAN*	A. Ireland *GBR*	F. Colberg *USA*
1924 J. Delarge *BEL*	H. Mendez *ARG*	D. Lewis *CAN*
1928 E. Morgan *NZL*	R. Landini *ARG*	R. Smillie *CAN*
1932 E. Flynn *USA*	E. Campe *GER*	B. Ahlberg *FIN*
1936 S. Suvio *FIN*	M. Murach *GER*	G. Petersen *DEN*
1948 J. Torma *TCH*	H. Herring *USA*	A. d'Ottavio *ITA*
1952 Z. Chychla *POL*	S. Shcherbakov *URS*	V. Jørgensen *DEN* & G. Heidemann *GER*
1956 N. Linca *ROM*	F. Tiedt *IRL*	K. Hogarth *AUS* & N. Gargano *GBR*
1960 G. Benvenuti *ITA*	Y. Radonyak *URS*	L. Drogosz *POL* & James Lloyd *GBR*
1964 M. Kasprzyk *POL*	R. Tamulis *URS*	P. Purhonen *FIN* & S. Bertini *ITA*
1968 M. Wolke *GDR*	J. Bessala *CMR*	V. Masalimov *URS* & M. Guilloti González *ARG*
1972 E. Correa *CUB*	J. Kajdi *HUN*	D. Murunga *KEN* & J. Valdez *USA*

Light Middleweight

Not held before 1952. Weight limit 71kg (156lb 8½oz).

Gold	Silver	Bronze
1952 L. Papp *HUN*	T. van Schalkwyk *SAF*	B. Tishin *URS* & E. Herrera *ARG*
1956 L. Papp *HUN*	J. Torres *USA*	J. McCormack *GBR* & Z. Pietrzykowski *POL*
1960 W. McClure *USA*	C. Bossi *ITA*	B. Lagutin *URS* & W. Fisher *GBR*
1964 B. Lagutin *URS*	J. Gonzales *FRA*	N. Maiyegun *NGR* & J. Grzesiak *POL*
1968 B. Lagutin *URS*	R. Garbey *CUB*	J. Baldwin *USA* & G. Meier *GER*
1972 D. Kottysch *GER*	W. Rudkowski *POL*	A. Minter *GBR* & P. Tiepold *GDR*

Middleweight

Not held before 1904. In 1904–8 weight limit 71.67kg (158lb); 1920–36 72.57kg (160lb); 1948 73kg (169lb 15oz); from 1952 75kg (165lb 5¾oz).

Gold	Silver	Bronze
1904 C. Mayer *USA*	B. Spradley *USA*	
1908 J. Douglas *GBR*	R. Baker *AUS*	W. Philo *GBR*

Gold	Silver	Bronze
1912 *Not held*		
1920 H. Mallin *GBR*	G. A. Prud'homme *CAN*	M. H. Herscovitch *CAN*
1924 H. Mallin *GBR*	J. Elliott *GBR*	J. Beecken *BEL*
1928 P. Toscani *ITA*	J. Heřmánek *TCH*	L. Steyaert *BEL*
1932 C. Barth *USA*	A. Azar *ARG*	E. Pierce *SAF*
1936 J. Despeaux *FRA*	H. Tiller *NOR*	R. Villareal *ARG*
1948 L. Papp *HUN*	J. Wright *GBR*	I. Fontana *ITA*
1952 F. Patterson *USA*	V. Tita *ROM*	B. Nikolov *BUL* & K. Sjölin *SWE*
1956 G. Shatkov *URS*	R. Tapia *CHI*	G. Chapron *FRA* & V. Zalazar *ARG*
1960 E. Crook *USA*	T. Walasek *POL*	·I. Monea *ROM* & Y. Feofanov *URS*
1964 V. Popenchenko *URS*	E. Schulz *GER*	F. Valla *ITA* & T. Walasek *POL*
1968 C. Finnegan *GBR*	A. Kiselyov *URS*	A. Zaragoza *MEX* & A. Jones *USA*
1972 V. Lemechev *URS*	R. Virtanen *FIN*	P. Amartey *GHA* & M. Johnson *USA*

Light Heavyweight

Not held before 1920. Weight limit 1920–36 79.38kg (175lb); 1948 80kg (176lb 6oz); from 1952 81kg (178lb 9oz).

Gold	Silver	Bronze
1920 E. Eagan *USA*	S. Sørsdal *NOR*	H. Franks *GBR*
1924 H. Mitchell *GBR*	T. Petersen *DEN*	S. Sørsdal *NOR*
1928 V. Avendaño *ARG*	E. Pistulla *GER*	K. L. Miljon *HOL*
1932 D. Carstens *SAF*	G. Rossi *ITA*	P. Jørgensen *DEN*
1936 R. Michelot *FRA*	R. Vogt *GER*	F. Risiglione *ARG*
1948 G. Hunter *SAF*	D. Scott *GBR*	M. Cia *ARG*
1952 N. Lee *USA*	A. Pacenza *ARG*	A. Perov *URS* & H. Siljander *FIN*
1956 J. F. Boyd *USA*	G. Negrea *ROM*	C. Lucas *CHI* & R. Murauskas *URS*
1960 C. Clay *USA*	Z. Pietrzykowski *POL*	A. Madigan *AUS* & G. Saraudi *ITA*
1964 C. Pinto *ITA*	A. Kiselyov *URS*	A. Nicolov *BUL* & Z. Pietrzykowski *POL*
1968 D. Poznyak *URS*	I. Monea *ROM*	G. Stankov *BUL* & S. Dragan *POL*
1972 M. Parlov *YUG*	G. Carrillo *CUB*	I. Ikhouria *NGR* & J. Gortat *POL*

Heavyweight

Not held before 1904. In 1904–8 weight limit over 71.67kg (158lb); 1920–36 79.38kg (175lb); 1948 80kg (176lb 6oz); from 1952 81kg (178lb 9oz).

Gold	Silver	Bronze
1904 S. Berger *USA*	C. Mayer *USA*	
1908 A. L. Oldham *GBR*	S. C. H. Evans *GBR*	F. Parks *GBR*
1912 *Not held*		
1920 R. Rawson *GBR*	S. Petersen *DEN*	X. Eluère *FRA*
1924 O. von Porat *NOR*	S. Petersen *DEN*	A. Porzio *ARG*
1928 A. R. Jurado *ARG*	N. Ramm *SWE*	M. J. Michaelsen *DEN*
1932 S. Lovell *ARG*	L. Rovati *ITA*	F. Feary *USA*
1936 H. Runge *GER*	G. Lovell *ARG*	E. Nilsen *NOR*
1948 R. Iglesias *ARG*	G. Nilsson *SWE*	J. Arthur *SAF*
1952 H. E. Sanders *USA*	*Not awarded*	A. Nieman *SAF* & I. Koski *FIN*
1956 T. P. Rademacher *USA*	L. Mukhin *URS*	D. Bekker *SAF* & G. Bozzano *ITA*
1960 F. de Piccoli *ITA*	D. Bekker *SAF*	J. Nemec *TCH* & G. Siegmund *GER*
1964 J. Frazier *USA*	H. Huber *GER*	G. Ros *ITA* & V. Yemelyanov *URS*
1968 G. Foreman *USA*	I. Chepulis *URS*	G. Bambini *ITA* & J. Rocha *MEX*
1972 T. Stevenson *CUB*	I. Alexe *ROM*	P. Hussing *GER* & H. Thomsen *SWE*

Canoeing *Men*

Canadian Singles

Course 1,000m (1,094yd). Not held before 1936.

Gold	Silver	Bronze
1936 F. Amyot *CAN* 5min 32.1sec	B. Karlik *TCH* 5min 36.9sec	E. Koschik *GER* 5min 39.0sec
1948 J. Holeček *TCH* 5min 42.0sec	D. Bennett *CAN* 5min 53.3sec	R. Boutigny *FRA* 5min 55.9sec
1952 J. Holeček *TCH* 4min 56.3sec	J. Parti *HUN* 5min 03.6sec	O. Ojanperä *FIN* 5min 08.5sec
1956 L. Rotman *ROM* 5min 05.3sec	I. Hernek *HUN* 5min 06.2sec	G. Bukharin *URS* 5min 12.7sec
1960 J. Parti *HUN* 4min 33.93sec	A. Silayev *URS* 4min 34.41sec	L. Rotman *ROM* 4min 35.87sec
1964 J. Eschert *GER* 4min 35.14sec	A. Igorov *ROM* 4min 37.89sec	Y. Penyaev *URS* 4min 38.31sec

	Gold	Silver	Bronze
1968	T. Tatai *HUN* 4min 36.14sec	D. Lewe *GER* 4min 38.31sec	V. Galkov *URS* 4min 40.42sec
1972	I. Patzaichin *ROM* 4min 08.94sec	T. Wichmann *HUN* 4min 12.42sec	D. Lewe *GER* 4min 13.63sec

Canadian Pairs
Course 1,000m (1,094yd). Not held before 1936.

	Gold	Silver	Bronze
1936	TCH 4min 50.1sec	AUT 4min 53.8sec	CAN 4min 56.7sec
1948	TCH 5min 07.1sec	USA 5min 08.2sec	FRA 5min 15.2sec
1952	DEN 4min 38.3sec	TCH 4min 42.9sec	GER 4min 48.3sec
1956	ROM 4min 47.4sec	URS 4min 48.6sec	HUN 4min 54.3sec
1960	URS 4min 17.94sec	ITA 4min 20.77sec	HUN 4min 20.89sec
1964	URS 4min 04.64sec	FRA 4min 06.52sec	DEN 4min 07.48sec
1968	ROM 4min 07.18sec	HUN 4min 08.77sec	URS 4min 11.30sec
1972	URS 3min 52.60sec	ROM 3min 52.63sec	BUL 3min 58.10sec

Kayak Singles
Course 1,000m (1,094yd). Not held before 1936.

	Gold	Silver	Bronze
1936	G. Hradetzky *AUT* 4min 22.9sec	H. Cämmerer *GER* 4min 25.6sec	J. Kraaier *HOL* 4min 35.1sec
1948	G. Fredriksson *SWE* 4min 33.2sec	J. F. Kobberup Andersen *DEN* 4min 39.9sec	H. Eberhardt *FRA* 4min 41.4sec
1952	G. Fredriksson *SWE* 4min 07.9sec	T. Strömberg *FIN* 4min 09.7sec	L. Gantois *FRA* 4min 20.1sec
1956	G. Fredriksson *SWE* 4min 12.8sec	I. Pisarev *URS* 4min 15.3sec	L. Kiss *HUN* 4min 16.2sec
1960	E. Hansen *DEN* 3min 53.0sec	I. Szöllősi *HUN* 3min 54.02sec	G. Fredriksson *SWE* 3min 55.89sec
1964	R. Peterson *SWE* 3min 57.13sec	M. Hesz *HUN* 3min 57.28sec	A. Vernescu *ROM* 4min 00.77sec
1968	M. Hesz *HUN* 4min 02.63sec	A. Shaparenko *URS* 4min 03.58sec	E. Hansen *DEN* 4min 04.39sec
1972	A. Shaparenko *URS* 3min 48.06sec	R. Peterson *SWE* 3min 48.35sec	G. Csapo *HUN* 3min 49.38sec

Kayak Pairs
Course 1,000m (1,094yd). Not held before 1936.

	Gold	Silver	Bronze
1936	AUT 4min 03.8sec	GER 4min 08.9sec	HOL 4min 12.2sec
1948	SWE 4min 07.3sec	DEN 4min 07.5sec	FIN 4min 08.7sec
1952	FIN 3min 51.1sec	SWE 3min 51.1sec	AUT 3min 51.4sec
1956	GER 3min 49.6sec	URS 3min 51.4sec	AUT 3min 55.8sec
1960	SWE 3min 34.73sec	HUN 3min 34.91sec	POL 3min 37.34sec
1964	SWE 3min 38.54sec	HOL 3min 39.30sec	GER 3min 40.69sec
1968	URS 3min 37.54sec	HUN 3min 38.44sec	AUT 3min 40.71sec
1972	URS 3min 31.23sec	HUN 3min 32.00sec	POL 3min 33.83sec

Kayak Fours
Course 1,000m (1,094yd). Not held before 1964.

	Gold	Silver	Bronze
1964	URS 3min 14.67sec	GER 3min 15.39sec	ROM 3min 15.51sec
1968	NOR 3min 14.38sec	ROM 3min 14.81sec	HUN 3min 15.10sec
1972	URS 3min 14.02sec	ROM 3min 15.07sec	NOR 3min 15.27sec

Slalom – Canadian Singles
Not held before 1972.

	Gold	Silver	Bronze
1972	R. Eiben *GDR* 315.84 pts	R. Kauder *GER* 327.89 pts	J. McEwan *USA* 335.95 pts

Slalom – Canadian Pairs
Not held before 1972.

	Gold	Silver	Bronze
1972	GDR 310.68 pts	GER 311.90 pts	FRA 315.10 pts

Slalom – Kayak Singles
Not held before 1972.

	Gold	Silver	Bronze
1972	S. Horn *GDR* 268.56 pts	N. Sattler *AUT* 270.76 pts	H. Gimpel *GDR* 277.95 pts

Canoeing *Women*
Kayak Singles
Course 500m (547yd). Not held before 1948.

	Gold	Silver	Bronze
1948	K. Hoff *DEN* 2min 31.9sec	A. van der Anker-Doedans *HOL* 2min 32.8sec	F. Schwingl *AUT* 2min 32.9sec
1952	S. Saimo *FIN* 2min 18.4sec	G. Liebhart *AUT* 2min 18.8sec	N. Savina *URS* 2min 21.6sec
1956	E. Dementieva *URS* 2min 18.9sec	T. Zenz *GER* 2min 19.6sec	T. Søby *DEN* 2min 22.3sec
1960	A. Seredina *URS* 2min 08.08sec	T. Zenz *GER* 2min 08.22sec	D. Pilecka (Walkowiakówna) *POL* 2min 10.46sec
1964	L. Khvedosyuk *URS* 2min 12.87sec	H. Lauer *ROM* 2min 15.35sec	M. Jones *USA* 2min 15.68sec
1968	L. Pinaeva *URS* 2min 11.09sec	R. Breuer *GER* 2min 12.71sec	V. Dumitru *ROM* 2min 13.22sec
1972	Y. Ryabchinskaya *URS* 2min 03.17sec	M. Jaapies *HOL* 2min 04.03sec	A. Pfeffer *HUN* 2min 05.50sec

Kayak Pairs
Course 500m (547yd). Not held before 1960.

	Gold	Silver	Bronze
1960	URS 1min 54.76sec	GER 1min 56.66sec	HUN 1min 58.22sec
1964	GER 1min 56.95sec	USA 1min 59.16sec	ROM 2min 00.25sec
1968	GER 1min 56.44sec	HUN 1min 58.60sec	URS 1min 58.61sec
1972	URS 1min 53.50sec	GDR 1min 54.30sec	ROM 1min 55.01sec

Slalom – Kayak Singles
Not held before 1972.

	Gold	Silver	Bronze
1972	A. Bahmann *GDR* 364.50 pts	G. Grothaus *GER* 398.15 pts	M. Wunderlich *GER* 400.50 pts

Cycling
1,000 Metres Sprint
In 1896–1900 the distance was 2,000m. From 1924 only times over the last 200m have been recorded.

	Gold	Silver	Bronze
1896	P. Masson *FRA* 4min 56.0sec	S. Nikolopoulos *GRE* 5min 00.2sec	L. Flameng *FRA* nda
1900	G. Taillandier *FRA* 2min 52.0sec	F. Sanz *FRA* nda	Lake *USA* nda
1904	*Not held*		
1908	*Final declared void because time limit was exceeded.*		
1912	*Not held*		
1920	M. Peeters *HOL* 1min 38.3sec	H. T. Johnson *GBR* nda	H. Ryan *GBR* nda
1924	L. Michard *FRA* 12.8sec	J. Meijer *HOL*	J. Cugnot *FRA*
1928	R. Beaufrand *FRA* 13.2sec	A. Mazairac *HOL*	W. Falck-Hansen *DEN*
1932	J. van Egmond *HOL* 12.6sec	L. Chaillot *FRA*	B. Pellizzari *ITA*
1936	T. Merkens *GER* 11.8sec	A. van Vliet *HOL*	L. Chaillot *FRA*
1948	M. Ghella *ITA* 12.0sec	R. Harris *GBR*	A. Schandorff *DEN*
1952	E. Sacchi *ITA* 12.0sec	L. Cox *AUS*	W. Potzernheim *GER*
1956	M. Rousseau *FRA* 11.4sec	G. Pesenti *ITA*	R. Ploog *AUS*
1960	S. Gaiardoni *ITA* 11.1sec	L. Sterckx *BEL*	V. Gasparella *ITA*
1964	G. Pettenella *ITA* 13.69sec	S. Bianchetto *ITA*	D. Morelon *FRA*
1968	D. Morelon *FRA* 10.68sec	G. Turrini *ITA*	P. Trentin *FRA*
1972	D. Morelon *FRA* 11.69sec	J. M. Nicholson *AUS*	O. Pkhakadze *URS*

1,000 Metres Time Trial
Not held before 1928.

	Gold	Silver	Bronze
1928	W. Falck-Hansen *DEN* 1min 14.4sec	G. D. H. Bosch van Drakestein *HOL* 1min 15.2sec	E. Gray *AUS* 1min 15.6sec
1932	E. Gray *AUS* 1min 13.0sec	J. van Egmond *HOL* 1min 13.3sec	G. Rampelberg *FRA* 1min 13.4sec
1936	A. van Vliet *HOL* 1min 12.0sec	P. Georget *FRA* 1min 12.8sec	R. Karsch *GER* 1min 13.2sec
1948	J. Dupont *FRA* 1min 13.5sec	P. Nihant *BEL* 1min 14.5sec	T. Godwin *GBR* 1min 15.0sec
1952	R. Mockridge *AUS* 1min 11.1sec	M. Morettini *ITA* 1min 12.7sec	R. Robinson *SAF* 1min 13.0sec
1956	L. Faggin *ITA* 1min 09.8sec	L. Fouček *TCH* 1min 11.4sec	A. Swift *SAF* 1min 11.6sec
1960	S. Gaiardoni *ITA* 1min 07.27sec	D. Gieseler *GER* 1min 08.75sec	R. Vargashkin *URS* 1min 08.86sec
1964	P. Sercu *BEL* 1min 09.59sec	G. Pettenella *ITA* 1min 10.09sec	P. Trentin *FRA* 1min 10.42sec
1968	P. Trentin *FRA* 1min 03.91sec	N. C. Fredborg *DEN* 1min 04.61sec	J. Kierzkowski *POL* 1min 04.63sec
1972	N. C. Fredborg *DEN* 1min 06.44sec	D. Clark *AUS* 1min 06.87sec	J. Schütze *GDR* 1min 07.02sec

4,000 Metres Pursuit *Individual*
Not held before 1964.

	Gold	Silver	Bronze
1964	J. Daler *TCH* 5min 04.75sec	G. Ursi *ITA* 5min 05.96sec	P. Isaksson *DEN* 5min 01.90sec
1968	D. Rebillard *FRA* 4min 41.71sec	M. F. Jensen *DEN* 4min 42.43sec	X. Kurmann *SUI* 4min 39.42sec
1972	K. Knudsen *NOR* 4min 45.74sec	X. Kurmann *SUI* 4min 51.96sec	H. Lutz *GER* 4min 50.80sec

4,000 Metres Pursuit *Team*
Not held before 1920.

	Gold	Silver	Bronze
1920	ITA 5min 20.0sec	GBR nda	SAF nda
1924	ITA 5min 15.0sec	POL nda	BEL nda
1928	ITA 5min 01.8sec	HOL 5min 06.2sec	GBR 5min 02.4sec

	Gold	Silver	Bronze
1932	ITA 4min 53.0sec	FRA 4min 55.7sec	GBR 4min 56.0sec
1936	FRA 4min 45.0sec	ITA 4min 51.0sec	GBR 4min 53.6sec
1948	FRA 4min 57.8sec	ITA 5min 36.7sec	GBR 5min 55.8sec
1952	ITA 4min 46.1sec	SAF 4min 53.6sec	GBR 4min 51.5sec
1956	ITA 4min 37.4sec	FRA 4min 39.4sec	GBR 4min 42.2sec
1960	ITA 4min 30.90sec	GER 4min 35.78sec	URS 4min 34.05sec
1964	GER 4min 35.67sec	ITA 4min 35.74sec	HOL 4min 38.99sec
1968	DEN 4min 22.44sec	GER 4min 18.92sec	ITA 4min 18.35sec
1972	GER 4min 22.14sec	GDR 4min 25.25sec	GBR 4min 23.78sec

2,000 Metres Tandem

Not held before 1908. From 1928 only times over the last 200m have been recorded.

1908	FRA 3min 07.6sec	GBR nda	GBR nda
1912	*Not held*		
1920	GBR 2min 49.4sec	SAF nda	HOL nda
1924	FRA 2min 40.0sec	DEN nda	HOL nda
1928	HOL 11.8sec	GBR	GER
1932	FRA 12.0sec	GBR	DEN
1936	GER 11.8sec	HOL	FRA
1948	ITA 11.3sec	GBR	FRA
1952	AUS 11.0sec	SAF	ITA
1956	AUS 10.8sec	TCH	ITA
1960	ITA 10.7sec	GER	URS
1964	ITA 10.75sec	URS	GER
1968	FRA 9.83sec	HOL	BEL
1972	URS 10.52sec	GDR	POL

Road Race *Individual*

In 1896 the distance was 87 km (54 miles); in 1912 320 km (199 miles); in 1920 175km (109 miles); in 1924 188km (117 miles); in 1928 169km (105 miles); in 1932 and 1936 100km (62 miles); in 1948 199.6km (124 miles); in 1952 190.4km (118 miles); in 1956 187.7km (117 miles); in 1960 175.4km (109 miles); in 1964 194.8km (121 miles); in 1968 196.2km (122 miles); in 1972 182.4km (113 miles).

1896	A. Konstantinidis *GRE* 3hr 22min 31.0sec	A. Goedrich *GER* 3hr 42min 18.0sec	F. Battel *GBR* nda
1900–1908	*Not held*		
1912	R. Lewis *SAF* 10hr 42min 39.0sec	F. Grubb *GBR* 10hr 51min 24.2sec	C. Schutte *USA* 10hr 52min 38.8sec
1920	H. Stenqvist *SWE* 4hr 40 min 01.8sec	H. J. Kaltenbrun *SAF* 4hr 41min 26.6sec	F. Canteloupe *FRA* 4hr 42min 54.4sec
1924	A. Blanchonnet *FRA* 6hr 20min 48.0sec	H. Hoevenaers *BEL* 6hr 30min 27.0sec	R. Hamel *FRA* 6hr 30min 51.6sec
1928	H. Hansen *DEN* 4hr 47min 18.0sec	F. W. Southall *GBR* 4hr 55min 06.0sec	G. Carlsson *SWE* 5hr 00min 17.0sec
1932	A. Pavesi *ITA* 2hr 28min 05.6sec	G. Segato *ITA* 2hr 29min 21.4sec	B. Britz *SWE* 2hr 29min 45.2sec
1936	R. Charpentier *FRA* 2hr 33min 05.0sec	G. Lapébie *FRA* 2hr 33min 05.2sec	E. Nievergelt *SUI* 2hr 33min 05.8sec
1948	J. Beyaert *FRA* 5hr 18min 12.6sec	G. P. Voorting *HOL* 5hr 18min 16.2sec	L. Wouters *BEL* 5hr 18min 16.2sec
1952	A. Noyelle *BEL* 5hr 06min 03.4sec	R. Grondelaers *BEL* 5hr 06min 51.2sec	E. Ziegler *GER* 5hr 07min 47.5sec
1956	E. Baldini *ITA* 5hr 21min 17.0sec	A. Geyre *FRA* 5hr 23min 16.0sec	A. Jackson *GBR* 5hr 23min 16.0sec
1960	V. Kapitonov *URS* 4hr 20min 37.0sec	L. Trapè *ITA* 4hr 20min 37.0sec	W. van den Berghen *BEL* 4hr 20min 57.0sec
1964	M. Zanin *ITA* 4hr 39min 51.63sec	K. Å. Rodian *DEN* 4hr 39min 51.65sec	W. Godefroot *BEL* 4hr 39min 51.74sec
1968	P. Vianelli *ITA* 4hr 41min 25.24sec	L. Mortensen *DEN* 4hr 42min 49.71sec	G. Pettersson *SWE* 4hr 43min 15.24sec
1972	H. Kuiper *HOL* 4hr 14min 37.0sec	K. C. Sefton *AUS* 4hr 15min 04.0sec	*Not awarded*

Road Race *Team*

Although team medals were awarded from 1912, a separate team event was not held until 1960. From 1960 it has been a 100-km (62-miles) time trial.

1912	SWE 44hr 35min 33.6sec	GBR 44hr 44min 39.2sec	USA 44hr 47min 55.5sec
1920	FRA 19hr 16min 43.2sec	SWE 19hr 23min 10.0sec	BEL 19hr 28min 44.4sec
1924	FRA 19hr 30min 14.0sec	BEL 19hr 46min 55.4sec	SWE 19hr 59min 41.6sec
1928	DEN 15hr 09min 14.0sec	GBR 15hr 14min 49.0sec	SWE 15hr 27min 49.0sec
1932	ITA 7hr 27min 15.2sec	DEN 7hr 38min 50.2sec	SWE 7hr 39min 12.6sec
1936	FRA 7hr 39min 16.2sec	SUI 7hr 39min 20.4sec	BEL 7hr 39min 21.0sec
1948	BEL 15hr 58min 17.4sec	GBR 16hr 03min 31.6sec	FRA 16hr 08min 19.4sec
1952	BEL 15hr 20min 46.6sec	ITA 15hr 33min 27.3sec	FRA 15hr 38min 58.1sec
1956	FRA 22 pts (16hr 10min 36sec)	GBR 23 pts (16hr 10min 46sec)	GER 27 pts (16hr 11min 10sec)

	Gold	Silver	Bronze
1960	ITA 2hr 14min 33.53sec	GER 2hr 16min 56.31sec	URS 2hr 18min 41.67sec
1964	HOL 2hr 26min 31.19sec	ITA 2hr 26min 55.39sec	SWE 2hr 27min 11.52sec
1968	HOL 2hr 07min 49.06sec	SWE 2hr 09min 26.60sec	ITA 2hr 10min 18.74sec
1972	URS 2hr 11min 17.8sec	POL 2hr 11min 47.5sec	*Not awarded*

Equestrian Sports

Show Jumping *Individual*

Not held before 1900.

1900	A. Haegeman (Benton II) *BEL* 2min 16.0sec	G. van der Poele (Windsor Squire) *BEL* 2min 17.6sec	de Champsavin (Terpsichore) *FRA* 2min 26.0sec
1904–1908	*Not held*		
1912	J. Cariou (Mignon) *FRA* 186 pts	R. W. von Kröcher (Dohna) *GER* 186 pts	E. de Blommaert (Clonmore) *BEL* 185 pts
1920	T. Lequio (Trebecco) *ITA* 2 flts	A. Valerio (Cento) *ITA* 3 flts	G. Lewenhaupt (Mon Coeur) *SWE* 4 flts
1924	A. Gemuseus (Lucette) *SUI* 6 flts	T. Lequio (Trebecco) *ITA* 8.75 flts	A. Królikiewicz (Picador) *POL* 10 flts
1928	F. Ventura (Eliot) *TCH* 0 flts	P. Bertran de Balanda (Papillon) *FRA* 2 flts	C. Kuhn (Pepita) *SUI* 4 flts
1932	T. Nishi (Uranus) *JPN* 8 flts	H. Chamberlin (Show Girl) *USA* 12 flts	C. von Rosen (Empire) *SWE* 16 flts
1936	K. Hasse (Tora) *GER* 4 flts	H. Rang (Delfis) *ROM* 4 flts	J. von Platthy (Sellö) *HUN* 8 flts
1948	H. Mariles- Cortés (Arete) *MEX* 6.25 flts	R. Uriza (Hatvey) *MEX* 8 flts	J. F. d'Orgeix (Sucre de Pomme) *FRA* 8 flts
1952	P. J. d'Oriola (Ali Baba) *FRA* 8 flts	O. Cristi (Bambi) *CHI* 8 flts	F. Thiedemann (Meteor) *GER* 8 flts
1956	H. G. Winkler (Halla) *GER* 4 flts	R. d'Inzeo (Merano) *ITA* 8 flts	P. d'Inzeo (Uruguay) *ITA* 11 flts
1960	R. d'Inzeo (Posillipo) *ITA* 12 flts	P. d'Inzeo (The Rock) *ITA* 16 flts	D. Broome (Sunsalve) *GBR* 23 flts
1964	P. J. d'Oriola (Lutteur B) *FRA* 9 flts	H. Schridde (Dozent) *GER* 13.75 flts	P. Robeson (Firecrest) *GBR* 16 flts
1968	W. Steinkraus (Snowbound) *USA* 4 flts	M. Coakes (Stroller) *GBR* 8 flts	D. Broome (Mister Softee) *GBR* 12 flts
1972	G. Mancinelli (Ambassador) *ITA* 8 flts	A. Moore (Psalm) *GBR* 8 flts	N. Shapiro (Sloopy) *USA* 8 flts

Show Jumping *Team* (Nations' Cup)

Not held before 1912.

1912	SWE 545 pts	FRA 538 pts	GER 530 pts
1920	SWE 14 flts	BEL 16.25 flts	ITA 18.75 flts
1924	SWE 42.5 flts	SUI 50 flts	POR 53 flts
1928	ESP 4 flts	POL 8 flts	SWE 10 flts
1932	*Not awarded (no nation completed the course with three riders)*		
1936	GER 44 flts	HOL 51.5 flts	POR 56 flts
1948	MEX 34.25 flts	ESP 56.5 flts	GBR 67 flts
1952	GBR 40.75 flts	CHI 45.75 flts	USA 52.25 flts
1956	GER 40 flts	ITA 66 flts	GBR 69 flts
1960	GER 46.5 flts	USA 66 flts	ITA 80.5 flts
1964	GER 68.50 flts	FRA 77.75 flts	ITA 88.50 flts
1968	CAN 102.75 flts	FRA 110.50 flts	GER 117.25 flts
1972	GER 32.00 flts	USA 32.25 flts	ITA 48.00 flts

Dressage *Individual*

Not held before 1912.

1912	C. Bonde (Emperor) *SWE* 15 flts	G. A. Boltenstern (Neptun) *SWE* 21 flts	H. von Blixen-Finecke (Maggie) *SWE* 32 flts
1920	J. Lundblad (Uno) *SWE* 27.937 pts	B. Sandström (Sabel) *SWE* 26.312 pts	H. von Rosen (Running Sister) *SWE* 25.125 pts
1924	E. Linder (Piccolomini) *SWE* 276.4 pts	B. Sandström (Sabel) *SWE* 275.8 pts	F. X. Lesage (Plumard) *FRA* 265.8 pts
1928	C. F. Frhr von Langen (Draufgänger) *GER* 237.42 pts	P. Marion (Linon) *FRA* 231.00 pts	R. Olson (Günstling) *SWE* 229.78 pts
1932	F. X. Lesage (Taine) *FRA* 343.75 pts	P. Marion (Linon) *FRA* 305.42 pts	H. Tuttle (Olympic) *USA* 300.50 pts

	Gold	Silver	Bronze
1936	H. Pollay (Kronos) GER 1,760.0 pts	F. Gerhard (Absinth) GER 1,745.5 pts	A. Podhajsky (Nero) AUT 1,721.5 pts
1948	H. Moser (Hummer) SUI 492.5 pts	A. Jousseaume (Harpagon) FRA 480.0 pts	G. A. Boltenstern (Trumf) SWE 447.5 pts
1952	H. St Cyr (Master Rufus) SWE 561.0 pts	L. Hartel (Jubilee) DEN 541.5 pts	A. Jousseaume (Harpagon) FRA 541.0 pts
1956	H. St Cyr (Juli) SWE 860 pts	L. Hartel (Jubilee) DEN 850 pts	L. Linsenhoff (Adular) GER 832 pts
1960	S. Filatov (Absent) URS 2,144 pts	G. Fischer (Wald) SUI 2,087 pts	J. Neckermann (Asbach) GER 2,082 pts
1964	H. Chammartin (Woermann) SUI 1,504 pts	H. Boldt (Remus) GER 1,503 pts	S. Filatov (Absent) URS 1,486 pts
1968	I. Kizimov (Ikhor) URS 1,572 pts	J. Neckermann (Mariano) GER 1,546 pts	R. Klimke (Dux) GER 1,537 pts
1972	L. Linsenhoff (Piaff) GER 1,229 pts	E. Petushkova (Pepel) URS 1,185 pts	J. Neckermann (Venetia) GER 1,177 pts

Dressage *Team*
Not held before 1928.

	Gold	Silver	Bronze
1928	GER 669.72 pts	SWE 650.86 pts	HOL 642.96 pts
1932	FRA 2,818.75 pts	SWE 2,678.00 pts	USA 2,576.75 pts
1936	GER 5,074 pts	FRA 4,856 pts	SWE 4,660.5 pts
1948	FRA 1,269 pts	USA 1,256 pts	POR 1,182 pts
1952	SWE 1,597.5 pts	SUI 1,579.0 pts	GER 1,501.0 pts
1956	SWE 2,475 pts	GER 2,346 pts	SUI 2,346 pts
1960	Not held		
1964	GER 2,558 pts	SUI 2,526 pts	URS 2,311 pts
1968	GER 2,699 pts	URS 2,657 pts	SUI 2,547 pts
1972	URS 5,095 pts	GER 5,083 pts	SWE 4,849 pts

Three-Day Event *Individual*
Not held before 1912.

	Gold	Silver	Bronze
1912	A. Nordlander (Lady Artist) SWE 46.59 pts	H. von Rochow (Idealist) GER 46.42 pts	J. Cariou (Cocotte) FRA 46.32 pts
1920	H. Mörner (Germania) SWE 1,775 pts	Å. Lundström (Yrsa) SWE 1,738.75 pts	E. Caffaratti (Traditore) ITA 1,733.75 pts
1924	A. D. C. van der Voort van Zijp (Silver Piece) HOL 1,976 pts	F. Kirkebjerg (Meteor) DEN 1,873.5 pts	S. Doak (Pathfinder) USA 1,845.5 pts
1928	C. F. Pahud de Mortanges (Marcroix) HOL 1,969.82 pts	G. P. de Kruyff (Va-t-en) HOL 1,967.26 pts	B. Neumann (Ilja) GER 1,944.42 pts
1932	C. F. Pahud de Mortanges (Marcroix) HOL 1,813.83 pts	E. F. Thomson (Jenny Camp) USA 1,811 pts	C. von Rosen (Sunnyside Maid) SWE 1,809.42 pts
1936	L. Stubbendorf (Nurmi) GER 37.70 flts	E. F. Thomson (Jenny Camp) USA 99.90 flts	H. M. Lunding (Jason) DEN 102.20 flts
1948	B. Chevalier (Aiglonne) FRA +4 pts	F. Henry (Swing Low) USA 21 flts	R. Selfelt (Claque) SWE 25 flts
1952	H. von Blixen-Finecke (Jubal) SWE 28.33 flts	G. Lefrant (Verdun) FRA 54.50 flts	W. Büsing (Hubertus) GER 55.50 flts
1956	P. Kastenman (Iluster) SWE 66.53 flts	A. Lütke-Westhues (Trux von Kamax) GER 84.87 flts	F. Weldon (Kilbarry) GBR 85.48 flts
1960	L. Morgan (Salad Days) AUS +7.15 pts	N. Lavis (Mirrabooka) AUS 16.50 flts	A. Bühler (Gay Spark) SUI 51.21 flts
1964	M. Checcoli (Surbean) ITA 64.40 pts	C. Moratorio (Chalan) ARG 56.40 pts	F. Ligges (Donkosak) GER 49.20 pts
1968	J. J. Guyon (Pitou) FRA 38.86 flts	D. Allhusen (Lochinvar) GBR 41.61 flts	M. Page (Foster) USA 52.31 flts
1972	R. Meade (Laurieston) GBR 57.73 pts	A. Argenton (Woodland) ITA 43.33 pts	J. Jonsson (Sarajevo) SWE 39.67 pts

Three-Day Event *Team*
Not held before 1912.

	Gold	Silver	Bronze
1912	SWE 139.06 pts	GER 138.48 pts	USA 137.33 pts
1920	SWE 5,057.5 pts	ITA 4,735 pts	BEL 4,560 pts
1924	HOL 5,297.5 pts	SWE 4,743.5 pts	ITA 4,512.5 pts
1928	HOL 5,865.68 pts	NOR 5,395.68 pts	POL 5,067.92 pts
1932	USA 5,038.083 pts	HOL 4,689.083 pts	
1936	GER 676.65 flts	POL 991.70 flts	GBR 9,195.50 flts
1948	USA 161.50 flts	SWE 165.00 flts	MEX 305.25 flts
1952	SWE 221.94 flts	GER 235.49 flts	USA 587.16 flts

	Gold	Silver	Bronze
1956	GBR 355.48 flts	GER 475.91 flts	CAN 572.72 flts
1960	AUS 128.18 flts	SUI 386.02 flts	FRA 515.71 flts
1964	ITA 85.80 flts	USA 65.86 pts	GER 56.73 pts
1968	GBR 175.93 flts	USA 245.87 flts	AUS 331.26 flts
1972	GBR 95.53 pts	USA 10.81 pts	GER −18.00 flts

Fencing *Men*
Foil *Individual*

	Gold	Silver	Bronze
1896	E. Gravelotte FRA 4 wins	H. Callot FRA 3 wins	P. Mavromichalis Pierrakos GRE 2 wins
1900	E. Coste FRA 6 wins	H. Masson FRA 5 wins	J. Boulenger FRA 4 wins
1904	R. Fonst CUB nda	A. Van Zo Post CUB nda	C. Tatham CUB nda
1908	Not held		
1912	N. Nadi ITA 7 wins	P. Speciale ITA 5 wins	R. Verderber AUT 4 wins
1920	N. Nadi ITA 10 wins	P. Cattiau FRA 9 wins	R. Ducret FRA 9 wins
1924	R. Ducret FRA 6 wins	P. Cattiau FRA 5 wins	M. van Damme BEL 4 wins
1928	L. Gaudin FRA 9 wins	E. Casmir GER 9 wins	G. Gaudini ITA 9 wins
1932	G. Marzi ITA 9 wins	J. Levis USA 6 wins	G. Gaudini ITA 5 wins
1936	G. Gaudini ITA 7 wins	E. Gardère FRA 6 wins	G. Bocchino ITA 4 wins
1948	J. Buhan FRA 7 wins	C. d'Oriola FRA 5 wins	L. Maszlay HUN 4 wins
1952	C. d'Oriola FRA 8 wins	E. Mangiarotti ITA 6 wins	M. di Rosa ITA 5 wins
1956	C. d'Oriola FRA 6 wins	G. Bergamini ITA 5 wins	A. Spallino ITA 5 wins
1960	V. Zhdanovich URS 7 wins	Y. Sisikin URS 4 wins	A. Axelrod USA 3 wins
1964	E. Franke POL 3 wins	J. C. Magnan FRA 2 wins	D. Revenu FRA 1 win
1968	I. Drimba ROM 4 wins	J. Kamuti HUN 3 wins	D. Revenu FRA 3 wins
1972	W. Woyda POL 5 wins	J. Kamuti HUN 4 wins	C. Noël FRA 2 wins

Foil *Team*
Not held before 1920, except in 1904 when there was a competition won by Cuba from an international team.

	Gold	Silver	Bronze
1920	ITA	FRA	USA
1924	FRA	BEL	HUN
1928	ITA	FRA	ARG
1932	FRA	ITA	USA
1936	ITA	FRA	GER
1948	FRA	ITA	BEL
1952	FRA	ITA	HUN
1956	ITA	FRA	HUN
1960	URS	ITA	GER
1964	URS	POL	FRA
1968	FRA	URS	POL
1972	POL	URS	FRA

Épée *Individual*
Not held before 1900.

	Gold	Silver	Bronze
1900	R. Fonst CUB nda	L. Perrée FRA nda	L. Sée FRA nda
1904	R. Fonst CUB nda	C. Tatham CUB nda	A. Van Zo Post CUB nda
1908	G. Alibert FRA 5 wins	A. Lippmann FRA 4 wins	E. Olivier FRA 4 wins
1912	P. Anspach BEL 6 wins	I. Osiier DEN 5 wins	P. Le Hardy de Beaulieu BEL 4 wins
1920	A. Massard FRA 9 wins	A. Lippmann FRA 7 wins	G. Buchard FRA 6 wins
1924	C. Delporte BEL 8 wins	R. Ducret FRA 7 wins	N. Hellsten SWE 7 wins
1928	L. Gaudin FRA 8 wins	G. Buchard FRA 7 wins	G. Calnan USA 6 wins
1932	G. Cornaggia-Medici ITA 8 wins	G. Buchard FRA 8 wins	C. Agostini ITA 7 wins
1936	F. Riccardi ITA 5 wins	S. Ragno ITA 6 wins	G. Cornaggia-Medici ITA 6 wins
1948	L. Cantone ITA 7 wins	O. Zappelli SUI 5 wins	E. Mangiarotti ITA 5 wins
1952	E. Mangiarotti ITA 7 wins	D. Mangiarotti ITA 6 wins	O. Zappelli SUI 6 wins

	Gold	Silver	Bronze
1956	C. Pavesi *ITA* 5 wins	G. Delfino *ITA* 5 wins	E. Mangiarotti *ITA* 5 wins
1960	G. Delfino *ITA* 5 wins	A. Jay *GBR* 5 wins	B. Khabarov *URS* 4 wins
1964	G. Kriss *URS* 2 wins	W. Hoskyns *GBR* 2 wins	G. Kostava *URS* 1 win
1968	G. Kulcsár *HUN* 4 wins	G. Kriss *URS* 4 wins	G. Saccaro *ITA* 4 wins
1972	C. Fenyvesi *HUN* 4 wins	J. La Degaillerie *FRA* 3 wins	G. Kulcsár *HUN* 3 wins

Épée *Team*
Not held before 1908.

	Gold	Silver	Bronze
1908	FRA	GBR	BEL
1912	BEL	GBR	HOL
1920	ITA	BEL	FRA
1924	FRA	BEL	ITA
1928	ITA	FRA	POR
1932	FRA	ITA	USA
1936	ITA	SWE	FRA
1948	FRA	ITA	SWE
1952	ITA	SWE	SUI
1956	ITA	HUN	FRA
1960	ITA	GBR	URS
1964	HUN	ITA	FRA
1968	HUN	URS	POL
1972	HUN	SUI	URS

Sabre *Individual*

	Gold	Silver	Bronze
1896	I. Georgiadis *GRE* 4 wins	T. Karakalos *GRE* 3 wins	H. Nielsen *DEN* 2 wins
1900	G. de la Falaise *FRA* nda	L. Thiébaut *FRA* nda	S. Flesch *AUT* nda
1904	M. De Diaz *CUB* nda	W. Grebe *USA* nda	A. Van Zo Post *CUB* nda
1908	J. Fuchs *HUN* 6 wins	B. Zulavsky *HUN* 6 wins	V. Goppold de Lobsdorf *BOH* 4 wins
1912	J. Fuchs *HUN* 6 wins	B. Békéssy *HUN* 5 wins	E. Mészáros *HUN* 5 wins
1920	N. Nadi *ITA* 11 wins	A. Nadi *ITA* 9 wins	A. E. W. de Jong *HOL* 7 wins
1924	S. Posta *HUN* 5 wins	R. Ducret *FRA* 5 wins	J. Garai *HUN* 5 wins
1928	Ö. Tersztyánszky *HUN* 9 wins	A. Petschauer *HUN* 9 wins	B. Bini *ITA* 8 wins
1932	G. Piller *HUN* 8 wins	G. Gaudini *ITA* 7 wins	E. Kabos *HUN* 5 wins
1936	E. Kabos *HUN* 7 wins	G. Marzi *ITA* 6 wins	A. Gerevich *HUN* 6 wins
1948	A. Gerevich *HUN* 7 wins	V. Pinton *ITA* 5 wins	P. Kovács *HUN* 5 wins
1952	P. Kovács *HUN* 8 wins	A. Gerevich *HUN* 7 wins	T. Berczelly *HUN* 5 wins
1956	R. Kárpáti *HUN* 6 wins	J. Pawłowski *POL* 5 wins	L. Kuznetsov *URS* 4 wins
1960	R. Kárpáti *HUN* 5 wins	Z. Horváth *HUN* 4 wins	W. Calarese *ITA* 4 wins
1964	T. Pézsa *HUN* 2 wins	C. Arabo *FRA* 2 wins	U. Mavlikhanov *URS* 1 win
1968	J. Pawłowski *POL* 4 wins	M. Rakita *URS* 4 wins	T. Pésza *HUN* 3 wins
1972	V. Sidiak *URS* 4 wins	P. Maroth *HUN* 3 wins	V. Nazlymov *URS* 3 wins

Sabre *Team*
Not held before 1908.

	Gold	Silver	Bronze
1908	HUN	ITA	BOH
1912	HUN	AUT	HOL
1920	ITA	FRA	HOL
1924	ITA	HUN	HOL
1928	HUN	ITA	POL
1932	HUN	ITA	POL
1936	HUN	ITA	GER
1948	HUN	ITA	USA
1952	HUN	ITA	FRA
1956	HUN	POL	URS
1960	HUN	POL	ITA
1964	URS	ITA	POL
1968	URS	ITA	HUN
1972	ITA	URS	HUN

Fencing *Women*

Foil *Individual*
Not held before 1924.

	Gold	Silver	Bronze
1924	E. Osiier *DEN* 5 wins	G. M. Davis *GBR* 4 wins	G. Heckscher *DEN* 3 wins
1928	H. Mayer *GER* 7 wins	M. Freeman *GBR* 6 wins	O. Oelkers *GER* 4 wins
1932	E. Preis *AUT* 8 wins	J. H. Guiness *GBR* 8 wins	E. Bogen *HUN* 7 wins
1936	I. Elek *HUN* 6 wins	H. Mayer *GER* 5 wins	E. Preis *AUT* 5 wins
1948	I. Elek *HUN* 6 wins	K. Lachmann *DEN* 5 wins	E. (Preis) Müller *AUT* 5 wins
1952	I. Camber *ITA* 5 wins	I. Elek *HUN* 5 wins	K. Lachmann *DEN* 4 wins
1956	G. Sheen *GBR* 6 wins	O. Orban *ROM* 6 wins	R. Garilhe *FRA* 5 wins
1960	H. Schmid *GER* 6 wins	V. Rastvorova *URS* 5 wins	M. Vicol *ROM* 4 wins
1964	I. (Ujlaki) Rejtö *HUN* 2 wins	H. Mees *GER* 2 wins	A. Ragno *ITA* 2 wins
1968	Y. Novikova *URS* 4 wins	P. Roldan *MEX* 3 wins	I. Rejtö *HUN* 3 wins
1972	A. (Ragno) Lonzi *ITA* 4 wins	I. Bobis *HUN* 3 wins	G. Gorokhova *URS* 3 wins

Foil *Team*
Not held before 1960.

	Gold	Silver	Bronze
1960	URS	HUN	ITA
1964	HUN	URS	GER
1968	URS	HUN	ROM
1972	URS	HUN	ROM

Gymnastics *Men*

Combined Exercises *Individual*
Not held before 1900.

	Gold	Silver	Bronze
1900	G. Sandras *FRA* 302 pts	N. Bas *FRA* 295 pts	L. Démanet *FRA* 295 pts
1904	J. Lenhart *AUT* 69.80 pts	W. Weber *GER* 69.10 pts	A. Spinnler *SUI* 67.99 pts
1908	A. Braglia *ITA* 317 pts	S. W. Tysal *GBR* 312 pts	L. Ségura *FRA* 297 pts
1912	A. Braglia *ITA* 135 pts	L. Ségura *FRA* 132.5 pts	A. Tunesi *ITA* 131.5 pts
1920	G. Zampori *ITA* 88.35 pts	M. Torrès *FRA* 87.62 pts	J. Gounot *FRA* 87.45 pts
1924	L. Štukelj *YUG* 110.340 pts	R. Pražák *TCH* 110.323 pts	B. Supčik *TCH* 106.930 pts
1928	G. Miez *SUI* 247.500 pts	H. Hänggi *SUI* 246.625 pts	L. Štukelj *YUG* 244.875 pts
1932	R. Neri *ITA* 140.625 pts	I. Pelle *HUN* 134.925 pts	H. Savolainen *FIN* 134.575 pts
1936	A. Schwarzmann *GER* 133.100 pts	E. Mack *SUI* 112.334 pts	K. Frey *GER* 111.532 pts
1948	V. Huhtanen *FIN* 229.7 pts	W. Lehmann *SUI* 229.0 pts	P. Aaltonen *FIN* 228.8 pts
1952	V. Chukarin *URS* 115.70 pts	G. Shaginyan *URS* 114.95 pts	J. Stalder *SUI* 114.75 pts
1956	V. Chukarin *URS* 114.25 pts	T. Ono *JPN* 114.20 pts	Y. Titov *URS* 113.80 pts
1960	B. Shakhlin *URS* 115.95 pts	T. Ono *JPN* 115.90 pts	Y. Titov *URS* 115.60 pts
1964	Y. Endo *JPN* 115.95 pts	S. Tsurumi *JPN*, B. Shakhlin *URS* & V. Lisitski *URS* 115.40 pts	
1968	S. Kato *JPN* 115.90 pts	M. Voronin *URS* 115.85 pts	A. Nakayama *JPN* 115.65 pts
1972	S. Kato *JPN* 114.650 pts	E. Kenmotsu *JPN* 114.575 pts	A. Nakayama *JPN* 114.325 pts

Combined Exercises *Team*
Not held before 1904.

	Gold	Silver	Bronze
1904	USA 374.43 pts	USA 356.37 pts	USA 349.69 pts
1908	SWE 438 pts	NOR 425 pts	FIN 405 pts
1912	ITA 265.75 pts	HUN 227.25 pts	GBR 184.50 pts
1920	ITA 359.855 pts	BEL 346.785 pts	FRA 340.100 pts
1924	ITA 839.058 pts	FRA 820.528 pts	SUI 816.661 pts
1928	SUI 1,718.625 pts	TCH 1,712.250 pts	YUG 1,648.750 pts
1932	ITA 541.850 pts	USA 522.275 pts	FIN 509.995 pts
1936	GER 657.430 pts	SUI 654.802 pts	FIN 638.468 pts
1948	FIN 1,358.30 pts	SUI 1,356.70 pts	HUN 1,330.85 pts
1952	URS 574.40 pts	SUI 567.50 pts	FIN 564.20 pts
1956	URS 568.25 pts	JPN 566.40 pts	FIN 555.95 pts

	Gold	Silver	Bronze
1960	JPN 575.20 pts	URS 572.70 pts	ITA 559.05 pts
1964	JPN 577.95 pts	URS 575.45 pts	GER 565.10 pts
1968	JPN 575.90 pts	URS 571.10 pts	GDR 557.15 pts
1972	JPN 571.25 pts	URS 564.05 pts	GDR 559.70 pts

Floor Exercises
Not held before 1932.

	Gold	Silver	Bronze
1932	I. Pelle HUN 9.60 pts	G. Miez SUI 9.47 pts	M. Lertora ITA 9.23 pts
1936	G. Miez SUI 18.666 pts	J. Walter SUI 18.500 pts	K. Frey GER, E. Mack SUI 18.466 pts
1948	F. Pataki HUN 38.70 pts	J. Mogyorósi-Klencs HUN 38.40 pts	Z. Ružička TCH 38.10 pts
1952	W. Thoresson SWE 19.25 pts	T. Uesako JPN & J. Jokiel POL 19.15 pts	
1956	V. Muratov URS 19.20 pts	N. Aihara JPN, W. Thoresson SWE & V. Chukarin URS 19.10 pts	
1960	N. Aihara JPN 19.45 pts	Y. Titov URS 19.325 pts	F. Menichelli ITA 19.275 pts
1964	F. Menichelli ITA 19.45 pts	V. Lisitski URS 19.35 pts	Y. Endo JPN 19.35 pts
1968	S. Kato JPN 19.475 pts	A. Nakayama JPN 19.400 pts	T. Kato JPN 19.275 pts
1972	N. Andrianov URS 19.175 pts	A. Nakayama JPN 19.125 pts	S. Kasamatsu JPN 19.025 pts

Horizontal Bar

	Gold	Silver	Bronze
1896	H. Weingärtner GER	A. Flatow GER	
1900	Not held		
1904	A. Heida USA & E. Hennig USA 40 pts		G. Eyser USA 39 pts
1908–1920	Not held		
1924	L. Štukelj YUG 19.73 pts	J. Gutweniger SUI 19.236 pts	A. Higelin FRA 19.163 pts
1928	G. Miez SUI 19.17 pts	R. Neri ITA 19.00 pts	E. Mack SUI 18.92 pts
1932	D. Bixler USA 18.33 pts	H. Savolainen FIN 18.07 pts	E. Teräsvirta FIN 18.07 pts
1936	A. Saarvala FIN 19.367 pts	K. Frey GER 19.267 pts	A. Schwarzmann GER 19.233 pts
1948	J. Stalder SUI 39.7 pts	W. Lehmann SUI 39.4 pts	V. Huhtanen FIN 39.2 pts
1952	J. Günthard SUI 19.55 pts	J. Stalder SUI & A. Schwarzmann GER 19.50 pts	
1956	T. Ono JPN 19.60 pts	Y. Titov URS 19.40 pts	M. Takemoto JPN 19.30 pts
1960	T. Ono JPN 19.60 pts	M. Takemoto JPN 19.52 pts	B. Shakhlin URS 19.475 pts
1964	B. Shakhlin URS 19.625 pts	Y. Titov URS 19.55 pts	M. Cerar YUG 19.50 pts
1968	M. Voronin URS & A. Nakayama JPN 19.550 pts		E. Kenmotsu JPN 19.375 pts
1972	M. Tsukahara JPN 19.725 pts	S. Kato JPN 19.525 pts	S. Kasamatsu JPN 19.450 pts

Parallel Bars

	Gold	Silver	Bronze
1896	A. Flatow GER	J. A. Zutter SUI	H. Weingärtner GER
1900	Not held		
1904	G. Eyser USA 44 pts	A. Heida USA 43 pts	J. Duha USA 40 pts
1908–1920	Not held		
1924	A. Güttinger SUI 21.63 pts	R. Pražák TCH 21.61 pts	G. Zampori ITA 21.45 pts
1928	L. Vácha TCH 18.83 pts	J. Primožič YUG 18.50 pts	H. Hänggi SUI 18.08 pts
1932	R. Neri ITA 18.97 pts	I. Pelle HUN 18.60 pts	H. Savolainen FIN 18.27 pts
1936	K. Frey GER 19.067 pts	M. Reusch SUI 19.034 pts	A. Schwarzmann GER 18.967 pts
1948	M. Reusch SUI 39.50 pts	V. Huhtanen FIN 39.30 pts	C. Kipfer SUI & J. Stalder SUI 39.10 pts
1952	H. Eugster SUI 19.65 pts	V. Chukarin URS 19.60 pts	J. Stalder SUI 19.50 pts
1956	V. Chukarin URS 19.20 pts	M. Kubota JPN 19.15 pts	T. Ono JPN & M. Takemoto JPN 19.10 pts
1960	B. Shakhlin URS 19.40 pts	G. Carminucci ITA 19.375 pts	T. Ono JPN 19.35 pts
1964	Y. Endo JPN 19.675 pts	S. Tsurumi JPN 19.45 pts	F. Menichelli ITA 19.35 pts

	Gold	Silver	Bronze
1968	A. Nakayama JPN 19.475 pts	M. Voronin URS 19.425 pts	V. Klimenko URS 19.225 pts
1972	S. Kato JPN 19.475 pts	S. Kasamatsu JPN 19.375 pts	E. Kenmotsu JPN 19.250 pts

Pommelled Horse
In 1948 Zanetti (4th) and Figone (5th) received the silver and bronze medals respectively because it was not then the rule to pass over subsequent places when there was a tie for first place.

	Gold	Silver	Bronze
1896	J. A. Zutter SUI	H. Weingärtner GER	
1900	Not held		
1904	A. Heida USA 42 pts	G. Eyser USA 33 pts	W. Merz USA 29 pts
1908–1920	Not held		
1924	J. Wilhelm SUI 21.23 pts	J. Gutweniger SUI 21.13 pts	A. Rebetez SUI 20.73 pts
1928	H. Hänggi SUI 19.75 pts	G. Miez SUI 19.25 pts	H. Savolainen FIN 18.83 pts
1932	I. Pelle HUN 19.07 pts	O. Bonoli ITA 18.87 pts	F. Haubold USA 18.57 pts
1936	K. Frey GER 19.333 pts	E. Mack SUI 19.167 pts	A. Bachmann SUI 19.067 pts
1948	P. Aaltonen FIN, V. Huhtanen FIN & H. Savolainen FIN 38.7 pts	L. Zanetti ITA 38.30 pts	G. Figone ITA 38.20 pts
1952	V. Chukarin URS 19.50 pts	Y. Korolkov URS & G. Shaginyan URS 19.40 pts	
1956	B. Shakhlin URS 19.25 pts	T. Ono JPN 19.20 pts	V. Chukarin URS 19.10 pts
1960	E. Ekman FIN & B. Shakhlin URS 19.375 pts		S. Tsurumi JPN 19.150 pts
1964	M. Cerar YUG 19.525 pts	S. Tsurumi JPN 19.325 pts	Y. Tsapenko URS 19.20 pts
1968	M. Cerar YUG 19.325 pts	O. E. Laiho FIN 19.225 pts	M. Voronin URS 19.200 pts
1972	V. Klimenko URS 19.125 pts	S. Kato JPN 19.000 pts	E. Kenmotsu JPN 18.950 pts

Long Horse Vault

	Gold	Silver	Bronze
1896	C. Schuhmann GER	J. A. Zutter SUI	
1900	Not held		
1904	A. Heida USA & G. Eyser USA 36 pts		W. Merz USA 31 pts
1908–1920	Not held		
1924	F. Kriz USA 9.98 pts	J. Koutny TCH 9.97 pts	B. Mořkovsky TCH 9.93 pts
1928	E. Mack SUI 9.58 pts	E. Löffler TCH 9.50 pts	S. Derganc YUG 9.46 pts
1932	S. Guglielmetti ITA 18.03 pts	A. Jochim GER 17.77 pts	E. Carmichael USA 17.53 pts
1936	A. Schwarzmann GER 19.20 pts	E. Mack SUI 18.967 pts	M. Volz GER 18.467 pts
1948	P. Aaltonen FIN 39.1 pts	O. Rove FIN 39.0 pts	J. Mogyorosi-Klencs HUN, F. Pataki HUN & L. Sotornik TCH 38.5 pts
1952	V. Chukarin URS 19.20 pts	M. Takemoto JPN 19.15 pts	T. Uesako JPN & T. Ono JPN 19.10 pts
1956	H. Bantz GER & V. Muratov URS 18.85 pts		Y. Titov URS 18.75 pts
1960	T. Ono JPN & B. Shakhlin URS 19.35 pts		V. Portnoi URS 19.225 pts
1964	H. Yamashita JPN 19.660 pts	V. Lisitski URS 19.325 pts	H. Rantakari FIN 19.300 pts
1968	M. Voronin URS 19.000 pts	Y. Endo JPN 18.950 pts	S. Diomidov URS 18.925 pts
1972	K. Köste GDR 18.850 pts	V. Klimenko URS 18.825 pts	N. Andrianov URS 18.800 pts

Rings

	Gold	Silver	Bronze
1896	I. Mitropoulos GRE	H. Weingärtner GER	P. Persakis GRE
1900	Not held		
1904	H. Glass USA 45 pts	W. Merz USA 35 pts	E. Voight USA 32 pts
1908–1912	Not held		
1924	F. Martino ITA 21.553 pts	R. Pražák TCH 21.483 pts	L. Vácha TCH 21.430 pts
1928	L. Štukelj YUG 19.25 pts	L. Vácha TCH 19.17 pts	E. Löffler TCH 18.83 pts
1932	G. Gulack USA 18.97 pts	W. Denton USA 18.60 pts	G. Lattuada ITA 18.50 pts

	Gold	Silver	Bronze
1936	A. Hudec TCH 19.433 pts	L. Štukelj YUG 18.670 pts	M. Volz GER 18.670 pts
1948	K. Frei SUI 39.6 pts	M. Reusch SUI 39.1 pts	Z. Ružička TCH 38.5 pts
1952	G. Shaginyan URS 19.75 pts	V. Chukarin URS 19.55 pts	D. Leonkin URS & H. Eugster SUI 19.40 pts
1956	A. Azarian URS 19.35 pts	V. Muratov URS 19.15 pts	M. Takemoto JPN & M. Kubota JPN 19.10 pts
1960	A. Azarian URS 19.725 pts	B. Shakhlin URS 19.500 pts	V. Kapsazov BUL & T. Ono JPN 19.425 pts
1964	T. Hayata JPN 19.475 pts	F. Menichelli ITA 19.425 pts	B. Shakhlin URS 19.400 pts
1968	A. Nakayama JPN 19.450 pts	M. Voronin URS 19.325 pts	S. Kato JPN 19.225 pts
1972	A. Nakayama JPN 19.350 pts	M. Voronin URS 19.275 pts	M. Tsukahara JPN 19.225 pts

Gymnastics *Women*

Combined Exercises *Individual*

Not held before 1952.

	Gold	Silver	Bronze
1952	M. Gorokhovskaya URS 76.78 pts	N. Bocharova URS 75.94 pts	M. Korondi HUN 75.82 pts
1956	L. Latynina URS 74.933 pts	Á. Keleti HUN 74.633 pts	S. Muratova URS 74.466 pts
1960	L. Latynina URS 77.031 pts	S. Muratova URS 76.696 pts	P. Astakhova URS 76.164 pts
1964	V. Čáslavská TCH 77.564 pts	L. Latynina URS 76.998 pts	P. Astakhova URS 76.965 pts
1968	V. Čáslavská TCH 78.25 pts	Z. Voronina URS 76.85 pts	N. Kuchinskaya URS 76.75 pts
1972	L. Turishcheva URS 77.025 pts	K. Janz GDR 76.875 pts	T. Lazakovich URS 76.850 pts

Combined Exercises *Team*

Not held before 1928.

	Gold	Silver	Bronze
1928	HOL 316.75 pts	ITA 289.00 pts	GBR 258.25 pts
1932	Not held		
1936	GER 506.50 pts	TCH 503.60 pts	HUN 499.00 pts
1948	TCH 445.45 pts	HUN 440.55 pts	USA 422.63 pts
1952	URS 527.03 pts	HUN 520.96 pts	TCH 503.32 pts
1956	URS 444.80 pts	HUN 443.50 pts	ROM 438.20 pts
1960	URS 382.320 pts	TCH 373.323 pts	ROM 372.053 pts
1964	URS 380.890 pts	TCH 379.989 pts	JPN 377.889 pts
1968	URS 382.85 pts	TCH 382.20 pts	GDR 379.10 pts
1972	URS 380.50 pts	GDR 376.55 pts	HUN 368.25 pts

Beam

Not held until 1952.

	Gold	Silver	Bronze
1952	N. Bocharova URS 19.22 pts	M. Gorokhovskaya URS 19.13 pts	M. Korondi HUN 19.02 pts
1956	Á. Keleti HUN 18.800 pts	E. Bosáková TCH & T. Manina URS 18.633 pts	
1960	E. Bosáková TCH 19.283 pts	L. Latynina URS 19.233 pts	S. Muratova URS 19.232 pts
1964	V. Čáslavská TCH 19.449 pts	T. Manina URS 19.399 pts	L. Latynina URS 19.382 pts
1968	N. Kuchinskaya URS 19.650 pts	V. Čáslavská TCH 19.575 pts	L. Petrik URS 19.250 pts
1972	O. Korbut URS 19.400 pts	T. Lazakovich URS 19.375 pts	K. Janz GDR 18.975 pts

Asymmetrical Bars

•Not held before 1952.

	Gold	Silver	Bronze
1952	M. Korondi HUN 19.40 pts	M. Gorokhovskaya URS 19.26 pts	Á Keleti HUN 19.16 pts
1956	Á. Keleti HUN 18.966 pts	L. Latynina URS 18.833 pts	S. Muratova URS 18.800 pts
1960	P. Astakhova URS 19.616 pts	L. Latynina URS 19.416 pts	T. Lyukhina URS 19.399 pts
1964	P. Astakhova URS 19.332 pts	K. Makray HUN 19.216 pts	L. Latynina URS 19.199 pts
1968	V. Čáslavská TCH 19.650 pts	K. Janz GDR 19.500 pts	Z. Voronina URS 19.425 pts
1972	K. Janz GDR 19.675 pts	O. Korbut URS & E. Zuchold GDR 19.450 pts	

Horse Vault

Not held before 1952.

	Gold	Silver	Bronze
1952	Y. Kalinchuk URS 19.20 pts	M. Gorokhovskaya URS 19.19 pts	G. Minaicheva URS 19.16 pts

	Gold	Silver	Bronze
1956	L. Latynina URS 18.833 pts	T. Manina URS 18.800 pts	A. S. Colling SWE & O. Tass HUN 18.733 pts
1960	M. Nikolaeva URS 19.316 pts	S. Muratova URS 19.049 pts	L. Latynina URS 19.016 pts
1964	V. Čáslavská TCH 19.483 pts	L. Latynina URS 19.283 pts	B. Radochia GER 19.283 pts
1968	V. Čáslavská TCH 19.775 pts	E. Zuchold GDR 19.625 pts	Z. Voronina URS 19.500 pts
1972	K. Janz GDR 19.525 pts	E. Zuchold GDR 19.275 pts	L. Turishcheva URS 19.250 pts

Floor Exercises

Not held before 1952.

	Gold	Silver	Bronze
1952	Á. Keleti HUN 19.36 pts	M. Gorokhovskaya URS 19.20 pts	M. Korondi HUN 19.00 pts
1956	L. Latynina URS & Á. Keleti HUN 18.733 pts		E. Leuştean ROM 18.700 pts
1960	L. Latynina URS 19.583 pts	P. Astakhova URS 19.532 pts	T. Lyukhina URS 19.449 pts
1964	L. Latynina URS 19.599 pts	P. Astakhova URS 19.500 pts	A. Jánosi HUN 19.300 pts
1968	V. Čáslavská TCH & L. Petrik URS 19.675 pts		N. Kuchinskaya URS 19.650 pts
1972	O. Korbut URS 19.575 pts	L. Turishcheva URS 19.550 pts	T. Lazakovich URS 19.450 pts

Handball

Not held before 1972.

	Gold	Silver	Bronze
1972	YUG	TCH	ROM

Hockey

Not held before 1908.

	Gold	Silver	Bronze
1908	ENG	IRL	SCO & WAL
1912	Not held		
1920	ENG	DEN	BEL
1924	Not held		
1928	IND	HOL	GER
1932	IND	JPN	USA
1936	IND	GER	HOL
1948	IND	GBR	HOL
1952	IND	HOL	GBR
1956	IND	PAK	GER
1960	PAK	IND	ESP
1964	IND	PAK	AUS
1968	PAK	AUS	IND
1972	GER	PAK	IND

Judo

Lightweight

Weight limit 1964 68kg (149lb 14½oz); from 1972 63kg (138lb 14½oz). Not held before 1964.

	Gold	Silver	Bronze
1964	T. Nakatani JPN	E. Hänni SUI	O. Stepanov URS & A. Bogolubov URS
1968	Not held		
1972	T. Kawaguchi JPN	Not awarded	Y. I. Kim PRK & I. Mounier FRA

Welterweight

Weight limit 70kg (154lb 5oz). Not held before 1972.

	Gold	Silver	Bronze
1972	T. Nomura JPN	A. Zajkowski POL	D. Hoetger GDR & A. Novikov URS

Middleweight

Weight limit 80kg (176lb 6oz). Not held before 1964.

	Gold	Silver	Bronze
1964	I. Okano JPN	W. Hofmann GER	J. Bregman USA & E. T. Kim KOR
1968	Not held		
1972	S. Sekine JPN	S. L. Oh PRK	B. Jacks GBR & J. P. Cochet FRA

Light Heavyweight

Weight limit 93kg (205lb 0½oz). Not held before 1972.

	Gold	Silver	Bronze
1972	S. Khokhoshvili URS	D. C. Starbrook GBR	P. Barth GER & C. Ishii BRA

	Gold	Silver	Bronze

Heavyweight

Weight limit 1964 over 80kg (176lb 6oz); from 1972 over 93kg (205lb 0½oz). Not held before 1964.

	Gold	Silver	Bronze
1964	I. Inokuma JPN	A. H. Rogers CAN	A. Kiknadze URS & P. Chikviladze URS
1968	Not held		
1972	W. Ruska HOL	K. Glahn GER	G. Onashvili URS & M. Nishimura JPN

Open

No weight limit. Not held before 1964.

	Gold	Silver	Bronze
1964	A. Geesink HOL	A. Kaminaga JPN	K. Glahn GER & T. Boronovskis AUS
1968	Not held		
1972	W. Ruska HOL	V. Kusnetsov URS	A. Parisi GBR & J. C. Brondani FRA

Modern Pentathlon

The five events are horse-riding, fencing, pistol-shooting, swimming and cross-country running. From 1912 to 1952 a point for each place achieved in the separate events was awarded, i.e. 1 for the winner, 2 for the second, etc. In 1956 a scoring system evaluating performance rather than position in each event was introduced.

Modern Pentathlon *Individual*

Not held before 1912.

	Gold	Silver	Bronze
1912	G. Lilliehöök SWE 27 pts	G. Åsbrink SWE 28 pts	G. de Laval SWE 30 pts
1920	G. Dyrssen SWE 18 pts	E. de Laval SWE 23 pts	G. Runö SWE 27 pts
1924	B. Lindman SWE 18 pts	G. Dyrssen SWE 39.5 pts	B. Uggla SWE 45 pts
1928	S. Thofelt SWE 47 pts	B. Lindman SWE 50 pts	H. Kahl GER 52 pts
1932	J. Oxenstierna SWE 32 pts	B. Lindman SWE 35.5 pts	R. Mayo USA 38.5 pts
1936	G. Handrick GER 31.5 pts	C. Leonard USA 39.5 pts	S. Abba ITA 45.5 pts
1948	W. Grut SWE 16 pts	G. Moore USA 47 pts	G. Gärdin SWE 49 pts
1952	L. Hall SWE 32 pts	G. Benedek HUN 39 pts	I. Szondi HUN 41 pts
1956	L. Hall SWE 4,833 pts	O. Mannonen FIN 4,774.5 pts	V. Korhonen FIN 4,750 pts
1960	F. Németh HUN 5,024 pts	I. Nagy HUN 4,988 pts	R. Beck USA 4,981 pts
1964	F. Török HUN 5,116 pts	I. Novikov URS 5,067 pts	A. Mokeyev URS 5,039 pts
1968	B. Ferm SWE 4,964 pts	A. Balczó HUN 4,953 pts	P. Lednev URS 4,795 pts
1972	A. Balczó HUN 5,412 pts	B. Onishenko URS 5,335 pts	P. Lednev URS 5,328 pts

Modern Pentathlon *Team*

Not held before 1952.

	Gold	Silver	Bronze
1952	HUN 166 pts	SWE 182 pts	FIN 213 pts
1956	URS 13,690.5 pts	USA 13,482.0 pts	FIN 13,185.5 pts
1960	HUN 14,863 pts	URS 14,309 pts	USA 14,192 pts
1964	URS 14,961 pts	USA 14,189 pts	HUN 14,173 pts
1968	HUN 14,325 pts	URS 14,248 pts	FRA 13,289 pts
1972	URS 15,968 pts	HUN 15,348 pts	FIN 14,812 pts

Rowing

The course for all events has been 2,000m (1 mile 427 yd) since 1952. In 1904 it was 3,219m (2 miles); in 1908 2,414m (1½ miles); in 1948 1,880m (1 mile 296 yd). In 1928 third and fourth places were decided in a special race.

Single Sculls

Not held before 1900.

	Gold	Silver	Bronze
1900	H. Barrelet FRA 7min 35.6sec	A. Gaudin FRA 7min 41.6sec	St George Ashe GBR 8min 15.6sec
1904	F. Greer USA 10min 08.5sec	J. Juvenal USA 2 lengths	C. Titus USA 1 length
1908	H. Blackstaffe GBR 9min 26.0sec	A. McCulloch GBR 1 length	B. von Gaza GER & K. Levitzky HUN nda
1912	W. D. Kinnear GBR 7min 47.6sec	P. Veirman BEL 7min 56.0sec	E. B. Butler CAN & M. Kusik URS nda
1920	J. B. Kelly USA 7min 35.0sec	J. Beresford GBR 7min 36.0sec	C. H. d'Arcy NZL 7min 48.0sec
1924	J. Beresford GBR 7min 49.2sec	W. E. G. Gilmore USA 7min 54.0sec	J. Schneider SUI 8min 01.0sec
1928	H. Pearce AUS 7min 11.0sec	K. Myers USA 7min 20.8sec	T. D. Collet GBR 7min 19.8sec
1932	H. Pearce AUS 7min 44.4sec	W. Miller USA 7min 45.2sec	G. Douglas URU 8min 13.6sec
1936	G. Schäfer GER 8min 21.5sec	J. Hasenöhrl AUT 8min 25.8sec	D. Barrow USA 8min 28.0sec
1948	M. Wood AUS 7min 24.4sec	E. Risso URU 7min 38.2sec	R. Catasta ITA 7min 51.4sec
1952	Y. Tyukalov URS 8min 12.8sec	M. Wood AUS 8min 14.5sec	T. Kocerka POL 8min 19.4sec
1956	V. Ivanov URS 8min 02.5sec	S. Mackenzie AUS 8min 07.7sec	J. Kelly USA 8min 11.8sec
1960	V. Ivanov URS 7min 13.96sec	A. Hill GER 7min 20.21sec	T. Kocerka POL 7min 21.26sec
1964	V. Ivanov URS 8min 22.51sec	A. Hill GER 8min 26.24sec	G. Kottman SUI 8min 29.68sec
1968	H. J. Wienese HOL 7min 47.80sec	J. Meissner GER 7min 52.00sec	A. Demiddi ARG 7min 57.19sec
1972	Y. Malyshev URS 7min 10.12sec	A. Demiddi ARG 7min 11.53sec	W. Güldenpfennig GDR 7min 14.45sec

Double Sculls

Not held before 1904.

	Gold	Silver	Bronze
1904	USA 10min 03.2sec	USA nda	USA nda
1908–1912	Not held		
1920	USA 7min 09.0sec	ITA 7min 19.0sec	FRA 7min 21.0sec
1924	USA 6min 34.0sec	FRA 6min 38.0sec	SUI 3 lengths
1928	USA 6min 41.4sec	CAN 6min 51.0sec	AUT
1932	USA 7min 17.4sec	GER 7min 22.8sec	CAN 7min 27.6sec
1936	GBR 7min 20.8sec	GER 7min 26.2sec	POL 7min 36.2sec
1948	GBR 6min 51.3sec	DEN 6min 55.3sec	URU 7min 12.4sec
1952	ARG 7min 32.2sec	URS 7min 38.2sec	URU 7min 43.7sec
1956	URS 7min 24.0sec	USA 7min 32.2sec	AUS 7min 37.4sec
1960	TCH 6min 47.50sec	URS 6min 50.49sec	SUI 6min 50.59sec
1964	URS 7min 10.66sec	USA 7min 13.16sec	TCH 7min 14.23sec
1968	URS 6min 51.82sec	HOL 6min 52.80sec	USA 6min 54.21sec
1972	URS 7min 01.77sec	NOR 7min 02.58sec	GDR 7min 05.55sec

Coxless Pairs

Not held before 1900.

	Gold	Silver	Bronze
1900	BEL 7min 49.6sec	BEL 7min 52.4sec	FRA 8min 0.6sec
1904	USA 10min 57.0sec	USA nda	USA nda
1908	GBR 9min 41.0sec	GBR 2½ lengths	CAN nda
1912–1920	Not held		
1924	HOL 8min 19.4sec	FRA 8min 21.6sec	
1928	GER 7min 06.4sec	GBR 7min 08.8sec	USA 7min 20.4sec
1932	GBR 8min 00.0sec	NZL 8min 02.4sec	POL 8min 08.2sec
1936	GER 8min 16.1sec	DEN 8min 19.2sec	ARG 8min 23.0sec
1948	GBR 7min 21.1sec	SUI 7min 23.9sec	ITA 7min 31.5sec
1952	USA 8min 20.7sec	BEL 8min 23.5sec	SUI 8min 32.7sec
1956	USA 7min 55.4sec	URS 8min 03.9sec	AUT 8min 11.8sec
1960	URS 7min 02.00sec	AUT 7min 03.69sec	FIN 7min 03.80sec
1964	CAN 7min 32.94sec	HOL 7min 33.40sec	GER 7min 38.63sec
1968	GDR 7min 26.56sec	USA 7min 26.71sec	DEN 7min 31.84sec
1972	GDR 6min 53.16sec	SUI 6min 57.06sec	HOL 6min 58.70sec

Coxed Pairs

Not held before 1900.

	Gold	Silver	Bronze
1900	HOL 7min 34.2sec	FRA 7min 34.4sec	FRA 7min 57.2sec
1904–1912	Not held		
1920	ITA 7min 56.0sec	FRA 7min 57.0sec	SUI nda
1924	SUI 8min 39.0sec	ITA 8min 39.1sec	USA nda
1928	SUI 7min 42.6sec	FRA 7min 48.4sec	BEL 7min 59.4sec
1932	USA 8min 25.8sec	POL 8min 31.2sec	FRA 8min 41.2sec
1936	GER 8min 36.9sec	ITA 8min 49.7sec	FRA 8min 54.0sec
1948	DEN 8min 05.0sec	ITA 8min 12.2sec	HUN 8min 25.2sec
1952	FRA 8min 28.6sec	GER 8min 32.1sec	DEN 8min 34.9sec
1956	USA 8min 26.1sec	GER 8min 29.2sec	URS 8min 31.0sec
1960	GER 7min 29.14sec	URS 7min 30.17sec	USA 7min 34.58sec
1964	USA 8min 21.23sec	FRA 8min 23.15sec	HOL 8min 23.42sec
1968	ITA 8min 04.81sec	HOL 8min 06.80sec	DEN 8min 08.07sec
1972	GDR 7min 17.25sec	TCH 7min 19.57sec	ROM 7min 21.36sec

Coxless Fours

Not held before 1904.

	Gold	Silver	Bronze
1904	USA 9min 53.8sec	USA nda	
1908	GBR 8min 34.0sec	GBR 1½ lengths	
1912–1920	Not held		
1924	GBR 7min 08.6sec	CAN 1¼ lengths	SUI nda
1928	GBR 6min 36.0sec	USA 6min 37.0sec	ITA 6min 31.6sec
1932	GBR 6min 58.2sec	GER 7min 03.0sec	ITA 7min 04.0sec
1936	GER 7min 01.8sec	GBR 7min 06.5sec	SUI 7min 10.6sec
1948	ITA 6min 39.0sec	DEN 6min 43.5sec	USA 6min 47.7sec
1952	YUG 7min 16.0sec	FRA 7min 18.9sec	FIN 7min 23.3sec

	Gold	Silver	Bronze
1956	CAN 7min 08.8sec	USA 7min 18.4sec	FRA 7min 20.9sec
1960	USA 6min 26.26sec	ITA 6min 28.78sec	URS 6min 29.62 sec
1964	DEN 6min 59.30sec	GBR 7min 00.47sec	USA 7min 01.37sec
1968	GDR 6min 39.18sec	HUN 6min 41.64sec	ITA 6min 44.01sec
1972	GDR 6min 24.27sec	NZL 6min 25.64sec	GER 6min 28.41sec

Coxed Fours

Not held before 1900. In 1900 there was a dispute and two finals were held, (1) for the crews with the fastest times in the heats and (2) for the winners of the three heats.

	Gold	Silver	Bronze
1900	(1) FRA 7min 11.0sec	FRA 7min 18.0sec	GER 7min 18.2sec
	(2) GER 5min 59.0sec	HOL 6min 33.0sec	GER 6min 35.0sec
1904–1908	Not held		
1912	GER 6min 59.4sec	GBR 2 lengths	DEN nda
1920	SUI 6min 54.0sec	USA 6min 58.0sec	NOR 7min 02.0sec
1924	SUI 7min 18.4sec	FRA 7min 21.6sec	USA nda
1928	ITA 6min 47.8sec	SUI 7min 03.4sec	POL 7min 12.8sec
1932	GER 7min 19.0sec	ITA 7min 19.2sec	POL 7min 26.8sec
1936	GER 7min 16.2sec	SUI 7min 24.3sec	FRA 7min 33.3sec
1948	USA 6min 50.3sec	SUI 6min 53.3sec	DEN 6min 58.6sec
1952	TCH 7min 33.4sec	SUI 7min 36.5sec	USA 7min 37.0sec
1956	ITA 7min 19.4sec	SWE 7min 22.4sec	FIN 7min 30.9sec
1960	GER 6min 39.12sec	FRA 6min 41.62sec	ITA 6min 43.12sec
1964	GER 7min 00.44sec	ITA 7min 02.84sec	HOL 7min 06.46sec
1968	NZL 6min 45.62sec	GDR 6min 48.20sec	SUI 6min 49.04sec
1972	GER 6min 31.85sec	GDR 6min 33.30sec	TCH 6min 35.64sec

Eights

Not held before 1900.

	Gold	Silver	Bronze
1900	USA 6min 09.8sec	BEL 6min 13.8sec	HOL 6min 23.0sec
1904	USA 7min 50.0sec	CAN nda	
1908	GBR 7min 52.0sec	BEL 2 lengths	CAN nda
1912	GBR 6min 15.0sec	GBR 1 length	GER nda
1920	USA 6min 02.6sec	GBR 6min 05.0sec	NOR 6min 36.0sec
1924	USA 6min 33.4sec	CAN 6min 49.0sec	ITA nda
1928	USA 6min 03.2sec	GBR 6min 05.6sec	CAN 6min 03.8sec
1932	USA 6min 37.6sec	ITA 6min 37.8sec	CAN 6min 40.4sec
1936	USA 6min 25.4sec	ITA 6min 26.0sec	GER 6min 26.4sec
1948	USA 5min 56.7sec	GBR 6min 06.9sec	NOR 6min 10.3sec
1952	USA 6min 25.9sec	URS 6min 31.2sec	AUS 6min 33.1sec
1956	USA 6min 35.2sec	CAN 6min 37.1sec	AUS 6min 39.2sec
1960	GER 5min 57.18sec	CAN 6min 01.52sec	TCH 6min 04.84sec
1964	USA 6min 18.23sec	GER 6min 23.29sec	TCH 6min 25.11sec
1968	GER 6min 07.00sec	AUS 6min 07.98sec	URS 6min 09.11sec
1972	NZL 6min 08.94sec	USA 6min 11.61sec	GDR 6min 11.67sec

Shooting

Free Pistol

Range 50m (55yd).

	Gold	Silver	Bronze
1896	S. Paine USA 442 pts	V. Jensen DEN 285 pts	H. Nielsen DEN nda
1900	K. Röderer SUI 503 pts	A. Paroche FRA 466 pts	K. Staeheli SUI 453 pts
1904–1908	Not held		
1912	A. Lane USA 499 pts	P. Dolfen USA 474 pts	C. E. Stewart GBR 470 pts
1920	C. Frederick USA 496 pts	A. da Costa BRA 489 pts	A. Lane USA 481 pts
1924–1932	Not held		
1936	T. Ullman SWE 559 pts	E. Krempel GER 544 pts	C. des Jammonières FRA 540 pts
1948	E. Vasquez Cam PER 545 pts	R. Schnyder SUI 539 pts	T. Ullman SWE 539 pts
1952	H. Benner USA 553 pts	A. Léon Gozalo ESP 550 pts	A. Balogh HUN 549 pts
1956	P. Linnosvuo FIN 556 pts	M. Umarov URS 556 pts	O. Pinion USA 551 pts
1960	A. Gushchin URS 560 pts	M. Umarov URS 552 pts	Y. Yoshikawa JPN 552 pts
1964	V. Markkanen FIN 560 pts	F. Green USA 557 pts	Y. Yoshikawa JPN 554 pts
1968	G. Kosykh URS 562 pts	H. Mertel GER 562 pts	H. Vollmar GDR 560 pts
1972	R. Skanåker SWE 567 pts	D. Iuga ROM 562 pts	R. Dollinger AUT 560 pts

Moving Target (Running Boar)

Not held in its present form before 1972. Range 50m (55yd).

	Gold	Silver	Bronze
1972	L. Zhelezniak URS 569 pts	H. Bellingrodt COL 565 pts	K. Kynoch GBR 562 pts

Rapid-Fire Pistol

Range 25m (27yd 1ft).

	Gold	Silver	Bronze
1896	I. Frangudis GRE 344 pts	G. Orphanidis GRE 249 pts	H. Nielsen DEN nda
1900	M. Larrouy FRA 58 pts	L. Moreaux FRA 57 pts	E. Balme FRA 57 pts
1904	Not held		
1908	P. van Asbroeck BEL 490 pts	R. Storms BEL 487 pts	J. E. Gorman USA 485 pts
1912	A. Lane USA 287 pts	P. Palén SWE 286 pts	J. H. von Holst SWE 283 pts
1920	G. Paraense BRA 274 pts	R. Bracken USA 272 pts	F. Zulauf SUI 269 pts
1924	H. N. Bailey USA 18 pts	V. Carlberg SWE 18 pts	L. Hannelius FIN 18 pts
1928	Not held		
1932	R. Morigi ITA 36 pts	H. Hax GER 36 pts	D. Matteucci ITA 36 pts
1936	C. van Oyen GER 36 pts	H. Hax GER 35 pts	T. Ullman SWE 34 pts
1948	K. Takács HUN 580 pts	C. E. Diaz Sáenz Valiente ARG 571 pts	S. Lundqvist SWE 569 pts
1952	K. Takács HUN 579 pts	S. Kun HUN 578 pts	G. Lichiardopol ROM 578 pts
1956	S. Petrescu ROM 587 pts	Y. Cherkassov URS 585 pts	G. Lichiardopol ROM 581 pts
1960	W. McMillan USA 587 pts	P. Linnosvuo FIN 587 pts	A. Zabelin URS 587 pts
1964	P. Linnosvuo FIN 592 pts	I. Tripşa ROM 591 pts	L. Nacovsky TCH 590 pts
1968	J. Zapedski POL 593 pts	M. Roşca ROM 591 pts	R. Suleimanov URS 591 pts
1972	J. Zapedski POL 595 pts	L. Falta TCH 594 pts	V. Torshin URS 593 pts

Free Rifle

Range 300m except in 1924 when it was 400–800m.

	Gold	Silver	Bronze
1896	G. Orphanidis GRE 1,583 pts	I. Frangudis GRE 1,312 pts	V. Jensen DEN 1,305 pts
1900–1904	Not held		
1908	A. Helgerud NOR 909 pts	H. Simon USA 887 pts	O. Sæther NOR 883 pts
1912	P. Colas FRA 987 pts	L. J. Madsen DEN 981 pts	N. H. D. Larsen DEN 962 pts
1920	M. Fisher USA 997 pts	N. H. D. Larsen DEN 985 pts	O. Østensen NOR 980 pts
1924	M. Fisher USA 95 pts	C. T. Osburn USA 95 pts	N. H. D. Larsen DEN 93 pts
1928–1936	Not held		
1948	E. Grünig SUI 1,120 pts	P. Janhonen FIN 1,114 pts	W. Røgeberg NOR 1,112 pts
1952	A. Bogdanov URS 1,123 pts	R. Bürchler SUI 1,120 pts	L. Vainshtain URS 1,109 pts
1956	V. Borisov URS 1,138 pts	A. Erdman URS 1,137 pts	V. Ylönen FIN 1,128 pts
1960	H. Hammerer AUT 1,129 pts	H. Spillmann SUI 1,127 pts	V. Borisov URS 1,127 pts
1964	G. Anderson USA 1,153 pts	S. Kveliashvili URS 1,144 pts	M. Gunnarsson USA 1,136 pts
1968	G. Anderson USA 1,157 pts	V. Kornev URS 1,151 pts	K. Müller SUI 1,148 pts
1972	L. Wigger USA 1,155 pts	B. Melnik URS 1,155 pts	L. Pap HUN 1,149 pts

Smallbore Rifle   Prone

Not held before 1908. Range 50m (55yd) except in 1908 when range was 45.7 and 91.4m (50 and 100yd), 40 shots. In 1908–12 competitors could fire from any position; in 1920 standing; from 1924 prone.

	Gold	Silver	Bronze
1908	A. A. Carnell GBR 387 pts	H. R. Humby GBR 386 pts	G. Barnes GBR 385 pts
1912	F. Hird USA 194 pts	W. Milne GBR 193 pts	H. Burt GBR 192 pts
1920	L. A. Nuesslein USA 391 pts	A. Rothrock USA 386 pts	D. Fenton USA 385 pts
1924	P. C. de Lisle FRA 398 pts	M. Dinwiddie USA 396 pts	J. Hartmann SUI 394 pts
1928	Not held		
1932	B. Rönnmark SWE 294 pts	G. Huet MEX 294 pts	Z. Hradetzky-Sóos HUN 293 pts
1936	W. Røgeberg NOR 300 pts	R. Berzsenyi HUN 296 pts	W. Karaś POL 296 pts
1948	A. Cook USA 599 pts	W. Tomsen USA 599 pts	J. Jonsson SWE 597 pts
1952	I. Sarbu ROM 400 pts	B. Andreev URS 400 pts	A. Jackson USA 399 pts
1956	G. R. Quellette CAN 600 pts	V. Borisov URS 599 pts	G. S. Boa CAN 598 pts

	Gold	Silver	Bronze
1960	P. Kohnke GER 590 pts	J. Hill USA 589 pts	E. Forcella Pelliccioni VEN 587 pts
1964	L. Hammerl HUN 597 pts	L. Wigger USA 597 pts	T. Pool USA 596 pts
1968	J. Kurka TCH 598 pts	L. Hammerl HUN 598 pts	I. Ballinger NZL 597 pts
1972	H. J. Li PRK 599 pts	V. Auer USA 598 pts	N. Rotaru ROM 598 pts

Smallbore Rifle Three Positions

Not held before 1952. Range 50m (55yd), standing, kneeling, prone.

	Gold	Silver	Bronze
1952	E. Kongshaug NOR 1,164 pts	V. Ylönen FIN 1,164 pts	B. Andreev URS 1,163 pts
1956	A. Bogdanov URS 1,172 pts	O. Hořínek TCH 1,172 pts	N. J. Sundberg SWE 1,167 pts
1960	V. Shamburkin URS 1,149 pts	M. Niasov URS 1,145 pts	K. Zähringer GER 1,139 pts
1964	L. Wigger USA 1,164 pts	V. Khristov BUL 1,152 pts	L. Hammerl HUN 1,151 pts
1968	B. Klingner GER 1,157 pts	J. Writer USA 1,156 pts	V. Parkhimovich URS 1,154 pts
1972	J. Writer USA 1,166 pts	L. Bassham USA 1,157 pts	W. Lippoldt GDR 1,153 pts

Trap Shooting

Not held before 1900. 200 pigeons, except in 1908 when there were 80.

	Gold	Silver	Bronze
1900	R. de Barbarin FRA 17 pts	R. Guyot FRA 17 pts	J. de Clary FRA 17 pts
1904	*Not held*		
1908	W. H. Ewing CAN 72 pts	G. Beattie CAN 60 pts	A. Maunder GBR & A. Metaxas GRE 57 pts
1912	J. Graham USA 96 pts	A. Göldel GER 94 pts	H. Blau URS 91 pts
1920	M. Arie USA 95 pts	F. Troeh USA 93 pts	F. Wright USA 87 pts
1924	G. Halasy HUN 98 pts	K. Huber FIN 98 pts	F. Hughes USA 97 pts
1928–1948	*Not held*		
1952	G. P. Généreux CAN 192 pts	K. Holmqvist SWE 191 pts	H. Liljedahl SWE 190 pts
1956	G. Rossini ITA 195 pts	A. Smelczyński POL 190 pts	A. Ciceri ITA 188 pts
1960	I. Dumitrescu ROM 192 pts	G. Rossini ITA 191 pts	S. Kalinin URS 190 pts
1964	E. Mattarelli ITA 198 pts	P. Senichev URS 194 pts	W. Morris USA 194 pts
1968	J. R. Braithwaite GBR 198 pts	T. Garrigus USA 196 pts	K. Czekalla GDR 196 pts
1972	A. Scalzone ITA 199 pts	M. Carrega FRA 198 pts	S. Basagni ITA 195 pts

Skeet

Not held before 1968.

	Gold	Silver	Bronze
1968	Y. Petrov URS 198 pts	R. Garagnani ITA 198 pts	K. Wirnhier GER 198 pts
1972	K. Wirnhier GER 195 pts	Y. Petrov URS 195 pts	M. Buchheim GDR 195 pts

Swimming and Diving *Men*

100 Metres Freestyle

In 1904 the distance was 91.44m (100 yd).

	Gold	Silver	Bronze
1896	A. Hajós (Guttmann) HUN 1min 22.2sec	E. Choraphas GRE 1min 23.0sec	O. Herschmann AUT nda
1900	*Not held*		
1904	Z. von Halmay HUN 1min 02.8sec	C. Daniels USA nda	J. S. Leary USA nda
1908	C. Daniels USA 1min 05.6sec	Z. von Halmay HUN 1min 06.2sec	H. Julin SWE 1min 08.8sec
1912	D. P. Kahanamoku USA 1min 03.4sec	C. Healy AUS 1min 04.6sec	K. Huszagh USA 1min 05.6sec
1920	D. P. Kahanamoku USA 1min 01.4sec	P. K. Kealoha USA 1min 02.2sec	W. Harris USA 1min 03.0sec
1924	J. Weissmuller USA 59.0sec	D. P. Kahanamoku USA 1min 01.4sec	S. Kahanamoku USA 1min 01.8sec
1928	J. Weissmuller USA 58.6sec	I. Bárány HUN 59.8sec	K. Takaishi JPN 1min 00.0sec
1932	Y. Miyazaki JPN 58.2sec	T. Kawaishi JPN 58.6sec	A. Schwartz USA 58.8sec
1936	F. Csik HUN 57.6sec	M. Yusa JPN 57.9sec	S. Arai JPN 58.0sec
1948	W. Ris USA 57.3sec	A. Ford USA 57.8sec	G. Kádas HUN 58.1sec
1952	C. Scholes USA 57.4sec	H. Suzuki JPN 57.4sec	G. Larsson SWE 58.2sec

	Gold	Silver	Bronze
1956	J. Henricks AUS 55.4sec	J. Devitt AUS 55.8sec	G. Chapman AUS 56.7sec
1960	J. Devitt AUS 55.2sec	L. Larson USA 55.2sec	M. Dos Santos BRA 55.4sec
1964	D. Schollander USA 53.4sec	R. McGregor GBR 53.5sec	H. J. Klein GER 54.0sec
1968	M. Wenden AUS 52.2sec	K. Walsh USA 52.8sec	M. Spitz USA 53.0sec
1972	M. Spitz USA 51.22sec	J. Heidenreich USA 51.65sec	V. Bure URS 51.77sec

200 Metres Freestyle

Not held before 1900. In 1904 the distance was 201.17m (220yd).

	Gold	Silver	Bronze
1900	F. Lane AUS 2min 25.2sec	Z. von Halmay HUN 2min 31.0sec	K. Ruberl AUT 2min 32.0sec
1904	C. Daniels USA 2min 44.2sec	F. Gailey USA 2min 46.0sec	E. Rausch GER 2min 56.0sec
1908–1964	*Not held*		
1968	M. Wenden AUS 1min 55.2sec	D. Schollander USA 1min 55.8sec	J. Nelson USA 1min 58.1sec
1972	M. Spitz USA 1min 52.78sec	S. Genter USA 1min 53.73sec	W. Lampe GER 1min 53.99sec

400 Metres Freestyle

Not held before 1904. In 1904 the distance was 402.3m (440yd).

	Gold	Silver	Bronze
1904	C. Daniels USA 6min 16.2sec	F. Gailey USA 6min 22.0sec	O. Wahle AUT 6min 39.0sec
1908	H. Taylor GBR 5min 36.8sec	F. Beaurepaire AUS 5min 44.2sec	O. Scheff AUT 5min 46.0sec
1912	G. Hodgson CAN 5min 24.4sec	J. Hatfield GBR 5min 25.8sec	H. Hardwick AUS 5min 31.2sec
1920	N. Ross USA 5min 26.8sec	L. Langer USA 5min 29.0sec	G. Vernot CAN 5min 29.6sec
1924	J. Weissmuller USA 5min 04.2sec	A. Borg SWE 5min 05.6sec	A. Charlton AUS 5min 06.6sec
1928	A. Zorilla ARG 5min 01.6sec	A. Charlton AUS 5min 03.6sec	A. Borg SWE 5min 04.6sec
1932	C. Crabbe USA 4min 48.4sec	J. Taris FRA 4min 48.5sec	T. Oyokota JPN 4min 52.3sec
1936	J. Medica USA 4min 44.5sec	S. Uto JPN 4min 45.6sec	S. Makino JPN 4min 48.1sec
1948	W. Smith USA 4min 41.0sec	J. McLane USA 4min 43.4sec	J. Marshall AUS 4min 47.4sec
1952	J. Boiteux FRA 4min 30.7sec	F. Konno USA 4min 31.3sec	P. O. Östrand SWE 4min 35.2sec
1956	M. Rose AUS 4min 27.3sec	T. Yamanaka JPN 4min 30.4sec	G. Breen USA 4min 32.5sec
1960	M. Rose AUS 4min 18.3sec	T. Yamanaka JPN 4min 21.4sec	J. Konrads AUS 4min 21.8sec
1964	D. Schollander USA 4min 12.2sec	F. Wiegand GER 4min 14.9sec	A. Wood AUS 4min 15.1sec
1968	M. Burton USA 4min 09.0sec	R. Hutton CAN 4min 11.7sec	A. Mosconi FRA 4min 13.3sec
1972	B. Cooper AUS 4min 00.27sec	S. Genter USA 4min 01.94sec	T. McBreen USA 4min 02.64sec

1,500 Metres Freestyle

In 1896 the distance was 1,200m (1,310yd 1ft 5½in); in 1900 1,000m (1,093yd 1ft 10in); in 1904 1,609.34m (1 mile).

	Gold	Silver	Bronze
1896	A. Hajós HUN 18min 22.2sec	I. Andreou GRE 21min 03.4sec	E. Choraphas GRE nda
1900	J. Jarvis GBR 13min 40.2sec	O. Wahle AUT 14min 53.6sec	Z. von Halmay HUN 15min 16.4sec
1904	E. Rausch GER 27min 18.2sec	G. Kiss HUN 28min 28.2sec	F. Gailey USA 28min 54.0sec
1908	H. Taylor GBR 22min 48.4sec	T. S. Battersby GBR 22min 51.2sec	F. Beaurepaire AUS 22min 56.2sec
1912	G. Hodgson CAN 22min 00.0sec	J. Hatfield GBR 22min 39.0sec	H. Hardwick AUS 23min 15.4sec
1920	N. Ross USA 22min 23.2sec	G. Vernot CAN 22min 36.4sec	F. Beaurepaire AUS 23min 04.0sec
1924	A. Charlton AUS 20min 06.6sec	A. Borg SWE 20min 41.4sec	F. Beaurepaire AUS 20min 48.4sec
1928	A. Borg SWE 19min 51.8sec	A. Charlton AUS 20min 02.6sec	C. Crabbe USA 20min 28.8sec
1932	K. Kitamura JPN 19min 12.4sec	S. Makino JPN 19min 14.1sec	J. Cristy USA 19min 39.5sec
1936	N. Terada JPN 19min 13.7sec	J. Medica USA 19min 34.0sec	S. Uto JPN 19min 34.5sec
1948	J. McLane USA 19min 18.5sec	J. Marshall AUS 19min 31.3sec	G. Mitró HUN 19min 43.2sec
1952	F. Konno USA 18min 30.3sec	S. Hashizume JPN 18min 41.4sec	T. Okamoto BRA 18min 51.3sec
1956	M. Rose AUS 17min 58.9sec	T. Yamanaka JPN 18min 00.3sec	G. Breen USA 18min 08.2sec
1960	J. Konrads AUS 17min 19.6sec	M. Rose AUS 17min 21.7sec	G. Breen USA 17min 30.6sec
1964	R. Windle AUS 17min 01.7sec	J. Nelson USA 17min 03.0sec	A. Wood AUS 17min 07.7sec

	Gold	Silver	Bronze
1968	M. Burton *USA* 16min 38.9sec	J. Kinsella *USA* 16min 57.3sec	G. Brough *AUS* 17min 04.7sec
1972	M. Burton *USA* 15min 52.58sec	G. Windeatt *AUS* 15min 58.48sec	D. Northway *USA* 16min 09.25sec

100 Metres Backstroke
Not held before 1904. In 1904 the distance was 91.44m (100yd).

	Gold	Silver	Bronze
1904	W. Brack *GER* 1min 16.8sec	G. Hoffmann *GER* nda	G. Zacharias *GER* nda
1908	A. Bieberstein *GER* 1min 24.6sec	L. Dam *DEN* 1min 26.6sec	H. Haresnape *GBR* 1min 27.0sec
1912	H. Hebner *USA* 1min 21.2sec	O. Fahr *GER* 1min 22.4sec	P. Kellner *GER* 1min 24.0sec
1920	W. P. Kealoha *USA* 1min 15.2sec	R. Kegeris *USA* 1min 16.2sec	G. Blitz *BEL* 1min 19.0sec
1924	W. P. Kealoha *USA* 1min 13.2sec	P. Wyatt *USA* 1min 15.4sec	K. Bartha *HUN* 1min 17.8sec
1928	G. Kojac *USA* 1min 08.2sec	W. Laufer *USA* 1min 10.0sec	P. Wyatt *USA* 1min 12.0sec
1932	M. Kiyokawa *JPN* 1min 08.6sec	T. Irie *JPN* 1min 09.8sec	K. Kawatsu *JPN* 1min 10.0sec
1936	A. Kiefer *USA* 1min 05.9sec	A. Van de Weghe *USA* 1min 07.7sec	M. Kiyokawa *JPN* 1min 08.4sec
1948	A. Stack *USA* 1min 06.4sec	R. Cowell *USA* 1min 06.5sec	G. Vallerey *FRA* 1min 07.8sec
1952	Y. Oyakawa *USA* 1min 05.4sec	G. Bozon *FRA* 1min 06.2sec	J. Taylor *USA* 1min 06.4sec
1956	D. Theile *AUS* 1min 02.2sec	J. Monckton *AUS* 1min 03.2sec	F. McKinney *USA* 1min 04.5sec
1960	D. Theile *AUS* 1min 01.9sec	F. McKinney *USA* 1min 02.1sec	R. Bennett *USA* 1min 02.3sec
1964	*Not held*		
1968	R. Matthes *GDR* 58.7sec	C. Hickcox *USA* 1min 00.2sec	R. Mills *USA* 1min 00.5sec
1972	R. Matthes *GDR* 56.58sec	M. Stamm *USA* 57.70sec	J. Murphy *USA* 58.35sec

200 Metres Backstroke
Not held before 1900.

	Gold	Silver	Bronze
1900	E. Hoppenberg *GER* 2min 47.0sec	K. Ruberl *AUT* 2min 56.0sec	J. Drost *HOL* 3min 01.0sec
1904–1960	*Not held*		
1964	J. Graef *USA* 2min 10.3sec	G. Dilley *USA* 2min 10.5sec	R. Bennett *USA* 2min 13.1sec
1968	R. Matthes *GDR* 2min 09.6sec	M. Ivey *USA* 2min 10.6sec	J. Horsley *USA* 2min 10.9sec
1972	R. Matthes *GDR* 2min 02.82sec	M. Stamm *USA* 2min 04.09sec	M. Ivey *USA* 2min 04.33sec

100 Metres Breaststroke
Not held before 1968.

	Gold	Silver	Bronze
1968	D. McKenzie *USA* 1min 07.7sec	V. Kosinski *URS* 1min 08.0sec	N. Pankin *URS* 1min 08.0sec
1972	N. Taguchi *JPN* 1min 04.94sec	T. Bruce *USA* 1min 05.43sec	J. Hencken *USA* 1min 05.61sec

200 Metres Breaststroke
Not held before 1908.

	Gold	Silver	Bronze
1908	F. Holman *GBR* 3min 09.2sec	W. Robinson *GBR* 3min 12.8sec	P. Hansson *SWE* 3min 14.6sec
1912	W. Bathe *GER* 3min 01.8sec	W. Lützow *GER* 3min 05.0sec	K. Malisch *GER* 3min 08.0sec
1920	H. Malmroth *SWE* 3min 04.4sec	T. Henning *SWE* 3min 09.2sec	A. Aaltonen *FIN* 3min 12.2sec
1924	R. Skelton *USA* 2min 56.6sec	J. de Combe *BEL* 2min 59.2sec	W. Kirschbaum *USA* 3min 01.0sec
1928	Y. Tsuruta *JPN* 2min 48.8sec	E. Rademacher *GER* 2min 50.6sec	T. Yldefonso *PHI* 2min 56.4sec
1932	Y. Tsuruta *JPN* 2min 45.4sec	R. Koike *JPN* 2min 46.6sec	T. Yldefonso *PHI* 2min 47.1sec
1936	T. Hamuro *JPN* 2min 41.5sec	E. Sietas *GER* 2min 42.9sec	R. Koike *JPN* 2min 44.2sec
1948	J. Verdeur *USA* 2min 39.3sec	K. Carter *USA* 2min 40.2sec	R. Sohl *USA* 2min 43.9sec
1952	J. Davies *AUS* 2min 34.4sec	B. Stassforth *USA* 2min 34.7sec	H. Klein *GER* 2min 35.9sec
1956	M. Furukawa *JPN* 2min 34.7sec	M. Yoshimura *JPN* 2min 36.7sec	K. Yunichev *URS* 2min 36.8sec
1960	W. Mulliken *USA* 2min 37.4sec	Y. Osaki *JPN* 2min 38.0sec	W. Mensonides *HOL* 2min 39.7sec
1964	I. O'Brien *AUS* 2min 27.8sec	G. Prokopenko *URS* 2min 28.2sec	C. Jastremski *USA* 2min 29.6sec
1968	F. Muñoz *MEX* 2min 28.7sec	V. Kosinski *URS* 2min 29.2sec	B. Job *USA* 2min 29.9sec
1972	J. Hencken *USA* 2min 21.55sec	D. Wilkie *GBR* 2min 23.67sec	N. Taguchi *JPN* 2min 23.88sec

100 Metres Butterfly
Not held before 1968.

	Gold	Silver	Bronze
1968	D. Russell *USA* 55.9sec	M. Spitz *USA* 56.4sec	R. Wales *USA* 57.2sec
1972	M. Spitz *USA* 54.27sec	B. Robertson *CAN* 55.56sec	J. Heidenreich *USA* 55.74sec

200 Metres Butterfly
Not held before 1956.

	Gold	Silver	Bronze
1956	W. Yorzyk *USA* 2min 19.3sec	T. Ishimoto *JPN* 2min 23.8sec	G. Tumpek *HUN* 2min 23.9sec
1960	M. Troy *USA* 2min 12.8sec	N. Hayes *AUS* 2min 14.6sec	D. Gillanders *USA* 2min 15.3sec
1964	K. Berry *AUS* 2min 06.6sec	C. Robie *USA* 2min 07.5sec	F. Schmidt *USA* 2min 09.3sec
1968	C. Robie *USA* 2min 08.7sec	M. Woodroffe *GBR* 2min 09.0sec	J. Ferris *USA* 2min 09.3sec
1972	M. Spitz *USA* 2min 00.70sec	G. Hall *USA* 2min 02.86sec	R. Backhaus *USA* 2min 03.23sec

200 Metres Individual Medley
Not held before 1968. Order of strokes: butterfly, backstroke, breaststroke, freestyle.

	Gold	Silver	Bronze
1968	C. Hickcox *USA* 2min 12.0sec	G. Buckingham *USA* 2min 13.0sec	J. Ferris *USA* 2min 13.3sec
1972	G. Larsson *SWE* 2min 07.17sec	T. McKee *USA* 2min 08.37sec	S. Furniss *USA* 2min 08.45sec

400 Metres Individual Medley
Not held before 1964. Order of strokes: butterfly, backstroke, breaststroke, freestyle.

	Gold	Silver	Bronze
1964	R. Roth *USA* 4min 45.4sec	R. Saari *USA* 4min 47.1sec	G. Hetz *GER* 4min 51.0sec
1968	C. Hickcox *USA* 4min 48.4sec	G. Hall *USA* 4min 48.7sec	M. Holthaus *GER* 4min 51.4sec
1972	G. Larsson *SWE* 4min 31.98sec	T. McKee *USA* 4min 31.98sec	A. Hargitay *HUN* 4min 32.70sec

4 × 100 Metres Freestyle Relay
Not held before 1964.

	Gold	Silver	Bronze
1964	USA 3min 33.2sec	GER 3min 37.2sec	AUS 3min 39.1sec
1968	USA 3min 31.7sec	URS 3min 34.2sec	AUS 3min 34.7sec
1972	USA 3min 26.42sec	URS 3min 29.72sec	GDR 3min 32.42sec

4 × 200 Metres Freestyle Relay
Not held before 1908.

	Gold	Silver	Bronze
1908	GBR 10min 55.6sec	HUN 10min 59.0sec	USA 11min 02.8sec
1912	AUS 10min 11.6sec	USA 10min 20.2sec	GBR 10min 28.2sec
1920	USA 10min 04.4sec	AUS 10min 25.4sec	GBR 10min 37.2sec
1924	USA 9min 53.4sec	AUS 10min 02.0sec	SWE 10min 06.8sec
1928	USA 9min 36.2sec	JPN 9min 41.4sec	CAN 9min 47.8sec
1932	JPN 8min 58.4sec	USA 9min 10.5sec	HUN 9min 31.4sec
1936	JPN 8min 51.5sec	USA 9min 03.0sec	HUN 9min 12.3sec
1948	USA 8min 46.0sec	HUN 8min 48.4sec	FRA 9min 08.0sec
1952	USA 8min 31.1sec	JPN 8min 33.5sec	FRA 8min 45.9sec
1956	AUS 8min 23.6sec	USA 8min 31.5sec	URS 8min 34.7sec
1960	USA 8min 10.2sec	JPN 8min 13.2sec	AUS 8min 13.8sec
1964	USA 7min 52.1sec	GER 7min 59.3sec	JPN 8min 03.8sec
1968	USA 7min 52.3sec	AUS 7min 53.7sec	URS 8min 01.6sec
1972	USA 7min 35.78sec	GER 7min 41.69sec	URS 7min 45.76sec

4 × 100 Metres Medley Relay
Not held before 1960. Order of strokes: backstroke, breaststroke, butterfly, freestyle.

	Gold	Silver	Bronze
1960	USA 4min 05.4sec	AUS 4min 12.0sec	JPN 4min 12.2sec
1964	USA 3min 58.4sec	GER 4min 01.6sec	AUS 4min 02.3sec
1968	USA 3min 54.9sec	GDR 3min 57.5sec	URS 4min 00.7sec
1972	USA 3min 48.16sec	GDR 3min 52.1sec	CAN 3min 52.26sec

Highboard Diving
Not held before 1904. In 1904 and 1908 this was a combined highboard and springboard event. In 1928 Desjardins gained a superior aggregate of placings to Simaika although the latter gained more points.

	Gold	Silver	Bronze
1904	G. Sheldon *USA* 12.66 pts	G. Hoffmann *GER* 11.66 pts	F. Kehoe *USA* & A. Braunschweiger *GER* 11.33 pts
1908	H. Johansson *SWE* 83.75 pts	K. Malmström *SWE* 78.73 pts	A. Spångberg *SWE* 74.00 pts
1912	E. Adlerz *SWE* 73.94 pts	A. Zürner *GER* 72.60 pts	G. Blomgren *SWE* 69.56 pts
1920	C. Pinkston *USA* 100.67 pts	E. Adlerz *SWE* 99.08 pts	H. Prieste *USA* 93.73 pts
1924	A. White *USA* 97.46 pts	D. Fall *USA* 97.30 pts	C. Pinkston *USA* 94.60 pts
1928	P. Desjardins *USA* 98.74 pts	F. Simaika *EGY* 99.58 pts	M. Galitzen *USA* 92.34 pts
1932	H. Smith *USA* 124.80 pts	M. Galitzen *USA* 124.28 pts	F. Kurtz *USA* 121.98 pts

	Gold	Silver	Bronze
1936	M. Wayne *USA* 113.58 pts	E. Root *USA* 110.60 pts	H. Stork *GER* 110.31 pts
1948	S. Lee *USA* 130.05 pts	B. Harlan *USA* 122.30 pts	J. Capilla Pérez *MEX* 113.52 pts
1952	S. Lee *USA* 156.28 pts	J. Capilla Pérez *MEX* 145.21 pts	G. Haase *GER* 141.31 pts
1956	J. Capilla Pérez *MEX* 152.44 pts	G. Tobian *USA* 152.41 pts	R. Connor *USA* 149.79 pts
1960	R. Webster *USA* 165.56 pts	G. Tobian *USA* 165.25 pts	B. Phelps *GBR* 157.13 pts
1964	R. Webster *USA* 148.58 pts	K. Dibiasi *ITA* 147.54 pts	T. Gompf *USA* 146.57 pts
1968	K. Dibiasi *ITA* 164.18 pts	A. Gaxiola *MEX* 154.49 pts	E. Young *USA* 153.93 pts
1972	K. Dibiasi *ITA* 504.12 pts	R. Rydze *USA* 480.75 pts	F. Cagnotto *ITA* 475.83 pts

Springboard Diving

Not held before 1908.

	Gold	Silver	Bronze
1908	Albert Zürner *GER* 85.5 pts	K. Behrens *GER* 85.3 pts	G. Gaidzik *USA* 80.8 pts
1912	P. Günther *GER* 79.23 pts	H. Luber *GER* 76.78 pts	K. Behrens *GER* 73.73 pts
1920	L. Kuehn *USA* 675.40 pts	C. Pinkston *USA* 655.30 pts	L. Balbach *USA* 649.50 pts
1924	A. White *USA* 696.40 pts	P. Desjardins *USA* 693.20 pts	C. Pinkston *USA* 653.00 pts
1928	P. Desjardins *USA* 185.04 pts	M. Galitzen *USA* 174.06 pts	F. Simaika *EGY* 172.46 pts
1932	M. Galitzen *USA* 161.38 pts	H. Smith *USA* 158.54 pts	R. Degener *USA* 151.82 pts
1936	R. Degener *USA* 163.57 pts	M. Wayne *USA* 159.56 pts	A. Greene *USA* 146.29 pts
1948	B. Harlan *USA* 163.64 pts	M. Anderson *USA* 157.29 pts	S. Lee *USA* 145.52 pts
1952	D. Browning *USA* 205.29 pts	M. Anderson *USA* 199.84 pts	R. Clotworthy *USA* 184.92 pts
1956	R. Clotworthy *USA* 159.56 pts	D. Harper *USA* 156.23 pts	J. Capilla Pérez *MEX* 150.69 pts
1960	G. Tobian *USA* 170.00 pts	S. Hall *USA* 167.08 pts	J. Botella *MEX* 162.30 pts
1964	K. Sitzberger *USA* 159.90 pts	F. Gorman *USA* 157.63 pts	L. Andreasen *USA* 143.77 pts
1968	B. Wrightson *USA* 170.15 pts	K. Dibiasi *ITA* 159.74 pts	J. Henry *USA* 158.09 pts
1972	V. Vasin *URS* 594.09 pts	F. Cagnotto *ITA* 591.63 pts	C. Lincoln *USA* 577.29 pts

Water Polo

Not held before 1900.

	Gold	Silver	Bronze
1900	GBR	BEL	FRA
1904	USA	USA	USA
1908	GBR	BEL	SWE
1912	GBR	SWE	BEL
1920	GBR	BEL	SWE
1924	FRA	BEL	USA
1928	GER	HUN	FRA
1932	HUN	GER	USA
1936	HUN	GER	BEL
1948	ITA	HUN	HOL
1952	HUN	YUG	ITA
1956	HUN	YUG	URS
1960	ITA	URS	HUN
1964	HUN	YUG	URS
1968	YUG	URS	HUN
1972	URS	HUN	USA

Swimming and Diving *Women*

100 Metres Freestyle

Not held before 1912.

	Gold	Silver	Bronze
1912	F. Durack *AUS* 1min 22.2sec	W. Wylie *AUS* 1min 25.4sec	J. Fletcher *GBR* 1min 27.0sec
1920	E. Bleibtrey *USA* 1min 13.6sec	I. Guest *USA* 1min 17.0sec	F. Schroth *USA* 1min 17.2sec
1924	E. Lackie *USA* 1min 12.4sec	M. Wehselau *USA* 1min 12.8sec	G. Ederle *USA* 1min 14.2sec
1928	A. Osipowich *USA* 1min 11.0sec	E. Garatti *USA* 1min 11.4sec	J. Cooper *GBR* 1min 13.6sec
1932	H. Madison *USA* 1min 06.8sec	W. den Ouden *HOL* 1min 07.8sec	E. (Garatti) Saville *USA* 1min 08.2sec
1936	H. Mastenbroek *HOL* 1min 05.9sec	J. Campbell *ARG* 1min 06.4sec	G. Arendt *GER* 1min 06.6sec
1948	G. Andersen *DEN* 1min 06.3sec	A. Curtis *USA* 1min 06.5sec	M. L. Vaessen *HOL* 1min 07.6sec
1952	K. Szőke *HUN* 1min 06.8sec	J. Termeulen *HOL* 1min 07.0sec	J. Temes *HUN* 1min 07.1sec
1956	D. Fraser *AUS* 1min 02.0sec	L. Crapp *AUS* 1min 02.3sec	F. Leech *AUS* 1min 05.1sec
1960	D. Fraser *AUS* 1min 01.2sec	C. Von Saltza *USA* 1min 02.8sec	N. Steward *GBR* 1min 03.1sec
1964	D. Fraser *AUS* 59.5sec	S. Stouder *USA* 59.9sec	K. Ellis *USA* 1min 00.8sec
1968	J. Henne *USA* 1min 00.0sec	S. Pedersen *USA* 1min 00.3sec	L. Gustavson *USA* 1min 00.3sec
1972	S. Neilson *USA* 58.59sec	S. Babashoff *USA* 59.02sec	S. Gould *AUS* 59.06sec

200 Metres Freestyle

Not held before 1968.

	Gold	Silver	Bronze
1968	D. Meyer *USA* 2min 10.5sec	J. Henne *USA* 2min 11.0sec	J. Barkman *USA* 2min 11.2sec
1972	S. Gould *AUS* 2min 03.56sec	S. Babashoff *USA* 2min 04.33sec	K. Rothhammer *USA* 2min 04.92sec

400 Metres Freestyle

Not held before 1920. In 1920 the distance was 300m (328yd 4in).

	Gold	Silver	Bronze
1920	E. Bleibtrey *USA* 4min 34.0sec	M. Woodbridge *USA* 4min 42.8sec	F. Schroth *USA* 4min 52.0sec
1924	M. Norelius *USA* 6min 02.2sec	H. Wainwright *USA* 6min 03.8sec	G. Ederle *USA* 6min 04.8sec
1928	M. Norelius *USA* 5min 42.8sec	M. J. Braun *HOL* 5min 57.8sec	J. McKim *USA* 6min 00.2sec
1932	H. Madison *USA* 5min 28.5sec	L. Kight *USA* 5min 28.6sec	J. Makaal *SAF* 5min 47.3sec
1936	H. Mastenbroek *HOL* 5min 26.4sec	R. Hveger *DEN* 5 min 27.5sec	L. (Kight) Wingard *USA* 5min 29.0sec
1948	A. Curtis *USA* 5min 17.8sec	K. M. Harup *DEN* 5min 21.2sec	C. Gibson *GBR* 5min 22.5sec
1952	V. Gyenge *HUN* 5min 12.1sec	É. Novák *HUN* 5min 13.7sec	E. Kawamoto *USA* 5min 14.6sec
1956	L. Crapp *AUS* 4min 54.6sec	D. Fraser *AUS* 5min 02.5sec	S. Ruuska *USA* 5min 07.1sec
1960	C. Von Saltza *USA* 4min 50.6sec	J. Cederqvist *SWE* 4min 53.9sec	C. Lagerberg *HOL* 4min 56.9sec
1964	V. Duenkel *USA* 4min 43.3sec	M. Ramenofsky *USA* 4min 44.6sec	T. L. Stickles *USA* 4min 47.2sec
1968	D. Meyer *USA* 4min 31.8sec	L. Gustavson *USA* 4min 35.5sec	K. Moras *AUS* 4min 37.0sec
1972	S. Gould *AUS* 4min 19.04sec	N. Calligaris *ITA* 4min 22.44sec	G. Wegner *GDR* 4min 23.11sec

800 Metres Freestyle

Not held before 1968.

	Gold	Silver	Bronze
1968	D. Meyer *USA* 9min 24.0sec	P. Kruse *USA* 9min 35.7sec	M. T. Ramirez *MEX* 9min 38.5sec
1972	K. Rothhammer *USA* 8min 53.68sec	S. Gould *AUS* 8min 56.39sec	N. Calligaris *ITA* 8min 57.46sec

100 Metres Backstroke

Not held before 1924.

	Gold	Silver	Bronze
1924	S. Bauer *USA* 1min 23.2sec	P. Harding *GBR* 1min 27.4sec	A. Riggin *USA* 1min 28.2sec
1928	M. J. Braun *HOL* 1min 22.0sec	E. E. King *GBR* 1min 22.2sec	J. Cooper *GBR* 1min 22.8sec
1932	E. Holm *USA* 1min 19.4sec	P. Mealing *AUS* 1min 21.3sec	V. Davies *GBR* 1min 22.5sec
1936	D. Senff *HOL* 1min 18.9sec	H. Mastenbroek *HOL* 1min 19.2sec	A. Bridges *USA* 1min 19.4sec
1948	K. M. Harup *DEN* 1min 14.4sec	S. Zimmerman *USA* 1min 16.0sec	J. J. Davies *AUS* 1min 16.7sec
1952	J. Harrison *SAF* 1min 14.3sec	G. Wielema *HOL* 1min 14.5sec	J. Stewart *NZL* 1min 15.8sec
1956	J. Grinham *GBR* 1min 12.9sec	C. Cone *USA* 1min 12.9sec	M. Edwards *GBR* 1min 13.1sec
1960	L. Burke *USA* 1min 09.3sec	N. Steward *GBR* 1min 10.8sec	S. Tanaka *JPN* 1min 11.4sec
1964	C. Ferguson *USA* 1min 07.7sec	C. Caron *FRA* 1min 07.9sec	V. Duenkel *USA* 1min 08.0sec
1968	K. Hall *USA* 1min 06.2sec	E. Tanner *CAN* 1min 06.7sec	J. Swagerty *USA* 1min 08.1sec
1972	M. Belote *USA* 1min 05.78sec	A. Gyarmati *HUN* 1min 06.26sec	S. Atwood *USA* 1min 06.34sec

200 Metres Backstroke

Not held before 1968.

	Gold	Silver	Bronze
1968	L. Watson *USA* 2min 24.8sec	E. Tanner *CAN* 2min 27.4sec	K. Hall *USA* 2min 28.9sec
1972	M. Belote *USA* 2min 19.19sec	S. Atwood *USA* 2min 20.38sec	D. M. Gurr *CAN* 2min 23.22sec

100 Metres Breaststroke

Not held before 1968.

	Gold	Silver	Bronze
1968	D. Bjedov *YUG* 1min 15.8sec	G. Prosumenshchikova *URS* 1min 15.9sec	S. Wichman *USA* 1min 16.1sec

	Gold	Silver	Bronze
1972	C. Carr *USA* 1min 13.58sec	G. Stepanova *URS* 1min 14.99sec	B. Whitfield *AUS* 1min 15.73sec

200 Metres Breaststroke
Not held before 1924.

	Gold	Silver	Bronze
1924	L. Morton *GBR* 3min 33.2sec	A. Geraghty *USA* 3min 34.0sec	G. Carson *GBR* 3min 35.4sec
1928	H. Schrader *GER* 3min 12.6sec	M. Baron *HOL* 3min 15.2sec	L. (Hildesheim) Mühe *GER* 3min 17.6sec
1932	C. Dennis *AUS* 3min 06.3sec	H. Maehata *JPN* 3min 06.4sec	E. Jacobsen *DEN* 3min 07.1sec
1936	H. Maehata *JPN* 3min 03.6sec	M. Genenger *GER* 3min 04.2sec	I. Sørensen *DEN* 3min 07.8sec
1948	P. van Vliet *HOL* 2min 57.2sec	B. Lyons *AUS* 2min 57.7sec	É. Novák *HUN* 3min 00.2sec
1952	É. Székely *HUN* 2min 51.7sec	É. Novák *HUN* 2min 54.4sec	H. Gordon *GBR* 2min 57.6sec
1956	U. Happe *GER* 2min 53.1sec	É. Székely *HUN* 2min 54.8sec	E. M. Ten Elsen *GER* 2min 55.1sec
1960	A. Lonsbrough *GBR* 2min 49.5sec	W. Urselmann *GER* 2min 50.0sec	B. Göbel *GER* 2min 53.6sec
1964	G. Prosumenshchikova *URS* 2min 46.4sec	C. Kolb *USA* 2min 47.6sec	S. Babanina *URS* 2min 48.6sec
1968	S. Wichman *USA* 2min 44.4sec	D. Bjedov *YUG* 2min 46.4sec	G. Prosumenshchikova *URS* 2min 47.0sec
1972	B. Whitfield *AUS* 2min 41.71sec	D. Schoenfield *USA* 2min 42.05sec	G. Stepanova *URS* 2min 42.36sec

100 Metres Butterfly
Not held before 1956.

	Gold	Silver	Bronze
1956	S. Mann *USA* 1min 11.0sec	N. Ramey *USA* 1min 11.9sec	M. J. Sears *USA* 1min 14.4sec
1960	C. Schuler *USA* 1min 09.5sec	M. Heemskerk *HOL* 1min 10.4sec	J. Andrew *AUS* 1min 12.2sec
1964	S. Stouder *USA* 1min 04.7sec	A. Kok *HOL* 1min 05.6sec	K. Ellis *USA* 1min 06.0sec
1968	L. McClements *AUS* 1min 05.5sec	E. Daniel *USA* 1min 05.8sec	S. Shields *USA* 1min 06.2sec
1972	M. Aoki *JPN* 1min 03.34sec	R. Beier *GDR* 1min 03.61sec	A. Gyarmati *HUN* 1min 03.73sec

200 Metres Butterfly
Not held before 1968.

	Gold	Silver	Bronze
1968	A. Kok *HOL* 2min 24.7sec	H. Lindner *GDR* 2min 24.8sec	E. Daniel *USA* 2min 25.9sec
1972	K. Moe *USA* 2min 15.57sec	L. Colella *USA* 2min 16.34sec	E. Daniel *USA* 2min 16.74sec

200 Metres Individual Medley
Not held before 1968. Order of strokes: butterfly, backstroke, breaststroke, freestyle.

	Gold	Silver	Bronze
1968	C. Kolb *USA* 2min 24.7sec	S. Pedersen *USA* 2min 28.8sec	J. Henne *USA* 2min 31.4sec
1972	S. Gould *AUS* 2min 23.07sec	K. Ender *GDR* 2min 23.59sec	L. Vidali *USA* 2min 24.06sec

400 Metres Individual Medley
Not held before 1964. Order of strokes: butterfly, backstroke, breaststroke, freestyle.

	Gold	Silver	Bronze
1964	D. De Varona *USA* 5min 18.7sec	S. Finneran *USA* 5min 24.1sec	M. Randall *USA* 5min 24.2sec
1968	C. Kolb *USA* 5min 08.5sec	L. Vidali *USA* 5min 22.2sec	S. Steinbach *GDR* 5min 25.3sec
1972	G. Neall *AUS* 5min 02.97sec	L. Cliff *CAN* 5min 03.57sec	N. Calligaris *ITA* 5min 03.99sec

4 × 100 Metres Freestyle Relay
Not held before 1912.

	Gold	Silver	Bronze
1912	GBR 5min 52.8sec	GER 6min 04.6sec	AUT 6min 17.0sec
1920	USA 5min 11.6sec	GBR 5min 40.8sec	SWE 5min 43.6sec
1924	USA 4min 58.8sec	GBR 5min 17.0sec	SWE 5min 35.8sec
1928	USA 4min 47.6sec	GBR 5min 02.8sec	SAF 5min 13.4sec
1932	USA 4min 38.0sec	HOL 4min 47.5sec	GBR 4min 52.4sec
1936	HOL 4min 36.0sec	GER 4min 36.8sec	USA 4min 40.2sec
1948	USA 4min 29.2sec	DEN 4min 29.6sec	HOL 4min 31.6sec
1952	HUN 4min 24.4sec	HOL 4min 29.0sec	USA 4min 30.1sec
1956	AUS 4min 17.1sec	USA 4min 19.2sec	SAF 4min 25.7sec
1960	USA 4min 08.9sec	AUS 4min 11.3sec	GER 4min 19.7sec
1964	USA 4min 03.8sec	AUS 4min 06.9sec	HOL 4min 12.0sec
1968	USA 4min 02.5sec	GDR 4min 05.7sec	CAN 4min 07.2sec
1972	USA 3min 55.19sec	GDR 3min 55.55sec	GER 3min 57.93sec

4 × 100 Metres Medley Relay
Not held before 1960. Order of strokes: backstroke, breaststroke, butterfly, freestyle.

	Gold	Silver	Bronze
1960	USA 4min 41.1sec	AUS 4min 45.9sec	GER 4min 47.6sec
1964	USA 4min 33.9sec	HOL 4min 37.0sec	URS 4min 39.2sec
1968	USA 4min 28.3sec	AUS 4min 30.0sec	GER 4min 36.4sec
1972	USA 4min 20.75sec	GDR 4min 24.91sec	GER 4min 26.46sec

Highboard Diving
Not held before 1912. In 1924 Smith gained a superior aggregate of placings to Becker although the latter gained more points.

	Gold	Silver	Bronze
1912	G. Johansson *SWE* 39.90 pts	L. Regnell *SWE* 36.00 pts	I. White *GBR* 34.00 pts
1920	S. (Clausen) Fryland *DEN* 34.60 pts	E. Armstrong *GBR* 33.30 pts	E. Ollivier *SWE* 33.30 pts
1924	C. Smith *USA* 33.20 pts	E. Becker *USA* 33.40 pts	H. Töpel *SWE* 32.80 pts
1928	E. (Becker) Pinkston *USA* 31.60 pts	G. Coleman *USA* 30.60 pts	L. Sjöqvist *SWE* 29.20 pts
1932	D. Poynton *USA* 40.26 pts	G. Coleman *USA* 35.56 pts	M. Roper *USA* 35.22 pts
1936	D. (Poynton) Hill *USA* 33.93 pts	V. Dunn *USA* 33.63 pts	K. Köhler *GER* 33.43 pts
1948	V. Draves *USA* 68.87 pts	P. Elsener *USA* 66.28 pts	B. Christoffersen *DEN* 66.04 pts
1952	P. McCormick *USA* 79.37 pts	P. J. Myers *USA* 71.63 pts	J. Irwin *USA* 70.49 pts
1956	P. McCormick *USA* 84.85 pts	J. Irwin *USA* 81.64 pts	P. J. Myers *USA* 81.58 pts
1960	I. Krämer *GER* 91.28 pts	P. J. (Myers) Pope *USA* 88.94 pts	N. Krutova *URS* 86.99 pts
1964	L. Bush *USA* 99.80 pts	I. (Krämer) Engel *GER* 98.45 pts	G. Alekseeva *URS* 97.60 pts
1968	M. Duchková *TCH* 109.59 pts	N. Lobanova *URS* 105.14 pts	A. Peterson *USA* 101.11 pts
1972	U. Knape *SWE* 390.00 pts	M. Duchková *TCH* 370.92 pts	M. Janicke *GDR* 360.54 pts

Springboard Diving
Not held before 1920.

	Gold	Silver	Bronze
1920	A. Riggin *USA* 539.90 pts	H. Wainwright *USA* 534.80 pts	T. Payne *USA* 534.10 pts
1924	E. Becker *USA* 474.50 pts	A. Riggin *USA* 460.40 pts	C. Fletcher *USA* 436.40 pts
1928	H. Meany *USA* 78.62 pts	D. Poynton *USA* 75.62 pts	G. Coleman *USA* 73.38 pts
1932	G. Coleman *USA* 87.52 pts	K. Rawls *USA* 82.56 pts	J. Fauntz *USA* 82.12 pts
1936	M. Gestring *USA* 89.27 pts	K. Rawls *USA* 88.35 pts	D. (Poynton) Hill *USA* 82.36 pts
1948	V. Draves *USA* 108.74 pts	Z. A. Olsen *USA* 108.23 pts	P. Elsener *USA* 101.30 pts
1952	P. McCormick *USA* 147.30 pts	M. Moreau *FRA* 139.34 pts	Z. A. (Olsen) Jensen *USA* 127.57 pts
1956	P. McCormick *USA* 142.36 pts	J. Stunyo *USA* 125.89 pts	I. MacDonald *CAN* 121.40 pts
1960	I. Krämer *GER* 155.81 pts	P. J. (Myers) Pope *USA* 141.24 pts	E. Ferris *GBR* 139.09 pts
1964	I. (Krämer) Engel *GER* 145.00 pts	J. Collier *USA* 138.36 pts	P. Willard *USA* 138.18 pts
1968	S. Gossick *USA* 150.77 pts	T. Pogosheva *URS* 145.30 pts	K. O'Sullivan *USA* 145.23 pts
1972	M. King *USA* 450.03 pts	U. Knape *SWE* 434.19 pts	M. Janicke *GDR* 430.92 pts

Volleyball *Men*
Not held before 1964.

	Gold	Silver	Bronze
1964	URS	TCH	JPN
1968	URS	JPN	TCH
1972	JPN	GDR	URS

Volleyball *Women*
Not held before 1964.

	Gold	Silver	Bronze
1964	JPN	URS	POL
1968	URS	JPN	POL
1972	URS	JPN	PRK

Weightlifting

The official results are recorded in kilograms. In order to give approximate equivalents in pounds, we have followed the International Weightlifting Federation's system of converting from kilos to pounds to the nearest quarter pound below (because Imperial scales for weighing competitors and barbells weigh to the nearest quarter pound). Since in each case we have converted the total (of two lifts, or, in the early days, three lifts), the total as given in pounds is not quite the same as it would be if we had converted each lift separately into pounds, and therefore is only approximate.

Flyweight
Not held before 1972. Weight limit 52kg (114¼lb).

	Gold	Silver	Bronze
1972	Z. Smalcerz *POL* 337.5kg (744lb)	L. Szücs *HUN* 330.00kg (727½lb)	S. Holczreiter *HUN* 327.5kg (722lb)

Bantamweight

Not held before 1948. Weight limit 56kg (123¼lb).

	Gold	Silver	Bronze
1948	J. De Pietro *USA* 307.5kg (677¾lb)	J. Creus *GBR* 297.5kg (655¾lb)	R. Tom *USA* 295.0kg (650¼lb)
1952	I. Udodov *URS* 315.0kg (694¼lb)	M. Namdjou *IRN* 307.5kg (677¾lb)	A. Mirzai *IRN* 300.0kg (661¼lb)
1956	C. Vinci *USA* 342.5kg (755lb)	V. Stogov *URS* 337.5kg (744lb)	M. Namdjou *IRN* 332.5kg (733lb)
1960	C. Vinci *USA* 345.0kg (760½lb)	Yoshinobu Miyake *JPN* 337.5kg (744lb)	E. Elmkhah *IRN* 330.0kg (727½lb)
1964	A. Vakhonin *URS* 357.5kg (788lb)	I. Földi *HUN* 355.0kg (782½lb)	S. Ichinoseki *JPN* 347.5kg (766lb)
1968	M. Nassiri *IRN* 367.5kg (810lb)	I. Földi *HUN* 367.5kg (810lb)	H. Trebicki *POL* 357.5kg (788lb)
1972	I. Földi *HUN* 377.5kg (832lb)	M. Nassiri *IRN* 370.0kg (815½lb)	G. Chetin *URS* 367.5kg (810lb)

Featherweight

Not held before 1920. Weight limit 60kg (132¼lb).

	Gold	Silver	Bronze
1920	F. de Haes *BEL* 220.0kg (485lb)	A. Schmidt *EST* 212.5kg (486¼lb)	E. Ritter *SUI* 210.0kg (462¾lb)
1924	P. Gabetti *ITA* 402.5kg (887¼lb)	A. Stadler *AUT* 385.0kg (848¾lb)	A. Reinmann *SUI* 382.5kg (843¼lb)
1928	F. Andrysek *AUT* 287.5kg (633¾lb)	P. Gabetti *ITA* 282.5kg (622¾lb)	H. Wölpert *GER* 282.5kg (622¾lb)
1932	R. Suvigny *FRA* 287.5kg (633¾lb)	H. Wölpert *GER* 282.5kg (622¾lb)	A. Terlazzo *USA* 280.0kg (617¼lb)
1936	A. Terlazzo *USA* 312.5kg (688¾lb)	S. Soliman *EGY* 305.0kg (672¼lb)	I. Shams *EGY* 300.0kg (661¼lb)
1948	M. Fayad *EGY* 332.5kg (733lb)	R. Wilkes *TRI* 317.5kg (699¾lb)	J. Salmassi *IRN* 312.5kg (688¾lb)
1952	R. Chimishkian *URS* 337.5kg (744lb)	N. Saksonov *URS* 332.5kg (733lb)	R. Wilkes *TRI* 322.5kg (710¾lb)
1956	I. Berger *USA* 352.5kg (777lb)	Y. Minaev *URS* 342.5kg (755lb)	M. Zieliński *POL* 335.0kg (738½lb)
1960	Y. Minaev *URS* 372.5kg (821lb)	I. Berger *USA* 362.5kg (799lb)	S. Mannironi *ITA* 352.5kg (777lb)
1964	Yoshinobu Miyake *JPN* 397.5kg (876¼lb)	I. Berger *USA* 382.5kg (843¼lb)	M. Nowak *POL* 377.5kg (832lb)
1968	Yoshinobu Miyake *JPN* 392.5kg (865¼lb)	D. Zhanidze *URS* 387.5kg (854¼lb)	Yoshuyike Miyake *JPN* 385.0kg (848¾lb)
1972	N. Nurikyan *BUL* 402.5kg (887¼lb)	D. Zhanidze *URS* 400.0kg (881¾lb)	J. Benedek *HUN* 390.0kg (859¾lb)

Lightweight

Not held before 1920. Weight limit 67.5kg (148¾lb).

	Gold	Silver	Bronze
1920	A. Neuland *EST* 257.5kg (567½lb)	L. Williquet *BEL* 240.0kg (529lb)	F. Rooms *BEL* 230.0kg (507lb)
1924	E. Décottignies *FRA* 440.0kg (970lb)	A. Zwerina *AUT* 427.5kg (942¼lb)	B. Durdis *TCH* 425.0kg (936¾lb)
1928	K. Helbig *GER* & H. Haas *AUT* 322.5kg (710¾lb)		F. Arnout *FRA* 302.5kg (666¾lb)
1932	R. Duverger *FRA* 325.0kg (716½lb)	H. Haas *AUT* 307.5kg (677¾lb)	G. Pierini *ITA* 302.5kg (666¾lb)
1936	A. M. Mesbah *EGY* & R. Fein *AUT* 342.5kg (755lb)		K. Jansen *GER* 327.5kg (722lb)
1948	I. H. Shams *EGY* 360.0kg (793½lb)	A. Hamouda *EGY* 360.0kg (793½lb)	J. Halliday *GBR* 340.0kg (749½lb)
1952	T. Kono *USA* 362.5kg (799lb)	Y. Lopatin *URS* 350.0kg (771½lb)	V. Barberis *AUT* 350.0kg (771½lb)
1956	I. Rybak *URS* 380.0kg (837¾lb)	R. Khabutdinov *URS* 372.5kg (821lb)	C. H. Kim *KOR* 370.0kg (815½lb)
1960	V. Bushuev *URS* 397.5kg (876¼lb)	H. L. Tan *SIN* 380.0kg (837¾lb)	A. W. Aziz *IRQ* 380.0kg (837¾lb)
1964	W. Baszanowski *POL* 432.5kg (953½lb)	V. Kaplunov *URS* 432.5kg (953½lb)	M. Zieliński *POL* 420.0kg (925¾lb)
1968	W. Baszanowski *POL* 437.5kg (963½lb)	P. Jalayer *IRN* 422.5kg (931¼lb)	M. Zieliński *POL* 420.0kg (925¾lb)
1972	M. Kirzhinov *URS* 460.0kg (1,014lb)	M. Kuchev *BUL* 450.0kg (992lb)	Z. Kaczmarek *POL* 437.5kg (964½lb)

Middleweight

Not held before 1920. Weight limit 75kg (165¼lb).

	Gold	Silver	Bronze
1920	H. Gance *FRA* 245.0kg (540lb)	P. Bianchi *ITA* 237.5kg (523½lb)	A. Pettersson *SWE* 237.5kg (523½lb)
1924	C. Galimberti *ITA* 492.5kg (1,085¾lb)	A. Neuland *EST* 455.0kg (1,003lb)	J. Kikas *EST* 450.0kg (992lb)
1928	R. François *FRA* 335.0kg (738½lb)	C. Galimberti *ITA* 332.5kg (733lb)	A. Scheffer *HOL* 327.5kg (722lb)
1932	R. Ismayr *GER* 345.0kg (760½lb)	C. Galimberti *ITA* 340.0kg (749½lb)	K. Hipfinger *AUT* 337.5kg (744lb)
1936	K. S. el Touni *EGY* 387.5kg (854¼lb)	R. Ismayr *GER* 352.5kg (777lb)	A. Wagner *GER* 352.5kg (777lb)
1948	F. Spellman *USA* 390.0kg (859¾lb)	P. George *USA* 382.5kg (843¼lb)	S. J. Kim *KOR* 380.0kg (837¾lb)
1952	P. George *USA* 400.0kg (881¾lb)	G. Gratton *CAN* 390.0kg (859¾lb)	S. J. Kim *KOR* 382.5kg (843¼lb)
1956	F. Bogdanovski *URS* 420.0kg (925¾lb)	P. George *USA* 412.5kg (909¼lb)	E. Pignatti *ITA* 382.5kg (843¼lb)
1960	A. Kurinov *URS* 437.5kg (964½lb)	T. Kono *USA* 427.5kg (942¼lb)	G. Veres *HUN* 405.0kg (892¾lb)
1964	H. Zdražila *TCH* 445.0kg (981lb)	V. Kurentsov *URS* 440.0kg (970lb)	M. Ohuchi *JPN* 437.5kg (964½lb)
1968	V. Kurentsov *URS* 475.0kg (1,047lb)	M. Ohuchi *JPN* 455.0kg (1,003lb)	K. Bakos *HUN* 440.0kg (970lb)
1972	Y. Bikov *BUL* 485.0kg (1,069lb)	M. Trabulsi *LIB* 472.5kg (1,041½lb)	A. Silvino *ITA* 470.0kg (1,036lb)

Light Heavyweight

Not held before 1920. Weight limit 82.5kg (181¾lb).

	Gold	Silver	Bronze
1920	E. Cadine *FRA* 290.0kg (131½lb)	F. Hünenberger *SUI* 275.0kg (124½lb)	E. Pettersson *SWE* 272.5kg (124¼lb)
1924	C. Rigoulot *FRA* 502.5kg (1,107¾lb)	F. Hünenberger *SUI* 490.0kg (1,080¼lb)	L. Friedrich *AUT* 490.0kg (1,080¼lb)
1928	S. Nosseir *EGY* 355.0kg (782½lb)	L. Hostin *FRA* 352.5kg (777lb)	J. Verheijen *HOL* 337.5kg (744lb)
1932	L. Hostin *FRA* 365.0kg (804½lb)	S. Olsen *DEN* 360.0kg (793½lb)	H. Duey *USA* 330.0kg (727½lb)
1936	L. Hostin *FRA* 372.5kg (821lb)	E. Deutsch *GER* 365.0kg (804½lb)	I. Wasif *EGY* 360.0kg (793½lb)
1948	S. Stanczyk *USA* 417.5kg (920¼lb)	H. Sakata *USA* 380.0kg (837¾lb)	G. Magnusson *SWE* 375.0kg (826¾lb)
1952	T. Lomakhin *URS* 417.5kg (920½lb)	S. Stanozyk *USA* 415.0kg (914¾lb)	A. Vorobev *URS* 407.5kg (898¼lb)
1956	T. Kono *USA* 447.5kg (986½lb)	V. Stepanov *URS* 427.5kg (942¼lb)	J. George *USA* 417.5kg (920¼lb)
1960	I. Paliński *POL* 442.5kg (975½lb)	S. George *USA* 430.0kg (947¾lb)	J. Bochenek *POL* 420.0kg (925¾lb)
1964	R. Plyukfelder *URS* 475.0kg (1,047lb)	G. Tóth *HUN* 467.5kg (1,030½lb)	G. Veres *HUN* 467.5kg (1,030½lb)
1968	B. Selitski *URS* 485.0kg (1,069lb)	V. Belyaev *URS* 485.0kg (1,069lb)	N. Ozimek *POL* 472.5kg (1,041½lb)
1972	L. Jensen *NOR* 507.5kg (1,118¾lb)	N. Ozimek *POL* 497.5kg (1,096¾lb)	G. Horváth *HUN* 495.0kg (1,091¼lb)

Middle Heavyweight

Not held before 1952. Weight limit 90kg (198¼lb).

	Gold	Silver	Bronze
1952	N. Schemansky *USA* 445.0kg (981lb)	G. Novak *URS* 410.0kg (902¾lb)	L. Kilgour *TRI* 402.5kg (887¼lb)
1956	A. Vorobev *URS* 462.5kg (1,019½lb)	D. Sheppard *USA* 442.5kg (975½lb)	J. Debuf *FRA* 425.0kg (936¾lb)
1960	A. Vorobev *URS* 472.5kg (1,041½lb)	T. Lomakhin *URS* 457.5kg (1,008½lb)	L. Martin *GBR* 445.0kg (981lb)
1964	V. Golovanov *URS* 487.5kg (1,074¾lb)	L. Martin *GBR* 475.0kg (1,047lb)	I. Paliński *POL* 467.5kg (1,030½lb)
1968	K. Kangasniemi *FIN* 517.5kg (1,140¾lb)	Y. Talts *URS* 507.5kg (1,118¾lb)	M. Gołąb *POL* 495.0kg (1,091¼lb)
1972	A. Nikolov *BUL* 525.0kg (1,157¼lb)	A. Shopov *BUL* 517.5kg (1,140¾lb)	H. Bettembourg *SWE* 512.5kg (1,129¾lb)

Heavyweight

For results before 1972 see Super Heavyweight. Weight limit 110kg (242½lb).

	Gold	Silver	Bronze
1972	Y. Talts *URS* 580.0kg (1,278½lb)	A. Kraichev *BUL* 562.5kg (1,240lb)	S. Grützner *GDR* 555.0kg (1,223½lb)

Super Heavyweight

This class was described as Heavyweight until 1972. In 1896 and 1904 two separate competitions were held. (1) one-hand lift and (2) two-hand lift. Weight limits 1896–1904 open; 1920–48 over 82.5kg (181¾lb); 1952–68 over 90kg (198¼lb); from 1972 over 110kg (242½lb).

	Gold	Silver	Bronze
1896	(1) L. Elliott *GBR* 71.0kg (156½lb)	V. Jensen *DEN* 57.2kg (126lb)	A. Nikolopoulos *GRE* 57.2kg (126lb)
	(2) V. Jensen *DEN* 111.5kg (245¾lb)	L. Elliott *GBR* 111.5kg (245¾lb)	S. Versis *GRE* 100.0kg (220½lb)
1900	*Not held*		
1904	(1) O. P. Osthoff *USA* 48 pts	F. Winters *USA* 45 pts	F. Kungler *USA* 10 pts
	(2) P. Kakousis *GRE* 111.58kg (245lb)	O. P. Osthoff *USA* 84.36kg (185lb)	F. Kungler *USA* 79.83kg (175lb)
1908–1912	*Not held*		
1920	F. Bottino *ITA* 270.0kg (595¼lb)	J. Alzin *LUX* 255.0kg (562lb)	L. Bernot *FRA* 250.0kg (551lb)
1924	G. Tonani *ITA* 517.5kg (1,140¾lb)	F. Aigner *AUT* 515.0kg (1,135¼lb)	H. Tammer *EST* 497.5kg (1,096¾lb)
1928	J. Strassberger *GER* 372.5kg (821lb)	A. Luhaäär *EST* 360.0kg (793½lb)	J. Skobla *TCH* 357.5kg (788lb)
1932	J. Skobla *TCH* 380.0kg (837¾lb)	V. Pšenička *TCH* 377.5kg (832lb)	J. Strassberger *GER* 377.5kg (832lb)
1936	J. Manger *GER* 410.0kg (902¾lb)	V. Pšenička *TCH* 402.5kg (887¼lb)	A. Luhaäär *EST* 400.0kg (881¾lb)
1948	J. Davis *USA* 452.5kg (997½lb)	N. Schemansky *USA* 425.0kg (936¾lb)	A. Charité *HOL* 412.5kg (909¼lb)
1952	J. Davis *USA* 460.0kg (1,014lb)	J. Bradford *USA* 437.5kg (964½lb)	H. Selvetti *ARG* 432.5kg (953½lb)
1956	P. Anderson *USA* 500.0kg (1,102¼lb)	H. Selvetti *ARG* 500.0kg (1,102¼lb)	A. Pigaiani *ITA* 452.5kg (997½lb)

	Gold	Silver	Bronze
1960	Y. Vlasov URS 537.5kg (1,184$\frac{3}{4}$lb)	J. Bradford USA 512.5kg (1,129$\frac{3}{4}$lb)	N. Schemansky USA 500.0kg (1,102$\frac{1}{4}$lb)
1964	L. Zhabotinski URS 572.5kg (1,262lb)	Y. Vlasov URS 570.0kg (1,256$\frac{1}{2}$lb)	N. Schemansky USA 537.5kg (1,184$\frac{3}{4}$lb)
1968	L. Zhabotinski URS 572.5kg (1,262lb)	S. Reding BEL 555.0kg (1,223$\frac{1}{2}$lb)	J. Dube USA 555.0kg (1,223$\frac{1}{2}$lb)
1972	V. Alekseev URS 640.0kg (1,410$\frac{3}{4}$lb)	R. Mang GER 612.0kg (1,344$\frac{3}{4}$lb)	G. Bonk GDR 572.5kg (1,262lb)

Wrestling Freestyle

Not held before 1904. Weight limit 1904 47.6kg (105lb); from 1972 48kg (105lb 13oz). In 1909 this weight category was called 'Flyweight'.

	Gold	Silver	Bronze
1904	R. Curry USA	J. Heim USA	G. Thiefenthaler USA
1908–1968	*Not held*		
1972	R. Dmitriev URS	O. Nikolov BUL	E. Javadpour IRN

Flyweight

Not held before 1904. Weight limit 1904 52.16kg (115lb); from 1948 52kg (114lb 10oz). In 1904 this weight category was called 'Bantamweight'.

	Gold	Silver	Bronze
1904	G. Mehnert USA	G. Bauers USA	M. Nelson USA
1908–1936	*Not held*		
1948	L. Viitala FIN	H. Balamir TUR	T. Johansson SWE
1952	H. Gemici TUR	Y. Kitano JPN	M. Mollaghassemi IRN
1956	M. Tsalkalamanidze URS	M. Khojastehpour IRN	H. Akbaş TUR
1960	A. Bilek TUR	M. Matsubara JPN	M. Saifpour Saidabadi IRN
1964	Y. Yoshida JPN	C. S. Chang KOR	S. Aliaakbar Haydari IRN
1968	S. Nakata JPN	R. Sanders USA	S. Sukhbaatar MGL
1972	K. Kato JPN	A. Alakhverdiev URS	H. K. Gwong PRK

Bantamweight

Not held before 1904. Weight limit 1904 56.80kg (125lb); 1908 54kg (119lb); 1924–36 56kg (123lb 7$\frac{1}{4}$oz); from 1948 57kg (125lb 10$\frac{1}{2}$oz). In 1904 this weight category was called 'Featherweight'.

	Gold	Silver	Bronze
1904	I. Niflot USA	A. Wester USA	Z. Strebler USA
1908	G. Mehnert USA	W. J. Press GBR	B. A. Côté CAN
1912–1920	*Not held*		
1924	K. Pihlajamäki FIN	K. E. Mäkinen FIN	B. Hines USA
1928	K. E. Mäkinen FIN	E. Spapen BEL	J. Trifunov CAN
1932	R. Pearce USA	Ö Zombori HUN	A. Jaskari FIN
1936	Ö Zombori HUN	R. Flood USA	J. Herbert GER
1948	N. Akkar TUN	G. Leeman USA	C. Kouyos FRA
1952	S. Ishii JPN	R. Mamedbekov URS	K. S. Jadav IND
1956	M. Dagistanli TUR	M. Yaghoubi IRN	M. Shakhov URS
1960	T. McCann USA	N. Zalev BUL	T. Trojanowski POL
1964	Y. Uetake JPN	H. Akbaş TUR	A. Ibragimov URS
1968	Y. Uetake JPN	D. Behm USA	A. Gorgori IRN
1972	H. Yanagida JPN	R. Sanders USA	L. Klinga HUN

Featherweight

Not held before 1904. Weight limit 1904 61.24kg (135lb); 1908 60.30kg (133lb); 1920 60kg (132lb 4$\frac{1}{2}$oz); 1924–36 61kg (134lb 7$\frac{1}{2}$oz); 1948–60 62kg (136lb 11oz); 1964–68 63kg (138lb 12oz); from 1972 62kg (136lb 11oz). In 1904 this weight category was called 'Lightweight'.

	Gold	Silver	Bronze
1904	B. Bradshaw USA	T. McLear USA	B. C. Clapper USA
1908	G. Dole USA	J. Slim GBR	W. McKie GBR
1912	*Not held*		
1920	C. Ackerley USA	S. Gerson USA	P. W. Bernard GBR
1924	R. Reed USA	C. Newton USA	K. Naito JPN
1928	A. Morrison USA	K. Pihlajamäki FIN	H. Minder SUI
1932	K. Pihlajamäki FIN	E. Nemir USA	E. Karlsson SWE
1936	K. Pihlajamäki FIN	F. Millard USA	G. Jönsson SWE
1948	G. Bilge TUR	I. Sjölin SWE	A. Müller SUI
1952	B. Şit TUR	N. Guivehtchi IRN	J. Henson USA
1956	S. Sasahara JPN	J. Mewis BEL	E. Penttilä FIN
1960	M. Dagistanli TUR	S. Ivanov BUL	V. Rubashvili URS
1964	O. Watanabe JPN	S. Ivanov BUL	N. Khokhashvili URS
1968	M. Kaneko JPN	E. Todorov BUL	S. Seyed-Abassy IRN
1972	Z. Abdulbekov URS	V. Akdag TUR	I. Krastev BUL

Lightweight

Not held before 1904. Weight limit 1904 65.77kg (145lb); 1908 66.60kg (146lb 13$\frac{1}{4}$oz); 1920 67.50kg (148lb 13oz); 1924–36 66kg (145lb 8oz); 1948–60 67kg (147lb 11$\frac{1}{4}$oz); 1964–68 70kg (154lb 5oz); from 1972 68kg (149lb 14$\frac{1}{2}$oz). In 1904 this weight category was called 'Light Middleweight'.

	Gold	Silver	Bronze
1904	O. Roehm USA	S. R. Tesing USA	A. Zirkel USA
1908	G. de Relwyskow GBR	W. Wood GBR	A. Gingell GBR
1912	*Not held*		
1920	K. Anttila FIN	G. Svensson SWE	P. Wright GBR
1924	R. Vis USA	V. Vikström FIN	A. Haavisto FIN
1928	O. Käpp EST	C. Pacôme FRA	E. Leino FIN
1932	C. Pacôme FRA	K. Kárpáti HUN	G. Klarén SWE
1936	K. Kárpáti HUN	W. Ehrl FIN	H. Pihlajamäki FIN
1948	C. Atik TUR	G. Frändfors SWE	H. Baumann SUI
1952	O. Anderberg SWE	J. T. Evans USA	D. Tovfighe IRN
1956	E. Habibi IRN	S. Kasahara JPN	A. Bestaev URS
1960	S. Wilson USA	V. Sinyavski URS	E. Dimov (Valchev) BUL
1964	E. Valchev BUL	K. J. Rost GER	I. Horiuchi JPN
1968	A. Movahed Ardabili IRN	E. Valchev JPN	S. Danzandarjaa MGL
1972	D. Gable USA	K. Wada JPN	R. Ashuraliev URS

Welterweight

Not held before 1904. Weight limit 1904 71.67kg (158lb); 1924–36 72kg (158lb 11$\frac{1}{2}$oz); 1948–60 73kg (160lb 15oz); 1964–68 78kg (171lb 15$\frac{1}{4}$oz); from 1972 74kg (163lb 2$\frac{1}{4}$oz). In 1904 this weight category was called 'Middleweight'; in 1924 it was called 'Light Middleweight'.

	Gold	Silver	Bronze
1904	C. Erikson USA	W. Beckmann USA	J. Winholtz USA
1908–1920	*Not held*		
1924	H. Gehri SUI	E. Leino FIN	O. Müller SUI
1928	A. J. Haavisto FIN	L. O. Appleton USA	M. E. Letchford CAN
1932	J. Van Bebber USA	D. MacDonald CAN	E. Leino FIN
1936	F. Lewis USA	T. Andersson SWE	J. Schleimer CAN
1948	Y. Dogu TUR	R. Garrard AUS	L. Merrill USA
1952	W. Smith USA	P. Berlin SWE	A. Modjtabavi IRN
1956	M. Ikeda JPN	I. Zengin TUR	V. Balavadze URS
1960	D. Blubaugh USA	I. Ogan TUR	M. Bashir PAK
1964	I. Ogan TUR	G. Sagaradze URS	M. A. Sanatkaran IRN
1968	M. Atalay TUR	D. Robin FRA	D. Purev MGL
1972	W. Wells USA	J. Karlsson SWE	A. Seger GER

Middleweight

Not held before 1908. Weight limit 1908 73kg (161lb); 1920 75kg (165lb 5$\frac{1}{2}$oz); 1924–60 79kg (174lb 2$\frac{3}{4}$oz); 1964–68 87kg (191lb 12$\frac{3}{4}$oz); from 1972 82kg (180lb 12$\frac{1}{2}$oz).

	Gold	Silver	Bronze
1908	S. Bacon GBR	G. de Relwyskow GBR	F. Beck GBR
1912	*Not held*		
1920	E. Leino FIN	V. Penttala FIN	C. Johnson USA
1924	F. Hagmann SUI	P. Ollivier BEL	V. F. Pekkala FIN
1928	E. Kyburz SUI	D. P. Stockton CAN	S. Rabin GBR
1932	I. Johansson SWE	K. Luukko FIN	J. Tunyogi HUN
1936	E. Poilvé FRA	R. Voliva USA	A. Kireççi TUR
1948	G. Brand USA	A. Candemir TUR	E. Lindén SWE
1952	D. Tsimakuridze URS	G. R. Takhti IRN	G. Gurics HUN
1956	N. Stanchev BUL	D. Hodge USA	G. Skhirtladze URS
1960	H. Güngör TUR	G. Skhirtladze URS	H. Y. Antonsson SWE
1964	P. Gardshev BUL	H. Güngör TUR	D. Brand USA
1968	B. Gurevich URS	M. Jigjid MGL	P. Gardshev BUL
1972	L. Tediashvili URS	J. Peterson USA	V. Jorga ROM

Light Heavyweight

Not held before 1920. Weight limit 1920 82.5kg (181lb 8oz); 1924–60 87kg (191lb 12$\frac{3}{4}$oz); 1964–68 97kg (213lb 13$\frac{1}{2}$oz); from 1972 90kg (198lb 6$\frac{3}{4}$oz).

	Gold	Silver	Bronze
1920	A. Larsson SWE	C. Courant SUI	W. Maurer USA
1924	J. Spellman USA	R. Svensson SWE	C. Courant SUI
1928	T. Sjöstedt SWE	A. Bögli SUI	H. Lefebvre FRA
1932	P. Mehringer USA	T. Sjöstedt SWE	E. Scarf AUS
1936	K. Fridell SWE	A. Neo EST	E. Siebert GER
1948	H. Wittenberg USA	F. Stöckli SUI	B. Fahlkvist SWE
1952	V. Palm SWE	H. Wittenberg USA	A. Atan TUR
1956	G. R. Takhti IRN	B. Kulaev URS	P. S. Blair USA
1960	A. Atli TUR	G. R. Takhti IRN	A. Albul URS
1964	A. Medved URS	A. Ayik TUR	S. Mustafov BUL
1968	A. Ayik TUR	S. Lomidze URS	J. Csatári HUN
1972	B. Peterson USA	G. Strakhov URS	K. Bajko HUN

Heavyweight

Not held before 1904. Weight limit 1904 over 71.67kg (158lb); 1908 over 73kg (161lb); 1920 over 82.5kg (181lb 14oz); 1924–60 over 87kg (191lb 12$\frac{3}{4}$oz); 1964–68 over 97kg (213lb 13$\frac{1}{2}$oz); from 1972 under 100kg (200lb 7$\frac{1}{4}$oz).

	Gold	Silver	Bronze
1904	B. Hansen USA	F. Kungler USA	F. Warmbold USA
1908	G. C. O'Kelly GBR/IRL	J. Gundersen NOR	E. Barrett GBR/IRL
1912	*Not held*		
1920	R. Roth SUI	N. Pendleton USA	E. Nilsson SWE & F. Meyer USA
1924	H. Steele USA	H. Wernli SUI	A. McDonald GBR
1928	J. Richthoff SWE	A. Sihvola FIN	E. Dame FRA
1932	J. Richthoff SWE	J. Riley FIN	N. Hirschl AUT
1936	K. Palusalu EST	J. Klapuch TCH	H. Nyström FIN
1948	G. Bóbis HUN	B. Antonsson SWE	J. Armstrong AUS
1952	A. Mekokishvili URS	B. Antonsson SWE	K. Richmond GBR
1956	H. Kaplan TUR	H. Mekhmedov BUL	T. Kangasniemi FIN
1960	W. Dietrich GER	H. Kaplan TUR	S. Tsarasov URS
1964	A. Ivanitski URS	L. Djiber BUL	H. Kaplan TUR

	Gold	Silver	Bronze
1968	A. Medved *URS*	O. Duralyev *BUL*	W. Dietrich *GER*
1972	I. Yarygin *URS*	K. Baianmunkh *MGL*	J. Csatári *HUN*

Super Heavyweight

Not held before 1972. Weight limit over 100kg (220lb 7¼oz).

	Gold	Silver	Bronze
1972	A. Medved *URS*	O. Duralyev *BUL*	C. Taylor *USA*

Wrestling Greco-Roman Style

Light Flyweight

Not held before 1972. Weight limit under 48kg (105lb 13oz).

	Gold	Silver	Bronze
1972	G. Berceanu *ROM*	R. Aliabadi *IRN*	S. Anghelov *BUL*

Flyweight

Not held before 1948. Weight limit under 52kg (114lb 10¼oz).

	Gold	Silver	Bronze
1948	P. Lombardi *ITA*	K. Olcay *TUR*	R. Kangasmäki *FIN*
1952	B. Gurevich *URS*	I. Fabra *ITA*	L. Honkala *FIN*
1956	N. Solovyev *URS*	I. Fabra *ITA*	D. A. Egribas *TUR*
1960	D. Pirvulescu *ROM*	O. Sayed *EGY*	M. Paziraye *IRN*
1964	T. Hanahara *JPN*	A. Kerezov *BUL*	D. Pirvulescu *ROM*
1968	P. Kirov *BUL*	V. Bakulin *URS*	M. Zeman *TCH*
1972	P. Kirov *BUL*	K. Hirayama *JPN*	G. Bognanni *ITA*

Bantamweight

Not held before 1924. Weight limit 1924–28 under 58kg (128lb); 1932–36 under 56kg (123lb 7½oz); from 1948 under 57kg (125lb 10½oz).

	Gold	Silver	Bronze
1924	E. Pütsep *EST*	A. Ahlfors *FIN*	V. Ikonen *FIN*
1928	K. Leucht *GER*	J. Maudr *TCH*	G. Gozzi *ITA*
1932	J. Brendel *GER*	M. Nizzola *ITA*	L. François *FRA*
1936	M. Lőrincz *HUN*	E. Svensson *SWE*	J. Brendel *GER*
1948	K. Pettersén *SWE*	A. M. Hassan *EGY*	H. Kaya *TUR*
1952	I. Hódes *HUN*	Z. Khihab *LIB*	A. Terian *URS*
1956	K. Vyrupaev *URS*	E. Vesterby *SWE*	F. Horvat *ROM*
1960	O. Karavaev *URS*	I. Cernea *ROM*	P. Dinko *BUL*
1964	M. Ichiguchi *JPN*	V. Trostyanski *URS*	I. Cernea *ROM*
1968	J. Varga *HUN*	I. Baciu *ROM*	I. Kochergin *URS*
1972	R. Kazakov *URS*	H. J. Veil *GER*	R. Bjoerlin *FIN*

Featherweight

Not held before 1912. Weight limit 1912–20 60kg (132lb 4½oz); 1924–28 62kg (136lb 11oz); 1932–36 61kg (134lb 7¾oz); 1948–60 62kg (136lb 11oz); 1964–68 63kg (138lb 14½oz); from 1972 62kg (136lb 11oz).

	Gold	Silver	Bronze
1912	K. Koskelo *FIN*	G. Gerstacker *GER*	O. Lasanen *FIN*
1920	O. Friman *FIN*	H. Kähkönen *FIN*	F. Svensson *SWE*
1924	K. Anttila *FIN*	A. Toivola *FIN*	E. Malmberg *SWE*
1928	V. Väli *EST*	E. Malmberg *SWE*	G. Quaglia *ITA*
1932	G. Gozzi *ITA*	W. Ehrl *GER*	L. Koskela *FIN*
1936	Y. Erkan *TUR*	A. Reini *FIN*	E. Karlsson *SWE*
1948	M. Oktav *TUR*	O. Anderberg *SWE*	F. Tóth *HUN*
1952	Y. Punkin *URS*	I. Polyák *HUN*	A. Rashed *EGY*
1956	R. Mäkinen *FIN*	I. Polyák *HUN*	R. Zhneladze *URS*
1960	M. Sille *TUR*	I. Polyák *HUN*	K. Vyrupaev *URS*
1964	I. Polyák *HUN*	R. Rurura *URS*	B. Martinović *YUG*
1968	R. Rurura *URS*	H. Fujimoto *JPN*	S. Popescu *ROM*
1972	G. Markov *BUL*	H. H. Wehling *GDR*	K. Lipień *POL*

Lightweight

Not held before 1908. Weight limit 1908 66.6kg (147lb); 1912–28 67.5kg (148lb 13oz); 1932–36 66kg (145lb 8oz); 1948–60 67kg (147lb 11¼oz); 1964–68 70kg (154lb 5oz); from 1972 68kg (149lb 14½oz).

	Gold	Silver	Bronze
1908	E. Porro *ITA*	N. Orlov *RUS*	A. (Lindén) Linko *FIN*
1912	E. Väre *FIN*	G. Malmström *SWE*	E. Matiasson *SWE*
1920	E. Väre *FIN*	T. Tamminen *FIN*	F. Andersen *NOR*
1924	O. Friman *FIN*	L. Keresztes *HUN*	K. Westerlund *FIN*
1928	L. Keresztes *HUN*	E. Sperling *GER*	E. Westerlund *FIN*
1932	E. Malmberg *SWE*	A. Kurland *DEN*	E. Sperling *GER*
1936	L. Koskela *FIN*	J. Herda *TCH*	V. Väli *EST*
1948	G. Freij *SWE*	A. Eriksen *NOR*	K. Ferencz *HUN*
1952	S. Safin *URS*	G. Freij *SWE*	M. Athanasov *TCH*
1956	K. Lehtonen *FIN*	R. Dogan *TUR*	G. Tóth *HUN*
1960	A. Koridze *URS*	B. Martinović *YUG*	G. Freij *SWE*
1964	K. Ayvaz *TUR*	V. Bularca *ROM*	D. Gvantseladze *URS*
1968	M. Munemura *JPN*	S. Horvath *YUG*	P. Galaktopoulos *GRE*
1972	S. Khisamutdinov *URS*	S. Apostolov *BUL*	G. M. Ranzi *ITA*

Welterweight

Not held before 1932. Weight limit 1932–36 72kg (158lb 11¾oz); 1948–60 73kg (160lb 15oz); 1964–68 78kg (171lb 15½oz); from 1972 74kg (163lb 2¼oz).

	Gold	Silver	Bronze
1932	I. Johansson *SWE*	V. Kajander *FIN*	E. Gallegati *ITA*
1936	R. Svedberg *SWE*	F. Schäfer *GER*	E. Virtanen *FIN*
1948	G. Andersson *SWE*	M. Szilvási *HUN*	H. Hansen *DEN*
1952	M. Szilvási *HUN.*	G. Andersson *SWE*	K. Taha *LIB*
1956	M. Bayrak *TUR*	V. Maneev *URS*	P. Berlin *SWE*
1960	M. Bayrak *TUR*	G. Maritschnigg *GER*	K. Schiermeyer *FRA*
1964	A. Koleslov *URS*	C. Todorov *BUL*	B. Nyström *SWE*
1968	R. Vesper *GDR*	D. Robin *FRA*	K. Bajkó *HUN*
1972	V. Macha *TCH*	P. Galaktopoulos *GRE*	J. Karlsson *SWE*

Middleweight

Not held before 1908. Weight limit 1908 73kg (161lb); 1912–28 75kg (165lb 5¾oz); 1932–60 79kg (174lb 2¾oz); 1964–68 87kg (191lb 12¾oz); from 1972 82kg (180lb 12½oz). In 1912 this weight category was called 'Middleweight A'; in 1928 'Welterweight'.

	Gold	Silver	Bronze
1908	F. Mårtensson *SWE*	M. Andersson *SWE*	A. Andersen *DEN*
1912	C. Johansson *SWE*	M. Klein *RUS*	A. Asikainen *FIN*
1920	C. Westergren *SWE*	A. Lindfors *FIN*	M. Perttilä *FIN*
1924	E. Westerlund *FIN*	A. Lindfors *FIN*	R. Steinberg *EST*
1928	V. Kokkinen *FIN*	L. Papp *HUN*	A. Kuznets *EST*
1932	V. Kokkinen *FIN*	J. Földeák *GER*	A. Cadier *SWE*
1936	I. Johansson *SWE*	L. Schweikert *GER*	J. Palotás *HUN*
1948	A. Grönberg *SWE*	M. Tayfur *TUR*	E. Gallegati *ITA*
1952	A. Grönberg *SWE*	K. Rauhala *FIN*	N. Belov *URS*
1956	G. Kartozia *URS*	D. Dobrev *BUL*	R. Jansson *SWE*
1960	D. Dobrev *BUL*	L. Metz *GDR*	I. Taranu *ROM*
1964	B. Simić *YUG*	J. Kormanik *TCH*	L. Metz *GER*
1968	L. Metz *GDR*	V. Olenik *URS*	B. Simić *YUG*
1972	C. Hegedus *HUN*	A. Nazarenko *URS*	M. Nenadić *YUG*

Light Heavyweight

Not held before 1908. Weight limit 1908 93kg (205lb); 1912–28 82.5kg (181lb 14oz); 1932–60 87kg (191lb 12¾oz); 1964–68 97kg (213lb 13¾oz); from 1972 90kg (198lb 6¾oz). In 1912 this weight category was called 'Middleweight B'; in 1928 'Middleweight'.

	Gold	Silver	Bronze
1908	V. Weckman *FIN*	Y. Saarela *FIN*	C. Jensen *DEN*
1912	*Not awarded*	A. Ahlgren *SWE* & I. Böhling *FIN*	B. Varga *HUN*
1920	C. Johansson *SWE*	E. Rosenqvist *FIN*	J. Eriksen *DEN*
1924	C. Westergren *SWE*	J. R. Svensson *SWE*	O. Pellinen *FIN*
1928	I. Mustafa *EGY*	A. Riger *GER*	O. Pellinen *FIN*
1932	R. Svensson *SWE*	O. Pellinen *FIN*	M. Gruppioni *ITA*
1936	A. Cadier *SWE*	E. Bietags *LIT*	A. Neo *EST*
1948	K. E. Nilsson *SWE*	K. Gröndahl *FIN*	I. Orabi *EGY*
1952	K. Gröndahl *FIN*	S. Shikhladze *URS*	K. E. Nilsson *SWE*
1956	V. Nikolaev *URS*	P. Sirakov *BUL*	K. E. Nilsson *SWE*
1960	T. Kiş *TUR*	K. Bimbalov *BUL*	G. Kartozia *URS*
1964	B. Radev (Aleksandrov) *BUL*	P. Svensson *SWE*	H. Kiehl *GER*
1968	B. Radev *BUL*	N. Yakovenko *URS*	N. Martinescu *ROM*
1972	V. Rezantsev *URS*	J. Corak *YUG*	C. Kwieciński *POL*

Heavyweight

Weight limit 1896 none; 1908 over 93kg (205lb); 1912–28 over 82.5kg (181lb 14oz); 1932–60 over 87kg (191lb 12¾oz); 1964–68 over 97kg (213lb 13¾oz); from 1972 under 100kg (220lb 7¼oz).

	Gold	Silver	Bronze
1896	C. Schuhmann *GER*	G. Tsitas *GRE*	S. Christopoulos *GRE*
1900–1904	*Not held*		
1908	R. Weisz *HUN*	A. Petrov *RUS*	S. M. Jensen *DEN*
1912	Y. Saarela *FIN*	J. Olin *FIN*	S. M. Jensen *DEN*
1920	A. Lindfors *FIN*	P. Hansen *DEN*	M. Nieminen *FIN*
1924	H. Deglane *FRA*	E. Rosenqvist *FIN*	R. Badó *HUN*
1928	J. R. Svensson *SWE*	H. E. Nyström *FIN*	G. Gehring *GER*
1932	C. Westergren *SWE*	J. Urban *TCH*	N. Hirschl *AUT*
1936	K. Palusalu *EST*	J. Nyman *SWE*	K. Hornfischer *GER*
1948	A. Kireçÿi *TUR*	T. Nilsson *SWE*	G. Fantoni *ITA*
1952	Y. Kotkas *URS*	J. Ružička *TCH*	T. Kovanen *FIN*
1956	A. Parfenov *URS*	W. Dietrich *GER*	A. Bulgarelli *ITA*
1960	I. Bogdan *URS*	W. Dietrich *GER*	B. Kubat *TCH*
1964	I. Kozma *HUN*	A. Roshchin *URS*	W. Dietrich *GER*
1968	I. Kozma *HUN*	A. Roshchin *URS*	P. Kment *TCH*
1972	N. Martinescu *ROM*	N. Iakovenko *URS*	F. Kiss *HUN*

Super Heavyweight

Not held before 1972. Weight over 100kg (220lb 7¼oz).

	Gold	Silver	Bronze
1972	A. Roshchin *URS*	A. Tomov *BUL*	V. Dolipschi *ROM*

Yachting

5.5 Metres

Not held before 1952.

	Gold	Silver	Bronze
1952	USA 5,751 pts	NOR 5,325 pts	SWE 4,554 pts
1956	SWE 5,527 pts	GBR 4,050 pts	AUS 4,022 pts
1960	USA 6,900 pts	DEN 5,679 pts	SUI 5,122 pts
1964	AUS 5,981 pts	SWE 5,254 pts	USA 5,106 pts
1968	SWE 8.0 pts	SUI 32.0 pts	GBR 39.8 pts
1972	*Not held*		

Tempest

Not held before 1972.

	Gold	Silver	Bronze
1972	URS 28.1 pts	GBR 34.4 pts	USA 47.7 pts

	Gold	Silver	Bronze

Soling
Not held before 1972.

| 1972 | USA 8.7 pts | SWE 31.7 pts | CAN 47.1 pts |

Flying Dutchman
Not held before 1960.

1960	NOR 6,774 pts	DEN 5,991 pts	GER 5,882 pts
1964	NZL 6,255 pts	GBR 5,556 pts	USA 5,158 pts
1968	GBR 3.0 pts	GER 43.7 pts	BRA 48.4 pts
1972	GBR 22.7 pts	FRA 40.7 pts	GER 51.1 pts

Dragon
Not held before 1948.

1948	NOR 4,746 pts	SWE 4,621 pts	DEN 4,223 pts
1952	NOR 6,130 pts	SWE 5,556 pts	GER 5,352 pts
1956	SWE 5,723 pts	DEN 5,723 pts	GBR 4,547 pts
1960	GRE 6,733 pts	ARG 5,715 pts	ITA 5,704 pts
1964	DEN 5,854 pts	GER 5,826 pts	USA 5,523 pts
1968	USA 6.0 pts	DEN 26.4 pts	GDR 32.7 pts
1972	AUS 13.7 pts	GDR 41.7 pts	USA 47.7 pts

Star
Not held before 1932.

1932	USA 46 pts	GBR 35 pts	SWE 28 pts
1936	GER 80 pts	SWE 64 pts	HOL 63 pts
1948	USA 5,828 pts	CUB 4,949 pts	HOL 4,731 pts
1952	ITA 7,635 pts	USA 7,216 pts	POR 4,903 pts
1956	USA 5,876 pts	ITA 5,649 pts	BAH 5,223 pts
1960	URS 7,619 pts	POR 6,665 pts	USA 6,269 pts
1964	BAH 5,664 pts	USA 5,585 pts	SWE 5,527 pts
1968	USA 14.4 pts	NOR 43.7 pts	ITA 44.7 pts
1972	AUS 28.1 pts	SWE 44.0 pts	GER 44.4 pts

Finn
Not held before 1924. This single-handed class was not for Finn boats until 1952; before then it was for various types.

1924	L. Huybrechts *BEL* 2 pts	H. Robert *NOR* 7 pts	H. Dittmar *FIN* 8 pts
1928	S. Thorell *SWE* nda	H. Robert *NOR* nda	B. Broman *FIN* nda
1932	J. Lebrun *FRA* 87 pts	A. L. J. Maas *HOL* 85 pts	S. A. Cansino *ESP* 76 pts
1936	D. M. J. Kagchelland *HOL* 163 pts	W. Krogmann *GER* 150 pts	P. M. Scott *GBR* 131 pts
1948	P. Elvstrøm *DEN* 5,543 pts	R. Evans *USA* 5,408 pts	J. H. de Jong *HOL* 5,204 pts
1952	P. Elvstrøm *DEN* 8,209 pts	C. Currey *GBR* 5,449 pts	R. Sarby *SWE* 5,051 pts
1956	P. Elvstrøm *DEN* 7,509 pts	A. Nelis *BEL* 6,254 pts	J. Marvin *USA* 5,953 pts
1960	P. Elvstrøm *DEN* 8,171 pts	A. Chuchelov *URS* 6,520 pts	A. Nelis *BEL* 5,934 pts
1964	W. Kuhweide *GER* 7,638 pts	P. Barrett *USA* 6,373 pts	H. Wind *DEN* 6,190 pts
1968	V. Mankin *URS* 11.7 pts	H. Raudaschl *AUT* 53.4 pts	F. Albarelli *ITA* 55.1 pts
1972	S. Maury *FRA* 58.0 pts	I. Hatzipavlis *GRE* 71.0 pts	V. Potapov *URS* 74.7 pts

Biathlon   Luge
Bobsleighing   Figure Skating *Men*
Ice Hockey   Figure Skating *Women*

Gold	Silver	Bronze

The Winter Games

Before the first Winter Games at Chamonix, winter sports were held at the Olympic Games in London (1908) and Antwerp (1920). At each there were official competitions in figure skating (for men, women and pairs). At Antwerp there was also a competition in ice hockey.

Biathlon

20-km (12½-mile) cross-country race with four shooting exercises. Not held before 1960.

Gold	Silver	Bronze
1960 K. Lestander *SWE* 1hr 33min 21.6sec	A. Tyrväinen *FIN* 1hr 33min 57.7sec	A. Privalov *URS* 1hr 34min 54.2sec
1964 V. Melanin *URS* 1hr 20min 26.8sec	A. Privalov *URS* 1hr 23min 32.5sec	O. Jordet *NOR* 1hr 24min 38.8sec
1968 M. Solberg *NOR* 1hr 13min 45.9sec	A. Tikhonov *URS* 1hr 14min 40.4sec	V. Gundartsev *URS* 1hr 18min 27.4sec
1972 M. Solberg *NOR* 1hr 15min 55.50sec	H. Knauthe *GDR* 1hr 16min 07.60sec	L. Arwidson *SWE* 1hr 16min 27.03sec

Biathlon Relay

4 x 7.5km (4⅔ miles) with two shooting exercises. Not held before 1968.

Gold	Silver	Bronze
1968 URS 2hr 13min 02.4sec	NOR 2hr 14min 50.2sec	SWE 2hr 17min 26.3sec
1972 URS 1hr 51min 44.92sec	FIN 1hr 54min 37.25sec	GDR 1hr 54min 57.67sec

Bobsleighing

Two-Man Bob

Not held before 1932.

Gold	Silver	Bronze
1932 USA I 8min 14.74sec	SUI II 8min 16.28sec	USA II 8min 29.15sec
1936 USA I 5min 29.29sec	SUI II 5min 30.64sec	USA II 5min 33.96sec
1948 SUI II 5min 29.20sec	SUI I 5min 30.40sec	USA II 5min 35.30sec
1952 GER I 5min 24.54sec	USA I 5min 26.89sec	SUI I 5min 27.71sec
1956 ITA I 5min 30.14sec	ITA II 5min 31.45sec	SUI I 5min 37.46sec
1960 *Not held*		
1964 GBR I 4min 21.90sec	ITA II 4min 22.02sec	ITA I 4min 22.63sec
1968 ITA I 4min 41.54sec	GER I 4min 41.54sec	ROM I 4min 44.46sec
1972 GER II 4min 57.07sec	GER I 4min 58.84sec	SUI I 4min 59.33sec

Four-Man Bob

Not held before 1924.

Gold	Silver	Bronze
1924 SUI II 5min 45.54sec	GBR II 5min 48.83sec	BEL I 6min 02.29sec
1928 USA II 3min 20.50sec	USA I 3min 21.00sec	GER II 3min 21.90sec
1932 USA I 7min 53.68sec	USA II 7min 55.70sec	GER I 8min 00.04sec
1936 SUI II 5min 19.85sec	SUI I 5min 22.73sec	GBR I 5min 23.41sec
1948 USA II 5min 20.10sec	BEL I 5min 21.30sec	USA I 5min 21.50sec
1952 GER I 5min 07.84sec	USA I 5min 10.48sec	SUI I 5min 11.70sec
1956 SUI I 5min 10.44sec	ITA II 5min 12.10sec	USA I 5min 12.39sec
1960 *Not held*		
1964 CAN I 4min 14.46sec	AUT I 4min 15.48sec	ITA II 4min 15.60sec
1968 ITA I 2min 17.39sec	AUT I 2min 17.48sec	SUI I 2min 18.04sec
1972 SUI I 4min 43.07sec	ITA I 4min 43.83sec	GER I 4min 43.92sec

Ice Hockey

Gold	Silver	Bronze
1920 CAN	USA	TCH
1924 CAN	USA	GBR
1928 CAN	SWE	SUI
1932 CAN	USA	GER
1936 GBR	CAN	USA
1948 CAN	TCH	SUI
1952 CAN	USA	SWE
1956 URS	USA	CAN
1960 USA	CAN	URS
1964 URS	SWE	TCH
1968 URS	TCH	CAN
1972 URS	USA	TCH

Luge

Single-Seater *Men*

Not held before 1964.

Gold	Silver	Bronze
1964 T. Köhler *GER* 3min 26.77sec	K. Bonsack *GER* 3min 27.04sec	H. Plenk *GER* 3min 30.15sec
1968 M. Schmid *AUT* 2min 52.48sec	T. Köhler *GDR* 2min 52.66sec	K. Bonsack *GDR* 2min 53.33sec
1972 W. Scheidel *GDR* 3min 27.58sec	H. Ehrig *GDR* 3min 28.39sec	W. Fiedler *GDR* 3min 28.73sec

Two-seater *Men*

Not held before 1964.

Gold	Silver	Bronze
1964 AUT 1min 41.62sec	AUT 1min 41.91sec	ITA 1min 42.87sec
1968 GDR 1min 35.85sec	AUT 1min 36.34sec	GER 1min 37.29sec
1972 ITA & GDR 1min 28.35sec		GDR 1min 29.16sec

Single-seater *Women*

Not held before 1964.

Gold	Silver	Bronze
1964 O. Enderlein *GER* 3min 24.67sec	I. Geisler *GER* 3min 27.42sec	H. Thurner *AUT* 3min 29.06sec
1968 E. Lechner *ITA* 2min 28.66sec	C. Schmuck *GER* 2min 29.37sec	A. Dünhaupt *GER* 2min 29.56sec
1972 A. M. Müller *GDR* 2min 59.18sec	U. Rührold *GDR* 2min 59.49sec	M. Schumann *GDR* 2min 59.54sec

Figure Skating *Men*

Gold	Silver	Bronze
1908 U. Salchow *SWE* 1,886.5 pts	R. Johansson *SWE* 1,826.0 pts	P. Thorén *SWE* 1,787.0 pts
1920 G. Grafström *SWE* 2,838.50 pts	A. Krogh *NOR* 2,634.00 pts	M. Stixrud *NOR* 2,561.00 pts
1924 G. Grafström *SWE* 2,575.25 pts	W. Böckl *AUT* 2,518.75 pts	G. Gautschi *SUI* 2,223.50 pts
1928 G. Grafström *SWE* 2,698.25 pts	W. Böckl *AUT* 2,682.50 pts	R. van Zeebroeck *BEL* 2,578.75 pts
1932 K. Schäfer *AUT* 2,602.0 pts	G. Grafström *SWE* 2,514.5 pts	M. Wilson *CAN* 2,448.3 pts
1936 K. Schäfer *AUT* 2,959.0 pts	E. Baier *GER* 2,805.3 pts	F. Kaspar *AUT* 2,801.0 pts
1948 R. Button *USA* 1,720.6 pts	H. Gerschwiler *SUI* 1,630.1 pts	E. Rada *AUT* 1,603.2 pts
1952 R. Button *USA* 1,730.3 pts	H. Seibt *AUT* 1,621.3 pts	J. Grogan *USA* 1,627.4 pts
1956 H. A. Jenkins *USA* 1,497.75 pts	R. Robertson *USA* 1,492.15 pts	D. Jenkins *USA* 1,465.41 pts
1960 D. Jenkins *USA* 1,440.2 pts	K. Divin *TCH* 1,414.3 pts	D. Jackson *CAN* 1,401.0 pts
1964 M. Schnelldörfer *GER* 1,916.9 pts	A. Calmat *FRA* 1,876.5 pts	S. Allen *USA* 1,873.6 pts
1968 W. Schwartz *AUT* 1,904.1 pts	T. Wood *USA* 1,891.6 pts	P. Pera *FRA* 1,864.5 pts
1972 O. Nepela *TCH* 2,739.1 pts	S. Chetverukhin *URS* 2,672.4 pts	P. Pera *FRA* 2,653.1 pts

Figure Skating *Women*

Gold	Silver	Bronze
1908 M. Syers (-Cave) *GBR* 1,262.5 pts	E. Rendschmidt *GER* 1,055.0 pts	D. Greenhough Smith *GBR* 960.5 pts
1920 M. Julin-Mauroy *SWE* 913.50 pts	S. Norén *SWE* 887.75 pts	T. Weld *USA* 898.00 pts
1924 H. Plank-Szabo *AUT* 2,094.25 pts	B. S. Loughran *USA* 1,959.0 pts	E. Muckelt *GBR* 1,750.50 pts
1928 S. Henie *NOR* 2,452.25 pts	F. Burger *AUT* 2,248.50 pts	B. Loughran *USA* 2,254.50 pts
1932 S. Henie *NOR* 2,302.5 pts	F. Burger *AUT* 2,167.1 pts	M. Vinson *USA* 2,158.5 pts
1936 S. Henie *NOR* 2,971.4 pts	C. Colledge *GBR* 2,926.8 pts	V. A. Hultén *SWE* 2,763.2 pts
1948 B. A. Scott *CAN* 1,467.7 pts	E. Pawlik *AUT* 1,418.3 pts	J. Altwegg *GBR* 1,405.5 pts
1952 J. Altwegg *GBR* 1,455.8 pts	T. Albright *USA* 1,432.2 pts	J. du Bief *FRA* 1,422.0 pts
1956 T. Albright *USA* 1,866.39 pts	C. Heiss *USA* 1,848.24 pts	I. Wendl *AUT* 1,753.91 pts
1960 C. Heiss *USA* 1,490.1 pts	S. Dijkstra *HOL* 1,424.8 pts	B. Roles *USA* 1,414.9 pts
1964 S. Dijkstra *HOL* 2,018.5 pts	R. Heitzer *AUT* 1,945.5 pts	P. Burka *CAN* 1,940.0 pts
1968 P. Fleming *USA* 1,970.5 pts	G. Seyfert *GDR* 1,882.3 pts	H. Masková *TCH* 1,828.8 pts
1972 B. Schuba *AUT* 2,751.5 pts	K. Magnussen *CAN* 2,673.2 pts	J. Lynn *USA* 2,663.1 pts

Figure Skating *Pairs*

Gold	Silver	Bronze
1908 A. Hübler & H. Burger *GER* 56.0 pts	P. W. Johnson & J. H. Johnson *GBR* 51.5 pts	M. Syers (-Cave) & E. Syers *GBR* 48.0 pts
1920 L. Jakobsson (-Eilers) & W. Jakobsson *FIN* 80.75 pts	A. Bryn (-Schøyen) & Y. Bryn *NOR* 72.75 pts	P. W. Johnson & B. Williams *GBR* 66.25 pts
1924 H. Engelmann & A. Berger *AUT* 74.50 pts	L. Jakobsson (-Eilers) & W. Jakobsson *FIN* 71.75 pts	A. Joly & P. Brunet *FRA* 69.25 pts
1928 A. Joly & P. Brunet *FRA* 100.50 pts	L. Scholz & O. Kaiser *AUT* 99.25 pts	M. Brunner & L. Wrede *AUT* 93.25 pts

	Gold	Silver	Bronze
1932	A. Brunet & P. Brunet FRA 76.7 pts	B. Loughran & S. Badger USA 77.5 pts	E. Rotter & L. Szollás HUN 76.4 pts
1936	M. Herber & E. Baier GER 103.3 pts	I. Pausin & E. Pausin AUT 102.7 pts	E. Rotter & L. Szollás HUN 97.6 pts
1948	M. Lannoy & P. Baugniet BEL 123.5 pts	A. Kékessy & E. Király HUN 122.2 pts	S. Morrow & W. Diestelmeyer CAN 121.0 pts
1952	R. Falk & P. Falk GER 102.6 pts	K. E. Kennedy & M. Kennedy USA 100.6 pts	M. Nagy & L. Nagy HUN 97.4 pts
1956	E. Schwartz & K. Oppelt AUT 101.8 pts	F. Dafoe & N. Bowden CAN 101.9 pts	M. Nagy & L. Nagy HUN 99.3 pts
1960	B. Wagner & R. Paul CAN 80.4 pts	M. Kilius & H. J. Bäumler GER 76.8 pts	N. Ludington & R. Ludington USA 76.2 pts
1964	L. Belousova & O. Protopopov URS 104.4 pts	M. Kilius & H. J. Bäumler GER 103.6 pts	D. Wilkes & G. Revell CAN 98.5 pts
1968	L. Belousova & O. Protopopov URS 315.2 pts	T. Yukchesternava & A. Gorelik URS 312.3 pts	M. Glockshuber & W. Danne GER 304.4 pts
1972	I. Rodnina & A. Ulanov URS 420.4 pts	L. Smirnova & A. Suraikin URS 419.4 pts	M. Gross & U. Kagelmann GDR 411.8 pts

Speed Skating *Men*

500 Metres
Not held before 1924.

	Gold	Silver	Bronze
1924	C. Jewtraw USA 44.0sec	O. Olsen NOR 44.2sec	R. M. Larsen NOR & C. Thunberg FIN 44.8sec
1928	C. Thunberg FIN & B. Evensen NOR 43.4sec		J. O. Farrell USA, R. M. Larsen NOR & J. Friman FIN 43.6sec
1932	J. A. Shea USA 43.4sec	B. Evensen NOR nda	A. Hurd CAN nda
1936	I. Ballangrud NOR 43.4sec	G. Krog NOR 43.5sec	L. Freisinger USA 44.0sec
1948	F. Helgesen NOR 43.1sec	K. Bartholomew USA, T. Byberg NOR & R. Fitzgerald USA 43.2sec	
1952	K. Henry USA 43.2sec	D. McDermott USA 43.9sec	A. Johansen NOR & G. Audley CAN 44.0sec
1956	Y. Grishin URS 40.2sec	R. Grach URS 40.8sec	A. Gjestvang NOR 41.0sec
1960	Y. Grishin URS 40.2sec	W. Disney USA 40.3sec	R. Grach URS 40.4sec
1964	R. McDermott USA 40.1sec	Y. Grishin URS, V. Orlov URS & A. Gjestvang NOR 40.6sec	
1968	E. Keller GER 40.3sec	M. Thomassen NOR & R. McDermott USA 40.5sec	
1972	E. Keller GER 39.44sec	H. Börjes SWE 39.69sec	V. Muratov URS 39.80sec

1,500 Metres
Not held before 1924.

	Gold	Silver	Bronze
1924	C. Thunberg FIN 2min 20.8sec	R. M. Larsen NOR 2min 22.0sec	S. O. Moen NOR 2min 25.6sec
1928	C. Thunberg FIN 2min 21.1sec	B. Evensen NOR 2min 21.9sec	I. Ballangrud NOR 2min 22.6sec
1932	J. A. Shea USA 2min 57.5sec	A. Hurd CAN nda	W. F. Logan CAN nda
1936	C. Mathiesen NOR 2min 19.2sec	I. Ballangrud NOR 2min 20.2sec	B. Wasenius FIN 2min 20.9sec
1948	S. Farstad NOR 2min 17.6sec	Å. Seyffarth SWE 2min 18.1sec	O. Lundberg NOR 2min 18.9sec
1952	H. Andersen NOR 2min 20.4sec	W. van der Voort HOL 2min 20.6sec	R. Aas NOR 2min 21.6sec
1956	Y. Grishin URS & Y. Mikhailov URS 2min 08.6sec		T. Salonen FIN 2min 09.4sec
1960	R. Aas NOR & Y. Grishin URS 2min 10.4sec		B. Stenin URS 2min 11.5sec
1964	A. Antson URS 2min 10.3sec	C. Verkerk HOL 2min 10.6sec	V. Haugen NOR 2min 11.2sec
1968	C. Verkerk HOL 2min 03.4sec	A. Schenk HOL & I. Eriksen NOR 2min 05.0sec	
1972	A. Schenk HOL 2min 02.96sec	R. Grønvold NOR 2min 04.26sec	G. Claesson SWE 2min 05.89sec

5,000 Metres
Not held before 1924.

	Gold	Silver	Bronze
1924	C. Thunberg FIN 8min 39.0sec	J. Skutnabb FIN 8min 48.4sec	R. M. Larsen NOR 8min 50.2sec
1928	I. Ballangrud NOR 8min 50.5sec	J. Skutnabb FIN 8min 59.1sec	B. Evensen NOR 9min 01.1sec
1932	I. Jaffee USA 9min 40.8sec	E. S. Murphy USA nda	W. F. Logan CAN nda
1936	I. Ballangrud NOR 8min 19.6sec	B. Vasenius FIN 8min 23.3sec	A. Ojala FIN 8min 30.1sec
1948	R. Liaklev NOR 8min 29.4sec	O. Lundberg NOR 8min 32.7sec	G. Hedlund SWE 8min 34.8sec
1952	H. Andersen NOR 8min 10.6sec	C. Broekman HOL 8min 21.6sec	S. Haugli NOR 8min 22.4sec
1956	B. Shilkov URS 7min 48.7sec	S. Ericsson SWE 7min 56.7sec	O. Goncharenko URS 7min 57.5sec
1960	V. Kosychkin URS 7min 51.3sec	K. Johannesen NOR 8min 00.8sec	J. Pesman HOL 8min 05.1sec
1964	K. Johannesen NOR 7min 38.4sec	P. I. Moe NOR 7min 38.6sec	F. A. Maier NOR 7min 42.00sec
1968	F. A. Maier NOR 7min 22.4sec	C. Verkerk HOL 7min 23.2sec	P. Nottet HOL 7min 25.5sec
1972	A. Schenk HOL 7min 23.61sec	R. Grønvold NOR 7min 28.18sec	S. Stensen NOR 7min 33.39sec

10,000 Metres
Not held before 1924.

	Gold	Silver	Bronze
1924	J. Skutnabb FIN 18min 04.8sec	C. Thunberg FIN 18min 07.8sec	R. M. Larsen NOR 18min 12.2sec
1928	*Event officially annulled because of the condition of the ice.*		
1932	I. Jaffee USA 19min 13.6sec	I. Ballangrud NOR nda	F. Stack CAN nda
1936	I. Ballangrud NOR 17min 24.3sec	B. Vasenius FIN 17min 28.2sec	M. Stiepl AUT 17min 30.0sec
1948	Å. Seyffarth SWE 17min 26.3sec	L. Parkkinen FIN 17min 36.0sec	P. Lammio FIN 17min 42.7sec
1952	H. Andersen NOR 16min 45.8sec	C. Broekman HOL 17min 10.6sec	C. E. Asplund SWE 17min 16.6sec
1956	S. Ericsson SWE 16min 35.9sec	K. Johannesen NOR 16min 36.9sec	O. Goncharenko URS 16min 42.3sec
1960	K. Johannesen NOR 15min 46.6sec	V. Kosychkin URS 15min 49.2sec	K. Bäckman SWE 16min 14.2sec
1964	J. Nilsson SWE 15min 50.1sec	F. A. Maier NOR 16min 06.0sec	K. Johannesen NOR 16min 06.3sec
1968	J. Höglin SWE 15min 23.6sec	F. A. Maier NOR 15min 23.9sec	Ö. Sandler SWE 15min 31.8sec
1972	A. Schenk HOL 15min 01.35sec	C. Verkerk HOL 15min 04.70sec	S. Stensen NOR 15min 07.08sec

Speed Skating *Women*

500 Metres
Not held before 1960 although there were three demonstration events for women speed skaters in 1932.

	Gold	Silver	Bronze
1960	H. Haase GER 45.9sec	N. Donchenko URS 46.0sec	J. Ashworth USA 46.1sec
1964	L. Skoblikova URS 45.0sec	I. Yegorova URS 45.4sec	T. Sidorova URS 45.5sec
1968	L. Titova URS 46.1sec	M. Meyers USA, D. Holum USA & J. Fish USA 46.3sec	
1972	A. Henning USA 43.33sec	V. Krasnova URS 44.01sec	L. Titova URS 44.45sec

1,000 Metres
Not held before 1960.

	Gold	Silver	Bronze
1960	K. Guseva URS 1min 34.1sec	H. Haase GER 1min 34.3sec	T. Rylova URS 1min 34.8sec
1964	L. Skoblikova URS 1min 33.2sec	I. Yegorova URS 1min 34.3sec	K. Mustonen FIN 1min 34.8sec
1968	C. Geijssen HOL 1min 32.6sec	L. Titova URS 1min 32.9sec	D. Holum USA 1min 33.4sec
1972	M. Pflug GER 1min 31.40sec	A. Keulen-Deelstra HOL 1min 31.61sec	A. Henning USA 1min 31.62sec

1,500 Metres
Not held before 1960.

	Gold	Silver	Bronze
1960	L. Skoblikova URS 2min 25.2sec	E. Seroczynska POL 2min 25.7sec	H. Pilejczyk POL 2min 27.1sec
1964	L. Skoblikova URS 2min 22.6sec	K. Mustonen FIN 2min 25.5sec	B. Kolokoltseva URS 2min 27.1sec
1968	K. Mustonen FIN 2min 22.4sec	C. Geijssen HOL 2min 22.7sec	C. Kaiser HOL 2min 24.5sec
1972	D. Holum USA 2min 20.85sec	C. Baas-Kaiser HOL 2min 21.05sec	A. Keulen-Deelstra HOL 2min 22.05sec

Gold	Silver	Bronze

3,000 Metres
Not held before 1960.

	Gold	Silver	Bronze
1960	L. Skoblikova URS 5min 14.3sec	V. Stenina URS 5min 16.9sec	E. Huttunen FIN 5min 21.0sec
1964	L. Skoblikova URS 5min 14.9sec	V. Stenina URS & P. H. Han PRK 5min 18.5sec	
1968	J. Schut HOL 4min 56.2sec	K. Mustonen FIN 5min 01.0sec	C. Kaiser HOL 5min 01.3sec
1972	C. Baas-Kaiser HOL 4min 52.14sec	D. Holum USA 4min 58.67sec	A. Keulen-Deelstra HOL 4min 59.91sec

Alpine Skiing *Men*
Downhill
Not held as a separate competition before 1948.

	Gold	Silver	Bronze
1948	H. Oreiller FRA 2min 55.0sec	F. Gabl AUT 2min 59.1sec	K. Molitor & R. Olinger SUI 3min 00.3sec
1952	Z. Colò ITA 2min 30.8sec	O. Schneider AUT 2min 32.0sec	C. Pravda AUT 2min 32.4sec
1956	A. Sailer AUT 2min 52.2sec	R. Fellay SUI 2min 55.7sec	A. Molterer AUT 2min 56.2sec
1960	J. Vuarnet FRA 2min 06.0sec	H. P. Lanig GER 2min 06.5sec	G. Perillat FRA 2min 06.9sec
1964	E. Zimmermann AUT 2min 18.16sec	L. Lacroix FRA 2min 18.90sec	W. Bartels GER 2min 19.48sec
1968	J. C. Killy FRA 1min 59.85sec	G. Perillat FRA 1min 59.93sec	J. D. Dätwyler SUI 2min 00.32sec
1972	B. Russi SUI 1min 51.43sec	R. Collombin SUI 1min 52.07sec	H. Messner AUT 1min 52.40sec

Giant Slalom
Not held before 1952.

	Gold	Silver	Bronze
1952	S. Eriksen NOR 2min 25.0sec	C. Pravda AUT 2min 26.9sec	T. Spiss AUT 2min 28.8sec
1956	A. Sailer AUT 3min 00.1sec	A. Molterer AUT 3min 06.3sec	W. Schuster AUT 3min 07.2sec
1960	R. Staub SUI 1min 48.3sec	J. Stiegler AUT 1min 48.7sec	E. Hinterseer AUT 1min 49.1sec
1964	F. Bonlieu FRA 1min 46.71sec	K. Schranz AUT 1min 47.09sec	J. Stiegler AUT 1min 48.05sec
1968	J. C. Killy FRA 3min 29.28sec	W. Favre SUI 3min 31.50sec	H. Messner AUT 3min 31.83sec
1972	G. Thoeni ITA 3min 09.62sec	E. Bruggmann SUI 3min 10.75sec	W. Mattle SUI 3min 10.99sec

Slalom
Not held before 1948.

	Gold	Silver	Bronze
1948	E. Reinalter SUI 2min 10.3sec	J. Couttet FRA 2min 10.8sec	H. Oreiller FRA 2min 12.8sec
1952	O. Schneider AUT 2min 00.00sec	S. Eriksen NOR 2min 01.2sec	G. Berge NOR 2min 01.7sec
1956	A. Sailer AUT 3min 14.7sec	C. Igaya JPN 3min 18.7sec	S. Sollander SWE 3min 20.2sec
1960	E. Hinterseer AUT 2min 08.9sec	M. Leitner AUT 2min 10.3sec	C. Bozon FRA 2min 10.4sec
1964	J. Stiegler AUT 2min 11.13sec	W. W. Kidd USA 2min 11.27sec	J. F. Heuga USA 2min 11.52sec
1968	J. C. Killy FRA 1min 39.73sec	H. Huber AUT 1min 39.82sec	A. Matt AUT 1min 40.09sec
1972	F. F. Ochoa ESP 1min 49.27sec	G. Thoeni ITA 1min 50.28sec	R. Thoeni ITA 1min 50.30sec

Alpine Skiing *Women*
Downhill
Not held before 1948.

	Gold	Silver	Bronze
1948	H. Schlunegger SUI 2min 28.3sec	T. Beiser AUT 2min 29.1sec	R. Hammerer AUT 2min 30.2sec
1952	T. Jochum-Beiser AUT 1min 47.1sec	A. Buchner GER 1min 48.0sec	G. Minuzzo ITA 1min 49.0sec
1956	M. Berthod SUI 1min 40.7sec	F. Dänzer SUI 1min 45.4sec	L. Wheeler CAN 1min 45.9sec
1960	H. Beibl GER 1min 37.6sec	P. Pitou USA 1min 38.6sec	G. Hecher AUT 1min 38.9sec
1964	C. Haas AUT 1min 55.39sec	E. Zimmermann AUT 1min 56.42sec	G. Hecher AUT 1min 56.66sec
1968	O. Pall AUT 1min 40.87sec	I. Mir FRA 1min 41.33sec	C. Haas AUT 1min 41.41sec
1972	M. T. Nadig SUI 1min 36.68sec	A. M. Pröll AUT 1min 37.00sec	S. Corrock USA 1min 37.68sec

Giant Slalom
Not held before 1952.

	Gold	Silver	Bronze
1952	A. (Mead) Lawrence USA 2min 06.8sec	D. Rom AUT 2min 09.0sec	A. Buchner GER 2min 10.0sec

	Gold	Silver	Bronze
1956	O. Reichert GER 1min 56.5sec	J. Frandl AUT 1min 57.8sec	D. Hochleitner AUT 1min 58.2sec
1960	Y. Rügg SUI 1min 39.9sec	P. Pitou USA 1min 40.0sec	G. (Minuzzo) Chenal ITA 1min 40.2sec
1964	M. Goitschel FRA 1min 52.24sec	C. Goitschel FRA & J. Saubert USA 1min 53.11sec	
1968	N. Greene CAN 1min 51.97sec	A. Famose FRA 1min 54.61sec	F. Bochatay SUI 1min 54.74sec
1972	M. T. Nadig SUI 1min 29.90sec	A. M. Pröll AUT 1min 30.75sec	W. Drexel AUT 1min 32.35sec

Slalom
Not held before 1948.

	Gold	Silver	Bronze
1948	G. Fraser USA 1min 57.2sec	A. Meyer SUI 1min 57.7sec	E. Mahringer AUT 1min 58.0sec
1952	A. (Mead) Lawrence USA 2min 10.6sec	O. Reichert GER 2min 11.4sec	A. Buchner GER 2min 13.3sec
1956	R. Colliard SUI 1min 52.3sec	R. Schöpf AUT 1min 55.4sec	Y. Sidorova URS 1min 56.7sec
1960	A. Heggtveit CAN 1min 49.6sec	B. Snite USA 1min 52.9sec	B. Henneberger GER 1min 56.6sec
1964	C. Goitschel FRA 1min 29.86sec	M. Goitschel FRA 1min 30.77sec	J. Saubert USA 1min 31.36sec
1968	M. Goitschel FRA 1min 25.86sec	N. Greene CAN 1min 26.15sec	A. Famose FRA 1min 27.89sec
1972	B. Cochran USA 1min 31.24sec	D. Debernard FRA 1min 31.26sec	F. Steurer FRA 1min 32.69sec

Nordic Skiing *Men*
15 Kilometres Cross-Country
Not held before 1924. From 1924 to 1952 it was decided over 18km (11.18 miles).

	Gold	Silver	Bronze
1924	T. Haug NOR 1hr 14min 31.0sec	J. Grøttumsbraaten NOR 1hr 15min 51.0sec	T. Niku FIN 1hr 26min 26.0sec
1928	J. Grøttumsbraaten NOR 1hr 37min 01.0sec	O. Hegge NOR 1hr 39min 01.0sec	R. Ødegaard NOR 1hr 40min 11.0sec
1932	S. Utterström SWE 1hr 23min 07.0sec	A. T. Wikström SWE 1hr 25min 07.0sec	V. Saarinen FIN 1hr 25min 24.0sec
1936	E. A. Larsson SWE 1hr 14min 38.0sec	O. Hagen NOR 1hr 15min 33.0sec	P. Niemi FIN 1hr 16min 59.0sec
1948	M. Lundström SWE 1hr 13min 50.0sec	N. Östensson SWE 1hr 14min 22.0sec	G. Eriksson SWE 1hr 16min 06.0sec
1952	H. Brenden NOR 1hr 1min 34.0sec	T. Mäkelä FIN 1hr 2min 09.0sec	P. Lonkila FIN 1hr 2min 20.0sec
1956	H. Brenden NOR 49min 39.0sec	S. Jernberg SWE 50min 14.0sec	P. Kolchin URS 50min 17.0sec
1960	H. Brusveen NOR 51min 55.5sec	S. Jernberg SWE 51min 58.6sec	V. Hakulinen FIN 52min 03.0sec
1964	E. Mäntyranta FIN 50min 54.1sec	H. Grønningen NOR 51min 34.8sec	S. Jernberg SWE 51min 42.2sec
1968	H. Grønningen NOR 47min 54.2sec	E. Mäntyranta FIN 47min 56.1sec	G. Larsson SWE 48min 33.7sec
1972	S. Å. Lundbäck SWE 45min 28.24sec	F. Simashov URS 46min 00.84sec	I. Førmø NOR 46min 02.68sec

30 Kilometres Cross-Country
Not held before 1956.

	Gold	Silver	Bronze
1956	V. Hakulinen FIN 1hr 44min 06.0sec	S. Jernberg SWE 1hr 44min 30.0sec	P. Kolchin URS 1hr 45min 45.0sec
1960	S. Jernberg SWE 1hr 51min 03.9sec	R. Rämgård SWE 1hr 51min 16.9sec	N. Anikin URS 1hr 52min 28.2sec
1964	E. Mäntyranta FIN 1hr 30min 50.7sec	H. Grønningen NOR 1hr 32min 02.3sec	I. Voronchikhin URS 1hr 32min 15.8sec
1968	F. Nones ITA 1hr 35min 39.2sec	O. Martinsen NOR 1hr 36min 28.9sec	E. Mäntyranta FIN 1hr 36min 55.3sec
1972	V. Vedenin URS 1hr 36min 31.15sec	P. Tyldum NOR 1hr 37min 25.30sec	J. Harviken NOR 1hr 37min 32.44sec

50 Kilometres Cross-Country
Not held before 1924.

	Gold	Silver	Bronze
1924	T. Haug NOR 3hr 44min 32.0sec	T. Strømstad NOR 3hr 46min 23.0sec	J. Grøttumsbraaten NOR 3hr 47min 46.0sec
1928	P. E. Hedlund SWE 4hr 52min 03.0sec	G. Jonsson SWE 5hr 05min 30.0sec	V. Andersson SWE 5hr 05min 46.0sec
1932	V. Saarinen FIN 4hr 28min 00.0sec	V. Liikkanen FIN 4hr 28min 20.0sec	A. Rustadstuen NOR 4hr 31min 53.0sec
1936	E. Wiklund SWE 3hr 30min 11.0sec	A. Wikström SWE 3hr 33min 20.0sec	N. J. Englund SWE 3hr 34min 10.0sec
1948	N. Karlsson SWE 3hr 47min 48.0sec	H. Eriksson SWE 3hr 52min 20.0sec	B. Vanninen FIN 3hr 57min 28.0sec
1952	V. Hakulinen FIN 3hr 33min 33.0sec	E. Kolehmainen FIN 3hr 38min 11.0sec	M. Estenstad NOR 3hr 38min 28.0sec
1956	S. Jernberg SWE 2hr 50min 27.0sec	V. Hakulinen FIN 2hr 51min 45.0sec	F. Terentyev URS 2hr 53min 32.0sec

	Gold	Silver	Bronze
1960	K. Hämäläinen *FIN* 2hr 59min 06.3sec	V. Hakulinen *FIN* 2hr 59min 26.7sec	R. Rämgård *SWE* 3hr 02min 46.7sec
1964	S. Jernberg *SWE* 2hr 43min 52.6sec	A. Rönnlund *SWE* 2hr 44min 58.2sec	A. Tiainen *FIN* 2hr 45min 30.4sec
1968	O. Ellefsæter *NOR* 2hr 28min 45.8sec	V. Vedenin *URS* 2hr 29min 02.5sec	J. Haas *SUI* 2hr 29min 14.8sec
1972	P. Tyldum *NOR* 2hr 43min 14.75sec	M. Myrmo *NOR* 2hr 43min 29.45sec	V. Vedenin *URS* 2hr 44min 00.19sec

4 × 10 Kilometres Relay

Not held before 1936.

	Gold	Silver	Bronze
1936	FIN 2hr 41min 33.0sec	NOR 2hr 41min 39.0sec	SWE 2hr 43min 03.0sec
1948	SWE 2hr 32min 08.0sec	FIN 2hr 41min 06.0sec	NOR 2hr 44min 33.0sec
1952	FIN 2hr 20min 16.0sec	NOR 2hr 23min 13.0sec	SWE 2hr 24min 13.0sec
1956	URS 2hr 15min 30.0sec	FIN 2hr 16min 31.0sec	SWE 2hr 17min 42.0sec
1960	FIN 2hr 18min 45.6sec	NOR 2hr 18min 46.4sec	URS 2hr 21min 21.6sec
1964	SWE 2hr 18min 34.6sec	FIN 2hr 18min 42.4sec	URS 2hr 18min 46.9sec
1968	NOR 2hr 08min 33.5sec	SWE 2hr 10min 13.2sec	FIN 2hr 10min 56.7sec
1972	URS 2hr 04min 47.94sec	NOR 2hr 04min 57.06sec	SUI 2hr 07min 00.06sec

Ski Jumping

70 Metres Jump

Not held before 1924. 1924–60 held on one hill.

	Gold	Silver	Bronze
1924	J. T. Thams *NOR* 18.960 pts	N. Bonna *NOR* 18.689 pts	T. Haug *NOR* 18.000 pts
1928	A. Andersen *NOR* 19.208 pts	S. Ruud *NOR* 18.542 pts	R. Burkert *TCH* 17.937 pts
1932	B. Ruud *NOR* 228.1 pts	H. Beck *NOR* 227.0 pts	K. Wahlberg *NOR* 219.5 pts
1936	B. Ruud *NOR* 232.0 pts	S. Eriksson *SWE* 230.5 pts	R. Andersen *NOR* 228.9 pts
1948	P. Hugsted *NOR* 228.1 pts	B. Ruud *NOR* 226.6 pts	T. Schjelderup *NOR* 225.1 pts
1952	A. Bergmann *NOR* 226.0 pts	T. Falkanger *NOR* 221.5 pts	K. Holmström *SWE* 219.5 pts
1956	A. Hyvärinen *FIN* 227.0 pts	A. Kallakorpi *FIN* 225.0 pts	H. Glass *GER* 224.5 pts
1960	H. Recknagel *GER* 227.2 pts	N. Halonen *FIN* 222.6 pts	O. Leodolter *AUT* 219.4 pts
1964	V. Kankkonen *FIN* 229.9 pts	T. Engan *NOR* 226.3 pts	T. Brandtzäg *NOR* 222.9 pts
1968	J. Raska *TCH* 216.5 pts	B. Bachler *AUT* 214.2 pts	B. Preiml *AUT* 212.6 pts
1972	Y. Kasaya *JPN* 244.2 pts	A. Konno *JPN* 234.8 pts	S. Aochi *JPN* 229.5 pts

90 Metres Jump

In 1964 the hill was 80m (87yd 1ft).

	Gold	Silver	Bronze
1964	T. Engan *NOR* 230.7 pts	V. Kankkonen *FIN* 228.9 pts	T. Brandtzäg *NOR* 227.2 pts
1968	V. Beloussov *URS* 231.3 pts	J. Raska *TCH* 229.4 pts	L. Grini *NOR* 214.3 pts
1972	W. Fortuna *POL* 219.9 pts	W. Steiner *SUI* 219.8 pts	R. Schmidt *GDR* 219.3 pts

Nordic Combined

15-km (9.3 miles) cross-country and jumping. Not held before 1924. After 1928 the scoring system was altered.

	Gold	Silver	Bronze
1924	T. Haug *NOR* 18,906 pts	T. Strømstad *NOR* 18,219 pts	J. Grøttumsbraaten *NOR* 17,854 pts
1928	J. Grøttumsbraaten *NOR* 17,833 pts	H. Vinjarengen *NOR* 15,303 pts	J. Snersrud *NOR* 15,021 pts
1932	J. Grøttumsbraaten *NOR* 446.00 pts	O. Stenen *NOR* 436.05 pts	H. Vinjarengen *NOR* 434.60 pts
1936	O. Hagen *NOR* 430.30 pts	O. Hoffsbakken *NOR* 419.80 pts	S. Brodahl *NOR* 408.10 pts
1948	H. Hasu *FIN* 448.80 pts	M. Huhtala *FIN* 433.65 pts	S. Israelsson *SWE* 433.40 pts
1952	S. Slåttvik *NOR* 451.621 pts	H. Hasu *FIN* 447.500 pts	S. Stenersen *NOR* 436.335 pts
1956	S. Stenersen *NOR* 455.000 pts	B. Eriksson *SWE* 437.400 pts	F. Gron-Gąsienica *POL* 436.800 pts
1960	G. Thoma *GER* 457.952 pts	T. Knutsen *NOR* 453.000 pts	N. Gusakov *URS* 452.000 pts
1964	T. Knutsen *NOR* 469.28 pts	N. Kiselev *URS* 453.04 pts	G. Thoma *GER* 452.88 pts
1968	F. Keller *GER* 449.04 pts	A. Kälin *SUI* 447.94 pts	A. Kunz *GDR* 444.10 pts

	Gold	Silver	Bronze
1972	U. Wehling *GDR* 413.340 pts	R. Miettinen *FIN* 405.505 pts	K. H. Luck *GDR* 398.800 pts

Nordic Skiing *Women*

5 Kilometres Cross-Country

Not held before 1964.

	Gold	Silver	Bronze
1964	K. Boyarskikh *URS* 17min 50.5sec	M. Lehtonen *FIN* 17min 52.9sec	A. Kolchina *URS* 18min 08.4sec
1968	T. Gustafsson *SWE* 16min 45.2sec	G. Kulakova *URS* 16min 48.4sec	A. Kolchina *URS* 16min 51.6sec
1972	G. Kulakova *URS* 17min 00.50sec	M. Kajosmaa *FIN* 17min 05.50sec	H. Sikolová *TCH* 17min 07.32sec

10 Kilometres Cross-Country

Not held before 1952.

	Gold	Silver	Bronze
1952	L. Wideman *FIN* 41min 40.0sec	M. Hietamies *FIN* 42min 39.0sec	S. Rantanen *FIN* 42min 50.0sec
1956	L. Kosyreva *URS* 38min 11.0sec	R. Yeroshina *URS* 38min 16.0sec	S. Edström *SWE* 38min 23.0sec
1960	M. Gusakova *URS* 39min 46.6sec	L. (Kosyreva) Baranova *URS* 40min 04.2sec	R. Yeroshina *URS* 40min 06.0sec
1964	K. Boyarskikh *URS* 40min 24.3sec	E. Mekshilo *URS* 40min 26.6sec	M. Gusakova *URS* 40min 46.6sec
1968	T. Gustafsson *SWE* 36min 46.5sec	B. Mørdre *NOR* 37min 54.6sec	I. Aufles *NOR* 37min 59.9sec
1972	G. Kulakova *URS* 34min 17.82sec	A. Olunina *URS* 34min 54.11sec	M. Kajosmaa *FIN* 34min 56.45sec

3 × 5 Kilometres Relay

Not held before 1956.

	Gold	Silver	Bronze
1956	FIN 1hr 9min 01.0sec	URS 1hr 9min 28.0sec	SWE 1hr 9min 48.0sec
1960	SWE 1hr 4min 21.4sec	URS 1hr 5min 02.6sec	FIN 1hr 6min 27.5sec
1964	URS 59min 20.2sec	SWE 1hr 1min 27.0sec	FIN 1hr 2min 45.1sec
1968	NOR 57min 30.0sec	SWE 57min 51.0sec	URS 58min 13.6sec
1972	URS 48min 46.15sec	FIN 49min 19.37sec	NOR 49min 51.49sec

257

Rules of the International Olympic Committee

The rules of the IOC give yet another insight to the Movement. Below we publish, with the permission of the IOC, an extract, giving those which are informative and omitting those relating to internal procedure and instructions to cities applying for the Games.

Olympic Rules and Regulations
Citius Altius Fortius
1975 (Approved in Vienna 1974)
Comité International Olympique, Château de Vidy, 1007 Lausanne

A – RULES

I – Fundamental Principles

1 The aims of the Olympic Movement are to promote the development of those fine physical and moral qualities which are the basis of amateur sport and to bring together the athletes of the world in a great quadrennial festival of sports thereby creating international respect and goodwill and thus helping to construct a better and more peaceful world.

2 The Olympic Games celebrate an Olympiad or period of four successive years. The first Olympiad of modern times was celebrated in Athens in 1896, and subsequent Olympiads and Games are numbered consecutively from that year, even though it has been impossible to hold the Games in any Olympiad.

3 The Olympic Games take place every four years. They unite Olympic competitors of all nations in fair and equal competition. The IOC shall secure the widest possible audience for these Games. No discrimination in them is allowed against any country or person on grounds of race, religion or politics.

4 The International Olympic Committee directs the Olympic Movement and retains all rights to the Olympic Games and to the Olympic Winter Games. Its constitution and powers are stated in the present Rules and Regulations.

The honour of holding the Olympic Games is entrusted to a city and not to a country or area. The choice of a city for the celebration of an Olympiad lies solely with the International Olympic Committee.

Application to hold the Games is made by the official authority of the city concerned with the approval of the National Olympic Committee which must guarantee that the Games will be organized to the satisfaction of and in accordance with the requirements of the International Olympic Committee and which must be responsible for all commitments undertaken by the elected city.

5 A separate cycle of Olympic Winter Games is held, comprising competitions in winter sports. The Olympic Winter Games are held in the same calendar year as the Olympic Games.

The first Olympic Winter Games were held in 1924 during the VIIIth Olympiad. They are numbered in rotation as they are held.

The term Olympiad is not used in connection with the Winter Games.

6 . . . *Legal protection*
The IOC takes the proper steps to ensure the international protection of the Olympic symbol and emblems. It also supports the efforts undertaken by the NOCs to ensure this protection within the framework of their national jurisdiction, and endeavours to obtain international protection of the Olympic symbol.
. . .

8 Only citizens of a country or area in which a National Olympic Committee recognized by the IOC operates, are qualified to compete in the Olympic Games under the colours of that country or area.

Recognition of a National Olympic Committee in such a country or area:
A. does not imply political recognition;
B. is dependent on the country or area having had a stable

government for a reasonable period.

9 The Games are contests between individuals and not between countries or areas.

10 The Olympic Games and the Winter Games are the exclusive property of the International Olympic Committee, which owns all rights over their organization and exploitation and over their reproduction by any means whatsoever. The IOC may grant concessions or licences in respect of these rights. Any surplus derived from the holding of the Olympic Games must be applied to the promotion of the Olympic Movement or to the development of amateur sport.

II – The International Olympic Committee

Juridical status, objects and powers
11 The International Olympic Committee was created by the Congress of Paris on June 23rd 1894; it was entrusted with the control and development of the modern Olympic Games.

It is a body corporate by international law having juridical status. Its duration is unlimited. Its headquarters are in Switzerland. It is formed not for profit and has as its aim:
A. the regular celebration of the Games;
B. making the Games ever more worthy of their glorious history and of the high ideals which inspired their revival by Baron Pierre de Coubertin and his associates;
C. encouraging the organization and development of amateur sport and sport competitions;
D. inspiring, and leading sport within the Olympic ideal, thereby promoting and strengthening friendship between the sportsmen of all countries.

Membership
12 The International Olympic Committee is a permanent organization. It selects such persons as it considers qualified to be members, provided that they speak French or English and are citizens of and reside in a country which possesses a National Olympic Committee recognized by the International Olympic Committee, and welcomes them into membership with a brief ceremony during which they accept the required obligations and responsibilities. There shall be only one member in any country except in the largest and most active in the Olympic Movement, and in those countries where the Olympic Games have been held, where there may be two.

Members of the International Olympic Committee are representatives of the IOC in their countries and not delegates of their country to the IOC. They may not accept from the Governments of their countries, or from any organization or individual, instructions which will in any way bind them or interfere with the independence of their vote.

Members with long and active service in the IOC who wish to resign, may be elected to honorary membership. Such honorary members may attend the Olympic Games under the same conditions as the IOC members.

13 A member:
A. may resign at any time;
B. if elected after 1965, must retire after reaching the age of 72;
C. shall cease to be a member if he changes his nationality or no longer lives permanently in his country; fails to attend meetings, or to take any active part in IOC affairs for two years, or if his subscription is more than one year in arrears; or by reason of circumstances that may arise, is not in a position properly to carry out his duties as a member;
D. is not responsible out of his personal property;
E. may be expelled by resolution of the IOC if in the IOC's opinion he has betrayed or neglected its interest or has been guilty of unworthy conduct.

Organization
14 *A – President*
The International Olympic Committee elects a President for

eight years from among its members by secret ballot and by an absolute majority of those present. He is eligible for re-election for successive terms of four years.

The newly elected President shall assume office at the end of the Session, or in the case of a Session held during the Olympic Games, after the closing of the Games. However the newly elected President attends meetings of the Executive Board immediately after his election.

If the President is unable to fulfil the duties of his office, the senior Vice-President in this capacity acts until a new President is elected at the next IOC Session. This new President thus nominated holds office only for the remainder of the term of the person whose place he takes until the IOC Session at the next Olympic Games. He is eligible for re-election as under para 1 of this rule.

B – Vice-Presidents

The International Olympic Committee also elects three Vice-Presidents (one at least from Europe) to hold office for only one period of four years.

If a Vice-President is unable to fulfil the duties of his office, the IOC elects a new Vice-President at the next IOC Session. This new Vice-President holds office only for the remainder of the term of the person whose place he takes. He is eligible for immediate re-election.

Vice-Presidents and members of the Executive Board shall assume office immediately after the end of the Session.

The President and the Vice-Presidents are *de jure* members of all commissions and sub-committees.

When an election is to be held, nominations in writing signed by at least three members shall be made and announced the day before. This refers also to the Executive Board elections.

C – Executive Board

The Executive Board is composed of the President, three Vice-Presidents, and five additional members.

The five additional members are elected to hold office until the main IOC Session which will be held in the fourth year after their election. They retire in rotation.

A retiring member from the Executive Board is not eligible for re-election in the year of his retirement. This does not apply to promotion to Vice-President or President.

If a member dies, resigns, is unable to fulfil the duties of his office, or if a vacancy occurs, a new member is elected by the IOC at its next meeting to take his place, but the new member holds office only for the remainder of the term of the person whose place he takes. A member so elected is, however, eligible for immediate re-election upon retirement.

15 For the management of the International Olympic Committee's current affairs, the Executive Board performs those duties that are assigned to it by the IOC, in particular:

It must ensure that the Rules and Regulations are observed;

It prepares the agenda for the meetings of the International Olympic Committee;

It submits to the IOC the names of the persons whom it recommends for election;

It is responsible for the management of the IOC's finances and makes an annual report;

It appoints the Directors;

It accepts the ultimate responsibility for the administration;

It keeps the IOC's records.

Secretaries, interpreters and other employees will be engaged according to the approved establishment and on such terms as the Executive Board decides.

16 The President may take action or make a decision where circumstances do not permit it to be taken by the International Olympic Committee or its Executive Board. Such action or decision is subject to ratification by the IOC at its next meeting.

Meetings

17 A. The Executive Board will hold conferences with all International Federations whose sports are included in the Olympic Games. Each International Federation is entitled to be represented at such conferences by two delegates.

The Executive Board may also invite other International Federations whose rules are accepted as conforming to those of the IOC for the purpose of considering general questions affecting these sports in relation to the Olympic Games. Each International Federation thus invited to attend such a conference is entitled to be represented by two delegates.

B. The Executive Board will also hold conferences at least every two years with all National Olympic Committees to hear reports on progress of the Olympic Movement in their countries and areas, to discuss their problems with them, and hear suggestions for strengthening the Olympic Movement and the Games. Each National Olympic Committee is entitled to be represented by two delegates.

. . .

Sessions

18 The International Olympic Committee meets when summoned by the President. He must convoke a meeting called Session at any time upon the written request of not less than one third of the members.

Normally, the place of the Session is decided by the IOC.

Notice of a Session must be accompanied by the agenda which should reach the members at least one month before the meeting. An item not on the agenda may be discussed with the Chairman's permission.

19 At a Session of the IOC, the President or in his absence one of the Vice-Presidents, takes the chair. In the absence of the President and Vice-Presidents the meeting selects one of its members to be Chairman. The quorum at a Session of the International Olympic Committee is thirty-five.

Resolutions (except a resolution under Rule 22) are passed if a majority of votes cast are in favour. Every member who is present at a meeting has one vote. Proxies are not allowed. A secret ballot is taken, if the Chairman so decides or if one member demands it. If the voting is tied the Chairman must cast the deciding vote.

All matters of procedure at Sessions of the International Olympic Committee not prescribed by these Rules are decided by the Chairman of the meeting.

Although French and English are the official languages of the International Olympic Committee, simultaneous translation shall also be provided for Russian, Spanish and German in all IOC Sessions.

In case of discrepancy between the French and English texts of these Rules and Regulations, the French text will prevail.

Postal Vote

20 The President may submit a resolution to the members by post in case of urgency, and if a majority of those who reply vote in favour of the resolution (other than a change of rules when rule 22 applies), and not less than thirty-five members in all vote, the resolution is carried. The result shall be reported to the IOC at its next session.

Resources

21 The International Olympic Committee fixes the amount of the annual subscription payable by members of the IOC on the recommendation of its Executive Board. Subscriptions fall due on the 1st January each year in advance.

The International Olympic Committee may accept gifts and may seek to obtain funds from any other source which will enable it to fulfil the task it has taken upon itself.

Cities entrusted with the organization of the Olympic Games or the Winter Games shall be liable to pay to the IOC whatever sum the IOC shall have fixed.

All sums arising out of the celebration of the Olympic Games or the Olympic Winter Games belong to the International Olympic Committee. It reserves the right to grant a portion to the Organizing Committee and to allocate a portion to the International Federations and the National Olympic Committees.

Alterations of Rules and Official Text

22 These Rules and Regulations may be altered only if two-thirds, and not less than twenty-five of the members present at a session vote in favour of the alteration. Bye-laws may be altered by simple majority. If requested by a member the vote must be secret.

Supreme Authority

23 The International Olympic Committee is the final authority on all questions concerning the Olympic Games and the Olympic Movement. It delegates, however, to the International Federations the technical control of the sports which they govern. In all other respects the powers of the IOC are paramount.

III — The National Olympic Committees

24 A. Only National Olympic Committees recognized and approved by the International Olympic Committee can enter competitors in the Olympic Games and the qualifying rounds. Therefore, in order that contestants from a country or geographical area can participate in the Olympic Games, a National Olympic Committee must be composed of at least five National Federations. These Federations in turn must be active members of the International Federations governing their sport on the Olympic programme. The National Olympic Committees must also conduct their activities in accordance with the Olympic Rules and Regulations and the high ideals of the Olympic Movement in order to be recognized by the International Olympic Committee.

B. National Olympic Committees have as their purpose the development and protection of the Olympic Movement and of amateur sport. They shall co-operate with the national amateur sport governing bodies (National Federations), affiliated to the International Federations recognized by the International Olympic Committee, in guarding and enforcing the eligibility rules. It is their duty, in co-operation with the National Federations, to organize and control the representatives of their country at the Olympic Games. They arrange to equip, transport and house these representatives.

They are organizations formed not for pecuniary profit, but devoted to the promotion and encouragement of the physical, moral and cultural education of the youth of the nation, for the development of character, good health and good citizenship.

C. National Olympic Committees must not associate themselves with affairs of a political or commercial nature.

D. The Rules and Regulations of the International Olympic Committee shall be incorporated in the Rules and Regulations of National Olympic Committees and shall be enforced by them in their respective countries or areas.

E. The IOC will consult the National Olympic Committees on the basic problems concerning the Olympic Movement in general and the activities of the NOCs in particular. The latter can make proposals to the IOC concerning the progress of the Olympic Movement and the sound organization and operation of the Olympic Games. All important problems connected with the NOCs will first be discussed with them and then submitted to the Sessions of the IOC.

F. A National Olympic Committee must not recognize more than one National Federation in each sport and that Federation must be affiliated to the International Federation recognized by the International Olympic Committee.

G. Because of the importance of National Olympic Committees which are in complete charge of the Olympic Movement in their countries, great care must be exercised in choosing members, who should be citizens of the country and men of good standing, of upright character, sound judgement and independent mind, with a knowledge of and a belief in Olympic principles.

They must include in their membership:

    a. the members of the International Olympic Committee for that country, if any, who shall be voting members of the Executive Board (or its equivalent);

    b. representatives of the National Federations, which are members of International Federations whose sport is included in the Olympic programme. These Federation representatives shall be of their own choice and must constitute a voting majority of the National Olympic Committee.

The following are not eligible to serve on a National Olympic Committee:

    1. a person who has ever competed as a professional;

    2. a person engaged in or connected with sport for personal profit (it is not intended to exclude individuals occupying purely administrative positions in connection with amateur sport);

    3. a person who has ever coached sports competitors for payment.

Exceptions may be made in the above categories by the Executive Board of the International Olympic Committee in special circumstances on the recommendation of the National Olympic Committee concerned.

H. Officers or members of a National Olympic Committee or the members of its Executive Board (or its equivalent) shall be elected at least every four years, at a National Olympic Committee meeting held expressly for that purpose. Governments cannot designate members of National Olympic Committees.

National Olympic Committees may co-opt to the Committee delegates of other amateur sport organizations or persons who have rendered or can render exceptional service to the Olympic Movement, subject to the restriction in clause b (above). Members of National Olympic Committees shall accept no salary or fee of any kind in respect of their position. They may, however, accept reimbursement for transportation, lodging and other proper expenses incurred by them in connection with their duties.

I. National Olympic Committees are responsible for the behaviour of all members of their delegations.

They make all arrangements for taking part in the Olympic Games.

All communications on such matters shall be addressed to them.

J. In order to obtain recognition, a certified copy of the Rules and Regulations of a National Olympic Committee with, if necessary, a translation in French or English, certified correct, must be approved by the International Olympic Committee. Subsequent changes of these Rules must be reported to and approved by the International Olympic Committee. Certified copies of the minutes of National Olympic Committee meetings at which the members and officers are elected or changed must be submitted to the IOC on request.

K. In the event of any regulations or actions of the National Olympic Committee conflicting with International Olympic Committee Rules, or of any political interference in its operations, the International Olympic Committee member in that country must report on the situation to his President for appropriate action. If there is no International Olympic Committee member in the country, it is the duty of the members of the National Olympic Committee to report to the International Olympic Committee, whose President has the power to appoint a member from another country to investigate and report.

25 National Olympic Committees must be completely independent and autonomous and must resist all political, religious or commercial pressure.

National Olympic Committees that do not conform to the Rules and Regulations of the International Olympic Committee forfeit their recognition and consequently their right to send participants to the Olympic Games.

IV — The Olympic Games

Eligibility Code

26 To be eligible for participation in the Olympic Games, a competitor must:

A. Observe and abide by the Rules and Regulations of the IOC and in addition the Rules and Regulations of his or her International Federation, as approved by the IOC, even if the Federation rules are more strict than those of the IOC.

B. Not have received any financial rewards or material benefit in connection with his or her sports participation, except as permitted in the bye-laws to this rule.

Medical

27 A. Doping is forbidden. The IOC will prepare a list of prohibited drugs.

B. All Olympic competitors are liable to medical control and examination in conformity with the rules of the Medical Commission.

C. Any Olympic competitor refusing to take a doping test or who is found guilty of doping shall be eliminated.

If the Olympic competitor belongs to a team, the match or competition in question shall be forfeited by that team.

After the explanations of the team have been considered and the case discussed with the International Federation concerned, a team in which one or more members have been found guilty of doping may be disqualified from the Olympic Games.

In sports in which a team may no longer compete after a member has been disqualified, the remaining members may compete on an individual basis in agreement with the IOC.

D. Competitors in sports restricted to women must comply with the prescribed tests for femininity.

E. A medal may be withdrawn by order of the Executive Board on a proposal of the Medical Commission.

F. A Medical Commission may be set up to implement these rules. Members of this commission may not act as Team Doctors.

G. The above regulations shall in no way effect further sanctions by the International Federations.

Necessary conditions for wearing the colours of a country

28 A. Only citizens of a country can represent that country in the Olympic Games (subject to the exceptions below).

B. If a competitor has represented a country in the Olympic Games or Regional Games or World or Area Championships he may not represent another country in the Olympic Games. Except:

1. where his former country has been incorporated in another state;

2. when he represented the former country, he did so because his native land at that time had no NOC;

3. where he has become a naturalized citizen of another country and at least three years have elapsed from the date of his application for such naturalization;

4. after one year from the date on which he last represented his former country, but in this case only with the agreement of the two National Sports Federations and the approval of the relevant International Federation and the permission of the International Olympic Committee;

5. in the case of a woman, if she changes her nationality by marriage, she may represent her husband's country.

C. Citizens of colonies or dominions wishing to represent the mother country.

Citizens born in a dominion or colony can represent the mother country if the dominion or colony has no NOC.

D. Interchange between citizens of dominions, colonies and mother country.

Provided that:

1. they have lived at least three years from the date in which they last represented their former country in the dominion, colony or mother country which they wish to represent:

2. they have lived at least one year from the date on which they last represented their former country in the dominion, colony or mother country which they wish to represent;

that in this case:

a. it is legally impossible to become a naturalized citizen of the country which they wish to represent;

b. the agreement of two National Sports Federations and the approval of the International Federation concerned and the permission of the International Olympic Committee have all first been obtained.

E. A person born abroad in a different country to the country of which his parents have citizenship can compete for the country of his parents.

Provided that:

1. he has established the nationality/citizenship of his parents, and

2. has not previously represented the country of his birth.

Age Limit

29 No age limit for competitors in the Olympic Games is stipulated by the International Olympic Committee.

International Sports Federations

30 The following International Sports Federations governing Olympic sports are recognized by the International Olympic Committee:

International Archery Federation; International Amateur Athletic Federation; International Amateur Basketball Federation; International Bobsleigh and Tobogganing Federation; International Amateur Boxing Association; International Canoeing Federation; International Amateur Cyclists Federation; International Equestrian Federation; International Fencing Federation; International Football Federation; International Gymnastics Federation; International Amateur Handball Federation; International Hockey Federation; International Ice Hockey Federation; International Judo Federation; International Luge Federation; International Union for Modern Pentathlon and Biathlon; International Rowing Federation; International Shooting Union; International Skating Union; International Skiing Federation; International Amateur Swimming Federation; International Volleyball Federation; International Weight-Lifting Federation; International Amateur Wrestling Federation; International Yacht Racing Union.

Programme

31 The official programme shall include at least fifteen of the following sports:

Archery; Athletics; Basketball; Boxing; Canoeing; Cycling; Equestrian Sports; Fencing; Football; Gymnastics; Handball; Hockey; Judo; Modern Pentathlon; Rowing; Shooting; Swimming, Diving and Water-polo; Volleyball; Weight-Lifting; Wrestling; Yachting.

The number of sports shall be the accepted maximum.

Participation of Women

32 Women are allowed to compete in Archery, Athletics, Basketball, Canoeing, Diving, Equestrian Sports, Fencing, Gymnastics, Handball, Hockey, Luge, Rowing, Shooting, Figure and Speed Skating, Skiing, Swimming, Volleyball and Yachting, according to the rules of the International Federation concerned.

Admission of Sports

33 Only sports widely practised in at least forty countries and three continents may be included in the programme of the Olympic Games.

Only sports widely practised by men in at least twenty-five countries and two continents may be included in the programme of the Olympic Winter Games.

Only sports widely practised by women in twenty-five countries and two continents may be included in the programme of the Olympic Games, and sports practised in twenty countries and two continents in the programme of the Olympic Winter Games.

Note:

These standards only apply to new sports. For those sports

which are already on the Olympic programme, 8 years will be given to reach the standards.

Widely practised means:

a) National Championships of cups permanently organized by the respective National Sports Federation;

b) international participation and the holding of Regional and World Championships in the respective sports.

Events

The International Olympic Committee in consultation with the International Federations concerned will decide the events which shall be included in each sport, in bearing with the global content and aspect of the Olympic programme and on the basis of statistical data referring to the number of participating countries in each event of the Olympic programme, of the World Championships, of Regional Games and all other competitions under the patronage of the IOC and the patronage of the IFs, for a period of one Olympiad (4 years).

Team Sports

There shall be 12 teams for sports in which only men participate.

There shall be 18 teams for sports in which men and women compete provided that the number of women's teams is not less than 6.

It is the duty of the International Federation concerned to determine the number of men's and women's teams within the prescribed limits.

Olympic Winter Games

The programme for the Olympic Winter Games may include: Biathlon, Bobsleigh, Ice Hockey, Luge, Skating and Skiing. In each sport, the events are governed by the technical rules of the International Federation concerned. The medals and diplomas must be different from those of the Olympic Games. The Olympic Winter Games are governed by the Rules and Regulations of the Olympic Games except where special provision is made.

Establishment and Revision of the Olympic Programme

The programme of sports will be fixed by the International Olympic Committee at the time the invitations to stage the Games are considered and no changes are permitted thereafter.

The International Olympic Committee revises after each Olympic Games (4 years) the Olympic programme and has the right to eliminate sports in which there is insufficient international interest, according to the above-mentioned standards for the admission of sports, or not properly controlled according to Olympic Regulations.

National Fine Arts

34 The Organizing Committee shall arrange, subject to the approval of the International Committee, exhibitions and demonstrations of the national Fine Arts (Architecture, Literature, Music, Painting, Sculpture, Photography and Sport Philately) and fix the dates during which these exhibitions and demonstrations shall take place. The programme may also include theatrical, ballet, opera performances, or Symphony concerts. This section of the programme should be of the same high standard as the sports events and be held concurrently with them in the same vicinity. It shall receive full recognition in the publicity released by the Organizing Committee.

35 . . . The entry form must contain the eligibility rules for the Olympic Games and the following statement, to be signed by the competitor:

I, the undersigned, declare on my honour that I have studied all the rules and comply with the Eligibility Code of the Olympic Games as specified on this form.

The National Federation and National Olympic Committee shall also sign this form to confirm that they have brought all the rules to the competitor's attention.

Entries are not valid unless the above rules are observed.

No commercial advertising is permitted on equipment used in the Games nor on the uniforms or numbers worn by contestants or officials, in fact nothing may be worn on the uniforms of contestants or officials except the flag or emblem of the National Olympic Committee, which must meet with the approval of the National Olympic Committee.

Number of Entries

36 The maximum number of entries from each National Olympic Committee in each event is fixed by the International Olympic Committee in consultation with the appropriate International Federation. The following numbers cannot be exceeded:

A. for individual events, three competitors from each country (without reserves) in both Olympic and Olympic Winter Games (except in skiing where four are permitted);

B. for team sports, one team per country, the number of reserves to be decided by the International Olympic Committee in consultation with the International Federation concerned.

. . .

Penalties in case of fraud

43 A competitor proved to have transgressed the Olympic Rules knowingly shall be disqualified and lose any position that he may have gained. If this competitor's National Olympic Committee or National Federation is proved to have been party to the fraud, the entire team in the sport involved shall also be disqualified.

Final Court of Appeal

44 The Executive Board of the International Olympic Committee decides all matters of controversy of a non-technical nature concerning the Games. (Such matters may be submitted only by National Olympic Committees, International Federations or the Organizing Committee.) In addition the Executive Board may intervene in all questions of a non-technical nature.

Prizes

45 The prizes of the Olympic Games shall be provided by the Organizing Committee for distribution by the International Olympic Committee. They consist of medals and diplomas. In individual events the first prize shall be a silver-gilt medal and a diploma, the second prize a silver medal and a diploma, the third prize a bronze medal and a diploma. The medals must bear the name of the sport concerned and shall be attached in a removable fashion to a chain or ribbon, which may be hung around the neck of the competitor. Diplomas but not medals shall also be given for the fourth, fifth and sixth places. All participants in a tie will be entitled to receive a medal and a diploma. . . . The names of all winners shall be inscribed upon the walls of the stadium where the Games have taken place. . . . If an Olympic competitor is disqualified, his medal must be returned. If this is not done, the National Olympic Committee runs the risk of suspension.

. . .

Information Media

49 *In order to ensure the widest possible audience for the Olympic Games, and subject to the rights of the International Olympic Committee, the necessary steps shall be taken to allow representatives of all forms of mass media to attend and report on the events and ceremonies accompanying the Games, in observance of the rights of the IOC.

Without prejudice to the granting of exclusive rights as defined hereafter, the showing, without payment of royalties, of newsreels covering the Games is authorized within the framework of regular news programmes in which the actual news element constitutes the main feature, whether in cinemas, over the whole of a television network or on a single station, but is limited to three reports of three minutes each, separated by an interval of at least three hours.

The International Olympic Committee may, subject to pay-

Note: see also bye-laws.

ment of broadcasting rights, grant the right to broadcast and/or distribute reports on the Olympic Games. The total amount of the broadcasting and distribution rights shall be paid to the International Olympic Committee by the bodies to which these rights have been granted.

The International Olympic Committee may grant a television company the exclusive right to broadcast the Games in a given territory. In this case no other television company may broadcast on such territory the coverage of any Olympic event before the company that has acquired the exclusive rights for that country has completed the whole of its news broadcasts for the day, on the day it broadcasts its coverage of aforesaid event. This prohibition shall cease at the latest forty-eight hours after the end of the event or ceremony.

Each Olympic Games shall be recorded for posterity by the Olympic Film, the exclusive rights for which shall be the property of the International Olympic Committee, and by technical films which the International Federations will be authorized to make on their respective sports.

50 The rules affecting the administration and organization of the Olympic Games may not be changed at the two Sessions prior to the year of the organization of the Games. This rule will not apply to the bye-laws.

V – The Olympic Protocol

51 The International Olympic Committee selects the city in which the Olympic Games take place at a meeting in a country having no city as candidate. . . .

Time and Duration of the Olympic Games

53 The Olympic Games must take place during the first year of the Olympiad which they are to celebrate (e.g. in 1912 for the Vth Olympiad, 1972 for the XXth). They cannot be postponed to another year. Their non-celebration during this first year entails the non-celebration of the Olympiad and involves the annulment of the rights of the city chosen. These rights cannot be carried forward to the next Olympiad without the approval of the International Olympic Committee.

The time of year when the Olympic Games are held is not permanently fixed but will be proposed to the International Olympic Committee by the Organizing Committee for approval.

The International Olympic Committee alone makes the decision.

The period of the Games must not exceed fifteen days, including the opening day. If there is no competition on Sundays, the duration can be extended accordingly. The Olympic Winter Games must be confined to ten days. The official ending of the Games is when the Olympic flame is extinguished.

Olympic City

54 The events must all take place in or as near as possible to the city chosen and preferably at or near the main stadium. The city chosen cannot share its privilege with another nor can it permit any deviation from the programme or from the Olympic Regulations.

No other international events may be scheduled in or near the Olympic City during the period of the Games, or during the preceding or following week.

55 *Programme*

For all the technical arrangements of the Games, the Organizing Committee must consult the International Federations concerned. It must see that all the different branches of sport are placed on the same footing. . . .

Advertising, propaganda

Every kind of demonstration or propaganda, whether political, religious or racial, in the Olympic areas is forbidden.

Commercial installations and advertising signs shall not be permitted inside the stadium or other sports arenas.

The display of any clothing or equipment such as shoes, skis, handbags, hats, etc. marked conspicuously for advertising

purposes in any Olympic venue (training grounds, Olympic Village, or fields of competition), by participants either competitors, coaches, trainers or anyone else associated with an Olympic team in official capacity, will normally result in immediate disqualification or withdrawal of credentials.

Emblem

The Organizing Committee cannot use the Olympic emblem (see Rule 16) for publicity or commercial purposes. Any use shall be submitted to the IOC in advance for approval. It will ensure the protection of the Olympic emblem and the emblem of the Games by the government of its country for the IOC and the Organizing Committee. It cannot authorize the use of the emblem of the Games for publicity or commercial purposes in the countries or territories of any other NOC, without the permission of that NOC and the approval of the IOC.

During the Games and for the period of preparation for them and for the two years after they have ended, the Organizing Committee is authorized to exploit the official emblems and all badges, posters, objects and documents which it designs, creates, publishes or reproduces for the purpose of the Games.

The Organizing Committee shall take all steps that may be required in order to ensure all rights and property of the official emblems of the Games and other things mentioned above, for the benefit of the IOC and to ensure their necessary protection.

The same directives apply to the Organizing Committee of the Session for all printed material and other items as mentioned above.

Responsibilities prior to and following the Games

Publicity for any Olympic Games should not be released before the conclusion of the preceding Olympic Games.

A final report and recommendations shall be presented to the IOC by the Organizing Committee, during the Session following the Games. These reports shall include the audited accounts.

. . .

B – BYE-LAWS

I – To Rule 26

A. A Competitor may:

1. Be a physical education or sports teacher who gives elementary instruction.

2. Accept, during the period of preparation and actual competition which shall be limited by the rules of each International Federation:

a) Assistance administered through his or her National Olympic Committee or National Federation for:

Food and lodging; cost of transport; pocket money to cover incidental expenses; insurance cover in respect of accidents, illness, personal property and disability; personal sports equipment and clothing; cost of medical treatment, physiotherapy and authorized coaches.

b) Compensation, authorized by his or her National Olympic Committee or National Federation, in case of necessity, to cover financial loss resulting from his or her absence from work or basic occupation, on account of preparation for, or participation in, the Olympic Games and international sports competitions. In no circumstances shall payment made under this provision exceed the sum which the competitor would have earned in the same periods. The compensation may be paid with the approval of the National Federations or the National Olympic Committees at their discretion.

3. Accept prizes won in competition within the limits of the rules established by the respective International Federations.

4. Accept academic and technical scholarships.

B. A Competitor must not:

1. Be or have been a professional athlete in any sport, or contracted to be so before the official closing of the Games.

2. Have allowed his person, name, picture or sports performance to be used for advertising, except when his or her

International Federation, National Olympic Committee or National Federation enters into a contract for sponsorship or equipment. All payments must be made to the International Federation, National Olympic Committee or National Federation concerned, and not to the individual.

3. Carry advertising material on his person or clothing in the Olympic Games, World or Continental Championships and Games under patronage of the IOC, other than trade marks on technical equipment or clothing as agreed by the IOC with the International Federations.

4. Have acted as a professional coach or trainer in any sport.

C. Eligibility Commission

A commission may be appointed to enforce Rule 26 and these Bye-Laws, together with Rules 1 and 3 (fundamental principles), 8 (citizenship), 28 (special conditions), 35 (affiliation), 49 (reporting).

II – To Rule 49

After consulting the International Federation concerned, the Organizing Committee shall place at the disposal of the radio, cinema, television and press the space necessary for the proper coverage of the Games. The number and position of the places reserved for the mass-media personnel, photographers, and radio, cinema and television equipment, may be limited only for reasons directly concerning the organization of the events unless the Executive Board shall otherwise agree.

The Organizing Committee shall exercise control over the use of all cameras set up in the stadia and stands. Cameras used privately for strictly non-commercial purposes in the enclosures reserved for spectators shall not however be subject to any restriction.

Accreditation

The Organizing Committee shall issue an accreditation card to the representatives of the different forms of mass media, officially accredited either by the National Olympic Committee of their respective country, or directly by the Organizing Committee, subject in each case to the International Olympic Committee's approval.

The accreditation card will give representatives of the written and spoken press, radio, television, newsreels and photographers, free and unrestricted admission to the events and official ceremonies.

Under no circumstances, throughout the duration of the Olympic Games, may any participating athlete, trainer, official, etc. be accredited as a journalist.

Broadcasting rights

The term 'broadcasting' means informing the public of the official events and ceremonies within the Olympic Games, by all radio and audio-visual forms of mass media (cinema, radio, television, closed-circuit programmes, video-cassette, etc.).

With the authority of the International Olympic Committee and subject to its approval, the Organizing Committee may against payment therefor grant concessions for the broadcasting and distribution rights for the coverage of the Olympic Games.

Subject to the preceding provisions of this bye-law, the right to show the Olympic Games on television may only be granted by the Organizing Committee (acting under powers delegated to it by the International Olympic Committee, and subject always to approval of any relevant contracts by the Executive Board of the International Olympic Committee) directly to television organizations in respect of their respective national territories or to the national or international associations of such organizations.

The contracts entered into between the Organizing Committee and the broadcasting and distribution companies for the purchase of such rights to be exercised solely by the purchasers and within their respective territories – shall be submitted to the Executive Board of the International Olympic Committee for its approval.

A representative of the International Olympic Committee shall be entitled to attend all discussions concerning the drafting of such contracts. Every contract shall stipulate that the International Olympic Committee's Rules and Regulations shall be deemed to be incorporated in the contract and shall be binding on all parties to it.

The total amount of the television rights is to be paid to the International Olympic Committee, either directly or through the intermediary of the Organizing Committee.

Photograph and film pools

The Organizing Committee in collaboration with the television companies, newsreel producers and photographic agencies, and at the expense of the latter, shall set up photograph and film pools. The material thus obtained may not be re-used for making a special Olympic programme of any kind or for audio-visual programmes on either the Games or the athletes competing in the Games.

A copy of all original films taken by the pools shall be given free of charge to the International Olympic Committee for its archives. The same applies to all still photographs taken by the pools.

*Olympic Film and technical films**

The Organizing Committee shall take all necessary steps to ensure that the Games are recorded on a film comprising shots of each individual sport.

All rights in this film shall at all times remain the exclusive property of the International Olympic Committee. However, for a period of four years commencing with the end of the Games, the International Olympic Committee shall grant the right to exploit this film to the Organizing Committee of the Olympic Games subject to the payment of a royalty based on the gross receipts.

Once the film is released, a complete copy together with the master negative is to be given free of charge to the International Olympic Committee.

The International Federations and National Olympic Committees may obtain, at cost price, copies of this film for private showing to their members only.

The International Federations will be authorized to make 16-mm technical films of their respective events intended for schools, athletic clubs or other similar bodies in return for payment.

A copy of all technical films taken during the Olympic Games must be given to the IOC for its archives.

The National Olympic Committees may buy copies of these films from the Organizing Committee for showing under the same conditions as the International Federations.

Distribution: The Olympic film and technical films must be distributed according to the internationally accepted practices of the film industry.

C – INSTRUCTIONS

. . .

III – Ceremony of Introduction for New Members

After his election, the new member is received officially, with a short speech of welcome, by the President and the Committee in full assembly.

He then makes the following declaration:

Recognizing the responsibilities that go with the great honour of serving as (one of) the representative(s) of the International Olympic Committee in my country, (name of his country), *I bind myself to promote the Olympic Movement to the best of my ability and to guard and preserve its fundamental principles as conceived by the Baron Pierre de Coubertin, keeping myself as a member free from all political, sectarian or commercial influence.*

After this declaration the neophyte is introduced to each member of the International Olympic Committee present. He then expresses briefly his thanks and his appreciation of his predecessor and takes the place reserved for him. . . .

* This paragraph will be reviewed by the IOC.

The abbreviations given here and in other sections of the book for names of countries are the official ones used by the IOC. The dates given are those of recognition by the IOC (dates earlier than 1935 are the dates of foundation).

Afghanistan (AFG) 1936
National Olympic Federation of
Afghanistan
Kabul

Albania (ALB) 1959
Comité Olympique de la République
Populaire d'Albanie
Rruga Abdi Toptani 3, Tirana

Algeria (ALG) 1964
Comité National Olympique Algérien
Rue de la Liberté 24, Algiers

Argentina (ARG) 1927
Comité Olímpico Argentino
Carlos Pellegrini 1362, Buenos Aires

Australia (AUS) 1895
Australian Olympic Federation
14 McKillop Street, Melbourne 3000
Victoria

Austria (AUT) 1912
Österreichisches Olympisches Comité
Prinz Eugen-Strasse 12, 1040 Vienna

Bahamas (BAH) 1952
Bahamas Olympic Association
P.O. Box 6250, Nassau

Barbados (BAR) 1955
Barbados Olympic Association
Box 659, Bridgetown

Belgium (BEL) 1906
Comité Olympique Belge
Avenue de Bouchant 1020, Brussels

Bermuda (BER) 1936
Bermuda Olympic Association
P.O. Box 1665, Hamilton, Bermuda

Bolivia (BOL) 1936
Comité Olímpico Boliviano
Casilla 4481, La Paz

Brazil (BRA) 1935
Comité Olímpico Brasileiro
Avenida Rio Branco 156-30 andar-Sala
3020–ZC–21
Rio de Janeiro

British Honduras (HBR) 1967
Belize Olympic and Commonwealth
Games Association
P.O. Box 103, Belize City
British Honduras

Bulgaria (BUL) 1923
Comité Olympique Bulgare
Rue Marin Drinov 19, Sofia

Burma (BIR) 1947
Burma Olympic Committee
Aungsan Memorial Stadium, Rangoon

Cambodia (KHM) 1961
Comité National Olympique Khmer
Vithei Oknha Keth 1, B.P. 101
Phnom-Penh

Cameroons (CMR) 1963
Comité Olympique Camerounais
B.P. 528, Yaoundé

Canada (CAN) 1907
Canadian Olympic Association
Olympic House, Cité du Havre
Montréal 103, P.Q.

Central Africa (CAF) 1965
Comité Olympique Centrafricain
B.P. 573, Bangui, R.C.A.

Chad (CHA) 1964
Comité Olympique Tchadien
B.P. 2206, Fort-Lamy

Chile (CHI) 1896
Comité Olímpico de Chile
Casilla 2239, Santiago

China, Republic of (ROC) 1960
Republic of China Olympic Committee
P.O. Box 17–51, Taipei

Colombia (COL) 1948
Comité Olímpico Colombiano
Centro Administrativo Nacional
Edificio del Ministerio de Educación
Nacional, Can, Mineducación Nacional
Piso 30, Bogotá

Congo Republic (CGO) 1964
Comité Olympique Congolais
B.P. 2061, Brazzaville

Costa Rica (CRC) 1954
Comité Olímpico de Costa Rica
Apartado 5388, San José

Cuba (CUB) 1954
Comité Olímpico Cubano
Hôtel Habana Libre, Habana

Czechoslovakia (TCH) 1920
Československý Olympijský Výbor
Národní Třida 33, 112 93 Prague

Dahomey (DAH) 1962
Comité Olympique Dahoméen
B.P. 437, Porto-Novo

Denmark (DEN) 1905
Danmarks Olympiske Komité
Idrættens Hus, Brøndbyvester
pr. 2600 Glostrup

Dominican Republic (DOM) 1962
Comité Olímpico Dominicano
3er Piso, Centro Olimpico Juan Pablo
Duarte, Apartado Postal 406
Santo Domingo

Ecuador (ECU) 1959
Comité Olímpico Ecuatoriano
Apartado de Correos 204, Guayaquil

Egypt (EGY) 1910
Comité Olympique Égyptien
Rue Kasr-el-Nil 13, P.O. Box 2055, Cairo

Ethiopia (ETH) 1954
Comité Olympique Éthiopien
B.P. 3241, Addis Abbaba

Fiji (FIJ) 1955
Fiji Amateur Sports Association and
National Olympic Committee
P.O. Box 331, Suva

Finland (FIN) 1919
Finnish Olympic Committee
Topeliuksenkatu 41a, Helsinki 25

France (FRA) 1894
Comité National Olympique et Sportif
Français
Rue d'Anjou 23, 75008 Paris

Gabon (GAB) 1967
Comité Olympique Gabonais
B.P. 2266, Libreville

German Democratic Republic
(GDR) 1955
Nationales Olympisches Komitee der
Deutschen Demokratischen Republik
Behrenstrasse 40/41, 108 Berlin

German Federal Republic (GER) 1950
Nationales Olympisches Komitee
für Deutschland
Otto-Fleck-Schneise 12, Postfach 710 130
6000 Frankfurt-am-Main 71

Ghana (GHA) 1952
Ghana Olympic and Overseas Games
Committee, P.O. Box 1272, Accra

Great Britain (GBR) 1905
The British Olympic Association
12 Buckingham Street, London
WC2N 6DJ

Greece (GRE) 1894
The Hellenic Olympic Committee
4 Kapsali Street, Athens 138

Guatemala (GUA) 1947
Comité Olímpico Guatemalteco
Palacio de Deportes, Guatemala C.A.

Guinea (GUI) 1965
Comité Olympique Guinéen
B.P. 262, Conakry

Guyana (GUY) 1948
Guyana Olympic, International and
British Commonwealth Games Assn
P.O. Box 30, Georgetown

Haiti (HAI) 1924
Comité Olympique Haïtien
P.O. Box 537, Port-au-Prince

Honduras (HON) 1956
Comité Olímpico Hondureño
Tegucigalpa D.C., Honduras, C.A.
Apartado Postal 36 C

Hong Kong (HKG) 1951
Amateur Sports Federation and Olympic
Committee of Hong Kong
Prince's Building 908, Hong Kong

Hungary (HUN) 1895
Comité Olympique Hongrois
Rosenberg Hàzaspár U. 1, Budapest V

Iceland (ISL) 1935
Iceland Olympic Committee
P.O. Box 864, Reykjavik

India (IND) 1924
Indian Olympic Association
c/o Joint Director General, Border

Security Force, Ministry of Home Affairs
Room 11, North Block, New Delhi 11001

Indonesia (INA) 1952
Komite Olympiade Indonesia
c/o Koni Pusat, Senajan, Djakarta

Iran (IRN) 1947
Iranian National Olympic Committee
Kakhe Varzesh, Teheran

Iraq (IRQ) 1948
Iraq Olympic Committee
Youth Township, Ministry of Youth
P.O. Box 441, Baghdad

Ireland (IRL) 1923
Olympic Council of Ireland
National Stadium, South Circular Road
Dublin 8

Israel (ISR) 1952
Olympic Committee of Israel
6 Ha'arbaa Street, Tel Aviv 64739

Italy (ITA) 1915
Comitato Olympico Nazionale Italiano
Foro Italico, Rome

Ivory Coast (CIV) 1963
Comité Olympique Ivoirien
B.P. 1872, Abidjan

Jamaica (JAM) 1936
Jamaica Olympic Association
P.O. Box 80, Kingston

Japan (JPN) 1912
The Japanese Olympic Committee
Kishi Memorial Hall, 1–1–1 Jinnan
Shibuya-Ku, Tokyo

Jordan (JOR) 1963
Jordan Olympic Committee
P.O. Box 1794, Amman

Kenya (KEN) 1955
Kenya Olympic Association
P.O. Box 46888, Nairobi

Korea (KOR) 1947
Korean Olympic Committee
I.O.P. Box 1106, Seoul

Korea, Democratic People's Republic of
(PRK) 1957
National Olympic Committee of the
Democratic People's Republic of Korea
Pyong-Yang

Kuwait (KUW) 1966
Kuwait Olympic Committee
P.O. Box 795, Kuwait

Lebanon (LIB) 1948
Comité Olympique Libanais
B.P. 5419 or 4300, Beirut

Lesotho (LES) 1972
Lesotho Olympic Committee
P.O. Box 138, Maseru

Liberia (LBR) 1955
Liberian Olympic Games Association
P.O. Box 502, Monrovia

Libya (LBA) 1963
Comité Olympique Lybien
B.P. 879, Tripoli

Liechtenstein (LIE) 1936
Comité Olympique de Liechtenstein
Städtle 22, 9490 Vaduz

Luxembourg (LUX) 1908
Comité Olympique Luxembourgeois
B.P. 2335, Luxembourg-Gare

Madagascar (MAD) 1964
Comité Olympique Malagasy
B.P. 4188, Tananarive

Malaysia (MAL) 1954
Olympic Council of Malaysia
Stadium Negara, Jalan Davidson
Kuala Lumpur

Malawi (MAW) 1968
Olympic and Commonwealth Games
Association of Malawi
P.O. Box 867, Blantyre

Mali (MLI) 1963
Comité Olympique Malien
B.P. 88, Bamako

Malta (MLT) 1936
Malta Olympic Committee
Oak Everest, Clover Hill
San Tomaso, Marsascala

Mauritius (MRI) 1972
Mauritius Olympic Committee
22 Lislet Geoffroy Street, Port Louis

Mexico (MEX) 1923
Comité Olímpico Mexicano
Apartado Postal 36–24, Ave. del
Conscripto y Anillo Periférico
Mexico 10 D.F.

Monaco (MON) 1953
Comité Olympique Monégasque
4 rue des Iris, Monte Carlo

Mongolia (MGL) 1962
Comité National Olympique de la
République Populaire de Mongolie
Baga Toirog 55, Oulan Bator

Morocco (MAR) 1959
Comité National Olympique Marocain
B.P. 1207, Rabat Principal
Rue Soumayah, Rabat Agdal

Nepal (NEP) 1963
National Olympic Committee of Nepal
Bag Durbar, Kathmandu

Netherlands (HOL) 1912
Nederlandsch Olympisch Comité
Surinamestraat 33, The Hague

Netherlands Antilles (AHO) 1950
Nederlands Antilliaans Olympisch
Comité, Santa Rosaweg 22
Willemstad, Curaçao

New Zealand (NZL) 1911
New Zealand Olympic and British
Commonwealth Games Association
P.O. Box 643, Wellington

Nicaragua (NCA) 1959
Comité Olímpico Nicaragüense
P.O. Box 786, Managua

Niger (NIG) 1964
Comité Olympique Nigérien
B.P. 626, Niamey

Nigeria (NGR) 1951
Nigeria Olympic Association
P.O. Box 3156, Lagos

Norway (NOR) 1900
Norwegian Olympic Committee
Sognsveien 75, Oslo 8

Pakistan (PAK) 1948
Pakistan Olympic Association
Olympic House, 2 Temple Road, Lahore

Panama (PAN) 1947
Comité Olímpico de Panamá
Apartado 2927, Panama 3

Papua New Guinea (PAP) 1974
Papua New Guinea Olympic Committee
P.O. Box 89, Port Moresby

Paraguay (PAR) 1968
Comité Olímpico Paraguayo
Esadio Comuneros, Av. Republica y 15
de Agosto, Asunción, Casilla Postal 1420

Peru (PER) 1936
Comité Olímpico Péruano
Estadio Nacional, Puerta 29, 3er Piso
Lima

Philippines (PHI) 1929
Philippines National Olympic Committee
c/o P.A.A.F., P.O. Box 2272, Manila

Poland (POL) 1919
Comité Olympique Polonais
4 rue Frascati, Warsaw 45

Portugal (POR) 1909
Comité Olimpico Portugues
Rua Braamcamp 12, R. C. Lisbon

Puerto Rico (PUR) 1948
Comité Olímpico de Puerto Rico
G.P.O. Box 4722, San Juan
Puerto Rico 00936

Rhodesia (RHO) 1959
National Olympic Committee
of Rhodesia
P.O. Box 1720, Bulawayo

Romania (ROM) 1914
Comité Olympique Roumain
Str. Vasile Conta 16, Bucharest

Salvador, El (SAL) 1962
Comité Nacional Olímpico
Apartado Postal 759, San Salvador

San Marino (SMR) 1959
Comitato Olimpico Nazionale
Sammarinese, San Marino

Saudi Arabia (ARS) 1965
Saudi Arabia Olympic Committee
P.O. Box 956, Riyadh

Senegal (SEN) 1963
Comité Olympique Sénégalais
Rue de Boufflers 1, Dakar

Sierra Leone (SLE) 1964
Sierra Leone Olympic and Overseas
Games Committee

c/o The National Sports Council
of Sierra Leone,
P.O. Box 1181, Tower Hill, Freetown

Singapore (SIN) 1948
Singapore National Olympic Council
P.O. Box 2941, Sports House
Rutland Road, Singapore 8

Somalia (SOM) 1972
The Somali National Olympic
Committee
P.O. Box 523, Mogadishu

Spain (ESP) 1924
Comité Olímpico Español
Av. de Martin Fierro
s/n., Madrid 3

Sri Lanka (SRI) 1937
Sri Lanka National Olympic and
Commonwealth Games Association
3/2 Melder Place, Nugegoda

Sudan (SUD) 1959
Sudanese Olympic Committee
P.O. Box 1938, Khartoum

Surinam (SUR) 1959
Surinaams Olympisch Comité
Herman Snostraat 9
Paramaribo-Surinam

Swaziland (SWZ) 1972
Swaziland Commonwealth and
Games Association
P.O. Box 835, Mbabane

Sweden (SWE) 1913
Sveriges Olympiska Kommitté
Box 1216, 111 82 Stockholm

Switzerland (SUI) 1912
Comité Olympique Suisse
Ch. du Boisy 2, 1004 Lausanne

Syria (SYR) 1948
Syrian Olympic Committee
P.O. Box 3375, Damascus

Tanzania (TAN) 1968
Tanzania Olympic Committee
P.O. Box 2182, Dar-es-Salaam

Thailand (THA) 1950
Olympic Committee of Thailand
Army Officer Club, Sri Ayuthaya Road
Tavest, Bangkok

Togo (TOG) 1965
Comité Olympique Togolais
B.P. 1320, Lomé

Trinidad and Tobago (TRI) 1962
Trinidad and Tobago Olympic
Association, P.O. Box 529
Port of Spain, Trinidad

Tunisia (TUN) 1957
Comité Olympique Tunisien
Rue Pierre-de-Coubertin 2 bis
Tunis

Turkey (TUR) 1924
Turkish Olympic Committee
P.O. Box 90, Tesvikiye, Emlâk Cad. 21
Nisantasi, Istanbul

Uganda (UGA) 1956
Uganda Olympic Committee
P.O. Box 2610, Kampala

Upper Volta (VOL) 1972
Comité National Olympique Voltaïque
B.P. 772, Ouagadougou

Uruguay (URU) 1932
Comité Olímpico Uruguayo
Casilla de Correos 161, Montevideo

USA (USA) 1895
United States Olympic Committee
Olympic House, 57 Park Avenue
New York, N.Y. 10016

USSR (URS) 1951
Comité Olympique d'U.R.S.S.
Skatertny Pereulok 4, Moscow

Venezuela (VEN) 1935
Comité Olímpico Venezolano
Apartado Postal 193, Caracas

Viet Nam (VNM) 1951
Comité National Sportif et
Olympique du Viet-Nam
Rue Hông Thâp Tu 37, Saigon 1

Virgin Islands (ISV) 1967
Virgin Islands Olympic Committee
P.O. Box 668, St Thomas,
Virgin Islands 00801

Yugoslavia (YUG) 1920
Comité Olympique Yougoslave
Terazije 35/11, Belgrade

Zaire (ZAI) 1968
Comité National Olympique Zaïrois
B.P. 6232, Kinshasa VI

Zambia (ZAM) 1963
National Olympic Committee of Zambia
P.O. Box 1268, Chingola

Acknowledgments and Notes on Illustrations

The publishers are indebted to the following for permission to quote from their publications: the International Olympic Committee for the extracts from their Rules and Regulations on pages 258–64, and for the many extracts from the *Olympic Review*, other publications, press releases and minutes which appear throughout the book; the Swedish Olympic Committee for the quotation on page 118 from the Official Report of the Olympic Games of 1912; the Japanese Olympic Committee for the quotation on page 163 from the introduction to KonIchikawa's film, *Tokyo Olympiad*. The quotation on page 95 is from an interview between Sam Balter and the writer of the article and is reproduced with Sam Balter's permission. The translation from the French of Coubertin's *Ode to Joy* reproduced on pages 161–2 by John G. Dixon originally appeared in *The Olympic Idea: Discourses and Essays*, edited by the Carl-Diem-Institut, published by Editions Internationales Olympia, Lausanne, and Olympischer Sport-Verlag, Stuttgart, and is reproduced with their permission. We should also like to acknowledge the help of M. Geoffroy de Navacelle in supplying us with photographs of his uncle, Coubertin, and in giving us permission to reproduce many of his writings, some previously unpublished.

The editors of this book would like to express their grateful thanks to all the contributors and many others who provided or suggested sources of information and illustrations; in particular the officials and staff of the International Olympic Committee, of many International Sports Federations, National Olympic Committees and National Sports Associations; and many individuals. We should also like to express our gratitude to previous Olympic historians, in particular Dr Ferenc Mező, author of *The Modern Olympic Games* (English edition 1956; originally published in 1930) and Erich Kamper, author of *Encyclopaedia of the Olympic Winter Games* (1964), *Encyclopaedia of the Olympic Games* (1972) and *Who's Who at the Olympics* (1975), whose books have been invaluable references.

The producers are also indebted to the following for assistance: Max Ammann, Krystyna Baran, Georges Croses, Marianne Dumartheray, Raymond Kaye, Celia Ratzman, Tony Raven, Vicki Robinson and Margaret Smithers; and also all those who are indicated by the following list of illustrations, especially the staffs of the agencies and libraries and individual owners of photographs. Every effort has been made to trace the primary source of illustrations; in one or two cases where it has not been possible, the producers wish to apologize if the acknowledgment proves to be inadequate; in no case is such inadequacy intentional and if any owner of copyright who has remained untraced will communicate with the producers a reasonable fee will be paid and the required acknowledgment made in future editions of the book.

Colour Illustrations
Page
33 Jean-Paul Maeder
34 Sportsworld, Don Morley
67 a. Popperfoto. b. Gerry Cranham
68 a. and b. Gerry Cranham
101 Gerry Cranham
102 Gerry Cranham
135 Kishimoto
136 Colorsport
185 Gerry Cranham
186–7 Kishimoto
188 Kishimoto
221 Kishimoto
222–3 Kishimoto
224 Gerry Cranham

Monochrome Illustrations
Title page Final of 5,000 metres, 1964. E. D. Lacey

Page
4 Judo, 1964. Popperfoto
5 a. Boxing, 1964. Popperfoto
5 b. Fencing, 1936. British Olympic Association; John R. Freeman Ltd
6 Wrestling, 1936. British Olympic Association; John R. Freeman Ltd
15 a. Jean-Paul Maeder. b. British Olympic Association; John R. Freeman Ltd
16 a. National Postal Museum, London. b. and c. British Olympic Association; John R. Freeman Ltd
19 a. and b. Associated Press. c. Johnny Morris, courtesy International Olympic Committee
21 Keystone
23 a. Popperfoto. b. Mexican National Olympic Committee
25 a. Museum of Olympia; photo N. Tombazi, Psychico-Athens, courtesy Otto Szymiczek. b. British Olympic Association; photo John R. Freeman Ltd
26 German Archaeological Institute, Athens, courtesy Otto Szymiczek
28 a. International Olympic Committee. b. Otto Szymiczek
31 a. Presse Sports. b. London Electrotype Agency. c. Presse Sports
32 Missouri Historical Society
35 British Olympic Association; John R. Freeman Ltd
36 a. Missouri Historical Society. b. London Electrotype Agency
38 Canadian Public Archives, courtesy Doug Gilbert
39 a. and b. British Olympic Association; John R. Freeman Ltd
40 British Olympic Association; John R. Freeman Ltd
41 Radio Times Hulton Picture Library
42 British Athletics Publicity and Information Unit
43 British Olympic Association; John R. Freeman Ltd
45 R. Wilsher, courtesy E. R. L. Powell
46 British Olympic Association; John R. Freeman Ltd
47 British Olympic Association; John R. Freeman Ltd
49 R. Wilsher, courtesy E. R. L. Powell
50 ANP, Amsterdam
52 a. and b. ANP, Amsterdam
53 US National Olympic Committee; John R. Freeman Ltd, courtesy British Olympic Association
54 Associated Press
56 British Olympic Association; John R. Freeman Ltd
57 a. and b. Library of Congress
58 British Olympic Association; John R. Freeman Ltd
61 Keystone
63 Racecourse Technical Services Ltd
65 a. and b. PA Photos
66 Ministry of Sports, Luxembourg
69 Popperfoto
70 Melbourne Herald-Sun
71 Melbourne Herald-Sun
73 Italian National Olympic Committee
74 Popperfoto
75 Keystone
77 Popperfoto
78 Popperfoto
79 E. D. Lacey
80 Mexican National Olympic Committee
82 Syndication International, London
83 Horst Müller
84 E. D. Lacey
85 a. Radio Times Hulton Picture Library. b. Associated Press
87 Colorsport
89 a. From Matthew Walbancke, *Annalia Dubrensia* (1636), courtesy the British Library Board. b. Courtesy Museum of Fine Arts, Boston (Attic Red-figured Kylix, H. L. Pierce Fund 98.876)
91 British Olympic Association; John R. Freeman Ltd
92 Associated Press
93 Horst Müller
94 Popperfoto
96 E. D. Lacey
97 Sport and General
98 Radio Times Hulton Picture Library
99 Popperfoto
103 British Olympic Association; John R. Freeman Ltd
104 Italian National Olympic Committee
105 British Olympic Association; John R. Freeman Ltd
106 a. United Press International. b. E. D. Lacey
108 British Olympic Association; John R. Freeman Ltd
109 Popperfoto
110 Melbourne Herald-Sun
111 Colorsport
112 Colorsport
113 ANP, Amsterdam
114 Associated Press
116 Kishimoto
117 Horst Müller
119 British Olympic Association; John R. Freeman Ltd

120 Melbourne Herald-Sun
121 Radio Times Hulton Picture Library
122 Reproduction Jean-Paul Maeder
124 Missouri Historical Society
125 Netherlands National Olympic Committee; John R. Freeman Ltd, courtesy British Olympic Association
126 Melbourne Herald-Sun
127 Popperfoto
129 Popperfoto
130 Popperfoto
131 Associated Press
132 Popperfoto
133 British Olympic Association; John R. Freeman Ltd
134 Popperfoto
137 E. D. Lacey
139 Geoffroy de Navacelle
140 Geoffroy de Navacelle
142 a. Geoffroy de Navacelle. b. Mansell Collection
145 Jean-Paul Maeder
146 Jean-Paul Maeder
148 Jean-Paul Maeder
150 Jean-Paul Maeder
151 Jean-Paul Maeder
154 Syndication International, London
155 Presseamt der Stadt Kiel
157 British Olympic Association; John R. Freeman Ltd
158 Reproduction Jean-Paul Maeder
160 C. Megaloconomou, Greek Photo News; courtesy Otto Szymiczek
163 a. British Olympic Association; John R. Freeman Ltd. b. Netherlands National Olympic Committee; John R. Freeman Ltd, courtesy British Olympic Association. c. Presse Bilderdienst Kindermann
164 Japanese National Olympic Committee
165 a., b. and c. Leni Riefenstahl-Produktion
171 British Olympic Association; John R. Freeman Ltd
175 Holmenkollen Ski Museum
177 a. Presse Sports. b. Reproduction Jean-Paul Maeder
178 Presse Sports
179 a. KUR und Verkehrsverein, St Moritz. b. Associated Press. c. Mansell Collection
180 a. NTB Photo. b. Photopress Zurich
181 a. and b. Popperfoto
182 Votava
183 George Konig
184 Colorsport
190 Presse-Seeger
191 a. Frischauf-Bild. b. Presse Sports
192 a. Votava. b. Colorsport
195 a. Keystone. b. Votava
196 Presse-Seeger
197 Kishimoto
198 a. Associated Press. b. Presse-Seeger
199 Colorsport
201 a. Parry O'Brien (USA), 1956. Associated Press. b. Mary Peters (GBR), 1972. Keystone. c. Nikolai Avilov (URS), 1972. Associated Press. d. Waldemar Baszanowski (POL), 1964. Pop-perfoto. e. Jesse Owens (USA), 1936. Keystone. f. Marjorie Gestring (USA), 1936. Library of Congress. g. Vera Čáslavská (TCH), 1964. Kishimoto. h. Ludwig Stubbendorf (GER) riding Nurmi, 1936. British Olympic Association; John R. Freeman Ltd. i. Marie-Thérèse Nadig (SUI), 1972. Colorsport. j. Pierre Trentin (FRA), 1968. Pop-perfoto
202 Kishimoto
205 Associated Press
206 Keystone
207 Radio Times Hulton Picture Library
208 Tony Duffy
211 British Olympic Association; John R. Freeman Ltd
213 Missouri Historical Society
214 Syndication International, London
216 Tony Duffy
217 Kishimoto
218 Novosti
219 Missouri Historical Society
220 Horst Müller
226 Associated Press
228 Presse Sports

Index

Killanin, Lord, and Rodda, John
Rodda

(s) Olympic Games.